THE MEASUREMENT AND BEHAVIOR OF UNEMPLOYMENT

NATIONAL BUREAU OF ECONOMIC RESEARCH

Special Conference Series

1. Problems in the Study of Economic Growth (not published)
2. Conference on Business Cycles
3. Conference on Research in Business Finance
4. Regularization of Business Investment
5. Business Concentration and Price Policy
6. Capital Formation and Economic Growth
7. Policies to Combat Depression
8. The Measurement and Behavior of Unemployment

The Measurement and Behavior of Unemployment

A CONFERENCE OF THE
UNIVERSITIES–NATIONAL BUREAU COMMITTEE
FOR ECONOMIC RESEARCH

A REPORT OF THE
NATIONAL BUREAU OF ECONOMIC RESEARCH, NEW YORK

PUBLISHED BY
PRINCETON UNIVERSITY PRESS, PRINCETON
1957

L.C. CARD 57-5442

Printed in the United States of America
by Princeton University Press, Princeton, New Jersey

RELATION OF NATIONAL BUREAU DIRECTORS TO PUBLICATIONS REPORTING CONFERENCE PROCEEDINGS

Since the present volume is a record of conference proceedings, it has been exempted from the rules governing submission of manuscripts to, and critical review by, the Board of Directors of the National Bureau. It has, however, been reviewed and accepted for publication by the Director of Research.

(Resolution adopted July 6, 1948 and revised November 21, 1949)

Universities–National Bureau Committee For Economic Research

This Committee is a cooperative venture of universities and the National Bureau. Its guiding objective is the encouragement of economic research on problems susceptible of objective treatment and of sufficiently broad scope to merit attention by institutions serving a scientific and public interest.

CONTENTS

THE MEASUREMENT AND BEHAVIOR OF UNEMPLOYMENT

INTRODUCTION

CLARENCE D. LONG
COUNCIL OF ECONOMIC ADVISERS

ALTHOUGH the economic writings of recent decades have manifested deep concern over the problem of unemployment, that concern has not included a strong interest in its measurement and behavior. This is doubtless traceable to a belief that the remedy for unemployment lies basically in monetary and fiscal action, and thus requires no detailed knowledge of its behavior—only a general awareness that at any given date it is high or low. Such a belief was understandable, and even forgivable, in view of the dearth of reliable statistics of unemployment up to 1940. But in recent years a vast storehouse of information on the structure of unemployment has been opened up by the United States censuses of 1940 and 1950; a prompt monthly record of unemployment in the nation as a whole has been supplied by the Census Bureau in its sample labor force estimates; and a monthly, and even weekly, record of unemployment in the various states, industries, and labor market areas has been made available by the federal-state unemployment insurance system through its unemployment claims data.

This Conference was projected in the belief that a sound treatment of unemployment requires not a miracle drug but a deep understanding of its causes, and that the time has come for a full exploration of the available statistics. For this exploration, a Conference on the Measurement and Behavior of Unemployment—a theme suggested by Leo Wolman—was planned by a committee consisting of A. Ross Eckler, Richard A. Lester, Lloyd G. Reynolds, Charles D. Stewart, and Clarence D. Long (Chairman). In making these plans, the Committee benefited from the assistance of E. J. Eberling and Meredith B. Givens and from the counsel of Leo Wolman. The Conference, held in Princeton on September 17 and 18, 1954, was attended by about ninety experts, including representatives from twenty-eight universities, the Dominion Bureau of Statistics, the Bureau of the Census, the Agricultural and Marketing Service, the Budget Bureau, the Bureau of Employment Security, the Bureau of Labor Statistics, the Council of Economic Advisers, the Department of Defense, the Federal Reserve Board, the Library of Congress, the Office of Defense Mobilization, the National Bureau of Economic Research, the National Industrial Conference Board, the Congress of Industrial Organizations, and the American Federation of Labor. The Secretary of the Con-

Note: Mr. Long has since returned to The Johns Hopkins University.

ference was Phillip Cagan. In preparing the material for publication, we had the help of the National Bureau's editorial staff. H. Irving Forman made the charts.

The papers and discussions that were put before this Conference do not, of course, solve the problem of unemployment; nor do they clear up all confusion about its definition. But they should serve to eliminate any notion that unemployment can be prevented or eliminated without close knowledge of what it is, where it is, and what it is like. Although investigators can never be made to observe rigid jurisdictional lines, it seemed feasible to divide the papers into two parts: Part I dealing with meaning and measurement, and Part II with behavior.

Part I consists of five papers. The first, by Albert Rees, deals not so much with unemployment as with full employment—the question of what is the minimum level of frictional unemployment.

Rees does not offer a measure of full employment, but he does show that the various criteria of full employment used in the past would not furnish a consistent guide to economic policy. He demonstrates from recent British statistics that Lord William Beveridge's famous "verbal" definition of full employment—more vacant jobs than unemployed persons—has not been very consistent with his numerical definition: that full employment exists when the number of unemployed is equal to or less than 3 per cent. He also believes that price behavior is not an adequate criterion of full employment and points to several instances in the United States when prices fell while employment was still rising; in the most recent, the turning point of prices led that of employment by nearly two and one-half years. He concludes with the wise observation that modern economies may be too complex to be guided by any single rule and that there may be no escape from reliance on judgment and discretion in counter-cyclical policy.

The other papers in Part I differ widely in their approaches to both definition and measurement. Gertrude Bancroft, who has had a great deal to do with the pioneering development of the census sample monthly unemployment estimate, is nevertheless quite candid in suggesting that the present concept has been largely based on pragmatic, not logical or analytical, considerations; that the census measure leaves out many groups with a better claim to the status of unemployed than some of the groups which it covers; and that the present concept does not yield a clear-cut measure of the effects of production cutbacks, frictions or dislocations in the economic system, wasted manpower, or need for income. In order to remedy these defects and thus to arrive at a concept more useful to current policy needs, Miss Bancroft offers a new arrangement, and suggests some notable inclusions and exclusions. In particular, she calls for the collection of "reasons for part-time employment" every month (as is now done in Canada) instead of every three months; for the shifting of "temporarily laid-off" workers from the "employed" to the "unemployed" category; for the setting up of a new category, "those who work less than full time for business reasons"; and, finally, for no longer counting as unemployed certain persons who say they did not look for work because they believed there was none available. This last proposal of Miss Bancroft is part of her search for more objective criteria of unemployment. It will nevertheless be challenged by many students who, like Miss Bancroft, favor a rigidly objective test of work seeking *in principle,* but who also feel that *in practice* the small modification involved in this change is not worth exposing the census series to the formal charge that the estimates of the future will no longer be comparable with the estimates of the past. Miss Bancroft, a Census Bureau official, absolves her agency from responsibility for these views; but Robert W. Burgess, Director of the Census, in commenting on her paper, states that Miss Bancroft's recommendations will be given serious consideration by the Census Bureau in planning future improvements in its concepts and measurements.

The paper by Herbert S. Parnes does not criticize the census concept of unemployment, but instead compares the census measure, as is, with the alternative measures of unemployment currently available in the United States, particularly those of the federal-state unemployment insurance system. He presents some interesting statistical comparisons, which demonstrate that, although concepts and coverages are quite different, and the ratio of insured to total unemployment has ranged widely, the two unemployment series have moved in the same direction for about two out of every three months between 1949 and 1954. Moreover, some adjustments can be made in each series, which do not reconcile them completely, but which do bring them closer together.

An analyst's concept of unemployment is apt to depend on the problems he faces in his daily work. Margaret J. Hagood and Louis J. Ducoff of the Department of Agriculture, who have long been concerned with the surplus of inadequately employed workers in nonindustrial rural areas, point to the results of two sample surveys of open-country households that were made in certain low-income rural areas of eastern Kentucky and southeastern Oklahoma in 1952. These surveys show that only two-thirds of males fourteen and older in those areas were employed even as many as 180 full-time days a year. Yet these males indicated only a low degree of availability for out-of-area employment, a finding that is in some conflict with the historical fact that large numbers of persons left these areas during the decade 1940-1950. The authors concede that it is difficult to test a person's availability for work without making him an actual job offer, but they also feel that the census-type test does not reveal this disguised unemployment. It has no way of eliciting the extent to which better training, improved labor mobility, and expanded work opportunities would persuade many people to seek work who are at present inactive because they feel unemployable or believe that the search for work is useless. The authors would thus measure unemployment by *developing*, rather than by *static*, standards.

This is what Richard C. Wilcock is also urging in a very different type of analysis when he asks that more attention be turned to discovering the characteristics and behavior of people attached only irregularly, inactively, or subjectively, to the labor force, a group he calls the secondary labor force. On the other hand, in the discussion of Wilcock's paper, Gladys L. Palmer, who has carried a major part of the burden of developing American labor force and unemployment measures, suggests that most faith be placed in what people do, rather than in what they say in answers to hypothetical questions. She proposes that queries designed to bring in people now classed outside the labor force be balanced by queries designed to identify a substantial number of persons who may have only a tenuous right to classification as unemployed or who may be on the brink of leaving the labor force.

The papers of Part II cannot escape some problems of measurement, but they deal primarily with unemployment behavior. Stanley Lebergott presents his revised estimates of average annual labor force, employment, and unemployment from 1900 to 1954 and endeavors to make them comparable in concept with the sample survey estimates collected by the Works Progress Administration and the Census Bureau in the years since 1940. He has relied primarily on the decennial census for bench marks and has estimated unemployment in the intervening years by subtracting interpolated estimates of employment from interpolated estimates of labor force. Unemployment so estimated is subject to great potential miscalculation, since a relatively small error in the employment estimate and a relatively small error in the labor force estimate may combine to form a relatively large error in the unemployment estimate. His data—revisions of the long-established National Industrial Conference Board estimates—modify our knowledge of past unemployment behavior in the United States; they would, for example, make the 1929-1930 rise more severe than the 1937-1938 rise, rather than the reverse, as indicated by the N.I.C.B. But he points out that the broad picture shows no startling change in the way we are accustomed to consider this period. Such has been the paucity of information on unemployment that seldom have we been afforded an insight into the ancient question of whether unemployment has been increasing in recent generations. Lebergott thinks that the answer to this question must not be made without pondering whether workers may be more willing to admit being unemployed now than in 1900 or in 1930, and whether the practice of granting vacations, which has been growing, permits slack in the labor force to exist without a corresponding amount of unemployment. Nevertheless, he concludes that during 1900 to 1950, unemployment was 4 or 5 per cent as an annual average and that, on the whole, high-level employment has characterized the performance of the American economy in the past half-century.

Philip M. Hauser finds great differences in the amount of unemployment among persons of different age and sex, marital status, family responsibility, and industry and occupational group; but he also observes that these differences have been stable. One notable difference, for example, has been the consistently higher unemployment rate of women than of men, of young persons than of older persons, and of nonwhite than of white persons. On the other hand, these differences may be deceptive. Notably, the higher unemployment rate of women may be due to a greater tendency not necessarily to lose their jobs but rather to alter their desire to work, for in every month large numbers of women leave the labor force and large numbers of other women enter. Those entering take time to locate new jobs and in the meantime are unemployed. Thus Hauser finds that less than half of the female additions to unemployment originated in previous employment (in "disemployment") and one-half originated in a previous non-labor-force status; as thus measured by disemployment rates it would seem that women are less liable than men to unemployment. Hauser calls for more and better information on gross changes in the labor force by various types of characteristics, information which would enable us to compute disemployment rates cross-classified by age, sex, marital status, industry, and occupation, and thus to learn much more about the differential vulnerability of these classes to factors beyond their control. Such conclusions obviously have great significance for any policy aimed at remedying unemployment.

David L. Kaplan, studying the attachment of the unemployed person to three major United States industries—manufacturing, construction, and trade—finds that many unemployed and employed persons change their industry of attachment even in intervals as short as a month. He indicates that each industry may have a well-established labor force with which it plays a steady game of "put-and-take," but that the industry-attachment of the unemployed does not have the same importance as the age, sex, race, and occupational characteristics.

The remaining paper on the behavior of unemployment in the United States, by Louis Levine, deals with the wide differences in unemployment that may exist at any given time between one local labor market area and another. A local labor market is an area within which a worker can change jobs without changing residence. Unfortunately, there are no current counts, or even sample surveys, of total unemployment in each of the various areas. Estimates are currently made by the state employment security agencies, under general instructions from the United States Bureau of Employment Security. However, these agencies have little data upon which to base their estimates of unemployed persons who have just entered or re-entered the labor market, who are moving from one area to another, or who have exhausted their benefit rights; and there is no way to check the accuracy of such data except from the single comparison with the 1950 census, the only one to collect complete information on unemployment in local labor market areas as now defined. Levine feels that such a comparison is not very helpful, because even the complete census estimates are themselves subject to criticism. One may well question whether such estimates of local unemployment could be regarded as superior to the data which the Census Bureau gathers by visiting every house. But in any case, Levine's study brings out a clear need for better-founded estimates of unemployment in local areas. The urgency of the need is highlighted by the wide differences he finds in economic condition among different localities at any given time. For example, the 1949 unemployment rate in Bridgeport, Connecticut was more than 12 per cent, and in South Bend, Indiana was 20 per cent, whereas in 1954 the picture was almost the reverse.

The studies of Warren W. Eason, on the one hand, and Walter Galenson and Arnold Zellner, on the other, illuminate for us the behavior of unemployment abroad. Eason has not been able to say how much unemployment there is in the Soviet Union, because officially there is no unemployment in that nation and because the labor-force information that would enable us to hunt for hidden unemployment has been largely suppressed since 1929 (when about 18 per cent of the then small number of wage and salary workers were unemployed). He does tell us, however, some things about Soviet planning that are of significance to the question of unemployment—such as the fact that there was a change of labor force almost overnight from one largely self-employed to one entirely under control of state and cooperative organizations, and that we must look for unemployment in the actual dislocations in the national economy, in seasonal fluctuations, in time lags of workers going from one job to another, and in workers seeking work for the first time. In addition to these insights into Russian unemployment offered by Eason, we have those of the late Eugene M. Kulischer, whose death on April 2, 1956 the members of this Conference deeply regret. He suggested that the great overpopulation and underemployment that always existed in Soviet agriculture before 1939, but were wiped out by the great manpower losses in World War II, have since recurred because the rapid development of agricultural technology cut the need for labor.

Finally, we have Galenson's and Zellner's valuable appraisal of unemployment in nine Western nations (excluding this country). The authors—recognizing that any comparison for a given year would provide results that could be expected to be at the mercy of the particular economic conditions—have taken on the formidable task of tracing the course of unemployment in each of the countries over a long-time period. In most of the countries the data begin before World War I, and in four countries (Denmark, Germany, Norway, and the United Kingdom) they begin in 1904 or earlier. The authors recognize that unemployment is not defined in precisely the same way in any two countries. But they feel that the statistics are more uniform than the list of differences in concept and coverage would suggest. For in most Western countries, the unemployment statistics were compiled by trade unions under the so-called Ghent system. These unions usually gathered the data as part of the administration of payments for out-of-work benefits or of waiver of dues during unemployment. They used simple techniques in order to save processing time and tended to copy each other's methods, thus leading to a certain uniformity. Moreover, the trade union officials were in a position to know the unemployment of their members in a way that is not ordinarily open to government officials or house-to-house canvassers. The statistics are not, of course, without deficiencies. On the one hand, skilled workers, who are, other things equal, less likely to be unemployed, tend to be represented disproportionately, thus giving the data a downward bias. On the other hand, building construction and mining industries, which are rather unstable industries, tend to be disproportionately represented; and agriculture, government, and rail transport, which are typically stable industries, are ordinarily excluded. Moreover, the number of unions reporting varies from one country to another and from one time to another. Despite these defects, the authors feel that the data offer a reasonable basis for comparison between different countries and provide a fairly accurate gauge of trend, if not of absolute level. Their conclusions from these elaborate endeavors are modest but important. They show that unemployment has not followed a simple trend, but that it was low before the start of World War I (except in Denmark, where they feel unemployment was overstated) and that it has been low since the end of World War II. The great wave of unemployment that has left such an impress on modern thinking seems to have been a phenomenon confined to the period between the end of World War I and the beginning of World War II, and especially to the decade of the 1930's. What were the circumstances and the policies that could have produced such a phenomenon? This is not the least of the provocative questions arising out of this conference volume to which future economic investigation might do well to turn attention.

PART I

THE MEANING AND MEASUREMENT OF UNEMPLOYMENT AND FULL EMPLOYMENT

THE MEANING AND MEASUREMENT OF FULL EMPLOYMENT

ALBERT REES

UNIVERSITY OF CHICAGO

1. Introduction

THE prevention of mass unemployment is now universally considered a primary goal of economic policy. Most of the literature on full employment has been concerned with policies by which full employment can be reached or maintained. This paper will not cover such policies. Rather, it will deal first with the definition and measurement of full employment, with ways of determining when full employment has been reached and when departures from it begin. The second part of the paper will deal with factors that affect the level of full employment as defined and measured in a specific way. These factors can change full-employment levels over time and cause them to differ from one economy to another. Looked at in another way, the problem of this paper is to measure frictional unemployment. Frictional unemployment must here be defined broadly enough to include all unemployment, not excepting seasonal, that exists in the presence of "adequate" total demand for commodities and labor in the economy.

At the outset, I recognize that not everyone thinks it desirable to define or measure full employment precisely. Beardsley Ruml has taken this position, holding that full employment should, like liberty and justice, be a broadly conceived goal of a democratic society.[1] Others have taken the view that the definition of full employment is primarily a political matter. Thus Allan G. B. Fisher feels that in practice, governments will be content to define full employment as "avoiding that level of unemployment, whatever it may happen to be, which there is good reason to fear may provoke an inconvenient restlessness among the electorate."[2]

Although such views may have merit, I feel that economic and sta-

Note: While preparing this paper, I was a Research Associate of the National Bureau of Economic Research. I am indebted to several members of the staff of the National Bureau for valuable assistance. Geoffrey Moore, Clarence D. Long, Phillip Cagan, and Leo Wolman have read a previous draft and made helpful suggestions; Millard Hastay gave advice on some statistical problems, and Harry Eisenpress did the seasonal adjustments.

[1] *Full Employment Act of 1945, Hearings,* Senate Committee on Banking and Currency. 79th Cong., 1st sess., 1945, p. 398.

[2] A. G. B. Fisher, *International Aspects of Full Employment in Great Britain,* London, Royal Institute of International Affairs, 1946, p. 19.

tistical definitions of full employment are valuable for two purposes. First, they may serve as one guide, though not usually as the sole guide, to government and central bank policy in monetary and fiscal matters, and to public and private policy in other areas of decision-making related to employment. This is, of course, the primary motive for interest in full employment. Second, measures of full employment are of interest for analytical purposes, in defining conditions of tight or balanced labor markets and their consequences. In this sense, measures of full employment cannot be replaced by measures of cyclical peaks, which may fail to reach full employment. The peak of 1937 is an example. It is also conceivable that in a period of very tight labor markets there could be a mild cyclical trough that never fell below a full-employment level according to some definition.

Some aspects of the concept of full employment are still, on occasion, sources of confusion. The concept, as it is generally used, is not analogous to the concept of capacity for physical plant. The full-employment level does not indicate the maximum number of man-hours of gainful employment that can be obtained from a given population, since it assumes that labor-force participation is voluntary and that hours of work are not abnormally high. Under unusual conditions, such as total war, both labor-force participation and hours of work can be raised much above peacetime full-employment levels by a combination of incentives and legal requirements.

A closely related aspect of the full-employment concept is that not all reductions in labor input at full employment create departures from full employment. In the usual sense of full employment and its sense in this paper, such departures arise only from decreases in demand or the failure of demand to grow as rapidly as supply. A decrease in supply will be considered as altering the full-employment level, except to the extent that it is induced by a change in demand.

This implies that the definition of full employment does not involve the knotty problem of the shape of the supply curve of labor for the economy as a whole, or the shape of the underlying indifference surfaces relating leisure to real income. Thus if at a given level of real wages workers choose to increase the time they devote to leisure and to decrease the time they devote to productive employment, the shape or position of the supply schedule is altered without creating a departure from full employment. A departure from full employment exists only when involuntary idleness rises above its full-employment level, when more workers seek employment at the current level of wages and cannot find it. In practice, however, it may sometimes be difficult to distinguish between voluntary and involuntary idleness.

A complication would arise if the level of real wages of fully employed workers fell during periods of less than full employment. In such circumstances there might be workers who were unwilling to work at the current level of real wages but were willing to work at the full-employment level. Their unemployment would not be involuntary in the usual sense, but it would be involuntary in the sense that it would arise from a cyclical change in real wages and not from an autonomous change in tastes that placed a higher value on leisure.

However, it is usually true that the real wages of fully employed workers tend to rise in business contractions, since money wages are generally less flexible downward than consumer prices. Unemployment arising in business contractions is therefore involuntary whether it is defined at the current or the full-employment level of wages and whether wages are defined in real or money terms.[3]

Given the demand for labor and the size of the labor force, an increase in labor turnover or a decrease in the efficiency of the labor market in handling turnover (effecting job transfers) will also cause a fall in employment and a rise in frictional unemployment. Since it does not result from a decrease in demand, this rise in frictional unemployment is also considered a change in the full-employment level rather than a departure from it.

It would be comforting to declare with confidence that there is some one best definition and measure of full employment, and to defend this declaration successfully. I cannot see my way clear to do so. Rather, there seem to be a number of possible measures, each having advantages and disadvantages. Since I know of no systematic exploration of these possibilities, some clearing away of underbrush seems to be needed more than an attempt to blaze the one best trail. In connection with each measure discussed, an example or illustration will be presented from the employment statistics of the United States or Great Britain.

This discussion of measures of full employment is not intended to be exhaustive. A great many measures and definitions of full employment have been advanced, and it is not possible to explore all of them here. Those included are intended to cover the important general cases; most of the omitted measures are variants of those included.

Definitions of full employment can be classified on at least two bases. The first is the extent to which the avoidance of unemployment is given priority over other and possibly competing objectives of economic policy. The second is the technical basis of the definition: What

[3] For further discussion of this point, see my "Wage Determination and Involuntary Unemployment," *Journal of Political Economy*, April 1951, pp. 143-153.

kind of statistical series does it employ and how does it employ them? These two bases are not entirely independent. It is possible at times to follow alternative statistical paths to the same objectives; at other times the technical nature of a definition has definite implications for its policy orientation. The discussion here will proceed on the basis of a technical classification of definitions, with implications for policy pointed out along the way whenever possible.

2. *Measures of Full Employment*

MINIMUM UNEMPLOYMENT APPROACH

The measures discussed in this section all define full employment as existing when unemployment is at a minimum. This minimum is determined historically; it is the lowest unemployment previously reached. Such measures are probably the most widely used of all measures of full employment. Often they are the real basis of definitions that seem at first to be based on something else.

The basic advantage of the minimum unemployment concept is its relative simplicity and freedom from ambiguity. It gives a very low estimate of the unemployment permissible under a full-employment policy, which accounts for part of its popularity. However, a minimum unemployment concept rules out the possibility of overfull employment, and considers minimum and optimum unemployment the same; anything more is considered less than full employment. The historical minimum of unemployment in a given economy may be associated with inflation or with labor shortages, but these are not taken into account. Thus, as a guide to policy, minimum unemployment definitions seem to imply necessarily what Viner has called "full employment at whatever cost."[4] The same is true of the maximum employment definitions that will be discussed later.

To turn the concept of minimum unemployment into an operational definition, certain limits must be specified. Firstly, are any circumstances or conditions to be ruled out in selecting the minimum? I assume that there is general agreement that periods of total war should be excluded; for example the years from 1941 through 1945 in the United States or 1939 through 1945 in Great Britain should not be used in selecting a minimum unemployment figure. The labor market conditions produced by total war cannot be duplicated in peacetime, and no one would want to duplicate them merely to reduce unemployment. On the other hand, it is not clear that partial or limited war, such as the Korean War, should be excluded, and I have not excluded it. The

[4] Jacob Viner, "Full Employment at Whatever Cost," *Quarterly Journal of Economics*, August 1950, pp. 385-407.

degree of tightness in labor markets created by the Korean War could probably have been created by peacetime monetary and fiscal policies.

Secondly, how far back in time should one go to find a minimum? In principle, it can be argued that the period should be limited to two or three decades; there can be such fundamental changes in labor market structure over longer periods that earlier minima would no longer be meaningful. In practice, the problem does not arise for either the United States or Great Britain, because of the lack of available statistics. Except in section 2, the data used in this paper begin with January 1946 whenever possible.

Thirdly, over what time period should the minimum be taken? The longer the time period allowed, the greater is the spread of the data around their trough, and the higher the resulting estimate of the minimum. It would seem unreasonable to base a definition on the experience of one month or a few months, even if the data for these months are seasonally adjusted. I have used a period of twelve months in selecting minima because it eliminates errors that might arise from faulty seasonal adjustment.

Finally, what measure of unemployment is to be minimized? Several alternatives are examined in the following sections.

Minimum Total Unemployment. For the United States, the series most frequently used is the Bureau of the Census series on unemployment.[5] This series is obtained from the monthly sample survey of the labor force, taken for one week in each month.[6] Those counted as un-

[5] The alternative is the Bureau of Employment Security's series on insured unemployment. This series has advantages for some purposes, as well as some special disadvantages. I will not discuss these here, since the focus of this paper is differences in concepts of full employment rather than alternative measures for any given concept.

[6] For a thorough discussion of the methods used in these surveys, see Louis J. Ducoff and Margaret J. Hagood, *Labor Force Definition and Measurement: Recent Experience in the United States*, Social Science Research Council, Bull. 56, 1947, and *Current Population Reports*, Bureau of the Census, Series P-23, No. 2, July 30, 1954.

The sample used contains 24,000 to 26,000 dwelling units and other living quarters, and completed interviews are obtained from 20,000 to 22,000 households each month. Estimates based on this sample differ from the results of a complete enumeration because of sampling variability. The Bureau of the Census estimates that for unemployment, the chances are about nineteen out of twenty that sampling variability is less than approximately 8 per cent.

In January 1954, the Bureau began to use a new sample containing the same number of households as the old one but taken from a larger number of geographical areas (230 rather than 68). For January 1954, there was a discrepancy of 728,000 between the estimates of unemployment based on the two samples. This is approximately 24 per cent of the larger estimate. For discussion of the sources of this discrepancy, see the paper by Gertrude Bancroft in this volume and the

employed are those "who did not work at all during the survey week and were looking for work. Also included as unemployed are persons who would have been looking for work except that (1) they were temporarily ill, (2) they expected to return to a job from which they had been laid off for an indefinite period, or (3) they believed no work was available in their line of work or in the community."[7]

The top line of Chart 1 shows unemployment as just defined as a percentage of the civilian labor force, both seasonally adjusted. The ratio to the civilian labor force rather than an absolute number is used to avoid a rise in minimum unemployment over time as a result of labor-force growth.

The minimum unemployment for any twelve-month period is 2.3 per cent of the civilian labor force for the twelve months ending October 1953. Prior to the business contraction of 1949, the minimum for any twelve-month period was 3.3 per cent for the twelve months ending October 1948. In January 1949 the seasonally adjusted monthly series rose sharply above this level.

It has been suggested that for purposes of defining full employment, the unemployment data should include certain subcategories of the category "with a job and not at work." These subcategories cover persons temporarily laid off with definite instructions to return to work within thirty days and persons waiting to start a new job or business to which they were scheduled to report within the following thirty days.[8] The suggestion concerning temporary layoffs conforms to British practice which includes in unemployment the partially corresponding category, "temporarily stopped."

The Bureau of the Census considers the temporary layoff group as employed because they have jobs, and although they are not working at them, they are not seeking work, and new jobs need not be found for them. It is pointed out that the scheme of classification used by the census gives priority to "unemployed" over "temporary layoff"; thus any worker on temporary layoff who distrusted the promise of rehire sufficiently to seek other work would be counted as unemployed.[9]

---

mimeographed report of the Special Advisory Committee on Employment Statistics, August 1954.

In the charts that accompany this paper the segments labeled "new" show data from the new (230 area) sample.

[7] Quoted from the official definition of the Bureau of the Census.

[8] See Russ Nixon, "Correction of Census Bureau Estimates of Unemployment," *Review of Economics and Statistics*, February 1950, pp. 50-55; and T. K. Hitch, "The Meaning and Measurement of Full or Maximum Employment," *Review of Economics and Statistics*, February 1951, pp. 1-11.

[9] See Charles D. Stewart, "The Definition of Unemployment," *Review of Economics and Statistics*, February 1950, p. 58.

On the other hand, the loss of work by this group resembles unemployment because it is involuntary, and its rather clear inverse conformity to the business cycle suggests that a principal cause of temporary layoffs is lack of demand. Data for this group are available

CHART 1

Percentage of the Civilian Labor Force Unemployed or on Temporary Layoff, 1946-1954

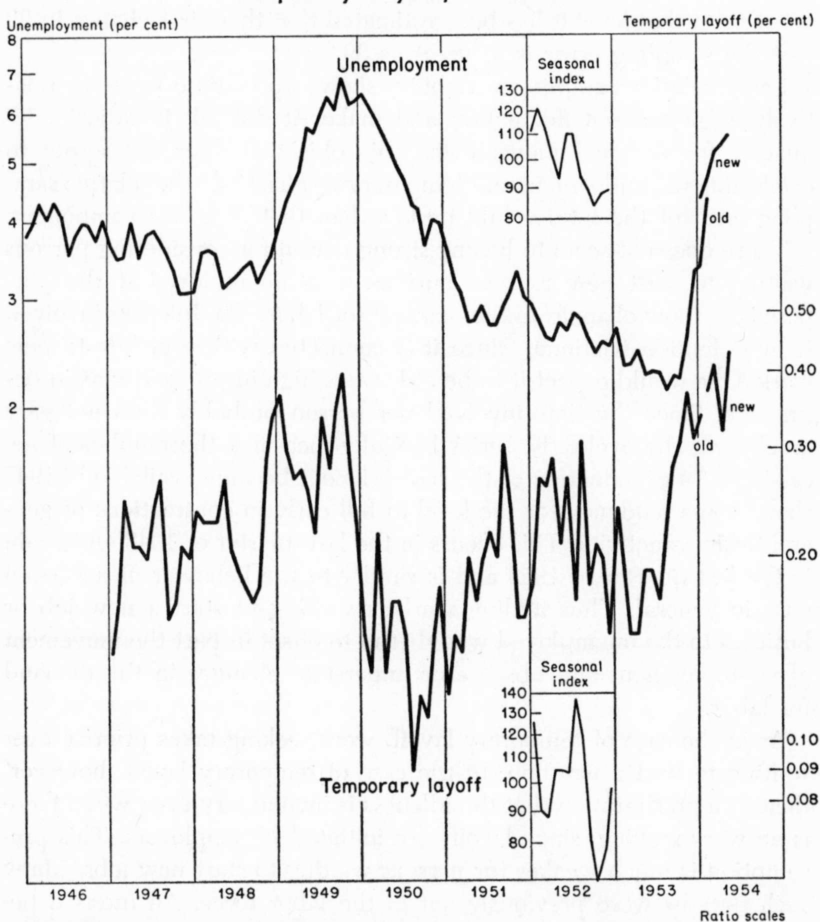

since 1947 and are shown, seasonally adjusted, on the bottom line of Chart 1. The number of persons on temporary layoffs rises significantly from September 1948 to October 1949, and again in the last half of 1953. This series seems to lead unemployment at its troughs. Thus in 1948 it rose sharply from October to December, when the rise in unemployment was too small to be considered very meaningful;

similarly in 1953 it rose sharply from July to October, though unemployment in October was still below the July level.

Conceptually, there is a fairly strong case for including this group in the unemployed, or at least for considering both in defining full employment. The principal objection to considering them separately is a practical one. In sample statistics, the amount of sampling variability grows relative to the estimated size of a group as estimated size decreases. The temporary layoff group is often in the neighborhood of 100,000. At that level it has been estimated that there is 1 chance in 20 that the sampling error is as great as 39,000.[10]

Large relative sampling variability shows up in time series as relatively large random fluctuation and makes it difficult to adjust adequately for seasonal movements. This objection does not apply to combining unemployment and temporary layoffs, since the relative sampling error of the total would be less than that of either component.

There does not seem to be any strong reason for considering persons waiting to start new jobs or businesses as unemployed if the purpose is to show changes in the demand for labor. The idleness involved is by definition frictional, since it is connected with transfers to new work. One would expect it to be at least as high in prosperity as in depression. Since the time involved per person probably does not vary much over the cycle, the series basically measures the number of accessions. An examination of the series since it became available in 1947 shows some tendency for the level to fall early in contractions of general business activity. This occurs in the last quarter of 1948 and again in the last quarter of 1953 and is similar to the behavior of accession data in general. Thus adding workers waiting to start a new job or business to the unemployed would tend to offset in part the movement of unemployment and obscure or understate changes in the demand for labor.

As in the case of temporary layoff, work-seeking takes priority over waiting to start a new job. In the case of temporary layoff, however, there is a presumption that the idleness is involuntary even when there is no work-seeking, since layoffs are initiated by employers. This presumption is much weaker for persons waiting to start new jobs. Many such persons were previously not in the labor force. An interval between getting a job and starting work could often be requested by the employee rather than by the employer.

Minimum Total and Partial Unemployment. The data on total unemployment discussed above include only persons who did not work

[10] This estimate is an older one than that for unemployment given in note 6; it is based on data for 1948-1950. It is probable that an estimate comparable with that of note 6 would be higher.

at all during the survey week. It is frequently suggested that in measuring full employment, changes in partial unemployment should be taken into account. In census statistics, partially unemployed persons can be defined as those who worked at least one hour, but involuntarily worked less than a full week. These persons are now counted as employed. Theoretically, the increase in this group during a business contraction could be enormous. If, in response to a decline in demand, most employers were to reduce labor input by work sharing rather than by layoffs, millions of man-weeks of employment could be lost each week in involuntary idleness without appearing at all in the unemployment statistics.

It is unquestionably true that a significant amount of work sharing does take place in business contractions, and that it results in partial unemployment. It does not follow, however, that the statistics on total unemployment, as usually interpreted, understate the increase in total plus partial idleness during business contractions. This is because each new wholly unemployed worker is generally considered as adding a full workweek to the time lost in involuntary idleness, which is not always true. Some of the new wholly unemployed workers were previously part-time workers. Thus the usual way of looking at unemployment involves two errors working in opposite directions: it overlooks increases in partial unemployment and at the same time overweights increases in unemployment arising from the loss of jobs by part-time workers. It is not possible to state a priori which error will predominate.

Partial unemployment will be used here to mean the time not worked by involuntary part-time workers, or the amount by which time worked falls short of a full workweek. A full workweek is taken as 40 hours.[11] Following Hitch,[12] involuntary part-time workers are defined as (1) those who regularly work part time, yet prefer and could accept full-time work, and (2) those who usually work full time but were working part time during the census survey week because they had begun or

[11] The use of a constant full workweek greatly simplifies the calculations in this section. Forty hours is somewhat below the average number of hours worked by all persons in the labor force, including self-employed workers, agricultural workers, and persons with more than one job. This average has fluctuated between 41 and 42 hours since 1949. However 40 hours has been by far the most common single workweek; in 1949 more than 36 per cent of the labor force worked 40 hours in each survey week not containing a holiday; since then the percentage has risen to more than 40, reaching 46 in January 1954. Forty hours is also the standard workweek set in the Fair Labor Standards Act. It is thus reasonable to think of a person working 40 hours as working a full week even though in some cases he is working less than is normal for him. The choice of 41 or 42 hours as the full workweek would not make any appreciable difference for the analysis that follows.

[12] Hitch, *op.cit.*, p. 8.

ended a job during the week, or because of slack work, layoff, or repairs to plant and equipment. Those part-time workers not considered involuntary will be called "other part-time workers." They include (1) voluntary part-time workers, who usually work part time and do not prefer or could not accept full-time work; and (2) workers who usually work full time but worked part time during the survey week because of vacation, illness, bad weather, industrial disputes, and various personal reasons.

The error involved in overlooking increases in involuntary part-time work will be exactly offset by overweighting the loss of work by other part-time workers if the time not worked by all part-time workers, involuntary and other, remains constant. More generally, the cyclical increase in persons wholly unemployed, considered as representing full weeks of work lost, will correctly state, understate, or overstate the actual increase in time lost from partial plus total unemployment according as the time not worked by all part-time workers does not vary with the cycle, varies directly with the cycle, or varies inversely with the cycle.[13]

With this principle in mind, the available data can be examined to see what kind of bias is actually involved in the usual failure to consider partial unemployment in measuring full employment. The data consist of a monthly series on time not worked by all part-time workers and information on time not worked by involuntary part-time workers and other part-time workers for 15 months in which special surveys were made. The fifteen special surveys of part-time work are spread irregularly over the period from September 1947 to December 1953. Following census usage of the term "part time," the data refer to workers who worked less than 35 hours a week. Time not worked is computed from the number of workers in each of four intervals of hours and is expressed in units of 40-hour weeks. Thus each week of time lost in involuntary part-time work can be considered the equivalent of one wholly unemployed worker seeking full-time work.[14]

The data on time not worked by part-time workers are shown in Chart 2. The bottom line of this chart shows time not worked by involuntary part-time workers at the dates of the special surveys. This series shows marked conformity to the cycle in its general shape, and taken by itself might be the basis for contending that overlooking partial unemployment will cause a serious understatement of increases in the involuntary loss of work. In the total time not worked by all part-time workers (top line of Chart 2), no corresponding conformity

[13] For an algebraic proof of this proposition, see Appendix Note 1.
[14] For details of the derivation of these series, see Appendix Note 2.

CHART 2
Time Not Worked by Part-Time Workers, 1946-1954

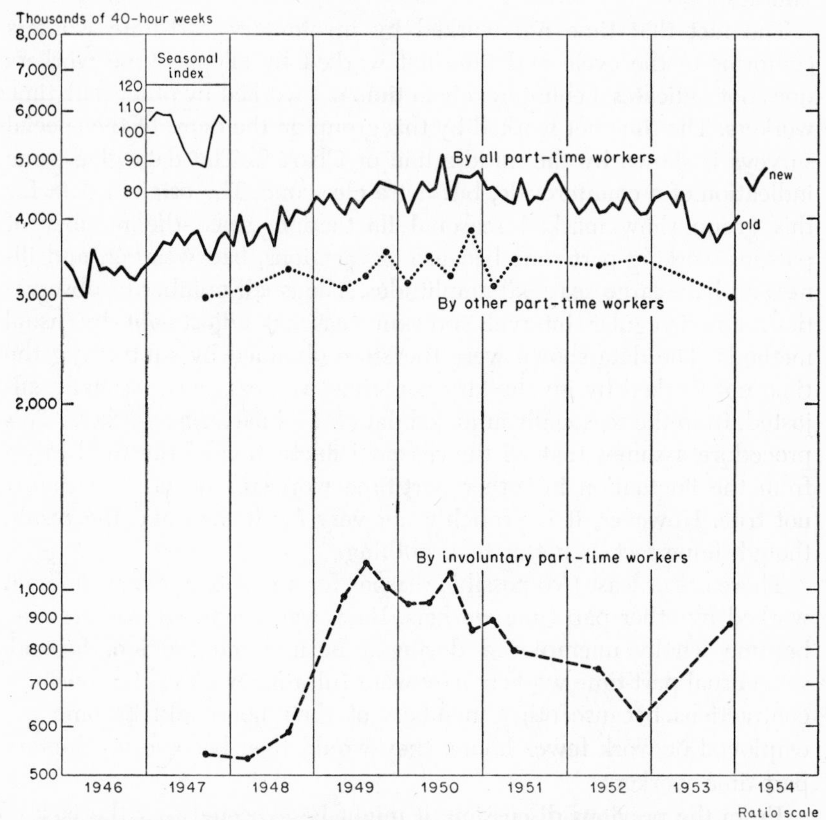

to the cycle is apparent. Judgments about the conformity of this series are more reliable than those about the series on involuntary part-time work because it is based on monthly data and it covers a longer period. Starting in 1946, the series rises steadily to a peak in December 1950.[15] The rate of rise does not increase perceptibly during the reference contraction of November 1948 to October 1949. After December 1950 the series falls, and the fall is accentuated rather than broken by the contraction in the last half of 1953. The data from the new sample for early

[15] The apparent peak in July 1950 is the result of imperfect seasonal adjustment; the survey week contained the Independence Day holiday. All or part of the rise in this series in the early years may be spurious, and results from the use of a constant full-time workweek. Average hours worked declined steadily from 1946 through 1949, and much of this decline was probably due to reductions in the standard workweek in some industries. The understatement of time not worked is therefore somewhat greater in the earlier years, but this defect would not prevent the series from reflecting any cyclical increase in time not worked.

1954 show a higher level of time not worked. It is not clear whether this represents a cyclical change or simply a difference between the two samples.

The fact that time not worked by involuntary part-time workers conforms to the cycle and time not worked by all part-time workers does not indicates a countercycle in time not worked by other part-time workers. The time not worked by this group on the dates of the special surveys is shown by the middle line of Chart 2. The data give some indication of a countercycle, but not a clear one. The original data for this group show marked seasonal fluctuation, since the number of persons working part time because of vacations, bad weather, and illness all have large seasonal amplitudes. The small number of observations and irregular intervals prevent seasonal adjustment by usual methods. The data shown were therefore obtained by subtracting the time not worked by involuntary part-time workers, not seasonally adjusted, from the seasonally adjusted data for all part-time workers. This procedure assumes that all the seasonal fluctuation of the total arises from the fluctuation in "other part-time workers," which is certainly not true. However, it is probably not very far wrong, and the result, though imperfect, is better than nothing.

There are at least two possible reasons for a countercycle in time not worked by other part-time workers. First, some of these workers may become wholly unemployed during a business contraction. Second, some usual part-time workers may want full-time work during business contractions because other members of their household become unemployed or work fewer hours; they would then become involuntary part-time workers.

From the previous discussion, it might be expected that the lack of conformity to the reference contraction in time not worked by all part-time workers in 1948-1949 demonstrates that the change in the wholly unemployed, considered as representing full weeks of involuntary time lost, is an approximately correct measure of the change in involuntary time lost. Before this can be asserted, an additional complication must be taken into account.

An increase in time not worked by "other part-time workers" has been treated as not involuntary because it does not arise from lack of demand. This is clearly true when the increase arises from an increase in the number of such workers. It is not equally true if the increase in time not worked arises from a decrease in the average hours worked, which might occur involuntarily through lack of demand even for a worker whose basic decision to work part time rather than full time was voluntary.

Changes in time not worked by "other part-time workers" are accounted for almost entirely by changes in the number of workers rather than changes in average hours worked. Average hours worked shows a slight seasonal pattern but no trace of a cyclical pattern. For the eleven special surveys starting with May 1949 the average hours of this group vary between 19.4 and 19.9 per week except for two August figures of 20.2 and 20.9.[16]

The data therefore seem to support the view that changes in the wholly unemployed viewed as representing full weeks of involuntary time lost are an approximately correct measure of the absolute amount of change in time lost in partial and total unemployment during the contraction of 1949. This conclusion is somewhat at variance with that of T. K. Hitch. A comparison of his methods with those used here may be found in Appendix Note 3.

It should be noted that the discussion above applies to changes in partial unemployment, not to levels. The number of wholly unemployed as a percentage of the civilian labor force does understate the amount of total plus partial unemployment. The understatement arises in two ways: (1) the numerator excludes partial unemployment, and (2) the denominator includes as full units the members of the part-time labor force. This understatement is offset in very small part by including as full units in the numerator the wholly unemployed seeking part-time work.

The understatement is present at all phases of the business cycle, and seems to be greater at peaks than at troughs. Correcting it would involve largely getting used to new magnitudes and would probably lead to smaller rather than larger estimates of the extent of departures from full employment.

Concepts that do not understate the amount of partial and total unemployment can be developed. One might be called full-time equivalent unemployment as a percentage of the full-time equivalent labor force. This would count people having or seeking full-time jobs as whole units. Persons holding part-time jobs by choice and seeking part-time jobs would be counted in appropriate fractions of full-time jobs. Persons involuntarily working part-time would be counted as full units in the denominator, and their time lost would be counted in appropriate fractions of full workweeks in the numerator. This measure can now be computed only for the dates of the special surveys of part-time work for May 1949 and after and cannot be seasonally adjusted.

For May 1949 full-time equivalent unemployment was 7.0 per cent

[16] Prior to May 1949, data are not available. Data for November 1952 are excluded since they are affected by the occurrence of Election Day during the survey week.

of the full-time equivalent labor force, and in May 1951 it was 3.9 per cent.[17] The corresponding figures for unemployment as a percentage of the civilian labor force (not seasonally adjusted) are 5.6 and 2.7. The relative decline is greater in the usual measure. Similar results can be obtained for other dates during the period from 1949 to 1953. They seem to indicate that partial unemployment varies less than total unemployment over the cycle, and adding it to estimates of total unemployment would decrease the relative amplitude of unemployment cycles.

The concepts involved in the present data on partial unemployment are subject to question. The question asked of usual part-time workers "Do you prefer and could you accept full-time work?" relates to attitudes and not, like most census questions, to behavior. The question "Are you seeking full-time work?" would be consistent with other census concepts. The Canadian labor force survey has recently begun to ask this question of part-time workers. The change in concepts involved would undoubtedly reduce the level of estimates of partial unemployment. What it would do to their movement over time can only be conjectured.

To conclude, the available evidence suggests that failure to consider partial unemployment does not lead to underestimates of the cyclical rise in total plus partial unemployment. However, this evidence leaves much to be desired. Better data on part-time work collected more frequently and regularly would be very valuable, and could reverse these conclusions.

Minimum Long-Duration Unemployment. The unemployment data that have been discussed are mixtures of frictional unemployment and cyclical unemployment, becoming almost purely frictional in the neighborhood of their troughs. To detect departures from full employment, it would be desirable to have some way of statistically separating frictional unemployment from cyclical unemployment.

At first thought, one might seek to do this by inquiring into the reasons for the loss of jobs. A person who quits a job voluntarily might be called frictionally unemployed while he seeks other work; a person who is laid off because of slack trade might be called cyclically unemployed. Further reflection reveals fatal weakness in this distinction. Even during full employment individual firms, industries, and localities may experience declines in demand. No one has suggested that maintaining full employment means maintaining every worker indefinitely in his own particular job.[18] This point was well stated by Lord Beveridge

[17] In this calculation, 40 hours is again taken as the full-time workweek.

[18] Lord Beveridge has gone so far as to suggest "the need for stabilizing the demand for labour, not merely in total, but in each of its main categories," William H. Beveridge, *Full Employment in a Free Society*, Norton, 1945, p. 269.

in 1909 when he wrote "The cause of a man's being unemployed is not that which led him to lose his last job but that which prevents him from getting another job now."[19] Loss of a job for any cause results in frictional unemployment if there are other jobs available reasonably well suited to the worker's abilities.

This line of reasoning suggests the duration of unemployment as a possible device for distinguishing frictional unemployment from other types. Unemployment might be considered frictional whenever the worker succeeds in finding a new job in a short period of time. Unfortunately, this is not precisely the information given by statistics of unemployment by duration. We would like the total duration of unemployment from start to end, and, to be thoroughly unreasonable, we would like to know this duration at the start. What we get, of course, is the duration up to the time the statistics are collected. Thus there is no way of telling currently how much short-duration unemployment is the beginning of long-duration unemployment.[20]

Nevertheless, the available statistics on unemployment by duration are of some value. I have taken unemployment of over 10 weeks as long-duration unemployment. The term is used by the Bureau of the Census to refer to unemployment of 15 weeks and over. Fifteen weeks seems a long period for the purpose of separating out frictional unemployment, but the major differences between long- and short-term unemployment can be shown about equally well by several possible dividing lines.

For the period since 1947 Chart 3 shows unemployment of over 10 weeks duration, and unemployment of 10 weeks duration and under, seasonally adjusted and expressed as a percentage of the civilian labor force. Published data on duration for prior years are classified by months and are therefore not comparable. The minimum long-duration unemployment for a twelve-month period occurs in the twelve months ending November 1953, when it was 0.5 per cent of the civilian labor force. Prior to the 1949 recession, the minimum for a twelve-month period was 0.8 per cent of the civilian labor force for the twelve months ending December 1948. In February 1949, the monthly series, seasonally adjusted, rises sharply above this level.

The series on long-duration unemployment has a much larger amplitude in the 1949 contraction than either short-duration unemployment or total unemployment. This, of course, is because it excludes most

[19] William H. Beveridge, *Unemployment: A Problem of Industry*, 2nd ed., London, Longmans, 1930, p. 114.

[20] This point is made with vehemence by H. W. Singer (*Unemployment and the Unemployed*, London, King, 1940, pp. 3-5). Singer also points out that "short duration" unemployment may start when a long period of unemployment is broken by a brief job.

CHART 3
Percentage of the Civilian Labor Force Unemployed, by Duration of Unemployment, 1947-1954

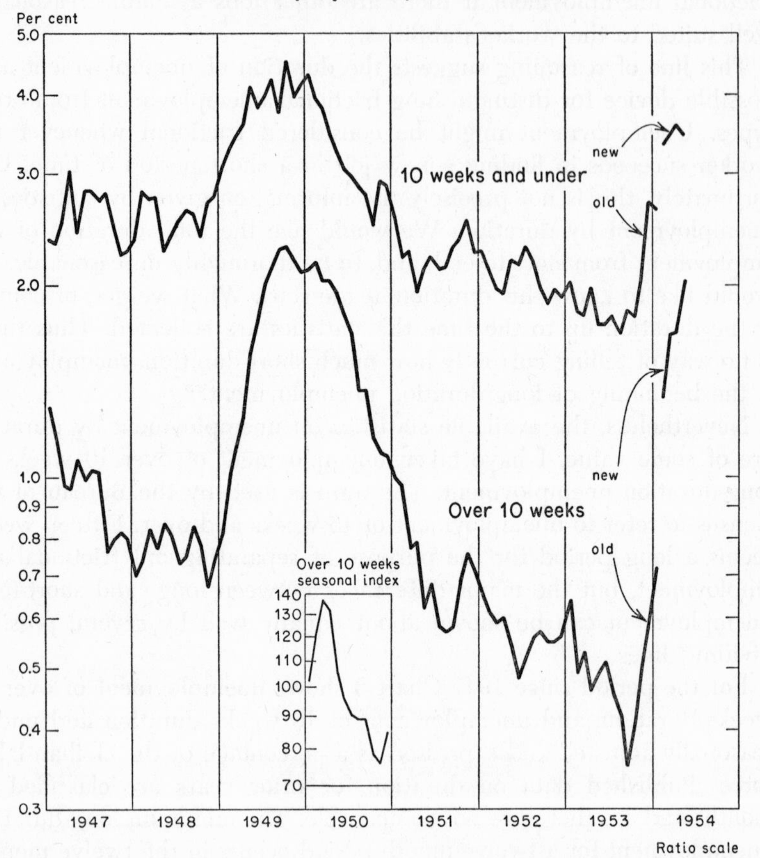

frictional unemployment. However, it does not represent only cyclical unemployment, for even at peaks in general business activity it includes between one-fifth and one-fourth of all unemployment. Long-duration unemployment at cyclical peaks represents largely the more stubborn frictions, those created by declining industries and localities. This kind of unemployment is sometimes called "structural." A second, though probably much less important, source of long-duration unemployment at cyclical peaks is the inclusion of marginal workers who are induced to seek work by tight labor market conditions but are nevertheless regarded by employers as unemployable. In American census statistics, the worker's concept of his own employability, as expressed in work-seeking activity, controls his inclusion.

The rise in short-duration unemployment during the contraction of 1948-1949 shows that this series includes some unemployment that is not frictional, because an unemployed worker must pass through this category to reach the long-duration category. For the same reason, one would expect the long-duration series to lag behind the short-duration series. Although this lag shows clearly in the seasonal patterns of the two series, it is not so evident at the cyclical turning points. The lag of long-duration unemployment at the trough in 1948 is too great to be explained on these grounds, and the two peaks coincide in 1949. At the trough in the fall of 1953, the one-month lag of long-duration unemployment is consistent with the reasoning above.

In addition to its greater cyclical amplitude, the long-duration series conforms more closely to the business cycle in its timing in 1948 than do short-duration or total unemployment. The trough in long-duration unemployment in November 1948 coincides with the peak in general economic activity as determined by the reference dates of the National Bureau of Economic Research. The trough in total unemployment leads the reference peak by eleven months; the trough in short-duration unemployment leads by twelve months. The series on long-duration unemployment is not used by the Bureau in setting reference dates; total unemployment is used.

The limited evidence available tends to support the conclusion that long-duration unemployment is a more reliable indicator of cycles in general business activity than total unemployment. It may therefore be more useful in formulating full-employment goals. It would probably be less useful for the quick detection of changes in business activity, since over a number of cycles long-duration unemployment might tend to lag at the reference turns.

MAXIMUM EMPLOYMENT APPROACH

The terms maximum employment and minimum unemployment are sometimes used interchangeably. By definition, employment plus unemployment equals the civilian labor force. The maximum ratio of employment to the population of working age would always coincide with the minimum ratio of unemployment to the population of working age if the rate of participation in the civilian labor force were always the same. Since it is not always the same, differences in timing between maximum employment and minimum unemployment are possible. However, only the effect of changes in the civilian labor force need be considered here, since in all other respects using maximum employment as a basis for defining full employment gives the same result as using minimum total unemployment.

As mentioned earlier, an autonomous reduction in labor-force participation is not considered a departure from full employment, but a change in the full-employment level. However, a change in labor-force participation induced by a reduction in demand should be considered capable of causing a departure from full employment. Here two kinds of effects are theoretically possible. The first is that predicted by the theory known as the "additional worker theory."[21] This theory holds that a depression increases the size of the labor force because the unemployment of primary wage earners (husbands and fathers) forces dependents to seek work. Exactly the opposite theory was widely advanced in the autumn and winter of 1953-1954. This theory holds that a decline in the demand for labor discourages some job seekers and induces them to leave the labor force.[22] The conflict between these theories concerns the direction of the net change in the labor force during contractions, since it is generally accepted that declining employment will produce some gross change in both directions. It is also possible that the net change would differ in direction at different stages of a contraction.

Since both theories regard the full-employment labor force as normal, neither would, if accepted, cause any change in the estimates of full-employment levels reached by the minimum total unemployment approach. Acceptance of either theory would, however, cause a change in the size of a departure from full employment as estimated from unemployment data. Although these theories are opposite in their basic content, each has been used to show that unemployment was underestimated by the statistics current at the time the theory was advanced. In 1940, when the additional worker theory was put forward, unemployment was estimated by subtracting employment estimates based on establishment reports from an estimate of the normal labor force extrapolated from the decennial census. If the estimate of the labor force was too low, so was the estimate of unemployment. At present, unemployment and employment are both estimated directly from household sample statistics. If a fall in the labor force is induced by lack of demand, the unemployment figure excludes an additional "disappearance of jobs" shown by the fall in employment.

The evidence concerning the effect of changes in demand on the labor force has been thoroughly reviewed by Clarence D. Long.[23] He

[21] See the literature cited by Clarence D. Long in "Impact of Effective Demand on the Labor Supply," *American Economic Review*, May 1953, p. 459, note 3.

[22] For one of numerous examples of this view see the letter by Emil Rieve, Chairman, C.I.O. Committee on Economic Policy, in the *New York Times*, January 21, 1954, p. 30.

[23] Long, *op.cit.*, and references cited therein.

concludes that the depression of the thirties caused a decline in labor-force participation of about 2 per cent of population in the United States, and that the business contraction of 1948-1949 caused no significant change in either direction. The series on civilian labor force used in this paper confirms Long's conclusion for 1948-1949.[24] Chart 4 shows no significant drop in labor-force participation during the 1948-1949 contraction.

CHART 4

Percentage of Civilian Noninstitutional Population Fourteen and Over in the Civilian Labor Force, 1946-1954

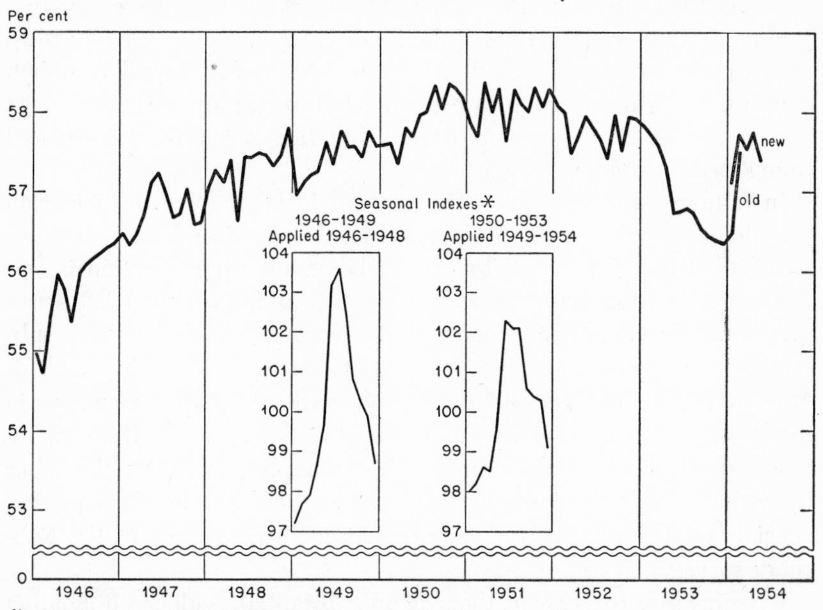

* Scale for plotting seasonal indexes is chosen so that 1 unit is equal to 1/2 unit in the series plotted, which results in approximately equal percentage changes.

The scale chosen is very large, to enable the detection of even a slight drop. This makes prominent the random fluctuation caused by imperfect seasonal adjustment and sampling variability. There is no reason to believe, however, that these sources of error would entirely obscure any cyclical pattern.[25]

[24] Long's data are quarterly and his seasonal adjustment is based on the years 1946-1948. The data used here are monthly and the seasonal adjustments are based on the years 1946-1949 and 1950-1953.

[25] The Bureau of the Census has estimated that the chances are about 19 out of 20 that the sampling variability of an estimate of the civilian labor force is less than approximately 1.2 per cent. The chances of error persisting over several months are smaller than the chances of error in a single month (see Long, *op.cit.*, p. 464).

The decline in labor-force participation which began in April 1953 and continued throughout the year gave rise to the theory that unemployment estimates understated the decline in the demand for labor late in the year. The theory, however, fails to explain why falling demand should cause falling labor-force participation in 1953, but not in 1949. The labor-force participation of women and of men 14 to 17 was slightly higher in March 1953 than in March 1948, but these differences seem insufficient to account for the differences in the subsequent behavior of this series. The theory that discouragement with the lack of job opportunities was the reason for withdrawal from the labor force in 1953 also fails to explain why workers were so easily discouraged. They apparently left the labor force too quickly to show up even briefly in unemployment statistics. The theory would be much more plausible if advanced to explain a fall in employment concurrent with a smaller rise in unemployment, but this is not what happened from April to August.[26]

In January and February 1954, the fall in labor-force participation was sharply reversed, and the general level of 1952 and the first quarter of 1953 was regained. This rise in labor-force participation is evident in data from both the old (68 area) and the new (230 area) samples. The rise in labor-force participation coincided with a substantial rise in unemployment, suggesting that it was not the result of increased demand. Nor did it coincide with any striking change in foreign relations or military commitments. It may result from an intensified effort of enumerators to get a complete count of the labor force; because of the January discrepancies between the two samples, special training sessions for enumerators were held prior to the February survey.

It seems safe to say that there is no substantial evidence upholding the view that labor-force participation declines when there are moderate decreases in the demand for labor. Therefore, in the absence of further evidence, there is no clear conceptual advantage in using employment data rather than unemployment data to measure the extent of departures from full employment, except in periods of severe de-

[26] The drop in labor-force participation in 1953 is discussed at some length in the *Economic Report of the President*, January 1954 (pp. 149-151). This discussion points to evidence that the demand for labor was still strong in the months when labor-force participation dropped most. It seeks to relate the drop to the "yielding of China on the prisoner-repatriation issue on March 28," and points to a similar drop under somewhat analogous circumstances in 1945.

Members of the staff of the Bureau of the Census regard this decline as an error of measurement rather than a real phenomenon. They point out that a large part of the decline in employment took place among government workers, for which there is no explanation.

pression.[27] Further evidence on the cause of changes in labor-force participation such as those of 1953-1954 might be obtained from seasonally adjusted monthly data on labor-force participation by sex and age groups.

TURNOVER APPROACH

Lack of adequate turnover data prevents using this approach to measure full employment. Nevertheless, it is worth exploring for the additional insights it gives into the full-employment concept.

The amount of unemployment can be considered as the product of two factors: the number of accessions (one measure of turnover), and the length of the period of work-seeking that precedes each accession.[28] The advantage of considering unemployment in this way is that it partially reduces reliance on historical minima that characterizes the definitions of full employment discussed previously. Full employment can now be defined as existing when the average duration of work-seeking per accession is at a minimum. A departure from full employment would arise if this duration increased (as shown later, this is not the same as the average duration of unemployment reported in unemployment statistics), but a departure would not arise if unemployment increased solely because the number of accessions rose, while average duration remained constant. This would mean only an increase in frictional unemployment arising from an increased amount of friction to be overcome. It could take place because of a greater inclination on the part of workers to change jobs or to move in and out of the labor force, which cannot be condemned as inherently bad.

[27] This statement is intended to apply to employment and unemployment data of equal accuracy. For some purposes, employment data based on establishment reports may be more accurate than sample-survey data on unemployment.

[28] Accessions rather than separations are the appropriate measure of turnover, since each accession can be thought of as preceded by a period of job-seeking. At the limit the length of this period is zero when no working time is lost between jobs, or a new entrant to the labor force begins work as soon as he enters. It is not true even in this sense that every separation is followed by a period of job-seeking, since many separations occur when workers die, retire, or leave the labor force for other reasons. Although a "common-sense" notion of unemployment views it as caused by layoffs and discharges, it is actually quite difficult to approach the number of instances of unemployment from the separations side. To do so we should have to take the total number of separations, subtract those occasioned by withdrawal from the labor force, and add the number of entries into the labor force. In approaching the problem from the accessions side, it is necessary to omit unemployment that is terminated by withdrawal from the labor force.

Other writers who use the turnover approach have not specified the concept of turnover involved; they speak simply of "job changes" (see Alvin H. Hansen, *Economic Policy and Full Employment*, McGraw-Hill, 1947, p. 108; Beveridge, *Full Employment in a Free Society*, pp. 127-128; and A. C. Pigou, *Unemployment*, London, Williams & Norgate, 1913, p. 29).

The number of accessions would be measured currently from turnover data; only the duration of work-seeking per accession would need to be taken as a historical minimum. The result would be a concept of minimum unemployment that changed through time with the amount of friction to be overcome. The unchanging portion of the concept can be viewed as the maximum efficiency previously achieved in overcoming given amounts of friction.

Two types of data on accessions are available for the United States, and neither is well suited to the purpose of this section. The Bureau of Labor Statistics publishes accession rates for manufacturing and for a few nonmanufacturing industries. These are conceptually correct for our purpose, but both incomplete in coverage and of somewhat doubtful accuracy as to level. The Bureau of the Census in its series on gross changes in the labor force estimates total additions to nonagricultural employment. These are complete in coverage but concern additions to nonagricultural employment taken as a whole, rather than accessions to the work force of individual employers. Thus shifts from unemployment, agricultural employment, and outside the labor force to nonagricultural employment are included in total additions to nonagricultural employment, but shifts from one employer to another within nonagricultural employment are excluded unless at least a week of unemployment or time spent outside the labor force intervenes between jobs. Complete turnover coverage could be obtained by adding questions to the monthly survey of the labor force. Each employed worker whose status as now defined had not changed since the preceding month would have to be asked whether he had changed employers, and each worker who had changed employers or become employed since the preceding month would have to be asked how long he had been without work while looking for his new job. From these answers, including the instances where the duration of work-seeking was zero, an average duration could be computed.

The possible use of such data can best be illustrated by a hypothetical example such as that shown in Table 1. This table assumes a labor market in which all separations and all accessions take place on the first day of each month. In "full-employment equilibrium" the workers hired are those who became unemployed on the first day of the preceding month, so that the average duration of unemployment is one month. This is the situation shown for month 1. In the succeeding months, a larger volume of unemployment is generated by a reduction in the number of accessions, then absorbed again as accessions rise. It is assumed that the first workers to become unemployed are the first to be rehired.

TABLE 1

A Hypothetical Example Showing the Relation of Turnover to Unemployment

Month (1)	Number of Separations (2)	Number of Accessions (3)	Number Unemployed During Month (4)	Average Duration of Completed[a] Unemployment (Months) (5)
1	100	100 (0)	100 (1)	1
2	100	50 (1)	50 (1)	
			100 (2)	
			150	1
3	100	0	50 (1)	
			100 (2)	
			100 (3)	
			250	. . .
4	100	50 (1)	100 (2)	
			100 (3)	
			100 (4)	
			300	3
5	100	100 (2)	100 (3)	
			100 (4)	
			100 (5)	
			300	3
6	100	100 (3)	100 (5)	
		100 (4)	100 (6)	
		200	200	2.5
7	100	100 (5)		
		100 (6)		
		200	100 (7)	1.5
8	150	100 (7)	150 (8)	1
9	150	150 (8)	150 (9)	1

[a] Derived from the detail of column 3. These figures refer to the average duration of unemployment of those hired in each month.

Note: Figures in parentheses refer to the month in which workers were separated from their previous jobs.

Starting with month 8, the number of separations rises to 150, and the number of accessions rises correspondingly starting with month 9. This increases the level of unemployment; however, it does not represent a new departure from full employment, as might be inferred from the number of unemployed alone. This can be seen by looking at the average duration of unemployment, which does not rise. The average duration figures of this example show completed duration, unlike usual duration data, which show duration up to the time of a count of the unemployed. Completed duration data would also differ in practice by including the instances of zero duration (which do not occur in the example). These, of course, cannot be obtained from a count of the unemployed.

Only statistics of completed duration can be combined with the number of accessions to produce a volume of unemployment. In practice, however, similar conclusions could be drawn from the usual duration data. A rise in unemployment without a rise in its average duration implies increased turnover even though the corresponding turnover data are not available. Hence the collection of complete turnover data may not be worth the costs involved. The concept is nevertheless useful in clarifying the problem of measuring full employment.

UNFILLED VACANCIES APPROACH

This approach to the measurement of full employment is suggested by the definition of Lord Beveridge that full employment "means having always more vacant jobs than unemployed men."[29] Definitions based on a ratio of unemployment to unfilled vacancies are completely free from the dependence on historical experience that is present in the definitions discussed previously. Instead, the standard is taken from the kind of balance that is desired in the labor market. Whereas a historical minimum provides a unique standard, the unfilled vacancies approach permits selection from a broad continuum of standards. At one extreme are large and constant excesses of vacancies over unemployed workers, in the middle is an approximate equality between the two, and at the other extreme are excesses of unemployed workers over vacancies not exceeding specified limits. The choice of a standard along this continuum will depend on the relative strength of the desires to avoid unemployment and to avoid inflation.

The measurement of ratios of unemployment to vacancies requires data on the number of unfilled vacancies—the best source of these is an extensive and widely used system of public employment offices. For the United States, no data are available.[30]

Canada publishes complete data on the unfilled vacancies listed at

[29] Beveridge, *Full Employment in a Free Society*, p. 18.

[30] Data are published on the number of unfilled vacancies "in clearance," i.e. those of which notice was sent to employment service offices other than the one where they originated because they could not be filled locally. These are only a part of the total number of listed vacancies, which in turn are only a small part of the vacancies in the economy.

employment service offices. However, as in the United States, the use of the employment service is voluntary for employers and is by no means universal. Hence even in years of low unemployment, the number of unemployed greatly exceeds the number of listed vacancies. For 1951, a year of very low unemployment in Canada, the average number of unemployed at the dates of the quarterly surveys of the labor force was 109,000. For the four first of the month dates closest to these surveys, the average number of unfilled vacancies was only 55,000. Despite the incompleteness of Canadian data on vacancies, they have been used to compute a series of ratios of unfilled vacancies to applications for employment;[31] the results do not seem to be very useful in defining levels of full employment, although the movements of the series are informative.

For Great Britain, it is possible to compute ratios of unemployed workers to unfilled vacancies for the period since late 1947. During most of this period, the listing of vacancies with employment exchanges was compulsory for most employers. During the rest of the period, use of the exchanges was voluntary, but so widespread that the changes from a compulsory to a voluntary basis and back to a compulsory basis again produce only minor breaks in the series.

The top line of Chart 5 shows the number of wholly unemployed per 100 unfilled vacancies, seasonally adjusted, for Great Britain since October 1947. The series is shown in three segments: during the first period, from October 1947 to February 1950, the amended Control of Engagements Order was in effect; during the second period, from March 1950 to February 1952, there was no compulsion to list vacancies; during the third period, from March 1952 on, the Notification of Vacancies Order was in effect. The height of the breaks between segments shows the approximate effect of these administrative changes. Workers who are temporarily stopped have been excluded from the unemployment data, since they are presumably not seeking new jobs.[32] The number of vacancies listed is less than the total number of vacancies in Great Britain even for the periods of compulsory listing. This is true for two reasons: (1) some industries and some groups of workers are excluded from the provisions of the Notification of Vacancies Order, and (2) some employers give standing orders to the employment exchanges to refer all suitable applicants without specifying a number of vacancies. The extent of the resulting understatement of vacancies cannot be estimated from published data but could perhaps be esti-

[31] See Emile Benoit-Smullyan, "On the Meaning of Full Employment," *Review of Economic Statistics*, May 1948, p. 132.

[32] For further details on the derivation of this series, see Appendix Note 5.

CHART 5

Number Wholly Unemployed and Wholly Unemployed per 100 Unfilled Vacancies, Great Britain, 1947-1954

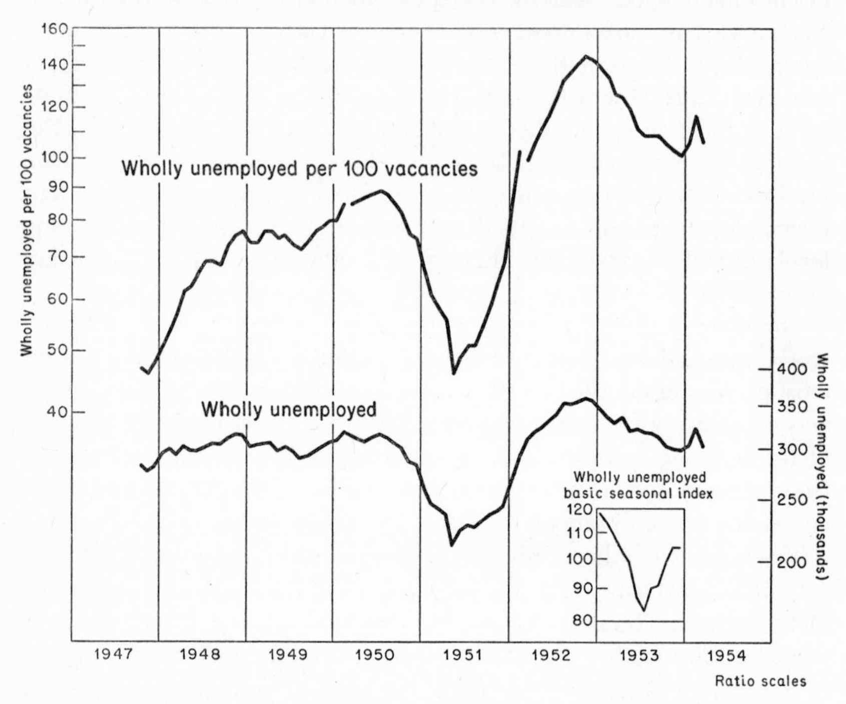

mated by the Ministry of Labour. Despite the understatement of vacancies, the number of unemployed per 100 unfilled vacancies was consistently below 100 from September 1947 to January 1952.

The bottom line of Chart 5 shows the number of wholly unemployed, seasonally adjusted. The general shape of the two series is very similar, but the relative amplitude of fluctuations in the ratio of unemployed to vacancies is much greater than that of fluctuations in unemployment. This extreme sensitivity of the ratio arises because it records changes in the labor market simultaneously from both sides; the same forces that produce a rise in unemployment also produce a fall in unfilled vacancies, and the ratio reflects them in both terms. Users of such a ratio must take care that its sensitivity does not create undue concern over what are really small changes in labor market conditions. However, this sensitivity does not seem to create erratic or random fluctuation; on the contrary, the series of ratios is smoother than either of the component series, indicating a tendency for random movements of one component to be cancelled or damped by movements of the other.

This series of ratios permits a comparison of Lord Beveridge's verbal definition of full employment with his numerical definition, and with the official definition of the government of the United Kingdom. Beveridge's numerical definition is that full employment exists when the number of unemployed does not exceed 3 per cent of the number of employees.[33] This includes an allowance for seasonal unemployment. The official definition is in effect the same; the full-employment standard is "a level of unemployment of 3 per cent at the seasonal peak."[34] Statistics consistent in concept with this definition are not published for the United Kingdom but are published for Great Britain. Since the definition is stated in terms of the seasonal peak, only data for the peak month of unemployment (January) can be compared with the definition. If the definition had been stated in terms of seasonally adjusted data, it would not be subject to this limitation.

Since the ratios presented here are based on an incomplete reporting of vacancies, the condition of Beveridge's verbal definition that the number of vacancies exceed the number of unemployed will still be satisfied when the ratio stands at or perhaps somewhat above 100. It was not this high at any time from September 1947 to January 1952. In February 1952 it reached 103. In this month, when seasonal unemployment is near its peak, the unadjusted unemployment rate for Great Britain was 1.9 per cent. In January 1953, the ratio was 139; the unemployment rate, 2.2. In January 1954, the ratio was 105; the unemployment rate, 1.8. These ratios show less than full employment by Beveridge's verbal definition, unless the number of unreported vacancies was large. At the same time, there was more than full employment by the 3 per cent definition. It seems probable that for Great Britain, Beveridge's verbal definition of full employment would never permit as much as 3 per cent unemployment at the seasonal peak. However, at the time that he first used it, available statistics did not permit its translation into numerical terms by the means used here.

PRICE APPROACH

The fear has frequently been expressed that full employment, as defined in many of the ways previously discussed, could be attained only at the cost of inflation. Very low levels of unemployment can be

[33] Beveridge, *Full Employment in a Free Society*, pp. 126-128.

[34] Reply of the Government of the United Kingdom in *Problems of Unemployment and Inflation, 1950 and 1951* (United Nations, 1951, p. 80). This official standard was announced in Parliament on March 22, 1951. The concept differs from that of unemployment as a percentage of the civilian labor force by excluding from the base the self-employed and unpaid family workers. On the larger base, it would be about 0.025 per cent less. The numerator includes the "temporarily stopped."

reached by creating a vast demand for goods and services, which eliminates all unemployment except frictional and reduces the amount of frictional unemployment by shortening the time needed to find jobs. However, the creation of a vast demand for goods and services must also tend to raise prices. Recent experience in a number of countries seems to show that this is more than a theoretical problem. In the post-war years, Australia, Sweden, and the United Kingdom, among other countries, have experienced a combination of extremely low unemployment and very sharp increases in the price level.

The selection of a definition of full employment that would not be inflationary if adopted as a guide to policy can be made in several ways. A historical minimum of unemployment can be used as a starting point, but increased by an arbitrary allowance to reduce the danger of inflation if the previous minimum of unemployment was reached under conditions of rising prices. A ratio of unemployed workers to unfilled vacancies can be selected that is high enough to reduce the dangers of inflation. Finally, specifications about price behavior can be written into the definition of full employment. The last approach is the one chosen by Bertil Ohlin, who defines full employment as "the degree of employment that exists when the aggregate demand for commodities is at the highest level that is compatible with the condition that demand at existing prices is balanced by current domestic supply."[35]

This definition is one of a large family of possible definitions in which the goals of maximum employment or minimum unemployment are subjected to various kinds of constraints. For the constraint of stable prices could be substituted, for example, prices declining at specified rates, a constant or slowly rising quantity of money, or the maintenance of a fixed rate of exchange with some foreign currency. The question naturally arises whether such definitions are definitions of full employment in anything more than a purely formal sense; that is, do they imply reasonably low levels of unemployment? The discussion here will be restricted to the constraint of stable prices, both because it arises out of dangers that may be inherent in some unconstrained definitions of full employment, and because there is reason to believe that it does not restrict the concept of full employment so severely as to make it such in form but not in fact.

One would naturally expect some relation between the cyclical movements of employment and prices, because both are influenced by the general level of demand. The question is really how closely are the two

[35] Bertil Ohlin, *The Problem of Employment Stabilization*, Columbia University Press, 1949, p. 6. The word "domestic" precludes obtaining the necessary supply from abroad by means of foreign credits or the depletion of gold or foreign exchange reserves. The word "current" precludes obtaining it by drawing down inventories.

movements related.[36] In particular, does large scale unemployment persist during business expansions once prices have regained the level at which they are to be stabilized? If Ohlin's definition implies a policy of "choking off" some expansions, at what point does this occur?

In order to investigate these questions, some of the terms of the definition must be specified more precisely; these specifications are not necessarily the ones that Ohlin would have chosen. First, a way of measuring prices must be specified. I have chosen a general index of wholesale prices, largely because wholesale prices are more flexible than retail prices.[37]

The selection of a price index permits a search for data that will help in clarifying the cyclical relation of prices to unemployment. The data required are a monthly index of wholesale prices and a monthly series showing unemployment or employment. There should be no breaks in the statistical continuity of the series. The period should cover several business cycles, including some whose peaks reach high levels of employment, and it should exclude such extraneous disturbances as major wars.

These requirements are difficult to meet. In the postwar period, normal relationships between prices and employment have been distorted in many countries by direct price controls and currency devaluations. No major free economy had high levels of employment during most of the 1930's, and the further back in time one goes, the fewer are the countries for which adequate data on both prices and employment are available.

I have selected the following countries, time periods, and statistical series as offering the best available tests of the relationships between prices and employment or unemployment at high employment levels:

1. *Great Britain, 1887-1913.* The Sauerbeck wholesale price index and the seasonally adjusted percentage of unemployment among trade unionists[38]

[36] This question was of great interest to Irving Fisher. For some pioneering investigation of this area, see his "Employment and the Price Level" in *Stabilization of Employment*, C. F. Roos, editor, Principia Press, 1933; and "A Statistical Relation between Unemployment and Price Changes," *International Labour Review*, June 1926, pp. 785-792.

[37] The literature on price stabilization as a guide to counter-cyclical policy contains several discussions of the characteristics of a desirable index to stabilize (see Irving Fisher, *Stabilizing the Dollar*, Macmillan, 1925, pp. 149ff.; Henry C. Simons, "Rules versus Authorities in Monetary Policy," *Journal of Political Economy*, February 1936, pp. 12-13; and Lloyd W. Mints, *Monetary Policy for a Competitive Society*, McGraw-Hill, 1950, p. 129). These writers all conclude that wholesale price indexes are the best available indexes to use as guides to stabilization policy.

[38] Both series have serious defects for this purpose. The Sauerbeck price index is overweighted with imported commodities, and the trade union unemployment rate covers only a small and cyclically unstable portion of the economy. Against

2. *United States, 1919-1929.* The BLS wholesale price index and the BLS index of factory employment, seasonally adjusted

3. *United States, 1946-1953.* The BLS wholesale price index, and unemployment as a percentage of the civilian labor force, seasonally adjusted

The last period is included despite its shortness because it is of the greatest current interest, and the data are the most adequate.

For periods 1 and 2 the dates of the peaks and troughs in prices and employment are shown in Table 2. The expected general correspondence is clearly present. There is a cycle in unemployment or employment for every cycle in prices. The converse is also true, except that there is nothing in the wholesale price series corresponding to the sharp but brief rise in unemployment in Great Britain from May to November of 1897. There is a generally close correspondence in timing between the peaks in wholesale prices and the peaks in employment or in unemployment inverted. At the troughs, the correspondence in timing is usually not close.

Before examining further the relevance of these data to Ohlin's definition of full employment, it is necessary to specify more precisely another term in the definition. The definition speaks of "existing prices" without any time referent. If prices are stabilized at a time of widespread unemployment the result will not be full employment in any meaningful sense. Widespread unemployment could probably not be eliminated without some increase in the price level. "Existing prices" should refer to those existing in a period of high employment. However, one cannot use the concept of high employment in the definition without making it completely circular. I have therefore substituted for "existing prices" the previous peak in the price index, relying on the correspondence in peaks between prices and employment to insure that this defines a price level compatible with high levels of employment.[39] The Ohlin rule as thus interpreted would not require a full-employ-

---

these disadvantages must be set the great advantage of consistent series covering a long period unbroken by major extraneous disturbances. For a discussion of this unemployment series, see Beveridge, *Unemployment: A Problem of Industry*, pp. 16-23. For discussion of the price series, see the *Journal of the Royal Statistical Society*, March 1921, pp. 255-277.

[39] The rule is generally a reasonable one, but may produce undesirable results in two cases. The first is that in which wholesale prices at their last peak were temporarily abnormally high, as in 1920. The second is that in which wholesale prices at their peak are below a former well-established level, and unemployment is still high, as in 1937. In some such cases, the level of the next to the last peak would be used; this might have been appropriate in 1939 and 1940. In other such cases, a maximum permissible price level would have to be chosen arbitrarily; this would have been necessary in 1922.

TABLE 2

Peaks and Troughs in Prices and Employment, Great Britain, 1887-1913, and United States, 1919-1929

GREAT BRITAIN, 1887-1913				UNITED STATES, 1919-1929			
Wholesale Prices		*Trade Union Unemployment Rate, Inverted*		*Wholesale Prices*		*Index of Factory Employment*	
Peaks	*Troughs*	*Peaks*	*Troughs*	*Peaks*	*Troughs*	*Peaks*	*Troughs*
	June 1888				Feb. 1919		March 1919
Dec. 1889	July 1896	Jan. 1890	Dec. 1892	May 1920	Jan. 1922	Jan. 1920	July 1921
		May 1897	Nov. 1897	March 1923	June 1924	June 1923	July 1924
July 1900	Nov. 1902	Oct. 1899	May 1904	Nov. 1925	June 1927	Jan. 1926	Jan. 1928
May 1907	Feb. 1909	April 1907	Oct. 1908	Sept. 1928		Aug. 1929	
March 1913		Nov. 1912					

ment policy to undo past inflation but would require it to prevent future inflation, in the sense of prices that reach new high levels.

The paired price and unemployment series can now be used to form a rough notion of the amount of unemployment compatible with the definition. This is done by discovering the instances in which prices regained a former peak and observing the level and trend of unemployment when this price level was regained. Too much importance should not be attached to the exact point when this occurs, since if prices were stabilized at this level, employment might continue to rise for a time, though perhaps not as rapidly as it would have if prices had continued to rise.

The British series from 1887 to 1913 (Chart 6) afford three instances when peaks in wholesale prices were regained. The first of these occurred in January 1900, when prices regained their December 1889 level. The seasonally adjusted trade union unemployment rate for January 1900 was 1.9 per cent; its low of 1.8 per cent had been reached three months previously. Prices continued to rise until July 1900, and during this period the unemployment rate rose to 2.5 per cent. Monetary and fiscal policy that would have held down prices during this period might therefore have accelerated the rise in unemployment. The trade union unemployment rate was still relatively low at the end of the period. In three depressions between 1885 and 1913 it reached 9 per cent.

The second instance of a regained peak in prices occurred in April 1906, when prices regained the peak of July 1900. The unemployment rate for April 1906 was 3.6 per cent; its trough was 3.1 per cent in April 1907. The same level was also reached in September 1906. A policy that held down prices during 1906 and the early months of 1907 would probably have prevented the unemployment rate from falling this low.

The third instance of a regained peak in prices occurred in February 1912, when prices regained the level of May 1907. The unemployment rate in February 1912 was 2.9 per cent. The trough of 1.7 per cent was reached in November, and a policy of holding down prices would again have prevented the trough from being so low.

It can be concluded that employment in Great Britain was overfull in three instances during this period, according to this definition, but that the levels of unemployment implied by the definition would nevertheless have been reasonably low. In the United States from 1919 to 1929 employment was never overfull, since wholesale prices never surpassed their previous peaks.

The last instance of a regained peak in wholesale prices occurred

CHART 6

Unemployment and Wholesale Prices, Great Britain, 1887-1913

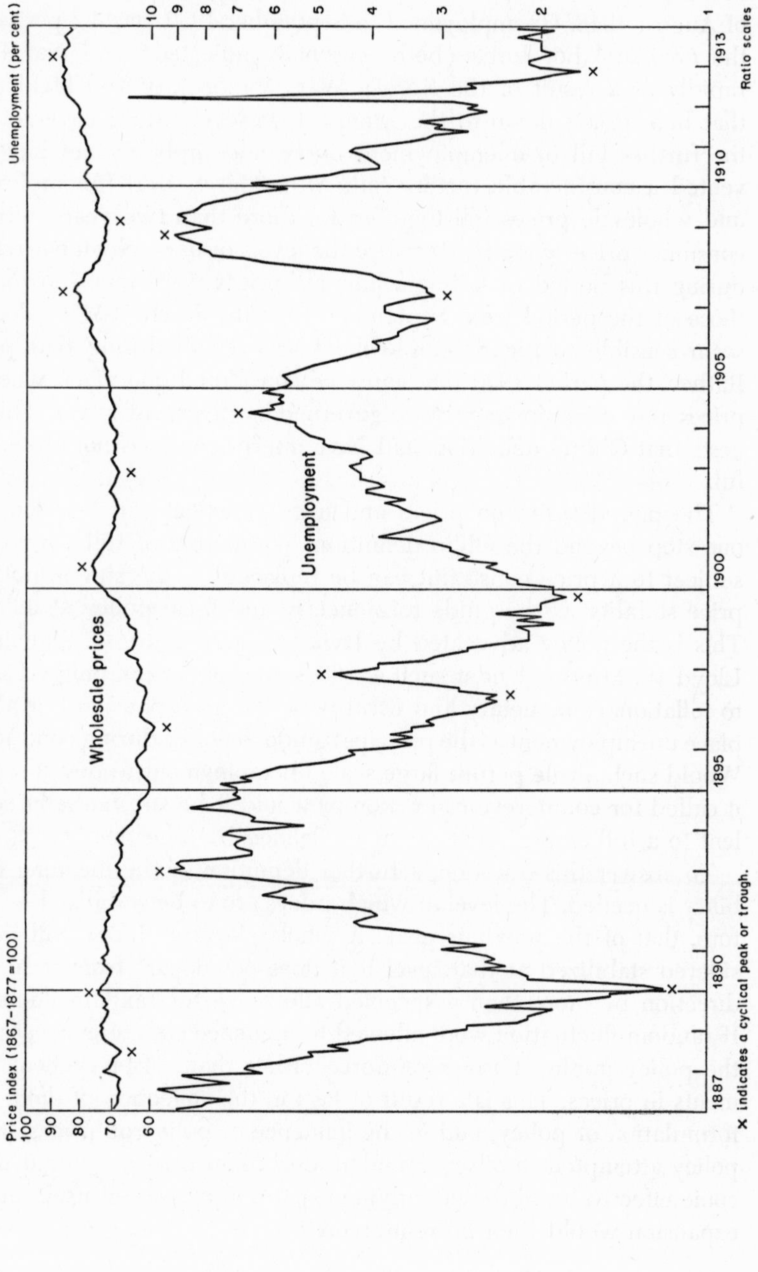
Price index (1867-1877=100)
100
90
80
70
60
Unemployment (per cent)
10
9
8
7
6
5
4
3
2
1
Wholesale prices
Unemployment
1887
1890
1895
1900
1905
1910
1913
Ratio scales
x indicates a cyclical peak or trough.

in the United States in September 1950, when prices regained the level of August 1948. Unemployment in September 1950 was 4.2 per cent of the civilian labor force (both seasonally adjusted) and was falling rapidly as a result of the Korean War. A monetary and fiscal policy that held prices down to the August 1948 level would have retarded the further fall in unemployment but would probably not have prevented a considerable further fall. After March 1951, unemployment and wholesale prices fell together for more than two years, although consumer prices were rising. Since the levels of unemployment reached during this period of falling wholesale prices were much lower than those of the period from September 1950 to March 1951, it does not seem sensible to regard employment as overfull during that period. Rather, the period 1950-1953 must be considered one when wholesale prices and unemployment were governed by divergent forces. This suggests that Ohlin's definition, as I have interpreted it, is not always useful.

The paired series on prices and unemployment can be used to go one step beyond the Ohlin definition. The notion of full employment subject to a price constraint can be replaced by the simple notion of price stability as the guide to monetary and fiscal policy at all times. This is the policy advocated by Irving Fisher, Henry C. Simons, and Lloyd W. Mints.[40] Under such a rule, stable prices not only set a limit to inflationary monetary and fiscal policy in an expansion but also replace unemployment as the principal guide to policy during contractions. Would such a rule permit large-scale unemployment to develop before it called for countercyclical action or would it be substantially equivalent to a full-employment policy as defined by other methods?

To answer this question, a further definition of the meaning of stability is needed. The level at which prices are to be stabilized is, as before, that of the previous peak. A wholesale price index will be considered stabilized at that level if it does not depart from it in either direction by more than a specified allowance for random fluctuation. If random fluctuation were allowed to influence countercyclical policy, the policy might at times reinforce rather than offset cyclical movements in prices. This is a result of lags in the collection of data, in the formulation of policy, and in the influence of policy on prices. Thus if policy attempted to offset a random decline in prices, it might not become effective until the underlying expansion reasserted itself, and this expansion would then be reinforced.[41]

[40] See the works cited in note 37.

[41] For fuller discussion of this point, see Mints, *op.cit.*, p. 140, and Milton Friedman, "A Monetary and Fiscal Framework for Economic Stability," *American Economic Review*, June 1948, pp. 254-258.

I have determined the allowance for random movement for each series by examining such random movements[42] over the period for which it was used. For the Sauerbeck index for Great Britain, 1885-1913, an allowance of 4 per cent was necessary, because of the small coverage of the index and the high proportion of sensitive prices included. Two random rises and one random decline during the period exceeded this allowance. For the BLS wholesale price index for the United States, an allowance of 3 per cent was made for the period 1919-1929, and 2 per cent for 1946-1953. No random movements during these periods exceeded these allowances.

The effect of a stable price policy during contractions can be roughly estimated by determining the points at which declines in wholesale prices clearly become more than random, and observing the level and trend of unemployment of these points. The instances that will permit the most unemployment under such a policy are those when the peak in prices lags behind the trough in unemployment (the peak in unemployment inverted). Three lags of more than one month are shown in Table 2. In Great Britain, the peak in wholesale prices of July 1900 lagged 9 months behind the trough in unemployment. The decline in wholesale prices exceeded the allowance for random fluctuation in January 1901, when the unemployment rate had reached 2.9 per cent. A lag of 4 months in the peak of prices behind the trough in unemployment occurred in 1913. The decline in prices exceeded the allowance for random fluctuation in March 1914, when the unemployment rate was 2.2 per cent. The third substantial lag shown on the table occurs in the United States in 1920. The decline in prices exceeded the allowance for random fluctuation in August 1920. From January to August the seasonally adjusted index of factory employment declined from 116 to 106 (1923-1925=100) but in August it was still at a relatively high level.[43] The final instance of a lag is not shown in Table 2; in 1948 in the United States the peak in wholesale prices lagged nine months behind the trough in unemployment. By December 1948 the decline in wholesale prices exceeded the allowance for random fluctuation. Unemployment in December 1948 was 3.5 per cent of the civilian labor force, compared with 3.1 per cent at its trough in December 1947 (see Chart 7), and an average of 3.3 per cent for the 12 months ending October 1948 (then the lowest 12 month average since World War II).

These four cases suggest that using wholesale prices as a principal guide to countercyclical policy would not delay action in contractions

[42] As used here, a random movement means a movement that does not constitute a specific cycle in the method of analyzing cycles used by the National Bureau of Economic Research.

[43] The rule was probably not appropriate during this contraction (see note 39).

CHART 7
Wholesale Prices and Percentage of Civilian Labor Force Unemployed, United States, 1946-1954

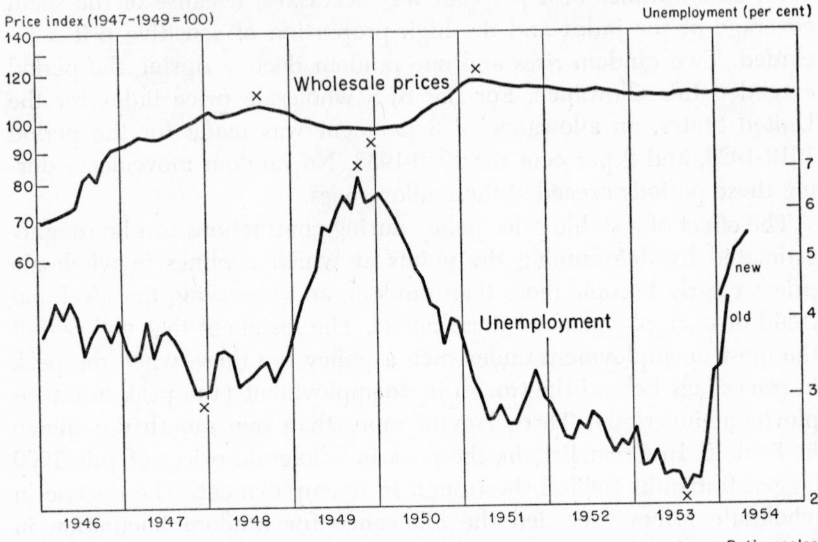

to a point where large amounts of unemployment were tolerated. The real anomalies created by the price stability rule lie in the opposite direction, and occur when the peak in wholesale prices leads the trough in unemployment. Two instances of long leads have occurred in the United States since 1919. The first occurred when the peak in wholesale prices in September 1928 led the peak in factory employment by 11 months (see Chart 8). The decline in wholesale prices exceeded the allowance for random fluctuation in February 1929. In this month the index of factory employment stood at 105, its highest level since 1923, and it continued to rise to 108 in August. The second instance occurred when the peak in wholesale prices in March 1951 led the tentative trough in unemployment of August 1953 by 29 months. The decline in wholesale prices exceeded the allowance for random fluctuation in July 1951. In this month unemployment was 2.7 per cent of the civilian labor force, the lowest since World War II, and it continued to fall thereafter. In these two instances, a policy of preventing declines in the wholesale price level would have resulted in still tighter labor markets, and probably in unintended rises in consumer prices and in wages. This dilemma could perhaps be averted by selecting some lower level of prices as the goal of price stabilization, but only at the cost of permitting greater unemployment in other contractions.

CHART 8
Index of Factory Employment and Wholesale Price Index, United States, 1919-1930

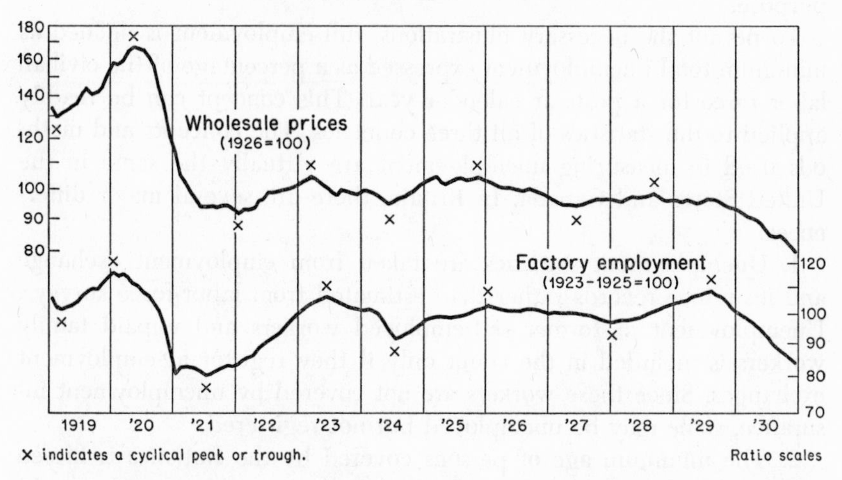

This analysis has been designed more to suggest methods of further exploration than to provide any definitive statement of the relations between prices and unemployment. It has suggested that Ohlin's definition of full employment may be a reasonable one. However, the further departure from usual concepts of full employment implied in the Fisher-Simons-Mints rule leads to new difficulties. Some definitions of full employment raise problems by implying that monetary and fiscal policy should be guided by unemployment to the point of becoming useless as weapons against inflation; similarly the Fisher-Simons-Mints rule may mean concentration on wholesale prices to the point of ignoring important contraindications in employment and elsewhere. It appears that modern economies are too complex to be guided by any one simple rule; the alternatives are a set of rules more complicated than those that I have tried to test, some reliance on judgment and discretion in counter-cyclical policy, or complete reliance on "built in stabilizers."

3. *Factors Affecting the Level of Full Employment*

The third section of this paper will consider briefly the sources of differences that develop over time or exist between countries in the level of full employment as defined and measured in some one way. For purposes of illustrating these differences, comparisons will be made between the United States and Great Britain, and between the United States and Canada. The illustration of differences over time in full-employment levels in the United States is not possible, because such differences develop slowly, and the relevant statistics for widely separated points in time cannot be made sufficiently comparable for the purpose.

To permit the necessary illustrations, full employment is defined as minimum total unemployment expressed as a percentage of the civilian labor force for a postwar calendar year. This concept can be readily applied to the statistics of all three countries. The concepts and methods used in measuring unemployment are virtually the same in the United States and Canada. In Britain, there are several major differences:

1. Unemployment statistics are taken from employment exchange and insurance records rather than estimated from labor-force surveys. Unemployment of former self-employed workers and unpaid family workers is included in the count only if they register at employment exchanges. Since these workers are not covered by unemployment insurance, some may be unemployed but not registered.

2. The minimum age of persons covered by the statistics is fifteen years rather than fourteen years.

3. The statistics include all persons registered as seeking work on a given *day*. Canadian and United States statistics cover persons who did not work as much as one hour for a full *week*.

Differences 1 and 2 would lead to a lower count of unemployment in Great Britain than in the other two countries. Difference 3 would lead to a higher count, and is by far the most important. On grounds of differences in concept alone, one would therefore expect minimum levels of unemployment to be higher in Great Britain than in the United States or Canada.

The postwar calendar year of lowest unemployment in the United States was 1953. Since all of the data for 1953 needed in making international comparisons are not yet available, I have used 1952, when unemployment was 2.7 per cent of the civilian labor force in the United States. For Great Britain, the postwar calendar year of lowest unemployment was 1951, when the wholly unemployed were 1.1 per cent of the civilian labor force (working population).[44] In Canada, 1947 and 1951 were the two years of lowest unemployment, with 2.0 and 2.1 per cent unemployed respectively. As this difference is too small to be of much significance, I have used 1951 to keep the comparisons closer together in time.

The year 1952 in the United States and the year 1951 in Canada and

[44] This estimate was obtained by dividing the mid-monthly figures for the wholly unemployed by simple averages of adjacent end-of-month figures for the civilian working population.

Great Britain were years of intense demand. There is no assurance, however, that this intensity of demand was exactly equal in the three cases. This may create differences in the minimum unemployment rates that cannot be taken into account in the discussion that follows.

COMPOSITION OF THE LABOR FORCE

The composition of the labor force by race, age, sex, industry, and class of worker influences the minimum rate of unemployment, because different categories of workers have different minimum unemployment rates. If the minimum unemployment rate for each category remained the same, that for the whole economy could change through shifts in the distribution of workers among the various categories. The structure of minimum unemployment rates for various types of workers is rooted in differences that for the most part seem persistent and present in many economies. Several examples can be given. Very young workers have high unemployment rates because they move in and out of the labor force frequently, and their lack of experience makes it harder for them to find work. Construction workers have high unemployment rates because their work is seasonal and turnover is frequent. Self-employed workers have very low unemployment rates, since lack of demand usually affects them through reduced earnings rather than loss of work. Thus in 1952 the unemployment rate in the United States was 2.4 per cent for all males, 3.1 per cent for all females, and 7.6 for males 14 to 19 years of age. In 1952 the unemployment rate for the experienced civilian labor force (which excludes work seekers who never held full-time civilian jobs) was 2.4 per cent; for construction workers it was 5.5 per cent, and for self-employed workers, 0.9 per cent.

The extent to which differences in the composition of the labor force are responsible for differences in the minimum unemployment levels of the three countries can be estimated by determining what the United States unemployment rate for 1952 would have been if its labor force composition had been like that of Canada or Great Britain in 1951. In other words, the United States unemployment rates for various categories are reweighted by the weights appropriate to the other countries.

For Great Britain, weights by age, sex, and major industry group can be obtained for 1951. Class of worker is not available, and race is not relevant. When the United States 1952 unemployment rate for the experienced labor force (2.4 per cent) is weighted by the 1951 industry distribution of British employment it rises to 2.5.[45] When the

[45] The categories used are mining; transportation, utilities, and communication; agriculture and fisheries; manufacturing; construction; distribution; finance and services; and government. The British data exclude the unemployed and include the self-employed.

United States unemployment rate for the civilian labor force in 1952 (2.7 per cent) is weighted by the age and sex composition of British wage and salary workers and unemployed, it rises to 2.8.[46] The principal cause of the difference is the larger proportion of young workers in the British labor force, despite the 15-year minimum age in British employment statistics.

Measurable differences in labor force composition between Great Britain and the United States thus fail to explain the differences in minimum unemployment rates. It is possible, though not likely, that unmeasurable differences in class of worker and detailed industry composition would work in the opposite direction.

For Canada, data for 1951 are available by major industry group, class of worker, and sex, but not by age. These data are averages of four quarterly labor force surveys, except that employment in nonagricultural industries was not available for the November survey. The averages of the other three surveys had to be used as estimates of the annual averages. When the unemployment rate of the United States experienced labor force for 1952 (2.4 per cent) is weighted by the Canadian distribution by industry and class of worker it drops to 2.2.[47] When the United States rate for the civilian labor force in 1952 (2.7 per cent) is weighted by the sex distribution of the Canadian labor force it drops to 2.6. These differences account for roughly half of the difference in minimum unemployment rates between the United States and Canada.

Trends in the composition of the United States labor force do not suggest any clear direction of future change in minimum unemployment rates. The secular increase in labor force participation by women and the secular decrease in the importance of agriculture may tend to raise minimum unemployment rates. This may be offset to some extent by the secular rise in the age at which workers enter the labor force.

LABOR TURNOVER

For any given composition of the labor force, changes in the minimum unemployment rate over time, or differences in it between coun-

[46] The rate for United States workers aged fourteen to nineteen was weighted by the number of British workers aged fifteen to nineteen.

[47] In making these estimates, assumptions had to be made about the distribution by class of worker of 32,000 Canadian workers in fishing and trapping, and 118,000 in forestry. It was assumed that all of the former were self-employed, and all of the latter were wage and salary workers. These assumptions both involve errors, although the errors are offsetting to some extent.

An unemployment rate for the United States for government and services combined was obtained by weighting the separate rates by employment of full- and part-time employees as estimated by the National Income Division of the Department of Commerce (*Survey of Current Business*, July 1953, p. 20).

tries will depend largely on labor turnover. In this is included both the number of accessions and the length of time needed to find a job. The first depends on the net rate of growth of the labor force, the rate of gross addition to the labor force, and the rate of mobility within the labor force. The second depends on the intensity of demand and the efficiency with which the labor market is organized. The extent of seasonal fluctuation in industry affects both gross additions to the labor force and mobility within the labor force, which in turn is influenced by the desire of workers to move, by changes in technology, and changes in the composition of demand.

Many of the factors just listed cannot be measured with available statistics for any one country, much less compared between countries. The net growth of the labor force, a relatively minor factor, is available for all three countries. For the United States from January 1952 to January 1953 the civilian labor force grew 1.0 per cent. In Great Britain, the civilian working population grew 0.4 per cent from December 31, 1950 to December 31, 1951. In Canada, the civilian labor force grew 1.3 per cent from March 3, 1951 to March 1, 1952. These data explain a very small part of the lower unemployment rate in Great Britain.

Data on the accession rate in all manufacturing are available for the United States and Great Britain. For 1952, the annual average monthly accession rate for United States manufacturing was 4.4 per hundred workers; for British manufacturing it was 3.2.[48] The real difference is probably larger than these figures indicate. There is a considerable understatement of accessions in manufacturing by the United States data, arising from sampling bias.[49] A corresponding understatement may be present in British data but must be very much smaller, since these data are based on reports from all employers in manufacturing with more than 10 employees. A second source of understatement is present in the British data but not in the American. The British data do not show accessions of workers who were separated later in the same reporting period (4 to 6 weeks). On the whole, the degree of understatement is probably less, perhaps much less, in the British data.

I can only speculate on the sources of lower turnover in Great Britain. They may include less seasonal fluctuation, since Britain has milder winters and cooler summers than much of the United States; less willingness to move on the part of British workers; smaller shifts in the

[48] This figure is based on data covering the 53 weeks starting December 31, 1950 and ending January 5, 1952. The 53 weeks are divided into twelve periods: one of 6 weeks, three of 5 weeks, and eight of 4 weeks. To obtain a monthly average, the accession rate for each period was multiplied by the number of weeks in the period, and the sum of the products was divided by 52.

[49] See Jeanette G. Siegel, "Measurement of Labor Turnover," *Monthly Labor Review*, Dept. of Labor, May 1953, pp. 519-522.

composition of British demand; and perhaps less shifting in and out of the labor force by British workers, especially women and younger workers.

In addition to having less turnover than the United States, Britain handles a larger proportion of its turnover through public employment exchanges, and this would seem on the whole to mean that it is handled more efficiently. In the absence of data on the total amount of turnover, no demonstration of this point is possible.

Neither is it possible to say anything about secular trends in turnover in the United States. The series on turnover in manufacturing are available back to 1919, but both concepts and coverage have changed too much to permit trustworthy comparisons of present levels with those of the 1920's. Reductions in the minimum level of unemployment could take place either through a reduction over time in the amount of turnover, or through more efficient handling of it. The former would be desirable if it resulted from a decrease in the seasonal fluctuations in the demand for labor. However, reduction in turnover from other causes is not necessarily desirable, except where such turnover arises from lack of knowledge. Consumers are usually the best judges of the necessity for shifts in the pattern of demand, and workers are usually the best judges of the necessity for voluntarily quitting a job to seek another. It is not for the economist to say whether consumers and workers should want more or less mobility in the future.

On the other hand, an increase in the efficiency with which a given volume of turnover is handled is always to be desired. Perhaps this can be achieved by further improvement of public employment services. If so, the level of unemployment corresponding to any concept of full employment may be lower in the future than it is now.

4. *Summary*

The selection of a definition of full employment depends both on the nature of policy goals and the availability of statistical tools. This paper does not attempt to state what relative importance should be attached to competing goals of policy. It has, however, attempted to classify definitions of full employment to reveal their policy implications.

Some definitions clearly imply the priority of avoiding unemployment over other goals. This is true of the minimum unemployment and maximum employment approaches. To a slightly lesser extent it is true of the turnover approach as defined here. Within the general framework of these approaches the degree of priority given to avoiding unemployment can be increased by broadening the definition of unemployment.

Other definitions of full employment clearly imply that at times the cost of further reductions in unemployment is too high in terms of competing policy objectives. This is true of the price approach, and other approaches having the same implication could be devised.

Finally, some approaches are flexible enough so that they can be used to give either a very high or a rather low priority to the avoidance of unemployment. This is true of the unfilled vacancies approach.

The approaches discussed can also be summarized in terms of their statistical practicability. Since the United States and many other countries have reasonably good statistics on unemployment, employment, and prices, the minimum unemployment, maximum employment, and price approaches do not present serious statistical difficulties. The unfilled vacancy approach is practicable for Great Britain and for some other countries, but not for the United States or Canada. Its use depends on the existence of good statistics of unfilled vacancies. The turnover approach requires information of a kind that is nowhere available at present.

By means of some international comparisons it has been pointed out that the same approach will produce different numerical results in different economies, because of underlying dissimilarities in their labor forces and labor markets.

Appendix

NOTE 1. PROOF OF A PROPOSITION CONCERNING PARTIAL UNEMPLOYMENT

Let:

$N =$ total labor force
$F =$ number fully employed
$I =$ number of involuntary part-time workers
$P =$ number of other part-time workers
$U =$ number of wholly unemployed

Let N remain constant over time, and for the other variables let the subscripts 0 and 1 refer to two points in time between which unemployment is rising. Net movement over time is assumed to take place between F and U, between F and I, and between P and U. To simplify the problem, no net change is assumed to take place between P and F or between P and I.

Time worked is expressed in full workweeks. For F it is 1, for U it is 0, and for I and P it is a and b respectively, where a and b are constant fractions.

First, find an expression for the increase in involuntary time lost. Involuntary time lost can increase in three ways:

1. By movement from F to U. Each such move involves the loss of

one workweek. The increase in time lost arising here is expressed as the increase in U, minus that part of the increase in U resulting from movement from P to U, or the decrease in P. This expression is $(U_1 - U_0) - (P_0 - P_1)$.

2. By movement from P to U. Each such move involves a loss of time equal to the time worked by P, or b. The increase in time lost arising here is b times the decrease in P, or $b\ (P_0 - P_1)$.

3. By movement from F to I. Each such move involves a loss of time equal to the time not worked by I, or $(1 - a)$. The increase in time lost arising here is $(1 - a)$ times the increase in I, or $(1 - a)\ (I_1 - I_0)$.

The total increase in involuntary time lost is therefore $(U_1 - U_0) - (P_0 - P_1) + b(P_0 - P_1) + (1 - a)\ (I_1 - I_0)$.

To see when the increase in U considered as representing full weeks of time lost is just equal to the actual increase in involuntary time lost, set the expression for the increase in involuntary time lost equal to the increase in U:

(1)

$$(U_1 - U_0) - (P_0 - P_1) + b(P_0 - P_1) + (1 - a)\ (I_1 - I_0) = (U_1 - U_0)$$

This equation is satisfied when total time not worked by all part-time workers (I and P) does not change. This condition can be expressed in two ways:

$$(1 - a)\ (I_1 - I_0) + (1 - b)\ (P_1 - P_0) = 0 \quad (2)$$

$$(1 - a)\ (I_1 - I_0) = (1 - b)\ (P_0 - P_1) \quad (2a)$$

Substituting (2a) in (1) we get:

(3)

$$(U_1 - U_0) - (P_0 - P_1) + b(P_0 - P_1) + (1 - b)\ (P_0 - P_1) = (U_1 - U_0)$$

$$0 = 0$$

In exactly similar fashion it can be shown that when time not worked by all part-time workers increases, the increase in U is less than the total increase in involuntary time lost, and when time not worked by all part-time workers decreases, the increase in U is greater than the total increase in involuntary time lost.

NOTE 2. DERIVATION OF TIME NOT WORKED BY PART-TIME WORKERS

Data on the time not worked by all part-time workers for March 1947 and thereafter are derived from the number of workers who worked 1 to 14 hours, 15 to 21 hours, 22 to 29 hours, and 30 to 34 hours. The time not worked for each class is taken as 40 hours minus the midpoint of the interval. For the period from January 1946 through February 1947, the published data are divided into only three hours classes (1 to 14, 15 to 29, and 30 to 34). These classes were handled in the same way. The effect of this break could be measured by combining data for the months following February 1947 into three classes. It proved to be slight, and the totals for the whole period 1946-1953 were therefore treated as a continuous series.

This series is very much affected by holidays which sometimes fall in the survey week in July, September, or November. In adjusting the series for seasonal variation, a ratio to a modified 12-month moving total was used. This modified total included interpolated values for months containing holidays; the interpolations were based on relationships to adjacent months in years when no holiday fell in the survey week. Separate seasonal adjustments were then made for these months for years when the survey week contained a holiday and years when it did not. These adjustments were based on separate averages of ratios of original data to the modified moving total. The result is generally satisfactory, except that July 1950 is substantially undercorrected. November 1950, when Armistice Day fell on Saturday of the survey week was not considered a month containing a holiday in the survey week.

The series on time lost by involuntary and other part-time workers were derived from numbers in the four hours classes listed above. However, prior to May 1949, no breakdowns by hours were published in the special surveys of part-time workers. The number of involuntary part-time workers usually working full time and usually working part time were therefore distributed into hours classes for the special surveys of September 1947, March 1948, and September 1948. This distribution was based on the average percentage distribution of the same classes of workers for the next six special surveys (not counting November surveys, in which the distribution was somewhat disturbed by Armistice Day holidays).

The special survey of September 1947 did not divide usual part-time workers preferring full-time work into those who could and who could not accept full-time work. This division was estimated from the average of the next two special surveys, the only two containing data suitable for this purpose.

NOTE 3. METHOD OF ANALYZING PARTIAL UNEMPLOYMENT USED BY T. K. HITCH

Hitch analyzed data on partial unemployment for 1947, 1948, and 1949, using the same source used in this paper. He concluded tentatively that "the volume of [involuntary] part-time work increases somewhat faster than unemployment, at least in the early stages of a depression."[50]

The logic of Hitch's method takes into account in part the offsetting nature of increases in involuntary part-time work and decreases in other part-time work. This is done by not assuming that each additional wholly unemployed person represents an additional full week of involuntary time lost. Instead, he uses data from the special surveys of part-time work to estimate the average hours of work sought by the wholly unemployed. This estimate is based on (1) the number of wholly unemployed persons seeking full-time and part-time work, and (2) the average hours worked by all part-time workers.[51]

This method allows for the fact that some wholly unemployed workers are former voluntary part-time workers and assumes that when such workers become unemployed, they seek part-time work. No allowance is made for the fact that of the unemployed who formerly had full-time jobs, some would have been "other part-time workers" in any given week while they were employed. When such a worker moves from "other part-time work" to "unemployed" he is counted as losing a full week of work involuntarily. The workers in question are those who lose time while employed because of illness, vacation, industrial disputes, bad weather, and personal reasons. This treatment of these workers may involve a slight overestimate of increases in involuntary time lost, although the point is debatable. It is clear that full-time jobs are being lost, and only the use of man-hours as a unit of measurement creates a problem.

Another problem is created by Hitch's unit of measurement. Stated fully, this unit is man-hours lost in total and partial unemployment as a percentage of man-hours constituting total labor force time. The base of this percentage varies with average hours worked. A reduction in overtime that caused average hours to fall from 43 to 41 would cause this measure of unemployment to rise, even though the time lost in total and partial unemployment was unchanged. To use the historical minimum of this percentage as a definition of optimum employment implies that overtime work is always desirable. This contradicts the

[50] Hitch, *op.cit.*, p. 8. The quotation refers to only one group of involuntary part-time workers. However, Hitch finds that the other large group maintains a stable relationship to the volume of unemployment, and hence the conclusion quoted must apply also to the total.

[51] The average hours of actual part-time workers must be used, since those seeking part-time work are not asked how many hours of work they are seeking. It would seem more logical to use the average hours of those who usually work part time by preference instead of the average hours of all part-time workers. This would reduce somewhat Hitch's estimates of time lost by the wholly unemployed.

views that underlie the Fair Labor Standards Act and most collective agreements.

So far, we have examined the concepts involved in Hitch's method. Perhaps these are less important than the practical problems involved. Hitch's estimates rely very heavily on the infrequent and irregular surveys of part-time work. This is a weakness in itself and, in addition, precludes any seasonal adjustments. Hitch appears to use the data on all part-time workers only as a means of interpolating in the series on involuntary part-time workers between special survey dates. This paper has attempted to use the data on all part-time workers as an independent check on the special survey data.

NOTE 4. DERIVATION OF THE NUMBER OF WHOLLY UNEMPLOYED PER 100 UNFILLED VACANCIES FOR GREAT BRITAIN

The derivation of this series involves a number of practical problems. Data on the number of unfilled vacancies refer to every fourth Wednesday, while those for unemployment refer to the Monday nearest the middle of each month. These two dates can be separated by 2, 5, 9, or 12 days. I have computed the ratio of corresponding observations as they stand when they are separated by 2 or 5 days. When they are separated by 9 or 12 days, I have taken the ratio of unemployment to the average of the preceding and the following observation for unfilled vacancies. The unemployment data then refer to a day separated by 2 or 5 days from the midpoint of the averaged period. The 5-day periods in both cases always include a weekend. A more elegant interpolation based on an actual count of days would be possible, but would involve assumptions about the extent to which changes in the state of the labor market can take place on Saturdays and Sundays. I do not know what assumptions would be appropriate.

The two series were seasonally adjusted separately before the ratio was computed. Because the unfilled vacancies series is broken into three segments by administrative change, the usual method of seasonal adjustment by ratios to 12-month moving totals could not be used. The link relative method was used instead to minimize the loss of observations at the breaks. The seasonal adjustment of unemployment is by the method of ratios to moving totals. Since the amplitude of the seasonal movement in this series was not constant, a correction for amplitude was made by the method used by Kuznets.[52]

The series on the number of persons wholly unemployed includes all registered unemployed, whether or not insured. Prior to June 1948, the

[52] Simon Kuznets, *Seasonal Variations in Industry and Trade*, National Bureau of Economic Research, 1933, p. 324.

unemployed registered but not insured were not divided into "wholly unemployed" and "temporarily stopped." After June 1948, the figures for insured and uninsured unemployed were combined, and the total was so divided. For June 1948, it can be computed that 99 per cent of the uninsured unemployed were wholly unemployed. This percentage was used in calculating the total number of wholly unemployed prior to June 1948.

In January 1948, 8,000 persons formerly considered disqualified for employment were added to the number of unemployed, and such persons were counted as unemployed thereafter. I have added 8,000 to the number of unemployed for the last three months of 1947 to produce a continuous series.

NOTE 5. SOURCES OF DATA

Except as otherwise noted, all United States data used in this paper are from the *Current Population Reports: Labor Force*, Bureau of the Census, Series P-57, P-59, and P-50, various dates; and *Labor Force Bulletin*, No. 7, April 1947. The data on wholesale prices and accession rates in manufacturing appear in the monthly issues of the *Monthly Labor Review*, Dept. of Labor.

For Great Britain, except as otherwise noted, all data are from the monthly issues of the *Ministry of Labour Gazette*, and for Canada all data are from the monthly issues of the *Labour Gazette*.

The Sauerbeck wholesale price index for Great Britain, 1887-1913, was published annually in the *Journal of the Royal Statistical Society*. The seasonally adjusted series on trade union unemployment in Great Britain was taken from the business cycle files of the National Bureau of Economic Research. The original data appeared in the (British) *Labour Gazette*, predecessor of the present *Ministry of Labour Gazette*.

The seasonally adjusted Bureau of Labor Statistics index of factory employment for the United States for 1919-1929 was adjusted by the Board of Governors of the Federal Reserve System and appeared in various issues of the *Federal Reserve Bulletin*.

COMMENT

ELMER C. BRATT, Lehigh University

Albert Rees has brought us much closer to an understanding of the full-employment concept. Although he has not elaborated on it, I believe that he implicitly accepts a full-employment goal founded on broad social considerations and on elimination of the waste involved in unlimited departure from effective output rates.

Rees concludes that at present no single way of defining or measuring full employment is sufficient. However, he points to two promising possibilities related to business-cycle policy: minimum unemployment and maximum duration of work-seeking. I wish to point to certain problems connected with the use of either measure.

With regard to minimum unemployment, it appears dangerous to minimize partial employment as much as Rees appears to minimize it. The recessions in the period checked were so mild that the possible burden of partial unemployment is not highlighted. His Chart 2 shows the great relative increase in involuntary part-time workers in 1949, even though their absolute increase appears unimportant. In a more serious depression the increase in the number of part-time workers might well be substantial.

Rees has performed an important service in developing the maximum duration of work-seeking as a concept of full employment, but a simple mean duration figure would appear to represent deviation from full employment less effectively than a distribution. Those out of work no more than a week do not significantly detract from full employment and perhaps should be considered separately from figures representing more serious dislocations. Further, those lying in the upper ranges of the distribution may represent special situations rather than characteristic cyclical changes in the aggregate situation. Possibly a positional mean would best characterize the problem.

The particular advantage of the maximum-duration-of-work-seeking concept is that it relates to seeking work and finding a job rather than to the number who admit unemployment. It represents a measure of the effectiveness of the process of finding work. From the point of view of social considerations, interest is centered on how effective this process is. This is a positive concept, in contrast to the negative connotations connected with the number of unemployed. Also, it is founded on actual activity (length of unemployment and number of accessions), while the number of unemployed is founded on judgments of interviewees. It seems to me that the problem of defining and measuring full employment is so important that the lack of the actual data required for measuring duration of work-seeking should not keep us from seeking the most effective method of measurement. When actual data become available, experience may, of course, force us to revise our ideas regarding the usefulness of the concept.

The danger of inflation makes it impossible to ignore the movement of prices as a constraint on any concept of full employment adopted. This applies to duration of work-seeking as well as to proportionate unemployment. Lack of faith in the price mechanism and the anomalies found in price history militate against the use of stable prices to represent full-employment levels. Sensitivity in the movement of the number of unemployed per vacancy indicates that such a figure may be useful as another constraint. Extremes may be found critically indicative. But this figure scarcely provides the basis for a definition or a direct measure of full employment. Neither the unemployed nor the number of vacancies represents actual activity measures. The latter is unimportant unless the vacancies lead to placements; thus we can argue that accessions are more important as an indicator.

CURRENT UNEMPLOYMENT STATISTICS OF THE CENSUS BUREAU AND SOME ALTERNATIVES

GERTRUDE BANCROFT
BUREAU OF THE CENSUS

1. *Introduction*

In the recent technical discussion of the measurement of unemployment most of the emphasis has been on statistical problems—the adequacy of the collection of the official statistics and the reasonableness of the concepts and definitions used. It is my intention in this paper to examine these questions as they relate to the Census Bureau data. First, however, a brief review of the general problem of concepts might serve as a useful introduction.

What are the criteria for selecting an unemployment concept? Presumably, an economist would ask for a measurement of unemployment in his terms, that is, the surplus or unused supply of labor under current market conditions. A statistician, given the assignment of providing data to measure this unused supply, has many decisions to make. For example, should he count the number of persons who want but cannot find jobs or only the number who have lost jobs because of declining business activity? What shall be the tests of inability to find jobs? Should unemployment be measured by man-hours lost instead of by number of persons out of work? Should partial employment, in terms of hours, or underemployment, in terms of income in relation to skill, be included in the measure? Does unemployment exist when a worker is assigned below his maximum skill level or when his service is wasted because of inefficient methods of production?

It does not seem possible to select a concept of unemployment in a vacuum. The choice must be made with some knowledge of the uses of the resulting measurement and the methods of deriving it. In the past, the issue has usually been settled, not by the economist in the light of his own analytical needs, but by those who have the job of advising policy makers. For example, the concept of unemployment used by the Census Bureau gives a measure of the number of job applicants—persons without work and seeking new jobs. This concept had its origin in a period of mass unemployment when public policy was

Note: The opinions expressed in this paper are those of the author and do not necessarily reflect the position of the Census Bureau.

directed toward providing work relief for employable persons who were in need and out of work. A count of all jobless persons seeking employment would obviously provide an upper limit for such a program.

At the present time, public policy needs are less clear cut. It is true that the statistics on total unemployment are examined when the unemployment compensation system is being evaluated but there is no legal or automatic, administrative tie-up. To a large extent, the total unemployment figures today are used as an economic indicator or as a signal of distress to warn that consumer income and standards of living may be falling in certain segments of the population.

For such uses, the figures on unemployment should be derived objectively and should reflect quickly and accurately the results of changes in economic activity that affect demands for manpower. They should also mirror changes in the demand for jobs associated with labor-force expansion or contraction. It should be possible, in addition, to distinguish various types of unemployment within the total, according to severity of impact on the family or individual, occupational and industrial characteristics, and other qualitative factors. (Most of these requirements point to a count of persons, rather than to man-hours lost, or some other derived measure.) The present concept used by the Census Bureau meets some but not all of these needs. The criticisms that have been advanced and some of the alternatives suggested will be discussed later in this paper.

Finally, it should be emphasized that the formulation of a satisfactory concept must take into account the method of measurement as well as the uses of the measurement itself. Because of the peculiar characteristics of the state of being unemployed, however defined, the problem of measurement takes on great importance in any realistic discussion of concepts. Therefore, it has seemed desirable to summarize here the experience with measuring the Census concept in order that the concept itself, as well as the alternatives, may be properly evaluated.

2. The Census Concept of Unemployment

According to the Census Bureau, the number of unemployed workers means the number of persons who did no work at all for pay or profit or in a family enterprise during a specified calendar week but who were reported as looking for work. In addition to the active work seekers (including those waiting to hear the results of some job-seeking activity made during the last sixty days) certain "inactive" groups are also included, in recognition of some of the special conditions of the labor market. These are persons who would have been looking for work except that they were temporarily ill, they were waiting to be called back to a job from which they had been laid off on an indefinite basis, or they believed no work was available in their line of work or in the community.

DEVELOPMENT OF CONCEPT

The history of the development of this concept is by now familiar. Briefly, the depression of the thirties gave rise to an urgent need for an administratively useful measure of unemployment. It also stimulated a recurring, bitter controversy over the appropriate methods of definition and classification. Then, as now, political attitudes and economic interests colored the popular discussions and may even have affected somewhat the technical work. Efforts to measure the number of employables out of work, the number able and willing to work, or the number for whom jobs should be provided, all came close to foundering on the rocks of controversy over techniques and definitions. Toward the end of the decade, various experiments pointed to a middle-of-the-road solution—that is, a current activity test. Thus, if a person has no job but is currently making an active search for work, it could be agreed that he is unemployed.

In a period of long-term unemployment, however, "current activity" seemed an unnecessarily restrictive test for a person who had unsuccessfully searched for work in his occupation for many months, or who had lived in a depressed one-industry town where common knowledge of the job market made it abundantly clear that there were no jobs available. Similarly, persons who thought they would be called back to their old jobs after a layoff might be expected not to seek other jobs actively in the interim. Again, persons whose search for work was interrupted by temporary illness should, nevertheless, be included in the count of the unemployed.

Accordingly, three types of "inactive" work seekers were added to the pure group of "active" unemployed (along with those on emergency work programs) and the combined total came to be generally accepted as a good measure of the jobless.

It appears now that the acceptability of this concept was largely based on pragmatic, not logical or analytical, considerations. The Works Progress Administration had given impetus to much of the experimental work in its surveys of unemployment. In that research, and developing from the Enumerative Check of the 1937 Census of Unemployment, the use of a set of direct interviews with samples of the population had come to be considered the most economical, comprehensive means of measurement. Generally, these surveys had to be conducted by only moderately well trained interviewers, recruited on an *ad hoc* basis and unlikely to be able to classify individuals correctly on the basis of complex responses. It was believed, however, that they could adequately record the answers to a few simple, direct questions, which could be designed to elicit objective information. In other words, the concept was useful because it was measurable. So far as anyone knew at that date, the measurement of this concept was almost entirely objective, and would, therefore, produce "unbiased" results, regardless of operating conditions.

This operational definition, as is well known, was used in the 1940 Census of Population and in the Monthly Report on Unemployment, the monthly sample survey of the population inaugurated in 1940 by the Works Progress Administration. That survey, which was transferred to the Census Bureau in August 1942, and rechristened the Monthly Report on the Labor Force and later the Current Population Survey, has been the source of the estimates of total unemployment for more than fourteen years. Throughout these years, the definition of unemployment has remained unchanged, although methods of measurement have altered somewhat. From time to time, as we shall see, doubts have been cast on both the concept and the measurement, and both are under official review again at this time.

MEANING OF CONCEPT

Starting with an operational definition of unemployment, can we find any theoretical justification for its use? What are we measuring? It has been said that unemployment as currently defined represents the number of people without jobs who are exerting some pressure on the free labor market for jobs.[1] Is this equivalent to the unused supply of labor under current demand conditions?

At some points, changes in the number of persons looking for work have no relation to the demand for workers and the level of employment, except perhaps in a remote sense. For example, the end of the school year in June brings into the unemployed group thousands of temporary vacation workers and persons beginning their working life who would not be in the labor force under a different school calendar. The traditional availability of such workers may affect staffing patterns of industries with summer peaks (agriculture, construction, forestry, recreation and service industries, etc.), but the initial impetus for the expansion of unemployment at the beginning of the summer and its contraction at the end of the summer, is from the supply side.

[1] Charles Stewart, unpublished memorandum, Interagency Committee on Labor Supply, Employment and Unemployment Statistics, Bureau of the Budget, February 4, 1945.

Again, the number of people looking for work during a given calendar week must be very wide of the mark in measuring unused labor supply, if, as we have seen, thousands of potential workers can be recruited from outside the labor force into jobs without seeking work for any substantial period. Each month during 1951 and 1952, an average of almost 3 million people were found to be employed who had not been seeking work as recently as the month before; some had looked for work between the two survey dates but many had gone straight into jobs. Conversely, millions moved from employment to some activity outside the labor force, without looking for other jobs in the meantime. Supply, therefore, must have to be defined and measured by some other indicator.

Perhaps then the best that can be claimed for the present concept of unemployment is that it furnishes a rough guide to the short-term immediate demand for new jobs, or conversely, measures the immediate (one-week's) supply of workers with no present job attachment. Its utility may be less as a tool of economic analysis and more as an index of short-run dislocation of manpower or of the volume of available manpower that has no present job connection.

As a prelude to a better understanding of the Census figures, let us examine what is included in this totality of persons labeled "unemployed." In that classification might be found any of the types of persons listed below if they were reported as looking for work, actively or inactively (the list, although not exhaustive, covers most of the different major groups):

1. Persons who have lost jobs in industry or business because of economic factors beyond their control
2. Persons who are temporarily unable to work at their jobs because of labor disputes in other industries or because of interruptions to production due to natural disasters, breakdowns, etc.
3. Persons who have been fired from their jobs for personal reasons
4. Persons who have quit their jobs to try to improve their economic status
5. Persons who have quit their jobs from dissatisfaction for a variety of reasons; floaters
6. Persons who have retired voluntarily or involuntarily from their jobs because of old age but who still prefer to work
7. Persons looking for their first job after leaving school or college
8. Persons looking for part-time or temporary jobs to earn pin money
9. Persons entering (or re-entering) the labor market to supplement

the earnings of the chief wage earner in the family or to substitute for him in times of illness, depression, etc.

10. Recently discharged military personnel seeking civilian jobs
11. Persons who are actually unable to work, but who nevertheless try to find employment
12. Seasonal workers re-entering the labor market at the opening of the period of seasonal activity
13. Seasonal workers who could not be placed in their community during the off season and whose unemployment reflects either climatic or business conditions

On the other hand, the label "unemployed" as developed from this concept does not, and cannot under present interpretations, include any of the following, who might well be considered "unemployed" for some purposes:

1. Partially employed, working at their regular jobs but at reduced hours because of economic difficulties
2. Underemployed, working below grade or below usual wage level because of layoffs from regular jobs
3. Self-employed, working full time but at marginal types of work that provide less than a minimum standard of living for themselves and their families
4. Unpaid workers who help in the family enterprise on a full-time basis because they cannot find paid jobs
5. Persons who have become discouraged in their search for work and indicate no current interest in employment
6. Persons with needed skills who are not free to take a job or not interested in the going wage rates but who, for some purposes, such as mobilization, might be considered part of the labor supply and unemployed
7. Persons whose search for work is limited to "signing for unemployment compensation checks"
8. Seasonal workers in the off season who do not seek other jobs
9. Other persons not working at their jobs or businesses for a variety of reasons but not seeking new jobs

In summary, then, the present concept of unemployment yields a measurement of the number of job applicants, regardless of reason for seeking work. It does not yield a clear-cut measurement of the effects of production cutbacks, or frictions or dislocations in the economic system, because it excludes the underemployed and includes voluntary job shifting and other labor force movement. Even less is the concept a measure of wasted manpower or of need for income, since it takes no account of earnings, skill utilization, or living standards among the employed.

3. *Experience with Measurement of Unemployment*

Up to this point, the discussion of the present concept of unemployment has been presented without reference to the method of measurement. The current procedures could undoubtedly be adapted to measure many other concepts, but the survey method itself has certain kinds of limitations that we do not yet know how to remove.

In summarizing here some of the accumulated information on the problems that have arisen in the measurement of the concept of unemployment, my purpose, as indicated earlier, is to provide background for the final assessment of the unemployment measurement furnished by the Census statistics. It is necessary, in this process, to point out weaknesses and areas of inaccuracy. But in compensation for these and the other controversial features of the data, there is a flexibility in the population survey technique, as well as a rich variety of results for analysis, that does not exist in measurements arising from administrative statistics. Some of these compensating features will be discussed in Section 4.

MEASUREMENT PROCEDURE

To summarize briefly the current Census Bureau procedures for measuring unemployment: Each month, a group of part-time interviewers calls upon a sample of approximately 25,000 addresses, to ask questions of all resident persons fourteen years of age and over regarding their activity during the preceding week, the week containing the eighth of the month. These addresses are selected from maps, lists, etc. of living quarters located in 230 sample areas.[2] The sample is a probability sample—that is, each dwelling unit has a known probability of coming into the sample—and the sampling errors can be computed from the sample itself. Each household is interviewed for a period of four months, dropped from the sample for eight months, and interviewed again for a second four-month period. One-eighth of the sample each month is completely new, one-eighth returning for its second four-month period.

Relatively few questions are asked each month to determine employment status. (The personal characteristics of each member of the household at the sample address are recorded the first month the

[2] For up-to-date description of the sample and estimation procedure, see "Concepts and Methods Used in the Current Labor Force Statistics Prepared by the Bureau of the Census," *Current Population Reports*, Series P-23, No. 2, July 30, 1954.

household is interviewed and are transcribed to the schedule which is sent to Washington each month. As persons leave or are added to the households in the sample dwelling units, reports for them are eliminated or added. Age and marital status are kept up-to-date for persons remaining in the sample households.) The employment status questions currently in use consist of a series of sorter questions, as follows:

1. What was this person doing most of last week, working, keeping house (or going to school) or something else? For all persons reporting some status other than working or being unable to work because of long-term illness or disability, the next three questions apply:
2. Did this person do any work at all last week, not counting work around the house?
3. If NO in 2: Was he looking for work?
4. If NO in 3: Even though he didn't work last week, does he have a job or business from which he was temporarily absent? If YES, reason for absence is entered in a pre-coded box: illness, vacation, labor dispute, bad weather, layoff with definite instructions to return in thirty days of layoff, waiting to start new job or business in thirty days, and all other.

Persons reported as working in questions 1 or 2 are asked the number of hours they worked during the week, and occupation, industry, and class of worker of job (private wage or salary worker, government worker, own account, or unpaid family worker). Occupation, industry, and class of worker are also reported for persons with a job but not at work and not looking for work. These two constitute the employed.

Persons reported as not working but looking for work are asked the number of weeks they have been looking for work, and the occupation, industry, and class of worker of their last full-time job of two weeks or more.

These actual questions are by design as simple and brief as possible, in order to permit a speedy, inexpensive interview and to avoid imposing too much on the respondent, who, it is hoped will be a cooperative and voluntary member of the survey panel for eight interviews. The instructions to the interviewers on concepts and definitions are contained in a detailed manual together with instructions for all the other phases of the survey. The questions as worded are generally understood and appear to obtain correct answers in the vast majority of cases; for respondents who do not understand or who raise questions, the interviewer is supposed to be familiar with the detailed definitions and able to probe and interpret the facts related to him so that he can correctly classify the respondent, or bring the problem to the attention of his supervisor.

EXPERIENCE WITH MEASUREMENT OF CERTAIN PROBLEM GROUPS

Marginal cases have always presented problems in the measurement of unemployment by direct surveys as well as in the determination of unemployment for benefit purposes. For the first five years of the operation of the Census sample survey, separate identification was made of persons actively seeking work, and of the three types of inactive unemployed: those on indefinite layoff, those not seeking work because of temporary illness or the belief that no work was available in their line of work or in the community. Until the termination of the work relief programs in 1943, persons on work relief were also counted among the unemployed. Identification was accomplished by specifying that all persons not at work on a regular or government job and not actively seeking work were to be asked the reason they were not seeking work. Codes were supplied the interviewers for labeling the inactive unemployed and the persons on work relief.

The distribution of the total unemployed into the specified categories is shown in Table A-1 for the years during which these identifications were made. It will be seen that most categories of unemployed workers decreased rapidly with the defense and war production programs. The number of active work seekers dropped continually except for a seasonal pickup in the summer months when students came into the labor market. The "inactive" groups, except those not looking for work because of illness, showed a higher rate of decline than did the work seekers through 1943. In the last two years of the war, the figures reflecting layoffs began to show a moderate rise, which may, in fact, have occurred, although the sampling error on such numbers does not permit a firm conclusion. The relative stability in the number of persons not actively seeking work because of temporary illness arouses some suspicion about the meaning of this category. Certainly it would not be expected to approach the number of able-bodied, active work seekers, as it does some months. Rather, in a period of labor shortage and rising family incomes, it is likely that persons too ill to look for a job would have actually been able to withdraw from the labor force.

As experience with the survey accumulated, it began to appear that there was some failure to obtain a full count of persons in the labor force, particularly the employed sector. Supplementary questions directed toward persons classified as not in the labor force had the effect of increasing the count of the labor force temporarily. It was believed that interviewers had been ignoring the specified questions for persons they assumed to be nonworkers. These experiences led to further experimentation with question wording and to the adoption in July 1945 of a set of questions substantially like those in current use. Although conclusive proof could never be adduced, it was generally believed that the question on reason for not looking for work month after month had had two unfortunate results: (1) interviewers began to assume the answers to this and other questions in order to avoid irritation of the respondent and (2) there was a tendency on the part of some respondents to rationalize their inactivity when asked why they were not looking for work by saying they were ill, particularly in a period of wartime manpower shortages. Accordingly, the revised schedule eliminated the question on the reason for not looking for work, but the concept of unemployment remained the same. The interviewers were instructed to classify as among those "looking for work" anyone who on the basis of information furnished, appeared to meet the definition of inactive unemployed.

There has always remained some uneasiness about this method of handling the problem, and if unemployment had become a serious problem in the postwar period, it is hoped that some better method would have been devised.

RELIABILITY OF MEASUREMENT

Sources of Error. It should be obvious even from this drastically condensed description of the survey that the procedures currently used cannot produce highly refined, precise results. Although the series of Census Bureau publications presenting the data have been heavy with cautions about the possibilities of various types of errors, there is a surprising number of users, both technical and nontechnical, who have ignored these cautions. Let me restate them:

1. All estimates from the sample are subject to sampling variability, which may be large on the smaller numbers. With unemployment at about the 3 million level, the chances are one in three that sampling error may be as high as 4 per cent; in one case out of twenty, the sampling error may be as high as 8 per cent. At the 3 million level, if the sample estimates show unemployment at 5 per cent of the labor force, the chances are one in three that the sampling error could be as high as 0.19 percentage points. In other words, the chances are about two out of three that the rate based on a complete count would fall within the range of 4.81 and 5.19 per cent, and nineteen out of twenty that it would fall within the range of 4.62 and 5.38 per cent. Estimates of the amount of change in unemployment from one month to the next have a somewhat smaller error because 75 per cent of the households in the sample are identical between two successive months. The

current estimation procedure, introduced in February 1954, was developed to take advantage of this fact.[3]

2. Another type of error arises not because of sampling but because of the enumerative process. These errors have their source in the lack of precise knowledge on the part of the respondent about the activities of other members of the household; lack of understanding of the questions; failure of interviewers to ask the questions properly or to interpret the answers correctly. In short, a second interview by another person or even by the same person would not always produce the same answers. This type of error tends to be larger in the case of unemployment than in the case of some other employment status categories, as will be discussed later. Despite years of census and survey experience, little is known about how to control these errors, within reasonable bounds of cost.

3. The processes of listing the land areas from which the sample dwelling units are drawn, selecting the sample, identifying all the individuals associated with those sample dwelling units, and completing all interviews may give rise to errors. A systematic check of completeness of coverage has shown that interviewers miss about 1.3 per cent of the population because of failure to list completely all living quarters in the designated areas and miss another 0.5 per cent in the quarters they visit. Failure to make contacts in occupied dwelling units by the end of the survey period averages about 3 to 5 per cent of the total occupied sample units a month. Adjustments for these errors are made in the final step of the estimation procedure, when the sample results are weighted up to independent estimates of the population by age, sex, and color, based on projections of the latest Decennial Census counts.

4. Errors can arise in the coding, editing, and tabulating of the survey results. These are fairly easy to control and have never proved to be serious.

5. Errors arise also, not from the sampling process or from imperfect performance of other activities, but from the difficulties of applying definitions. As in all fields of human behavior, there are situations in which a clear-cut classification cannot be made. These borderline cases are particularly troublesome in the interpretation of the present unemployment concept and give rise at least to instability in the results, if not error. An example is the case of a fisherman who works on shares nine months of the year and does no other work during the remaining three months because no other work exists in his area. Is he to be classified as unemployed or not in the labor force during the off season? His traditional labor force pattern is nine months of work and three

[3] *Ibid.*, p. 6.

months of inactivity. If other work were to be had in the off season, he might attempt to find it, but under conditions that he knows, he would say that he was not looking for work. Has he been "laid off" from his job? Or is he in the category of inactive unemployed who would be looking for work except that he believes no work is available in his line or in the community?

The case of the fisherman, if put to a vote of the major users of the data, would probably result in a classification of seasonally unemployed. Assume, however, that the marginal case is that of a housewife who works in the local vegetable cannery as long as there are any products to be processed. The canning season is considerably shorter than the fishing season, in this case. When the season is over, she can find no other work in the community, and becomes a full-time housewife again. Has she left the labor force or is she unemployed for the rest of the year? Or, consider the familiar case of the housewife who takes a temporary job in a department store before Christmas to earn money for the family gifts. If, after Christmas, she leaves her name with the employment office of the store to be called for a part-time job, does this constitute looking for work, even though she takes no other steps to find a job? Does this action justify her inclusion among the unemployed in later months—February, March, etc.? Questions of this kind have plagued the operators of labor force surveys everywhere because of the areas of vagueness in the concepts.

Measurement of Error. The labor force concepts introduced in 1940 with the Census of Population and the Monthly Unemployment Survey were hailed as a great advance in objectivity and measurability. Moreover, it was thought that the Decennial Census count of employment and unemployment could serve to evaluate the sample survey data and that if the sample estimates were sufficiently close to the truth, the survey would become a satisfactory vehicle for intercensal estimates. Complete count data would provide the true levels.

When the preliminary sample data from the Decennial Census became available, the comparisons with the as yet unpublished estimates from the WPA forty-one-county sample were made. Unexpectedly, the survey estimate of unemployment was higher than the Census count, and apparently closer to the truth (Table A-2). Partial evidence of this was adduced from comparisons of the figures on emergency workers with official figures.[4] At a later date, when the early sample estimates

[4] An interagency group spent considerable time analyzing the differences between the two sets of estimates and examining the procedures of the WPA survey. Census data for the forty-one counties in the WPA sample were weighted up to national estimates, using the WPA weighting scheme, in order to determine whether the differences were due to the estimation procedure. This test gave substantially the same count of unemployment as did the Census 5 per cent sample. A matching

were revised to bring them into line with the estimates from the sixty-eight-area sample introduced by the Census Bureau in 1943, they were tied to a Census bench mark, but the Census figures used were those adjusted for misclassification of emergency workers and other defects.

The notion that a figure derived from a sample survey could be more nearly correct than a complete count received confirmation again in the 1950 Census comparisons. The Census count of employment was 5 per cent below the survey estimate and the count of unemployment 20 per cent below (Table A-3). With a greater degree of sophistication ten years later, advance plans had been made for a detailed investigation of probable Census-survey differences. The Census reports for the current survey sample households were matched with the survey reports. In addition, a second sample of households was drawn in the sixty-eight Current Population Survey areas which had not previously been included in the monthly survey, and these were interviewed independently by survey enumerators after the Census schedule had been filled, in order to examine differences for respondents who had not been previously "conditioned" by the survey interviews. An elaborate check was also made of the coverage of households and population in the sample survey. Final analysis, taking into account both response and coverage differences, is incomplete, but some conclusions can be drawn by examining the data for persons interviewed in both the 1950 Census and the CPS.

Briefly, these data show that the survey interviewers, who had more training and experience than the temporary Census enumerators, seemed to do a somewhat more careful job of asking the employment status questions, although this was not always true. Survey experience has generally shown that a higher count of the labor force reflects better interviewing, since more detailed questioning is required to uncover marginal and occasional workers. Comparisons of the two reports for the unemployed sector are difficult to interpret because the Census enumeration extended over a longer period and did not always refer to the same week. For a characteristic as volatile as unemployment, the time reference difference may be serious. However, when the data are examined for persons interviewed for the same calendar

---

study of WPA and Census returns for the same persons was proposed but apparently never completed. It is amusing to read the record of these discussions in the light of subsequent history. At that date, the Census Bureau representatives disagreed with the position that differences in enumerator performance were responsible for the different results, and they strongly opposed any public statement to that effect. For contrast, see the text of any report of the 1950 Census of Population and Housing.

week, the differences are larger, not smaller, in the case of unemployment and agricultural employment; the estimates based on the reports of the Census enumeration of the matched cases are 24 per cent lower for unemployment and 16 per cent lower for agricultural employment (Table A-4). (Agricultural employment was rising seasonally during April and the later enumerations had the effect of raising the Census level, making it appear closer to the original CPS level than was actually the case.) The relative differences in the estimates of unemployment were equally great for men and women; for employed persons, the two results were much closer for men than for women (2.1 per cent versus 7.5 per cent).

Gross differences as well as net differences are shown in Table A-5, for the unemployed. Even for persons enumerated at the same date, the matched returns indicate that the two sets of enumerators classified differently in more than half of the cases. The CPS interviewers appeared to have been somewhat more conscientious in asking the probing questions, although there was some failure on their part too. To what extent the difference in results was due to inadequate performance by the interviewers, to incomplete information supplied by the householder, or to vagueness of concept, cannot, of course, be determined from these data.

It seems to me, as a result of these experiences in 1940 and 1950, that it is clear now that the "true" level of unemployment as currently defined cannot be measured by a complete census. There is even some question—and this must be resolved before too long—as to whether the labor force concepts are suitable at all for a population census taken under the conditions that are customary in the United States.

It may be noted that the differences between the survey estimates and the Decennial Census data were considerably larger in 1950 than in 1940. It may be that Census enumerators were more skilled in 1940 than in 1950, or that the survey enumerators were less skilled in 1940 than in 1950. Sampling errors cannot be computed for the WPA sample. The comparison for the two dates, however, indicates that even when unemployment is widespread, there is much greater variability in its measurement under the present concept than is the case for the measurement of employment.

Is there any other method of arriving at the "true" level of unemployment against which to measure the reliability of any particular figure? Do the data from the unemployment insurance system more nearly approximate the truth than do the complete census data? The insured unemployment data differ so much in concept and method of compilation from the current Census estimates, as Parnes has carefully shown in his paper, that it is almost astonishing to find the two series moving together at any given point in time. No method so far devised has been found to make the two series comparable, except on an extremely rough basis. The legal eligibility for benefits of persons reported as looking for work to the Census interviewers cannot be determined with any reliability in the regular interview process. Conversely, the insurance system by its very nature will obtain a report on availability for work from a person seeking to establish eligibility for payment that is bound to differ on occasion from what would have been reported to a survey interviewer.

Thus, although there must be areas of agreement in the two measurements, and, in fact, they do tend to move together at critical turning points, the statistics arising from the operation of the insurance system do not appear to offer real possibility for establishing "truth" for any part of the Census count.

Evidence of this was furnished directly after the end of World War II when the Census figures on the unemployment of women and World War II veterans fell below the figures on claims and veterans readjustment allowances for some period of time. Research conducted jointly by the Census Bureau and the United States Employment Service and the State Employment Security offices in a number of areas in 1946 showed that a considerable proportion of persons claiming benefits did not report themselves to Census interviewers as looking for work. During that postwar period, many women were in the process of leaving the labor force and many veterans were in a transition stage between military service and civilian employment. Thus, although they were registered as available for placement with a public employment agency, and met the requirements for eligibility for benefits, they did not report themselves to the Census interviewers as actively seeking jobs, even though many of the women probably would have gone back to their war jobs. These findings caused concern but they did serve to emphasize the difference between the two concepts. Whether or not there should be a difference between the two is one of the problems being currently considered. From some points of view, it is reassuring that the American public, apparently, did not regard "the Government" as a monolithic power with whose various representatives it was necessary to act and talk with a high degree of circumspection and consistency at all times.

In the absence of acceptable, independent measurements of the "true" level of unemployment, some work has been done to try to determine from the survey itself what the errors of response might be. This work has consisted of special, supplementary inquiries to attempt a measurement of the possible number of unemployed according to the present concept who were not being revealed by the more limited regular questions.[5]

These studies were conducted in August 1946, May and June 1947, February and June 1948, May 1949, January and June 1950. They fell into two groups. The first approached the problem of checking the unemployed classification by seeking to identify recent labor force members who perhaps would have been classified as unemployed if appropriate additional questions had been asked to determine why they were not looking for work—a modification of the procedures used from 1940 to 1945. There was some evidence that further questioning on reasons for not looking for work had the effect of encouraging types of responses that suggested attachment to the labor force. The more questions asked, apparently, the more likely the respondent was to furnish affirmative answers, perhaps because it was thought such answers were desired by the government, perhaps because the added questions actually clarified the respondent's thinking. A second group of surveys experimented with the approach of asking persons not in the labor force who had recently looked for work whether they still wanted work and could have accepted jobs at the time of the survey. Most of the results of these surveys have been published, but for convenience, the major findings are summarized in Tables A-6 and A-7.

In all these experiments except the first, in August 1946, the additional questions were asked at the time of the original interview and were therefore limited in number and scope. Throughout the program of experimentation, a major objective was to find a simple device for modifying the "current activity" test, so that it would be possible to count persons who are on the "fringe" of the current labor force and really applicants for job openings but who are not caught by the regular questioning process. In order not to jettison altogether the current activity test for identifying job applicants, it seemed important to include just those whose search for work might be assumed to be only briefly interrupted. Unfortunately for the cause of statistical measurement, the sharp reduction in unemployment after mid-1950 removed the pressure for further work on this problem, at the time when funds for this type of research became seriously limited.

Clearly the method of questioning had some bearing on the number of "fringe" unemployed who were sorted out of the group originally reported as not in the labor force. In the August 1946 survey, the probing questions were directed to the very large group who had been in

[5] In two surveys, an attempt was also made to discover whether there were any persistent errors in the other direction, i.e. persons classified as unemployed who in fact were not really looking for work. Very few persons (under 100,000) were found among the unemployed who could not report some form of job seeking that met the definition.

the labor force at some time during the past year (or who were World War II veterans) but who were not in the labor force at the time the questions were asked—some 7.7 million (Table A-6). This time period included the months of cutbacks in war production and the demobilization period when the extra workers recruited for war demands were leaving the labor force, some voluntarily and some not. Many would have continued happily to work at their old jobs and rates of pay had this been possible. Hence it is not surprising that a large number (about 400,000) reported that the reason for not seeking work was the belief that none was available.

In more normal times, perhaps close to the maximum possible number of potential work seekers is elicited by the question "Does this person want a job?" In June 1947, about 2.9 million persons outside the labor force were reported as wanting a job; this compares with 2.6 million unemployed reported for that date. When the further question was asked on why those desiring jobs had not looked for work, about four-fifths gave reasons that indicated they were not available to take work or had very little enthusiasm for job-seeking. This proportion would probably have increased further if some test had been applied such as intentions of seeking work in the near future.

The next five surveys, conducted in the period 1948-1950 used almost identical questions, starting with a sorter question to separate recent work seekers from the rest of the nonworkers, using a period of a month prior to the survey week as the time period. "Current activity" was thus modified from a week to several weeks. Persons who as recently as this looked for work were asked if they still wanted and could take a job. This simple, two-stage test combining both activity and attitude appears to have given fairly consistent results, judging by the limited observations available (Table A-7).

All the studies from 1946 on demonstrated that the marginal, or fringe, unemployed are preponderantly women and young workers, groups with alternative activities in the form of keeping house or going to school which impel them to move into and out of the labor force from time to time or to which they return on a full-time basis when the job situation deteriorates. On the average, one-half of these fringe workers were women eighteen years old or over and one-quarter were youngsters under eighteen years of age, some of whom had never worked before.

Changes in the number of fringe workers during the period surveyed seem to have been determined more by the factors that affect seasonal labor force activity than by general business conditions, but the evidence is inconclusive. Table 1 shows total unemployment and the estimates of fringe workers, by sex, for available months. The data for

TABLE 1

Comparison of Total Unemployed as Reported and Number of Fringe Unemployed According to Special Surveys, by Sex, Selected Dates, 1946-1950

(thousands of persons, 14 years old and over)

MONTH AND YEAR	BOTH SEXES			MALE			FEMALE		
	Unemployed (1)	*Fringe Workers* (2)	*Ratio of (2) to (1)* (3)	*Unemployed* (4)	*Fringe Workers* (5)	*Ratio of (5) to (4)* (6)	*Unemployed* (7)	*Fringe Workers* (8)	*Ratio of (8) to (7)* (9)
August 1946[a]	2,060	1,500	72.8	1,600	358	22.4	460	1,142	248.3
May 1947	1,960	220	11.2	1,420	94	6.6	540	126	23.3
June 1947	2,555	563	22.0	1,707	212	12.4	848	351	41.4
February 1948	2,639	494	18.7	1,889	147	7.8	750	347	46.3
June 1948	2,184	386	17.7	1,375	122	8.9	809	264	32.6
May 1949	3,289	525	16.0	2,366	165	7.0	923	360	39.0
January 1950	4,480	667	14.9	3,262	215	6.6	1,218	452	37.1
June 1950	3,384	720	21.3	2,200	308	14.0	1,184	412	34.8

[a] Not comparable with later data.

August 1946 are included, although they were based on procedures entirely dissimilar to those for other months and cannot be considered comparable.

The estimates are subject to a high sampling error; nevertheless it appears that for male workers, the number of fringe workers has about the same ratio to total unemployment throughout, except in the early summer months, when a large number of youngsters are looking for work, on and off. For female workers, the pattern is erratic, but there is no conclusive evidence that the number of fringe workers changes proportionately with reported unemployment. In February 1948, the ratio of fringe workers to reported unemployment was 46.3, while in January 1950 after total unemployment had risen by about 60 per cent but fringe workers by only 30 per cent, the ratio was down to 37.1 per cent. To the extent that fluctuations are not due to sampling variability, they suggest that there may be a constant amount of unemployment among women that is intermittent in character and varying to some extent with the availability of temporary jobs, which is not uncovered by the present question. This may vary between 250,000 and 350,000—an amount which is small in relation to the size of the labor force, but not small in relation to reported unemployment. The problem apparently arises either because women in this group do not respond positively to the question "Were you looking for work?" since their activity is intermittent, or because there is some failure on the part of interviewers to observe prescribed procedures.

To be measurable, a concept like unemployment should be so defined that it is reproducible, that is, the same procedures used again and again should give the same results. Although in practice the ideal is seldom achieved in surveys of this kind, the techniques aimed for should be such that, given adequately trained interviewers, it makes no serious difference who asks the questions and who answers them, approximately the same results are achieved. We have already seen in the comparison of survey and Decennial Census data that this condition was not met in those two measurements.

A much more unexpected and troublesome demonstration was furnished by the change in the current survey sample design in early 1954. From 1943 on, the CPS estimates had been based on a sample of 25,000 households located in sixty-eight sample areas. These sample areas comprised 125 counties and independent cities and the District of Columbia. The desirability of spreading the sample over more areas in order to reduce the sampling variability of the estimates had long been recognized, and as soon as the 1950 Census of Population data became available, the redesign of the sample got under way. Selection of the new set of areas was completed in mid-1952, using the same basic principles of sampling as before, but taking advantage of more up-to-date information for purposes of stratification.

In the new sample, the number of sample households was to remain the same (roughly 25,000) but the households were to be selected in 230 rather than sixty-eight sample areas covering approximately 450 counties. In order to operate the greater number of areas within the limits of the budget, the field staff organization was to be revised, and the number of supervisory offices consolidated from sixty-three to thirty-four.

Although the selection of sample counties was completed in 1952 (and was used for the collection of retail trade statistics beginning in early 1953) the new sample could not be introduced into the Current Population Survey until funds were available for recruitment and training of the new staff of interviewers. In mid-summer of 1953, it became possible to go ahead with this work. It was planned to continue the operation of the sixty-eight-area sample intact as the basis for the published figures until February 1954, and to activate the new areas and new interviewers gradually. One-third of the new sample was to be introduced on a trial basis in November 1953, one-third in December, and the final third in January 1954. After another month, the sixty-eight-area sample was to be dropped.

The experience of the 1940 and 1950 Censuses, and other surveys, had revealed the difficulties of obtaining adequate measures of employment and unemployment with relatively untrained field personnel.

Consequently, in the sample changeover, the greatest possible attention was given to the task of training the new staff, while the old interviewers received the minimum of attention.

When the first results of the complete new sample became available for study after the January enumeration, it looked as if a statistical calamity had occurred. The new sample estimates of employment were almost identical with those from the sixty-eight-area sample, but the estimate of unemployment (and consequently of the civilian labor force) was about 700,000 higher. According to the sixty-eight-area sample, 3.8 per cent of the labor force was unemployed, according to the 230-area sample, 4.9 per cent. The change in sample areas could not have contributed much more than 300,000 to 400,000 of this difference in the level of unemployment and presumably somewhat less.[6] In this case, some differences were noted in all age-sex groups, not just those where marginal or intermittent workers are expected.

Both sets of estimates for January were published on a preliminary basis while the problem was under study, in order that the public might become aware of the possibility that the level of unemployment might be considerably higher than earlier estimates had indicated. A great deal of publicity was given to the two sets of figures, and this publicity was at its height during the special interviewer training sessions that were held for both old and new interviewers just prior to the February survey. It is possible that as a result, unusually zealous efforts were made to obtain a complete count of unemployed persons; indeed, there may have been some overcounting in the sense of reporting all marginal cases as unemployed.

In any event, the February unemployment estimates were within 300,000 of each other, a difference of the order of magnitude that might have been expected to arise from the change in sample counties. Because the 230-area sample was a more efficient design, the sixty-eight-area sample was dropped after the February enumeration. Ideally, it might have been desirable to continue the old sample for a much longer period in order to establish with greater certainty whether differences of the same magnitude would have persisted, and to provide more light on the reasons for difference. Unfortunately, resources for supervision of the field staff had been stretched to the limit, and there was no possibility of improvising either staff or funds to keep both operations going. Evidence was accumulating that the sixty-eight-area estimates had begun to deteriorate during the fall of 1953 when it was

[6] A Special Advisory Committee on Employment Statistics, under the chairmanship of Frederick F. Stephan of Princeton University, was appointed by the Secretary of Commerce to investigate the problem of the old versus the new sample (see the report of that committee for an intensive review of the evidence analyzed).

necessary to devote an increasingly large proportion of time to the new 230-area operation. The absence of usual attention from their supervisors and the possibility of loss of jobs may have caused the experienced interviewers to become somewhat perfunctory in their work. The new interviewers, on the other hand, were entering on their jobs just as the discussions of the developing severity of unemployment began to hit the press and radio. Their attitudes may have differed substantially from those of the old staff.

It is not intended here to review all the factors that gave rise to the difficulties associated with the introduction of the new sample or to present the vast body of evidence that was accumulated in the months of analysis. Rather, the point to be made is that unforeseen or unforeseeable circumstances can affect the satisfactory measurement of the present concept of unemployment, despite the utmost care in planning. There should have been no differences between the old and the new sample estimates beyond those attributable to the change in sample counties and in sample households. The expected range of this difference was calculable. It had been recognized that there was a risk in assuming that the new interviewers would be adequately trained by February 1954, but it was not realized that the sixty-eight-area estimates were in jeopardy because of the withdrawal of supervisory attention. Whether any concept of unemployment is sufficiently reproducible to be measurable under similar circumstances is a question that demands the consideration of both consumers and producers of statistics in this field.

Work is now in process at the Census Bureau to develop a technique for checking the quality of the work of individual interviewers and measuring the over-all reliability of the national estimates themselves. For many years, the supervisory field staff had used the device of reinterviewing households to check the original returns, but no systematic program was followed. Beginning in February 1954, part of their regular duties became the reinterview of a small subsample of the work under their jurisdiction, using the same procedures as in the original interview. The households to be checked are designated by the Washington office each month. The results showed substantial gross but small net differences in the categories of persons at work part time, persons with a job but not at work, and persons reported as unemployed. These differences appeared to narrow as the check continued into later months. The difficulty of determining which classification was the correct one, and how much of the difference could be explained by a time lag, or memory lapse, led to the extension of the reinterview process to include a reconciliation of discrepancies between the two interviews, wherever possible.

Concurrently with this experimentation, the device of a highly detailed reinterview is being tested—a procedure which does not aim at determining what the classification of the population would have been had the original interviewer followed the prescribed procedures without error, but rather seeks to develop all the information necessary to arrive at the "true" classification. This is the first attempt, as far as employment status measurement is concerned, to construct a "true" employment status distribution of the population. The Post-Enumeration Survey of the 1950 Census of Population and Housing was a pioneer effort to measure the errors in the original data on the size of the population and some of its characteristics—age, education, residence, occupation, industry, income, etc. It did not include, however, any check of employment status because of the lapse of time between the Census enumeration and the date of the Post-Enumeration Survey. In that check survey, the principle was used of asking more detailed questions on the original subject and then trying to explain why the two reports differed, in order to arrive at the true report. The aim of the present research is to develop some instrument of quality control and check that will be sufficiently sharp to detect the kind of drift in a series of data that apparently occurred in late 1953, in order to institute corrective action before a serious bias develops. Such a device would represent a prodigious advance in measurement technique and would give some promise of distinguishing between errors arising from the performance of the interviewers and those due to the ambiguity of the concepts used.

4. Some Alternative Measures of Lack of Work

POSSIBLE ALTERNATIVE MEASURES BASED ON CENSUS DATA

The preceding sections have outlined some of the evidence on the adequacy of the present Census measurement of unemployment. Despite all these problems of meaning and measurement, a statistical series is produced that seems to provide a reasonably good guide to changes taking place in the labor market. Undoubtedly, errors of various kinds have been too large for complete safety, at certain points in time; both levels and amounts of month-to-month change in the series have occasionally appeared to vary too far from the "unmeasurable," true amount. Nevertheless, the number of people in a small sample of the population responding affirmatively to a question on looking for work has been highly correlated with other indicators of economic activity, showing turning points that are roughly coincident with business cycle peaks and troughs.[7] It is well to remember this in looking over possible substitutes.

[7] For a brief summary of the extensive analysis underlying this statement see

One of the leading analysts of labor force data has remarked that as long as the measurement in use confirms general opinion of what is happening in the economy and agrees substantially with measurements from other sources, little attention is paid to the nature of the concepts. This is generally true, as far as the casual users of employment and unemployment statistics are concerned. But over the years, a variety of proposals for improving the Census figures on unemployment have been made by the specialized users of the data who for one reason or another are dissatisfied with the present concepts and their measurement. In some cases, these proposals have been based on considerations of logic, symmetry of classification, or intuitive beliefs on how the labor force behaves. In other cases, they appear to have been dictated by special interests of one kind or another. Whatever their motives, the critics have given impetus to expanding the types of detail made available by the Census Bureau from the monthly survey and can claim credit for the existence of so many different statistical building blocks.

Most of the discussions have centered around levels of unemployment, based on one concept or another, at a single point in time. Too little attention has been given to the effect on measurement of change from one point in time to another of the inclusion or exclusion of particular groups in the unemployment figures. If the categories in dispute are small in size, or remain constant over time, or change in the same way as does the present unemployment total, it obviously makes no difference how they are treated, as far as the usefulness of the unemployment figures as an economic indicator is concerned, once consumers are accustomed to the new levels. To the extent that the data are available or can be estimated, some of the more popular alternatives have been lined up here so that their changes over time may be examined. This review will show, I believe, that the movement of the present unemployment series would have been slightly dampened or magnified by some of the proposed adjustments but that, for the most part, the pattern originally recorded is largely unaffected.

The present labor force classification scheme includes among the employed some groups who, although attached to jobs, are by no means fully employed. For example, anyone who did any work for pay or in his own business, profession or farm, during the survey week is labeled as at work, regardless of how little he worked or how little he earned. Similarly, persons who performed some work without pay in their family business or farm, over and above incidental chores (defined as less than fifteen hours during a week) are labeled at work. Certain

---

Geoffrey Moore, "Analyzing Business Cycles," *American Statistician*, April-May 1954, pp. 13-19.

persons who did not work at all are also considered employed if they had jobs or businesses from which they were absent throughout the week and were not looking for other jobs: persons absent because of illness or other personal reasons, vacation, labor dispute, bad weather, or because they were on short-term (less than thirty-day) layoff, with definite instructions to return to work. Persons who were waiting to start work on new jobs within thirty days are also classified as employed during the survey week.

Among these groups with jobs or job attachments but little or no work during the survey week, there are a number of candidates for inclusion among the unemployed. The most popular are persons working part time because work is slack, persons on temporary layoff, and persons whose jobs have not yet started. These, it is believed, are affected by the same economic dislocations as are the job seekers. Other candidates for the unemployed include individuals whose failure to work full time may be attributed to external causes such as the weather or labor disputes rather than to personal or family reasons.

Thus, critics of the present concept who think statistics on unemployment which measure only the volume of job applicants are too restrictive tend to move toward a measurement of number of persons affected by the malfunctioning of the economic system; that is to say economic unemployment. A still more far-reaching concept is that of unemployment as a state of complete or partial idleness because of involuntary factors. Such factors range all the way from lack of jobs to any situation causing an interruption of full-time work other than one originating with the worker himself. This concept can be expanded even to include lack of work arising from illness. The count of unemployed would thus include all persons in the labor force able and willing to work full time who do not have full-time jobs at a given point in time.

Going still further, another modification of the present concept seeks to include in the labor force and the unemployed all persons who would be seeking work if they thought they could find a suitable job. It will be remembered that the present definition of unemployment classifies as an "inactive work seeker" a person who would have been seeking work except that he believes there is none available in his line of work or in the community. As we have seen, this is the most elusive category to isolate for accurate measurement. It was introduced originally to comprise only persons in stranded occupations or stranded areas who knew from frustrating experience that there were no longer any jobs to be had. Many kinds of seasonal workers and workers who come into the labor force on an occasional basis in response to special inducement or to meet special peak demands also may believe no work is available at other times. Therefore, it is argued, these too should be classified as unemployed when they are not working. By an extension of this reasoning, it is possible to include a substantial part of the population that works at any time during the year, or during any period of high employment. During 1953, for example, about 71 million persons worked at some time. Of this number, over 8 million were not in the labor force during the survey week in January 1954, 2 million of whom were women who had worked at some time during the year in agriculture. Apart from those who had become disabled, had definitely retired, or had returned to full-time school, none of these 8 million recent workers, it is sometimes argued, have voluntarily left the labor force in any real sense. Would they not be looking for some particular kind of job, if they thought it was available?

Unfortunately, this question can be answered at this point only by dogma, not data. Although we have made great advances in our knowledge of how the labor force changes, we are still only at the primitive stages in the understanding and measurement of individual motives for change. Accordingly, no attempt will be made here to speculate on variations in the volume of unemployment were it defined to include, in effect, all persons available for some kind of job.

It should be noted that none of the proponents of an expansion of the present concept to include persons who are involuntarily working less than full time would apply the test of "involuntariness" to the group now classified as unemployed. Reasons for looking for work obviously may be as diverse or as mixed as reasons for not working full time in any given week. Among the current job seekers are those who lost their last jobs for all sorts of reasons that have nothing to do with business conditions as well as those who were dissatisfied and left their last jobs voluntarily. Anyone who has tried to investigate why people change jobs knows the frustrations and pitfalls of classification, not to mention the problems of collecting meaningful data in the first place.

Whether or not they are aware of such difficulties, the major proponents of a more restrictive concept tend toward a definition based on activity and family characteristics rather than on motive. It is argued that active work seekers who are major breadwinners constitute the group of unemployed toward whom public concern and governmental programs should be directed. These critics are impatient with the omnibus character of the unemployment statistics. They regard the present unemployment figure as a large, undifferentiated total of family heads, primary workers, would-be baby sitters, floaters, unemployables, etc., and, therefore, seriously misleading as an economic indicator or a guide to the evaluation of the seriousness of the real problem. They also see few gains and some actual losses of precision in trying to broaden the "actively seeking work" test to include any jobless whose search for a new job may have been interrupted, postponed, or given up in discouragement.

In addition to the critics that would broaden or narrow the concept by adding or subtracting already identifiable classes in the present structure, there are those who believe that the present system either should be abandoned in favor of something else or supplemented by a totally different approach. One of these proposals, which could not be met with present statistical tools, is that the measurement of unemployment should be a measurement of unused human resources—that is, all persons who would like to work at jobs consistent with their training and experience, who are prevented from doing so because such opportunities are not available. Although none exists now, it is possible that research and experimentation could produce a satisfactory measurement of this concept.

Measurement of *time lost* as a result of total or partial unemployment is perhaps more frequently urged, to supplement the present approach. Counting as employed both a man who has only two days work a week and one who is working 8 hours of overtime, giving the same weight to each in the total, is not only illogical, it is argued, but tends to distort seriously any judgments on the "fullness" of employment. As a partial answer to the demand, it is possible to make rather rough estimates of time lost on the basis of currently available data, and more refined estimates might be feasible with a small amount of additional data. The results of such computations are discussed below.

The preceding list of alternatives is only suggestive of some that might be examined; an exhaustive list would include many other combinations of present data, as well as an unknown number of other proposals.

COMPARISON OF CHANGES IN TOTAL UNEMPLOYMENT AND IN ALTERNATIVE MEASURES OF LACK OF WORK

Differentiation of Total Unemployed. In Table A-8 and Chart 1, the figures on total unemployment have been broken down to show a series of components:

1. Adult unemployed workers of both sexes excluding those past retirement age (persons twenty-five to sixty-four years).
2. Adult male unemployed workers (twenty-five to sixty-four years). This component approximates a "major breadwinner" group and has the advantage of comprising those persons whose status of being unemployed is most susceptible to accurate measurement. For this group, the activity of "looking for work" generally accompanies the status of being "out of work."

CHART 1

Unemployed Persons of Specified Types, Monthly, 1948-1954

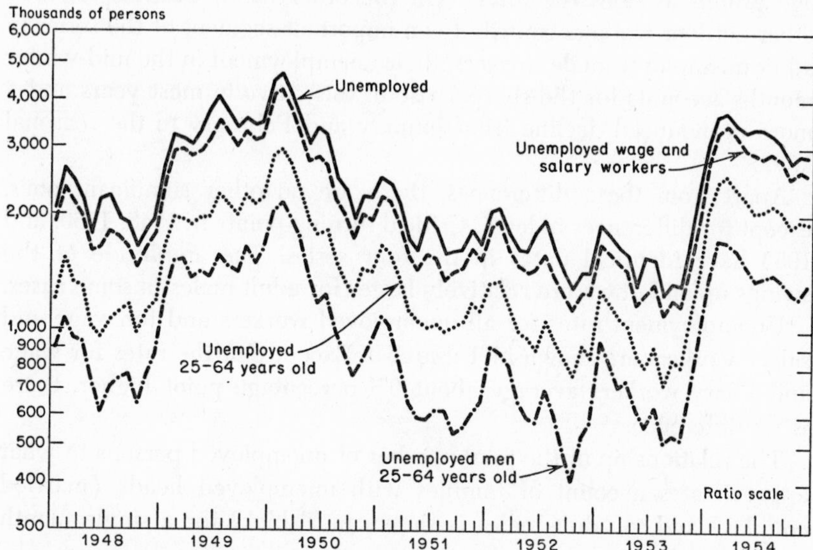

Note: September 1953 – January 1954 figures revised to correct for differences between 68-area and 230-area samples.

3. Unemployed wage and salary workers. It has been contended that the unemployment (and unemployment rates) of this component are much more sensitive than the total because of the elimination of the self-employed.

4. Unemployed family heads or married couples with husband unemployed. Information on marital status and family composition of the population is obtained through the CPS in April of each year (for March in 1950). Data on the number of unemployed family heads are available only for four of the past seven years. For each year, 1948-1953, the number of married couples in which the husband is unemployed has been tabulated, however, and this is very close to the number of unemployed heads (Table A-8). (A family head, as defined by the Census Bureau, is the head of any group of two or more persons related by blood, marriage, or adoption and residing together. Married couples are not all separate families; those living as part of a larger related group of persons are sub-families.)

None of the various monthly series described has been adjusted for seasonal variation. Had it been possible to do so, many of the differences revealed would have been almost eliminated. In the total unemployment figures are, of course, new workers and young vacation-time workers who account for the larger peaks in the mid-summer months. (Persons who never had a full-time job are excluded from the wage and salary figures, but otherwise those figures relate to the same age groups as does the total.) On the other hand, construction and other outdoor workers contribute an important segment of the series in adult unemployed male workers; their unemployment in the mid-winter months accounts for the sharper rise in this curve in most years and a more pronounced decline from January and February to the seasonal low.

Apart from these differences, there are no other significant ones, except for differences in level. Critical turning points in 1948, 1950, and 1953 have identical dates in the four series. The amplitude of the swings up and down are relatively larger for adult males in some cases.

Unemployment rates for all unemployed workers and for wage and salary workers are shown in Table A-9. Except that the rates for wage and salary workers average about 0.5 percentage point higher, there is no difference.

The relationship of the total number of unemployed persons to what approximates a count of families with unemployed heads (married couples) and to adult males is shown in Table 2 for a single month

TABLE 2

Comparison of Total Unemployed, Unemployed Adult Males, and Married Couples with Husband Unemployed, Selected Dates 1948-1954

(number in thousands; April 1948 = 100)

MONTH AND YEAR	TOTAL UNEMPLOYED		UNEMPLOYED MALES 25-64 YEARS OLD		MARRIED COUPLES, HUSBAND UNEMPLOYED[a]	
	Number	*Index*	*Number*	*Index*	*Number*	*Index*
April 1948	2,193	100.0	928	100.0	712	100.0
April 1949	3,016	137.5	1,369	147.5	1,115	156.6
March 1950	4,123	188.0	1,980	213.4	1,503	211.1
April 1951	1,744	79.5	651	70.2	480	67.4
April 1952	1,612	73.5	646	69.6	464	65.2
April 1953	1,582	72.1	744	80.2	564	79.2
April 1954	3,465	158.0	1,635	176.2	1,328	186.5

[a] For available months, the number of unemployed family heads is very close to this number: April 1949, 1,151,000; March 1950, 1,579,000; April 1951, 568,000; April 1952, 504,000.

of each year. These rather scanty data suggest that the rise in unemployment both in 1949-1950 and in 1954 was more severe for the group approximating family heads or major breadwinners than for other workers.

Additions to Total Unemployed. Table A-10 and Chart 2 show the data for various groups and various combinations of groups that might supplement the present measurement of unemployment. Because of

CHART 2

Unemployed Persons and Selected Groups of Employed Persons, Quarterly Averages, 1948-1954

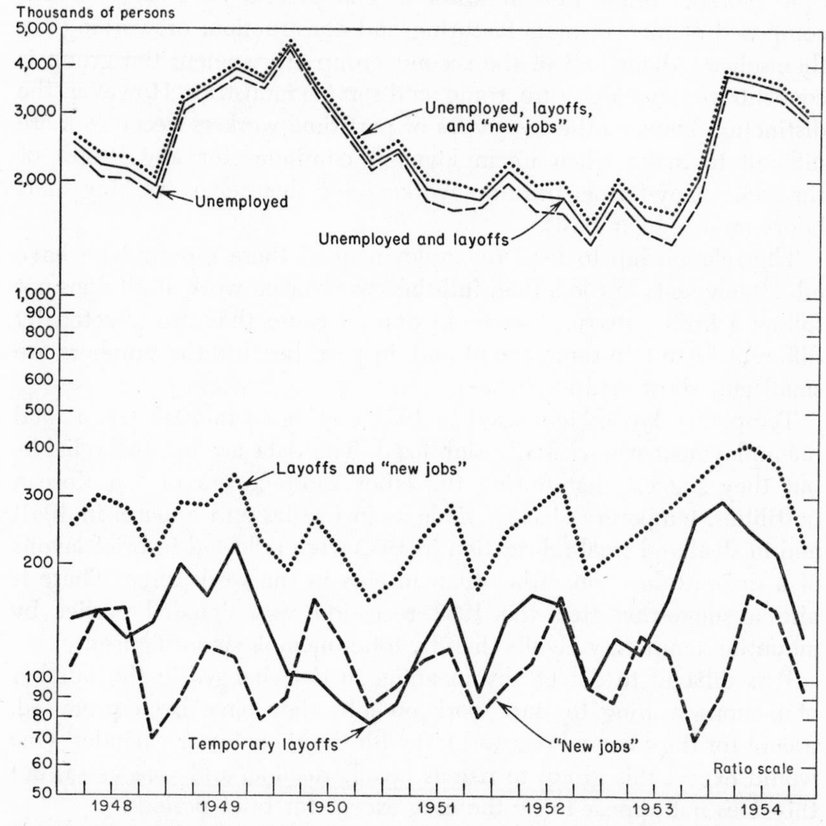

Note: September 1953 – January 1954 figures revised to correct for differences between 68-area and 230-area samples.

the instability of the small numbers, quarterly averages (averages of three months' observations) have been charted, where available.

1. Temporary layoffs: Persons not looking for work who have been laid off from their jobs with definite instructions to return within thirty days.

2. "New jobs": Persons waiting to start new jobs within thirty days.

3. Partially employed: Currently, information is obtained once a quarter about these groups, but between 1951 and 1953, data are available only infrequently.[8] (a) Regular full-time workers working part-time (less than thirty-five hours for economic reasons—slack work,

[8] See various reports on "Part-time Workers," *Current Population Reports*, Series P-50, Nos. 7, 12, 17, 18, 21, 25, 26, 28, 33, 34, 46, 52, and 53.

material shortage, job turnover, etc.): "economic part-time workers"; and (b) regular part-time workers who prefer and could accept full-time jobs: "involuntary part-time workers." These two groups of part-time workers differ in composition. The first is to a large extent composed of men in manufacturing and construction, or working for themselves. About half of the second group are women; the group is concentrated in agriculture, trade, and service industries. However, the distinction between the two types of part-time workers becomes more difficult to make when unemployment continues for any length of time and many former full-time workers find themselves working short hours on a regular basis.

The relationship to total unemployment of these groups who have job attachments but less than full-time work or no work at all does not follow a fixed pattern. This is, in part, because they are affected by different factors to some extent and, in part, because the numbers are small and show erratic changes.

Temporary layoffs increased in 1951 and again in 1952 when total unemployment was virtually stabilized. The data are not too reliable, but they suggest that during the labor shortage era of the Korean hostilities, temporary slack periods as in textiles and apparel in 1951, and in steel and steel fabrication in 1952 were reflected in brief layoffs of a definite duration rather than in cuts in the work force. There is also a suggestion that the 1953 recession was signaled earlier by mounting temporary layoffs than by total unemployment figures.

It is difficult to detect any meaning in the changes in the number of persons waiting to start work on jobs they have been promised, except for the seasonal rise and fall with the school year calendar. One would expect this group to rise as layoffs decline, and vice versa, but this does not appear to be the case except for brief periods.

The addition to the unemployed of temporary layoffs alone, or of temporary layoffs and persons waiting to start their new jobs, raises the total slightly but obviously cannot affect very much the direction of movement because of the relatively small numbers involved. To the extent that the number of persons on temporary layoff has any distinctive meaning as a measure of a special type of labor market situation or as a prediction of unemployment to come, the meaning is lost in a combined figure.

Turning to partial employment as defined here, we find there is some indication that cutting back hours of full-time workers may precede cuts in staff or mass layoffs. Also, total unemployment and hours cutbacks seem to reach their maxima at slightly different dates; for regular full-time workers in nonagricultural industries, however, the agreement appears to be quite close in 1954, although not in 1949-1950

(Table A-11). The absence of monthly figures over a period of years is a serious handicap in the analysis and permits only a tentative conclusion that this type of partial employment is not the same phenomenon as total unemployment.

The size of the group of regular part-time workers who have less work than they want is affected by seasonal factors as well as other changes in business conditions. The high points among these observations were reached in the August surveys, 1949, 1950, and 1954.

The effect of adding partially employed workers to those completely unemployed for the dates on which the information is available is shown in Table 3. With few exceptions the changes are magnified by adding partially employed persons. Decreases as well as increases are larger in the combined total, except in the few months when partial employment increased seasonally but unemployment declined or remained stable (notably September 1948, August 1950, and August 1954).

Whether there are any gains for the analyst or the policy maker in the alternative measure perhaps should not be decided on the basis of nineteen observations taken over a period of seven years. There seem to be reasons for continuing to regard total unemployment and partial employment as different types of maladjustments, requiring different remedies. Until more is known about how these phenomena are related, it may be a more satisfactory technical procedure to continue to make the data available separately.

Time Lost by Unemployment and Partial Employment. Estimates of man-hours of work provided by the economy and man-hours of time lost through unemployment and "underemployment" are available for the years 1947-1949, prepared by Thomas K. Hitch,[9] for the most part on the basis of Census data. Briefly, the computation consists of assuming that the unemployed and persons on temporary layoff or waiting to start new jobs had lost approximately forty hours of work on the average, and that the number of man-hours lost by the partially employed (i.e., those full-time workers working less than thirty-five hours because of economic reasons and other part-time workers who prefer full-time work) was equal to the difference between what they actually worked and approximately forty hours.

The number of man-hours of work provided by the economy was estimated by adding man-hours actually worked to the imputed hours that presumably were available to persons on vacation, ill, out for reasons of bad weather or personal factors for all or part of the survey week. Many of the factors entering into these computations were fairly

[9] Thomas K. Hitch, "Meaning and Measurement of 'Full' or 'Maximum' Employment," *Review of Economics and Statistics*, February 1951.

TABLE 3

Changes in Total Unemployment and Partial Employment between Selected Dates, 1948-1954

(number in thousands)

MONTH AND YEAR	CHANGE IN UNEMPLOYMENT		CHANGE IN PARTIAL EMPLOYMENT		CHANGE IN UNEMPLOYMENT PLUS PARTIAL EMPLOYMENT	
	Number	*Per Cent*	*Number*	*Per Cent*	*Number*	*Per Cent*
1948:						
March						
September	−541	−22.2	+147	+12.1	−394	−10.8
1949:						
May	+1,390	+73.2	+1,097	+80.7	+2,487	+76.3
August	+400	+12.2	+98	+4.0	+498	+8.7
November	−280	−7.6	−203	−7.9	−483	−7.7
1950:						
February	+1,275	+37.4	−269	−11.4	+1,006	+17.5
May	−1,627	−34.7	+72	+3.5	−1,555	−23.0
August	−557	−18.2	+202	+9.4	−355	−6.8
November	−260	−10.4	−550	−23.3	−810	−16.7
1951:						
February	+167	+7.5	+164	+9.1	+331	+8.2
May	−798	−33.2	−174	−8.8	−972	−22.2
1952:						
May	−7	−0.4	−75	−4.2	−82	−2.4
November	−184	−11.5	−324	−18.8	−508	−15.3
1953:						
May	−112	−7.9	−12[a]	−0.9	−124	−4.4
December	+1,007[b]	+77.1	+854[b]	+61.6	+1,861	+69.1
1954:						
March	+1,412	+61.0	+516	+23.0	+1,928	+42.3
May	−420	−11.3	−164	−6.0	−584	−9.0
August	−60	−1.8	+455	+17.6	+395	+6.7
November	−352	−10.8	−468	−15.4	−820	−13.0

[a] Estimated by applying the distribution of part-time workers by type in each hours-worked category in November 1952 to hours-worked categories for May 1953.
[b] Revised to correct for differences between 68-area and 230-area samples.

firmly based on direct surveys by the Census Bureau of part-time workers; others had to be assumed. The percentage of labor force time lost because of unemployment and related types of idleness was only slightly higher than the traditional unemployment rate and showed almost the same pattern of movement; no real significance could be attributed to any differences. Moreover, the computation of labor force time provided on an actual or imputed basis involves so many assumptions about the hours that could have been worked by various types of workers that the resultant numbers are, to say the least, synthetic. Finally, the assumption of a fixed number of man-hours lost (forty) by the unemployed and the "with a job" group means that the relative severity of joblessness will seem to decrease as the number of man-hours actually worked by the employed sector of the labor force rises. Thus, to some extent hours lost by the unemployed are offset by overtime hours, just as with the traditional unemployment rate, unadjusted for seasonal variation, the severity of unemployment may appear to diminish simply because agricultural employment is temporarily rising.

The key to most of the computations made by Hitch was the information derived from the Census Bureau's special surveys of part-time workers, which were conducted quarterly from May 1949 through May 1951. As indicated earlier they were conducted only occasionally between 1951 and 1954. No satisfactory method has been found to interpolate for the long gaps between surveys. For purposes of comparison with other measures, examination of man-hours lost must be limited to dates when statistics for part-time workers are available.

A slightly different method of computing man-hours lost has been used here, in order to reflect the changing distribution of hours worked during the period. It involves the following steps:

1. Assume that there is no involuntary part-time work or partial employment for economic reasons and add into the man-hours actually worked the estimated man-hours lost by these two groups of part-time workers.

2. Recompute average hours worked, dividing the adjusted man-hours worked by the total number of persons at work.

3. Assume that the unemployed and those persons on temporary layoff or waiting to start new jobs would have averaged this adjusted number of hours had they actually worked; multiply the number of persons in these three groups by the average computed in step two. (The estimate obtained is 2 to 4 per cent higher than any derived by taking account of the industrial composition of the unemployed and "with a job" groups and computing man-hours lost, industry by industry. Unfortunately, detailed data are available for this more refined calculation only in the months since September 1953.)

4. Add to (3) the estimated man-hours lost by the part-time workers. This sum equals the estimated man-hours lost because of unemployment, partial employment, temporary layoffs, and time spent waiting for new jobs to start.

Changes in this aggregate are compared with changes in total unemployment and in total unemployment plus partial employment, etc. in Table A-12. In Table 4, the same data are shown in relation to November 1952, the lowest *observed* point for the combined measure.

The index of man-hours lost obviously is very close in most months to that for the number of persons affected by unemployment and lack of work arising from the other specified causes. This follows from the method of estimation, in which the only factor which could cause difference is the amount of time lost by the partially employed.

Total unemployment alone is more sensitive than these aggregate measures, or at least has relatively sharper changes from low to high. In the 1950 peak, the index of total unemployment was 330.3 compared with 229.3 for aggregate number of persons affected by the various factors combined and 258.1 for aggregate man-hours lost. In March 1954, the differences were not so large but still noteworthy (262.7 as

TABLE 4

Indexes of Number of Persons Affected and Man-Hours Lost by Unemployment, Partial Employment, Temporary Layoffs, and "New Jobs," Selected Months, 1949-1954

(November 1952 = 100)

Month and Year	*Total Unemployment*	*Total Unemployment plus Partial Employment plus Temporary Layoffs and "New Jobs"*	*Man-hours Lost by Total Unemployment, Partial Employment, Temporary Layoffs and "New Jobs"*
1949:			
May	231.9	199.8	209.4
August	260.2	218.3	236.4
November	240.4	198.2	209.7
1950:			
February	330.3	229.3	258.1
May	215.6	181.2	192.4
August	176.3	166.8	171.0
November	158.0	139.0	145.6
1951:			
February	169.7	150.7	153.0
May	113.5	119.7	118.3
1952:			
May	113.0	118.2	116.0
November	100.0	100.0	100.0
1953:			
May[a]	92.1	98.1	97.6
December[b]	163.1	163.1	161.4
1954:			
March	262.7	225.9	230.1
May	233.1	208.4	211.2
August	228.8	218.5	218.3
November	204.0	189.9	189.4

[a] Partial employment estimated on the basis of November 1952 data.
[b] Revised to correct for differences between 68-area and 230-area samples.

compared with 225.9 and 230.1). Except for the greater amplitude of change noted, they all tell much the same story. However, a global concept of unemployment that included in a single total all these forms of lack of work, some of which do not always reflect changing business conditions, might actually be less useful as a barometer than is the present concept.

5. *Tentative Recommendation*

To stimulate discussion, I should like to propose, as a possible compromise, a new arrangement of the current monthly labor force data. Needless to say, this represents my own personal preference, and not the official position of the Census Bureau. Several changes would be required:

1. Attempts should be abandoned to include among the unemployed each month those inactive work seekers who would have been seeking work except for temporary illness or belief no work was available. The state of unemployment is a matter largely of attitude in these cases. Since no way has been found as yet to provide accurate measurements of changing attitudes with present procedures, I suggest that the concept be changed, at least until techniques are developed. Instead, special surveys on a quarterly or semiannual basis might be used to provide an approximate measure of this elusive segment of the labor supply.

2. Data on reasons for part-time work should be collected every month, as is done in Canada.

3. A new, major category would be introduced, comprising those persons who worked less than full-time during the survey week because of business conditions (the groups now labeled "economic" and "involuntary" part-time workers). Throughout the preceding discussion they have been called the "partially employed" to be consistent with current terminology. However, for a three-way breakdown of the labor force, a more convenient term and one that would more clearly distinguish them from the employed would be "partially unemployed."

4. The unemployed category (or better, the totally unemployed) would consist of two subgroups:

a. Persons actively seeking work (including specifically those registered at public employment offices).

b. Persons who had been laid off either temporarily or indefinitely from their jobs and were waiting to be called back rather than looking for new jobs. It might be necessary to impose a time limit on the length of layoff in order to eliminate persons who, in fact, had withdrawn from the labor force for a long period. Persons waiting to start new jobs, however, would remain in the employed, because trends in their number seem to bear no relation to the changes in the unemployed and they appear to be typically labor force entrants.

The following employment status distribution of the civilian population could then be provided each month:

- Civilian labor force
  - Employed
    - At work
    - With a job but not at work
  - Partially unemployed
  - Totally unemployed
    - Seeking work
    - Waiting recall to job
- Not in labor force

I believe that these modifications might meet several needs without serious loss of content or disruption of the continuity of the data on total unemployment. Obviously, it would be necessary to test in advance the effect on the level and movement of the unemployment count of discontinuing the inclusion of the two inactive groups and adding in those on temporary layoff who are now classified as employed. It is possible that the two changes might offset each other, if accompanied by a clarification and sharpening of the question on looking for work. In any case, it appears to me that the resulting figures on total unemployment would describe a relatively homogeneous group, and that the two components could be measured satisfactorily. Possible losses in the scope of the concept might be compensated for by a greater objectivity and precision in the monthly figures.

6. *Summary and Conclusions*

1. The present Census concept of unemployment provides a measure of the number of job applicants who have no other work during a calendar week.

2. Because job applicants seek work with varying degrees of activity and persistence, it is difficult to obtain a complete count with present survey procedures.

3. No source of the "true" level of unemployment as currently defined has been found. Complete counts of the population are defective because of enumeration problems, and efforts to measure errors from the survey itself have been only partially successful. Such efforts do suggest that the number of unemployed who may be incorrectly classified as outside the labor force does not vary directly with economic conditions.

4. Alternative concepts that are frequently suggested are of two

main groups (a) breakdowns of the unemployed to find a measure that reflects only changes in economic conditions and reflects them as accurately as possible and (b) expansions of the present concept to include all persons who are affected by shortage of work, whether or not they have jobs.

5. Although it may always fall short in terms of level, the present unemployment series is the most sensitive of the various alternatives except a series based on the number of unemployed adult males. Other possible variations raise the level but do not substantially alter the pattern of change, except in a few instances.

6. The figures on partial employment (or partial unemployment) are the most valuable of the supplementary indexes, since they do more than mirror the total unemployment figures and may have predictive value. It would be very desirable to collect them every month.

7. Except for political uses, it is generally advantageous to maximize the significant breakdowns of the labor force and minimize the use of global terms and concepts. Unfortunately, the reliability of the breakdowns is not always adequate from the standpoint of sampling error.

8. A relatively simple solution to some of the conceptual and measurement problems might be achieved if a third category of partially unemployed were distinguished in the labor force and if the totally unemployed group were separated into job seekers and persons awaiting recall to their old jobs. Attempts to measure other possible segments of the labor supply might better be made as special surveys.

Appendix

TABLE A-1

Estimates of Unemployed Workers by Type, Quarterly Months, 1940-1945

Month and Year		Total	Emergency Workers[a]	Nonemergency Workers						
						Inactive Unemployed				
							Reason for Not Seeking Work			
				Total	*Actively Seeking Work*	*Total*	*No Work Available*	*Layoff— Indefinite or Seasonal*	*Illness*	*Other*[b]
		Thousands of Persons, 14 Years Old and Over								
1940	July	7,413	2,163	5,250	4,200	1,050	333	310	240	167
	October	6,531	2,351	4,180	3,390	790	239	116	333	102
1941	January	6,801	2,657	4,144	3,212	932	175	345	335	77
	April	5,814	2,398	3,416	2,521	895	103	362	353	77
	July	5,235	1,723	3,512	3,077	435	65	91	279	
	October	3,462	1,519	1,943	1,559	384	67	81	236	
1942	January	3,893	1,417	2,476	2,015	461	37	188	236	
	April	2,738	1,218	1,520	1,237	283	28	76	179	
	July	2,427	714	1,713	1,448	265	14	74	177	
	October	1,451	472	979	782	197	11	47	139	
1943	January	1,370	364	1,006	748	258	5	52	201	
	April	950	159	791	573	218	7	39	172	
	July	1,290		1,290	949	341	5	54	282	
	October	910		910	529	381	14	51	316	
1944	January	1,079		1,079	555	524	15	148	361	
	April	776		776	440	336	16	50	270	
	July	995		995	616	379	8	95	276	
	October	633		633	312	321	10	47	264	
1945	January	839		839	438	401	11	103	287	
	April	764		764	380	384	3	108	273	
	July	1,087		1,087	612	475	3	129	343	

(continued on next page)

TABLE A-1 (continued)

MONTH AND YEAR		TOTAL	EMERGENCY WORKERS[a]	NONEMERGENCY WORKERS						
						Inactive Unemployed				
							Reason for Not Seeking Work			
				Total	Actively Seeking Work	Total	No Work Available	Layoff—Indefinite or Seasonal	Illness	Other[b]
				Percentage Distribution of Nonemergency Workers						
1940	July			100.0	80.0	20.0	6.4	5.9	4.6	3.2
	October			100.0	81.1	18.9	5.7	2.8	8.0	2.4
1941	January			100.0	77.5	22.5	4.2	8.3	8.1	1.9
	April			100.0	73.8	26.2	3.0	10.6	10.3	2.3
	July			100.0	87.6	12.4	1.9	2.6	7.9	
	October			100.0	80.2	19.8	3.4	4.2	12.2	
1942	January			100.0	81.4	18.6	1.5	7.6	9.5	
	April			100.0	81.4	18.6	1.8	5.0	11.8	
	July			100.0	84.5	15.5	0.8	4.3	10.4	
	October			100.0	79.9	20.1	1.1	4.8	14.2	
1943	January			100.0	74.4	25.6	0.5	5.1	20.0	
	April			100.0	72.4	27.6	0.9	4.9	21.8	
	July			100.0	73.6	26.4	0.4	4.2	21.8	
	October			100.0	58.1	41.9	1.6	5.6	34.7	
1944	January			100.0	51.4	48.6	1.4	13.7	33.5	
	April			100.0	56.7	43.3	2.1	6.4	34.8	
	July			100.0	61.9	38.1	0.8	9.5	27.8	
	October			100.0	49.3	50.7	1.6	7.4	41.7	
1945	January			100.0	52.2	47.8	1.3	12.3	34.2	
	April			100.0	49.7	50.3	0.4	14.1	35.8	
	July			100.0	56.4	43.6	0.3	11.8	31.5	

[a] Official figures of persons on WPA, CCC, NYA (except students), and other work programs.

[b] Until April 1941, persons not seeking work for other reasons were divided into those who appeared to be in the labor force and those who did not. It proved impossible to make this decision satisfactorily, and the group was treated as not in the labor force.

Note: Data not revised for schedule change in July 1945.

TABLE A-2

Comparison of Statistics on Employment Status from the WPA Monthly Report of Unemployment and the 1940 Census of Population, March 24-30, 1940

(millions of persons, 14 years old and over)

Employment Status	*WPA Monthly Report of Unemployment* (1)	*1940 Census of Population*[a] (2)	*Difference (1) — (2)* (3)	*Per Cent Difference (3) ÷ (1)* (4)
Civilian noninstitutional population	99.4	99.4	0	
In labor force	53.9	52.5	1.4	2.6
Employed	45.1	45.0	0.1	0.2
At work	43.7	43.7	0	
With a job but not at work	1.4	1.3	0.1	7.1
Unemployed	8.8	7.5	1.3	14.8
On public emergency work	2.7	2.4	0.3	11.1
Other unemployed	6.1	5.1	1.0	16.4
Not in labor force	45.4	45.1	0.3	0.7
Keeping house	29.4	28.8	0.6	2.0
In school	9.3	9.1	0.2	2.2
Unable to work	5.1	5.2	—0.1	—2.0
Other	1.6	2.0	—0.4	—25.0
Not ascertainable	0.1	1.8	—1.7	

[a] Data from a 5 per cent sample of returns of 1940 Census of Population.

Source: "Changes in Employment, Unemployment, and the Labor Force between June and July 1941, with Estimates for the Period April 1940 to July 1941," Monthly Report of Unemployment, mimeographed, Federal Works Agency, Work Projects Administration, undated.

TABLE A-3

Comparison of Statistics on Employment Status from Current Population Survey for April 1950 and the 1950 Census of Population, by Sex

(thousands of persons, 14 years old and over)

Employment Status and Sex	*CPS*[a] (1)	*Census*[b] (2)	*Difference* *(1) – (2)* (3)	*Per Cent Difference* *(3) ÷ (1)* (4)
Both Sexes:				
Civilian noninstitutional population	109,928	109,928	0	
In labor force	62,675	59,072	3,603	5.7
Employed	59,131	56,239	2,892	4.9
In agriculture	7,259	6,885	374	5.2
At work	7,007	6,718	289	4.1
With a job but not at work	252	167	85	33.7
In nonagricultural industries	51,873	49,354	2,519	4.9
At work	50,264	47,701	2,563	5.1
With a job but not at work	1,609	1,653	–44	–2.7
Unemployed	3,543	2,832	711	20.1
Not in labor force	47,254	50,856	–3,602	–7.6
Keeping house	33,182	32,180	1,002	3.0
Unable to work	2,359	4,566	–2,207	–93.6
In school, other, and not reported	11,713	14,110	–2,397	–20.5
Male:				
Civilian noninstitutional population	53,478	53,478	0	
In labor force	44,543	42,599	1,944	4.4
Employed	41,890	40,519	1,371	3.3
In agriculture	6,332	6,297	35	0.6
At work	6,125	6,171	–46	–0.8
With a job but not at work	207	126	81	39.1
In nonagricultural industries	35,558	34,222	1,336	3.8
At work	34,532	33,160	1,372	4.0
With a job but not at work	1,026	1,062	–36	–3.5
Unemployed	2,653	2,079	574	21.6
Not in labor force	8,936	10,879	–1,943	–21.7
Keeping house	96	286	–190	
Unable to work	1,573	2,754	–1,181	–75.1
In school, other, and not reported	7,267	7,839	–572	–7.9
Female:				
Civilian noninstitutional population	56,450	56,450	0	
In labor force	18,132	16,473	1,659	9.1
Employed	17,241	15,720	1,521	8.8
In agriculture	927	588	339	36.6
At work	882	547	335	38.0
With a job but not at work	45	41	4	8.9
In nonagricultural industries	16,315	15,132	1,183	7.3
At work	15,733	14,541	1,192	7.6
With a job but not at work	582	591	–9	–1.5
Unemployed	890	753	137	15.4
Not in labor force	38,318	39,977	–1,659	–4.3
Keeping house	33,086	31,894	1,192	3.6
Unable to work	786	1,812	–1,026	
In school, other, and not reported	4,446	6,270	–1,824	–41.0

[a] Adjusted, by sex, to the 1950 census levels of the civilian noninstitutional population, 14 years old and over.

[b] Complete count data except for "at work" and "with a job" breaks; these are estimated from a 3⅓ per cent sample.

TABLE A-4

Comparison of Estimates of Employment Status Based on Reports for Identical Persons Enumerated in the Same Week by Current Population Survey and 1950 Census Enumerators, by Sex, April 1950

(thousands of persons, 14 years old and over)

Employment Status and Sex	*Based on CPS Enumeration* (1)	*Based on Census Enumeration* (2)	*Difference (1) — (2)* (3)	*Per Cent Difference (3) ÷ (1)* (4)
Both Sexes:				
Civilian noninstitutional population	109,928	109,928	0	
In labor force	63,081	59,983	3,098	4.9
Employed	59,204	57,036	2,168	3.7
In agriculture	7,715	6,488	1,227	15.9
In nonagricultural industries	51,489	50,548	941	1.8
Unemployed	3,877	2,947	930	24.0
Not in labor force	46,847	49,945	–3,098	–6.6
Male:				
Civilian noninstitutional population	53,478	53,478	0	
In labor force	45,145	43,584	1,561	3.5
Employed	42,283	41,392	891	2.1
In agriculture	6,709	6,048	661	9.9
In nonagricultural industries	35,574	35,344	230	0.6
Unemployed	2,862	2,192	670	23.4
Not in labor force	8,333	9,894	–1,561	–18.7
Female:				
Civilian noninstitutional population	56,450	56,450	0	
In labor force	17,936	16,399	1,537	8.6
Employed	16,921	15,644	1,277	7.5
In agriculture	1,006	440	566	56.3
In nonagricultural industries	15,915	15,204	711	4.5
Unemployed	1,015	755	260	25.6
Not in labor force	38,514	40,051	–1,537	–4.0

TABLE A-5

Gross Differences in Employment Status for Unemployed Persons Enumerated in the Same Week by Current Population Survey and 1950 Census Enumerators, by Sex, April 1950

(thousands of persons, 14 years old and over)

Employment Status	*Unemployed in CPS, Not Unemployed in Census*	*Unemployed in Census, Not Unemployed in CPS*	*Difference*
Both sexes	1,976	1,046	930
	Census Status	*CPS Status*	
Employed in agriculture	31	45	–14
Employed in nonagricultural industries	801	388	413
Not in labor force	1,144	613	531
Male	1,336	666	670
	Census Status	*CPS Status*	
Employed in agriculture	31	45	–14
Employed in nonagricultural industries	654	359	295
Not in labor force	651	262	389
Female	640	380	260
	Census Status	*CPS Status*	
Employed in agriculture			
Employed in nonagricultural industries	147	29	118
Not in labor force	493	351	142

TABLE A-6

Reason for Not Looking for Work at Survey Date, Specified Groups Not in the Labor Force, by Sex, August 1946, and May and June 1947
(thousands of persons, 14 years old and over)

Reason and Sex	*August 1946*[a]	*May 1947*[b]	*June 1947*[c]
Both sexes	7,681	1,854	2,892
Reasons suggesting attachment to labor force	1,500	220	563
Believe no work available	363	99	352
Temporarily ill	619	43	84
On layoff; off season	338	25	10
Awaiting results of previous job application	180	53	117
Other reasons	6,181	1,634	2,329
Busy with home responsibilities	2,156	361	550
School	1,277	260	792
Do not want work, or resting	1,640	385	229
All other	1,108	628	758
Male	2,197	591	1,113
Reasons suggesting attachment to labor force	358	94	212
Believe no work available	149	55	119
Temporarily ill	147	15	47
On layoff; off season	9	4	3
Awaiting results of previous job application	53	20	43
Other reasons	1,839	497	901
Busy with home responsibilities	23	7	34
School	926	168	507
Do not want work, or resting	487	127	119
All other	403	195	241
Female	5,484	1,263	1,779
Reasons suggesting attachment to labor force	1,142	126	351
Believe no work available	214	44	233
Temporarily ill	472	28	37
On layoff; off season	329	21	7
Awaiting results of previous job application	127	33	74
Other reasons	4,342	1,137	1,428
Busy with home responsibilities	2,133	354	516
School	351	92	285
Do not want work, or resting	1,153	258	110
All other	705	433	517

[a] Persons not in the labor force who had worked or looked for work during the past year and World War II veterans.

[b] Persons not in the labor force who had worked or looked for work during the past two months.

[c] Persons not in the labor force who wanted a job.

TABLE A-7

Persons Not in the Labor Force Who Had Recently Looked for Work, by Sex and Availability for Work, Selected Dates, 1948-1950
(thousands of persons, 14 years old and over)

Sex and Availability for Work	*Feb. 1948*	*June 1948*	*May 1949*	*Jan. 1950*	*June 1950*
Both sexes	662	494	736	1,018	861
Still wanted work at time of survey	539	423	664	705	773
Could take a job	494[a]	386	525	667	720
Wanted full-time work	n.a.	n.a.	n.a.	334	536
Wanted part-time work	n.a.	n.a.	n.a.	333	184
Could not take a job	45	38	138	38	53
No longer wanted work	106	61	63	313	88
Not reported	17	8	10		
Male	213	162	270	344	346
Still wanted work at time of survey	162	136	247	232	325
Could take a job	147[a]	122	165	215	308
Wanted full-time work	n.a.	n.a.	n.a.	72	217
Wanted part-time work	n.a.	n.a.	n.a.	143	91
Could not take a job	15	14	82	17	17
No longer wanted work	46	22	19	112	21
Not reported	5	3	5		
Female	449	332	466	674	515
Still wanted work at time of survey	377	287	417	473	448
Could take a job	347[a]	264	360	452	412
Wanted full-time work	n.a.	n.a.	n.a.	262	319
Wanted part-time work	n.a.	n.a.	n.a.	190	93
Could not take a job	30	24	56	21	36
No longer wanted work	60	39	44	201	67
Not reported	12	5	5		

[a] Information was not obtained in February 1948 as to whether those reported as still wanting work could also have taken a job at that time. This number is estimated from detailed distributions by age and sex shown in the June 1948 and May 1949 surveys.

n.a. = not available.

Note: "Recently" was specified as since Christmas 1947, for the February 1948 survey, and since the first of the preceding month, for the other four surveys.

TABLE A-8

Unemployed Persons of Specified Types, Monthly, 1948-1954

(*thousands*)

Month and Year	*Total Unemployed*	*Unemployed 25-64 Years Old*	*Unemployed Men 25-64 Years Old*	*Unemployed Wage and Salary Workers*	*Married Couple with Husband Unemployed*
1948:					
January	2,065	1,198	898	1,896	
February	2,639	1,522	1,072	2,369	
March	2,440	1,322	945	2,149	
April	2,193	1,295	928	1,972	712
May	1,761	1,007	707	1,598	
June	2,184	957	605	1,640	
July	2,227	1,058	712	1,808	
August	1,941	1,110	749	1,743	
September	1,899	1,165	764	1,635	
October	1,642	981	636	1,446	
November	1,831	1,116	766	1,650	
December	1,941	1,184	868	1,773	
1949:					
January	2,664	1,634	1,236	2,433	
February	3,221	1,975	1,514	2,928	
March	3,167	1,935	1,521	2,935	
April	3,016	1,873	1,369	2,816	1,115
May	3,289	1,957	1,409	2,905	
June	3,778	1,960	1,370	3,130	
July	4,095	2,248	1,578	3,504	
August	3,689	2,126	1,462	3,284	
September	3,351	1,997	1,412	2,979	
October	3,576	2,253	1,665	3,287	
November	3,409	2,138	1,494	3,107	
December	3,489	2,213	1,612	3,194	
1950:					
January	4,480	2,823	2,061	4,152	
February	4,684	2,947	2,162	4,287	
March	4,123	2,713	1,980	3,776	1,503
April	3,515	2,343	1,759	3,194	
May	3,057	1,937	1,372	2,762	
June	3,384	1,787	1,183	2,806	
July	3,213	1,810	1,246	2,690	
August	2,500	1,494	981	2,185	
September	2,341	1,348	860	2,019	
October	1,940	1,229	759	1,733	
November	2,240	1,466	839	2,014	
December	2,229	1,434	956	1,951	

(continued on next page)

TABLE A-8 (continued)
(*thousands*)

Month and Year	Total Unemployed	Unemployed 25-64 Years Old	Unemployed Men 25-64 Years Old	Unemployed Wage and Salary Workers	Married Couples with Husband Unemployed
1951:					
January	2,503	1,674	1,093	2,249	
February	2,407	1,589	1,020	2,179	
March	2,147	1,381	816	1,899	
April	1,744	1,138	651	1,562	480
May	1,609	1,056	595	1,431	
June	1,980	1,022	585	1,578	
July	1,856	1,040	622	1,538	
August	1,578	994	618	1,346	
September	1,606	1,024	538	1,420	
October	1,616	1,050	560	1,452	
November	1,828	1,170	612	1,638	
December	1,674	1,128	654	1,514	
1952:					
January	2,054	1,334	906	1,870	
February	2,086	1,340	874	1,930	
March	1,804	1,144	810	1,610	
April	1,612	1,002	646	1,478	464
May	1,602	962	592	1,414	
June	1,818	890	576	1,454	
July	1,942	1,064	706	1,582	
August	1,604	942	602	1,378	
September	1,438	848	482	1,250	
October	1,284	768	408	1,130	
November	1,418	914	530	1,260	
December	1,412	856	582	1,246	
953:					
January	1,892	1,288	946	1,694	
February	1,788	1,182	830	1,592	
March	1,674	1,086	712	1,500	
April	1,582	1,036	744	1,438	564
May	1,306	866	623	1,172	
June	1,562	806	566	1,248	
July	1,548	910	634	1,332	
August	1,240	732	510	1,104	
September[a]	1,321	845	535	1,207	
October[a]	1,301	807	521	1,164	
November[a]	1,699	1,106	705	1,540	
December[a]	2,313	1,444	969	2,030	
954:					
January	3,087	2,037	1,381	2,770	
February	3,671	2,454	1,717	3,308	
March	3,725	2,526	1,716	3,442	
April	3,465	2,357	1,635	3,208	1,328
May	3,305	2,226	1,490	2,961	
June	3,347	2,056	1,373	2,903	
July	3,346	2,063	1,388	2,843	
August	3,245	2,123	1,403	2,905	
September	3,099	2,067	1,364	2,791	
October	2,741	1,880	1,253	2,498	
November	2,893	1,931	1,229	2,603	
December	2,838	1,915	1,325	2,567	

[a] Revised to correct for difference between 68-area and 230-area samples.

TABLE A-9

Unemployment Rates for All Unemployed Workers and for Unemployed Wage and Salary Workers, Monthly, 1948-1954

(*per cent*)

Unemployed Workers	*Jan.*	*Feb.*	*Mar.*	*Apr.*	*May*	*June*	*July*	*Aug.*	*Sept.*	*Oct.*	*Nov.*	*Dec.*
1948:												
All	3.5	4.4	4.1	3.6	2.9	3.4	3.5	3.1	3.1	2.7	3.0	3.2
Wage and salary	4.0	5.0	4.5	4.1	3.4	3.3	3.6	3.5	3.4	3.0	3.4	3.6
1949:												
All	4.4	5.3	5.2	5.0	5.3	6.0	6.4	5.8	5.3	5.7	5.4	5.6
Wage and salary	5.1	6.1	6.1	5.9	6.0	6.5	7.1	6.5	6.0	6.5	6.2	6.5
1950:												
All	7.3	7.6	6.7	5.7	4.9	5.2	5.0	3.9	3.7	3.0	3.5	3.6
Wage and salary	8.4	8.6	7.6	6.4	5.6	5.5	5.3	4.2	4.0	3.4	3.9	3.8
1951:												
All	4.1	3.9	3.4	2.8	2.6	3.1	2.9	2.5	2.5	2.5	2.9	2.7
Wage and salary	4.5	4.3	3.7	3.1	2.8	3.1	3.0	2.6	2.8	2.8	3.2	2.9
1952:												
All	3.3	3.4	2.9	2.6	2.6	2.8	3.0	2.5	2.3	2.0	2.2	2.2
Wage and salary	3.7	3.8	3.2	2.9	2.8	2.8	3.0	2.6	2.4	2.2	2.4	2.4
1953:												
All	3.0	2.9	2.7	2.5	2.1	2.4	2.4	1.9	2.1[a]	2.0[a]	2.7[a]	3.7[a]
Wage and salary	3.3	3.1	2.9	2.8	2.3	2.4	2.6	2.1	2.3[a]	2.2[a]	2.9[a]	3.9[a]
1954:												
All	4.9	5.8	5.8	5.4	5.1	5.1	5.1	5.0	4.8	4.2	4.5	4.5
Wage and salary	5.3	6.3	6.5	6.1	5.6	5.5	5.4	5.4	5.3	4.7	4.9	4.9

[a] Revised to correct for difference between 68-area and 230-area samples.

Note: Unemployment rates are unemployed as a percentage of the civilian labor force, and unemployed whose last job was as a wage or salary worker as a percentage of all wage and salary workers (employed and unemployed).

TABLE A-10

Unemployed Persons and Selected Groups of Employed Persons, Monthly, 1948-1954

(thousands of persons, 14 years old and over)

MONTH AND YEAR	TOTAL UNEMPLOYED (1)	PERSONS ON TEMPORARY LAYOFF OR WAITING TO START NEW JOB			PARTIALLY EMPLOYED			SUMMARY		
		Total (2)	*On Temporary Layoff* (3)	*Waiting to Start New Job* (4)	*Total* (5)	*"Economic" Part-time Workers*[a] (6)	*Involuntary Part-time Workers*[b] (7)	*(1)+(3)* (8)	*(1)+(2)* (9)	*(1)+(2)+(5)* (10)
1948:										
Jan.	2,065	306	180	126	n.a.	n.a.	n.a.	2,245	2,371	n.a.
Feb.	2,639	212	129	83	n.a.	n.a.	n.a.	2,768	2,851	n.a.
Mar.	2,440	236	122	114	1,213	712	511	2,562	2,676	3,889
Q. av.	2,382	252	144	108	n.a.	n.a.	n.a.	2,526	2,634	n.a.
Apr.	2,193	251	146	105	n.a.	n.a.	n.a.	2,339	2,444	n.a.
May	1,761	267	170	97	n.a.	n.a.	n.a.	1,931	2,028	n.a.
June	2,184	390	138	252	n.a.	n.a.	n.a.	2,322	2,574	n.a.
Q. av.	2,046	302	151	151	n..a	n.a.	n.a.	2,197	2,348	n.a.
July	2,227	319	163	156	n.a.	n.a.	n.a.	2,390	2,546	n.a.
Aug.	1,941	337	133	204	n.a.	n.a.	n.a.	2,074	2,278	n.a.
Sept.	1,899	184	87	97	1,360	814	546	1,986	2,083	3,443
Q. av.	2,023	280	128	152	n.a.	n.a.	n.a.	2,151	2,303	n.a.
Oct.	1,642	126	75	51	n.a.	n.a.	n.a.	1,717	1,768	n.a.
Nov.	1,831	234	139	95	n.a.	n.a.	n.a.	1,970	2,065	n.a.
Dec.	1,941	272	207	65	n.a.	n.a.	n.a.	2,148	2,213	n.a.
Q. av.	1,804	210	140	70	n.a.	n.a.	n.a.	1,944	2,014	n.a.

(continued on next page)

TABLE A-10 (continued)
(*thousands of persons, 14 years old and over*)

MONTH AND YEAR	TOTAL UNEMPLOYED (1)	PERSONS ON TEMPORARY LAYOFF OR WAITING TO START NEW JOB			PARTIALLY EMPLOYED			SUMMARY		
		Total (2)	*On Temporary Layoff* (3)	*Waiting to Start New Job* (4)	*Total* (5)	*"Economic" Part-time Workers*[a] (6)	*Involuntary Part-time Workers*[b] (7)	(1)+(3) (8)	(1)+(2) (9)	(1)+(2)+(5) (10)
1949:										
Jan	2,664	369	286	83	n.a.	n.a.	n.a.	2,950	3,033	n.a.
Feb.	3,221	268	168	100	n.a.	n.a.	n.a.	3,389	3,489	n.a.
Mar.	3,167	229	146	83	n.a.	n.a.	n.a.	3,313	3,396	n.a.
Q. av.	3,017	289	200	89	n.a.	n.a.	n.a.	3,217	3,306	n.a.
Apr.	3,016	269	182	87	n.a.	n.a.	n.a.	3,198	3,285	n.a.
May	3,289	276	167	109	2,457	1,571	886	3,456	3,565	6,022
June	3,778	311	143	168	n.a.	n.a.	n.a.	3,921	4,089	n.a.
Q. av.	3,361	285	164	121	n.a.	n.a.	n.a.	3,525	3,646	n.a.
July	4,095	385	292	93	n.a.	n.a.	n.a.	4,387	4,480	n.a.
Aug.	3,689	336	209	127	2,555	1,474	1,081	3,898	4,025	6,580
Sept.	3,351	301	175	126	n.a.	n.a.	n.a.	3,526	3,652	n.a.
Q. av.	3,711	340	225	115	n.a.	n.a.	n.a.	3,936	4,051	n.a.
Oct.	3,576	247	171	76	n.a.	n.a.	n.a.	3,747	3,823	n.a.
Nov.	3,409	213	139	74	2,352	1,387	965	3,548	3,622	5,974
Dec.	3,489	230	144	86	n.a.	n.a.	n.a.	3,633	3,719	n.a.
Q. av.	3,491	230	151	79	n.a.	n.a.	n.a.	3,642	3,721	n.a.

(continued on next page)

TABLE A-10 (continued)

(*thousands of persons, 14 years old and over*)

MONTH AND YEAR	TOTAL UNEMPLOYED (1)	PERSONS ON TEMPORARY LAYOFF OR WAITING TO START NEW JOB: *Total* (2)	*On Temporary Layoff* (3)	*Waiting to Start New Job* (4)	PARTIALLY EMPLOYED: *Total* (5)	*"Economic" Part-time Workers*[a] (6)	*Involuntary Part-time Workers*[b] (7)	SUMMARY: (1)+(3) (8)	(1)+(2) (9)	(1)+(2)+(5) (10)
1950:										
Jan.	4,480	219	118	101	n.a.	n.a.	n.a.	4,598	4,699	n.a.
Feb	4,684	144	72	72	2,083	1,095	988	4,756	4,828	6,911
Mar.	4,123	219	120	99	n.a.	n.a.	n.a.	4,243	4,342	n.a.
Q. av.	4,429	194	103	91	n.a.	n.a.	n.a.	4,532	4,623	n.a.
Apr.	3,515	192	86	106	n.a.	n.a.	n.a.	3,601	3,707	n.a.
May	3,057	249	110	139	2,155	1,087	1,068	3,167	3,306	5,461
June	3,384	353	110	243	n.a.	n.a.	n.a.	3,494	3,737	n.a.
Q. av.	3,318	265	102	163	n.a.	n.a.	n.a.	3,420	3,583	n.a.
July	3,213	268	131	137	n.a.	n.a.	n.a.	3,344	3,481	n.a.
Aug.	2,500	171	65	106	2,357	1,245	1,112	2,565	2,671	5,028
Sept.	2,341	198	63	135	n.a.	n.a.	n.a.	2,404	2,539	n.a.
Q. av.	2,684	212	86	126	n.a.	n.a.	n.a.	2,770	2,896	n.a.
Oct.	1,940	137	46	91	n.a.	n.a.	n.a.	1,986	2,077	n.a.
Nov.	2,240	142	72	70	1,807	986	821	2,312	2,382	4,189
Dec.	2,229	209	114	95	n.a.	n.a.	n.a.	2,343	2,438	n.a.
Q. av.	2,136	162	77	85	n.a.	n.a.	n.a.	2,213	2,298	n.a.

(continued on next page)

TABLE A-10 (continued)
(*thousands of persons, 14 years old and over*)

MONTH AND YEAR	TOTAL UNEMPLOYED (1)	PERSONS ON TEMPORARY LAYOFF OR WAITING TO START NEW JOB			PARTIALLY EMPLOYED			SUMMARY		
		Total (2)	*On Temporary Layoff* (3)	*Waiting to Start New Job* (4)	*Total* (5)	*"Economic" Part-time Workers*[a] (6)	*Involuntary Part-time Workers*[b] (7)	*(1)+(3)* (8)	*(1)+(2)* (9)	*(1)+(2)+(5)* (10)
1951:										
Jan.	2,503	180	93	87	n.a.	n.a.	n.a.	2,596	2,683	n.a.
Feb.	2,407	165	87	78	1,971	1,123	848	2,494	2,572	4,543
Mar.	2,147	205	80	125	n.a.	n.a.	n.a.	2,227	2,352	n.a.
Q. av.	2,352	183	87	96	n.a.	n.a.	n.a.	2,439	2,535	n.a.
Apr.	1,744	215	133	82	n.a.	n.a.	n.a.	1,877	1,959	n.a.
May	1,609	203	110	93	1,797	978	819	1,719	1,812	3,609
June	1,980	296	131	165	n.a.	n.a.	n.a.	2,111	2,276	n.a.
Q. av.	1,777	238	125	113	n.a.	n.a.	n.a.	1,902	2,015	n.a.
July	1,856	300	190	110	n.a.	n.a.	n.a.	2,046	2,156	n.a.
Aug.	1,578	258	148	110	n.a.	n.a.	n.a.	1,726	1,836	n.a.
Sept.	1,606	300	156	144	n.a.	n.a.	n.a.	1,762	1,906	n.a.
Q. av.	1,680	286	165	121	n.a.	n.a.	n.a.	1,845	1,966	n.a.
Oct.	1,616	168	104	64	n.a.	n.a.	n.a.	1,720	1,784	n.a.
Nov.	1,828	196	78	118	n.a.	n.a.	n.a.	1,906	2,024	n.a.
Dec.	1,674	156	98	58	n.a.	n.a.	n.a.	1,772	1,830	n.a.
Q. av.	1,706	173	93	80	n.a.	n.a.	n.a.	1,799	1,879	n.a.

(continued on next page)

TABLE A-10 (continued)
(*thousands of persons, 14 years old and over*)

MONTH AND YEAR	TOTAL UNEMPLOYED (1)	PERSONS ON TEMPORARY LAYOFF OR WAITING TO START NEW JOB			PARTIALLY EMPLOYED			SUMMARY		
		Total (2)	*On Temporary Layoff* (3)	*Waiting to Start New Job* (4)	*Total* (5)	*"Economic" Part-time Workers*[a] (6)	*Involuntary Part-time Workers*[b] (7)	*(1)+(3)* (8)	*(1)+(2)* (9)	*(1)+(2)+(5)* (10)
1952:										
Jan.	2,054	224	142	82	n.a.	n.a.	n.a.	2,196	2,278	n.a.
Feb.	2,086	272	154	118	n.a.	n.a.	n.a.	2,240	2,358	n.a.
Mar.	1,804	234	142	92	n.a.	n.a.	n.a.	1,946	2,038	n.a.
Q. av.	1,981	243	146	97	n.a.	n.a.	n.a.	2,127	2,224	n.a.
Apr.	1,612	258	188	70	n.a.	n.a.	n.a.	1,800	1,870	n.a.
May	1,602	238	142	96	1,722	1,014	708	1,744	1,840	3,562
June	1,818	340	174	166	n.a.	n.a.	n.a.	1,992	2,158	n.a.
Q. av.	1,677	279	168	111	n.a.	n.a.	n.a.	1,845	1,956	n.a.
July	1,942	262	150	112	n.a.	n.a.	n.a.	2,092	2,204	n.a.
Aug.	1,604	370	230	140	n.a.	n.a.	n.a.	1,834	1,974	n.a.
Sept.	1,438	336	94	242	n.a.	n.a.	n.a.	1,532	1,774	n.a.
Q. av.	1,661	323	158	165	n.a.	n.a.	n.a.	1,819	1,984	n.a.
Oct.	1,284	220	92	128	n.a.	n.a.	n.a.	1,376	1,504	n.a.
Nov.	1,418	198	98	100	1,398	826	572	1,516	1,616	3,014
Dec.	1,412	152	94	58	n.a.	n.a.	n.a.	1,506	1,564	n.a.
Q. av.	1,371	190	95	95	n.a.	n.a.	n.a.	1,466	1,561	n.a.

(continued on next page)

TABLE A-10 (continued)
(*thousands of persons, 14 years old and over*)

MONTH AND YEAR	TOTAL UNEMPLOYED (1)	PERSONS ON TEMPORARY LAYOFF OR WAITING TO START NEW JOB: *Total* (2)	*On Temporary Layoff* (3)	*Waiting to Start New Job* (4)	PARTIALLY EMPLOYED: *Total* (5)	*"Economic" Part-time Workers*[a] (6)	*Involuntary Part-time Workers*[b] (7)	SUMMARY: (1)+(3) (8)	(1)+(2) (9)	(1)+(2)+(5) (10)
1953:										
Jan.	1,892	274	194	80	n.a.	n.a.	n.a.	2,086	2,166	n.a.
Feb.	1,788	198	110	88	n.a.	n.a.	n.a.	1,898	1,986	n.a.
Mar.	1,674	176	84	92	n.a.	n.a.	n.a.	1,758	1,850	n.a.
Q. av.	1,785	216	129	87	n.a.	n.a.	n.a.	1,914	2,001	n.a.
Apr.	1,582	204	100	104	n.a.	n.a.	n.a.	1,682	1,786	n.a.
May	1,306	264	126	138	1,386[c]	811[c]	575[c]	1,432	1,570	2,956[c]
June	1,562	270	122	148	n.a.	n.a.	n.a.	1,684	1,832	n.a.
Q. av.	1,483	246	116	130	n.a.	n.a.	n.a.	1,599	1,729	n.a.
July	1,548	222	144	78	n.a.	n.a.	n.a.	1,692	1,770	n.a.
Aug.	1,240	302	170	132	n.a.	n.a.	n.a.	1,410	1,542	n.a.
Sept.[d]	1,321	313	172	141	n.a.	n.a.	n.a.	1,493	1,634	n.a.
Q. av.	1,370	279	162	117	n.a.	n.a.	n.a.	1,532	1,649	n.a.
Oct.[d]	1,301	282	193	89	n.a.	n.a.	n.a.	1,494	1,583	n.a.
Nov.[d]	1,699	346	273	73	n.a.	n.a.	n.a.	1,972	2,045	n.a.
Dec.[d]	2,313	363	316	47	2,240	1,680	560	2,629	2,676	4,916
Q. av.	1,771	331	261	70	n.a.	n.a.	n.a.	2,032	2,102	n.a.

(continued on next page)

TABLE A-10 (continued)
(*thousands of persons, 14 years old and over*)

MONTH AND YEAR	TOTAL UNEMPLOYED (1)	PERSONS ON TEMPORARY LAYOFF OR WAITING TO START NEW JOB			PARTIALLY EMPLOYED			SUMMARY		
		Total (2)	*On Temporary Layoff* (3)	*Waiting to Start New Job* (4)	*Total* (5)	*"Economic" Part-time Workers*[a] (6)	*Involuntary Part-time Workers*[b] (7)	*(1)+(3)* (8)	*(1)+(2)* (9)	*(1)+(2)+(5)* (10)
1954:										
Jan.	3,087	507	427	80	n.a.	n.a.	n.a.	3,514	3,594	n.a.
Feb.	3,671	324	216	108	n.a.	n.a.	n.a.	3,887	3,995	n.a.
Mar.	3,725	328	236	92	2,756	1,878	878	3,961	4,053	6,809
Q. av.	3,494	386	293	93	n.a.	n.a.	n.a.	3,787	3,880	n.a.
Apr.	3,465	404	216	188	n.a.	n.a.	n.a.	3,681	3,869	n.a.
May	3,305	385	294	91	2,592	1,644	948	3,599	3,690	6,282
June	3,347	456	229	227	n.a.	n.a.	n.a.	3,576	3,803	n.a.
Q. av.	3,372	415	246	169	n.a.	n.a.	n.a.	3,618	3,787	n.a.
July	3,346	436	298	138	n.a.	n.a.	n.a.	3,644	3,782	n.a.
Aug.	3,245	294	143	151	3,047	1,861	1,186	3,388	3,539	6,586
Sept.	3,099	364	198	166	n.a.	n.a.	n.a.	3,297	3,463	n.a.
Q. av.	3,230	365	213	152	n.a.	n.a.	n.a.	3,443	3,595	n.a.
Oct.	2,741	222	136	86	n.a.	n.a.	n.a.	2,877	2,963	n.a.
Nov.	2,893	253	120	133	2,579	1,506	1,073	3,013	3,146	5,725
Dec.	2,838	201	137	64	n.a.	n.a.	n.a.	2,975	3,039	n.a.
Q. av.	2,824	225	131	94	n.a.	n.a.	n.a.	2,955	3,049	n.a.

[a] Regular full-time workers working part time because of economic factors (slack work, job turnover, material shortages, and repairs to plant or equipment).
[b] Regular part-time workers who prefer and could accept full-time work.
[c] Estimated by applying distribution of part-time workers by type in each hours-worked category in November 1952 to hours-worked categories for May 1953.
[d] Revised to correct for differences between 68-area and 230-area samples.
n.a. = not available since not collected in this survey.

TABLE A-11

Unemployed Persons and Partially Employed Persons in Non-Agricultural Industries, Selected Months, 1949-1954
(thousands of persons, 14 years old and over)

MONTH AND YEAR	TOTAL UNEMPLOYED	PARTIALLY EMPLOYED	
		"Economic" Part-time Workers[a]	*Involuntary Part-time Workers*[b]
1949:			
May	3,289	1,530	786
August	3,689	1,191	952
November	3,409	1,244	865
1950:			
February	4,684	993	908
May	3,057	1,034	965
August	2,500	916	981
November	2,240	855	754
1951:			
February	2,407	1,033	806
May	1,609	918	694
1952:			
May	1,602	958	642
November	1,418	704	493
1953:			
December[c]	2,313	1,376	510
1954:			
March	3,725	1,712	794
May	3,305	1,547	866
August	3,245	1,451	1,059
November	2,893	1,285	935

[a] Regular full-time workers working part time because of economic factors (slack work, job turnover, material shortages, and repairs to plant or equipment).
[b] Regular part-time workers who prefer and could accept full-time work.
[c] Revised to correct for differences between 68-area and 230-area samples.

TABLE A-12

Comparison of Number of Persons Affected and Man-Hours Lost by Unemployment, Partial Employment, Temporary Layoffs, and "New Jobs," Selected Months, 1949-1954

(thousands of persons, 14 years old and over)

[M]onth and [Y]ear	Total Unemployment		Unemployment, Partial Employment, Temporary Layoffs, and "New Jobs"		Man-Hours Lost by Unemployment, Partial Employment, Temporary Layoffs, and "New Jobs"	
	Number	*Per Cent of Labor Force*	*Number*	*Per Cent of Labor Force*	*Number*	*Per Cent of Time Worked Plus Time Lost*
[1]949:						
May	3,289	5.3	6,022	9.7	195,618	7.3
August	3,689	5.8	6,580	10.3	220,887	8.4
November	3,409	5.4	5,974	9.5	195,863	7.4
[1]950:						
February	4,684	7.6	6,911	11.2	241,144	9.6
May	3,057	4.9	5,461	8.7	179,777	6.8
August	2,500	3.9	5,028	7.8	159,760	6.0
November	2,240	3.5	4,189	6.6	136,030	5.1
[1]951:						
February	2,407	3.9	4,543	7.4	142,968	5.8
May	1,609	2.6	3,609	5.7	110,501	4.1
[1]952:						
May	1,602	2.6	3,562	5.7	108,392	4.1
November	1,418	2.2	3,014	4.7	93,421	3.5
[1]953:						
May[a]	1,306	2.1	2,956	4.7	91,213	3.5
December[b]	2,313	3.7	4,916	7.8	150,762	5.8
[1]954:						
March	3,725	5.8	6,809	10.7	214,936	8.3
May	3,305	5.1	6,282	9.8	197,290	7.4
August	3,245	5.0	6,586	10.0	203,898	7.9
November	2,893	4.5	5,725	8.9	176,901	6.7

[a] Part-time workers estimated from November 1952 data.
[b] Revised to correct for difference between 68-area and 230-area samples.

COMMENTS

Nathan Keyfitz, Dominion Bureau of Statistics, Canada

The Canadian and United States labor force surveys have had somewhat parallel histories. The United States survey started in 1940, the Canadian in 1945. A game of leap frog has been played between the two surveys so far as technique is concerned, now one being ahead on some aspect, now the other, though at every stage Canadian progress has depended on our contacts with the Bureau of the Census. A year before our survey began Herbert Marshall and I visited the Bureau of the Census and Morris Hansen and his co-workers told us not only what they had done in creating the Current Population Survey but also what they would do if they were starting all over again. Some ten years before they were able to change their own survey, they suspected that the optimum number of areas within which the 25,000 households of the survey should be selected was more than the sixty-eight then in use. We accordingly started with 100 and have been slowly increasing the number since. We agreed also, ten years ago, that the completeness and accuracy of enumeration might be controlled without having a permanent office in each primary sampling unit, and Canada started with only six regional offices. The United States has adapted its organization to fewer offices this year, but because they did it more recently they have taken more care for the problem of control. However we are not quite sure either in Canada or the United States just what the most effective and economical method of enumeration control is; experiments are going on in both countries but more actively in the United States.

On the side of mechanics, the Canadian survey changed to mark-sense in the field early in 1951 and was followed in this by the United States survey. There is no question that speed, accuracy, and economy are gained through the use of a document that can be marked in the field. But no one contends that the method now being used in Canada and the United States is the last word, and the United States is actively searching for cheaper and more convenient methods.

A major difference in the mechanics of the two operations is the use of UNIVAC in the United States survey, IBM equipment in the Canadian. UNIVAC not only calculates survey results according to the original method of inflating the sample but also inflates by another method, comparing identical households of the given and the preceding month. Furthermore UNIVAC has enough electronic hardware to make variance calculations more frequently and on more realistic models than we can afford in Canada.

But perhaps of more interest to this group than enumeration and mechanical resemblances and differences between the United States and Canadian surveys are the concepts enumerated and estimated. First a semantic difference: the use of the term "unemployed" is prominent in your publications but not to be seen in the Canadian ones—or at least not in connection with any specific figure. In an attempt to get our public to see that there were different sorts of unemployed people we have issued figures of a number of categories, of which one is the "without a job and seeking work" during the reference week. There are signs that we are making progress towards convincing the public that different and equally legitimate points of view will require different combinations of categories for measurement. At the same time misunderstanding of the problem of measurement in public discussion remains a problem in Canada as in the United States.

Perhaps the matter of definition can be discussed in terms of a continuum, not the continuum of degrees of unemployment that has been referred to by other speakers but a continuum of precision in the specification of unemployment. At one extreme, as the sharpest possible definition, we might confine the series to family heads between twenty-five and sixty-four years of age who are wage and salary earners and so avoid all the difficulties of defining unemployment for persons who have been retired involuntarily, for housewives, for secondary workers of all sorts. On the other hand the total that one really wishes for purposes of analysis (whether the welfare of individuals or the productive labor supply of the community is concerned) is a broader group, in fact the whole adult population.

There is another dimension of sharpness, if we define sharpness to mean reproducibility of results. We could retain all age and sex groups but drop out of the unemployed those who would be looking for work except that they are sick or because they think that no work is available and confine the count of unemployed to active work seekers. Something of this kind is Miss Bancroft's suggestion, and this way of sharpening the result, even though it does make some sacrifice of categories which theory would urge us to include, is in line with the aim of statisticians in this field to avoid surveying intentions.

Ease of counting cannot be a decisive argument for choosing among concepts of unemployment. It is in some respects simplest to confine the count to persons without a job and seeking work all week, the "totally unemployed." If, however, the response of employers to a falling off in demand is to put their employees on short time, the number of totally unemployed will have diminishing significance. Miss Bancroft's aim is to secure the maximum inclusiveness consistent with a fairly high degree of reproducibility, and her proposals deserve our most careful consideration.

ROBERT W. BURGESS, Bureau of the Census

According to my point of view, the aim of the government statistician in analyzing employment and unemployment is to help everyone to understand these phenomena for all significant applications. I recognize the importance of such analysis in formulating and effectuating anticyclical measures but do not believe we should limit examination of certain aspects of unemployment, partial employment, or per capita productivity and income because they may not bear on such anticyclical thinking.

A major gain from such analysis would be improvement of basic concepts and working definitions. I am allergic to suggestions that we fall back on the broad and somewhat vague ideas appropriate to the pre-1940 data. I think we should give careful and sympathetic consideration to concepts like the secondary labor force, total potential labor supply, partial unemployment, and several others that have been mentioned.

Gertrude Bancroft has been with the Bureau of the Census since October 1943. During her service she has been chief of the unit and later the section which has had the major responsibility for directing the Current Population Survey. More recently she has been individually most concerned with reviewing the checks and recommendations connected with the recent critical study by the Secretary's Special Advisory Committee on Employment Statistics.

It may be noted that Miss Bancroft includes in her paper the usual and orthodox disclaimers that she is not presenting the official view of the Department of Commerce or the Census Bureau. While these statements are, of course, technically correct and are appropriate to insure that the paper and the remarks made to this audience reflect the speaker's own judgment, it should also be noted that Miss Bancroft's comments and recommendations are always given most serious consideration in the formulation of official Census Bureau policy.

UNEMPLOYMENT DATA FROM THE EMPLOYMENT SECURITY PROGRAM

HERBERT S. PARNES

THE OHIO STATE UNIVERSITY

FOR approximately the past decade and a half, there have been two major sources of current data on unemployment in the United States: the current population surveys conducted by the Bureau of the Census, and the administration of the federal-state employment security program. This paper analyzes the data which are made available by the operation of the employment security program and evaluates their usefulness as measures of unemployment.[1]

1. The Federal-State Employment Security Program

The administration of the employment security program in the United States is a federal-state partnership involving the Bureau of Employment Security in the Department of Labor and an employment security agency in each of the fifty-one states and territories (including the District of Columbia, Alaska, and Hawaii) which administers the state unemployment insurance law and operates a network of public employment offices.[2] A state unemployment insurance law must meet certain substantive and administrative standards imposed by the federal Social Security Act if employers in that state are to be eligible for the tax-offset allowed by the act and if the state is to receive federal grants for the administration of the program.

Among the requirements for the receipt of federal funds for administration is the making of such reports as may be required by the

Note: I am indebted to William Papier, Director, Division of Research and Statistics, Ohio Bureau of Unemployment Compensation, and to Louis Levine, Chief, Division of Reports and Analysis, Bureau of Employment Security, who read a preliminary draft of this paper and made numerous valuable suggestions. They do not, however, necessarily agree with all of my conclusions.

[1] It is noteworthy that data from public employment exchanges and/or unemployment insurance systems are a far more common source of unemployment statistics in other countries than labor force surveys. Of thirty countries that reported unemployment statistics to the International Labour Organization on a monthly or quarterly basis in 1952, only three derived the data from labor force surveys, as compared with twenty-one from employment exchanges and four from unemployment insurance systems (see *International Labour Review*, Statistical Supplement, November-December 1952, pp. 112-115).

[2] In addition to the state and territorial unemployment insurance laws there is a Veterans' Readjustment Assistance Act which provides unemployment compensation to veterans and a Railroad Unemployment Insurance Act which covers railroad employees. The former program is administered through the state employment security agencies with federal funds; the latter is administered by the Railroad Retirement Board.

BES. At the present time each state agency is required to make over twenty periodic reports to the Bureau. Thus, from the more than 1,600 full-time and approximately 2,000 part-time public employment offices throughout the country there is channeled through the state employment security agencies to the BES a wealth of statistical and descriptive data relating to the operation of the unemployment insurance programs and the public employment services and to labor market conditions in local areas. Some of these data, such as the number of applicants for jobs, and the number of persons claiming unemployment benefits, have been used as indicators of trends in unemployment.

Since much of the analysis in this paper involves a comparison of employment security with census data, it is desirable at this point to stress certain basic differences between the Bureau of the Census and the BES which significantly affect the nature of the data which each of these agencies collects. Perhaps the major difference in this context is that the Bureau of the Census is a statistical agency while the BES is not. The only limitations upon the types of unemployment data collected by the Census Bureau, therefore, are those imposed by considerations of feasibility and cost. The Census Bureau is free to use whatever concept of unemployment it regards as most useful, and to develop whatever measurement techniques appear to be most valid. On the other hand, since employment security data are almost exclusively by-products of the administration of unemployment insurance laws, definitions and procedures are in large measure imposed by the substantive and administrative characteristics of these laws. This means that an appraisal of BES data cannot realistically challenge the concepts and the techniques used, but must for the most part accept these as given and evaluate the usefulness of the results.

A second important difference between the Census Bureau and the BES is that although both are federal agencies, the former operates independently while the latter cooperates with fifty-one autonomous state or territorial administrative agencies. As a result, concepts and techniques for measuring and differentiating the labor force can be applied uniformly throughout the country by the Census Bureau, while the data received by the BES are affected by the wide diversity in both the substantive provisions and the administration of state unemployment insurance laws.

Third, in collecting employment and unemployment statistics the Census Bureau in effect goes to the people, and there are no legal restrictions on the segments of the population which can be surveyed. On the other hand, except for local area estimates of total unemployment, an individual is included in the data submitted to the BES only if he uses the services of the public employment offices and/or files a claim for unemployment benefits. This is significant in view of the rather substantial proportion of the labor force (which varies widely from state to state and among local areas within a state) which is for one reason or another ineligible for unemployment insurance.[3]

Finally, although a larger sample would enable Census Bureau techniques to yield estimates of employment and unemployment on a statewide or local area basis, the present sample permits only national estimates. On the other hand, the national statistics on claimants and job applicants compiled by the BES are summaries of data collected from local areas. Thus, the very nature of the employment security program yields statistics for local areas and states as well as for the nation as a whole.

There are four types of data resulting from the operation of the employment security program which either have been or are being used as indicators of unemployment: (1) the number of job applicants in the active files of local employment offices, (2) the number of initial claims filed under unemployment insurance laws, (3) the number of continued claims for unemployment insurance benefits, and (4) estimates of total unemployment in local areas made by labor market analysts on the basis of the foregoing and other data.

2. Active File Data As Indicators of Unemployment

When a person applies for work through a public employment office his application is put into an "active file" until he is placed in a job or until the application is canceled on the assumption that he has either found a job or is no longer in the labor force. The job applicant is supposed to report periodically to the employment service to indicate his continued availability for work. The "validity period" for the active file is a specified period of time, generally thirty or sixty days, during which a registration card is kept in the file without renewal by the applicant.

If unemployment is defined as a situation in which a person is not working but is looking for work, a count of the active file would be a valid measure of total unemployment at a given point of time to the extent that the following conditions existed: (1) all persons seeking work immediately registered with a public employment office, (2) no persons at work registered for other jobs with the public employment service, and (3) all registrants notified the employment office immediately after they had found work, and the employment office immediately removed the registration cards from the file.

[3] At the beginning of 1950, about 40 per cent of the national civilian labor force was not covered by state unemployment insurance laws.

It is known, of course, that none of these conditions actually obtains. In the first place, public employment offices are relatively little used by workers to find jobs as compared with the less formal methods of finding work through relatives and friends or through direct gate application.[4] To the extent that unemployed workers file claims for unemployment benefits they must, to be sure, register for work. But a significant proportion of the total labor force is not covered by unemployment insurance, and even some of those who are covered may not file claims, at least immediately. The downward bias in the active file figures which results from these factors is compensated only to a small degree by the fact that some persons who currently are working may register for other jobs. An inventory of the active files in ninety labor market areas in 1950 showed that the number of workers who had jobs and applied for others through the employment service was very small.[5]

Administrative factors are perhaps even more significant in preventing the active file from constituting a valid measure of unemployment. The validity period of the active file varies from state to state and also among local offices within a state. Moreover, since the primary function of the local employment office is to place workers in jobs rather than to develop unemployment statistics, it is reasonable to suppose that even within a single local employment office the diligence and regularity with which applications in the active file are canceled are inversely related to the pressure of other activities. For example, during the defense build-up of the latter part of 1941, the national count of the active file was well above the total unemployment estimate of the Monthly Report on Unemployment (the predecessor of the Monthly Report on the Labor Force and the Current Population Survey).[6] Similarly, from April 1951 to the end of 1953, the active file count was higher than the census estimate of total unemployment in almost every month (see Chart 1).

Prior to the development of the monthly labor force survey in 1940 there was some optimism about the usefulness of active file figures as an indicator of *trends* in unemployment and of the demographic *composition* of the unemployed.[7] Between 1934 and 1941 monthly series of

[4] For a review of the evidence on this point, see Herbert S. Parnes, *Research on Labor Mobility: An Appraisal of Research Findings in the United States*, Social Science Research Council, Bull. 65, 1954, pp. 162-165.

[5] "Job Seekers at Public Employment Offices, April 1950," BES, mimeographed, November 1950, p. 7.

[6] Loring Wood, "Statistical Data on Employment and Unemployment from Sources Other Than Labor Force Surveys," Appendix B in Louis J. Ducoff and Margaret J. Hagood, *Labor Force Definition and Measurement*, Social Science Research Council, 1947, p. 100.

[7] E. D. Hollander and J. F. Wellemeyer, Jr., "Can Employment Service Re-

CHART 1

Total Unemployment, Insured Unemployment, and Active File Count, 1950-1954

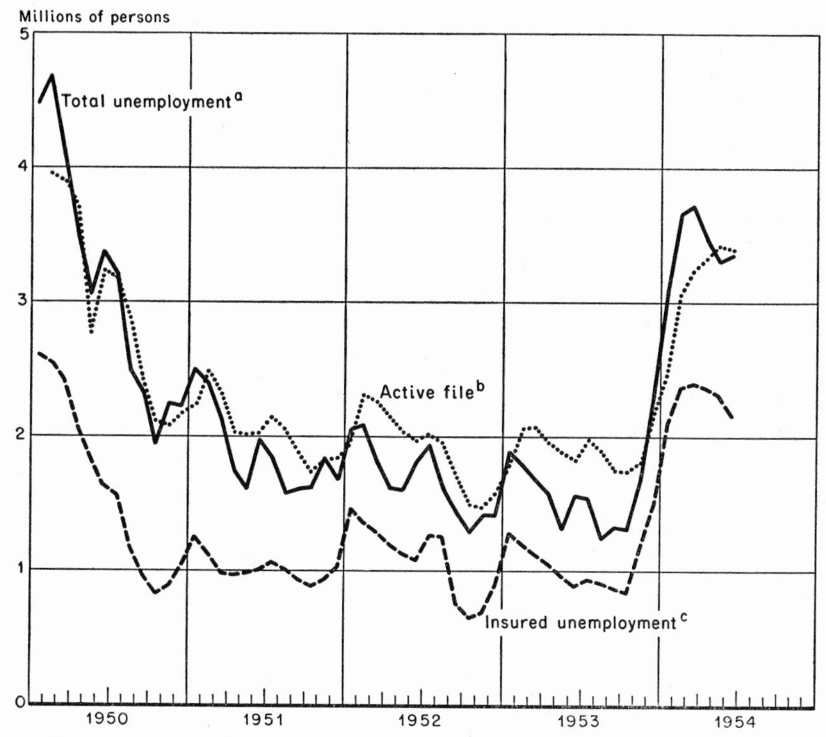

[a] Census estimates of total unemployment for the week including the eighth of the month. Estimates for September-December 1953 revised in light of the estimate yielded by the new 230-area sample in January 1954.

[b] Total active file at end of month plotted as of the week including the eighth of the following month.

[c] Total insured unemployment under veterans', railroad, and state unemployment insurance laws, including partial and part-total unemployment. Data for week including eighth of the month.

Source: Bureau of Employment Security.

state and national totals of the active file counts were compiled. From the very beginning, however, the data were affected by administrative factors. Mass registrations of workers occurred in 1933 and again in 1935 as the United States Employment Service became the placement agency first for the Civilian Works Administration and then for the

---

ports Be Used to Measure Unemployment?" Part I, *Monthly Labor Review,* June 1938, pp. 1456-1464; E. D. Hollander and E. D. Vinogradoff, "Can Employment Service Reports Be Used to Measure Unemployment?" Part II, *Monthly Labor Review,* July 1938, pp. 156-163.

Works Projects Administration programs. Registrations were also affected by the fact that in order to obtain relief in many areas families were required to show that all employable members were registered for work. Finally, sharp rises in the active file occurred when the payment of unemployment benefits (for which registration for work was a prerequisite) commenced in twenty-two states in 1938 and in the remaining states by the middle of 1939.[8]

Early in World War II the active file counts were abandoned, and by 1943 even the practice of maintaining an active file was largely in abeyance, as workers were channeled into abundant jobs without being required to file written applications. Since the fall of 1945, however, the practice of maintaining an active file has been resumed, and a count by sex and veteran status is included in a monthly report which each state agency is required to submit to the BES.

Several studies have been made to determine whether the active file gives a good representation of the characteristics of the unemployed. An early study comparing the active file with the Unemployment Census of 1937 found that the sex and race composition of the two sets of data were quite comparable, but that there were differences in the age and the occupational distributions. As compared with the Unemployment Census, the active file significantly understated the proportion of unemployed workers under 20; and it overrepresented manual workers and underrepresented white collar and farm workers.[9]

That the bias in the active file data with respect to age is persistent is suggested by the results of an inventory of the active file taken in April, 1950 in ninety major labor market areas. Comparison of the active file data with census data for that month shows that while less than 4 per cent of the active file registrants were under twenty years old, this age group accounted for almost 13 per cent of the unemployed workers reported by the census.[10] This underrepresentation of the very young workers in the active file might, of course, be expected. Young workers entering the labor force are not eligible for unemployment benefits and therefore do not have the same incentive to register for work as older workers who are more likely to have wage credits entitling them to benefits.

Unlike the situation in 1937, women were proportionately more numerous in the active file survey of 1950 than in the total unemploy-

[8] Wood, *op.cit.*, pp. 98-100.

[9] Hollander and Wellemeyer, *loc.cit.* The authors nevertheless concluded that if the active file distribution by sex, race, occupation, and industry had been applied to one of the standard estimates of total unemployment at the time, the results would have yielded substantially the same information as the Unemployment Census.

[10] "Job Seekers at Public Employment Offices, April 1950," pp. 5-6.

ment figure reported by the census. They comprised over a third of all the job applicants in the ninety areas, as compared with about a fourth of total unemployment reported by the census for the nation.[11] This difference may be in part attributable to the fact that labor force participation rates for women are higher in the metropolitan areas covered by the job applicant survey than in the nation as a whole. It may also be that some women who leave the labor force apply for unemployment benefits (and therefore register for work) despite the fact that they report to Census Bureau enumerators that they are not seeking work.

3. Claims Data as Indicators of Unemployment

Claims filed by workers for unemployment benefits are a second source of unemployment data yielded by the employment security program. There are two types of claims filed under unemployment insurance laws in the United States: initial claims and continued claims. An initial claim simply attests to the beginning of a period of unemployment, and theoretically should be filed by the worker immediately upon losing his job. It is used by the administrative agency to determine the potential eligibility of the claimant for benefits. A continued claim, on the other hand, is filed by the worker for completed weeks of unemployment subsequent to the filing of an initial claim. Continued claims may be either for waiting period credit or for compensable weeks. The waiting period is a non-compensable period of unemployment in which the worker is otherwise eligible for benefits.[12] Compensable claims are those continued claims which are filed after the completion of the waiting period, and represent requests for benefits. However, a continued claim, whether for waiting period credit or for benefit payment, certifies to the *completion* of a week or more of total or partial[13] unemployment, as contrasted with an initial claim,

[11] *Ibid.*

[12] The waiting period is required for only the first spell of unemployment during any benefit year. In 1952 the waiting period for total unemployment was one week in all but five states. Three of these required no waiting period, while two had a two-week period ("State Unemployment Insurance Laws, September 1, 1952," *Monthly Labor Review*, December 1952, pp. 623-625).

[13] All state laws provide for the payment of benefits for partial unemployment, which is almost universally defined as a week in which an individual's earnings, due to the involuntary loss of work, are less than his weekly benefit amount, that is, the amount of benefits he would receive were he totally unemployed. There is a technical distinction between "partial" and "part-total" unemployment. The former exists where an individual continues to work for his regular employer but is eligible for benefits because of a reduction in hours and earnings. The latter refers to a situation in which an individual loses his regular job and finds casual or part-time work. In the remainder of this paper "partial unemployment" will be used to refer to both of these situations.

which simply serves notice of the beginning of a period of unemployment.

The period for which continued claims are filed varies among the states in two respects which are significant for interpreting claims data. About half of the states require the filing of claims on a calendar week basis, which means that continued claims represent unemployment during a calendar week (from Sunday through Saturday). In the other half of the states a "flexible" week is used for claims purposes: a continued claim relates to unemployment during the seven consecutive days immediately preceding the day on which the claim is filed. Secondly, the administrative regulations of some states provide for the weekly filing of continued claims, while in others claims are taken biweekly.[14]

Data on initial claims and continued claims under the state unemployment insurance laws and the veterans' unemployment compensation program are reported by the state employment security agencies to the BES on a weekly and monthly basis. This makes possible the publication of weekly statistics on initial claims and insured unemployment not only for the nation as a whole, but with a breakdown by states. Moreover, the data are published by the BES within one week after the week in which the claims were filed.

INITIAL CLAIMS

Weekly statistics on initial claims have been regarded as valuable indicators of emerging unemployment.[15] If all members of the labor force who are out of jobs and looking for work were eligible for unemployment benefits, and if all such workers filed claims immediately upon losing their jobs (or upon entering the labor force, in the case of new entrants), the number of initial claims during a given week would constitute a perfect count of accessions to unemployment during that week. There are a number of factors, however, which prevent initial claims data from accurately reflecting changes in the number of newly unemployed workers. In the first place, the limited coverage of unemployment insurance laws obviously means that not all new unemployment is included in the data. Furthermore, even if rates of accession to unemployment were equal for covered and noncovered employments, changes in the volume of initial claims would not accurately reflect the percentage change in new unemployment from one

[14] Biweekly claims filing was adopted by many states during the fiscal year 1954 as the result of a severe budget cut. At the end of 1954 about twenty-nine states are taking claims on a weekly basis.

[15] Cf. Louis Levine, "Adaptations of the Unemployment Concept," *Review of Economics and Statistics*, February 1950, p. 67.

week to another. Workers newly entering the labor force without wage credits are ineligible for unemployment insurance and therefore do not ordinarily file claims. Consequently the seasonal increase in unemployment which occurs at the close of the school year as young workers enter the job market is not reflected in initial claims data.

Another limitation of data on initial claims lies in the fact that they are affected by legal and administrative factors which are quite independent of what may be happening to unemployment. Workers who exhaust their benefit rights in a given benefit year and remain unemployed may be eligible for benefits and may file initial claims at the beginning of a new benefit year. In such cases the initial claims clearly do not represent accessions to unemployment. The problem is complicated by the fact that ten states use a uniform benefit year (a twelve-month period that is the same for all claimants), while forty states have an individual benefit year (the fifty-two-week period beginning with each claimant's filing of a valid initial claim). In the former states, there is likely to be an increase in initial claims at the beginning of the benefit year which is independent of a change in unemployment. In the latter states there is likely to be some upward bias during the first month of each calendar quarter.[16]

The disqualification provisions of state unemployment insurance laws also limit the usefulness of initial claims data as a measure of new unemployment. For example, in those states in which workers who voluntarily quit their jobs without just cause are disqualified for the duration of their unemployment, many persons who leave jobs voluntarily probably do not apply for benefits. Moreover, even when there is no question as to the worker's eligibility, he may not immediately file an initial claim. There are indications that a lag of a week or more between the inception of unemployment and the filing of an initial claim is common.[17] It is possible, although there is no evidence on this point, that some eligible workers do not file claims at all during spells of unemployment, particularly when they are of relatively short duration.

A priori, a number of reasons can be suggested for a delay in filing initial claims, or for complete failure to do so. Some workers may still feel that a stigma attaches to the application for or the receipt of unemployment benefits and may therefore be reluctant to exercise their rights under the unemployment insurance laws except as a last resort. Among other workers there may be a disposition to regard their rights to unemployment benefits as a kind of "bank account" upon which they

[16] *The Labor Market and Employment Security*, BES, April 1954, p. 24.

[17] "Techniques for Estimating Unemployment," BES, mimeographed, July 1950, p. 10.

hesitate to draw at the beginning of a period of unemployment that they hope will be short. As they continue without work, however, they may re-assess the situation and file claims. Inertia and ignorance of their rights under the laws may be additional factors accounting for the failure of some workers to apply for unemployment benefits. Finally, in areas in which disqualification rates are high there may be a tendency for some unemployed workers to regard the filing of claims as a waste of time.[18]

INSURED UNEMPLOYMENT

The best known statistical series on unemployment obtained from the employment security program is called "insured unemployment," and is based upon the continued claims filed under the state unemployment insurance laws, the Veterans' Readjustment Assistance Act of 1952 (unemployment compensation for veterans), and the Railroad Unemployment Insurance Act. State employment security agencies are required to submit to the BES weekly and monthly reports on the "number of weeks of unemployment claimed" under both the state insurance and the veterans' unemployment compensation programs. These data are adjusted to represent the week in which unemployment occurred, rather than the week in which the claims were filed.[19] Thus, insured unemployment in any week represents the number of persons who, by filing continued claims for benefits or waiting period credit under the three unemployment insurance programs,[20] certify that they have been totally or partially unemployed during that week.

It is clear that data on insured unemployment cannot be used as a *measure* of total unemployment in the United States, if for no other reason, simply because of the limited coverage of unemployment insurance laws. On the other hand, it has been generally claimed that whatever their limitations, insured unemployment data have the very important advantages of being current and being available on a state,

[18] The entire question of the extent to which and the promptness with which eligible workers apply for unemployment benefits is one which requires research. The lag between layoffs and the filing of initial claims may be related to the state of the local labor market and be most pronounced when alternative job opportunities are still relatively abundant. Also, there may be local variations in the significance of the lag depending upon the industrial and occupational composition of employment, and upon the ethnic and cultural characteristics of the population. The degree of unionization in a local labor market may be an additional factor affecting the extent of failure to apply for benefits, for trade unions will probably have made their members more aware of their rights to benefits than nonmembers.

[19] For the nature of the adjustments required, see below, pp. 141-142.

[20] Some of the published data on insured unemployment relate only to claims filed under the state laws. In 1953, state insured unemployment accounted for over 90 per cent of total insured unemployment.

regional, and local as well as on a national basis.[21] In view of these advantages, it is important to inquire whether data on insured unemployment are a valid indicator of *changes* in the volume of total unemployment and of *differences* in unemployment rates between states or local areas. This question may be approached by comparing the definition of insured unemployment with the definition used by the Census Bureau in measuring total unemployment. Although such comparisons have been made frequently during the past several years, many of the differences between the two sets of data have been merely mentioned without being adequately explored.[22]

4. *Insured Unemployment and Census Unemployment*

Basically, the most serious limitation of insured unemployment data stems from the impossibility of stating precisely what it is they measure in terms that have economic (as distinguished from legal or administrative) significance. One can say that insured unemployment in a given week includes all persons who have filed claims under unemployment insurance laws certifying to total or partial unemployment during that week; but such a definition, although perfectly operational, lacks economic meaning in the absence of detailed knowledge about the content and administration of unemployment insurance laws and about the extent to which eligible workers avail themselves of their rights under these laws. Moreover, since the provisions of the unemployment insurance laws are variable over time as well as from state to state, and since administrative standards may vary even within a single state, insured unemployment may, from an economic point of view, mean quite different things at different times and in different places. The nature of some of these difficulties is shown in the following analysis of the differences between the coverage of insured unemployment data and census data on total unemployment.[23]

UNEMPLOYED WORKERS EXCLUDED FROM INSURED UNEMPLOYMENT

In terms of the census definition of unemployment, there are a number of categories of unemployed workers who are not included in insured unemployment statistics:

[21] See W. S. Woytinsky, *Employment and Wages in the United States*, Twentieth Century Fund, 1953, p. 402; Levine, *op.cit.*, p. 67; Wood, *op.cit.*, p. 104.

[22] See, for example, Gertrude Bancroft, "The Census Bureau Estimates of Unemployment," *Review of Economics and Statistics*, February 1950, pp. 59-65; Levine, *op.cit.*; *Hearings before the Joint Committee on the Economic Report*, 83d Cong., 2d sess., February 1-18, 1954, pp. 317-319.

[23] For the census definition of total unemployment, see Gertrude Bancroft, "Current Unemployment Statistics of the Census Bureau and Some Alternatives," in this volume.

Workers in Noncovered Employment. All state unemployment insurance laws exclude from coverage certain types of employments. Although there are variations from state to state, the most significant groups of workers excluded by all the laws are self-employed individuals, agricultural workers, domestic servants in private homes, employees of federal,[24] state, and local governments, and employees of non-profit organizations. (Railroad workers, excluded under state laws, are covered by the Railroad Unemployment Insurance Act.)

In addition to exclusions based upon type of employment, all but fifteen state laws exclude workers in establishments which have fewer than a specified minimum number of employees. In twenty-two states, which account for roughly a third of all covered employment, this minimum figure is eight employees; that is, only those establishments with eight or more workers are covered. Throughout the nation as a whole, the "size-of-firm limitations" of the state acts exclude about 3.4 million workers.[25] Total covered employment under state laws has been estimated as about 37 million workers, or approximately three-fourths of all wage and salary workers.[26]

The exclusion of the groups of workers noted above results from the fact that during their employment no tax contributions are paid in their behalf by their employers. Consequently, upon becoming unemployed they ordinarily will not have sufficient wage credits to be eligible for benefits. However, if an individual has sufficient wage credits in his base year from covered employment, he is not ineligible merely because his last job was in noncovered employment.

The coverage limitations of unemployment insurance laws not only prevent insured unemployment from being a complete measure of total unemployment as defined by the census but also prevent the ratio of insured unemployment to total covered labor force from being the same as the ratio of total unemployment to total labor force. There are differences in unemployment rates between covered employment on the one hand and specific segments of noncovered employment on the other. For example, census data show that unemployment rates among self-employed individuals are substantially lower than among

[24] By the act of Congress approved September 1, 1954, almost all civilian employees were brought under the unemployment insurance system beginning in 1955 (*Monthly Labor Review*, October 1954, p. 1102).

[25] *The Labor Market and Employment Security*, April 1954, p. 22. Beginning in 1956 the federal payroll tax for unemployment insurance will be applicable to employers of four or more workers. This change is expected to bring 1.3 million additional workers under coverage of state laws (*Monthly Labor Review*, October 1954, p. 1101).

[26] When the 1954 changes in the coverage of the program become fully effective, approximately 41 million of the 52 million wage and salary workers will be covered (*The Labor Market and Employment Security*, September 1954, p. 39).

wage and salary workers, both in agricultural and nonagricultural industries.[27] The exclusion of the self-employed from coverage of unemployment insurance laws would therefore tend to make the ratio of insured unemployment to covered labor force higher than the ratio of total unemployment to total labor force. Similarly, the exclusion of government workers would tend to have the same effect, since unemployment rates among government workers are generally lower than among private wage and salary workers.[28] On the other hand, the fact that unemployment rates were higher among agricultural than among nonagricultural wage earners between 1950-1952[29] would tend to create an opposite bias during this period.

The net effect of such differences in the incidence of unemployment between covered and noncovered workers is to cause the insured unemployment ratio to be higher than the total unemployment ratio. In 1948 and 1949, unemployment of wage and salary workers from covered industries accounted for three-fourths of total unemployment, but wage and salary employment in those industries comprised less than three-fifths of total employment.[30] In this connection it is noteworthy that the ratio of covered to total employment varies widely among the states, as well as among local labor market areas within a state.[31] Thus, variations in insured unemployment ratios among states or local areas do not necessarily reflect corresponding differences in total unemployment ratios.

The biases in insured unemployment ratios that result from the restricted coverage of unemployment compensation laws are not necessarily constant over time, and may prevent the insured unemployment series from reflecting the magnitude and direction of changes in the volume of total unemployment. For example, seasonal patterns of employment and unemployment in agriculture are different from those in most nonagricultural industries. Moreover, cyclical and secular variations in the relative importance of covered and noncovered employment would likewise disturb the similarity in movement between insured and total unemployment.

Workers without Sufficient Wage Credits. In addition to the unemployed persons who worked in noncovered employments and therefore

[27] *Annual Report on the Labor Force,* Bureau of the Census, 1952, p. 9.

[28] "Techniques for Estimating Unemployment," p. 20.

[29] *Annual Report on the Labor Force,* 1952, p. 9.

[30] "Techniques for Estimating Unemployment," p. 17.

[31] Current data on the ratio of covered to total labor force by state are not available. However, the BES has computed the ratios of covered employment to total nonagricultural employment for all but four states (for which estimates of nonagricultural employment are not available). In March 1954 these ratios ranged from 44 per cent in North and South Dakota to over 80 per cent in Connecticut, Massachusetts, Ohio, and Pennsylvania.

lack the necessary wage credits for eligibility, new entrants to the labor force or re-entrants whose previous jobs, even if in covered employment, were not sufficiently recent for them to have qualifying base year earnings are not included in the insured unemployment series.

Early in 1950, the ineligibility rate of new claimants for unemployment benefits was in the neighborhood of 15 per cent.[32] This figure, of course, does not measure the extent to which new entrants and re-entrants to the labor force are excluded from the insured unemployment total, because presumably the former do not file claims at all, and probably only those of the latter file whose employment experience has been sufficiently recent to give them some basis for believing they might be eligible.

The ineligibility of unemployed workers just entering the labor force has the same effect as the coverage limitations of the unemployment insurance laws: it not only prevents insured unemployment from being a complete measure of the unemployed, but it also prevents the magnitude and direction of month-to-month changes in total unemployment from being correctly registered. The rate of entry into the labor force is not constant from month to month. Moreover, the unemployment rate of new entrants is probably higher than that of workers who have been in the job market for some time. Thus, in months when larger-than-average numbers of workers are entering the labor force there is apt to be a downward bias in the percentage change in unemployment registered by insured unemployment data. This is the case, for example, during the summer months when young workers enter the labor force at the conclusion of the school year. To the extent that labor-force-participation rates increase during periods of high unemployment and/or during periods of supra-normal job opportunities, the same downward bias may exist during the trough and the peak of the business cycle.

Disqualified Workers. Even when an unemployed individual has sufficient base period wage credits to make him eligible for unemployment benefits, there are certain factors which may disqualify him. Although all state laws have disqualification provisions, there is wide variation in both the specific causes for disqualification and in the period for which it is effective. The principal reasons for disqualification, which appear in all state laws, are being unable to or unavailable for work, refusing to accept suitable work, discharge for misconduct, and voluntary quitting without just cause. All states likewise disqualify (at least for a limited period) workers whose unemployment results from a labor dispute in the establishment in which they are em-

[32] Levine, *op.cit.*, p. 68.

ployed. In some states the disqualification for benefits extends throughout the entire spell of unemployment. More frequently, disqualification is for a specified number of weeks, which may vary according to the cause of disqualification. Changes in state laws during 1953 have tended to make disqualification provisions more severe.[33]

In 1953, when there were 10,543,328 new spells of insured unemployment under state unemployment laws, there were a total of 1,207,326 disqualifications (excluding labor dispute disqualifications).[34] Although expressing disqualifications as a percentage of initial claims has certain limitations, if it is assumed that all of the disqualifications during the year applied to persons whose spells of unemployment began during the year, about 11 per cent of those who filed valid claims for new spells of unemployment were, for at least some part of the period of their unemployment, unrepresented in the insured unemployment statistics. It should be kept in mind, however, that many persons disqualified for being unavailable for work are perhaps not actually "seeking work," and therefore not unemployed in census terminology. On the other hand, it may be assumed that most persons who voluntarily quit their jobs or are discharged for misconduct do not bother to apply for unemployment benefits at least in those states which disqualify such workers for the entire spell of their unemployment.

Although it is not possible to estimate from available data the proportion of total unemployment (as defined by the census) that is excluded from insured unemployment statistics because of disqualifications, the foregoing analysis suggests that it is not negligible. Moreover, it is significant that the disqualification rate varies considerably from state to state, and among local areas of a given state,[35] thus limiting the usefulness of insured unemployment data for making interstate or interarea comparisons. In 1953 the disqualification rate ranged from a low of 5.8 per 1,000 claimant contacts in Kentucky to 46.7 per 1,000 in the District of Columbia. Since discharge for misconduct or voluntary quitting disqualify an individual at the beginning of a spell of unemployment, disqualifications for these reasons can meaningfully be

[33] See *Social Security Bulletin*, Social Security Administration, December 1953, pp. 19-20.

[34] Of these, 392,735 were for voluntarily quitting; 121,912 were for discharge for misconduct; 492,708 were for being unable to, or unavailable for, work; and 88,154 were for refusing suitable work. The remaining 111,817 were miscellaneous disqualifications which do not apply in all the states ("Disqualifications, by Issue, by State," BES, mimeographed table, March 1954).

[35] For example, in Ohio the number of disqualifications per 100 claimant contacts in 1953 averaged 3.6 for the state as a whole, but ranged between 2.1 and 7.3 among the eight largest labor market areas in the state (*Major Disqualification Issues and Rates, by Local Office of the Ohio State Employment Service, 1953*, Ohio Bureau of Unemployment Compensation, Table RS207-A).

expressed as ratios to new spells of unemployment. Disqualification for voluntarily quitting a job occurred in 37.2 out of every 1,000 new spells of unemployment in the nation as a whole, but the proportion ranged from 10.2 per 1,000 in New Jersey to 132.3 per 1,000 in South Carolina. Similarly, disqualification resulting from discharge for misconduct averaged 11.6 per 1,000 new spells of unemployment for the nation as a whole, but ranged from 1.4 in New York to 53.2 in South Carolina.[36]

Workers Who Have Exhausted Benefit Rights. All state unemployment insurance laws impose a maximum limit on the number of weeks that an individual may draw benefits during a period of fifty-two consecutive weeks. This ranges from sixteen weeks in four states to twenty-six weeks in about two dozen states,[37] with most of the remaining states having maximum benefit durations of twenty weeks.[38] When an individual exhausts his rights to benefits in a given benefit year, he is no longer included in the insured unemployment figures, despite the fact that he may continue to be unemployed. If he remains unemployed until a new benefit year begins, he may or may not be included in the figures at that time, depending upon whether he applies for benefits, and whether his earnings during the new base period make him eligible.

A number of studies have been made of persons exhausting their unemployment benefits,[39] and, as would be expected, the findings suggest substantial variation over time and from place to place in the duration of post-exhaustion unemployment. Among fourteen studies made during 1949-1950, the median duration of unemployment subsequent to the termination of benefit payments ranged between eight and twenty-three weeks.[40]

Analysis of the experience of workers exhausting unemployment benefits in Connecticut during 1949 indicated that 45 per cent of the exhaustees were re-employed sometime between the termination of their benefits and the date of the survey early in 1950. Of these only 10 per cent had found work within a week after benefit payments ceased, and another 26 per cent found jobs within a two- to five-week period. On the other hand, 40 per cent were without work for more

[36] "Disqualifications, by Issue, by State," mimeographed table.

[37] Maximum duration in Wisconsin is 26½ weeks.

[38] "Significant Benefit Provisions of State Unemployment Insurance Laws, December 1, 1953," *Monthly Labor Review*, March 1954, pp. 273-274. Slightly over a fourth of the states have uniform benefit durations. In the remaining states, however, not all workers are eligible for the maximum number of weeks specified in the law.

[39] For a bibliography, see "Adequacy of Benefits under Unemployment Insurance," BES, September 1952, pp. 33-36.

[40] *Ibid.*, p. 24.

than ten weeks after exhausting their benefits. The median duration of post-exhaustion unemployment for those who found jobs was nine weeks. Moreover, over a sixth of this group were again without work and looking for a job at the time of the survey.

Of the 55 per cent of the exhaustees in Connecticut who were not re-employed, somewhat under two-fifths were not seeking work in the survey period. The remaining 63 per cent, who were looking for jobs, had experienced an average (median) of nineteen weeks of unemployment since their benefit payments had ceased.[41]

The importance of exhaustions relative to total insured unemployment obviously varies with economic conditions, increasing as unemployment becomes more prevalent and of longer duration. The ratio of benefit exhaustions to first benefit payments during 1940 was about 50 per cent. This ratio declined continuously to less than 20 per cent in 1945, as first the defense build-up and then the war effort reduced unemployment to unprecedented lows. As a result of reconversion unemployment in 1946, the exhaustion ratio jumped to almost 40 per cent, then declined to the neighborhood of 30 per cent in each of the next four years. In 1951 the ratio dropped to about 20 per cent.[42] In fiscal year 1953 exhaustions were 18.8 per cent of first benefit payments, rising to 22.3 per cent in the fiscal year ending June 30, 1954.[43]

The effect of economic conditions upon the exhaustion ratio limits the usefulness of insured unemployment data for making comparisons between states with different levels of unemployment. In addition, the variation among the states in maximum benefit duration is a purely legal factor which likewise distorts such comparisons. If economic conditions were the same, the exhaustion ratio would be expected to vary inversely with the maximum duration of benefits. In 1953, when the exhaustion ratio was 20.8 per cent for the nation as a whole, it ranged between 8.6 per cent in Connecticut and 41.7 per cent in Louisiana.[44] The maximum benefit durations in these states are twenty-six weeks and twenty weeks, respectively.

Workers Who Do Not File Claims. In addition to those unemployed persons who, for one reason or another, are not eligible to receive unemployment benefits for a given week, eligible persons who do not file claims are also excluded from the insured unemployment total. Although the number who neglect to file claims at any time during an extended period of unemployment is probably relatively small, there is

[41] "What Happens After Exhaustions of Benefits," *The Labor Market and Employment Security*, May 1950, p. 29.

[42] "Adequacy of Benefits Under Unemployment Insurance," BES, mimeographed, September 1952, Table C-7.

[43] *The Labor Market and Employment Security*, September 1954, p. 40.

[44] *The Labor Market and Employment Security*, May 1954, p. 42.

evidence, as noted earlier, that a large proportion of those filing initial claims may have allowed a week or more to elapse between the inception of unemployment and the filing of their claims.

Initial claims are not included in insured unemployment data because theoretically such claims are filed at the beginning of a period of unemployment. When an individual has been unemployed for a week (or two weeks in states with biweekly filing), he is supposed to file a continued claim which certifies to the completion of a period of unemployment. If unemployment data are to include only those who have completed a week of unemployment, and if workers do in fact file initial claims immediately upon becoming unemployed, it is logical to exclude initial claims from the insured unemployment total. If, on the other hand, significant numbers of individuals delay filing initial claims, insured unemployment data might come closer to measuring the full extent of unemployment (as defined by the census) if initial claims were included. This is a question which empirical research might answer.

INSURED UNEMPLOYED EXCLUDED FROM CENSUS UNEMPLOYMENT

There are two categories of workers who may be included in insured unemployment statistics but who, by definition, are excluded from census data on unemployment:

Partially Unemployed Workers. All state laws provide for the payment of unemployment benefits to eligible individuals who are partially unemployed, and weeks of partial unemployment are not differentiated from weeks of total unemployment in deriving insured unemployment statistics.[45] On the other hand, the census includes among the unemployed only those who were without any remunerative work during the survey week. The relative importance of partial unemployment under unemployment insurance laws varies, of course, depending upon economic conditions. During most of 1946 it accounted for well under 5 per cent of total insured unemployment; in 1953 it amounted to almost one-tenth of the total.[46]

Variations among the states in the extent of insured partial unemployment may reflect differences in the benefit levels of their unemployment insurance laws as well as differences in economic conditions. A week of partial unemployment is defined in all the state laws as one in which an individual's earnings, as a result of involuntary loss of

[45] There are means of estimating the proportions of partial and total unemployment, however. State agencies submit to the Bureau of Employment Security a monthly report on benefit payments (Form ES-213) which indicates the number of weeks of unemployment compensated, with a subtotal for weeks of total unemployment.

[46] Data from BES.

work, are less than his weekly benefit amount. All other things being equal, therefore, a reduction of, say, 50 per cent in hours worked in a state with a high benefit level would give rise to more "partial unemployment" than an identical reduction in a state with a lower benefit level.

Workers with Jobs but Not at Work. The census definition of unemployment excludes persons who are neither working nor looking for work during the survey week, but who have a job from which they are absent because of temporary layoff, labor dispute, vacation, illness, or bad weather. While some of these individuals may be included in the insured unemployment total, most of them will not because of their ineligibility for benefits. For example, persons on paid vacations, and in some cases those on unpaid vacations, are not eligible for benefits; nor, in most states, are persons who are ill, since they are not able to work. Moreover, persons out of work as a direct result of a labor dispute in the establishment in which they work are disqualified for benefits, at least for a limited period of time, in all states. Persons on temporary layoff are included in the insured unemployment statistics only if they apply for benefits and if the administrative agency is willing to regard them as available for suitable work. In the twenty-six states which require a claimant to demonstrate that he is actively seeking work, such an individual who does not want to sever his attachment with his present employer would have at least to go through the motions of making a search for another job.

EFFECT OF ADMINISTRATIVE FACTORS ON CLAIMS DATA

There are a number of purely administrative factors which affect the validity of insured unemployment data as an indicator of changes in total unemployment. The effects of the uniform and the individual benefit years on initial claims have already been described, and somewhat the same effects are exerted on continued claims, from which the insured unemployment statistics are derived. The fact that some states use a calendar week while others use a "flexible" week for continued claims also creates some difficulty. In the former states, the weeks of unemployment claimed in the current week are used to represent insured unemployment in the preceding calendar week. In the latter states, the weeks of unemployment claimed in a given week are averaged with those in the preceding week and the result is used to represent insured unemployment in the preceding week. This adjustment has the effect of overstating unemployment during periods when unemployment is rising, and understating it when the trend is in the opposite direction.

In states where claims are taken on a biweekly rather than on a weekly basis the claims-taking load is generally distributed evenly over the working days of a two-week period, with each claimant reporting on a specified day. Consequently, in deriving the insured unemployment figure for a given week, the number of weeks of unemployment claimed by the group reporting in a given week is assumed to be equal to the number that would have been claimed if each individual had reported on a weekly basis. It may be that the extent to which eligible workers file claims differs between states that take claims weekly and those that take them biweekly. Although there are no data on this matter, it seems reasonable to suppose that an individual who is unemployed for a period of only slightly over one week will be more likely to file a claim in a state with weekly reporting than in one with biweekly reporting. In the latter case, the individual is already back at work at the time he is supposed to file his claim. Not only is it more difficult for him to get to the local employment office, but he may well believe that it is not worth the trouble, particularly if the week of unemployment which he might claim would serve only as waiting period credit rather than as a compensable week. To the extent that this occurs, there may be a downward bias in the insured unemployment statistics of states with biweekly reporting.

Finally, although this is not strictly speaking an administrative factor, it should be borne in mind that the criterion of "willingness to work" used in unemployment insurance laws is different from that used by the census. For unemployment insurance purposes the test is the availability of the worker for a suitable job as evidenced by his registration for work at a public employment office and his willingness to accept a referral to, or an offer of, a job. (Twenty-six states also require the individual to make an independent search for work.) In the case of the census, the individual's willingness to work is evidenced by a report to the Census Bureau enumerator, either by himself or by someone in his household, that he was looking for work during the survey week. It is clear that the administrative determination that an individual is available for suitable work is not equivalent to a report to a Census enumerator that the individual is seeking work.[47]

COMPARISON OF CENSUS AND INSURED UNEMPLOYMENT DATA, 1949-1954

In view of the numerous differences in coverage between census and insured unemployment data, it would be expected that the two series

[47] Studies conducted by the Bureau of the Census and the United States Employment Service during 1946 showed that significant proportions of unemployment benefit recipients were not reporting themselves as looking for work to Census enumerators (see Gertrude Bancroft, "Current Unemployment Statistics of the Census Bureau and Some Alternatives," in this volume).

not only give different counts of unemployment, but differ also in the month-to-month changes they indicate (see Table 1). In the sixty-six months between January 1949 and June 1954, the insured unemployment total (including the veterans' and the railroad programs) ranged between 40 and 89 per cent of total unemployment as measured by the census.[48] The median ratio of insured to total unemployment was 64 per cent, and the interquartile range was between 55 and 70. The month-to-month differences in the ratios were most pronounced in 1949, when they ranged between 56 per cent and 89 per cent,[49] and least pronounced in 1953 when the range was between 57 and 73 per cent. In the first five months of 1954, insured unemployment was a relatively constant proportion of total unemployment, ranging between 64 and 70 per cent.

There is no appreciable tendency for the variation among the ratios of insured to total unemployment to disappear when they are classified by month during the five-and-a-half-year period. In each of the twelve months the range between the highest and the lowest ratio is at least 21 percentage points, and in five months it is 30 or more.

Another way of analyzing the differences between the insured unemployment and the total unemployment series is in terms of the relative changes they show from month to month. Of the 65 month-to-month changes between January 1949 and June 1954, the two series agreed in *direction* in 46 and disagreed in 19. The differences in the magnitude of the month-to-month changes shown by the two sets of data ranged between almost 0 and 30 percentage points, the median difference being about 7 percentage points. The interquartile range of the differences was between about 3 and 13 percentage points.

It is difficult to see any pattern in the variation between the two series, except that the insured unemployment data invariably fail to register the sharp rise in unemployment shown by census data between May and June, when young workers (without wage credits under

[48] The variation would be even more pronounced if the immediate postwar years were included in the comparison. In each of the first ten months of 1946 insured unemployment actually exceeded total unemployment estimated by the Census Bureau. This was doubtless attributable at least in part to the heavy volume of veterans' claims, which accounted for half or more of all insured unemployment during most of the months of that year.

[49] The greater variation in 1949 is doubtless attributable in part to the wide variation in the number of veterans who filed claims under the Servicemen's Readjustment Act of 1944. During the first seven months of the year insured unemployment under the veterans' program ranged between about 490,000 and 680,000, or between about 20 and 25 per cent of total insured unemployment. In the last five months of the year, on the other hand, the range was between about 60,000 and 140,000, or between 3 and 6 per cent of total insured unemployment.

TABLE 1

Comparison of Census Unemployment and Total Insured Unemployment, 1949-1954

(*number in thousands of persons 14 years old and over*)

MONTH[a] AND YEAR	CENSUS TOTAL UNEMPLOYMENT		INSURED UNEMPLOYMENT[b]		INSURED UNEMPLOYMENT AS PER CENT OF CENSUS UNEMPLOYMENT
	Number	*Per Cent Change from Previous Month*	*Number*	*Per Cent Change from Previous Month*	
1949:					
January	2,664		2,108		79
February	3,221	+20.9	2,544	+20.7	79
March	3,167	−1.7	2,728	+7.2	86
April	3,016	−4.8	2,684	−1.6	89
May	3,289	+9.1	2,655	−1.1	81
June	3,778	+14.9	2,657	+0.1	70
July	4,095	+8.4	2,824	+6.3	69
August	3,689	−9.9	2,438	−13.7	66
September	3,351	−9.2	2,150	−11.8	64
October	3,576	+6.7	1,994	−7.3	56
November	3,409	−4.7	2,261	+13.4	66
December	3,489	+2.3	2,425	+7.3	70
1950:					
January	4,480	+28.4	2,611	+7.7	58
February	4,684	+4.6	2,548	−2.4	54
March	4,123	−12.0	2,417	−5.1	59
April	3,515	−14.7	2,051	−15.1	58
May	3,057	−13.0	1,837	−10.4	60
June	3,384	+10.7	1,638	−10.8	48
July	3,213	−5.1	1,560	−4.8	49
August	2,500	−22.2	1.178	−24.5	47
September	2,341	−6.4	954	−19.0	41
October	1,940	−17.1	820	−14.0	42
November	2,240	+15.5	889	+8.4	40
December	2,229	−0.5	1,059	+19.1	48
1951:					
January	2,503	+12.3	1,246	+17.7	50
February	2,407	−3.8	1,117	−10.4	46
March	2,147	−10.8	975	−12.7	45
April	1,744	−18.8	965	−1.0	55
May	1,609	−7.7	981	+1.7	61
June	1,980	+23.1	1,007	+2.7	51
July	1,856	−6.3	1,067	+6.0	57
August	1,578	−15.0	1,001	−6.2	63
September	1,606	+1.8	922	−7.9	57
October	1,616	+0.6	884	−4.1	55
November	1,828	+13.1	931	+5.3	51
December	1,674	−8.4	1,036	+11.3	62

(continued on next page)

TABLE 1 (continued)

(*number in thousands of persons 14 years old and over*)

MONTH[a] AND YEAR	CENSUS TOTAL UNEMPLOYMENT		INSURED UNEMPLOYMENT[b]		INSURED UNEMPLOYMENT AS PER CENT OF CENSUS UNEMPLOYMENT
	Number	*Per Cent Change from Previous Month*	*Number*	*Per Cent Change from Previous Month*	
1952:					
January	2,054	+22.7	1,466	+41.5	71
February	2,086	+1.6	1,350	−7.9	65
March	1,804	−13.5	1,284	−4.9	71
April	1,612	−10.6	1,182	−7.9	73
May	1,602	−0.6	1,127	−4.7	70
June	1,818	+13.5	1,087	−3.5	60
July	1,942	+6.8	1,268	+16.7	65
August	1,604	−17.4	1,257	−0.9	78
September	1,438	−10.3	743	−40.9	52
October	1,284	−10.7	647	−12.9	50
November	1,418	+10.4	690	+6.6	49
December	1,412	−0.4	898	+30.1	64
1953:					
January	1,892	+34.0	1,289	+43.5	68
February	1,788	−5.5	1,189	−7.8	66
March	1,674	−6.4	1,118	−6.0	67
April	1,582	−5.5	1,052	−5.9	66
May	1,306	−17.4	953	−9.4	73
June	1,562	+19.6	885	−7.1	57
July	1,548	−0.9	934	+5.5	60
August	1,240	−19.9	911	−2.5	73
September	1,321[c]	+6.5	862	−5.4	65
October	1,301[c]	−1.5	835	−3.1	64
November	1,699[c]	+30.6	1,183	+41.7	70
December	2,313[c]	+36.1	1,512	+27.8	65
1954:					
January	3,087	+33.5	2,119	+40.1	69
February	3,671	+18.9	2,368	+11.8	65
March	3,725	+1.5	2,399	+1.3	64
April	3,465	−7.0	2,361	−1.6	68
May	3,305	−4.6	2,308	−2.2	70
June	3,347	+1.2	2,145	−7.1	64

[a] Covers the week including the eighth of the month.

[b] Includes partial and part total unemployment as well as total unemployment under state, veterans', and railroad unemployment insurance laws.

[c] Revised estimates.

Source: Census data from Monthly Reports on the Labor Force, insured unemployment data from Bureau of Employment Security.

unemployment compensation laws) begin to look for work at the end of the school year. Thus, in 1949, 1950, 1952, and 1953 the census showed a substantial percentage increase in unemployment between May and June, while insured unemployment either declined or remained constant. In 1951 both series registered increases between these two months, but the rise in census unemployment was 23 per cent, while the increase in insured unemployment was only 3 per cent.

Attempts have been made to adjust both census and insured unemployment statistics so that the two series more nearly achieve a common definition of unemployment.[50] One set of adjustments which has been made involves (1) subtracting from census unemployment those unemployed persons who never had a full-time job or whose last reported job was in an industry apparently not covered by unemployment insurance, (2) subtracting from insured unemployment those persons drawing part-total or partial unemployment benefits, and (3) adding to census figures the number of persons on temporary layoff from nonagricultural jobs with definite instructions to return to work within thirty days. These adjustments do not reconcile all the differences between census and insured unemployment statistics.[51] Indeed, in view of the dependence of insured unemployment data on legal and administrative factors that are not only complex but also variable from state to state, it is clear that the two sets of data cannot be completely reconciled. Nevertheless, when the adjustments referred to above are made, the two series are closer in the amount of unemployment they indicate and also show a somewhat higher degree of correspondence in the direction and magnitude of month-to-month changes (see Table 2).

The differences in movement between the census and the insured unemployment series do not necessarily mean that the former are a more valid indicator than the latter of changes in levels of unemployment. Miss Bancroft has shown in her paper[52] the impossibility of determining "true" levels of unemployment against which a given series can be compared, and has described the sources of error in census data. Judgments about the relative validity of the two series, therefore, must in the last analysis rest upon evaluations of the respective concepts and techniques underlying them.

[50] See *Hearings before the Joint Committee on the Economic Report*, pp. 317-319 (see also Gertrude Bancroft, "The Census Bureau Estimates of Unemployment," as cited, p. 62).

[51] See Virginia Kyner, "Total and Insured Unemployment Estimates: A Criticism," and "A Rejoinder," by Gertrude Bancroft, *Review of Economics and Statistics*, November 1951, pp. 338-342.

[52] In this volume.

TABLE 2

Estimates of Completely Unemployed Persons in Industries Covered by Unemployment Insurance, Adjusted Census and Insured Unemployment, 1949-1953

(*thousands*)

	1949		1950		1951		1952		1953	
MONTH	*Census*	*Insured*	*Census*	*Insured*	*Census*	*Insured*	*Census*	*Insured*	*Census*	*Insured*
January	2,315	2,016	3,559	2,479	1,993	1,157	1,738	1,331	1,640	1,179
February	2,647	2,448	3,635	2,433	1,893	1,048	1,774	1,255	1,488	1,118
March	2,722	2,635	3,331	2,303	1,704	913	1,486	1,199	1,362	1,048
April	2,695	2,591	2,873	1,954	1,470	887	1,464	1,092	1,364	972
May	2,735	2,549	2,496	1,722	1,315	896	1,360	1,029	1,136	874
June	2,866	2,548	2,474	1,538	1,482	919	1,446	990	1,202	808
July	3,346	2,724	2,384	1,472	1,476	983	1,488	1,161	1,230	858
August	3,031	2,335	1,837	1,108	1,306	921	1,418	1,161	1,082	844
September	2,743	2,059	1,734	900	1,352	838	1,140	687	1,093	785
October	3,032	1,898	1,468	763	1,324	796	1,060	589	1,053	754
November	2,804	2,152	1,734	825	1,446	841	1,138	628	1,348	1,076
December	2,877	2,303	1,732	979	1,396	944	1,182	822	1,594	1,393

Adjustments: Census: Unemployed persons minus those who never had a full-time job or whose last reported job was in agriculture, government, domestic service, self-employment, or unpaid family work; added to the unemployed are persons laid off from nonagricultural jobs with instructions to return to work at a definite date within thirty days.

Insured unemployment: State-insured unemployment, unemployment compensation for veterans, and railroad unemployment program, minus estimated number who did any work during the week (partial and part-total employment). Proportion of weeks compensated during the month by the state unemployment insurance systems for total unemployment assumed to be proportion of benefit recipients who did no work.

Source: Bureau of the Census and Bureau of Employment Security (from *Hearings before the Joint Committee on the Economic Report*, 83d Cong., 2d Sess., Feb. 1-18, 1954, pp. 317-319).

5. Local Area Estimates of Total Unemployment

The BES has no legal responsibility for over-all unemployment estimates, and currently does not attempt to estimate total unemployment on a national basis. However, as part of the regular employment security reporting system, the Bureau does require such estimates on a local basis for 149 labor market areas accounting for about 70 per cent of nonagricultural employment in the United States.[53]

Estimates of unemployment are contained in a bimonthly labor market report (ES-219) which is prepared for each labor market area containing at least one city with a 1950 population of 50,000 or more, and for a few other areas with unusual labor market characteristics. The labor market area for which a report is made is defined as a central city or cities and the surrounding territory within reasonable commuting distance. So far as possible, boundaries of the Standard Metropolitan Areas are used.

The labor market report includes textual material describing labor market trends as well as statistical tables containing estimates of employment and unemployment, turnover, hours, and earnings. Recognizing that the estimates called for in the report require qualitative judgments on the part of the local analysts, the BES works with the state agencies on the development and improvement of needed sources of information and estimating techniques. It has prepared handbooks for the use of state and local employment agencies which suggest methods for making the estimates required by the report.[54] State agencies submit annual statements to the BES describing the techniques used for estimating employment, unemployment, and labor force changes. The Bureau periodically reviews the labor market reports from each area and submits written evaluations to the respective state agencies.

Data in the labor market reports are used for a number of purposes. According to the *Employment Security Manual*, their basic purpose is to aid in the planning, directing, and evaluation of the services of local employment offices. They are also used, however, as a basis for classifying labor market areas according to the relative adequacy of their labor supply.[55] Area classifications are "intended to provide a quick, convenient tool to measure comparative differences in the availability of labor (and general economic well-being) of the nation's major

[53] The area reporting program was initiated during the defense build-up prior to World War II. The number of areas included in the program has changed from time to time, being as high as 350 during the war.

[54] See, for example, "Techniques for Estimating Unemployment."

[55] See *Labor Market Developments in Major Areas*, published bimonthly in mimeographed form by the Bureau of Employment Security.

production and employment centers. . . . They have been widely used by Government agencies and private organizations in the introduction, administration, and evaluation of manpower programs and policies ever since the area classification program was first initiated in the early days of World War II."[56] Thus, the area classification program is conceived as useful in assisting employers with the location of new plants, and as a guide for government policies designed to alleviate unemployment.[57]

Although the extent of unemployment is not the sole criterion for classifying local labor market areas according to the relative adequacy of their labor supply, it is the most important one.[58] In view of the uses to which the classification of areas is put, it is desirable to inquire briefly into the nature of the estimates of total unemployment that are made. The concept of unemployment which local labor market analysts are instructed to use is almost identical with that employed by the Bureau of the Census.[59] The problem is thus one of utilizing the data which arise as by-products of the operation of the local employment office, together with whatever other materials are available, to arrive at such an estimate.

The general procedure, as well as some specific techniques for developing the unemployment estimate, have been suggested by the BES. The problem is broken down into three major segments: (1) estimating the number of unemployed workers from covered activities, (2) estimating the number of unemployed workers from noncovered activities, and (3) estimating the number of unemployed new entrants and re-entrants to the labor force as well as in-migrants to the local labor market area. Merely to state these problems is to indicate that their solution is, to say the least, a formidable task. For example, even to estimate the number of persons in the first of these three components of the unemployed would require knowledge about the extent to which there are delays in the filing of initial claims; the number of eligible workers who do not apply for benefits; the incidence of unem-

[56] "Criteria and Procedure Used in Classification of Labor Market Areas," statement introduced in *Hearings before the Joint Committee on the Economic Report*, p. 348.

[57] The availability of manpower, as indicated by the area classifications, is one of the criteria used by the Office of Defense Mobilization in the evaluation of applications for accelerated tax amortization assistance to new plants in selected defense industries. *Defense Manpower Policy No. 1*, Office of Defense Mobilization, August 2, 1951. Also, "it is the policy of the Federal Government to encourage the placing of contracts and facilities in areas of current or imminent labor surplus. . . ." *Defense Manpower Policy No. 4* (Revised), November 5, 1953.

[58] For a description of the classification criteria currently being used by the BES, see *Hearings before the Joint Committee on the Economic Report*, pp. 349-350.

[59] "Techniques for Estimating Unemployment," p. 6.

ployment among persons who have exhausted their rights to benefits; and the extent to which persons disqualified from the receipt of benefits are without jobs. Moreover, answers to these questions are clearly not constants. The amount of post-exhaustion unemployment is affected by the state of the labor market, and the same is probably true of the extent to which there is a lag in the filing of initial claims. This means that even for a given local area it is impossible to work out adjustment factors on the basis of a single study of each of these questions.

Space does not permit a description of the various techniques which have been recommended for estimating total unemployment on the basis of the data available to a labor market analyst in a local employment office. All of them have certain limitations, of which the BES is fully cognizant, and which arise because the employment security program unfortunately does not yield the types of data which are required. Moreover, some of the more refined techniques which the Bureau has recommended are so elaborate that it may reasonably be doubted that many local labor market analysts have the necessary combination of aptitude, diligence, staff, and time to apply them.

In view of the important purposes which local area estimates of unemployment serve, it would seem desirable to test the validity of those currently being made against the results of periodic household surveys similar to those which the Bureau of the Census now conducts on a national basis.[60] It might be possible for the Bureau of the Census and the BES to work out an arrangement in which the former agency would develop the sample within the local areas and the latter, in cooperation with the state agencies, would conduct the surveys, the results of which would be processed by the Census Bureau.

Such checks might indicate that the techniques currently employed yield estimates of total unemployment that are sufficiently accurate for the purposes which they are to serve, in which case the local labor force surveys might be discontinued. If, on the other hand, it should be established that employment security data do not yield valid estimates of unemployment, reliance would have to be placed exclusively on local labor force surveys.

[60] Attempts to compare BES estimates of total unemployment for local labor market areas with the unemployment counts obtained from the 1950 Census of Population encounter several difficulties. The Census Bureau has found that the 1950 census understated total unemployment as measured by the Current Population Survey by about 20 per cent. There are no data, however, on the extent of understatement by local area, which may vary from the national average. Moreover, the census data do not necessarily relate to the same week in April 1950 as the BES estimates. For these reasons, comparisons which have been made between the two sets of data for the fifteen largest labor market areas are not conclusive (letter from Louis Levine, Chief, Division of Reports and Analysis, BES, November 19, 1954).

6. Summary and Conclusions

1. The administration of the employment security program in the United States makes available several types of data which have some value as indicators of unemployment trends and possibly as bases for estimates of total unemployment.

2. The chief advantages of employment security data relating to unemployment are their currency and the fact that, unlike the data of the Bureau of the Census, they are available not only on a national basis but for regions, states, and local labor market areas as well. Moreover, the data are not subject to sampling variation, nor is the likelihood of response error as great as in the case of census data, since information is obtained directly from the worker rather than from someone in his household. Also, although administrative determinations of the availability of claimants for suitable work vary among states and local areas, the work test in all unemployment insurance laws perhaps provides a more objective criterion of attachment to the labor force than the "seeking work" criterion used by the Census Bureau.

3. On the other hand, the chief disadvantage of employment security data on unemployment is that it is impossible to define in terms that have economic (as distinguished from legal or administrative) significance precisely what it is that the data measure. This is true even of the active file figures and of the claims data that result from the operation of a single state program. The problem is made more complex by the diversity of the various unemployment insurance laws in their coverage, eligibility and disqualification provisions, and administrative features. This diversity, incidentally, qualifies to a considerable extent the advantages inherent in having state and local data. If interstate or interarea comparisons are to be made, it must be kept in mind that differences in the data may reflect differences in the unemployment insurance laws or their administration, as well as in rates of unemployment.

4. Initial claims data have some value as an indicator of incipient unemployment, but numerous legal and administrative factors must be considered in interpreting them. Although insured unemployment statistics, based on continued claims, show a rough correspondence in trend with total unemployment as defined and measured by the Bureau of the Census, there are rather pronounced variations in the ratio between insured and total unemployment. Nevertheless, there is an advantage in having unemployment data from two such different sources. For example, the high levels of insured unemployment relative to total unemployment in the fall and winter of 1953 suggested that the census data were understating total unemployment. This was con-

firmed when data based on the revised census sample became available in January 1954.

5. Claims data might have greater usefulness as an indicator of unemployment trends if more were known about the extent to which and the circumstances under which eligible workers fail to exercise their rights under unemployment insurance laws. Information is needed on the prevalence of delayed filing of initial claims under varying economic conditions and in areas with varying industrial structures. Similarly, it would be useful to know the extent of, and the reasons for, failure of eligible unemployed individuals to file for benefits at any time during spells of unemployment. Some of these problems are currently being investigated by state employment security agencies. Independent studies along similar lines would doubtless be worthwhile.

6. Estimates of total unemployment on a local area basis need to be checked by periodic labor force surveys. It is true that estimates of total unemployment based upon employment security data should be able to be made with greater confidence on a local than on a national basis. There is only one unemployment insurance law involved in the former case, and the labor market analyst is at least in a position to be intimately familiar with the character of the local labor market and with the administrative factors in the local office that are likely to affect active file and claims data. On the other hand, it remains to be demonstrated that even with these advantages employment security data provide a good basis for local area estimates of total unemployment.

COMMENT

NATHAN KEYFITZ, Dominion Bureau of Statistics, Canada

Like Herbert Parnes, I am a Bureau of Employment Security outsider. My remarks will be confined to some analogies and some differences between the United States and Canada in this field.

In both countries there is now extensive social security legislation; in the United States tied more closely to the individual states, in Canada to the federal government. I think that Parnes exaggerates the difficulties which arise from having forty-eight separate laws; Canada has but one Unemployment Insurance Act and yet most of the difficulties that he refers to are found in Canada.

The statisticians of the BES as well as the United States public appear to have concentrated their attention on initial claims, while in Canada there has been more emphasis on a series that we call unplaced applicants. Applicants include claimants since one condition for drawing benefit is being registered for employment, but in addition applicants include a proportion of the jobless who for one reason or another cannot claim benefit, a proportion which is in the nature of things unknown. These jobless include those attached to uncovered industries, persons who have exhausted their benefit rights, etc. The case for placing the main statistical emphasis on claimants rather than on applicants is partly that the former are subject to carefully worked out, sharply defined, and consistently administered legal requirements. This definiteness helps to prevent their being used to describe something which they are not, e.g. the whole of unemployment. However, since our own employment service people are not represented at this meeting I must be careful not to take up matters which would be contentious in Canada.

One special difficulty of Canadian figures of either applicants or claimants is that they do not indicate long-term trends. The coverage under the act has been steadily broadened in the fourteen years that it has been in operation and this fact increases the number of claimants and applicants. One type of extension of social security is the supplementary benefits for seasonally unemployed in our relatively difficult winter months.

In the several states cards are kept in the live files for from thirty to sixty days after the applicant was last seen in the office. This means that a man can have been working this long before his card is removed and there can be no question that this has an effect in exaggerating the number of cards in the file. The interest of Canadian authorities in getting statistics from the applicant files has shown itself in a reduction of this period to fifteen days; in principle the file is counted on Thursday of each week only for persons who were in contact with the office within the preceding fifteen days. In addition all persons who declared themselves to have a job are excluded for purposes of this count. As Parnes points out for the United States, we cannot be sure that the job applicants always state their existing job connections.

On the other hand, the number of persons entitled to benefit who failed to collect is mentioned several times by Parnes as a factor leading to understatement on the part of the statistics. I do not know whether Canadians are quicker to seize any money that may be due to them than are citizens of your country but we have never heard of this particular difficulty in Canada.

Parnes' statement that "the diligence and regularity with which applications in the active file are canceled are inversely related to the pressure of other activities" is probably part of the dynamics of any statistical compilation that is tied in with, and a subordinate element of, an administrative operation.

THE MEANING AND MEASUREMENT OF PARTIAL AND DISGUISED UNEMPLOYMENT

LOUIS J. DUCOFF AND MARGARET J. HAGOOD
AGRICULTURAL MARKETING SERVICE, DEPARTMENT OF AGRICULTURE

In a monograph published by the Social Science Research Council in 1947, the present writers devoted a chapter to the differentiation needed among the unemployed and the employed which would enhance the value of labor force statistics as indicators of the state of functioning of the economy.[1] Specifically it was felt that adequate statistics on the labor force and on the employed and unemployed components can come closer to revealing to what extent the economy approaches or departs from a full employment condition than any other statistical measure. Among the differentiations proposed, we outlined the need for separating from the employed those workers who were *inadequately* employed so as to identify and measure the size of the groups with definitely substandard employment. Two subclasses of the inadequately employed were singled out for further differentiation: (1) the underemployed who do not have a sufficient *amount* of work and (2) the employed who get substandard returns per hour of work because of its low productivity (mainly self-employed or unpaid family workers) or because they are employed at substandard wages. It was recognized that substandard wages might be the outward form of low productivity.

For most nonagricultural industries such differentiations can usefully be made in the monthly estimates of the employed which are based on the concept of a current week's activity. In agriculture, particularly for the self-employed, a longer time span, preferably a year's record on time worked and income received, is needed to evaluate the extent of underemployment or to determine the presence or absence of ineffective or unproductive employment.

1. *Formulations of the Concept of Underemployment*

Underemployment, partial unemployment, and disguised unemployment are various terms used to connote the several manifestations of inadequate employment opportunity or the underutilization of the actual or potential manpower resources. The difficulties of arriving at universally accepted definitions of full employment and of unemployment are well known. Because partial and disguised unemployment

[1] Louis J. Ducoff and Margaret J. Hagood, *Labor Force Definition and Measurement: Recent Experience in the United States,* Social Science Research Council, Bull. 56, 1947.

involve aspects related to considerations of full employment as well as to the nature of unemployment, it is important to review the concepts underlying the various terms used to describe partial and disguised unemployment.

A recent study by the United Nations refers to underemployment as:

> "employment in jobs which occupied only a part of the workers' available time or permit only the partial utilization of their capacities. The latter form of waste of human resources is sometimes called 'concealed' or 'disguised' unemployment, and may be created by any of the conditions which produce total unemployment, including structural maladjustments, cyclical fluctuations, or persistent deficiency of the general demand for labor . . . since the concept of underemployment includes employment which does not permit the workers to make their full potential contribution to the output of the community, full employment requires an occupational distribution of the labor force which is optimal from the standpoint of maximizing per capita output."[2]

This formulation of the concept of underemployment implies an evolutionary or developmental approach, as the optimal distribution and utilization of the labor force is, at any given stage of economic development, not an absolutely attainable goal, but rather an ideal construct indicating the direction in which changes should be sought.

Another writer, in examining the problem of underemployment as it manifests itself in Asia,[3] conceptualizes the problem by distinguishing between visible, disguised, and potential underemployment and treats these types as in fact three different stages in which labor may be released from a given economic sector because of its redundancy without reducing output in that sector. Thus visible underemployment is the excess of manpower available over manpower needed to carry out current production activities under existing methods and capital investment. The disguised unemployment, according to this writer, is the labor time or manpower potential that will be released if only simple changes in methods of production were made without any additional capital investment. Potential underemployment is the manpower that could be released from a given economic sector by a more fundamental change in methods of production, including substantial capital investment.

In a more theoretical treatment of the subject, Bishop conceptualizes

[2] *The Determinants and Consequences of Population Trends*, United Nations, Dept. of Social Affairs, Population Division, Population Studies No. 17, 1953, pp. 249-250.

[3] Chiang Hsieh, "Underemployment in Asia, I. Nature and Extent," *International Labor Review*, June 1952.

the problem of underemployment as follows: "Economic underemployment of labor exists when the real return which owners receive for the use of labor in the particular field of resource use is less than the real return which could be obtained for comparable resource services in other uses."[4] Since this concept is inconsistent with the rationality postulate, Bishop points out that underemployment arises out of (1) imperfect knowledge regarding employment opportunities or (2) barriers to the mobility of labor among uses, or both. Because the barriers to mobility may be of a psychic nature, Bishop is led to restate in the following terms the conditions he considers necessary for the existence of underemployment. "To determine whether labor is underemployed the relevant real income data must be expressed in levels of satisfaction rather than in terms of a particular bundle of goods and services. Underemployment of labor exists when the level of utility available to resource owners as a consequence of employing their labor in a particular use is less than the level of utility available to them by employment of labor in alternative uses."[5]

Even this limited review of efforts to conceptualize the problem of underemployment or partial unemployment suggests the complexity of devising operational definitions and measurement techniques. Nevertheless, the concept of underemployment has received increasing attention from two major directions in recent years. Problems of economic development with respect to underdeveloped countries have highlighted underemployment and ineffective employment as of greater importance than unemployment, as that concept is measured in industrialized countries. In more highly developed countries, the emphasis on the goal of full employment and progressively rising productivity and levels of living has increased efforts to identify groups, other than the totally unemployed, whose employment is inadequate because it is insufficient in amount, or below standard in productivity and returns, or both.

The concepts of underemployment and inadequate employment imply some standard or norm of employment which is not being met. If underemployment is to be measured, the standards must be explicitly formulated. These may vary with different cultures so that the measurement problem may have to be approached in different ways. Even within one country, the identification and measurement of underemployment may require different techniques for different groups of workers. The remainder of this paper is concerned chiefly with an exploration of these problems in the United States, and especially in the agricultural sector of the economy.

[4] Charles E. Bishop, "Underemployment of Labor in Southeastern Agriculture," *Journal of Farm Economics*, May 1954.
[5] *Ibid.*, p. 260.

2. Underemployment in the United States

Even though the United States economy has operated at relatively high levels in the last fifteen years, there has admittedly been less than "full" employment even when the number of totally unemployed was quite low. To approach the measurement of this departure empirically there have been proposals, particularly from organized labor groups, to recognize explicitly partial employment, or conversely partial unemployment, as a category in the current statistical series on the labor force. In such a formulation the partially unemployed would include (1) persons who worked part time during the survey week because of economic factors but who usually work full time and (2) persons who usually work part time but who prefer and would accept full-time work.

For most nonagricultural employees, labor force surveys could obtain information on time worked and wages earned in a current week, which, with supplementary questions on reasons for not working "full" weeks, would provide a basis for identifying underemployment or unremunerative employment. At present, the Census Bureau obtains data each month on time worked during the survey week and, at irregular intervals, on reasons for not working full weeks. These provide reasonably satisfactory data for identifying various groups of underemployed from the criterion of time worked. For the self-employed, however, and particularly for farm operators, the approach on the basis of a current week's activity and earnings is not satisfactory for identifying the inadequately employed.

In the United States, agriculture is a sector of the economy in which underemployment has been persistent and difficult to measure. The seasonal nature of most agricultural enterprises means that neither the labor input nor the money returns are spread evenly throughout the year. There may be practically no activity during certain weeks or months and very long working hours during other parts of the year. For example, on many one-crop farms, and especially on small cotton farms in the South, there may be practically no activity during the winter and again during the period between the last cultivation operations and the beginning of the harvest. Therefore, the information on time worked during a specific week does not have the same economic significance in the case of the farmer as it does in the case of the factory worker.

Also important, in addition to the insufficient hours worked by many underemployed farm operators, is the problem of substandard returns per hour of work because of low productivity. In some types of available data, it is often not possible to dissociate the factors of an insufficient amount of employment and the low returns per hour. Since the product of these two is measurable in the case of self-employed farm operators by annual income, most research workers in this field have used annual income as a criterion and designated as "underemployed" farm operators with annual incomes less than some specified amount, regardless of whether the low income resulted from an insufficient amount of work or substandard returns per hour of labor, or both. Thus, special tabulations from the 1950 Census of Agriculture show there were 1,622,000 farm-operator families with heads between the ages of twenty-five and sixty-five which had total family incomes of less than $2,000.[6] We have no information on the annual input of labor by these families, but it is believed that they averaged considerably less than full years of work and that the returns per hour averaged lower than the statutory minimum for most nonagricultural wage workers. Data on their land, machinery, livestock, etc., indicate that insufficient physical and capital resources were available for adequate employment of the manpower. From the standpoint of the agricultural sector of the United States economy, the problem of underemployment is mainly one of redundant or surplus manpower on the less productive farms. The levels of agricultural production achieved by the more productive sector of agriculture can adequately meet the existing domestic and export demands, including reasonable reserves of food and fiber.

Evidence of the redundance of manpower on farms at the beginning of World War II is the extensive out-migration of farm people to non-farm areas that occurred in the United States. Despite the substantial decline in number of farm workers and man-hours of farm labor input, total farm output in this decade increased by 20 per cent, while output per man-hour rose 62 per cent. The net migration from farms in this decade amounted to over 8½ million persons ten years of age and over, about evenly divided as between males and females. Sixty-one per cent of the males who migrated were between fifteen and fifty-nine years of age in 1940 and 33 per cent were under fifteen. The corresponding distribution of the female migrants was 54 and 40 per cent respectively (Table 1). Differentials in the rates of migration occurred as between different regions of the United States and different groups in the farm population. For example, the rate of out-migration from the South was greater than for the United States as a whole, reflecting the substantially greater out-migration of the nonwhite than of the white farm population in the South.

[6] *Long Range Farm Programs*, Technical Studies by the Dept. of Agriculture Relating to Selected Farm Price Support Proposals for the House of Representatives, Committee on Agriculture, 83d Cong., 2d sess., 1954, p. 160.

TABLE 1

Estimates of Net Migration from the Rural-Farm Population, 1940-1950

(number in thousands)

AREA AND AGE GROUP		TOTAL		MALE		FEMALE	
		Number	*Per Cent*	*Number*	*Per Cent*	*Number*	*Per Ce*
United States—all ages[a]		8,610	100.0	4,269	100.0	4,341	100.0
Age in 1940	*Age in 1950*						
Under 15	10-24	3,139	36.5	1,411	33.0	1,728	39.8
15-59	25-69	4,952	57.5	2,607	61.1	2,345	54.0
60 and over	70 and over	519	6.0	251	5.9	268	6.2
Rate of net migration:[b]							
United States			30.9		29.6		32.3
South			36.1		34.9		37.4
White			33.8		32.4		35.2
Nonwhite			42.4		41.7		43.1

[a] Net migration of persons from the rural-farm population between 1940 and 1950. Estimat relate to persons alive in both 1940 and 1950 and do not include estimates of migration of thos born or dying during the decade.

[b] Net migration expressed as a percentage of the expected survivors to 1950 of persons livin on rural farms in 1940.

Source: Dept. of Agriculture, Agricultural Marketing Service.

Information is not available by which to analyze in detail the full range of factors underlying this extensive population shift. Thus, for example, it would be revealing if information were available to show the areas to which the migration took place and the volume of such migration to each of the receiving areas. Much could be learned as to the causes and motivations for the migration if information were available on the particular economic circumstances of the individuals and families involved in the migration at the time that they left their farm communities. However, much of this migration was from low income or low production farms of people who were underemployed and who would have migrated earlier had employment opportunities existed. They were in large part people whose migration had been dammed up by the depressed economic conditions of the 1930 to 1940 decade. They responded rapidly to the employment opportunities that were created during the war and postwar years of prosperity in the next decade. Thus the swings of the economic cycle play an important role in determining the magnitude of the rural underemployment problem.

3. *Measurement of Underemployment*

Various approaches to identification of the underemployed by measurement of time worked during the entire year have been made in population censuses, in national sample surveys, and in special surveys in areas of rural underemployment. In the 1950 population census, a single question was asked (of a 20 per cent sample) on the number of weeks worked in 1949. Tabulations of the results by residence indicate a slightly higher prevalence of underemployment among rural-nonfarm than among urban or rural-farm workers. Among males who worked at some time during the year, the proportion who worked 40 or more weeks was 79.7 per cent for urban, 72.6 per cent for rural-nonfarm, and 79.4 per cent for rural-farm. Tabulations by industry from the decennial censuses and from current surveys for later years show that the high proportion among the rural-farm population is due largely to the high proportion of farmers reporting fifty weeks or more of work. For example, in 1953, the proportion of self-employed workers in agriculture reporting full-time year-round employment was 74.9 per cent, in contrast with 34.9 per cent for farm wage workers and 60.7 per cent for all in nonagricultural industries.[7]

The results seem to suggest fuller employment during the year for self-employed farmers than for a majority of nonagricultural occupations. There may be two types of inadequacies in this approach to the problem. One is the questionable value of the response to a single question to farm operators on the number of weeks they worked during the year. The other is the lack of information to cross-classify the amount of work performed with the value of the production achieved. In view of the known differences in efficiencies of time input and methods of production among farm operators in different economic size classes (which range from agricultural methods of past generations to modern-day scientific and mechanized farming), the inability to evaluate the time input by the product achieved severely limits interpretation of the data on "weeks worked."

The reality of the problem of underemployment in agriculture, however, can be perceived even through this barrier by noting results from a few studies in areas of concentration of low-income farm families.

4. *Special Studies of Rural Underemployment*

Two recent studies made cooperatively by the Department of Agriculture and the agricultural experiment stations of Kentucky and Oklahoma attempted a more refined approach to measurement of time input on an annual basis.[8] Interview sample surveys were made of

[7] "Work Experience of the Labor Force in 1953," Current Population Reports, Bureau of the Census, Series P-50, No. 54, August 4, 1954.

[8] Robert E. Galloway and Howard W. Beers, *Utilization of Rural Manpower in Kentucky*, Kentucky Agricultural Experiment Station and Bureau of Agricultural Economics, January 1953. James D. Tarver, *A Study of Rural Manpower in Southeastern Oklahoma*, Oklahoma Agricultural Experiment Station and Agricultural Marketing Service, September 1955.

the open-country households in economic area 8 in eastern Kentucky and economic area 9 in southeastern Oklahoma, both of which were areas of known low income and levels of living. In these studies, intensive questioning was made to ascertain as accurately as possible the work record during the year of all persons fourteen years of age and over in the open-country households. About twenty questions were used to get for each individual the information for the various seasons and types of work; the data were then converted into eight-hour days.

The results obtained are in several ways not exactly comparable with those obtained in the 1950 census, but even so the prevalence of greater-than-average underemployment is indicated. In Kentucky, of the rural-farm males fourteen years of age and over who were employed during the year ending March 1, 1952, only 66 per cent had 180 or more full-time days of work. This is substantially below the census figure already cited for rural-farm males in the United States in 1949—79 per cent reported forty weeks or more of work. In Oklahoma, 65 per cent reported 180 or more days.

The intermittent and seasonal character of the employment of hired farm workers and unpaid family workers is well known. Of a total hired farm work force of some 3 million individuals in 1952, only about 1 million had farm work as their chief activity during the year, averaging 212 days of work (including fifteen days of nonfarm work).[9] An additional 250,000 had nonfarm work as their chief activity, averaging 216 days of work. The remainder were chiefly housewives, school youths, and others who work on farms for only short periods. A similar picture is presented for 1953 for hired farm workers and unpaid family workers by the Current Population Surveys. Only 7.3 per cent of the unpaid family workers in agriculture and 34.9 per cent of the wage workers were full-time, year-round workers.[10]

To assess the problem of underemployment in a realistic way, it is necessary to consider the availability of underemployed workers for alternative opportunities, as well as the current stage of the business cycle in affording such opportunities. The pilot studies, made in co-operation with state and federal agencies, explored the availability of presumed underemployed workers in areas of low farm income, in areas which include the possibly underemployed seasonal hired farm workers, and in areas which depend mainly on migratory workers, whether imported or foreign.

The net result of these studies is not too positive in getting a measure of how many of these workers were really available for addi-

[9] Louis J. Ducoff, *The Hired Farm Working Force of 1952*, Bureau of Agricultural Economics, October 1953.

[10] "Work Experience of the Labor Force in 1953."

tional or more productive work. In relatively isolated areas of eastern Kentucky and southeastern Oklahoma, the respondents surveyed indicated a very low degree of availability of workers in open-country rural families for out-of-area employment. Only 14 per cent of the family heads surveyed in Kentucky and 4 per cent in Oklahoma said they would be willing to move to another location to take a year-round nonfarm job. This stands in sharp contrast to the actual record of migration from farms during the 1940-1950 decade. The farm population of the areas surveyed had net losses through migration equal to nearly 40 per cent of the farm population at the beginning of the decade for the Kentucky area and 45 per cent for the Oklahoma area. Age and possibly other types of selectivity in this high rate of migration during 1940-1950 may have left a less potentially mobile population remaining in the area. However, questions on availability are not always very meaningful or realistic in research projects of this type when the interviewer cannot offer to the interviewee anything in the way of a concrete job.

In contrast, much larger proportions of the persons surveyed deemed to be underemployed by arbitrary criteria expressed interest in additional employment in nonagricultural work within their own localities. Demographers, economists, and sociologists have for years advised that more new industry should be located in areas of rural underemployment. They have supplied maps and tables to highlight such recommendations, with little effect except when the industry, such as atomic energy and related plants, requires a vast expanse of space.

The special survey on availability revealed that the vast majority of the currently underemployed in the areas studied had little access to information on alternative opportunities. In March 1952, only about a fourth of the farm-family heads in the Kentucky area had heard of any farm or nonfarm jobs being available during the nearly two years after the outbreak of hostilities in Korea and the marked expansion in employment in defense industries.

5. *Implications*

The identification of partial and disguised unemployment is significant in any type of economy under any national employment conditions. In the United States, where the general levels of productivity and living standards are high, the existence of a substantial amount of underemployment in some sectors of the economy stands in contrast to the accepted norms and evokes inquiry as to what can be done about it. During the depression years of the 1930's, the identification and measurement of the unemployed and the underemployed led to various programs for temporary amelioration, but the lack of employment opportunity limited severely the transfer on a fairly permanent basis of the underutilized rural manpower to adequate and productive employment.

During World War II and the succeeding postwar years of prosperity, the problem shifted from a buyers' market to a sellers' market for labor. A tremendous relocation of manpower resources was the result. Net migration from the rural-farm population amounted to about 9 million during the decade of the 1940's, and most of this occurred without direction or assistance from governmental agencies. Voluntary mobility is a coveted feature of our American democratic economy, and underemployment of farm people was greatly reduced by the response of unemployed or inadequately employed farm workers to better employment opportunities in other jobs and locations.

Even under such favorable conditions for transfer of labor to more productive employment, the United States is still faced with a considerable surplus of inadequately employed workers, especially in nonindustrialized rural areas. The problems are accentuated in areas of low-income farms and areas in which mechanization is rapidly diminishing farm labor requirements. The areas are generally those in which the high level of birth rates in recent decades result in a higher rate of replacement of working adults than can be offset by deaths, retirements, or older men moving out of agricultural occupations.

Replacement ratios for rural-farm males of working age during the 1950-1960 decade are shown for state economic areas of the United States in Map 1.[11] The ratio indicates the number of young men who will be entering the working age for every 100 older men who will die or retire. The state economic areas of greatest potential population pressure during the next decade are largely in the southern Appalachian Mountains and interior plateaus, the South Atlantic coastal plain, a large contiguous area running from the southern high plains westward to the Colorado River and northward from there to southern Idaho, and portions of the Great Plains of the Dakotas. Many counties in these economic areas have replacement ratios of more than 200, indicating that more than twice as many young men as needed for replacement will reach working age in the farm population during the current decade. However, the replacement ratio has been substantially reduced in the last decade; for the United States as a whole it fell from 167 in the 1940-1950 decade to 135 for the present decade.

To date, the chief force operating to reduce underemployment has been sustained high levels of national employment and income which

[11] Gladys K. Bowles and Conrad Taeuber, *Replacement Rates for Rural-Farm Males of Working Age, 1950-60*, Agricultural Marketing Service and Bureau of the Census, 1956.

Map 1

Replacement Ratios of Rural-Farm Males Aged 25-69, for State Economic Areas, 1950-1960

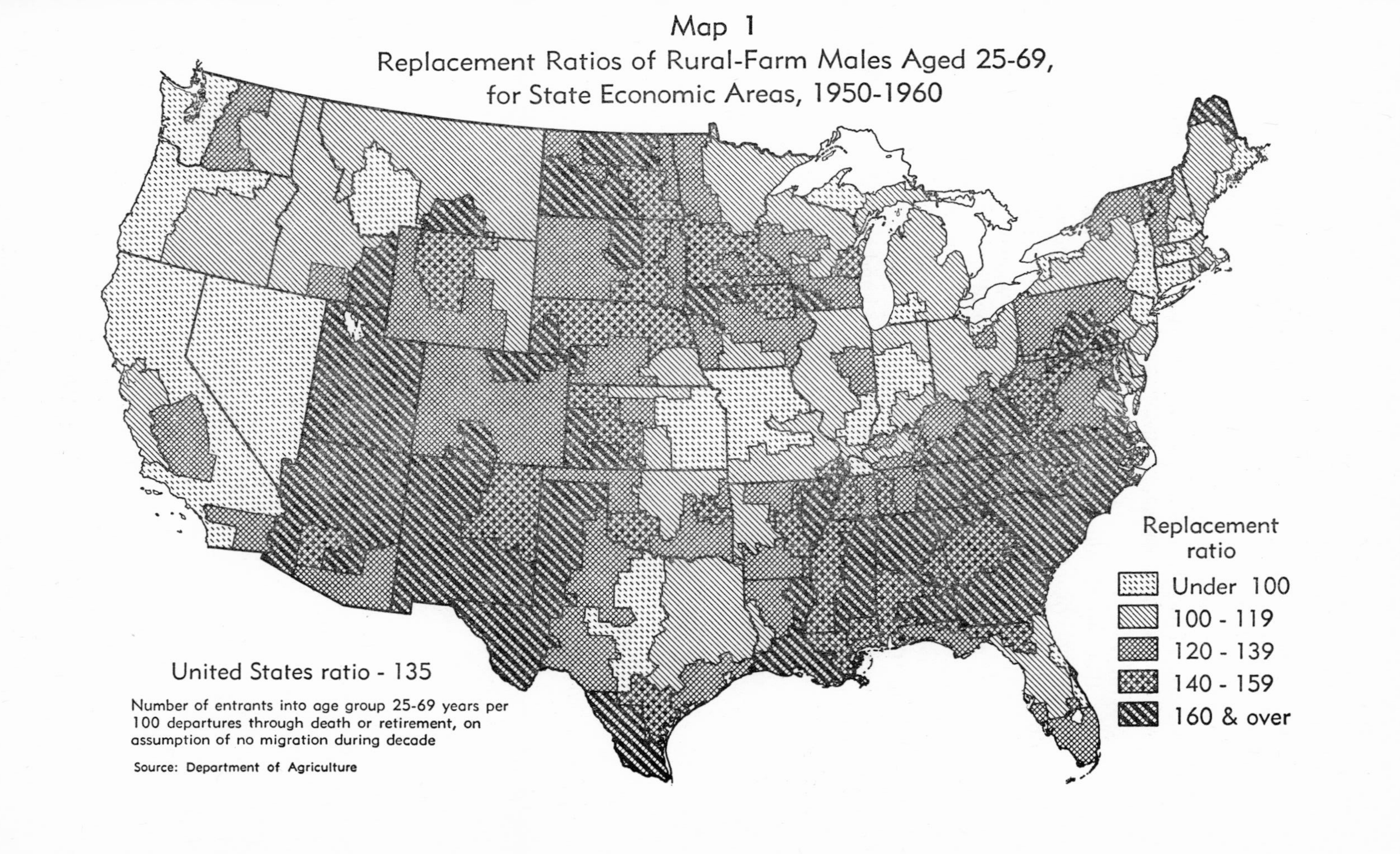

Source: Department of Agriculture

induce voluntary migration and shifts to more productive employment, rather than specific programs for areas of concentration of underemployment. However, there are still areas of concentration of underemployment, especially among low-income farm families. These areas, because of isolation and other factors, still have reserves of underutilized and ineffectively utilized manpower. In these same areas generally, farm youth are reaching working age in much larger numbers than are required for replacement needs. There is increasing public concern over the need for developing programs for vocational training of youths in nonfarm occupations, and for provision of retraining and nonfarm employment information for many adults. Development of programs by federal, state, and local agencies is impeded by lack of adequate statistics on the numbers, location, and characteristics of the underemployed, and especially on their availability and capacities for transfer into more productive employment. The problems of measurement have by no means been solved and research efforts must be intensified to develop better measures of partial employment and of underutilization of manpower resources.

THE SECONDARY LABOR FORCE AND THE MEASUREMENT OF UNEMPLOYMENT

RICHARD C. WILCOCK

INSTITUTE OF LABOR AND INDUSTRIAL RELATIONS,
UNIVERSITY OF ILLINOIS

THE central thesis of this paper is that differentiation in labor force statistics between those who are continuing or regular members of the labor force and those who are temporary or secondary members may be operationally feasible and if so would contribute to the analysis and understanding of employment and unemployment fluctuations in the American economy. In section 1 an attempt is made to define the concept of the secondary labor force. In section 2 an analysis of data from local labor market area studies and from the Current Population Survey of the Census Bureau is presented for the purpose of illustrating the expected advantages in labor force analysis of the proposed differentiation. In section 3 the problems of measurement are discussed, and a number of suggestions for further research and experimentation are made.

1. Secondary Workers and Labor Force Mobility

DEFINITIONS

Movement into and out of the labor force, or labor force mobility, can be classified into two basic types. One is an inevitable function of the human aging process and is characterized by movement into the labor force upon the completion of schooling and movement out when a worker retires or is retired because of age. The other consists of the entrances and exits of those persons who are not regularly or consistently in the labor force during the usual span of working years but who move into and out of the labor force intermittently or are in the labor force only once or twice for relatively short periods of time.

Although there have been significant changes in the conventional ages of labor force entry and retirement, changes in mobility of the first type are primarily long-run phenomena and do not exert great influence on short-run fluctuations in employment and unemployment.[1] The second type of labor force mobility is not only decidedly greater in volume of movement[2] but plays a vital role in short-run adjustments

[1] The increased participation of both young and old in World War II was primarily a short-run phenomenon of the second type of labor force mobility which temporarily reversed the secular trend of declining labor force participation rates on the part of teen-agers and older people.

[2] In 1952, for example, the total labor force averaged a net gain of 600,000

of labor supply to labor demand in American labor markets. All workers have to enter and leave at least once, but only some make a "practice" of going into and out of the labor force. This paper is concerned with those who do.

Data are available from the Census Bureau for recent years on gross movements into and out of agricultural and nonagricultural employment and unemployment, by previous status (employed, unemployed, or out of the labor force) and by sex, but these data unfortunately do not differentiate between those who are regularly members of the labor force and those who are mobile in respect to labor force participation.[3] To fill this need, this paper suggests a method of labor force classification which, while at present largely experimental, would if perfected and adopted make available for analytical and policy purposes data which would differentiate between the two categories of labor force attachment.

The value of such a differentiation will depend upon three factors: the advantages of the breakdown, the existence of any satisfactory alternative measurements, and the feasibility of measurement. The first two of these will be considered in section 2 of the paper and the third in section 3. Before presenting the evidence for the three factors, however, it is necessary to define as clearly as possible the terms being used.

Since there seem to be no satisfactory terms in the literature for the concepts being presented (see note 7), it is necessary to describe fully the terms used in the paper. Putting aside for the moment any questions about measurement, we can arbitrarily divide the adult, noninstitutional population into three main groups: those who have a steady and continuing labor force attachment; those who have had, are having, or are about to have a temporary labor force attachment; and those who have not had and are not likely to have any labor force attachment. The first group we shall designate as "primary workers"; the second group we shall call "secondary workers"; and the third group, "nonworkers."

Our interest here is in the characteristics and labor market behavior of persons in the second group, the secondary workers, but only those secondary workers whose labor market behavior is significant for analysis. A little reflection soon shows that attempted measurement of

---

persons over the 1951 average, but the monthly data show there were over 38 million "additions" to the labor force during the year. In each month, on the average, more than 3 million persons entered the labor force (cf. *Current Population Reports: Labor Force*, Bureau of the Census, Series P-50, No. 45, July 1953, pp. 1, 25).

[3] The "additions" and "reductions" represent the number of "status" changes from the census week in the previous month to the census week in the current month.

the entire "secondary worker" group, as such, without some limitation as to the degree and timing of the relationship to the labor force, would be a frustrating task—not only because of the amorphous nature of the group, since it could include any one who had ever been or might ever be in the labor force, but also because the resulting measurement would be an almost entirely useless bit of information for labor market analysis. A little further reflection shows, however, that since for any given period of time there are large numbers of secondary workers moving into or out of the labor force, this movement undoubtedly plays an important rôle in determining the size and composition both of the labor force and of its component parts, employment and unemployment.

We introduce, therefore, the concept of the secondary labor force. The secondary labor force consists of those secondary workers who during a given period of time, such as the census week, are in the labor force—that is, holding a job or actively seeking a job.[4] The primary labor force, then, would consist of those primary workers in the labor force at any given time—employed or seeking employment. Most primary workers are, of course, in the labor force continuously but, at any one time, there are always a certain number not in the labor force, usually through no fault of their own.[5]

Secondary workers may be further described as those who *typically* have some leeway in deciding whether to be in or out of the labor force while primary workers, until they retire, are *normally* in the labor force unless illness or other reason forces a temporary withdrawal. Put in another way, secondary workers have a primary attachment to a non-labor-force activity, such as homemaking, child care, school, or merely idleness, and when in the labor force are in temporarily; primary workers have gainful employment or the search for gainful employment as their principal activity and when out of the labor force are out temporarily.[6]

The use of the word "secondary" is, of course, not intended to imply in any sense a "second-class" status in respect to the labor force, nor to imply that social responsibility is limited to employment opportunities for primary workers. The secondary worker through his or her

[4] In section 3 of the paper the question is raised as to the proper categorization of secondary workers who at any given time are not seeking work solely because of their perception of the nonavailability of jobs (see p. 197 ff.).

[5] Table 1 below shows that even for civilian men not in institutions, in the age groups between twenty-five and fifty-four, there are several hundred thousand who do not work at all in the course of a year and an even larger number who are not in the labor force in any given month.

[6] Differentiating characteristics of primary and secondary members of the labor force are described in some detail in section 2 below.

mobility plays an important role in the economy as a major factor in the adjustment of labor supply to demand and when in the labor force is as much a part of it as the primary worker. The designation "secondary" is meant to indicate that the secondary worker, over the span of a working life, has a primary attachment to various non-labor-force activities. If a majority of secondary workers are women, this is testimony to the importance of their status in our society in essential activities not included in the labor force. As will be shown in section 2, most secondary workers, while in the labor force, either have—or have interrupted temporarily—time-consuming non-labor-force activities which according to the "norms" of our society usually preclude labor force service.

The term in labor force literature that comes closest perhaps to the secondary worker is "marginal worker," at least when marginal worker is used to mean one who shifts into and out of the labor force. The term has two objections, however. First, the word "marginal" applied to a worker seems to imply that the worker is on the fringe of employability. The great majority of secondary workers are, of course, employable in the sense of being acceptable to employers and efficient workers when employed. Secondly, the term "marginal worker" has been used with many different meanings—contrast its use in marginal productivity theory with its use in describing those who combine labor force activity with another activity—and would be misleading if used synonymously with the definition given for "secondary worker."[7]

Although we have now presented functional definitions of primary and secondary workers and primary and secondary labor force members, the question remains whether these groups can be differentiated in a way that is both operationally and analytically useful. An operational differentiation between primary and secondary attachment to the labor force has been attempted in two studies in local labor market areas.[8]

[7] The term "secondary worker" has also been used before but less frequently. Usually it has been employed as a short form of "secondary family worker," that is, a working member of a family other than the chief breadwinner. Secondary family workers for the most part would be "secondary workers." A secondary family worker, however, may have a continuous or primary labor force attachment; on the other hand, a secondary worker is not necessarily a secondary family worker. Similarly, several other terms in the literature cut across the terms used in this paper. A member of the "labor reserve" would be an experienced secondary worker who is not in the labor force and who might be expected to enter in a period of high labor demand. "Extra workers" usually means those potential or actual net additions to the labor force, regardless of prior experience, during a period of high labor demand. "Additional workers" has been used to mean both net additions when demand is high and net additions during a period of exceptionally low labor demand. None of these terms, therefore, would coincide with either the definition of "secondary worker" or "secondary labor force" as used in this paper.

[8] See Irvin Sobel and Richard C. Wilcock, "Secondary Labor Force Mobility in

In both of these studies the workers interviewed, all of whom were in the labor force, were classified as to primary or secondary labor force attachment. Those enumerated as primary members of the labor force met all of the following qualifications:

1. Had been in the civilian labor force continuously since 1945 *or* since first entrance into the labor force *or* had been out only for such reasons as illness, armed forces service, or short post-armed forces vacation, *and*

2. Would have been looking for work if did not have present job, *and*

3. Expected to remain in the labor force during a "normal working life."

Those classified as secondary labor force members were those who did not qualify as primary. In other words, their work histories and responses to questions showed

1. Voluntary movement into and out of the labor force since 1945, other than for military service or short vacations, *or*

2. An expectation of being out of the labor force (i.e. would not look for work) if did not have present job, *or*

3. An expectation of temporary labor force service, i.e. indicating an intention of leaving the labor force within a relatively short period of time and some time before the conventional age-range for retirement.

Only a small percentage of the individuals were difficult to classify. One type was the individual who was switching from a secondary to a primary attachment. A person with a history of voluntary separation from the labor force might indicate he or she would look for work if the present job ended and would stay in the labor force to age sixty-five or beyond. In the few situations like this, such information as "breadwinning status" or "ability to get along financially without a job" was decisive. The classification technique on the whole permitted a clear-cut differentiation between those with a primary and those with a secondary attachment.[9]

The workers in these survey samples, however, were all employed at the time they were interviewed. If the samples had included persons without jobs, the items for differentiation between primary and sec-

---

Four Midwestern Shoe Towns," *Industrial and Labor Relations Review*, April 1955, and by the same authors, *Labor Market Behavior in Nonmetropolitan Areas*, Institute of Labor and Industrial Relations, University of Illinois, 1956. The latter reports both on a field study in Kankakee, Illinois, conducted by the author of this paper in 1952 and the study in the four shoe towns, conducted by Irvin Sobel and the author in 1953.

[9] See the Appendix for the results of "machine coding" of type of labor force attachment contrasted to "hand and judgment" coding, and see section 3 for a suggested list of schedule items designed to obtain the necessary information for primary-secondary labor force differentiation.

ondary labor force membership would be the same with the exception of item 2. The individual would, of course, be asked if he was seeking a job to establish whether he was in the labor force.[10]

To sum up, the suggested operational definition of a secondary labor force member is a person who is in the labor force, as defined by the census,[11] but who has in recent years moved in and out or expects to leave the labor force voluntarily, either at some age short of the usual age of retirement or if he loses his job. The operational definition is essentially negative; that is, the secondary labor force member is one who does not meet one or more of the specifications for a primary attachment.[12]

In general, the secondary labor force draws upon the following groups for its membership: those women whose labor force attachment changes in response to changes in one or more of several factors such as marital status, home responsibilities, family income, and types of job openings available; a relatively small number of men who are neither young nor old but who do not wish to work continuously and can get away with it; those young men and women who move into and out of the labor force while completing their education; and those handicapped and older persons who are employable but seek or hold only temporary employment.

As to what proportion of the labor force consists of persons with a secondary attachment, any estimate would be hazardous. Woytinsky has estimated that in 1950 there were, on the average, 8 million persons in the labor force at any one time who were not in continuously during the year.[13] Since the criterion of noncontinuous service for "secondary labor force member" covers a period longer than one year, it is not surprising to obtain an estimate of average secondary labor force size for 1950 (based on proportions from the Kankakee and Shoe Town studies) several millions higher than the "marginal group" estimated by Woytinsky.

[10] An individual might be counted in the labor force, even if not actively seeking a job, if the only reason for not seeking work is the belief there are no jobs in his community or in his line of work (see the discussion on the fringe area between the labor force and non-labor force in section 3).

[11] Or, conceivably, under any revised definition of "in the labor force."

[12] For example, a person may have been in the labor force continuously since first entrance and would look for another job if necessary but expects to leave the labor force within two years at the age of 40.

[13] W. S. Woytinsky, *et al.*, *Employment and Wages in the United States*, Twentieth Century Fund, 1953, pp. 315-316, 326-327. He estimated also that there were 12 million people in a "marginal group" not in the labor force. For 1950, then, the estimate is that 20 million people had less-than-continuous labor force service, with roughly 8 million in at any one time. Table 1 shows that in 1952 the number of people employed at some time during the year exceeded the average number employed by more than 9 million.

Net additions and reductions to the secondary labor force can be estimated somewhat more precisely than the over-all size, but only if we assume that primary worker participation rates are stable. In April 1945, for example, there were almost 8 million more persons in the total labor force than there would have been if prewar trends had continued.[14] In 1951, on the average, there were almost 1 million more persons in the total labor force than there would have been under the 1949 labor force participation rate but almost 5 million fewer than called for by the 1944 participation rate.[15] These net changes represent changes in the size of the secondary labor force under the stated assumption (see also Table 1).

TABLE 1

1952 Work Experience Compared with Annual Average in Civilian Labor Force and Employed, by Age and Sex, in January 1953
(*thousands of persons, 14 years old and over*)

AGE AND SEX	WORKED DURING 1952		ANNUAL AVERAGE IN LABOR FORCE, 1952		ANNUAL AVERAGE EMPLOYED, 1952	
	Number	*Per Cent of Population*	*Number*	*Per Cent of Population*	*Number*	*Per Cent of Population*
ilian noninstitutional population	70,512	63.7	62,966	56.9	61,293	55.4
le	45,704	87.1	43,454	82.8	42,391	80.7
4-17	2,392	54.3	1,686	38.3	1,546	35.1
8-19	1,450	87.5	1,210	73.0	1,128	68.0
0-24	3,370	90.9	3,338	90.0	3,204	86.4
5-34	10,752	98.1	10,585	96.6	10,390	94.8
5-44	10,200	98.6	9,945	96.1	9,778	94.5
5-54	8,476	96.8	8,326	95.1	8,172	93.4
5-64	6,112	89.8	5,950	87.4	5,822	85.5
5 and over	2,952	50.3	2,415	41.2	2,351	40.1
nale	24,808	42.7	19,513	33.6	18,902	32.5
4-17	1,468	33.9	950	21.9	877	20.2
8-19	1,376	67.1	1,046	51.0	980	47.8
0-24	3,200	57.8	2,502	45.2	2,405	43.4
5-34	5,458	44.7	4,320	35.4	4,185	34.3
5-44	5,602	50.4	4,438	39.9	4,327	38.9
5-54	4,284	47.0	3,636	39.9	3,561	39.1
5-64	2,536	35.7	2,032	28.6	1,990	28.0
5 and over	884	13.2	590	8.8	579	8.7

ource: Computed from *Current Population Reports: Labor Force,* Bureau of the Census, ies P-50, No. 45, July 1953, Tables 3 and 4, and No. 48, November 30, 1953, Table B.

[14] John D. Durand, *The Labor Force in the United States, 1890-1960,* Social Science Research Council, 1948, p. 142.

[15] Computed from *Current Population Reports: Labor Force,* No. 19, March 1950, and No. 40, May 1952.

SOME PUBLIC POLICY AND SOCIAL SCIENCE QUESTIONS

Section 2 which follows endeavors to show some of the advantages of the proposed primary-secondary labor force differentiation. To set the stage, we list below a number of questions for public policy and social science research which are related to mobility in labor force participation.

1. If "movement into and out of the labor force frames all other forms of labor mobility," as Hauser suggests,[16] is it not desirable to have more analytically useful public data on labor force mobility, both for their relevance to public policy questions and as a reference point for research into the various kinds of factors—whether social, economic, political, or psychological—which influence labor force change?

2. If, as some research has indicated, wage rates are only one factor influencing labor force participation, what are the factors that determine mobility into and out of the labor force and how do they operate in the process of mobility choice? More specifically, what are the factors that determine stability or variation in labor force participation rates for the population, for primary and secondary workers, and for the various age-sex groups?

3. Is there a relationship between labor force mobility and the volume of unemployment? If there is, is the tendency to accentuate or to minimize unemployment? Also, is the effect on unemployment obscured by the techniques used in differentiating between the unemployed person and the nonworker?

4. Is there a relationship between labor force mobility and the size and industrial composition of local labor market areas? Is there also a relationship between changes in labor force participation rates and short-run changes in the demand for labor in local markets?

5. In general, do those who move into and out of the labor force (the "secondary workers" as defined) perform an important function in adjusting labor supply to labor demand or is this mobility quite independent of demand changes?

6. Finally, would data which differentiate between primary and secondary labor force attachment be contributory to workable estimates of labor force participation under various assumed conditions of economic change, such as those associated with a war emergency or an economic depression emergency? Or, assuming peacetime, nondepression conditions, would such a differentiation, if data so categorized were available, help to define "the breach between actual utilization and the capacities and desires of individuals, a policy problem sug-

[16] Philip M. Hauser, "Mobility in Labor Force Participation," in E. Wight Bakke, *et al.*, *Labor Mobility and Economic Opportunity*, Technology Press and Wiley, 1954, p. 11.

gested by the President in his message to the Congress on the Reorganization of the Council of Economic Advisers in 1953"?[17]

Possible answers to these questions are presented in the following propositions. In respect to each proposition, primary-secondary differentiation is examined as a method of analyzing the proposition's truth or falsity. In addition, head-of-household and age-sex group data are examined as alternative methods of analysis. No claim is made that other types of data are not pertinent to an examination of the propositions, but the analysis is in terms of labor force data, both national and local.

2. *The Secondary Labor Force as a Method of Analysis*

SOME PROPOSITIONS

Although the focus of this volume is on the behavior of unemployment, it is difficult to analyze problems of unemployment without considering them in the context of changes in employment and in the total labor force. The following propositions are centered upon mobility in labor force participation and are presented with the alleged justification that they are all intimately related to the nature and behavior of unemployment in the United States. The propositions are as follows:

On the Determinants of Labor Force Mobility. Labor force participation rates of primary workers are almost totally insensitive in the short run to such economic variables as labor demand and wage changes.[18] Labor force participation rates of secondary workers, on the other hand, are sensitive in the short run both to changes within the labor market (demand factors) and changes outside the market (supply factors).

1. Inward mobility of secondary workers is a function of both the known availability of suitable jobs and the relative desire to be employed, that is, the "need" for additional income or simply the desire to work.

2. Outward mobility results either from the loss of jobs accompanied by a perceived lack of other acceptable job opportunities or from the pressure of non-labor-force activities, such as child care, homemaking, or school.

[17] Charles D. Stewart, "Unemployment Statistics and Economic Policy Uses," mimeographed, delivered before the American Statistical Association, September 11, 1954, p. 9.

[18] Although rapid and substantial changes might hasten or retard initial labor force entry of young people or retirement of older people, the labor force participation rate of what might be called the "hard core" of the labor force—men between the ages of 25 and 64—changes almost imperceptibly with changes in economic activity and real incomes (see Clarence D. Long, "The Labor Force and Economic Change," in Richard A. Lester and Joseph Shister, *Insights into Labor Issues*, Macmillan, 1948, pp. 329-355).

Gross and Net Movements. Without a significant change in the level of labor demand, the gross movements of secondary workers into and out of the labor force tend to cancel each other out, except for the net change created by population increases.

1. When the demand for labor increases relative to population, the secondary worker participation rate increases, thus creating an increase in the over-all labor force participation rate. The increase in the rate results because the attraction of an increased number of suitable job openings[19] is a more powerful factor than the simultaneous falling off in the need for additional income, a factor working in the opposite direction.

2. When the demand for labor decreases, the net effect on participation rates may be small[20] because while the rates for some female age groups may increase[21] these are apt to be offset by net withdrawals within other groups, particularly on the part of young men and women. Here, the strong deterrent of job scarcity offsets the inducement to seek employment provided by declining real family incomes.

3. Real wage changes are not the most direct determinant of net short-run changes in the participation rates of secondary workers, although they represent one factor. An increase in labor demand, not accompanied by real wage changes per capita employed, would activate secondary workers; a decrease in labor demand, not accompanied by per employee real wage changes, would inactivate them. Changes in real family incomes resulting from the amount of employment in the family (both jobs and hours of work) are more significant, however, than changes in real wage rates per employed person, but the main effect is to check net labor force mobility. In other words, an influx of secondary workers increases household incomes and automatically reduces the pressure for secondary labor force participation.[22] Similarly, labor force withdrawals by some groups when labor demand declines may be offset by accessions stimulated by the attempt to maintain family incomes. Unless other factors are called into play,[23]

[19] The "suitableness" of job openings available to secondary workers involves a whole complex of factors, such as type of work, distance from place of residence, and type of fellow worker. It may also mean a fairly wide range of acceptable wage rates.

[20] Unless there is a retreat from an abnormally high position such as the declines experienced after World War II.

[21] It may be that housewives are "best buys" for many employers in terms of unit costs in periods of declining labor demand.

[22] A mother's job, for example, may allow a son or daughter to remain longer in school.

[23] As, for example, during World War II when patriotism and the absence of husbands, sons, and fathers who were in the armed forces helped to bring millions of additional secondary workers into the labor force. Wage controls, high income tax rates, and savings bond campaigns, it might be added, helped to hold down disposable family incomes.

therefore, income changes represent an equilibrating device in the collective decisions of secondary workers concerning labor force activity versus non-labor-force activities.[24]

Labor Force Participation Rates and Unemployment. It follows from the propositions above that the movement of secondary workers into and out of the labor force reduces the amplitude of unemployment fluctuations.

1. Since labor force participation rates for secondary workers increase with an increase in the number of job openings, but at a slower rate because of the dampening effect of higher family incomes, unemployment falls as labor demand increases but less than it would if there were no net influx of secondary workers.

2. After a period of abnormally high labor demand, labor force participation rates fall and unemployment may be considerably less than would otherwise be expected.[25]

3. Except for the case just cited, the over-all labor force participation rate changes little when labor demand declines. Thus, secondary labor force mobility in a recession period has little net effect on the volume of unemployment.

4. Secondary labor force mobility thus reduces the amplitude of unemployment fluctuations in the economy—for the most part by providing a floor rather than by establishing a ceiling.[26] As a result of labor force mobility, however, unemployment rates fall less rapidly for secondary than for primary labor force members when labor demand rises; on the other hand, when labor demand falls, unemployment rates rise less rapidly for secondary than for primary labor force members.[27]

Place-to-Place Differences. Secondary labor force participation rates are potentially more variable where there is little diversity in industrial composition.

1. In nonmetropolitan areas, an increase in demand (a new factory) can activate a substantial proportion of secondary workers and a

[24] Not considered here is the well-known inverse relationship between labor force participation and income level which exists at any instant in time. Long and others have suggested that the relationship over time can be the opposite of the static relationship (see Long, *op.cit.*, p. 343).

[25] The predictions of high unemployment after World War II resulted in part from underestimations of the volume of labor force withdrawals.

[26] This is undoubtedly beneficial to the economy, particularly in the upswing when the availability of secondary workers helps prevent labor "shortages."

[27] It is also possible that enumeration methods lead to an underestimation of unemployment at certain times. For example, in the initial stages of a recession secondary workers who are laid off but who are not ready to leave the labor force may not immediately seek other employment and be reported as out of the labor force. It is also possible that in such a period counting "temporary layoffs" as unemployed would give a more accurate picture (see Stanley Lebergott, "Those Unemployment Figures," *Illinois Business Review*, November 1954, p. 9).

decrease in demand (a factory closes) can inactivate a substantial proportion. The reasons include the reluctance of workers to leave the home community and the resulting underutilization of the population in many local market areas.[28]

2. The absence of job opportunities for secondary workers means low secondary labor force participation rates.[29]

3. In many local labor market areas, unemployment estimates fail to reflect the immediate availability of labor because of the large proportion of secondary workers out of the labor force.[30]

Supply-Demand Adjustment. Secondary labor force mobility tends to adjust labor supply to short-run changes in demand. Secondary labor force participation increased during World War II and during the Korean situation and fell off subsequently in both cases. In a recession, however, there is a general reluctance to withdraw from the labor force and recession unemployment may not be mitigated by net outward labor force mobility.

ADVANTAGES OF PRIMARY-SECONDARY DIFFERENTIATION IN LABOR FORCE ANALYSIS

The purpose of the paper is not to demonstrate conclusively the truth or falsity of any of the above propositions, since this is impossible with the data at hand. Instead, the purpose is a two-fold one of demonstrating the importance of the propositions in a number of aspects of labor force analysis and the usefulness of the primary-secondary differentiation as a method of analysis. For the most part the data used for illustration are those from the Census Bureau's Current Population Reports and from the two local labor market area studies previously mentioned.

The first advantage of the suggested differentiation is that it makes it possible to compare workers on the basis of whether they are mobile in respect to participation in the labor force in addition to the usual comparisons on the basis of sex and age. Some of the differences between primary and secondary labor force members, as shown by the data from the Kankakee and shoe town studies, can be quickly summarized. The differences in personal characteristics and aspects of labor market behavior shown in Tables 2 and 3 provide the background

[28] Geographic mobility is another factor in adjusting labor supply to demand in a local market area but is often much less important than labor force mobility.

[29] Many industries have, of course, made use of the labor "surplus" in smaller communities (see Richard C. Wilcock, "New Firms and the Labor Supply in Small Communities," *Current Economic Comment*, November 1954, pp. 3-15).

[30] Underemployment is also likely to be greater in small-population areas (see Louis J. Ducoff and Margaret J. Hagood, "The Meaning and Measurement of Partial and Disguised Unemployment," in this volume).

TABLE 2

Distribution of the Samples by Type of Labor Force Attachment, Kankakee, 1952, and Four Shoe Towns, 1953[a]

TYPE OF ATTACHMENT	BOTH SEXES		MALE		FEMALE		MEDIAN AGE (*years*)
	No.	*%*	*No.*	*%*	*No.*	*%*	
Kankakee:							
Primary	188	63	157	87	31	27	30.3
Secondary	108	37	24	13	84	73	26.3
Total	296	100	181	100	115	100	29.1
Shoe towns:							
Primary	388	59	182	98	206	43	40.0
Secondary	271	41	3	2	268	57	33.5
Total	659	100	185	100	474	100	37.3

[a] Both samples were deliberately selected in situations which would yield high proportions of secondary labor force members. The Kankakee sample was drawn in June and July 1952 from a universe of the recent "hires" (within the six-month period prior to the survey) in thirty-seven manufacturing, trade, and services companies in the Kankakee labor market area. At the time, Kankakee was a "tight" labor market and the "new hires" could be expected to include large proportions of young and of secondary workers. The universe for the shoe towns sample was the total nonsupervisory work forces of four shoe factories in as many small towns. In this case, a large proportion of secondary members was expected because of the known hiring practices of the shoe company which operated the four plants.

Source: Interviews (Kankakee) and questionnaires (shoe towns).

for subsequent discussion of labor force mobility. In some aspects of labor market behavior, not shown in Table 3, the primary and secondary workers differed very little. In both studies there were no significant differences in methods of job seeking—friends or relatives and direct application being the chief methods; in extent of job search—that is, in the number of places applied to for work; in expectation of finding a job meeting occupational preference, including job held at the time interviewed; in degree of satisfaction with their jobs; in knowledge about the labor market; and in knowledge about the company and the type of work before taking the job held at the time of the surveys.

Determinants of Secondary Labor Force Mobility. The two studies furnish some clues as to the determinants of inward and outward secondary labor force mobility suggested in the first proposition and tend to support the second and fourth propositions on net changes in labor force mobility. For inward mobility the data clearly indicate the combined effect of the "push" of certain kinds of personal circumstances and the "pull" of labor market changes. The push is illustrated

TABLE 3

Selected Comparisons between Primary and Secondary Labor Force Members, Kankakee and Four Shoe Towns

(*per cent*)

CHARACTERISTICS AND BEHAVIOR	KANKAKEE[a]		SHOE TOWNS[b]	
	Primary	*Secondary*	*Primary*	*Secondary*
Characteristics:				
Women	16	78	53	99
Under 25	43	63	15	34
Over 44	17	9	36	17
Widowed, divorced, or separated	11	3	13	4
Have 9 or more grades in school	62	89	38	56
Have 1 or more others in household working	49	89	54	84
Have a spouse who is working	c	c	39	66
Have no dependents	49	95	41	84
Behavior:				
Need to work for a living	80	5	78[e]	8[e]
Are "breadwinners"	76	8	97	8
Prefer factory to nonfactory jobs	59	23	46	25
Have been continuously in the labor force[d]	62	35	82	45
Would look for work if lost job[d]	90	14	84	46
Expect to stay in labor force during "normal working life"[d]	93	29	86	27

[a] N = 296. The number of respondents varies slightly between items.
[b] N = 659. The number of respondents varies slightly between items.
[c] No data.
[d] These items are related to the criteria for the primary-secondary differentiation.
[e] N = 109. Interview data.
Source: Interviews (Kankakee) and questionnaires and interviews (shoe towns).

by Table 4, which shows that a large proportion of those classified as secondary members expressed a need for higher family or personal income. The pull can be illustrated by the fact that in Kankakee more than a third of the "new hires" in manufacturing, trade, and services during a period of expanding employment were secondary members of the labor force.[31] In one of the shoe towns the factory had been shut down for two and one-half years and was reopened about a year before the survey was made. Sixty-five per cent of the respondents from this plant who were classified as secondary workers were labor force reentrants compared with only 34 per cent for the other three plants studied. Approximately one half of the secondary workers in the reopened plant were both labor force reentrants and company rehires.

[31] Extrapolating from the sample, some 1,250 secondary workers were hired into a nonfarm work force of some 15,000 in a six-month period during which estimated unemployment for the area was averaging between 400 and 500 persons.

TABLE 4

Primary and Secondary Workers, by Reason for Working, Kankakee and Four Shoe Towns

(*per cent*)

	KANKAKEE[a]			SHOE TOWNS[b]		
REASON	*Primary*	*Secondary*	*Total*	*Primary*	*Secondary*	*Total*
Need job for living	80	5	52	78	8	54
Help support family	13	59	30	14	62	30
Personal use	7	36	18	4	24	11
Other	0	0	0	4	6	5
Total	100	100	100	100	100	100

[a] N = 294.
[b] N = 109.
Source: Interviews (Kankakee) and interviews (shoe towns).

Another plant was only three years old and was located in the smallest and least industrialized of the four communities. Sixty-one per cent of the respondents in this plant were not in the labor force in the period preceding their employment by the company[32] compared with 43 per cent for the three other plants.

If the propensity to enter the labor force can be explained in terms of the desire for additional income and if entrance is related to the availability of job openings, what explains the temporary nature of the labor force attachment of secondary workers? The major explanation is found in the relative importance to these people of their non-labor-force activities and responsibilities. Table 5 illustrates the importance to secondary workers of major non-labor-force activities—"major" being interpreted to mean some activity consuming twenty hours or more a week. A third or more of the secondary worker respondents in each study had such a major non-labor-force responsibility while fully employed and roughly two-thirds in each sample had previously left the labor force at least once because of major home or school responsibilities.

Family responsibilities loom large in the analysis not only in explaining entrances (need for additional income) but also in explaining exits (need to care for family, particularly young children). The pendulum in many cases swings back and forth as the secondary worker makes decisions on the relative importance to self and family of being in or being out of the labor force. There is an element of choice, therefore, for the worker who does not have a continuously compelling economic necessity for working. As was indicated in Table 4, perhaps as many

[32] Thirty-four per cent entered the labor force for the first time and 27 per cent reentered.

TABLE 5

Non-Labor-Force Activities of Secondary Workers While in the Labor Force and When Out of the Labor Force, Kankakee and Four Shoe Towns

(*per cent*)

ACTIVITY AND REASON OUT OF LABOR FORCE	MAJOR REASON FOR PREVIOUS PERIODS OUT OF LABOR FORCE[a]		MAJOR NON-LABOR-FORCE ACTIVITY WHILE IN THE LABOR FORCE[b]		PROSPECTIVE ACTIVITY, IF LOST JOB	
	Kankakee[c]	*Shoe Towns*[d]	*Kankakee*[e]	*Shoe Towns*[f]	*Kankakee*[g]	*Shoe Towns*[h]
Major activity:						
In school	9	2	8	1	6	2
Housework and child care	55	62	86	91	37	29
Military service	2	0	n.a.	n.a.	0	0
Unpaid family work	n.a.	n.a.	6	8	n.a.	n.a.
Other activity or reason:						
Keeping house or staying at home	19	25	n.a.	n.a.	30	20
Vacation	7	2	n.a.	n.a.	10	3
Illness or other disability	4	9	n.a.	n.a.	n.a.	n.a.
Look for a job	n.a.	n.a.	n.a.	n.a.	14[i]	46[i]
Other	4	0	0	0	3	0
Total	100	100	100	100	100	100

[a] After first entrance and since World War II.

[b] At time of survey.

[c] N = 53.

[d] N = 119.

[e] N = 36—one-third of the secondary members had a major outside activity while holding a regular job.

[f] N = 98—36 per cent of the secondary members had a major outside activity while working.

[g] N = 108.

[h] N = 253.

[i] The larger proportion of the shoe workers who would look for work reflects the older age and lower family incomes of the respondents in that sample.

n.a. = not applicable.

Source: Interviews (Kankakee) and questionnaires (shoe towns).

as a fifth of all primary workers can make a reasonably free choice about continuation in the labor force but they are primary because they choose continuous labor force service. Almost all secondary workers have such a choice—although not necessarily every day or month—and they are secondary because they choose to move in and out. One interesting result in these studies, for example, is that almost as many of the primary women workers had children under 18 years of age as did the secondary women workers and they were primary workers because they saw no alternative to staying in the labor force.[33] Most secondary women workers with young children, on the other hand, had had fairly extensive periods out of the labor force during which they took care of their homes and children.[34]

As for outward labor force mobility, the secondary workers had both the ability and the propensity to withdraw from the labor force. The intent or expectation of leaving the labor force before the usual age range of retirement on the part of most secondary workers is shown in Table 6. Less than 30 per cent of the respondents in each of the samples who were classified as secondary expected to stay in the labor force until any usual retirement age and some of these undoubtedly did not expect to be in continuously until final retirement. In addition,

TABLE 6

Distribution of Primary and Secondary Members in Kankakee and Shoe Towns and of Men and Women in Shoe Towns, by Expectations as to Continuation of Labor Force Service

(*per cent*)

HOW LONG EXPECTS TO WORK	KANKAKEE[a]		SHOE TOWNS[b]			
	Primary	*Secondary*	*Primary*	*Secondary*	*Men*	*Women*
2 years or less	0	4	0	7	0	4
2-5 years	1	31	0	25	1	14
Over 5 years but less than working life	4	22	8	32	6	23
Working life	93	29	86	27	90	50
Don't know	2	14	6	9	3	9
Total	100	100	100	100	100	100

[a] N = 292.
[b] N = 538.
Source: Interviews (Kankakee) and questionnaires (shoe towns).

[33] Thirty-six per cent of the women in the Kankakee sample and 48 per cent of the female shoe factory respondents had children under eighteen living at home compared with a national average of 28 per cent for women in the labor force (cf. *Current Population Reports: Labor Force*, June 1953, Tables 1 and 4).

[34] These women might be said to conform more closely to the prevailing social norm under which it is not customary to continue two "full-time" responsibilities simultaneously.

as shown in Table 5, a majority of the secondary workers thought they would leave the labor force if they lost their jobs.

Mere intent is, of course, not enough, but the secondary workers demonstrated their ability to move into and out of the labor force both in their work histories and in their responses to questions about their ability to get along without a job. Thus, even though the secondary workers had important economic reasons for working, few of them were primary breadwinners at the time of the survey and few felt their job necessary "for a living." The secondary workers, therefore, had the ability to leave the labor force as well as the propensity.

Net Changes in Labor Force Mobility. Both inward and outward labor force mobility are to a large extent influenced by non-labor-force factors but they are also influenced by changes in the labor market. A key question for analysis, then, is whether there are net changes in labor force mobility under changing conditions in the demand for labor. Although the local labor market area studies under discussion do not offer conclusive proof, they do at least indicate that the secondary labor force in nonmetropolitan labor market areas is highly variable when there are significant, short-run changes in the demand for labor. Detailed discussions of this variability can be found in the references cited in note 8. In brief, the data from these studies show an apparent increase in the proportion of secondary workers in the labor force in Kankakee during a period when several new firms entered the area and when employment was additionally stimulated by the Korean situation, in one of the shoe towns when the shoe factory reopened after a two and one-half year shutdown, and in another of the shoe towns in the period after the shoe plant first opened in 1950. The work history data also indicate that when the shoe factory closed in one of the towns a substantial proportion of the secondary workers withdrew from the labor force for at least part of the two and one-half year period of shutdown.

Net changes in secondary labor force mobility can also be illustrated by data from the Current Population Survey of the Census Bureau, if the assumption is made that most of the net change in labor force participation rates for age-sex groups which presumably have substantial proportions of secondary members is caused by the labor force mobility of the secondary members. This assumption seems reasonable both in terms of the definitions of primary and secondary attachment and on the basis of the findings in Kankakee and the shoe towns. The brief analysis which follows is intended to illustrate, even though indirectly, some of the analytical advantages that would accrue if we had data that differentiated between primary and secondary labor force attachment.

Table 7 shows changes in labor force participation rates, by several age-sex groups, during a period of increasing demands on the labor of the American population—the Korean War period—and during two periods of fairly moderate decreases in labor demand—the 1949 and 1953-1954 recessions. Year-to-year changes are shown in order to eliminate most of the seasonal effect.[35]

The census data lend support to proposition 2 on gross and net movements into and out of the labor force. In 1952 the annual average for the participation of the adult population in the labor force was 58.7 per cent compared with 57.8 per cent in 1948, a year roughly comparable in levels of employment.[36] The increase in the rate between 1948 and 1952 can be explained largely in terms of the expansion of the armed forces.[37] The large amount of gross movement (about 67 million "additions" and "reductions" in the civilian labor force in the recession year of 1949 and almost 80 million in the high-employment-level year of 1951) does not, however, cancel itself out entirely nor does it occur without important changes in the age-sex composition of the labor force.

During the period of expansion in industrial output and employment in 1950 and 1951, when young men were entering the armed forces in relatively large numbers, there were substantial increases in the proportion of women 20 years old and over in the labor force. Since most of this increase came from women beyond the usual ages of labor force entry and since it was far above what could be accounted for by secular increases, it is reasonable to assume that the increase in rates was the result of a net addition to the secondary labor force. In addition, the rate for women under twenty years of age changed very little, checking momentarily the secular decline of participation by this group. Men sixty-five and over, however, continued to leave the labor force in increasing numbers, since apparently there was no increase in the demand for their services as had happened during World War II. The rate for civilian men under twenty declined, but this was probably the result of withdrawals to the armed forces in 1951 rather than the result of the secular decline in their participation because in the second half of 1950 their participation in the civilian labor force increased. What apparently happened in this period, then, was a slight

[35] These periods are used, even though the changes involved are relatively small and consequently the hazards of sampling errors and enumeration biases correspondingly high, because they are the only ones for which monthly data are available with detailed age-sex breakdowns.

[36] The unemployment rate in 1948 was 3.4; in 1952 it was 2.7.

[37] The total labor force was 58.8 per cent of adult population in 1951, up from 58.0 per cent in 1949, but the civilian labor force had actually dropped to 56.2 per cent in 1951 from 56.7 per cent in 1949.

TABLE 7

Selected Year-to-Year Changes in Indicators of Labor Demand and Civilian Labor Force Participation Rates, by Age-Sex Groups, Selected Periods of Labor-Demand Change, 1948-1954

PERIOD	INDICATORS OF LABOR-DEMAND CHANGE			CHANGES IN CIVILIAN LABOR FORCE PARTICIPATION RATES									
	Changes in Federal Reserve Board Index of Production[a]	*Change in Proportion of:*											
		Persons 14 and over Employed	*Men 20-54 Employed*	*Persons 14 and over*	*All Men*	*All Women*	*Men 14-19*	*Men 20-54*	*Men 65 and over*	*Women 14-19*	*Women 20-24*	*Women 25-34*	*Women 35 and over*
Period of increase in labor demand:													
Aug. 49-Aug. 50	25	1.5	1.7	0.4	0.3	0.6	2.2	0.1	—0.6	—0.4	—0.6	0.4	1.2
Dec. 49-Dec. 50	24	1.4	2.6	0.2	—0.1	0.9	1.1	0.4	—3.5	0.9	2.2	1.2	0.6
Apr. 50-Apr. 51	17	1.5	3.5	—0.1	—0.2	0.6	—1.8	0.2	—1.6	0.9	0.4	1.0	0.5
Aug. 50-Aug. 51	—4	0.7	2.0	—0.2	0.1	0.4	—0.1	0.6	—0.3	1.2	—0.1	1.1	0.2
Dec. 50-Dec. 51	—2	0.6	1.8	0.1	0.3	0.6	—1.5	1.0	—0.4	—1.0	—1.4	1.8	0.9
Apr. 49-Apr. 51	27	1.6	3.0	0.4	—0.4	1.8	—2.6	0.5	—2.1	—0.4	3.1	2.1	2.1
Period of decrease in labor demand:													
Aug. 48-Aug. 49	—8	—1.7	—2.2	—0.1	—0.7	0.5	—2.5	0.1	—1.0	—0.5	1.3	0.2	0.9
Dec. 48-Dec. 49	—6	—1.3	—2.1	0.1	—0.5	0.5	—1.1	0.1	—1.2	—1.0	2.3	—1.2	1.2
Apr. 53-Apr. 54	—12	—1.2	—2.1	0.5	—0.2	1.0	—2.3	0.5	—1.8	0.7	—0.7	1.5	1.3
Aug. 53-Aug. 54	—12	—1.7	—2.9	0.1	0.1	0.1	—0.5	n.c.	0.3	—2.7	1.7	1.4	—0.1
Aug. 52-Aug. 54	1	—1.6	—2.2	—0.2	—0.4	—0.3	—2.0	0.3	—1.2	—2.0	0.4	—2.1	0.6
Aug. 49-Aug. 54	27	—0.3	1.5	—0.8	—1.0	0.4	—4.9	1.2	—5.4	—3.1	—1.2	—0.4	2.1

[a] Index of industrial production—total—without seasonal adjustment.

n.c. = no change.

Source: Compiled from *Current Population Reports: Labor Force*, Bureau of the Census, Series P-57, monthly reports, various dates, and *Federal Reserve Bulletin*, Board of Governors, Federal Reserve System, December 1953, p. 1324, and October 1954, p. 1099.

increase in the total primary labor force as a result of some entries at younger ages and a more substantial increase in the secondary labor force in response to the increase in job openings available to secondary workers.

In two periods of moderate recession, the second half of 1949 and the first half of 1954, when demand fell from high peacetime levels, the civilian labor force changed insignificantly in proportion to population, but this seemed to occur because the decreases in participation of some age-sex groups were offset by increases on the part of others. The participation rates for both men and women under twenty years of age declined, partly as a result of a secular trend toward more years of schooling but partly, it seems probable, because when jobs are more scarce they are particularly so for this age group. The combination of secular trend and labor market practices also would explain the decline in rates for men aged sixty-five or over. For the female age groups other than the teen-age group, however, the over-all tendency was toward a slight increase in participation rates in the face of declining levels of employment. While these data are not adequate to support Woytinsky's hypothesis of a net influx of "secondary family workers" in response to the unemployment of the usual breadwinners, the data do show changes in rates which may be related to the changes in the level of labor demand. In each of the recession periods, the secular increase in the participation rates of women almost vanished.* It seems probable that the secular trend might have been reversed if women were in jobs as subject to layoff as those of men. As it was, these groups of women lost less in employment and suffered less from unemployment than did men** (see Table 8 below).

* Editor's Note: Mr. Wilcock does not present data in support of this statement and an examination of the seasonally adjusted data fails to verify it—at least insofar as females twenty-five to sixty-four are concerned. Aside from the usual random fluctuations (which cannot be ignored in a survey subject to both sampling and interview errors), no decrease in the labor force participation of females twenty-five to sixty-four could be detected in the 1949-1950 recession, either in absolute amount or in relation to the secular trend. There was a decline in relation to trend in the 1953-1954 downturn, but there is no way of telling whether it was in response to the recession or was a reaction to the high rate of participation during the Korean War. There is good reason to believe that female participation began to drop off when it became clear that the Korean War was ending, while unemployment was still declining.

** Editor's Note: A more precise test of these changes in labor force participation is had if the changes in employment or unemployment rates are added together to reveal the net changes in the labor force participation rate. If this is done for males twenty to fifty-four and for females twenty to twenty-four, twenty-five to thirty-four, and thirty-five and older, it will be found that, of the twelve comparisons for the three female age groups, six show a decline and six show a gain. The results do not indicate really systematic behavior for any of the three female groups for any of the comparisons.

In another period, mid-1951 to mid-1953, which might be termed "a return to normalcy," there was a net decline in labor force participation rates which was apparently the result of readjustment in labor force size after the higher levels achieved during the expansion related to the Korean War. During this period (not shown in Table 7) there was a net decline in employment rates, in spite of continuing increases in industrial output, and the civilian labor force participation rate fell off by 1.1 per cent (August 1951 to August 1953) because of labor force withdrawals in all of the age-sex groups containing substantial numbers of secondary labor force members except women 35 years old and over. One unusual result was that unemployment and employment rates fell off simultaneously.

The census data, therefore, indicate some relationship between participation rates and even moderate swings in the level of unemployment in the economy.* This relationship, it is suggested, would be shown more clearly if data were available that differentiated between primary and secondary labor force attachment. With such data it would be possible to analyze, for example, shifts in proportions of secondary members in the labor force in relation to various indicators of economic well-being.

In the propositions it was suggested that there is little direct relationship between real wage changes and changes in labor force participation, but that changes in real family incomes, as affected by the amount of employment which families have, may have an important effect in dampening net changes in labor force mobility. Although the data at hand are not adequate to support this hypothesis fully, the trends shown by the census data are consistent with the hypothesis and the data from the two local labor market area studies also tend to support it. In each of the periods under discussion real wages, as measured by Bureau of Labor Statistics data on net spendable weekly earnings adjusted for cost-of-living changes, increased. These increases in real wages apparently had little effect on inducing either a net increase or a net decrease in the secondary labor force. In periods when a larger number of families would have incomes of reduced size as a result of male unemployment, however, there was a tendency for increased participation in those female age groups which have a large proportion of women in families with growing children and heavy family expenses.**

* Editor's Note: It should be noted that this finding of a relationship between labor force participation rates and even moderate swings in employment is based partly on the Korean War experience. Rees finds no such relationship during the peacetime period which embraced the 1949 recession.

** Editor's Note: These conclusions should be treated with caution. Comparisons of labor force participation rates of August 1949 with those of August 1948, or of

Labor Force Participation Rates and Unemployment. Again using age-sex breakdowns as a substitute for data with a primary-secondary labor force differentiation, Table 8 gives some clues as to the relationship between secondary labor force mobility and unemployment. In 1950 and 1951, for example, unemployment rates declined much less rapidly for several groups than one would have expected in view of the increases in the employment rates. The cause was the net additions to the labor force in these groups. Between April 1949 and April 1951 the employment rate for women, aged twenty to twenty-four, jumped by 3.7 per cent, with 3.1 per cent accounted for by an increase in labor force participation and only 0.6 per cent resulting from a decrease in unemployment. The figures are similar for women between twenty-five and thirty-four and for those thirty-five years old and over. The unemployment rate for men, fourteen to nineteen, declined more rapidly because of the draft: in 1950, employment in this group rose more than unemployment fell because of an accelerated rate of entrance into the labor force, but in 1951 unemployment continued to fall even though the civilian employment rate leveled off and finally turned down. For men sixty-five and over the decline in unemployment was almost entirely the result of labor force withdrawals. The over-all result for this period of labor demand increase was an adaptation of labor supply to the increased demand through net inward labor force mobility. Without the net influx of secondary workers, unemployment would have been lower but very probably at a heavy cost of labor shortages and lost production.[38]

As the economy reached a more normal, but still high, level of employment after the peak of defense production passed, net mobility out of the labor force made it possible for unemployment rates to

---

those of December 1949 with those of December 1948 will show that there was no rise at all for women twenty-five to thirty-four and that increases for women twenty to twenty-four and thirty-five and over were very small considering the fact that there is a long-run upward trend in female labor force participation rates and that the data are subject to considerable sampling and response fluctuations.

[38] Longer hours of work and more efficiency per unit of labor would also increase labor supply. The longer hours, at least, did occur. Although the increase in labor supply in the second half of 1950 and in 1951 was in part the result of the secular increase in female labor force participation rates, this increase was apparently in excess of the secular movement. Since this was the Korean War period, the reasons for the increase are undoubtedly similar to those which apply to World War II experience. The census data, of course, do not reveal whether the more important factors are on the supply side—more women with fewer home responsibilities—or on the demand side—an increase in suitable job opportunities for women and changes in employer hiring practices. The Kankakee study data (summer of 1952) indicate that female labor force entrants were influenced by both supply and demand factors in a period of expanding employment opportunities.

TABLE 8

Selected Year-to-Year Changes in Employment and Unemployment Rates in the Civilian Labor Force, by Age-Sex Groups, Several Postwar Periods, 1949-1954

PERIOD	BOTH SEXES, 14 AND OVER		MEN 14-19		MEN 20-54		MEN 65 AND OVER		WOMEN 14-19		WOMEN 20-24		WOMEN 25-34		WOMEN 35 AND OVER	
	E	*U*	*E*	*U*	*E*	*U*	*E*	*U*	*E*	*U*	*E*	*U*	*E*	*U*	*E*	*U*
Period of increase in labor demand:																
Aug. 49-Aug. 50	1.5	–1.1	4.5	–2.3	1.7	–1.6	–0.1	–0.5	0.6	–1.0	1.3	–1.9	1.0	–0.6	1.5	–0.3
Dec. 49-Dec. 50	1.4	–1.2	3.4	–2.3	2.6	–2.2	–3.2	–0.3	1.6	–0.7	3.3	–1.1	1.7	–0.5	0.9	–0.3
Apr. 50-Apr. 51	1.5	–1.6	0.9	–2.7	3.5	–3.3	–0.8	–0.8	1.2	–0.3	1.3	–0.9	1.1	–0.1	0.8	–0.3
Aug. 50-Aug. 51	0.7	–0.9	1.5	–1.6	2.0	–1.4	0.6	–0.9	1.6	–0.4	0.5	–0.6	1.6	–0.5	0.5	–0.3
Dec. 50-Dec. 51	0.6	–0.5	–0.8	–0.7	1.8	–0.8	0.3	–0.7	–0.4	–0.6	–0.6	–0.8	1.7	0.1	1.0	–0.1
Apr. 49-Apr. 51	1.6	–1.2	–0.3	–2.3	3.0	–2.5	–1.1	–1.0	0.4	–0.8	3.7	–0.6	2.3	–0.2	2.1	n.c.
Period of "return to normalcy":																
Aug. 51-Aug. 52	–0.9	0.1	–5.2	0.2	0.2	n.c.	–3.6	0.3	–1.7	–0.2	–1.1	0.2	0.3	–0.1	0.1	n.c.
Dec. 51-Dec. 52	–0.2	–0.3	–2.3	0.1	0.4	–0.1	–1.4	–0.3	0.2	–0.4	–3.2	–0.1	–0.9	–0.6	1.1	–0.4
Apr. 52-Apr. 53	n.c.	–0.1	2.1	–0.7	–0.5	0.3	1.4	–0.6	–1.2	n.c.	1.4	–0.5	–0.3	–0.2	n.c.	–0.1
Aug. 52-Aug. 53	0.1	–0.4	–1.0	–0.5	0.7	–0.4	–0.9	–0.6	1.5	–0.8	–1.4	0.1	–3.1	–0.4	1.0	–0.3
Aug. 51-Aug. 53	–0.8	–0.3	–6.2	–0.3	0.9	–0.4	–4.5	–0.3	–0.2	–1.0	–2.5	0.3	–2.8	–0.5	1.1	–0.3
Period of decrease in labor demand:																
Dec. 52-Dec. 53	–1.5	0.4	–2.5	0.2	–1.1	0.9	–3.7	0.2	–3.6	n.c.	–2.2	0.2	–1.7	–0.1	–0.9	0.2
Apr. 53-Apr. 54	–1.2	1.7	–4.4	2.1	–2.1	2.4	–2.8	1.0	–0.7	1.4	–3.0	2.3	0.6	0.9	0.4	0.9
Aug. 53-Aug. 54	–1.7	1.8	–3.3	2.8	–2.9	2.9	–1.1	1.4	–4.6	1.9	1.0	0.7	0.1	1.3	–1.1	1.0
Aug. 52-Aug. 54	–1.6	1.4	–4.3	2.3	–2.2	2.5	–2.0	0.8	–2.9	0.9	–0.4	0.8	–3.0[a]	0.9	–0.1	0.7

[a] This figure is heavily influenced by net labor force withdrawals in late 1952 and early 1953.

E = employed, U = unemployed.

n.c. = no change.

Source: *Current Population Reports: Labor Force*, Bureau of the Census, Series P-57, monthly reports, various dates.

decline even though there was a net decrease in employment opportunities for the adult population. The low level of unemployment in 1952 and 1953 concealed quite sizable employment declines for men under twenty and over sixty-four and for women between the ages of twenty and thirty-four. Secular trends were reenforced by the decrease in the number of job openings for younger and older men. The participation rates for women under thirty-five declined, if the hypotheses are correct, both because job openings were fewer for women and because family incomes were not being cut into by high rates of male unemployment. Willingness and ability to withdraw from the labor force, therefore, helped make possible the low levels of unemployment during these years.

In the periods of general though moderate employment declines, 1949 and the first half of 1954, there was no net mobility outward to moderate the growth of unemployment. Examination of the age-sex group data, however, reveals some intriguing changes in employment and unemployment rates. For each of the age-sex groups with a substantial proportion of secondary members, unemployment increased less rapidly than it did for men between the ages of twenty and fifty-four, a group which presumably has a very small proportion of secondary members. For men under twenty and over sixty-four and for women under twenty this was caused largely by labor force withdrawals. Even for women twenty years old and over, however, where the tendency was to stay in the labor force or even increase the rate of participation, unemployment rates advanced less than they did for men, twenty to fifty-four, apparently because these groups of women had lower "disemployment rates," to use Hauser's term for unemployment that follows an employment status.

On the assumption that secondary labor force mobility is primarily responsible, the data tend to support the proposition that unemployment fluctuations are less volatile for the secondary labor force and that this reduces the amplitude of unemployment fluctuations for the total labor force. Chart 1 illustrates some of the effects on unemployment rates (as a percentage of each group's labor force) during successive periods of moderate labor force—and employment—expansion, moderate labor force contraction (with employment holding relatively steady in proportion to population), and labor force stability (with declining employment).

Other Advantages. The above analysis, it is contended, would be considerably improved if it were based on data that separated primary labor force attachment from secondary. Analysis by age-sex groups, however, gives some insight into the contributions which primary-secondary differentiations would make in analyzing changes in the

CHART 1

Unemployment Rates for Several Age-Sex Groups, April 1950–March 1955

(percentage of each group's labor force)

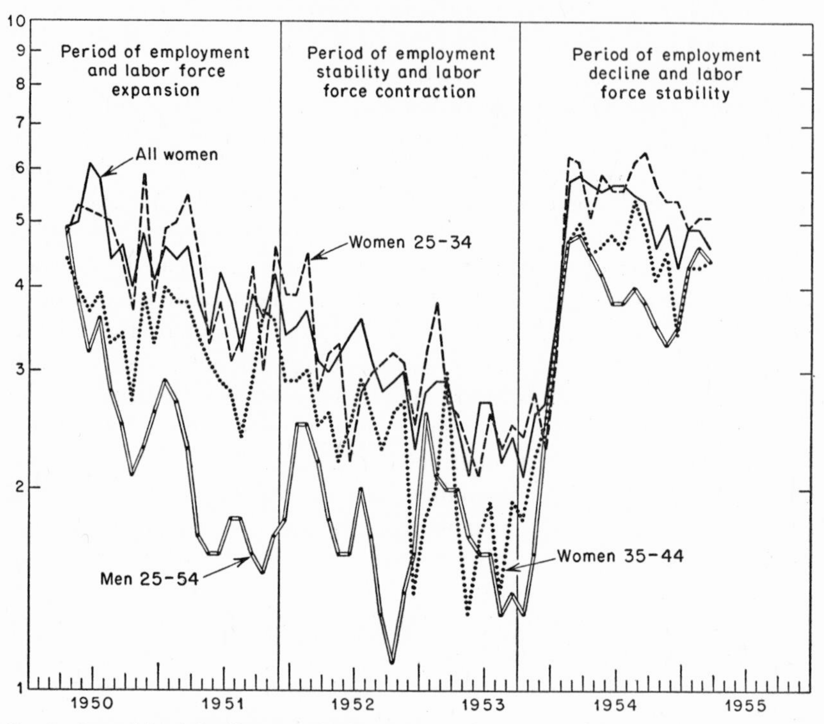

Source: *Current Population Reports: Labor Force*, Bureau of the Census, Series P-57, monthly reports.

employment and unemployment components of the labor force in relation to other changes in economic activity.

Without going into detail, it is possible to list several other areas of analysis in which the differentiation would be useful. Data on the behavior of the secondary labor force under varying economic conditions would be of particular value as additional data in formulating estimates of potential manpower under assumed conditions of high labor demand in national emergencies. Secondly, since most seasonal variations in the labor force are accounted for by secondary labor force mobility, secondary labor force data would contribute to the analysis of these seasonal shifts.[39] In the third place, secondary labor force data

[39] Charles D. Stewart has raised the question of "whether enumerators tend to assume that seasonal workers withdraw from the labor market without probing to discover whether they are seeking another job, thus contributing possibly to a substantial underestimate of those 'able, willing, and seeking to work'" (Stewart, *op.cit.*, p. 6).

would make it somewhat easier to distinguish between secular and short-run phenomena in labor force change. If, for example, female labor force participation rates increase in a given period, as they did for women twenty-five and over between April 1953 and April 1954, is the increase due to a secular trend or is it a net inflow of secondary workers in response to short-run labor market and family income changes? Has the secular increase in female participation been the result of a larger proportion of women with a primary attachment or a larger proportion with a secondary attachment to the labor force?

Fourth, the differentiation as a method of analysis can be used to advantage in special surveys of local labor market areas, particularly when rapid changes in employment have occurred or are imminent. Data from the 1950 census indicate rather large differences in labor force participation rates among areas, differences which seem to be related to the industrial composition in local labor markets. Some of the possibilities of analysis are illustrated in the two local area studies reported sketchily in this paper and more completely elsewhere.[40]

Finally, data on the secondary labor force might assist in determining the extent to which the economy is utilizing the man-hours available to it in the market. More adequate data on partial and disguised unemployment are perhaps more immediately important in this respect, but it seems probable that perfection of methods of estimating the secondary labor force would add to the labor force, under some conditions of demand, a number of people not seeking work because of a realistic recognition of the nonavailability of jobs.[41] Studies in nonmetropolitan areas indicate that in many of these areas the jobless residents who are able and ready to work will not search for jobs when they believe there are none to be had. The fact that they are reluctant to move to other communities is generally considered to be an indication that they like their "home towns" and are hopeful about job chances in the community and not that they do not wish to work.[42]

ALTERNATIVE METHODS OF ANALYSIS

The attempt made in the preceding pages to analyze secondary labor

[40] See references in note 8; Louis Levine, "Unemployment by Locality and Industry," in this volume; *Labor-Force Participation, Its Significance to Labor Market Analysis*, Bureau of Employment Security, June 1952, p. 37; Nedra Bartlett Belloc, "Labor-Force Participation and Employment Opportunities for Women," *Journal of the American Statistical Association*, September 1950, pp. 400-410; and Clarence D. Long, *The Labor Force in Wartime America*, National Bureau of Economic Research, Occasional Paper 14, 1944.

[41] See discussion below in section 3.

[42] In some respects, small towns and rural nonfarm areas are similar to the situation in Antigua, described by Rottenberg, where "no one 'actively' seeks work" (see Simon Rottenberg, "Labor Force Measurement in a Pre-Industrial Economy," *The Southern Economic Journal*, October 1951, p. 223).

force mobility on the basis of data categorized by age and sex shows that much can be done in the analysis of changes in the size and composition of employment and unemployment with this breakdown. The important question of the extent to which significant changes in employment and unemployment are brought about by changes in status of regular or temporary members of the labor force is left unanswered, except by inference. Age-sex breakdowns are vital to the analysis but it is suggested that a primary-secondary breakdown would add substantially to the successful interpretation of dynamic changes in the labor force and its components.

Data on employment and unemployment by "relationship to head of household" would also contribute greatly to the analysis of unemployment trends and their significance, particularly if such data were made available much more frequently than once in ten years.[43] Such data, while most useful, would be only the roughest kind of substitute for data categorized according to type of labor force attachment. The reason is that, although most heads of households are undoubtedly primary workers as defined in this paper, a sizable proportion of primary workers would not be heads of households. Similarly, while most secondary labor force members are members of households but not the heads, it is likely that a sizable number of secondary members are heads of households, even if in most cases heads of single-member households.

3. *Some Problems in Measurement*

With the concept of the secondary worker, the civilian, noninstitutional population can be categorized for any given period of time—at least in the abstract—as follows:

1. Primary labor force attachment:
   - Employed
   - Unemployed, actively seeking work
   - Unemployed, not actively seeking work because on either indefinite or temporary layoff,[44] because temporarily disabled, or because of belief that there is no work available in the community or in line of work[45]
2. Secondary labor force attachment:
   - Employed
   - Unemployed, actively seeking work

[43] See Philip Hauser, "Differential Unemployment and Characteristics of the Unemployed in the United States, 1940-1954," in this volume.

[44] See Gertrude Bancroft, "Current Unemployment Statistics of the Census Bureau and Some Alternatives," in this volume.

[45] See *Current Population Survey: Enumerator's Manual*, Bureau of the Census, January 1951, p. 67.

Unemployed, not actively seeking work for reasons cited above[46]

3. Not in the labor force:
   - Secondary workers not currently in the market
   - Nonworkers
     - Unable to work (would include some primary workers)
     - Not interested in working

DIFFERENTIATION WITHIN THE LABOR FORCE SECTOR

The local labor market area studies that experimented with primary-secondary differentiation suggest that differentiation within the labor force segment can be limited to evidence of continuous or noncontinuous labor force attachment prior to the time of data collection, labor force status at the time of survey (employed, unemployed, out of labor force), expectation of continuing in the labor force, and age.[47] On the basis of this as yet tentative conclusion, a conclusion which should be subjected to further research, some topics of inquiry are listed which might be used in a survey designed to separate respondents into primary and secondary labor force members. No attempt is made to suggest the precise wording of questions which might be used or to suggest the exact extent of inquiry required in such an area as prior labor force attachment. Questions necessary to establish whether a person is working, has a job, or does not have a job are not included here.

For those working, or with a job but not at work:

1. Whether, since a given date (an easy one to place such as "June 1950, when Korean conflict started"), has been a month or more without a job and not looking for work (yes, no)
2. If "yes": Length of time not looking and not seeking work; reason or reasons for not looking for work (school, housekeeping, housewife with children, vacation, illness, military service, other)[48]

[46] The borderline between unemployment and out of the labor force is discussed below, pp. 197ff.

[47] Other data would, of course, be essential for interpretation: sex, marital status, major non-labor-force activities, relationship to head of household, and number of workers in household. Age is relevant to the question of whether expected labor force withdrawal is or is not in the conventional range of retirement years. For example, if a sixty-three year old person expects to leave the labor force in two years, this expectation would not by itself be an indication of secondary labor force attachment.

[48] Differentiation between primary and secondary attachment, it is expected, could be accomplished automatically once the necessary combinations of responses are established. As noted in the Appendix, "reasons for being out of the labor force" probably cannot be used in the differentiation because primary workers may

3. Whether would look for work if did not have present job (yes, no—return to school, stay home, go into military service, other)
4. At what age expects to quit working for pay or income, or, if not sure, best guess as to how many years will continue working ("working life," less than two years, something over two years, doesn't know)

For those not working, without a job, and looking for work:

Items 1, 2, and 4 from above (included here would be those in the category recognized by the census as not actively seeking work solely because of the lack of suitable jobs).

Since labor force measurement is exceedingly complex and difficult, it is suggested that research into various phases of secondary labor force measurement and experimentation in such measurement (perhaps in selected local labor market areas) should be a prerequisite for any large-scale use of the secondary labor force concept. The problem areas, however, are apparent. In the first place, a reliable set of "ground rules" is needed for the minority of cases where secondary and primary labor force attachment shade into one another and for the shadowy area between unemployment and out of the labor force. The problem of measurement in these borderline areas has two parts. One is a question of policy related to the uses of labor force data; the other is a technical problem related to the ability to make clear-cut and consistent distinctions. If the technical problem is solved, the policy question may still remain.

The technical problem is whether it is possible to make sufficiently reliable distinctions between primary and secondary attachment and between unemployment and out of the labor force so that the data can be used with confidence. Subjective factors are involved and reliance must be placed on the consistency of answers. In the borderline area between primary and secondary attachment, subjective factors appear in the form of attitudes and degree of interest in continued employment for those who may be shifting or about to shift their labor force attachment. The goals of research in this area would be twofold: firstly, through intensive study of individual labor market activities and attitudes, to determine those factors which most reliably differentiate according to type of attachment; secondly, to determine whether responses would be sufficiently consistent from time to time and from place to place to permit valid measures of change.

If further research does confirm the feasibility of separating primary

have been out for almost any reason. The Appendix shows the results of automatic differentiation in the Kankakee sample using combinations of responses to four questions.

from secondary attachment, it might be expected that, over a period of time, the differentiation itself will contribute to the "reliability" of labor force interpretation, and particularly to the interpretation of unemployment figures. The reason is that the separation in the data of those with a temporary labor force attachment will make it possible, in comparing different periods, to show more precisely how unemployment is changing in relation to changes in employment. For example, when employment declines, data on the changes in the employed and unemployed components of the secondary labor force will show whether the decline is being absorbed by primary or secondary workers. When employment increases relative to population, the data should give a clearer picture of the source of the new employees—primary labor force unemployed, secondary labor force unemployed, or increases in the size of the secondary labor force.

The policy question for differentiation within the labor force sector of the population is simply whether it is in the public interest to have periodic estimates of the size and composition of the primary and secondary labor forces. Like any data, these could be misused, but the argument in favor of these additional data is similar to that in favor of the age-sex breakdowns which now are available—namely, that they would through careful analysis contribute to a better understanding of the workings of our economy.

THE BORDERLINE AREA BETWEEN UNEMPLOYMENT AND OUT OF THE LABOR FORCE

Probably few would question the existence of a borderline area between the labor force and non-labor-force segments of the economy, an area in which both the criteria for measurement and the techniques of measurement are important to the determination of who is or is not in the labor force. This borderline lies for the most part between the unemployed sector of the secondary labor force and secondary workers not in the labor force, because it is not particularly difficult to establish whether a primary worker is in the labor force.

At least two groups may be identified whose members may be difficult to classify in respect to type of labor force attachment. One consists of those who are more or less marginal in their attachment to the labor force because they are, or would be, less than average in their effectiveness as workers as a result of substantial mental or physical handicaps. In the second group are those who, as Ducoff and Hagood have expressed it: "*can* work at ordinary standards of efficiency but who may have difficulty finding employment because of hiring practices which discriminate against women, older persons, or racial and religious groups."[49] An unknown number of such people, otherwise able, willing and ready to work, may not be seeking employment because of such discrimination. Whether such people, most of whom would be secondary workers, should be counted in the labor force depends upon the criteria to be used.

It is not, perhaps unfortunately, a simple question of active search for work. The Census Bureau has already "compromised" its concept of "current activity" to include any person not looking for work because "he thinks there is no work available in the community or in his line of work,"[50] although it is questionable how many people in this category are actually counted as unemployed since much depends on the extent of the enumerator's probing. An active search for employment, therefore, has been officially recognized as not completely suitable as a criterion for determination of an unemployment status. Further research and experimentation, it is contended, are warranted in order to determine whether it would be operationally feasible to extend the area of "current availability" in measuring unemployment.

Even if it should be feasible, such an extension involves some policy decisions concerning the definition of unemployment. If we assume, however, that national policy is to achieve, as the Employment Act of 1946 puts it, "maximum production, employment, and purchasing power," without sacrificing such other goals as adequate leisure time, and if we assume further that the current level of demand is rarely the best base against which unemployment should be measured, a case can be made for expanding the area of "current availability" as a criterion for unemployment. In other words, if the "effective demand" does not draw into jobs or the active search for work some of those who desire employment and are both able and "ready" to accept employment, should not these people be considered as in the labor force?

Aside from the policy question, the problems of measurement are formidable and perhaps cannot even be defined accurately until more research has been undertaken and completed. Some of the questions to be asked, however, can be raised. When is a person (who is able to work) "ready" to take a job, that is, currently available? When he says that he is? These are questions perhaps for the social psychologist as well as for the economist. If a person is "ready," how much should he or she be allowed in the way of conditions under which a job would be acceptable and still be considered as realistically in the labor

[49] Louis J. Ducoff and Margaret J. Hagood, *Labor Force Definition and Measurement: Recent Experience in the United States*, Social Science Research Council Bull. 56, 1947, p. 46.

[50] *Current Population Survey: Enumerator's Manual*, p. 67. Persons not looking for work because of temporary disability or illness or because of an indefinite or more than 30-day layoff are also counted as unemployed.

market? Is a mother available for employment and in the labor force, for example, if she says she would be working if a day nursery were available? Is unwillingness to change one's place of residence to find employment a socially valid criterion for non-labor-force determination?

The few studies available in this area do not provide adequate answers to such questions but they do suggest that additional research has potential utility. In 1942, the Works Progress Administration made an attempt to estimate short-term availability for employment in terms of the number of people prepared to accept jobs for wages within the thirty-day period following the survey date. The estimate of 13 million people available for full- or part-time employment, even if the margin of error may have been fairly large, suggests at least that this borderline area may be fairly extensive.[51]

While any such measurements may exaggerate availability to the extent that they include people "on the verge" of entering the labor force who are offset by others *in* the labor force "on the verge" of leaving, it seems quite probable that a substantial number would be people not actively seeking work solely because of their perception of the nonavailability of jobs.

Several special surveys of the Census Bureau attacked the problem of whether supplementary questions would reveal a number of persons among those initially classified as out of the labor force who could have been classified as "seeking work." In each of the six such studies a different set of questions was used and the results, not surprisingly, showed the additional number varying between 11 per cent and 73 per cent of the reported number of unemployed. The Census Bureau concluded:

> ". . . the size of the marginal group identified in these studies should not be regarded as necessarily indicative of the number of 'omitted' workers. Not enough evidence has been accumulated . . . on the nature and motivation of persons in the marginal group to determine how many can be regarded as bona fide members of the labor force at the survey date. . . . In any event, there appears to be a need for further studies of this type. . . ."[52]

One thing that was clear was that the people in "the marginal group" were not entirely responsible for their own economic support and were, by the definition used in this paper, "secondary workers."

[51] *Monthly Report on Unemployment*, Works Progress Administration, April 22, 1942. Of the 13 million, 7.6 million were estimated as available for full-time employment—6.5 million housewives, 500,000 students, and 600,000 persons who were "unable or too old" to find work under "ordinary circumstances."

[52] *Labor Force Memorandum 4*, Bureau of the Census, February 21, 1950 (see the discussion of these studies in A. J. Jaffe and Charles D. Stewart, *Manpower Resources and Utilization*, Wiley, 1951, pp. 458-461).

In addition to the Census studies, two case studies were made in 1951, one in St. Paul, Minnesota, and one in Columbus, Ohio, on the question of the availability for work of nonworkers.[53] Although the samples were small, the wording of questions differed between the two studies, and one study employed interviews and the other questionnaires, some rough comparisons are possible between the findings of the two studies (see Table 9). It is quite possible, however, that the

TABLE 9

Comparison of Current Availability of Those Classified as "Not in Labor Force," Columbus, Ohio, and St. Paul, Minnesota, 1951

	COLUMBUS		ST. PAUL	
	Per Cent of Adult Population[a]	*Per Cent of Non-Labor Force*[b]	*Per Cent of Adult Population*[a]	*Per Cent of Non-Labor Force*[b]
Currently available, if necessary training provided	5	13		
Labor market reason only for not looking for work[c]			3	9
Total currently available, including "conditions for employment"[d]	11	28	11	33
Total number who "wish to work"[e]			14	42
Current availability range	5-11	13-28	3-11	9-33
Labor force participation rate, census definition	63		62	
Labor force participation rate, "current availability" definition	68-74		65-73	

[a] Adult population for Columbus includes "unable to work"; for St. Paul excludes "unable to work."

[b] Non-labor force means here not in the labor force, according to census definitions. Again data for Columbus include "unable to work," but for St. Paul exclude "unable to work."

[c] Could not get a job; could not get desired type of job; did not have enough training.

[d] Wanted part-time only, particular hours, a particular job, specified distance from home, and similar conditions.

[e] Those who answered "yes" to question: "Do you ever think you would like to take a job (go back to work)?"

Source: Derived from data in Kenneth E. Schnelle, *Manpower Resources in a Tight Labor Market,* Minnesota Division of Employment Security, 1952, and Samuel C. Kelley, *A Case Study in the Measurement of Manpower Resources,* The Ohio State University Research Foundation, 1951.

[53] Kenneth E. Schnelle, "Manpower Resources in a Tight Labor Market," Ph.D. thesis, University of Minnesota, Minnesota Division of Employment Security, mimeographed, 1952; Samuel C. Kelley, "A Case Study in the Measurement of Manpower Resources," mimeographed, The Ohio State University Research Foundation, 1951.

data from these studies exaggerate when they show roughly 3 to 5 per cent of the adult population and 9 to 13 per cent of those classified as out of the labor force under census definitions immediately ready to take jobs. Exaggeration may have resulted from the wording of questions, the respondents answering within a broader time reference than the census week, and the phenomenon previously mentioned that some people about to enter the labor force may be matched by others about to leave.[54] The significance of these studies, however, lies in the fact that they were both made in large metropolitan areas with diversified employment opportunities and high rates of labor force participation, in a period of high demand for labor. In spite of these conditions, significant numbers of people not in the labor force said they were ready to take jobs if they knew of jobs they could take.[55]

The results of these studies seem to suggest that additional research is warranted. Particular emphasis in such studies could be given to the reliability of response in the area of availability for employment and, perhaps more important, to the consistency of response over time; because if responses are consistent, there is hope for adequate measures of change.[56] In addition, an aim of research would be to establish what conditions for accepting employment can be included in a realistic concept of "in the labor market." Eventually, if the measurement problems are solved, it becomes a question of national policy to determine where to draw the line between the status of unemployment and a non-labor-force status.

DIFFERENTIATION WITHIN THE NON-LABOR-FORCE SECTOR

The Schnelle and Kelley studies and those which experimented with primary-secondary labor force differentiation suggest the additional possibility of experimentation in separating secondary workers from nonworkers in the non-labor-force sector of the population. Pertinent areas of inquiry for persons without a job and not looking for one would be: whether the person had ever had a job or owned a business;

[54] It is also possible that the entry of some of these people into employment would make it possible for others in the same households to leave the labor force. These comments are not intended to be criticisms of these studies because the authors were careful to point out some of the limitations and Schnelle even avoided any quantitative estimates for St. Paul on the basis of his study.

[55] In the St. Paul study, 12 per cent of the "non-labor-force" respondents said they would go to work in a national emergency. Apparently, the Korean War did not qualify as an emergency.

[56] It is noteworthy that criticism of the census measurement of unemployment has centered upon the type of people included or excluded each month and not upon inconsistencies in classification from one month to the next. Should the unemployment concept be broadened to include some categories not now included the most important question is whether these additional categories will be measured consistently.

whether he was physically able to work; his major activity (school, housekeeping, child care, other); his expectations of entering or returning to the labor force; and the conditions under which he would look for work or take a job.

Such research would contribute to our understanding of the factors involved in individual decisions to work for pay in our society and could conceivably lead to useful measurements, perhaps at irregular or infrequent intervals, of the composition of the adult population not in the labor force. Manpower analysis, for example, could benefit from data on secondary workers not in the labor force, particularly if breakdowns were available on previous labor force experience, present major activity, and conditions for labor force entrance. Such estimates probably could never be as accurate as breakdowns in the composition of the employed and unemployed now available, but the possibility exists that they could be sufficiently valid as measures of change over time.

4. Conclusions

A significant type of labor force mobility in the American economy consists of the non-age-connected entrances and exits of persons not regularly or consistently in the labor force during the customary span of a working life. This paper suggests that it would be both operationally feasible and analytically useful to differentiate within the labor force between persons with a regular or primary and those with a temporary or secondary attachment. Such a breakdown could be incorporated in labor force data without otherwise altering the definitions and techniques used by the census and without disturbing the continuity of total figures on employment and unemployment—although some alterations in the categories of employed and unemployed have been proposed elsewhere on other grounds.

The paper has presented some of the data from two local labor market area studies that experimented with the primary-secondary differentiation and has examined detailed age-sex group data from the census, using some assumptions on the age-sex characteristics of secondary labor force members in order to suggest some of the advantages of the proposed differentiation as a method of analysis. The belief is that it will supplement such other types of data, both existing and proposed, as the age-sex and "relationship to the head of the household" breakdowns already mentioned, number of workers in a household, multi-job holders, and hours of work.

Labor force data, with separate classifications for primary and secondary members made available periodically, would contribute, along with other relevant data, to the analysis of: the factors which influence inward and outward labor force mobility; the determinants of net change (and of stability) in labor force participation rates; the relationships among employment, unemployment, and nonworker statuses under changing economic conditions, as, for example, whether unemployment in a given period is arising from layoffs or labor force entrances; place-to-place differences in labor force participation rates and the relationship to differences in industrial composition; and seasonal and secular changes in the size and composition of the labor force. In addition, data on changes in the primary and secondary labor forces could contribute to the information needed as guides to monetary and fiscal policy decisions and in formulating estimates of manpower potential under emergency conditions of labor demand. Finally, techniques of secondary labor force measurement could be particularly useful in the analysis of local labor market areas where rapid changes in the demand for labor are taking place or are imminent. Such changes may become more common if for various reasons, including the "cold war," the geographic dispersion of industry is accelerated and nonmetropolitan areas attract more industry.

In addition to the discussion of differentiation within the labor force, as presently defined, the question has been raised of the utility of further examination and research in the borderline area between the status of being unemployed and that of being a nonworker. The suggestion is advanced that techniques could be developed, perhaps somewhat similar to those useful in measuring consumer expectations, that would permit an expansion of the concept of unemployment to include persons who are realistically in the labor market at a given period of time although not actively seeking work for the very realistic reason that they are convinced no work is available. The census, of course, already includes some people in this category as unemployed and agrees, in some of its publications, that further research is warranted.

Finally, the suggestion is made that experimentation and research might reveal some possibilities for adequate estimates of the number of secondary workers who at any given time are not in the labor force and for some data on the characteristics and labor force expectations of such secondary workers.

As Jaffe and Stewart have put it, "the labor force is an artifact,"[57] and as such it is subject to change. In the author's opinion, the technical possibilities of achieving change in the directions suggested are, in diminishing order: differentiation within the labor force; a more precise dividing line between unemployed status and nonworker status; and

[57] Jaffe and Stewart, *op.cit.*, p. 462.

differentiation in the non-labor-force sector between secondary workers and others. In any event, the possible advantages of secondary labor force and secondary worker data would seem to justify a recommendation for further research and experimentation on the part of university research groups, employment security agencies, and the Census Bureau.

Appendix

Mechanical Tabulation of Primary and Secondary Labor Force Attachment in Kankakee Sample, Using Combinations of Responses to Four Questions

Since the Kankakee study was experimental, and there were no models to follow in analyzing labor force mobility and primary and secondary labor force differentiation, the responses to most questions were categorized after the interviews were completed. The coding of labor force attachment was on the basis of responses to a number of questions and a considerable amount of experimentation took place in determining what combinations of responses would meet the definitions. The final coding was done through inspection of the data. Wherever necessary, relevant data from various parts of the interview schedule were used in making the final decision on each interviewee.

Quick and efficient coding of a much larger sample, periodically studied, would require automatic coding of labor force status. With this in mind, combinations of categories for four items of the coded Kankakee data were wired in an IBM "board" and the IBM machine was used to classify the sample according to labor force attachment (primary and secondary). The four items used were:

Items (columns)	*Categories (rows)*		
1. Length of time *not* in labor force since World War II or after first entrance	Only jobs, including interview job, summer or supplementary part-time[58]	In continuously	Several catego of length of tin out of labor fo
2. Periods of labor force participation	(same as above)	Several categories of "in continuously" according to when entered	Several catego of "in and out" cluding one fo "In World Wa and since Kor but not betwe

[58] From work history. "Supplementary part-time job" means holding a part-time job while the individual also has a major non-labor-force activity, such as school.

3. What respondent would be doing if not working	Looking for job; school	Vacation; home; travel	Housewife; military service; other
4. How long expects to work for living;[59] definite period under two years	Definite period two years or more	Indefinite period, over five years, but less than working life	Working life (to age sixty or beyond); doesn't know

The questions on which these items and categories are based are as follows:

1. (On the basis of month or more not working, from work history) Was there any part of this time when you were not looking for work? About how much of this time?
2. (From work history)
3. If you did not have a job *now* what would you be doing?
4. About how many years do you expect to keep on working (for pay or income)?

For the purpose of automatic classification the following combinations of categories on four items were set up to determine primary classification:

Combination 1

1, 2. In labor force continuously

3. If did not have interview job, would look for work, or take vacation, or enter military service

4. Expects to work for "normal working life," or for indefinite period but more than five years, or does not know

Combination 2

1, 2. In labor force continuously

3. Any answer but "housewife" on activity if did not have interview job

4. Expects to work "working life" or does not know.

Combination 3

1, 2. Out of labor force, one month or more, *except* those in World War II and since Korea but not between, and including those who never had a regular job

3. If did not have interview job, would look for work or enter military service

4. Expects to work "working life" or does not know

Combination 1, in which continuity in the labor force is the key item, accounts for 121 of the 183 (out of 188) automatic classifications which

[59] An adjustment for the age of the respondent was made in the coding of this item (see note 47).

agree with the original coding. Combination 2 discounts answers other than look for another job, on item 3, and makes continuous labor force service and expectation of staying in labor force the key factors. Only nine persons are covered by this combination. Combination 3 covers those primary workers who had been out of the labor force. Here, to be counted as primary, the individuals had to show, through their responses, *both* job hunting (or military service) if they did not have their interview job *and* expectation of remaining in the labor force. It might be noted that although primary workers tend to be out of the labor force for different reasons than do secondary, primary workers may have been out for any of the reasons categorized. Consequently, reasons for being out cannot be differentiated for purposes of automatic classification of labor force status. Combination 3 includes 53 of the 183 automatically classified as primary.

The following combinations of categories on four items were set up to determine secondary classification:

Combination 4

1, 2. Out of labor force, one month or more, *including* those in World War II and since Korea but not between, and including those who never had a regular job

3. Any answer on what would do if did not have interview job

4. Any answer on expectations of how long will work

Combination 5

1, 2. In labor force continuously or never had regular job

3. If did not have interview job, would look for work or enter military service

4. Expects to leave labor force in definite period of time, less than working life

Combination 6

1, 2. In labor force continuously, or never had regular job

3. Any answers, except "look for work," if did not have interview job

4. Any answer, except "working life," on how long will work

The IBM machine was wired to examine the cards for each combination, in order. Combinations 4, 5, and 6 therefore represent combinations which account for those interviewees not caught in combinations 1, 2, or 3. Combination 4 covers those who were in and out of the labor force and do not meet the conditions of combination 3 and classifies as secondary 65 of the 101 (out of 108) on which the machine agrees with the original coding. Combination 5 shows those cards which do not agree with item 4 on combinations 1 and 2. Only three are in this combination. Combination 6 represents those remaining after combinations 1 to 5 were examined and shows those who had been in continuously and neither would look for a job if did not have present one *nor* expect to stay in the labor force for "normal working life." Thirty-three are in this group.

Table A-1 shows the comparison with the original coding by inspection:

TABLE A-1

Comparison of Machine and Inspection Coding of Labor Force Attachment, Kankakee, 1952

A. Machine Coding

PRIMARY			SECONDARY		
Combination	*Agrees On*	*Disagrees On*	*Combination*	*Agrees On*	*Disagrees On*
1	121	2	4	65	3
2	9	3	5	3	2
3	53	2	6	33	0
Total	183	7[a]		101	5[b]

B. Inspection Coding

	Original Coding	*Machine Agrees On*	*Machine Disagrees On*	*Percentage Disagreement*	*Percentage Agreement*
Primary	188	183	5	2.7	97.3
Secondary	108	101	7	6.5	93.5
Total	296	284	12	4.1	95.9

[a] Represents those coded by machine as primary but originally coded as secondary.

[b] Represents those coded by machine as secondary but originally coded as primary.

The twelve "disagreements" are borderline cases. It is interesting to note that the five whom the machine classifies as secondary are all breadwinners, that is, primarily responsible for the income of their households. Three of the five also have dependents. None of the seven whom the machine classifies as primary are breadwinners. Four of the seven could "get along" indefinitely without a job. The twelve, in other words, were originally classified using data in addition to those represented by the four items given to the machine.

The results of the experiment are encouraging in terms of automatic classification. Further experimentation and research might reduce disagreements between machine coding and coding by inspection, where additional items of information are used, to a figure considerably smaller than the 4 per cent in this experiment. Including in the combinations responses on whether the person is primarily responsible for household income might reduce the percentage of disagreement, for example. Whether there are others in household working would be another item to consider in this respect. Consistency of responses on his activity if he did not have job and on his expectation of staying in the labor force also deserves additional study. The above results, as far as they go, show a consistent pattern of responses for most interviewees in terms of the original classification by labor force attachment. It would seem, then, that there is a good possibility that primary and secondary differentiation could be determined by machine, with special studies at times to determine whether the classifications deviate from those made with more complete data.

COMMENT

GLADYS L. PALMER, *University of Pennsylvania*

After the Employment Act of 1946 was passed, there was considerable discussion, both inside and outside of government circles, of the meaning of the phraseology "able and willing and seeking to work" and of the relation of the Current Population Survey's definitions to this concept. At about the same time, a major discrepancy between the counts of insured unemployment and Survey unemployment immediately after World War II precipitated a review of the Survey concepts by the Budget Bureau's interagency committee on labor supply, employment, and unemployment statistics. After lengthy discussion, it was agreed in 1948 to recommend no change. In my opinion, this decision was reached partly because the Survey concepts were believed to be the best available general-purpose measure and partly because the labor force categories in use had never been tested under conditions of marked changes in the level of business activity.

Since then there have been two downswings and one upswing in business activity, and we now have a better basis for judging the sensitivity of the series as well as their adequacy for a variety of purposes. Perhaps, also, the experience of a number of years of relatively high levels of employment has given us a better appreciation of the implications of possible goals envisaged by the Act. A second major review of the concepts is now under way, and I am sure that those of us from the Budget Bureau's committee welcome this opportunity to discuss important policy questions on the measurement of unemployment.

The two papers I am discussing suggest ways of identifying and measuring partial and "disguised" or "concealed" unemployment—one with respect to persons now counted in the labor force, the other, to both this group and to persons classified as nonworkers who may be considered available for employment. Both papers have the merit of citing experimental results and of directly or indirectly indicating the relative importance of their suggestions for amplification of current measures. If I interpret them correctly, Ducoff and Hagood believe that one of the first tasks of a "full employment" program is to give more hours of work or more productive employment to those already employed. Wilcock would plan for jobs first for the "primary" labor force (persons with relatively stable attachments to the labor market) and next for the "secondary" labor force (persons already in the labor force with temporary or irregular attachments to it and such non-workers as may indicate a desire for employment, for whom he suggests the title, "inactive unemployed").

All of us probably agree on the desirability of periodic measures of involuntary part-time work. Perhaps the only issues to be resolved are how often the measurement is to be done and how such workers are to be treated in a statistical series. We would also agree with Ducoff and Hagood that measures of time worked (whether of hours in a week or weeks in a year) are not so significant for agricultural as for nonagricultural workers and that special research rather than current statistical measurement is needed to identify the economic areas where labor surplus or low income problems are of long standing.

Both papers suggest that there are hazards in developing enumerative techniques for determining the availability for other employment of persons already at work or the availability for jobs of persons not actively in the labor market at any given time. This caution is substantiated by some of the experimental work undertaken at the Census Bureau as well as by local labor market studies. This group knows that complex social and economic forces influence an individual's behavior in the labor market at any point in time or over time. I am inclined to put more faith in the behavior patterns reflected in workers' actions over a period of time than in their responses to hypothetical questions about their availability for jobs. Nevertheless, I agree that this is a field for further research and experimental work.

If one thinks a full employment program should be geared to provide jobs for all who express a desire to work, one will not quarrel with Wilcock for broadening his definition of unemployment to include an inactive group who indicate this desire. Even if I were to accept this goal, however, I would quarrel with differentiating primary and secondary workers in a statistical series of labor force measurement. As a confirmed feminist, I object to the notion that it is anyone else's business how long I expect to be in the labor market or whether I am fully self-supporting or support others, especially if the answers to such questions are to be used for employment policy decisions. I had hoped that the basis for restriction of the employment of married women, for example, had gone with the depression of the 1930's. I think the suggested distinction is an invidious one for a government statistical series. This should not be interpreted to mean that I do not believe in analytical studies of the incidence of unemployment in families or in research on the regularity of attachment to the labor market of different groups of workers. Moreover, I believe that occasional or periodic measures of family employment and income yield useful data for a wide range of economic policy decisions. But I would give first priority in labor force statistics to amplification of the measures covering persons who are at work or looking for work at a given time.

PART II

THE BEHAVIOR OF UNEMPLOYMENT

ANNUAL ESTIMATES OF UNEMPLOYMENT IN THE UNITED STATES, 1900-1954

STANLEY LEBERGOTT

BUREAU OF THE BUDGET

The present paper is a preliminary report on estimates of unemployment for the period since 1900 intended to be consistent with the series currently reported by the Census Bureau in its Current Population Survey. These estimates have been derived as part of a broader project of estimating labor force and detailed employment and unemployment series for this period. Their function is to indicate the broad changes that have occurred over these decades, and mark the major year to year shifts in employment and unemployment. The discussion is focussed on four chief topics: the nature of unemployment measures; unemployment estimates as a measure of economic change; unemployment estimates as a measure of the level of unemployed manpower; and methods by which the present series was estimated.

1. *The Nature of Unemployment Measures*

Unemployment as measured in statistical series is a residual phenomenon. It reflects chiefly the number of persons who are disemployed *and remain without work*. Variations in the demand for labor do not *per se* produce unemployment. It is necessary for the needs and attitudes of those composing the labor force to complement these variations before unemployment is produced. Hence, a comparison of unemployment figures for, say, 1906 and 1946 will be a comparison, in part, of variations in demand and, in part, of variations in needs and attitudes of those in the labor force.

One of the most important single changes in the composition of the labor force over the past century has been the replacement of immigrant males and children by women. In 1900, 18 per cent of our labor was female. By 1952, the proportion was 31 per cent. A substantial part of the increased proportion tends to be in the labor force to supplement family incomes. The difference of 13 per cent, therefore, tends to give an unprecedented flexibility to the labor force. It was assumed previously that variations in the demand for labor would require com-

Note: The present estimates are unofficial and have no connection with the work of the Bureau of the Budget. They will differ somewhat from preliminary estimates that have been used in *Potential Economic Growth of the United States During the Next Decade*, Joint Committee on the Economic Report, 83d Cong., 2d sess., 1954, and are associated with different employment estimates than those used in the 1950 *Economic Report of the President*.

mensurate variations in unemployment. It has now become clear that because of the increased role of women in the labor force considerable variations in demand can be taken up without equally considerable variations in unemployment. When many of these women become disemployed, they do not, like the male labor force, become unemployed—they leave the labor force. The most spectacular example of this, of course, was the transition in 1945-1946. But even during such a stable year as 1952, roughly 10 million women who were not regular workers worked part of the year, withdrawing from the labor force at the end of their work.[1]

A second factor to be considered in historical comparisons partially offsets this tendency—namely the diminished role of farm employment. In 1900 farmers were more numerous than manufacturing employees; today they constitute less than a third. Since unemployment on the farm customarily tends to take the form of underemployment, the expected float of visible unemployment today would tend to be higher because of the shift to urban employment. (As a partial method of allowing for this, estimates are shown in Table 1 for the ratio of unemployment to the nonfarm employee labor force.)[2]

A third factor is the difference in social attitude. In 1900 we had no unemployment insurance system and no network of employment service offices. By 1954, we had an unemployment insurance system plus broad-scale unionization, a basically different orientation by business as to its own obligations and those which the government should assume. Instead of unemployment being considered primarily as a personal fault, it had come to be considered as one aspect of any large-scale complex economy. As a result of all this, we may get better reporting of actual unemployment now than in 1900. Housewives are less ashamed to admit to a Census Bureau enumerator that the family head is unemployed.[3] (Even since 1933 the reporting of unemployment may have been more adequate than previously—although this is very much of an a priori hypothesis.)

Experience suggests a greater reporting of unemployment during the depression, when there is greater sensitivity to it than at other times. As one indication one may note that the unemployment census of

[1] *Work Experience of the Population in 1952*, Bureau of the Census, Series P-50, No. 48, 1953. This estimate includes those who worked less than forty weeks during the year. One might properly include even more. The average level of unemployment over the year was both low and reasonably steady while the gross changes in unemployment revealed no sharp shifts.

[2] For a fuller discussion of this measure see the writer's "Earnings of Nonfarm Employees in the U.S., 1890-1946," *Journal of the American Statistical Association*, March 1948, pp. 87-88.

[3] The change is embodied in the shift from the characteristic phrase of the early depression—"some folks won't work"—to the 1945-1946 phrase, "the 52-20 Club."

TABLE 1

Unemployment, Annual Average, 1900-1954
(*number in thousands of persons 14 years old and over*)

Year	Number Unemployed	Change from Previous Year	Per Cent of Civilian Labor Force	Per Cent of Nonfarm Employees
1900	1,420		5.0	8.7
1901	710	–710	2.4	4.3
1902	800	90	2.7	4.5
1903	800	0	2.6	4.4
1904	1,490	690	4.8	7.9
1905	1,000	–490	3.1	5.1
1906	280	–720	0.8	1.4
1907	600	–320	1.8	2.9
1908	2,960	2,360	8.5	13.5
1909	1,870	–1,090	5.2	8.2
1910	2,150	280	5.9	9.1
1911	2,290	140	6.2	9.5
1912	1,960	–330	5.2	7.9
1913	1,680	–280	4.4	6.6
1914	3,110	1,430	8.0	11.9
1915	3,840	730	9.7	14.3
1916	1,920	–1,920	4.8	7.1
1917	1,920	0	4.8	7.0
1918	560	–1,360	1.4	2.1
1919	950	390	2.3	3.4
1920	1,670	720	4.0	5.8
1921	5,010	3,340	11.9	16.9
1922	3,220	–1,790	7.6	10.9
1923	1,380	–1,840	3.2	4.6
1924	2,440	1,060	5.5	8.0
1925	1,800	–640	4.0	5.9
1926	880	–920	1.9	2.8
1927	1,890	1,010	4.1	5.9
1928	2,080	190	4.4	6.4
1929	1,550	–530	3.2	4.7
1930	4,340	2,790	8.9	13.0
1931	8,020	3,680	15.9	23.3
1932	12,060	4,040	23.6	34.0
1933	12,830	770	24.9	35.3
1934	11,340	–1,490	21.7	30.6
1935	10,610	–730	20.1	28.4
1936	9,030	–1,580	17.0	23.9
1937	7,700	–1,330	14.3	20.0
1938	10,390	2,690	19.0	26.4
1939	9,480	–910	17.2	23.8

(continued on next page)

TABLE 1 (continued)

(number in thousands of persons 14 years old and over)

Year	*Number Unemployed*	*Change from Previous Year*	*Per Cent of Civilian Labor Force*	*Per Cent of Nonfarm Employees*
1940	8,120	–1,360	14.6	20.2
1941	5,560	–2,560	9.9	13.3
1942	2,660	–2,900	4.7	6.3
1943	1,070	–1,590	1.9	2.5
1944	670	–400	1.2	1.6
1945	1,040	370	1.9	2.5
1946	2,270	1,230	3.9	5.2
1947	2,140	–130	3.6	4.7
1948	2,064	–76	3.4	4.5
1949	3,395	1,331	5.5	7.3
1950	3,142	–253	5.0	6.6
1951	1,879	–1,263	3.0	3.8
1952	1,673	–206	2.7	3.4
1953	1,602	–71	2.5	3.2
1954	3,230	1,628	5.0	6.3

Source: 1900-1928, present estimates; 1929-1939, *Monthly Labor Review*, July 1948; 1940-1954, Bureau of the Census.

November 1937 found 11.0 million totally unemployed and emergency workers—or substantially above what the present estimates indicate.[4] Such an excess is not likely to appear in the current series but some tendency may recur.

A fourth significant factor is the extensive development of paid vacations. Summer declines in demand, seasonal shutdowns, and changes in models produced unemployment in earlier years. They still do today, but the growth in paid vacations provides a slack in the labor force without a corresponding amount of unemployment. A forced vacation is one thing; going fishing while on paid vacation is another. Some 4 million persons with jobs reported themselves on vacation in July 1951—3 million of them on paid vacations—while millions vacationed in other months.[5] Though no precise estimate can be made the data do indicate that vacations are ten times as common now as in 1900.[6]

[4] The 1937 average was 7.7 million and the 1938, 10.4. Since November was at the end of a recession beginning in June, one would expect the November figure to be somewhere between 7.7 and 10.4—perhaps about 9 million.

[5] Unpublished census data. Data for other recent years on vacations suggest similar results, but were not used because they include the effect of the Fourth of July holiday.

[6] This estimate is derived as follows. In the 1901 Cost of Living Survey of 24,402 families some 784 gave vacation as a cause of nonemployment, with an average duration of 2.61 weeks (*Eighteenth Annual Report of the Commissioner*

One would expect that the great improvements in public health and declines in mortality would lead to a decline in unemployment because of illness.[7] The data, however, suggest that the unemployment comparisons between the two dates are not much affected by this factor. Data for nonfarm male workers are available for several dates in the period. In 1900, an average of a week a year was lost in illness; in 1915-1917, about the same; and nationwide surveys in February 1949 and September 1950 again report a similar figure.[8] If valid, such similarity may indicate simply that the effects of improvements in general health have been offset by the decrease in the proportion of children and younger workers employed, the rise in the proportion of older workers, greater willingness to hire disabled workers, etc.

The various changes in the economic and social order which have accompanied changes in unemployment necessarily affect comparisons of unemployment over the years. But they do not vitiate the meaningfulness of such comparisons. For they represent a variation of the familiar index number problem and must be solved as the latter usually is by "looking the difficulty boldly in the face, and then passing on."

2. *Unemployment Estimates as a Measure of Economic Change*

How does the pattern of economic change indicated by the present unemployment series compare with that indicated by other series and other measures of economic change?

The comparative change in the present and other unemployment series is indicated in Table 2—where the series are presented—and in Table 3—where comparisons are made of year to year changes. The broad picture shows no startling changes in the way we are accustomed to considering this period: 1921 is still a year of major recession; 1908, 1914, 1924, 1927 are still years of recession. But the general magnitude of unemployment as measured by the present series never-

---

of Labor, Depts. of Commerce and Labor, 1903, pp. 287, 291). Had the same percentage of labor force time been spent in 1949 on vacations, we would have had an average number on vacation of 99,000. The actual figure was 1,361,000—or ten times as much (*Annual Report on the Labor Force, 1954*, Dept. of Commerce, Series P-59, Table A-11). A small number of persons reported "sickness and vacation" or "slack work and vacation," etc. in 1901.

[7] Present definitions include with the unemployed not all persons who are ill but those who were seeking work when they became temporarily ill.

[8] The 1900 estimate is based on data from the Cost of Living Survey. The 1915-1917 figures are based on Metropolitan Life Insurance Company surveys of policy holders in seven communities (cf. Ernest Bradford, *Industrial Unemployment*, Bureau of Labor Statistics, Bull. 310, 1922, p. 32, where other surveys in 1917, 1913, etc. report similar data).

The 1949-1950 data are reported by Theodore Woolsey (*Estimates of Disabling Illness Prevalent in the United States*, Public Health Monograph 4, 1952) and in unpublished census data.

TABLE 2

Selected Estimates of Unemployment, 1900-1930
(*number in thousands*)

Year	*Present Estimates* (1)	*NICB* (2)	*Douglas*[a] (3)	*Carson*[b] (4)	*Givens*[c] (5)	*Brookmire Economic Service* (6)	*Hart (per cent)*[d] (7)	*Weintrau[b] (per cent)*[e] (8)
1900	1,420	1,647	755					
1901	710	1,721	584					
1902	800	500	569				14.1	
1903	800	1,523	609				9.3	
1904	1,490	1,430	883				11.5	
1905	1,000	621	622				9.3	
1906	280	–143	577				5.5	
1907	600	756	695				6.0	
1908	2,960	2,296	1,654				14.8	
1909	1,870	719	925				8.6	
1910	2,150	553	774			0	6.5	
1911	2,290	1,571	1,025			496	10.8	
1912	1,960	920	775			0	9.6	
1913	1,680	1,018	936			267	9.3	
1914	3,110	2,214	1,899			2,027	15.8	
1915	3,840	2,355	1,822			1,479	16.0	
1916	1,920	187	774			112	7.1	
1917	1,920	–1,933	774			0	4.7	
1918	560	–3,099	719			58		
1919	950	–870	880			75		
1920	1,670	558	938	2,695	1,401	0		6
1921	5,010	4,754	2,913	6,085	4,270	3,653		25
1922	3,220	2,917	2,338	4,595	3,441	2,567		22
1923	1,380	749	1,010	2,880	1,532	0		11
1924	2,440	2,034	1,506	3,665	2,315	1,390		13
1925	1,800	817	1,120	2,855	1,775	387		13
1926	880	464	962	2,080	1,669	0		11
1927	1,890	1,620		2,380	2,055	1,466		12
1928	2,080	1,857		2,575				13
1929	1,550	429		1,910				10
1930	4,340	2,896		4,825				19

[a] Unemployment in manufacturing, transportation, building, and mining.
[b] Unemployment of wage and salary workers.
[c] Minimum unemployment.
[d] Unemployment as a percentage of nonagricultural workers.
[e] Unemployment as a percentage of labor supply.

Source: Column 2, *Economic Almanac, 1953-1954*, National Industrial Conference Boar[d], 1953, pp. 422-423; column 3, Paul Douglas, *Real Wages in the United States, 1890-192[6]*, Houghton Mifflin, 1930, p. 460; column 4, Daniel Carson, "Labor Supply and Employment," WPA, unpublished study, 1939, p. 357; column 5, Meredith Givens, in *Recent Econom[ic] Changes in the United States*, National Bureau of Economic Research, 1929, Vol. II, p. 47[8]; column 6, Brookmire Service, quoted in *ibid.*, p. 468; column 7, Hornell Hart, *Fluctuations [in] Employment in Cities of the United States, 1902 to 1917*, Trounstine Foundation, 1919, p. 4[?]; column 8, David Weintraub, *Technological Trends and National Policy*, National Resourc[es] Committee, 1937, p. 70.

theless differs significantly from that reported by earlier series. (So too does the ranking of individual years with respect to the severity of their unemployment.) Thus the present unemployment figures exceed the National Industrial Conference Board estimates for the three decades in the 1900-1930 period—by 8 per cent in the first decade, 555 per cent in the second (because the NICB shows negative unemployment for 1917-1919), and 35 per cent in the third.

Looking at the periods of rising unemployment, one may note that the present series shows larger gains during the three recessions before World War I but distinctly smaller rises during the nine recessions

TABLE 3

Changes in Unemployment, Selected Years, 1903-1954

(*number in thousands*)

	PRESENT ESTIMATES		NICB		DOUGLAS	
YEARS	*Number*	*Per Cent*	*Number*	*Per Cent*	*Number*	*Per Cent*
1903-1904	690	86	–97	–6	274	45
1907-1908	2,360	393	1,540	204	959	138
1913-1914	1,430	85	1,196	117	963	103
1919-1920	720	76	1,428	..	58	7
1920-1921	3,340	201	4,196	752	1,975	211
1923-1924	1,060	77	1,285	172	496	49
1926-1927	1,010	113	1,156	249		
1929-1930	2,790	180	2,467	575		
1930-1931	3,680	85	4,141	143		
1931-1932	4,040	50	4,348	162		
1932-1933	770	6	451	4		
1937-1938	2,690	35	3,393	53		
1945-1946	1,230	118				
1948-1949	1,331	65				
1953-1954	1,628	101				

Source: Based on Table 2.

after that war.[9] The difference in the postwar estimates reflects a difference in the sensitivity of the two series. The NICB *unemployment* series is necessarily more variable because the NICB *employment* series is more variable—and that for two reasons:

1. NICB estimates of employees in trade and service rest more largely on the use of manufacturing employment as an extrapolator—and manufacturing employment is one of the most sensitive employment series. The present estimates for these segments rest on more stable series.

2. NICB series for self-employed persons and domestic servants

[9] The present estimates show smaller percentage increases (8 instances) and smaller absolute increases (7 instances) in unemployment during these 9 postwar recessions.

generally are estimated to fluctuate with the number of employees in those groups. Present procedures rest on the assumption—made in the light of changes reported from population census to census, and data on annual changes since 1930—that the self-employment series is far less sensitive than that for employees.

Douglas' estimates, being limited to unemployment in four major industry groups, will naturally show smaller absolute changes in unemployment. With smaller absolute bases they can and do show much greater variations in percentage change.

A second point may be made. Not only is the present series generally less volatile, but the order of depression years in terms of severity is somewhat different. Thus the present estimates indicate the 1937-1938 recession to have been about as severe as 1929-1930—rather than substantially more severe, as the NICB data indicate. Also they indicate that the 1920-1921 rise in unemployment was clearly less than the 1930-1931 rise—rather than slightly more.

In addition to these general conclusions one may consider three specific examples of difference: 1920-1921, 1916-1917, and 1900-1901.

One of the most significant differences between the year-to-year trends shown by the NICB series and the present estimates is that for 1920-1921, when the NICB shows unemployment rising by 856,000 more than the present estimates do.

1. The difference arises chiefly because the NICB estimates a greater decline in trade and service employment to have occurred than the present series does.

2. The NICB decline for these groups is considerably larger than that indicated in a special survey conducted during 1923 for the National Bureau of Economic Research by Willford I. King.

The present estimates show a mild gain, reflecting the fact that the constant dollar volume of goods available for distribution in 1921 was about the same as in 1920.[10] The NICB figures, on the other hand, reflect the sharp drop in current dollar sales.[11] It is assumed that trade employment trends should more closely parallel trends in the real volume of goods than money sales.

The present estimates show a rise in domestic service and self-

[10] The volume data used for the present estimates were those of William Howard Shaw, *Value of Commodity Output since 1869*, National Bureau of Economic Research, 1947.

[11] The NICB used "the appropriate NY Federal Reserve Bank Index of distribution to extrapolate trade employment." The New York Bank index as reported by Norris Johnson in "New Indexes of Production and Trade" (*Journal of the American Statistical Association*, June 1938) is composed of less-than-carload lot carloadings data, department store sales, chain grocery sales, other chain sales, mail order sales, etc.

employment in service—both substantial groups in the service total. The NICB figures were derived from an estimating series dominated by manufacturing employment, and the latter fell by 25 per cent in this period.[12] Experience in the past quarter century, when we have reasonably reliable direct employment measures, indicates that total service employment in this category (and particularly self-employment) does not respond markedly to short-run cycle fluctuations, and shows little parallelism with the change in manufacturing employment.

For the 1920-1921 change in trade and service employment, and indeed in employment as a whole, one can refer to the estimates secured by W. I. King from direct employer reports.[13] While these data have limitations, they represent direct reports from a surprisingly large sample of employers. King's data indicate changes in the trade and service groups which are much more modest than the NICB data. His estimate of total employment shows a 1920-1921 drop of 3.2 million, almost equal to the present estimate of 3.3 million for the 1920-1921 rise in unemployment. (It is unlikely that three-quarters of a million additional workers entered the labor market during this period above and beyond the normal labor force growth—as would be necessary to make the NICB unemployment change consistent with King's employment change.)

For 1916-1917 NICB shows a far sharper fall in unemployment than the present estimates, and one which would a priori seem more likely in the light of the growth of war production. The difference arises chiefly because the NICB data for manufacturing employment (based on "a sample comprising 64 per cent of the total manufacturing employment in 1919") rose by 1.2 million[14]—while the present estimates report little gain since the deflated volume of manufacturing production as reported in Shaw's data shows only a small rise.[15] Douglas' direct employment series for manufacturing (based on BLS and New

[12] NICB and present figures for service components other than domestic and personal would not differ greatly in the amount of change. It is the domestic and personal group which would account for differences in change.

[13] In *Business Cycles and Unemployment*, National Bureau of Economic Research, 1923, p. 88.

[14] Because the NICB used manufacturing employment in estimating trade employment—and via trade, for service employment—the estimate for manufacturing becomes basic in determining this change. For a simple comparison between present and NICB estimates one should also note NICB includes the armed forces under the service total.

[15] Shaw shows a mild rise for total finished goods, and a drop in manufactured food, clothing, furniture, floor coverings, and miscellaneous house furnishings (Shaw, *op.cit.*, pp. 70, 72, 73). These latter data are used in the present procedure to estimate the trend for employment in trade and such service categories as dressmakers, etc.

York State) shows a gain of 537,000, much closer to the present 200,000 than to the NICB 1.2 million.[16]

As a final comparison one may take the 1900-1901 change. Here the present estimates show a marked decline in unemployment while the NICB figures actually rise slightly. The difference arises because of estimated differences in the trend of trade and service. The NICB series uses the combined movement of agricultural, mining, and manufacturing employment. The very substantial stability in agricultural employment over many decades and the lack of change in manufacturing employment during this year amounts to positing no change in the trade and service group.[17] The present series, on the other hand, reports a growth in employment assumed as resulting from (1) an increase of roughly 12 per cent in the volume of finished commodities (except producer durables) to be handled through the distribution system, and (2) the long-term upward trend of self-employment in these industries.

How do variations in unemployment as measured by the present estimates relate to variations in other measures of economic change? The question is as difficult to answer as it is interesting. The reason for the difficulty is simple. The present estimates were developed on the premise that the best possible employment and unemployment estimates were desired. This meant that the soundest procedure was to take advantage of the major advances in our knowledge of this period which are associated with the names of Shaw, Fabricant, Kuznets, and others who have laboriously developed basic production series for the National Bureau. Hence while a vast variety of other sources were used, together with quite independent data from censuses of prisons, reports of the Collector of Internal Revenue, lists of securities dealers, etc., substantial reliance was placed on these studies which worked the basic census of manufactures data into consistent detailed series. Similarly the employment estimates for construction rest on detailed estimates of deflated activity developed for the purpose at hand. Year-to-year changes in unemployment will closely reflect changes in employment. Individual employment series for key industries will in turn tend to reflect changes in production because of the method of estimate. However the frequency of bench-mark counts—quinquennial censuses of

[16] Paul Douglas, *Real Wages in the United States, 1890-1926*, Houghton Mifflin, 1930, p. 439. Douglas' sample covers some 15 per cent of manufacturing employment in 1914 and Berridge's combination of state data covered not much more as of 1914 or 1919. No information appears to be available concerning the sample used for the NICB estimates.

[17] Douglas shows a change similar to NICB—but since his data do not attempt to reflect trends in trade and service they are not inconsistent with present estimates.

manufacturing before the war and biennial after it—means fairly frequent checks on the combined productivity and hours factor interpolated between these dates. Hence even for these series changes from one bench-mark year to the next are independent of the production data.

While the relationship to production series therefore presents problems, the relationship to the national income estimates is less troublesome. This is because the Kuznets estimates that were used for 1919-1929 are derived chiefly by totaling the factor shares. Interest, rent, profits—these are certainly independent of the data used for the present estimates. And payrolls, the largest single component, are derived in most instances by applying ratios of pay to gross income, sales, or total outlays of the industry concerned. While for manufacturing, for example, that payroll data come from the same source, indeed the same reports, as do the employment data, so that there is likely to be a built-in consistency, the estimating process does not rest on the use of payroll estimates. For the 1930-1940 period the interrelationship of estimates is far less: beginning with 1936, reliance on the payroll totals from the independent body of tax reports filed under the Social Security system achieves a satisfactory degree of independence. For the 1940-1952 period the estimates are essentially independent in provenance. Deflated income data, however, are not available. Data on changes in deflated product were therefore used. The extremely close similarity between year-to-year changes in undeflated income and product justified such a step.[18]

With these qualifications one may review the pattern shown in Chart 1, where year-to-year changes in unemployment are matched against corresponding changes in deflated Gross National Product.[19] The relationship indicated is remarkably close. On the one hand we have estimates derived for the 1920-1940 period as a residual between labor force and employment totals. As such they are subject to the net resultant of errors in each series, with differences then calculated from these residuals. For the 1940-1952 period the series rests on reports from a continuously changing sample, consisting primarily of housewives reporting on the employment status of members of their family. On the other hand, the GNP totals represent the sum of a mass of component estimates developed from a hundred different sources, then deflated by a host of price data reported primarily by a vast sample

[18] The trend in employment is used in developing the trend in payrolls for domestic service but aside from this limited group there is nothing of note.

[19] Unemployment: present estimates. GNP: 1919-1929 from Simon Kuznets, *National Product since 1869*, National Bureau of Economic Research, 1946, p. 52, GNP wartime concept. GNP: 1930-1954, *National Income Supplement, 1954*, to, and July 1955 issue of, *Survey of Current Business*, Dept. of Commerce.

CHART 1

Changes in Unemployment and Deflated Gross National Product, 1920-1954

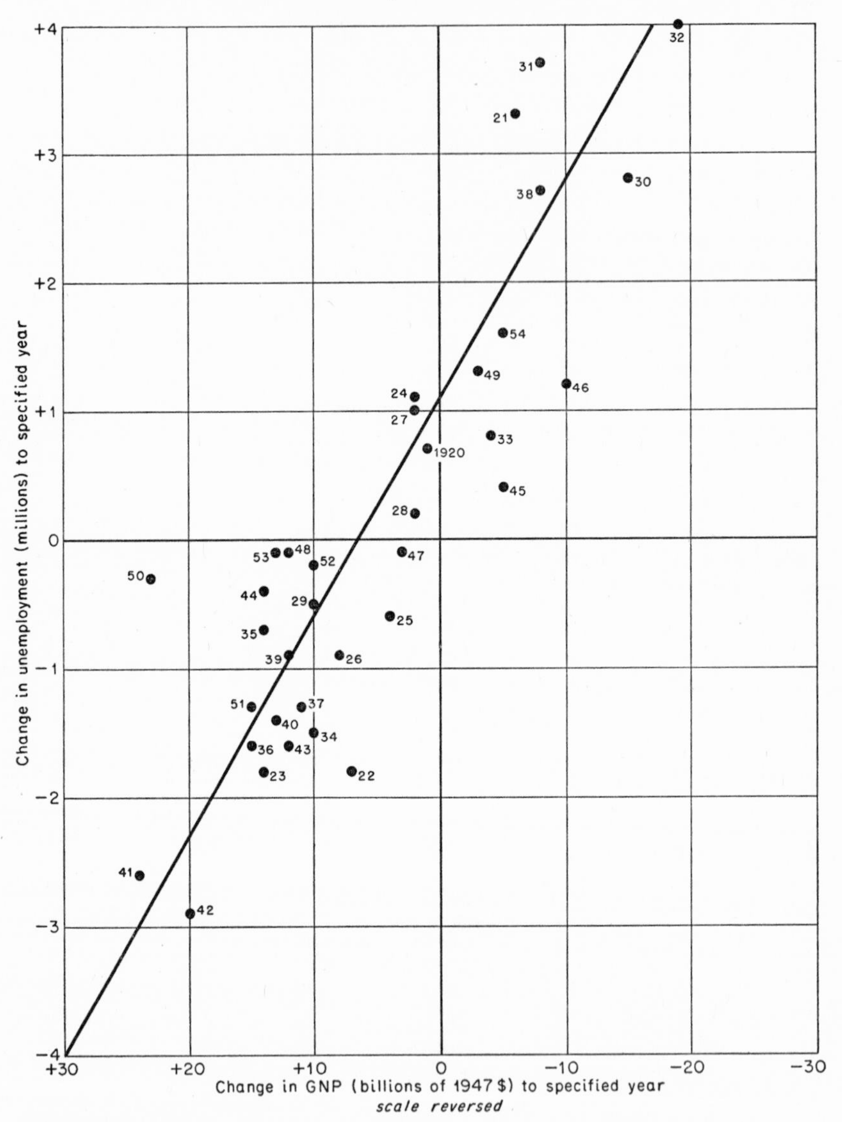

Note: GNP excludes military pay.

of retailers. Reporting errors of necessity exist in the production, the margin and the price data, while conceptual differences separate some of the data (particularly the price data) from those which are required for consistent estimating.

The relationship is nevertheless extremely close. The fact that it is so reflects three factors.

1. Year-to-year changes in unemployment tend to be mirror images of changes in employment. To judge from the 1940-1952 data the stability in the labor force totals from year to year is very great.[20] Despite sharp changes in worker rates for females and particular age groups the fact that most adult males are in the labor force year in and year out gives a considerable stability to the labor force totals.

2. Year-to-year changes in the employment estimates, though derived from a broad variety of sources, are dominated by variations in manufacturing employment (cf. Chart 2). Of necessity annual changes in employment are sensibly linked to changes in payrolls, in sales, and —with some stability in the distributive margin estimate—in final product values.

3. The GNP estimates were adjusted to exclude changes in military pay—an item which pretty well accounts for most of the changes in gross government product during the war years. This was done because variations in military payrolls had little current impact on the domestic productive economy.[21]

The sharp exceptions to this relationship are in many respects as interesting as the relationship itself. Perhaps the most striking are 1941, 1945, 1946, and 1950, all four associated with sharp changes in the mixture of peace and war characterizing our times. In 1941 and 1950 we became actively involved in wars—with sharp rises in GNP. An unemployment decline of nearly 5 million in each of these years (rather than 2.6 and 0.3) would have been required for these years to fit the regression line shown on the chart—a change whose magnitude is probably out of the question in a free labor market.[22]

In 1945 and 1946, on the other hand, there were drastic declines in government purchases, in production, and in manufacturing employment, with nothing like concomitant rises in unemployment. There were equally drastic changes in purchases during the war years, associated, however, with nothing like such a discrepancy. The explanation probably lies in our present measurement of unemployment. If we counted those receiving unemployment compensation (for total unemployment) as *per se* unemployed, then 1945 and 1946 would be

[20] Because the estimates before 1940 are interpolations they cast no direct light on this point.

[21] Data from *National Income Supplement, 1954*. Variations in government purchases, including those of food and clothing for the armed forces, are, of course, not excluded by this procedure.

[22] Moreover in 1950 negative unemployment would have been produced. This suggests that the function might include other variables—e.g. second differences in GNP.

CHART 2

Changes in Unemployment and Manufacturing Employment, 1920-1954

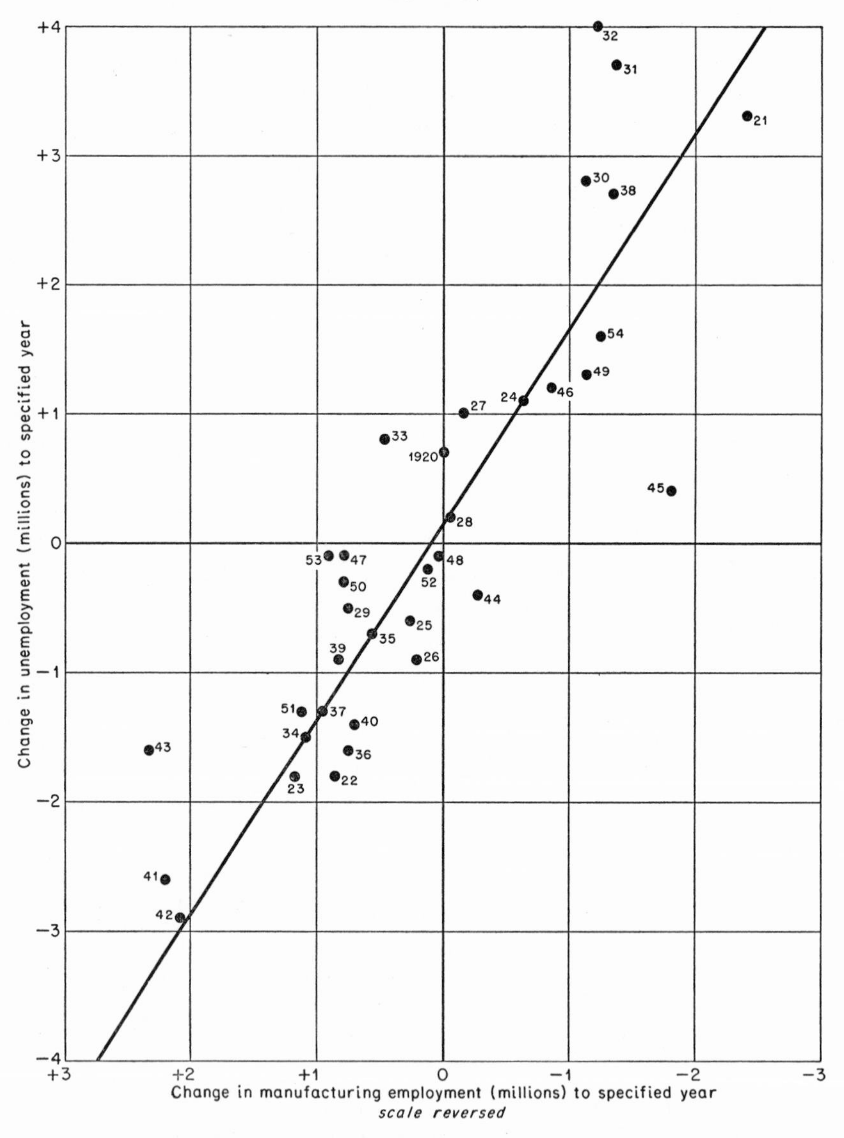

in line.[23] And in fact present procedures do define such receipt as unemployment but the information is not automatically sought—par-

[23] The desirability of doing so has, of course, nothing to do with the present discussion. The topic is discussed by the writer in *The Review of Economics and Statistics*, November 1954.

ticularly when, as after the war, many persons indicated that they were not in the labor force even though they might have been drawing unemployment compensation. Regardless of all this, the fact is that for the first time in the record a very substantial drop in employment, in GNP, in manufacturing employment did not produce anything like a proportionate rise in unemployment. The disemployed simply left the labor force or were absorbed by the boom on construction, trade, and other lines starved for help during the war.

How, it may be asked, do the variations in unemployment correspond with variations in business conditions as measured not by a single aggregate measure such as GNP but by a broad summary of measures not merely of products but prices, financial transactions, etc., which lie behind the NBER reference cycles? Given the array of data provided by Burns and Mitchell, we are able to determine for each year during the period how many months of that year were characterized by an expansion of economic activity, and how many, by contraction. In the table below, the years are classified into two groups—namely, those in which the National Bureau chronology reports more months of cyclical expansion than decline, and vice versa.[24] Each of these is then divided between those in which the percentage of the labor force employed, as measured by the current series, rose or fell.

YEARS IN WHICH NBER REPORTED MORE MONTHS OF:	YEARS IN WHICH PERCENTAGE OF LABOR FORCE EMPLOYED:			
	Rose		*Declined*	
Expansion than decline	1901	1922	1902	
	1905	1925	1908	
	1906	1926	1919	
	1909	1934	1924	
	1912	1935	1928	
	1915	1936	1933	
	1916	1939	1938	
	1918	1940		
Decline than expansion	1903		1904	1921
	1913		1907	1927
	1923		1910	1930
	1929		1911	1931
	1937		1914	1932
			1920	

Eleven years of all those in the period do not fall into the main diagonal. Of these the unemployment change for three (1902, 1903, and 1928) is so small as to be well within the margin of error.

[24] Arthur F. Burns and Wesley C. Mitchell, *Measuring Business Cycles*, National Bureau of Economic Research, 1946, Appendix A.

Concentrating on years with eight months or more in expansion, or contraction, gives us the following array:

YEARS WITH EIGHT MONTHS (OR MORE):	YEARS IN WHICH PERCENTAGE OF LABOR FORCE EMPLOYED:			
	Rose		*Declined*	
Expansion	1901	1925	1919	
	1905	1926	1928	
	1906	1934	1933	
	1909	1935		
	1912	1936		
	1915	1939		
	1916	1940		
	1922			
Decline	1903		1910	1927
	1913		1911	1930
			1914	1931
			1920	1932
			1921	

For 1919, the unemployment measure reflects the net impact of generally rising employment offset by a substantial rise in the civilian labor force attendant upon the return of the A.E.F. from France. Even a minor change in the 1903 figures—less than the likely margin of error—could change the direction of unemployment for those years. For the two other years, in which the mass of cycle indicators point to an economic change in one direction while the unemployment series move in the opposite direction, no single explanation is possible. It will, however, be recognized that relatively long series tend to conform less well to the cyclical indexes than short series, and for the pre-World War I years, the dating may not be finally established.[25]

3. Unemployment Estimates as a Measure of the Level of Unemployed Manpower

While one may concentrate chiefly on changes in unemployment for analysis, the administrator (and citizen) generally has an equal or greater interest in the level of unemployment. What does the record indicate as to the level of unemployment over the past? The number of years in the 1900-1954 period in which the percentage of the labor force unemployed was under 2 per cent, 2-2.9 per cent, etc., is as follows:

[25] Wesley Mitchell, *What Happens During Business Cycles,* National Bureau of Economic Research, 1951, p. 281. There must be few bits of testimony to inherent nobility of scholarship that equal Mitchell's labeling of the reference dates, after more than a quarter century of work, as "tentative."

Per Cent	*Number of Years*
Under 2	7
2-2.9	6
3-3.9	7
4-4.9	9
5-5.9	8
6-7.9	2
8-9.9	5
10-11.9	1
12-13.9	0
14-15.9	3
16 and over	7

The median year falls in the 4-4.9 per cent unemployment group, as does the mode.

These estimates for the years prior to 1940 are intended to measure the number of persons who are totally unemployed, having no work at all. For the 1930's this concept, however, does include one large group of persons who had both work and income from work—those on emergency work. In the United States we are concerned with measuring lack of regular work and do not minimize the total by excluding persons with made work or emergency jobs. This contrasts sharply, for example, with the German practice during the 1930's when persons in the labor force camps were classed as employed, and Soviet practice which includes employment in labor camps, if it includes it at all, as employment.

While total unemployment constitutes a useful measure of the extent to which our manpower is not fully utilized, it is not a complete measure and should not be used as such. Perhaps the most important element that is excluded is partial unemployment—the involuntary idleness during split weeks or short work days. Various pre-depression surveys showed from 10 to 15 per cent of urban wage earners working part time—most of them presumably desirous of full time work.[26] With the onset of the depression of the 1930's, however, the percentage increased abruptly. The immediate increase appeared to be greater than

[26] In 1915 an estimated 15 per cent of urban wage earners were underemployed (see Paul Brissenden, "Underemployment," *Business Cycles and Unemployment*, as cited, p. 68). In 1919 a survey of manufacturing industries reported 11 per cent of full time lost in idle hours (see Bradford, *op.cit.*, p. 28). In April 1930 the Census reported about 10 per cent of gainful workers on part time (*Census of Unemployment, 1930*, Vol. II, pp. 10, 357). King's data for 1921 gives a figure of about 8 per cent for factory workers in 1921 (*Business Cycles and Unemployment*, as cited, p. 95).

that in 1921. As one example, unemployment in Detroit about doubled from the census in the spring of 1930 to the January 1931 special unemployment census but part time employment increased more than 400 per cent.[27] By March 1932, according to a comprehensive survey of more than 6,000 companies with over 3 million employees, sponsored by the President's Organization on Unemployment Relief, 63 per cent of all employed manufacturing workers were on part time work.[28] No matter how this enormous percentage must be qualified, it is clear that it indicated a substantial quantity of underemployment among those with jobs. As the depression began to lift, the proportion on part-time declined. In November 1937 the proportion in manufacturing on part-time employment was about 20 per cent—or substantially down from the 63 per cent in early 1932.[29] By the postwar period the proportion was further reduced. The proportion of all persons in the labor force working part time in early 1948 was about 8 per cent—and only rose to 12 per cent near the peak of the 1949 recession.[30]

In summary, therefore, partial unemployment may have run to something like 10 per cent for most years, while during the depth of the depression something like half of all factory workers with jobs were on part-time work.

Employment is only one dimension of the economic welfare problem. A second is the number of hours worked, or partial employment. Other dimensions of this problem are the amount of income received and the skills utilized. The general problem of underemployment, however, is still more complex and has received separate discussion in this volume. It will therefore be sufficient here to emphasize that estimates of total unemployment do not include any direct allowance for this factor. The tremendous drop in the number of farmers and retail store keepers from 1940 to 1943 is one indication of the possible

[27] *Census of Unemployment, 1930*, Vol. II, pp. 139, 358, 482, 600.

[28] William J. Barrett, "Extent and Methods of Spreading Work," *Monthly Labor Review*, September 1932, p. 490. These companies reported a decline in employment from 1929 to March 1932 of 26.6 per cent. The decline for all manufacturing companies was about 32 per cent.

[29] The number partly unemployed as of November 1937 is estimated in the *Census of Partial Employment, Unemployment, and Occupations*, Vol. IV, *Final Report on Total and Partial Unemployment, 1937*, p. 20. Data from p. 125 of the same volume give a distribution by industry for the partly employed registrants. It was assumed that the 34 per cent proportion of manufacturing employees in this registrant group (combining manufacturing industry components shown) could be applied to the p. 20 survey total. The resultant figure was then related to the current (i.e. 1954) BLS estimate for 1937 manufacturing employment, after the latter had been adjusted to November levels by earlier BLS monthly indices.

[30] These data refer to all part-time work—only part of which, of course, was involuntary part-time work. Data from special census surveys for March 1948 and May and August 1949 suggest that the increase represented involuntary part-time work.

magnitude of such underemployment—even after allowing for the postwar return to higher levels in trade.

With this basic qualification in mind it may be appropriate to indicate how closely we came to achieving full employment over the past half century. Defining full employment is something like defining small business, low income, monopoly profit, or the just price. Definitions tend to be either imprecise or void of empirical reference. But if we think of the policy uses of the data we can define full employment in the light of what we have achieved in the past. Let us arbitrarily define "workable full employment"—to adapt an admirable phrase of J. M. Clark's—as the level achieved at least one year in four during the past half century. If we do so the percentage of the civilian labor force totally unemployed at full employment would be less than 3 per cent. (The percentage would have to be raised if our reference period were shorter, for it was achieved twice as frequently in the 1900-1925 period as in the 1926-1952.)[31] It has been asserted, however, that "full employment at high wages in a private enterprise economy is undesirable and self-destroying."[32] We may therefore wish to set a figure based on the assumption that full employment is less common. If we set the goal at that which prevailed in 10 per cent of the years, the ratio would run to 2 per cent or less. But one may take a less pessimistic approach. High level employment has characterized the performance of the American economy in the past half century. While even a level of 5 per cent unemployed would hardly be considered to present a major economic policy problem, such a level has been achieved in more than half this period. History does not indicate that our economy requires a substantial or continued high level of unemployment to operate effectively and without marked price rises.

4. *Methods by Which the Present Series Was Estimated*

The unemployment series for 1900-1930 was estimated by making direct bench-mark estimates of unemployment in 1900, 1910, and 1930, using the population census data on unemployment in those years, and interpolating intercensally by a provisional unemployment series. The provisional series was obtained by estimating civilian labor force and employment for the half century and deducting one series from the other.

BENCH-MARK ESTIMATES

1900. The estimate of unemployment in 1900 was based on data

[31] If, further, one excludes the war years, 3 per cent or less was achieved only twice in the latter period as against 9 times in the earlier.

[32] R. I. Nowell in *Journal of Farm Economics*, February 1947, p. 143.

collected in two enumerations. One was the 1900 Census of Population, which secured information on nonemployment during the year preceding the taking of the census. The second was an extensive survey made by the Commissioner of Labor of family income and expenditures that secured detailed information for about 25,000 families on cause and duration of unemployment during 1900-1901.

The starting point is the distribution of unemployment as shown in the 1900 Census of Population.[33] From the total shown there, the number of teachers, self-employed in agriculture, and others in occupations characteristically dominated by self-employment were excluded—to exclude periods of "unemployment" that were really periods not in the labor force.[34]

The distribution of male nonfarm employees by duration of unemployment derived in this fashion was adjusted to take account of the information provided by the 1901 Cost of Living Survey.[35] That survey reported for male heads of urban families in the wage-earner group the level and duration of unemployment by cause of unemployment.[36] Two adjustments were made on the basis of these data. First, an estimate was derived of the per cent of persons who should be excluded from each duration group because the causes of their idleness—e.g. no work wanted, drunkenness, old age, strike, vacation—would not currently be considered as justifying the classification of unemployment.[37] Secondly, it was assumed that the higher level of unemployment shown in the cost of living survey, based as it was on a detailed reckoning of the families' employment, income, and expenditure experience over the year, was likely to be more precise than the necessarily brief enumeration in a survey made only every ten years. The proportion unemployed shown in this survey was therefore first adjusted to allow for unemployment of nonfarm workers not covered by the survey—primarily those not heads of families[38] and then the differences between that propor-

[33] *Occupations*, Tables 1, 25.

[34] Such occupations include dentists, lawyers, boarding-house keepers, saloon keepers, etc.

[35] *Eighteenth Annual Report of the Commissioner of Labor, 1903.*

[36] *Ibid.*, pp. 290-291.

[37] The sickness and accident groups were also excluded on the assumption that most persons reporting sickness should be classed as not in the labor force. On the other hand, those for whom any of these causes was reported in combination with another cause were included. This was done because current procedures undoubtedly include some workers as unemployed who report these causes, particularly those who had been seeking work when they became temporarily ill.

[38] The ratio of employment rates among nonfarm gainful workers who were and were not family heads was estimated on the basis of 1930 relationships. These indicated the rate for singles was one-third greater (*Census of Population, 1930*, Vol. II, p. 848 and *Census of Unemployment, 1930*, Vol. II, p. 336). Adjustment for the relatively small portion of all nonfarm employees who were not within the

tion and the rate indicated by the census was used to adjust the census total unemployment figure upward. The adjustment was distributed into the various duration groups in the same way as the reported duration data of the cost of living survey indicate, which in fact implies that three-quarters of census omissions were in the lowest duration group—a reasonable implication since Census Bureau enumerators were likely to miss less of the hard core unemployment.

The average duration of unemployment in each duration group was computed from the very detailed interval data in the cost of living survey. Multiplying the number in each group by average duration and dividing by fifty to get estimated full-time unemployment gives a bench-mark figure for male nonfarm workers in 1900.

For female workers the census data were reduced to exclude data for teachers, agricultural pursuits, and other occupations, multiplied by average duration data (the same average within each duration group was used as above) and then converted to full time unemployment.

For male farm laborers the reported census total included unemployment of family workers. An estimate for wage earners alone was made as follows: In 1910, the unemployment percentage for male laborers not elsewhere specified building and hand trades was 34.8 compared to 11.5 for farm wage-earner laborers. The ratio of one to the other was applied to the laborer (domestic and personal service) rate of 44.3 in 1900 to give an estimate of 14.7 for male farm laborers (wage earners). (A similar procedure was used for females.) These were then distributed by duration as reported farm laborers.

1910. Although the census of 1910 secured data on unemployment of wage earners in the previous year, these data were not tabulated until 1948.

The 1910 data an unemployment are in the form of distributions for unemployed wage earners sixteen years and over by duration of unemployment.[39] By applying the distribution to the total for wage earners sixteen years and over, and deducting estimates made similarly for teachers and home farm laborers (wage earners) one secures a preliminary estimate for the number of unemployed wage earners by duration group. The resultant distribution was reduced to exclude unemployment which would not be counted by current definitions—using the same proportions within each group as indicated in the 1901 Cost of Living Survey—multiplying by the same average duration figures, within each group, as used for 1900 and computing man-years

scope of the survey was not attempted; it would make little difference in the results.

[39] These data were reproduced by the Census Bureau in a set of lithoprinted sheets, in 1948.

of unemployment. The resultant total was adjusted upward for under-enumeration.

This adjustment was derived as follows: A large scale survey on the employment and income of wage earners in selected industries in 1910 was conducted by the Immigration Commission. The survey provided data on duration of employment for 220,000 male wage earners (aged eighteen and over) in a broad range of industries.[40] Because the Commission was concerned with the foreign born the sample overrepresented foreign-born workers and those in certain industries. The separate distributions—e.g. males, native born of native father; white, employed in the agricultural implements industry; foreign born in bituminous coal mining, etc.—were therefore reweighted in accordance with the census gainful worker totals[41] to derive distributions for each industry of the male employees by employment duration. The resultant distributions, while covering all major mining and manufacturing industries (coal, cotton goods, furniture, meat packing, etc.) could not in themselves be taken as an adequate sample for a direct estimate of employment levels. They constitute, however, a very large sample with which to adjust the reported census unemployment data for the same industries. The ratio of adjusted to unadjusted totals for the sum of these industries was then used to adjust the grand total census figures estimated above.[42] There are two reasons for using the Immigration Commission survey to adjust the census reports. First, a detailed inquiry into family economic status was being made, with opportunity for a much more careful consideration of employment status during the previous year than would normally occur during the brief census interview. Second, the instructions in the Immigration Survey specifically required an explanation of lost time or low earnings, presumably leading to a more careful estimation of employment duration than the more general census interview where short duration figures would not be questioned.[43] The result of these differing pro-

[40] *Reports*, Immigration Commission, Vol. 23, 1911, Table 27.

[41] *Census of Population, 1910*, Vol. IV, Table VI.

[42] One example may be given. The Immigration Commission data indicate an average duration of employment in iron and steel manufacturing of 9.2 months for native white males of native parentage, 8.5 for native whites of foreign parentage, 7.9 for foreign born, and 10.8 for Negro. Weighting these by the Census gainful worker distributions gives an estimate of 8.5 for the industry—or 3.5 months unemployed. The census data for males in iron and steel indicate 9.1 weeks of unemployment for laborers and 8.4 for semi-skilled workers or, a weighted average of 9.0 weeks. Since these data relate to wage earners in mining and manufacturing in 1910, it is reasonably safe to equate periods of nonemployment with periods of unemployment, vacations being infrequent and periods of sickness being deducted in the earlier adjustment.

[43] *Reports*, Immigration Commission, Vol. 2, 1911, p. 703.

cedures is apparent in the data. Thus the census report shows 82-86 per cent of male employees in cotton goods with no unemployment in the previous year, whereas the Immigration Commission data show 63 per cent.[44] For coal mining the census shows 32 per cent of the operatives with a full year's employment while the Immigration Commission shows 15 per cent—a figure much more consistent with data on mine activity.[45] To the adjusted census data for unemployment among wage earners was added an allowance for unemployment among those classified as self-employed on the census day but who had periods in the labor force year during which they were seeking work as employees. The sum of the two figures then gives the 1910 unemployment bench mark.[46]

1918. Because of the unreasonable results which derive from a residual estimate for the war years, it is necessary to posit directly a level of unemployment in the peak war year of 1918. This was done by analogy from our actual experience during World War II, allowing for the generally lower level of unemployment in the years before World War I. The ratio of unemployment to nonfarm employees in 1943-1945 was as follows:

Year	*Per Cent*
1943	2.1
1944	1.6
1945	2.2

Since there was a more tightly organized labor market and production system in World War II, the peak war year, 1944, was excluded, and the 1943 and 1945 percentages were averaged to derive the 1918 estimate. Previous estimates arbitrarily posit an unemployment level for 1920.[47] It was felt preferable, however, not to estimate directly a

[44] Census data are not available for the industry but are shown for laborers, beamers, bobbin boys, spinners, and other occupations in cotton goods.

[45] *Mineral Resources of the U.S., 1911*, Geological Survey, Part 2, p. 45, 52. These data suggest the number of active days per year ran to about 200, roughly 29 days being lost in strikes in 1909.

[46] This procedure implicitly assumes the same unemployment rate among the wage earners as the self-employed. Such an assumption is consistent with census practice in 1890 and 1910, and allows for the fact that not only are some self-employed indistinguishable from wage earners—e.g. carpenters—but that some bona fide self-employed were wage earners for some period in the census year. For example, the unemployment rate for seamstresses and dressmakers was about the same in 1890 and 1910. If there were no unemployment among the self-employed in 1910, then the implicit rate of unemployment for wage earners was nearly double that for 1890—hardly a likely state of affairs.

[47] For example, the NICB assumed that the percentage unemployed by industry

level for a year of such mixed business activity as 1920 (with an unknown aftermath of the war affecting the level) but instead to estimate the level for 1918, a year of undoubtedly peak employment, using analogous data from World War II.[48]

Intercensal Estimates. Intercensal estimates were derived by interpolating between the unemployment figures for 1900, 1910, 1918, and 1929 by a preliminary unemployment series. That series was estimated by deducting employment from the labor force in each year. The derivation of the employment and labor force series was done in great detail and has been described elsewhere.[49]

They may, however, be briefly summarized. Independent employment series were developed for the key components of every major industry group. These series in turn were developed from movement series adjusted to census and other bench-mark dates whenever available. For manufacturing employees quinquennial census bench marks were available, with interpolation for 1899-1909 by an index of employment in selected states accounting for half of all manufacturing employees as of 1904, with interpolation between 1909 and 1914, and between 1914 and 1919 by Shaw's constant dollar data on the output of finished goods (except nonmanufactured foods) and construction materials. For 1919-1929 the Fabricant series, which utilizes biennial census data and Bureau of Labor Statistics series for interpolation, was used with the 1920-1921 change checked against a special field canvass made by Willford King. The self-employed count for census years was taken from the census of manufactures, with adjustments in 1904 and 1909 for omissions and changes in census enumeration practices, and for 1921-1929 for the census exclusion of small firms. For intercensal years estimates were derived from curves fitted to census dates, except that 1920 was assumed at the 1919 level.

Construction employees prior to 1920 were estimated by a regression against construction materials production (adjusted for inventory fluctuations in certain years) based on the relationship between the two series in the 1920-1940 period. For 1920-1929 estimates of contract activity were derived from estimates of total construction activity, for

group in 1920 could be interpolated between the percentages for 1900 and 1930 implicit in Population Census data.

[48] Douglas assumed a 3.5 per cent figure for 6 years, including 1918, and a slightly higher figure for 3 other years (Douglas, *op.cit.*, pp. 442-443), deriving his estimate by reducing somewhat the unemployment percentage for trade union members in Massachusetts manufacturing and transportation industries in April-June 1918.

[49] A summary of the preliminary results was presented at the 1950 Annual Meeting of the American Statistical Association. The methods used for 1930-1940 estimates were described briefly by the writer in the *Monthly Labor Review* for July 1948. It is hoped that a fuller description will be published at a later date.

major segments, and the contract series was then deflated by a specially developed series. This series was composed of two parts. One part consisted of materials prices (computed as the geometric mean of a fixed weighted series developed for this purpose and the regular variable weighted series). The other part consisted of average earnings (based on union data reweighted and adjusted to represent the movement of earnings of all employees. The two series were then combined, weighting them by a changing set of ratios of (1) payroll to (2) payroll plus materials costs, and the combined series was then divided by an index of average hours. Similar procedures were used to develop a labor requirements series for the 1929-1940 period which was used for interpolation between estimates for 1929, 1935, and 1939. Self-employed totals were extrapolated by this series.

For utilities a wide variety of data were used. Quinquennial census data for electric light and power, and for gas (biennial for gas during the 1920's) were interpolated from a growth curve to 1917, with data for a sample of private plants for later years. For manufactured gas, quinquennial and biennial census data were available, with interpolations by a regression against an output series. For telegraph employment Interstate Commerce Commission reports for 1926-1929, data supplied by Western Union for 1917-1926, and census of electrical industry data for earlier years were used. Separate estimates were made for other detailed utility and transport employment, using state data, tonnage of documented steam and motor vessels, etc.

For finance Comptroller of the Currency data for 1910, 1916, 1918, 1936, and 1940 make it possible to estimate employment per bank, which, when applied against the Comptroller's series for number of banks gives an extrapolating series for carrying back the BLS 1929 total.

A similar procedure was used for building and loan associations (employees per association times number of associations) and for brokers. Decennial counts of insurance employees and self-employed persons were interpolated by the number of life insurance policies, and decennial data for real estate brokers by the number of available nonfarm housing units.

For trade, decennial estimates of employees in each major line of business were derived by multiplying the number of dealers by the number of employees per dealer, with interpolation of the number of employees in each line by the relevant series for value of finished commodities destined for domestic consumption. For dealers separate estimates were similarly made, with saloon keepers and other groups separately estimated.

For service, separate estimates were made for physicians (salaried physicians estimated for census dates, interpolated by the ratio to hospital beds; self-employed physicians by the American Medical Association directory counts after the latter had been adjusted for various incomparabilities); dentists (interpolating decennial counts by adding graduations and deducting deaths in the profession); lawyers (decennial counts, interpolated by listings in Martindale's *American Law Directory*); nurses (adjusted census data for trained nurses interpolated by number of nursing graduates; adjusted census data for untrained nurses interpolated by the number of nonwhite births for 1920-1930 and total births for 1910-1920); hospitals (employment per hospital bed in 1900, 1910, 1923, and 1935 interpolated and applied to the number of hospital beds); hotels (decennial counts of proprietors interpolated linearly for 1900-1920, by number of hotels for 1920-1930; census counts of wage earners interpolated 1920-1930 by number of occupied hotel rooms, 1900-1920 by linear interpolation); amusement (employees per theatre, and employees per billiard parlor and bowling alley times estimated numbers of each; musicians by inventory of musical instruments); laundry, cleaning, etc. (quinquennial census counts interpolated by employment in trade using the close regression of one series against the other for seven years from 1900 to 1939); other service (half a dozen series, with decennial counts interpolated linearly in some components, by trade employment in others, subject to other adjustments); domestic service (detailed adjusted decennial census data directly interpolated, with the 1910 level carried to 1914, then reduced steadily to the 1920 level by 1918).

Government employment was estimated from Fabricant's series for federal employment (based on Civil Service Commission and other reports) and school employment, with other local employment interpolated between the selected dates shown by Fabricant by a regression of such employment against school employment.[50]

For agriculture, a variety of adjustments were made in decennial census totals. Family worker counts were interpolated 1900-1910, extrapolated 1910-1917 at the 1900-1910 annual rate of change, and interpolated for other years. For 1925 and subsequent years, data from the Department of Agriculture were used. For wage earners, decennial counts were interpolated by a moving average of a series for the size of aggregate farm enterprise, a measure of labor requirements.

The labor force totals were derived as follows: Unpublished estimates of population by age, sex, and color were adjusted to allow for the net immigration of workers. Worker rates for each group were derived from the decennial census data (as adjusted for the 1910 overcount)

[50] A final version of these estimates will utilize directly estimated series for each component of government employment. The differences are not such as to affect the unemployment estimates significantly except for 1919, which will be lowered.

and interpolated intercensally.[51] The population mulitplied by the rates gave the final civilian labor force figures. Similar interpolation procedures were used by the NICB, Douglas, Hart, and others except that the present estimates utilize revised census population data and make separate allowance not merely for age, sex, and color but also for nativity change in the population—the latter being particularly important in 1900-1910. A special estimate was made of the impact that additional participation by women in the labor force might have had on short-term changes in World War I, using a large-scale 1918 survey by the Women's Bureau. The result indicated no change in the unemployment total here estimated and a rise of only two-tenths of 1 per cent in the underlying labor force estimate for 1918.

The other likely period of irregular labor force change, the 1930's, is outside the scope of the present estimates. (However, it may be noted that the BLS figures were arrived at only after a special study of short-term changes for the 1930's had led to the conclusion that allowing for such changes would not affect "materially either the level or trend of employment for the years 1929-39.")[52]

COMMENT

Martin R. Gainsbrugh, National Industrial Conference Board

I regard Stanley Lebergott's paper highly as a piece of painstaking and exhaustive research. Despite the limited resources at his command, his care is really exemplary not only in assembling relevant data but even more in point, in directing the reader's attention to the assumptions behind the inevitable imputations, interpolations, and projections.

The results of his research, however, raise anew some basic questions on the meaning and significance of long-term historical (or "prehistoric") statistics on unemployment. These long-term data are necessarily constructed from estimates of the labor force and levels of employment drawn from various census materials (largely decennial) for 1940 and prior census periods. The basic information is static in character as compared with the dynamic concepts of labor force

[51] Despite adjustments by Alba Edwards and other experts there is little evidence to show that a gainful worker count secured different results because of January versus April or June enumeration. The subject is considered at length in a fuller report on the labor force estimates with the conclusion reached that cyclical variations—e.g. January 1920 representing a high level, postwar month—could more than have accounted for apparent incomparabilities in the labor force counts between 1900 and 1930.

[52] Cf. the writer's "Labor Force, Employment and Unemployment, 1929-39: Estimating Methods," *Monthly Labor Review*, July 1948.

incorporated in census or sample enumerations after the 1940 census. Most of my remarks pivot around this distinction in view of Lebergott's expressed intention to present estimates "consistent with the series currently reported by the Census Bureau in its Current Population Survey."

Since my subsequent comments may sound critical, I would not want them to imply the undertaking is not worth the effort. On the contrary, the fact that earlier and admittedly inadequate annual estimates by the Conference Board (and other "rash" researchers) are still employed, lacking better-based estimates, is itself justification. I find myself in welcome agreement with both Lebergott's "general preference for additional measurement series rather than improvements in existing series or data"[1] and the exception he rightly makes in this instance. Given the public interest in, and policy implications of, unemployment, it is important to wring from historical data whatever we can about its determinants, including fluctuations in the labor force and adjustments in employment to changing levels of productive activity. In this respect, Lebergott's research is probably definitive—expunging, among other things, the negative unemployment for earlier decades—and is therefore a real contribution. Nevertheless, I believe his results have limited analytical usefulness, primarily because the past data are inadequate for current purposes despite his diligence in rounding up source materials and imagination in putting them together.

Lebergott's figures on unemployment as presented in this paper are in general similar to the earlier estimates of the Conference Board, with respect both to level and cyclical change. This is personally gratifying but not surprising, since (for establishment of bench marks and for purposes of interpolation) the basic data that are common to both series of estimates considerably outweigh those that are unique in either. This initial gratification was replaced after reviewing Lebergott's procedures by this unhappy conclusion: his refinements and improvements are, unfortunately but necessarily, still superimposed on assumptions that "assume away" the answers to the following highly significant question about historical patterns of unemployment:

1. Unemployment statistics and collateral data on the labor force and employment[2] are widely used from the welfare point of view to measure the degree to which the economy succeeds or fails in providing jobs for those seeking work. This logically requires knowledge not only

[1] Stanley Lebergott, "Measurement for Economic Models," *Journal of the American Statistical Association*, June 1954, p. 213.

[2] A full description of Lebergott's estimates of the labor force and employment was presented in an earlier paper. The unemployment estimates presented here are derived from them and obviously cannot be evaluated independently of them.

of the size of the labor force but also of its dynamics, of how and why it changes. This new series is still static, resting primarily upon long-term demographic change. It is built up by interpolating average participation rates. It sheds little new light on short-run changes in and shifts within the labor force, in contrast to our current monthly reports on the labor force and unemployment.

2. This new series will also be used for purposes of business cycle analysis, to trace the impact of changing levels of economic activity upon levels of employment and unemployment. Actually, this historical employment series is projected in good part on the basis of physical activity and hence may reflect little more than the relative stability or volatility of activity among various industries. To what extent do variations in output affect labor requirements; how much of it is subsumed in hours, and how much in employment? Where independent series on physical activity and employment are available, answers to these questions are possible, but they are not provided, as yet, in this series.

3. A working definition of "full employment" for purposes of public policy is often attempted by reviewing relative levels of unemployment in the past. Lebergott directs himself to this point at some length. Earlier in his paper he had concluded: "Year-to-year changes in unemployment tend to be mirror images of changes in employment. To judge from the 1940-1952 [Monthly Report on the Labor Force] data, the stability in the labor force totals from year to year is very great." It would be interesting to test this conclusion against longer historical experience. Yet it is precisely at this point that the assumptions made necessary by gaps in the data are drawn primarily from 1940-1952 rather than earlier experience. This in turn conditions the unemployment estimates and leaves in doubt the distribution by years of the percentage of the labor force actually unemployed.

In summary, then, the historical labor force and employment series (and therefore the unemployment series) developed by Lebergott are "better" than those we have had heretofore. But they are still at best blunt instruments unsuited to the sharp analytical purposes to which unwary users will put them. Lebergott is alert to these reservations; his thoughtful remarks at the beginning of his paper and at various points throughout leave no doubt on that score. The key assumptions involved in interpolating labor force participation rates and projecting important areas of employment mean that his historical estimates of unemployment are still a discrete series from those subsequently derived since 1940—and ought to be so labeled and used.

DIFFERENTIAL UNEMPLOYMENT AND CHARACTERISTICS OF THE UNEMPLOYED IN THE UNITED STATES, 1940-1954

PHILIP M. HAUSER
UNIVERSITY OF CHICAGO

PUBLIC and professional interest in unemployment seems to be positively correlated with its incidence. Normally there is an appreciable lag, however, between increased levels of unemployment and its intensive analytical study. This Conference bears testimony to the prescience of its leaders. It provides a full-scale analysis of unemployment while we are still experiencing and, we hope, just as we are coming out of, our third postwar period of "economic adjustment." This timing is especially remarkable in that the Conference date was set about two years ago.

Most of us recall an even more intensive interest in unemployment about two decades ago. We were then in the midst of the most severe depression we have ever experienced. We knew that there was a large volume of joblessness but we did not know, and we were not to know for some eight years after the onset of the depression, just how many unemployed there were.[1] We knew little about the characteristics —demographic, social, or economic—of the unemployed. We did know something about the characteristics as well as the number of the unemployed on the relief rolls and on work relief programs.[2]

Our ability to hold this Conference to consider papers of the type prepared is a significant indication of the great progress which has been made since the thirties in the definition and measurement of unemployment. This is not to say that no further problems of concept or measurement exist. But the problems which plague us now are minor compared with those created by the almost complete ignorance of the thirties. The adoption by the Bureau of the Census of the labor force approach in the measurement of the nation's labor supply and the provision for the Current Population Survey giving monthly statistics on the total labor force, employment, and unemployment, have

Note: Grateful acknowledgment is made of the services of Dr. Evelyn M. Kitagawa, who assisted the writer in the preparation of several sections of this paper, and in its editing.

[1] Calvert L. Dedrick and Morris H. Hansen, *The Enumerative Check Census*, Census of Partial Employment, Unemployment and Occupations: 1937, Vol. IV, 1938.

[2] For example see Philip M. Hauser, *Workers on Relief in the United States, March 1935*, Works Progress Administration, 1938.

provided us with about fifteen years of current data on our labor supply and have illuminated vast areas of ignorance about its structure and dynamics. The knowledge we have gained has included information on the characteristics of the unemployed. Some of this information was summarized in a paper presented before the annual meetings of the American Statistical Association about five years ago.[3]

It was one of the conclusions of that paper that: "As already noted, the volume and rate of unemployment have fluctuated over a wide range during the past decade (1940-1949). However, especially if the war period is excluded, it has been essentially the same population groups, and the same economic groups, that repeatedly showed the highest incidence of unemployment."[4]

This conclusion is further bolstered by the analysis of unemployment data since 1949. We have experienced further changes in economic climate as a result of the partial remobilization incident to the increased temperature of the cold war and the Korean episode; and further demobilization during the period of the uneasy Korean truce and government economy measures. Unemployment rates declined after the recession highs of 1949 and increased again with the recession of 1953-1954. But the pattern of unemployment rates has remained essentially the same.

1. Unemployment, 1940-1954

An analysis of differential unemployment rates and the characteristics of the unemployed must be framed by a consideration of the volume and incidence of unemployment. Unemployment rates, as obtained by direct measurement since 1940, have varied on an annual average basis from a high of 14.6 per cent in 1940, to a low of 1.2 per cent in 1944 (see Table 1 and Chart 1). The high unemployment rate of 1940, based on an average volume of 8.1 million unemployed, represented, of course, a heritage from the depressed thirties. This unemployment heritage was dissipated, however, first with defense, and then with all-out war, production. By 1944, average unemployment for the year, under war-manpower controls, reached the remarkably low level of 700,000 and dropped to the unprecedented low rate of less than 1 per cent in October of that year.

With the war's end in 1945 and continued demobilization through 1946, unemployment increased. Annual average unemployment in 1945 and in 1946 was still relatively low, however, and far below the levels anticipated by many economists during the period of postwar readjust-

[3] Philip M. Hauser and Robert B. Pearl, "Who are the Unemployed?" *Journal of the American Statistical Association*, December 1950, pp. 479-500.
[4] *Ibid.*, p. 486.

TABLE 1

Unemployment Rates,[a] by Sex, Annual Average, 1940-1954
(*per cent*)

Year	*Both Sexes*	*Male*	*Female*
1940[b]	14.6	14.3	15.5
1941	9.9	9.5	11.2
1942	4.7	4.3	5.8
1943	1.9	1.5	2.7
1944	1.2	1.0	1.7
1945	1.9	1.8	2.2
1946	3.9	4.4	2.8
1947	3.6	3.7	3.2
1948	3.4	3.3	3.6
1949	5.5	5.5	5.4
1950	5.0	4.9	5.3
1951	3.0	2.6	3.9
1952	2.7	2.4	3.1
1953	2.4	2.3	2.6
1954 (June)	5.1	4.8	5.7

[a] Percentage of the total or appropriate part of the civilian labor force that is unemployed. This definition is used throughout this paper.

[b] Based on revised census data and estimates for January and February.

Source: Bureau of the Census.

ment. Average annual unemployment declined somewhat during 1947, and again in 1948, but increased appreciably during the recession experience in 1949 and 1950. With the partial mobilization occasioned by the Korean War, unemployment rates again declined during the three years 1951-1953, reaching a low of 2.4 per cent for the year 1953. Economic readjustment following the Korean truce, however, produced higher unemployment rates in the last months of 1953 and first half of 1954 (when this paper was written). In April of 1954, unemployment was at a level of about 5 per cent, approximately the same as that experienced in April 1949 and April 1950.

By reason of the availability of the Census Bureau's Current Population Survey—Monthly Report on the Labor Force—it is possible to measure not only the volume of unemployment, but also some broad characteristics of the unemployed throughout the period 1940 to the present time. It is thus possible to analyze unemployment rates and the characteristics of the unemployed in a variety of economic situations including relatively high-level depression unemployment (1940), low-level wartime unemployment under conditions of wartime manpower controls (1944), postwar adjustment unemployment (1949), low-level unemployment with partial remobilization for the Korean incident (1953), and increased levels of unemployment during the economic readjustment following the Korean truce (1953-1954).

CHART 1

Unemployment Rates, by Sex, Annual Average, 1940-1953

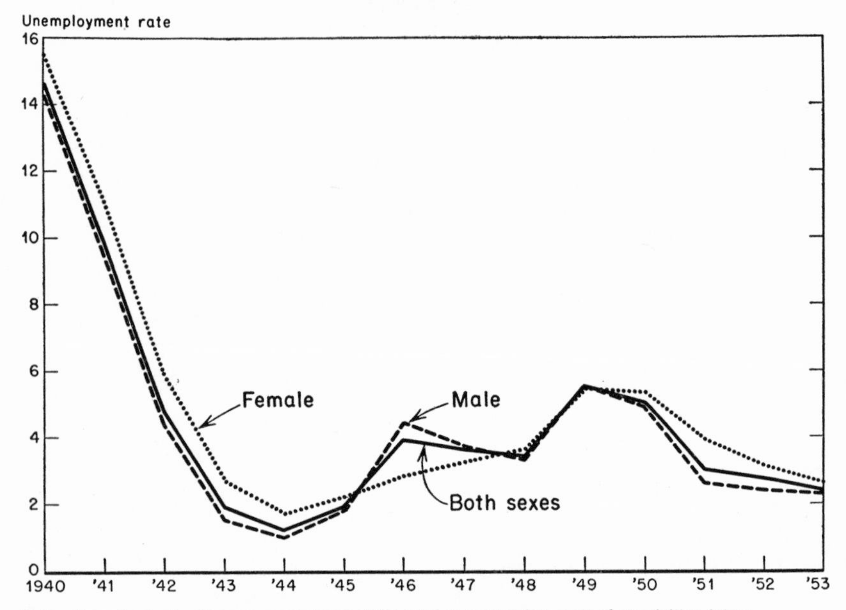

Note: Unemployment rates are percentages of the total or appropriate part of the civilian labor force that is unemployed.
Source: Table 1.

2. *Differential Unemployment Rates*

The incidence of unemployment varies among the different industrial and occupational sectors of the economy; and within occupational and industrial groupings has a differential impact on various segments of the population, classified by personal characteristics. Unemployment rates during the period 1940 to 1954 will be examined with two objectives in mind. The first is to ascertain the differential patterns that may be observed; the second is to see whether differential patterns of unemployment have varied under the different sets of economic conditions and fluctuating levels of unemployment outlined above.

SEX DIFFERENTIALS

Annual average unemployment rates for females exceeded those for male workers for eleven of the fourteen years in the annual series from 1940 through 1953. Only during the postwar years of 1946 and 1947, when female labor force participation rapidly decreased, and the recession year 1949, did female unemployment rates fall appreciably below those of male (see Table 1 and Chart 1).

The annual average female unemployment rate was about 8 per cent above the male rate in 1940. This gap increased each year to reach a high at which the female unemployment rate was 80 per cent above the male in 1943. During this period, however, total unemployment rates decreased considerably. At the same time, the number of females in the civilian labor force greatly increased while the number of males in the civilian labor force greatly decreased. The relatively higher female unemployment rates during this war period, then, reflect more the increase in female, and decrease in male, civilian labor force participation than differential vulnerability of employed persons to unemployment.

Subsequent to 1943, the gap between male and female unemployment rates declined through 1945. In 1945, annual average female unemployment rates were 22 per cent above male unemployment.

During 1946 and 1947, female unemployment rates fell below those of males. However, the female labor force was shrinking rapidly with the postwar contraction of the total labor force, while demobilized GIs were returning to the civilian labor force. Relatively low female unemployment during these years may reflect the female exodus from, and male return to, the civilian labor force rather than the differential vulnerability of employed persons to unemployment.

Female unemployment was higher than male in 1948, but lower in 1949. During both of these years, the number of the women in the labor force increased but the increase was greater between 1947 and 1948 than between 1948 and 1949.

Beginning with 1950 and the increase in female labor force participation with partial remobilization for the Korean incident, the gap between female and male unemployment rates again increased to reach a peak difference of about 50 per cent in 1951. It then gradually declined until 1953 when the female unemployment rate was 13 per cent above the male level.

The abnormal war and postwar conditions during the period from 1940 to date make it difficult to reach any conclusion about the differential vulnerability of employed persons, by sex, to unemployment. Large increases or decreases in the size of the female labor force and male transfers to and from military service to civilian employment distort the unemployment rate as a measure of such differential vulnerability.

It would seem that at least a tentative generalization about the differential vulnerability of male and female workers to unemployment may be drawn, however, from an analysis of the sex differences in unemployment at periods of relatively high levels of unemployment. During the period of observation, 1940 to 1954, there were five periods in which total unemployment reached a level of 5 per cent or more, namely 1940, 1941, 1949, 1950, and 1954 (the first half). In addition, reliable data are available for November 1937 at which time about a fifth of the labor force was unemployed.[5] In five of these six periods, female unemployment rates were well above those of the male, ranging from a level of 27 per cent above the male in 1937, to 8 per cent above the male in 1940 and in 1950. Only in 1949, with a total unemployment rate of 5.5 per cent, did the female unemployment rate (5.4 per cent) fail to exceed that of the male (5.5 per cent).[6]

However, this type of analysis also fails to indicate the differential vulnerability to unemployment of employed men and women. To obtain a measurement of the differential vulnerability to unemployment of the employed ("disemployment"), it is necessary to eliminate the portion of total unemployment that arises from reasons other than a shift from employment to unemployment; more specifically, from a change from non-labor-force status to unemployment. Fortunately, the availability of "gross change" statistics tabulated regularly by the Bureau of the Census since May 1948 makes such an analysis possible (see Table 2).

TABLE 2

Additions to Unemployment, by Previous Status and Sex, Annual Average, 1949-1952

(*per cent*)

Previous Status and Sex	*1949*	*1950*	*1951*	*1952*
Both sexes	100.0	100.0	100.0	100.0
Employed	68.8	62.9	59.0	63.2
Not in labor force	31.2	37.1	41.0	36.8
Male	100.0	100.0	100.0	100.0
Employed	79.1	74.3	71.0	74.5
Not in labor force	20.9	25.7	29.0	25.5
Female	100.0	100.0	100.0	100.0
Employed	47.3	43.1	42.8	44.8
Not in labor force	52.7	56.9	57.2	55.2

Source: Bureau of the Census.

As a prelude to this analysis, it is desirable to note that gross changes in labor force participation were much greater for women than for men. For example, in 1951 average monthly gross changes in labor

[5] Dedrick and Hansen, *op.cit.*, p. 20.

[6] By reason of sampling error the data for individual years are relatively unstable. The probability of female unemployment rates exceeding those of male for as many as five of the six years through chance alone, assuming no difference between male and female rates, is .109.

force participation (the average monthly number of additions to, and reductions from, the labor force), were 21.9 per cent of the average female labor force and only 5.5 per cent of the average male labor force.[7] Moreover, there is an important sex difference in the proportion of average monthly additions to unemployment that originate in employment in the previous month, as against previous non-labor-force status. In each of the years 1949 through 1952, the proportion of male additions to unemployment originating in a previous status of employment was appreciably greater than that for females (see Table 2). During this period about three-fourths of all male additions to unemployment originated in a previous status of employment and only a fourth from not in the labor force status. In contrast, less than half of the female additions to unemployment originated in previous employment and over half in a previous non-labor-force status.

A "disemployment rate" may be calculated by expressing the additions to unemployment from a previous employment status as a percentage of total employment. Such disemployment rates have been computed, by sex, for the years 1949 to 1952 and are presented in Table 3.

The pattern of disemployment rates differed from that of unemployment rates, by sex. In three of the four years, for which the data have been calculated, female disemployment rates were below those of male and in the fourth year (1951) it was approximately the same. In the two years of relatively high unemployment (1949 and 1950) the female disemployment rate was well below that of the male. As measured by disemployment rates it would seem that women are less vulnerable than men to unemployment.[8] Definitive conclusions, however, must await a longer and more stable series of disemployment rates.

AGE DIFFERENTIALS

Unemployment rates varied considerably by age for each of the sexes throughout the period under observation. Female unemployment rates by age showed less of a tendency to move upward past middle

[7] Philip M. Hauser, "Mobility in Labor Force Participation," E. Wight Bakke, *et al., Labor Mobility and Economic Opportunity*, Technology Press and Wiley, 1954, p. 35.

[8] This conclusion cannot, of course, be interpreted to mean more than that all employed women are less vulnerable to unemployment than all employed men. The observed differences in disemployment rates may arise from differences in industrial and occupational affiliation, age and other variables. To isolate the differentials by sex alone it would be highly desirable to have data available for the calculation of disemployment rates in which industry, occupation, and age structure are controlled. It might also be desirable to control other factors, depending on the purpose of the analysis.

TABLE 3

Employment, Disemployment, and Disemployment Rates by Sex, Twelve-Month Average,[a] 1949-1952
(*numbers in thousands*)

Employment and Disemployment, and Sex	*1949*	*1950*	*1951*	*1952*
Both sexes:				
Employment	58,783	59,811	60,946	61,293
Disemployment[b]	1,096	884	646	650
Disemployment rate[c]	1.9%	1.5%	1.1%	1.1%
Male:				
Employment	41,733	42,222	42,487	42,391
Disemployment[b]	854	663	446	476
Disemployment rate[c]	2.0%	1.6%	1.1%	1.1%
Female:				
Employment	17,050	17,589	18,459	18,902
Disemployment[b]	243	221	200	174
Disemployment rate[c]	1.4%	1.3%	1.1%	0.9%

[a] December-November for employment; January-December for disemployment.
[b] Disemployment figures are the average number of persons unemployed at the end of each monthly period who were employed at the beginning of the monthly period.
[c] Percentage of the total or appropriate part of the civilian labor force disemployed.
Source: Bureau of the Census.

age. Data are presented in Table 4 and Chart 2 showing unemployment rates by age and sex for five selected years, in two of which (1944 and 1953) unemployment reached relatively low levels.

Unemployment rates were relatively high for workers under twenty-five years of age and especially teen-agers. High unemployment rates for these age groups reflect in large measure the relatively high incidence of new entrants to the labor force.[9] Male unemployment rates consistently decreased at the more productive years and tended to increase at later ages beginning with about the age group forty-five years. The upturn in unemployment rates beyond middle age may reflect in part discriminatory practices toward older workers.

Unemployment rates for persons sixty-five years and over are especially difficult to interpret. In 1944 (and also in 1948 and 1951) during a relatively low level of unemployment the unemployment rate for males sixty-five and over was higher than that in the immediately preceding age interval. In 1940 and 1950, when unemployment rates were relatively high (and also in 1937), unemployment rates for males sixty-five and over, were below those of the preceding age group. In

[9] For age differentials in gross changes in labor force participation see *ibid.*, p. 35.

TABLE 4

Unemployment Rates, by Age and Sex, Annual Average, Selected Years, 1940-1953[a]

(*per cent*)

Age and Sex	*1940*	*1944*	*1949*	*1950*	*1953*
Both sexes, 14 and over	14.6	1.2	5.5	5.0	2.4
14 - 19	31.4	3.2	11.6	10.8	6.1
20 - 24	18.8	2.2	8.7	7.2	3.8
25 - 34	11.6	1.0	4.9	4.4	2.0
35 - 44	11.0	0.8	4.0	3.6	1.8
45 - 54	12.9	0.7	3.8	4.0	1.8
55 - 64	14.2	0.8	4.7	4.5	2.2
65 and over	8.8	1.0	4.6	4.3	1.8
Male, 14 and over	14.3	1.0	5.5	4.9	2.3
14 - 19	32.8	3.0	11.9	11.0	6.4
20 - 24	18.1	2.1	9.9	7.7	4.1
25 - 34	10.9	0.7	4.7	4.2	1.8
35 - 44	11.3	0.7	3.8	3.3	1.7
45 - 54	12.4	0.5	3.9	3.9	1.9
55 - 64	14.9	0.8	4.9	4.7	2.3
65 and over	10.0	1.1	4.9	4.6	2.0
Female, 14 and over	15.5	1.7	5.4	5.3	2.6
14 - 19	27.8	3.4	11.2	10.4	5.6
20 - 24	19.9	2.2	6.7	6.3	3.5
25 - 34	13.3	1.5	5.3	5.3	2.6
35 - 44	9.8	1.0	4.2	4.0	1.9
45 - 54	14.6	1.0	3.5	4.2	1.7
55 - 64	10.9	0.8	3.8	3.9	1.8
65 and over	2.1	0.7	3.4	3.4	1.3

[a] For 1944 and 1949, derived from weighted arithmetic means of the twelve monthly estimates. For 1940, estimated from revised 1940 census figures and less detailed age figures for remainder of year.

Source: Bureau of the Census.

1949, under similar relatively high levels of unemployment, the rate of males sixty-five and over was at the same level as that of the preceding age group.

It may be that the pattern of unemployment by age is more accurately described by the relationships in the years with relatively low levels of unemployment, which show a consistent rise in unemployment rates for persons sixty-five and over. The decrease in unemployment rates for older persons in the years with relatively high levels of unemployment may reflect the failure of the labor force measurement techniques to measure the incidence of unemployment among older workers in recession or depression periods. Under conditions of relatively high unemployment, older workers may tend to be reported as not in the labor force rather than as seeking work.

The apparent consistent difference in the relationship of unemploy-

CHART 2

Unemployment Rates, by Age and Sex, Annual Average, Selected Years, 1940-1953

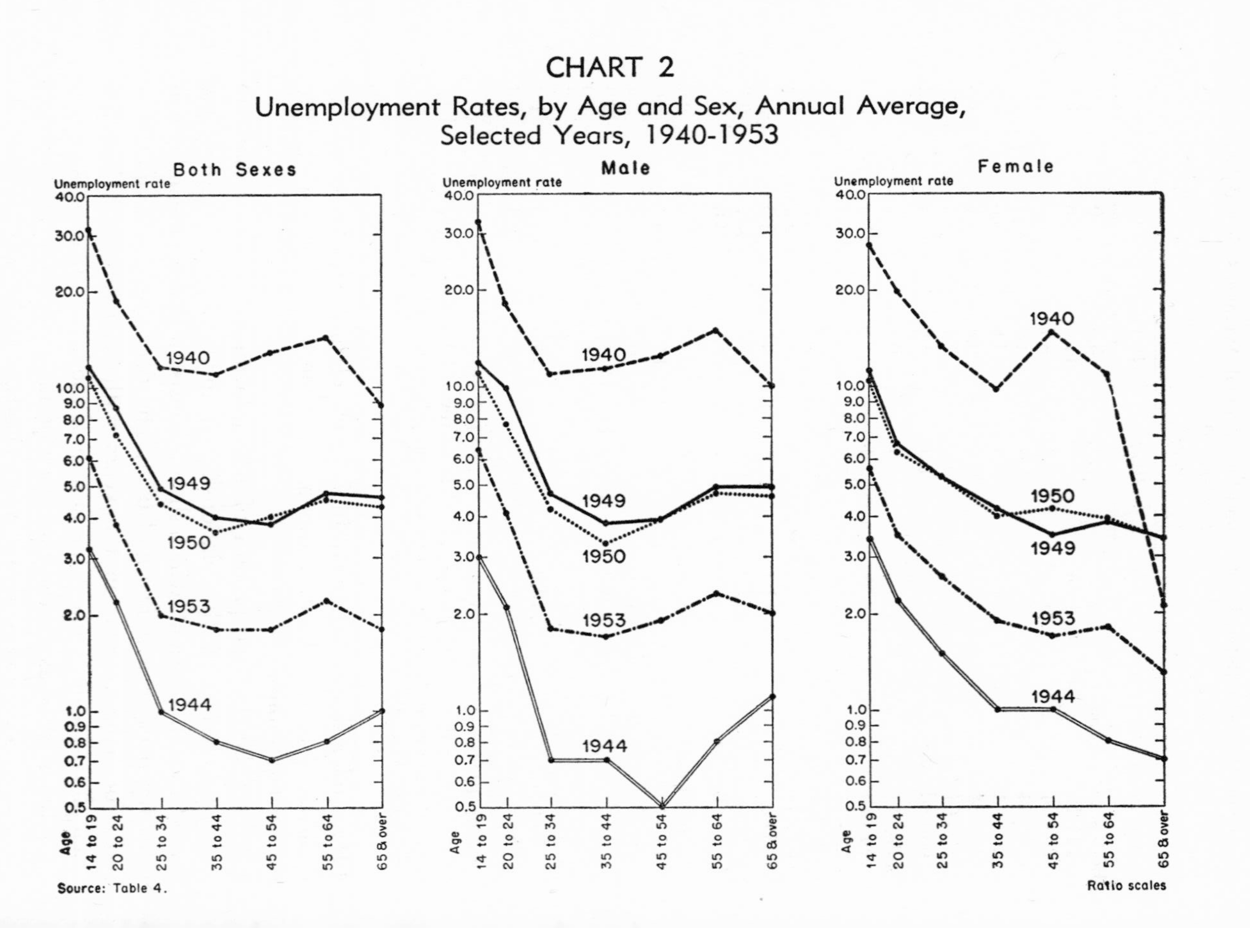

Source: Table 4.

ment rates for males sixty-five years and older and preceding age groups for years of relatively low and high unemployment, respectively, may tend to bolster this explanation. The pattern is not completely consistent, however. In 1953, a year of relatively low unemployment (total unemployment at level of 2.4 per cent), males sixty-five years and over had a lower unemployment rate than males in the preceding age group.

Unemployment rates for females, as for males, are highest among workers under twenty-five, especially teen-age workers. The rise of the rates for older workers was less marked among females than among males. The interpretation of the unemployment rates for females sixty-five and over are subject to the problems already referred to for males.

The differences in unemployment rates by age cannot be interpreted as indicating differential vulnerability to unemployment of the employed. Unfortunately, because of the unavailability of data disemployment rates cannot be calculated by age.[10]

COLOR DIFFERENTIALS

Because of the small size of the Current Population Survey sample, only limited data are available on a current basis on unemployment by color. Census statistics for 1940 and 1950 indicate that unemployment rates are considerably higher for nonwhite than for white workers. The unemployment rate of nonwhite workers for March 1940 is about 18 per cent; of whites 15 per cent. Unemployment in 1950 for nonwhite workers is 8.5 per cent; of white, 4.6 per cent.

During the war and postwar years this color differential in unemployment persisted (see Table 5). It is significant that nonwhite unemployment was considerably greater than white in periods of both high and low levels of total unemployment.[11] No pattern of change in differential unemployment by color was evident in the available data. However, the small size of the sample makes these relationships rather unstable and difficult to interpret.[12]

[10] Disemployment rates could be estimated from available data but only with considerable labor and relatively great error. It is to be hoped that the Bureau of the Census will be able, in the coming years, to provide "gross change" tabulations by labor force and non-labor-force status classified by age, sex, and color. Sampling errors will, of course, put limitations on cross tabulations but annual averages and a series build up over the years would undoubtedly provide valuable information.

[11] For an analysis of factors accounting for differentials in unemployment by color, see Ralph Turner, "Foci of Discrimination in the Employment of Nonwhite," *American Journal of Sociology*, November 1952, pp. 247-256; "The Relative Position of the Negro Male in the Labor Force of Large American Cities," *American Sociological Review*, August 1951. If nonagricultural workers alone are considered, color differentials are, of course, much more pronounced.

[12] Disemployment rates would be highly desirable in the analysis of color,

TABLE 5

Unemployment Rates, by Color and Sex, April, Selected Years, 1940-1953

(*per cent*)

Color and Sex	*1940*	*1944*	*1949*	*1950*	*1953*
Both sexes:					
White	15.0	1.1	4.7	4.9	2.1
Nonwhite	18.1	1.6	7.6	8.0	4.1
Male:					
White	15.5	n.a.	4.8	4.9	2.0
Nonwhite	19.3	n.a.	7.7	8.4	4.6
Female:					
White	13.5	n.a.	4.3	5.0	2.3
Nonwhite	16.8	n.a.	7.5	7.4	3.3

n.a. = not available.
Source: Bureau of the Census.

MARITAL STATUS DIFFERENTIALS

Statistics are available in the 1940 and 1950 Censuses of Population on unemployment by marital status. While the data for each of these census years relate to periods of relatively high unemployment, the level of unemployment in 1940 was considerably above the 1950 level.

For each sex, in both 1940 and 1950, unemployment rates were lower for married persons with spouses present than for other categories of marital status (see Table 6). Among females, married persons with spouse present also had lower unemployment rates in both 1940 and 1950. Unlike the males, however, white single females had lower unemployment rates than females of other marital status.

The patterns of marital status differentials in unemployment persist when the white and nonwhite populations are considered separately (see Tables 7 and 8). The difference in unemployment rates between married persons with spouse present and persons of other marital status was somewhat less for nonwhite than for white males, however, in both 1940 and 1950. Marital status made the least difference in unemployment rates for white females in 1950 than for any of the other groups studied. It is also worth noting that the marital status differentials in unemployment consistently held for each age group among males but was more erratic by age group among females. Single women of middle age and above tended to have unemployment rates as low as, or lower than, married women with spouse present.

---

marital status, relationship to head, and other differentials. Unfortunately such data are not yet available.

TABLE 6

Unemployment Rates by Marital Status, Age, and Sex, 1940 and 1950

(*per cent*)

AGE AND SEX	1940 Single	1940 Married, Spouse Present	1940 Other Status	1950 Single	1950 Married, Spouse Present	1950 Other Status
Male, 14 and over	22.3	11.0	19.0	9.7	3.3	9.2
14 - 17	29.2	19.7	19.1	10.5	7.4	4.5
18 - 19	32.8	21.1	31.9	11.6	6.6	17.5
20 - 24	21.9	14.9	22.4	10.3	4.8	13.0
25 - 29	16.5	11.3	18.8	8.8	3.4	11.2
30 - 34	16.6	9.9	18.1	8.0	2.8	9.4
35 - 44	18.4	9.7	19.7	8.1	2.8	9.6
45 - 54	21.6	11.1	20.3	8.7	3.2	9.2
55 - 64	22.5	13.2	21.0	9.6	3.8	9.0
65 - 74	14.6	9.9	12.7	8.3	4.4	6.9
75 and over	8.1	4.3	4.4	5.1	2.8	4.0
Female, 14 and over	16.0	6.8	16.3	5.1	3.6	6.2
14 - 17	38.5	15.1	33.1	12.7	14.9	19.0
18 - 19	31.0	13.9	29.9	7.5	7.2	18.9
20 - 24	16.3	7.4	21.1	5.1	4.6	11.0
25 - 29	9.6	5.8	18.1	4.0	4.1	8.5
30 - 34	7.5	5.3	17.4	3.6	3.7	7.4
35 - 44	7.4	6.5	16.9	3.0	3.1	5.9
45 - 54	7.9	8.0	15.9	2.4	3.0	5.3
55 - 64	8.8	9.5	15.1	2.9	2.9	5.0
65 - 74	6.9	6.8	7.8	3.3	2.9	4.0
75 and over	3.2	3.5	5.1	2.8	2.6	2.9

Source: Bureau of the Census.

DIFFERENTIALS BY RELATIONSHIP TO HEAD

The 1940 and 1950 census materials also permit an analysis of unemployment by relationship to head of household. The unemployment patterns reported above by marital status suggest that the incidence of unemployment is lowest among those with the greatest responsibility. This is indicated by the relatively low unemployment rates of married persons with spouse present, especially among males. This conclusion is bolstered by differential unemployment patterns by relationship to head of household and marital status.

In both 1940 and 1950, male unemployment rates are lower for heads of households than for all other categories of persons (see Table 9). The presence of a spouse made a difference in unemployment rates even for male heads of a household. It would be interesting to ascertain whether this differential is attributable to a difference in the responsibility of the male heads with wife present or reflects rather the economic as well as other powers of the wife. The differential patterns

TABLE 7

Unemployment Rates of the White Labor Force, by Marital Status, Age, and Sex, 1940 and 1950

(*per cent*)

	1940			1950		
AGE AND SEX	*Single*	*Married, Spouse Present*	*Other Status*	*Single*	*Married, Spouse Present*	*Other Status*
Male, 14 and over	22.3	10.6	18.5	9.4	3.1	8.7
14 - 17	31.8	20.7	18.0	10.6	7.8	4.4
18 - 19	33.4	22.6	32.9	11.2	6.3	17.1
20 - 24	21.7	15.1	21.9	9.9	4.5	12.0
25 - 29	16.2	10.9	18.5	8.4	3.1	10.2
30 - 34	16.1	9.5	17.7	7.6	2.5	8.8
35 - 44	18.0	9.2	19.0	7.9	2.6	9.0
45 - 54	21.4	10.7	19.8	8.5	3.0	9.0
55 - 64	22.6	13.0	20.9	9.5	3.7	8.8
65 - 74	14.5	9.8	12.5	8.3	4.3	6.7
75 and over	7.9	4.1	4.3	5.1	2.8	3.8
Female, 14 and over	15.6	6.4	16.3	4.7	3.2	5.6
14 - 17	42.6	15.4	43.7	12.6	13.9	16.1
18 - 19	31.1	12.9	30.1	6.9	6.6	17.5
20 - 24	15.9	6.6	21.4	4.3	4.0	9.5
25 - 29	9.0	5.2	17.7	3.5	3.5	7.1
30 - 34	6.9	4.9	17.2	3.4	3.3	6.5
35 - 44	6.9	6.2	17.0	2.8	2.7	5.6
45 - 54	7.8	7.9	16.3	2.3	2.8	5.0
55 - 64	8.8	9.7	15.4	3.0	2.8	5.0
65 - 74	7.1	7.5	7.7	3.1	2.3	3.9
75 and over	2.9	3.3	4.9	3.0	2.8	2.8

Source: Bureau of the Census.

of unemployment by relationship to head and marital status tended also to hold for both white and nonwhite populations and for each of the broad age classifications for which the data are available.

Unemployment patterns among women classified by relationship to head of household, differed from those of the men (see Table 10). The lowest unemployment rates, for both 1940 and 1950, were found among wives of heads of households. In contrast with male patterns of unemployment by marital status and relationship to head of household, single females who were head of households had lower unemployment rates than female heads with other marital status—that is, married, widowed, or divorced. Moreover, single female heads had even lower unemployment rates than wives of heads. This relationship held for each age group.

The patterns described tend to hold for the white and nonwhite

TABLE 8

Unemployment Rates of the Nonwhite Labor Force, by Marital Status, Age, and Sex, 1940 and 1950

(*per cent*)

	1940			1950		
AGE AND SEX	*Single*	*Married, Spouse Present*	*Other Status*	*Single*	*Married, Spouse Present*	*Other Status*
Male, 14 and over	22.6	14.9	21.6	12.1	5.7	11.2
14 - 17	18.3	a	a	9.5	b	b
18 - 19	27.3	15.1	28.6	14.1	8.6	18.7
20 - 24	23.6	14.2	23.8	14.1	7.2	15.8
25 - 29	21.0	14.5	19.5	12.5	6.8	13.9
30 - 34	21.1	14.2	20.0	11.2	5.8	11.4
35 - 44	22.2	14.8	22.9	9.9	5.1	11.3
45 - 54	24.5	16.3	23.6	10.5	5.2	10.0
55 - 64	21.4	16.4	22.4	10.3	6.0	10.3
65 - 74	16.3	10.6	14.4	7.0	5.7	8.9
75 and over	a	5.9	6.6	b	2.7	6.5
Female, 14 and over	19.6	8.8	16.3	10.7	6.6	8.1
14 - 17	21.5	14.8	21.8	13.8	18.7	b
18 - 19	29.3	16.6	29.6	15.8	12.0	22.8
20 - 24	21.2	11.1	20.4	12.3	10.1	15.0
25 - 29	15.5	9.0	18.9	8.8	7.8	11.8
30 - 34	14.4	7.7	18.0	6.0	6.5	9.5
35 - 44	13.5	8.0	16.5	6.5	5.7	6.6
45 - 54	11.8	8.5	14.4	5.5	5.0	6.4
55 - 64	9.1	8.3	13.7	4.7	4.6	5.5
65 - 74	2.2	3.9	8.1	6.9	7.8	4.9
75 and over	a	a	6.2	b	b	3.3

[a] Base less than 2,000.
[b] Base less than 3,000.
Source: Bureau of the Census.

populations and for each of the broad age groups, for which the data are presented in Tables 9 and 10. Although considerable speculation is possible to account for the patterns reported, the actual explanations must remain a matter for further research.

INDUSTRY DIFFERENTIALS

Data on the industrial affiliation of the unemployed are relatively limited. The 1940 census figures do not provide a good base for the analysis of subsequent changes in unemployment by industry because they provided industrial data for the total unemployed, including emergency workers, and did not show separate statistics for wage or salary workers. Comparable data, however, are available on unemployment rates for wage or salary workers by major industry group

TABLE 9

Male Unemployment Rates, by Relationship to Head of Household, Marital Status, Age, and Color, 1940 and 1950

(*per cent*)

RELATIONSHIP TO HEAD OF HOUSEHOLD, MARITAL STATUS, AND AGE	1940			1950		
	Total	*White*	*Nonwhite*	*Total*	*White*	*Nonwhite*
Total, 14 and over	14.7	14.3	17.9	4.9	4.6	7.9
In household	14.6	14.3	17.8	4.8	4.5	7.6
Head of household	11.1	10.8	14.8	3.3	3.1	5.7
Married, wife present	10.7	10.4	14.3	3.1	2.9	5.2
14 - 24	14.1	14.3	12.2	3.8	3.7	5.9
25 - 44	9.8	9.4	14.1	2.7	2.5	5.1
45 - 64	11.7	11.4	15.9	3.3	3.2	5.3
65 and over	9.1	9.0	9.9	4.1	4.1	5.1
Other	15.6	15.3	17.6	6.6	6.2	8.8
14 - 24	14.9	15.3	13.5	6.9	6.2	10.3
25 - 44	14.5	13.8	17.7	6.3	5.7	8.9
45 - 64	18.2	17.9	20.0	7.0	6.7	8.7
65 and over	9.9	9.7	11.3	6.0	5.8	7.8
Relative of head	23.8	23.8	23.6	10.0	9.7	12.1
Married, wife present	15.6	15.2	18.9	6.7	6.4	8.5
14 - 24	19.3	19.4	18.5	8.9	8.7	9.9
25 - 44	13.6	13.2	17.9	5.8	5.5	8.2
45 - 64	18.7	18.0	27.2	6.4	6.5	6.1
65 and over	16.3	16.0	[a]	7.1	7.1	7.6
Other	25.1	25.2	24.4	10.7	10.4	13.0
14 - 24	28.1	28.6	24.3	11.3	11.0	13.1
25 - 44	19.9	19.5	24.6	9.9	9.6	13.3
45 - 64	23.6	23.4	26.8	10.4	10.4	10.5
65 and over	13.6	13.5	16.2	6.3	6.1	9.0
Not relative of head	15.8	14.4	21.6	7.6	6.8	10.4
Married, wife present	16.2	14.1	20.6	8.1	7.4	9.3
14 - 24	16.2	14.3	20.5	7.2	7.0	7.6
25 - 44	14.4	12.0	18.8	8.3	7.4	9.5
45 - 64	21.0	18.6	29.2	8.2	7.6	9.7
65 and over	20.1	18.8	[a]	8.7	8.1	[b]
Other	15.8	14.5	21.8	7.6	6.7	10.8
14 - 24	12.0	10.7	18.9	7.1	6.1	11.8
25 - 44	14.3	12.5	21.2	7.1	5.9	10.6
45 - 64	21.6	20.9	26.3	8.5	8.0	10.7
65 and over	15.5	15.1	18.4	7.4	7.1	9.3

[a] Base less than 2,000.
[b] Base less than 3,000.
Source: Bureau of the Census.

TABLE 10

Female Unemployment Rates, by Relationship to Head of Household, Marital Status, Age, and Color, 1940 and 1950

(*per cent*)

RELATIONSHIP TO HEAD OF HOUSEHOLD, MARITAL STATUS, AND AGE	1940			1950		
	Total	*White*	*Nonwhite*	*Total*	*White*	*Nonwhite*
Total, 14 and over	13.3	13.1	14.6	4.7	4.2	8.0
In household	13.7	13.5	14.6	4.7	4.2	7.9
Head of household	14.9	14.7	15.7	4.9	4.5	7.1
Single	8.7	7.9	14.5	3.1	2.7	7.7
14 - 24	11.4	9.7	18.5	4.1	2.9	12.9
25 - 44	8.1	7.0	14.8	3.2	2.7	7.3
45 - 64	9.0	8.9	10.6	2.7	2.6	4.9
65 and over	6.3	6.5	a	3.6	3.4	b
Married, widowed, or divorced	17.3	17.8	15.9	5.5	5.2	7.0
14 - 24	21.1	22.3	19.1	10.4	8.3	16.4
25 - 44	19.0	19.5	17.8	6.3	5.7	7.6
45 - 64	17.0	17.7	14.1	5.1	4.9	6.2
65 and over	7.9	7.9	8.0	4.0	3.9	4.5
Wife of head	6.3	6.0	7.7	3.4	3.1	6.1
14 - 24	6.4	5.9	8.8	4.7	4.3	10.0
25 - 44	5.6	5.2	7.5	3.4	3.0	6.1
45 - 64	8.1	8.2	7.7	2.9	2.7	4.8
65 and over	6.3	7.0	3.4	2.8	2.2	7.2
Other relative of head	19.7	19.6	20.8	6.5	5.9	11.3
Married, husband present	9.4	8.5	14.1	4.8	4.1	9.0
14 - 24	13.1	11.7	19.6	6.1	5.3	11.3
25 - 44	7.2	6.7	10.6	4.0	3.4	7.7
45 - 64	10.1	9.9	11.0	4.0	3.5	7.2
65 and over	a	a	a	5.3	4.3	b
Other	20.4	20.3	21.5	6.6	6.1	11.6
14 - 24	27.1	27.2	25.6	8.3	7.6	14.9
25 - 44	11.6	11.2	16.2	5.0	4.4	9.0
45 - 64	13.3	13.2	14.7	4.6	4.4	6.7
65 and over	11.1	11.4	8.6	4.5	4.3	6.5
Not relative of head	7.7	6.2	14.4	4.3	3.4	7.8
Married, husband present	9.7	7.7	12.7	6.9	5.1	9.5
14 - 24	12.1	8.8	16.7	8.2	6.2	12.5
25 - 44	8.6	7.1	10.6	7.0	4.7	9.3
45 - 64	10.9	8.8	17.2	4.7	4.6	4.9
65 and over	a	a	a	b	b	b
Other	7.5	6.1	14.8	4.0	3.3	7.4
14 - 24	6.9	5.4	15.7	4.7	3.3	11.8
25 - 44	7.8	5.7	15.2	4.3	3.4	7.1
45 - 64	8.4	7.8	12.7	3.4	3.2	4.3
65 and over	5.4	5.4	6.1	2.6	2.6	3.2

[a] Base less than 2,000.
[b] Base less than 3,000.
Source: Bureau of the Census.

from 1948 through 1953 (see Table 11).[13] During two of these years, 1949 and 1950, unemployment was relatively high, whereas in the remaining years, 1948, 1951, 1952, and 1953, unemployment rates were relatively low.

In all of the years under observation, unemployment rates for wage or salary workers were above the average in the following industries:

TABLE 11

Unemployment Rates, by Major Industry Group, Annual Average, 1948-1953

(*per cent*)

Major Industry Group[a]	*1948*	*1949*	*1950*	*1951*	*1952*	*1953*
Total wage and salary workers	3.7	6.2	5.5	3.2	2.9	2.6
Agriculture, forestry, and fisheries	4.9	6.5	8.3	4.1	4.1	4.5
Mining	2.3	5.1[b]	6.2	3.3	3.1	3.9
Construction	7.4	11.7	10.7	6.0	5.5	5.7
Manufacturing	3.5	7.2	5.6	3.3	2.8	2.4
Durable goods	3.4	7.5	5.2	2.6	2.4	2.0
Nondurable goods	3.6	6.9	6.0	4.0	3.3	2.8
Transportation, communication, and other public utilities	3.0	5.2	4.1	1.9	1.9	1.7
Wholesale and retail trade	4.3	5.8	5.8	3.7	3.1	3.0
Wholesale trade	3.3	4.8	3.9	2.5	2.4	2.2
Retail trade	4.6	6.0	6.3	4.0	3.4	3.3
Service industries	3.2	5.5	4.5	2.8	2.4	2.1
Finance, insurance, and real estate	1.5	1.8	2.0	1.3	1.5	1.5
Business and repair services	4.1	6.1	5.7	3.2	2.9	2.9
Private households	4.0	6.6	6.4	4.4	3.7	2.9
Personal services except private household	4.6	7.4	7.7	4.6	3.8	3.6
Entertainment and recreation	9.9	10.7	9.9	7.1	6.0	5.3
Professional and related services	1.8	2.5	2.6	1.5	1.3	1.2
Public administration	2.0	2.9	2.8	1.6	1.1	1.2

[a] The industry categories shown for 1950 and prior years are based on the classification system used in the 1940 Census of Population, whereas those for 1951-1953 are based on the classification system used in the 1950 Census of Population, which differs slightly from the 1940 Census of Population.

[b] The month of October has been excluded in computing the rate for this industry; in October, during the work stoppage in the coal mines, a very large proportion of the miners were classified as unemployed because they were reported to be seeking substitute work. If this month were included, the resultant average rate would greatly exaggerate the typical situation during the rest of the year.

Source: Bureau of the Census.

[13] These data are presented to provide a framework for the data which follow on occupation. No special attempt is made to study the incidence of unemployment by industry because other papers in this volume are devoted to this subject, namely those by Kaplan and Levine.

agriculture, forestry, and fisheries; construction; retail trade (except in 1949); domestic service; personal service other than domestic; and amusement and recreation (see Chart 3). In all but one of these years (1948), unemployment rates were above average in nondurable goods manufacturing. If wage and salary workers in government are excluded from consideration, the lowest unemployment rates throughout the period of observation were to be found among wage or salary workers in finance, insurance, and real estate, and in the professional and related service industries.

In the two years of relatively high levels of unemployment, 1949 and 1950, the highest unemployment rates were found in the construction industry. In 1953, during which year the general level of unemployment was relatively low but toward the end of which our current recession developed, the construction industry also had the highest rate of unemployment. The construction industry had the highest rate of unemployment of any of the broad industry groups for the period under observation, 11.7 per cent (experienced in 1949). In three of the four years of relatively low levels of unemployment, the highest unemployment rates were found in entertainment and recreation.

These unemployment rates by industry do not, of course, take into account the unemployment of "new workers." Moreover, since they are available only for very broad groups, with a relatively large sampling error, very few generalizations are justified. An understanding, however, of differential rates of unemployment by industry must be regarded as a prerequisite to an understanding of the differential rates of unemployment among various population groupings. That is, differentials in the incidence of unemployment by age, sex, and color, for example, are undoubtedly in large measure to be accounted for by differentials in industrial employment of these various population groupings. Moreover, within the industrial sectors of the economy, differentials in unemployment by occupation also help to explain the differential impact in unemployment among various population groups.

OCCUPATIONAL DIFFERENTIALS

Data on unemployment rates by occupation are available in comparable form from 1940 through most of the intervening years to date. For comparability with the industrial statistics, statistics are presented for each of the years 1948 through 1953 (see Table 12). Occupational data are also presented for years 1940 and 1944 to provide comparability with statistics on differential unemployment rates by personal characteristics.

CHART 3

Deviations of Major Industry Groups from Average Unemployment Rates, Annual Average, 1948-1953

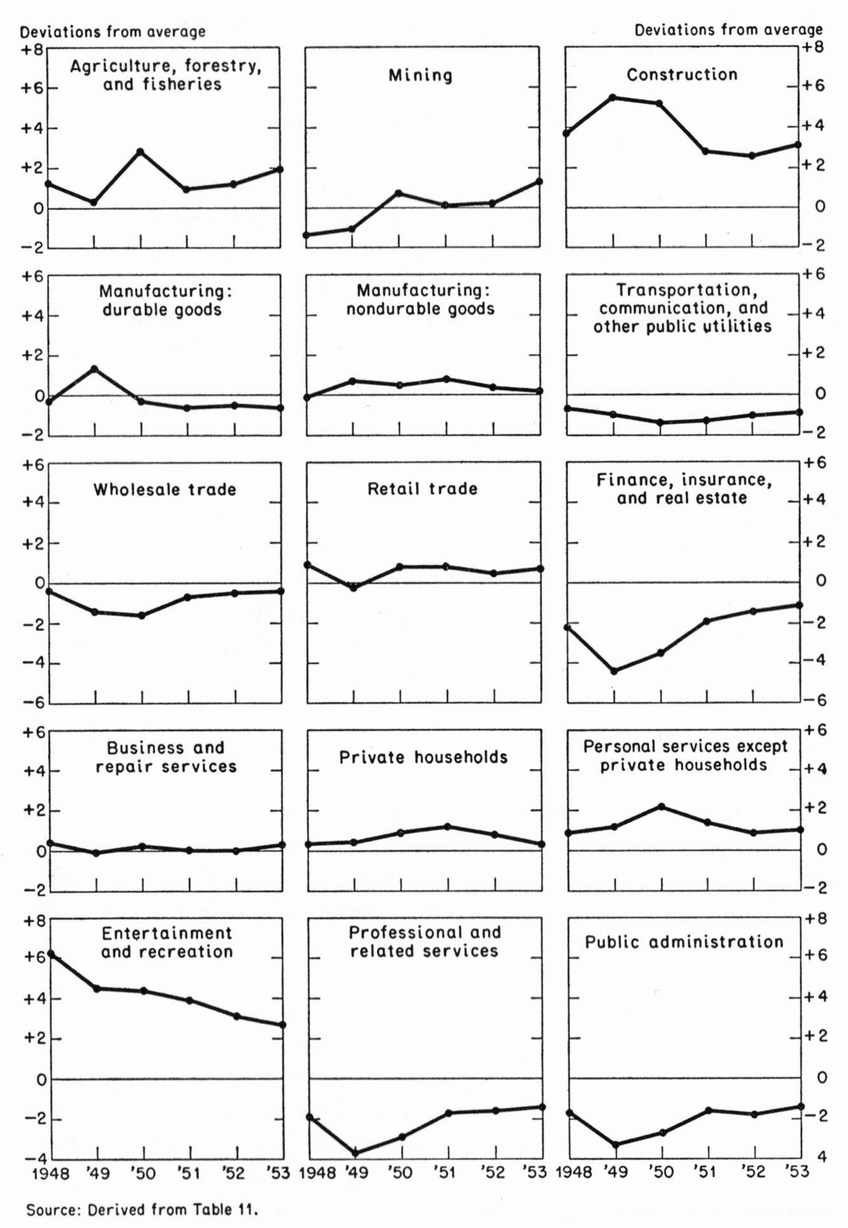

Source: Derived from Table 11.

TABLE 12

Unemployment Rates by Major Occupation Group and Sex, Selected Years, March 1940 and April 1944-1953

(per cent)

ajor Occupation Group and Sex[a]	*1940*[b]	*1944*[b]	*1948*	*1949*	*1950*	*1951*	*1952*	*1953*
h sexes	11.0	1.4	3.4	4.8	5.4	2.7	2.5	2.4
rofessional, technical, and kindred workers	5.5[c]	0.7[c]	1.5[c]	1.3[c]	2.2	1.4	0.7	0.8
armers and farm managers	3.0	[d]	0.2	0.2	0.3	0.5	0.2	0.1
anagers, officials, and proprietors, except farm	2.7	0.5	0.9	1.4	1.7	0.7	0.4	1.0
lerical and kindred workers	9.2	1.2	2.3	3.5	3.5	1.9	1.6	1.7
ales workers	8.9	1.0	3.3	3.4	4.0	2.9	1.7	2.9
raftsmen, foremen, and kindred workers	15.1	1.6	3.3	5.9	6.9	2.2	2.7	2.7
peratives and kindred workers	12.9	1.5	5.2	7.5	7.8	4.2	3.9	3.1
rivate household workers	10.1	3.4	2.5	4.4	4.7	3.5	3.0	2.4
ervice workers, except private household	9.7	2.1	5.3	5.9	7.1	4.6	3.6	3.9
arm laborers and foremen	12.5	1.4	2.4	3.4	5.4	1.8	3.3	2.3
aborers, except farm and mine	33.6	2.7	9.0	12.6	14.3	4.8	5.8	5.2
le	11.7	1.2	3.4	4.9	5.7	2.3	2.3	2.4
rofessional, technical, and kindred workers	6.1	0.4	1.2	1.0	2.7	1.3	0.8	0.6
armers and farm managers	3.0	[d]	0.2	0.2	0.3	0.5	0.2	0.1
anagers, officials, and proprietors, except farm	2.8	0.4	0.9	1.6	1.9	0.8	0.4	0.9
lerical and kindred workers	9.5	1.2	2.5	4.5	4.4	2.0	1.3	1.8
ales workers	8.5	0.4	3.1	3.5	3.5	2.0	1.6	2.4
raftsmen, foremen, and kindred workers	15.1	1.7	3.4	5.9	7.0	2.1	2.7	2.7
peratives and kindred workers	12.9	1.4	4.6	6.7	7.1	2.9	3.0	3.0
rivate household workers	11.9	4.2	2.2	3.2	12.1	7.5	5.0	7.1
ervice workers, except private household	9.2	1.6	5.9	6.1	7.9	4.2	3.6	4.5
arm laborers and foremen	13.2	1.1	2.8	4.2	6.7	2.1	4.4	2.8
aborers, except farm and mine	34.0	2.6	9.1	12.4	13.9	4.8	5.7	5.2
nale	8.7	1.8	3.4	4.5	4.6	3.5	2.8	2.4
rofessional, technical, and kindred workers	4.8	1.1	1.9	1.6	1.4	1.6	0.6	1.1
armers and farm managers	1.4	[d]	[d]	[d]	[d]	[d]	[d]	[d]
anagers, officials, and proprietors, except farm	1.8	0.9	1.3	0.3	0.8	0.2	0.4	1.1
lerical and kindred workers	9.0	1.2	2.2	2.9	2.8	1.9	1.7	1.6
ales workers	10.0	1.6	3.5	3.3	4.7	4.5	1.9	3.8
raftsmen, foremen, and kindred workers	10.7	0.8	[d]	6.8	1.1	2.8	2.4	2.2
peratives and kindred workers	13.0	1.7	6.8	9.5	9.4	7.0	6.2	3.5
rivate household workers	10.0	3.3	2.5	4.5	4.0	3.4	3.0	2.2
ervice workers, except private household	9.9	2.7	4.5	5.7	6.2	5.1	3.6	3.2
arm laborers and foremen	5.8	2.4	1.3	1.2	1.6	1.0	0.3	1.0
Laborers, except farm and mine	19.0	4.1	3.7	19.0	30.6	3.8	8.6	7.0

[a] The occupation categories shown for April 1950 and prior months are based on the ssification system used in the 1940 Census of Population, whereas those for April 1951-1953 based on the classification system used in the 1950 Census of Population, which differs htly from the 1940 Census of Population.

[b] These figures have not been revised to take account of improved enumeration procedures tituted in July 1945. They are based on the 1940 Census of Population and relate to the upation of the last full-time job for those looking for work and to the usual occupation for blic emergency workers.

[c] Excludes data for semiprofessional workers.

[d] Less than 0.05 per cent.

Source: Bureau of the Census.

In all of the years for which the data are presented, unemployment rates of nonfarm laborers and operatives were above those of the average unemployment of the experienced labor force (see Chart 4). In six of the eight years for which the data are presented, the incidence of unemployment was greater among craftsmen and foremen than for all of the experienced labor force. Only in 1948 and 1951 did the unemployment rate of this group fall below the average. In contrast, all of the categories of nonmanual workers, with the exception of sales workers in 1951 and 1953 had below average unemployment rates for each of the eight years.

The highest unemployment rates, by far, for each of the years except 1944, the wartime low in unemployment, were found among nonfarm laborers. In 1940, 1 in 3 laborers was unemployed as contrasted with 1 in 9 for all experienced workers; and in 1949 and 1950 about 1 in 8 laborers was unemployed as contrasted with 1 in 20 for all workers.

In general, the pattern described held for both men and women, with the exception that female service workers not in domestic service had higher than average unemployment rates for each of the years studied, and male sales workers had below average unemployment rates for seven of the eight years and just average rates for one of them (1953).

Sex differences in unemployment rates for each occupation provide interesting patterns, but they cannot be interpreted as indicating differential vulnerability to disemployment. Considering only those occupational groups in which appreciable concentrations of women appear, unemployment rates tend to be higher for female than male sales workers, and operatives and kindred workers; and lower for female than male workers among clerical and kindred workers and private household workers. No consistent pattern of sex differential unemployment rates obtained during the period studied for professional and technical and kindred workers, or service workers except in private households.

3. Composition of the Unemployed

Despite the relative stability of patterns of unemployment during the period studied, the actual composition of the unemployed varied considerably. This, of course, was the result of the great changes in the labor force participation rates of various population groups under the impact of World War II and its aftermath. Moreover, the changing pattern of industrial and occupational activity during this period also contributed to variations in the composition of the unemployed. To show extreme changes in the characteristics of unemployed workers

CHART 4

Deviations of Major Occupation Groups from Average Unemployment Rates, Selected Years, 1940-1953

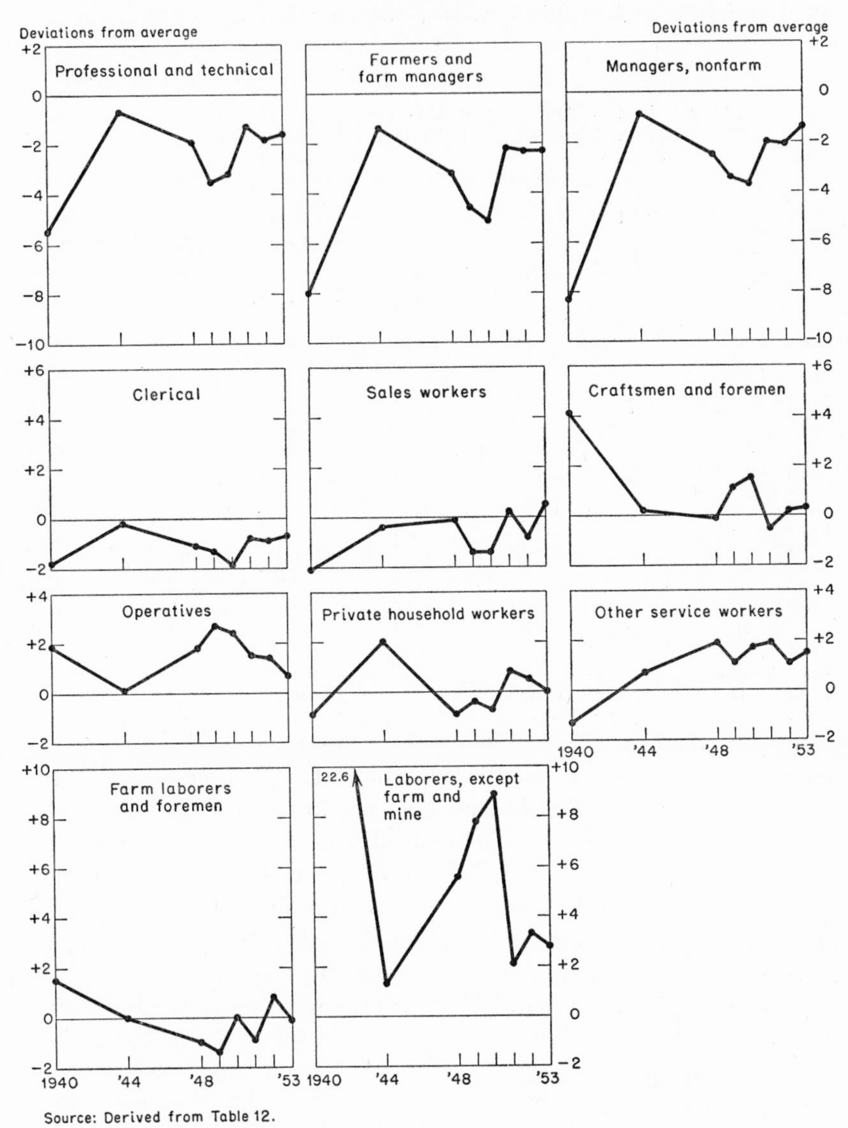

Source: Derived from Table 12.

as a group, data will be presented as far as possible for the selected years 1940, 1944, 1949, 1950, and 1953.

SEX COMPOSITION

The composition of the unemployed by sex changed greatly between 1940 and 1953 (see Table 13). In 1940, only 21.7 per cent of the unemployed were women. In 1944, in contrast, reflecting the relatively large increase in the female, and decrease in the male, civilian labor force, 42.9 per cent of the unemployed were female. Changes in the sex composition of the unemployed during the period under observation depended more on changes in the composition of the total labor force, as affected by war and postwar conditions, than on changes in sex differentials in the incidence of unemployment. At the time of the 1940 census, there was only about one woman for each three men among the jobless. With the great increase in the number of women in the labor force since the war, and the decrease of male workers in the civilian labor force, the number of female unemployed came close to equaling the number of male unemployed. With demobilization and the restoration of the more nearly normal sex ratio in the labor force, the proportion of females among the unemployed greatly decreased.

TABLE 13

Percentage Distribution of Unemployed, by Age and Sex, Selected Years, March 1940 and April 1944-1953

Age and Sex	*1940*	*1944*	*1949*	*1950*	*1953*
Both sexes, 14 and over	100.0	100.0	100.0	100.0	100.0
14 - 19	15.1	27.0	15.0	12.7	15.3
20 - 24	19.4	17.4	18.3	16.4	14.6
25 - 44	37.8	30.2	38.5	38.3	38.9
45 - 64	24.0	19.1	23.5	28.5	26.5
65 and over	2.4	6.4	4.6	4.1	4.7
Male, 14 and over	77.0	57.2	73.0	74.8	69.8
14 - 19	10.6	14.3	9.8	9.2	9.1
20 - 24	13.5	7.9	13.6	11.9	10.0
25 - 44	29.4	14.3	26.6	27.7	26.9
45 - 64	21.2	15.9	18.7	22.5	20.1
65 and over	2.3	4.8	4.3	3.5	3.7
Female, 14 and over	21.7	42.9	26.9	25.2	30.2
14 - 19	4.5	12.7	5.2	3.5	6.2
20 - 24	5.9	9.5	4.7	4.5	4.6
25 - 44	8.4	15.9	11.9	10.6	12.0
45 - 64	2.8	3.2	4.8	6.0	6.4
65 and over	0.1	1.6	0.3	0.6	1.0

Note: Details may not add up to totals because of rounding.
Source: Bureau of the Census.

A similar cycle, but of lesser magnitude, was observable in the increase in the proportion of women in the civilian labor force with the partial remobilization incident to the Korean episode.

AGE COMPOSITION

In 1940, 15.1 per cent of the unemployed were under twenty years of age (see Table 13). By 1944, the lowest point in unemployment during the period observed, 27 per cent of the unemployed were under twenty. This great increase was, of course, not attributable to the great increase in the unemployment rate of younger workers. It resulted rather from the great increase in the labor force participation rates of younger workers and their relatively greater importance in the total civilian labor force, on the one hand, and the relatively great decline in the unemployment rates of other workers, especially of the middle aged. By 1949, a year of relatively high unemployment, persons under twenty again made up 15.0 per cent of the jobless, and the rate was close to this figure in 1950 and 1953.

At the other extreme of the age scale, persons sixty-five years old and over, constituted 2.4 per cent of the jobless in 1940. By 1944, this proportion had almost tripled, reaching a level of 6.4 per cent. During the intervening period, however, as in the case of workers under twenty and all workers, unemployment rates of the older workers greatly declined. The increase of the proportion of the jobless who were older persons is attributable mainly to the increased labor force participation rates of older persons in the wartime civilian labor force, but also to the relatively great decline in the unemployment rates of persons of middle age.

Whereas the proportion of persons under twenty among the unemployed almost doubled and those sixty-five and over almost tripled in 1944, the proportion of the jobless who were between twenty and sixty-four years of age changed relatively little. Under peak war conditions, persons in these classes made up a smaller proportion of the unemployed in 1944 than in 1940, reflecting, of course, the greater participation of workers at the younger and older ends of the age scale.

The proportion of the jobless who were twenty to twenty-four years of age increased slightly in 1949 but decreased again in 1950 and 1953. The decrease was in large measure attributable to the decreased labor force participation rate of persons of this age resulting from the school attendance of demobilized GI's in the postwar years and from the increased preoccupation of women of this age group with marriage and reproduction.

It is evident that changes in the age composition of the unemployed, as well as changes in sex composition, cannot be interpreted as reflecting changes in unemployment rates. The changes are more the result of the important modifications in the composition of the total civilian labor force we have experienced under the impact of the war and postwar conditions.

COLOR COMPOSITION

Despite the fact that the differences in unemployment rates of white and nonwhite workers (see Table 14) must be cautiously interpreted,

TABLE 14

Percentage Distribution of Unemployed, by Color, Selected Years, March 1940 and April 1944-1953

Color	*1940*[a]	*1944*	*1949*	*1950*	*1953*
Total	100.0	100.0	100.0	100.0	100.0
White	88.1	82.7	84.9	84.4	79.1
Nonwhite	11.9	17.3	15.1	15.6	20.9

[a] Revised 1940 Census of Population data pertaining to week of March 24-30.
Source: Bureau of the Census.

particularly in the light of sampling error, it would seem that during the period under observation the net effect of shifts in the composition of the labor force and changing volumes of unemployment was a decrease in the proportion of the unemployed who were nonwhite in periods of high unemployment and an increase during periods of relatively low unemployment. It is possible that during periods of full employment, the white population is more successful than the nonwhite in reducing unemployment to minimal frictional levels. Another possible explanation for this phenomenon may be that during periods of full employment, mobility in labor force participation may be greater for nonwhite than white workers and may be reflected in relatively higher unemployment rates.

MARITAL COMPOSITION

Data on the marital composition of the unemployed, as in the case of unemployment rates, are available only for 1940 and 1950 (see Table 15). These data, in conjunction with the unemployment rates shown in Table 6 above, support two general conclusions: (1) In spite of the relatively low unemployment rates of married men with spouse present, they comprised one-half of all unemployed men in both years, because of their great preponderance in the labor force. (2) The fact that unemployment rates of single men decreased slightly more from 1940 to 1950 than those of men of "other" marital status probably accounts for part of the decrease in the proportion of the unemployed who were single. Specifically, the unemployment rate for single men was 2.3 times greater in 1940 than in 1950, while that for men of "other" marital status was 2.1 times greater.

Differences in the marital composition of unemployed women for 1940 and 1950 were much more marked. Single women constituted

TABLE 15

Percentage Distribution of Unemployed, by Marital Status and Sex, 1940 and 1950

Marital Status and Sex	*1940*	*1950*
Male, 14 and over	100.0	100.0
Single	41.8	37.1
Married, spouse present	49.2	49.6
Other status	9.0	13.3
Female, 14 and over	100.0	100.0
Single	58.9	35.5
Married, spouse present	15.4	35.9
Other status	25.6	28.7

Note: Details may not add up to totals because of rounding.
Source: Bureau of the Census.

almost 60 per cent of the unemployed in 1940, but only 36 per cent in 1950. The more than doubling of the relative importance of married women with spouse present among the unemployed reflects their increasing importance in the female labor force and also the sharper decrease in unemployment rates of single than married women. In 1940, the rate for single women was over three times as high as in 1950 while that for married women living with their spouses was only about twice as high.

COMPOSITION BY RELATIONSHIP TO HEAD

The composition of the unemployed according to their relationship to the head of the household also can be studied only for 1940 and 1950. On both dates, slightly more than one-half of the unemployed men were heads of households, and most of these unemployed heads had their wives living with them (see Table 16). The most striking fact about the distributions of unemployed men is their almost identical composition by relationship to head, marital status, and age in the two years studied. This is true for both whites and nonwhites.

The situation was quite different among women, however. A much lower proportion of unemployed women were heads of households (19 per cent in both years, see Table 17), and a much higher propor-

TABLE 16

Percentage Distribution of Unemployed Males, by Relationship to Head of Household, Marital Status, Age, and Color, 1940 and 1950

RELATIONSHIP TO HEAD OF HOUSEHOLD, MARITAL STATUS, AND AGE	1940			1950		
	Total	*White*	*Nonwhite*	*Total*	*White*	*Nonwhite*
Total, 14 and over in households	100.0	100.0	100.0	100.0	100.0	100.0
Head of household	52.3	52.3	52.1	53.3	53.9	49.8
Married, wife present	45.8	46.1	43.3	45.9	46.9	40.5
14 - 24	2.8	2.8	2.7	3.1	3.1	2.7
25 - 44	21.9	21.8	23.4	21.0	20.9	21.3
45 - 64	19.0	19.5	15.6	18.3	19.0	14.3
65 and over	2.1	2.1	1.6	3.6	3.8	2.2
Other	6.4	6.1	8.8	7.4	7.0	9.3
14 - 24	0.3	0.3	0.5	0.4	0.3	0.7
25 - 44	2.0	1.8	3.7	2.3	2.0	3.7
45 - 64	3.5	3.5	3.9	3.6	3.6	3.9
65 and over	0.6	0.6	0.6	1.1	1.1	1.0
Relative of head	41.2	42.3	33.1	40.8	41.3	37.4
Married, wife present	3.8	3.7	4.1	5.0	4.9	5.5
14 - 24	1.1	1.0	1.3	1.7	1.6	2.0
25 - 44	2.1	2.0	2.2	2.6	2.5	3.0
45 - 64	0.5	0.5	0.5	0.6	0.6	0.4
65 and over	0.1	0.1	[a]	0.1	0.1	0.1
Other	37.4	38.6	29.0	35.8	36.5	31.9
14 - 24	25.9	26.6	20.6	22.9	23.1	21.4
25 - 44	9.4	9.7	7.1	10.0	10.2	8.8
45 - 64	1.9	2.0	1.2	2.6	2.8	1.4
65 and over	0.2	0.2	0.1	0.4	0.4	0.2
Not related to head	6.5	5.5	14.8	6.0	4.8	12.8
Married, wife present	0.8	0.6	2.9	0.9	0.6	2.7
14 - 24	0.1	0.1	0.4	0.1	0.1	0.4
25 - 44	0.5	0.3	1.9	0.5	0.3	1.8
45 - 64	0.2	0.2	0.6	0.2	0.2	0.5
65 and over	[a]	[a]	[a]	[a]	[a]	[a]
Other	5.7	4.9	12.0	5.0	4.2	10.0
14 - 24	1.0	0.9	2.2	1.0	0.8	1.8
25 - 44	2.4	1.9	6.4	1.9	1.4	4.9
45 - 64	2.1	2.0	3.2	1.8	1.6	3.0
65 and over	0.2	0.2	0.3	0.3	0.3	0.4

[a] Less than 0.05 per cent.
Note: Details may not add up to totals because of rounding.
Source: Bureau of the Census.

TABLE 17

Percentage Distribution of Unemployed Females, by Relationship to Head of Household, Marital Status, Age, and Color, 1940 and 1950

RELATIONSHIP TO HEAD OF HOUSEHOLD, MARITAL STATUS, AND AGE	1940			1950		
	Total	*White*	*Nonwhite*	*Total*	*White*	*Nonwhite*
Total, 14 and over in households	100.0	100.0	100.0	100.0	100.0	100.0
Head of household	18.6	17.2	26.2	18.5	17.8	21.0
Single	3.0	2.9	3.6	3.1	3.2	2.7
14 - 24	0.4	0.3	0.8	0.4	0.3	0.7
25 - 44	1.4	1.2	2.3	1.3	1.2	1.5
45 - 64	1.1	1.2	0.5	1.1	1.3	0.4
65 and over	0.1	0.1	[a]	0.2	0.3	0.1
Married, widowed, or divorced	15.6	14.3	22.6	15.4	14.6	18.3
14 - 24	0.4	0.3	0.8	0.5	0.4	1.0
25 - 44	7.5	6.4	13.4	6.3	5.4	9.6
45 - 64	7.2	7.1	7.7	7.6	7.8	7.0
65 and over	0.5	0.4	0.6	1.0	1.0	0.7
Wife of head	12.1	11.5	15.3	32.2	32.8	29.7
14 - 24	1.5	1.3	2.3	5.5	5.8	4.4
25 - 44	7.0	6.5	9.7	18.7	18.5	19.2
45 - 64	3.5	3.5	3.2	7.6	8.2	5.7
65 and over	0.1	0.1	0.1	0.3	0.3	0.5
Other relative of head	61.5	65.3	41.0	42.9	44.3	37.9
14 - 24	45.2	48.4	27.9	27.2	28.2	23.4
25 - 44	12.9	13.3	10.9	11.6	11.5	11.7
45 - 64	3.2	3.4	2.1	3.7	4.0	2.5
65 and over	0.2	0.3	0.1	0.5	0.5	0.3
Not relative of head	7.8	6.0	17.5	6.5	5.1	11.3
Married, husband present	0.7	0.4	2.5	1.0	0.6	2.6
14 - 24	0.2	0.1	0.9	0.3	0.2	0.7
25 - 44	0.4	0.2	1.4	0.6	0.3	1.7
45 - 64	0.1	0.1	0.3	0.1	0.1	0.2
65 and over	[a]	[a]	[a]	[a]	[a]	[a]
Other	7.0	5.6	15.0	5.5	4.6	8.7
14 - 24	2.0	1.6	4.3	1.6	1.2	2.9
25 - 44	3.2	2.2	8.6	2.3	1.7	4.6
45 - 64	1.6	1.6	2.0	1.3	1.4	1.1
65 and over	0.2	0.2	0.1	0.2	0.3	0.1

[a] Less than 0.05 per cent.
Note: Details may not add up to totals because of rounding.
Source: Bureau of the Census.

tion were relatives of heads. Moreover, there was an important change in the composition of unemployed women *within* the group who were relatives of heads—in 1940, only 12 per cent of all unemployed women were wives of heads while in 1950 almost one-third were. This, too, is a reflection of the increased participation of wives of household heads in the female labor force, since the relative drop in unemployment rates from 1940 to 1950 was about the same for wives and other relatives of heads.

Roughly the same patterns of change in composition obtained among white and nonwhite women. However, in the case of the nonwhites, the marked increase in the proportion of wives of heads were offset by somewhat less marked decreases in two groups—other relatives of heads and women not related to the head of the household in which they lived.

INDUSTRY COMPOSITION

The industry composition of unemployed wage and salary workers who had previous employment is shown for April 1948 to April 1953 in Table 18. (The high over-all unemployment rates during this period were in 1949 and 1950—5.5 and 5.0 per cent, respectively—with rates between 2.4 and 3.4 for the other years [see Table 1].) No marked shifts in industry composition of the unemployed are evident for these years, especially if the range of sampling error of the Current Population Survey is taken into account. Manufacturing workers comprised roughly one-third of the unemployed throughout most of the period, workers in wholesale and retail trade accounted for about another fifth, service workers for about one-sixth of the unemployed, and construction workers for 11 to 16 per cent. The most significant characteristic of the unemployment rates (Table 11) and the industry composition of the unemployed (Table 19) is the stability of the ranks of the various industry groups with respect to both.

OCCUPATION COMPOSITION

The composition of unemployed persons by occupation of previous employment is available for March 1940 and 1944 as well as for April 1948 to April 1953. (As has been mentioned before, 1940 had the highest unemployment rate of the period under study, 14.6 per cent, and 1944 the lowest, 1.2 per cent.) The percentage of unemployed new workers—that is, persons who had never had full-time jobs—was greater in these two years than in any of the others (see Table 19). In 1940, this probably reflects the entry of more secondary family workers, without previous work experience, into the labor force in

TABLE 18

Percentage Distribution of Unemployed Wage and Salary Workers, by Major Industry Group, April 1948-1953

Major Industry Group[a]	*1948*	*1949*	*1950*	*1951*	*1952*	*1953*
Total wage and salary workers	100.0	100.0	100.0	100.0	100.0	100.0
Agriculture, forestry, and fisheries	3.8	3.8	5.0	3.3	4.9	4.0
Mining	0.5	1.3	1.7	2.9	1.2	4.0
Construction	13.5	12.6	13.4	11.1	16.4	15.4
Manufacturing	35.0	38.8	35.6	33.5	35.6	27.0
Durable goods	17.2	20.5	18.5	14.1	18.8	13.2
Nondurable goods	17.8	18.4	17.1	19.3	16.8	13.8
Transportation, communication, and other public utilities	9.6	9.9	6.9	5.5	5.5	5.3
Wholesale and retail trade	20.8	17.4	19.6	22.0	18.9	26.6
Wholesale trade	2.9	2.8	2.8	3.9	2.4	3.8
Retail trade	17.8	14.6	16.8	18.1	16.5	22.8
Service industries	13.8	14.2	14.9	20.0	15.4	16.1
Finance, insurance, and real estate	1.2	1.5	0.8	1.2	2.2	2.6
Business and repair services	2.6	2.1	1.8	1.3	1.6	1.8
Private households	2.4	3.5	3.4	5.6	4.6	4.3
Personal services, except private household	3.1	3.2	3.8	4.4	2.6	2.2
Entertainment and recreation	2.0	1.5	1.7	2.4	1.5	1.8
Professional and related services	2.6	2.5	3.5	5.1	3.0	3.3
Public administration	3.0	2.2	3.1	1.8	2.0	1.5

[a] The industry categories shown for April 1950 and prior months are based on the classification system used in the 1940 Census of Population, whereas those for April 1951-1953 are based on the classification system used in the 1950 Census of Population, which differs slightly from the 1940 Census of Population.

Note: Details may not add up to totals because of rounding.

Source: Bureau of the Census.

periods of high unemployment, in an attempt to supplement the family income. Similarly, the relatively high percentage in the middle of the war when unemployment rates were lowest, also reflects the recruitment of secondary workers to the labor force in the national emergency. These were, in the main, inexperienced very young workers and married women.

In 1940, when one-third of the laborers, except farm and mine, were unemployed (see Table 12), they constituted almost one-fourth of the unemployed (see Table 20). On the other hand, in 1944 when less than 3 per cent of this occupational group were unemployed they constituted less than 10 per cent of the unemployed. This is clear evidence that these laborers tended to constitute a lower proportion of the total unemployed as the volume of unemployment decreased. No

TABLE 19

Percentage Distribution of Unemployed, by Major Occupation Group, Selected Years, March 1940 and April 1944-1953

Major Occupation Group[a]	*1940*[b]	*1944*[b]	*1948*	*1949*	*1950*	*1951*	*1952*	*19*
Total unemployed	100.0	100.0	100.0	100.0	100.0	100.0	100.0	10
Professional, technical, and kindred workers	3.2	3.2	2.8	1.7	2.8	3.8	2.2	2
Farmers and farm managers	2.4	0.3	0.5	0.3	0.4	1.1	0.5	0
Managers, officials, and proprietors, except farm	1.6	2.6	2.7	2.9	3.2	2.5	1.5	3
Clerical and kindred workers	7.1	11.0	7.9	9.0	7.8	8.5	7.9	8
Sales workers	4.3	3.6	5.6	4.3	4.6	6.2	4.0	7
Craftsmen, foremen, and kindred workers	13.6	15.5	12.6	16.1	15.7	10.7	15.3	15
Operatives and kindred workers	18.6	23.7	30.9	31.1	28.6	31.2	30.9	26
Private household workers	3.6	7.7	2.1	2.8	2.7	4.0	3.5	2
Service workers, except private household	5.6	10.4	10.8	8.5	10.4	12.6	10.8	13
Farm laborers and foremen	6.7	5.0	2.9	3.2	3.9	2.5	4.5	3
Laborers, except farm and mine	23.4	9.4	14.8	15.9	15.0	11.1	13.6	12
Never had a full-time job	10.1	7.9	6.5	4.0	5.0	5.9	5.3	4

[a] The occupation categories shown for April 1950 and prior months are based on the classifi- tion system used in the 1940 Census of Population, whereas those for April 1951-1953 are ba on the classification system used in the 1950 Census of Population, which differs slightly fr the 1940 Census of Population.

[b] These figures have not been revised to take account of improved enumeration procedu instituted in July 1945. They are based on the 1940 Census of Population and relate to occupation of the last full-time job for those looking for work and to the usual occupation public emergency workers.

Note: Details may not add up to totals because of rounding.

Source: Bureau of the Census.

such tendency is evident in the other occupational groups. In fact, except for operatives and kindred workers, who became a larger proportion of the unemployed during the period studied, no pattern is evident in the variations in the occupational composition of the unemployed. With the exceptions noted, most of the fluctuations are minor, especially if account is taken of the sampling errors involved.

4. *Summary and Conclusion*

UNEMPLOYMENT RATES

With few exceptions, analysis of the differentials in unemployment rates from 1940 to 1954 revealed surprisingly stable patterns in the incidence of unemployment. Through varying levels of economic activity and total unemployment, the unemployment rates of women seemed to be consistently above those of men; those of young persons under twenty-five were consistently above those of older persons. Unemployment rates, especially for men, consistently decreased for persons up to forty-five years of age, then increased, although the rates of persons sixty-five years of age and over were erratic—perhaps partly as a result of problems of conceptual framework and measurement of the labor force.

The unemployment rates of nonwhite persons throughout the period of observation were higher than those of white. For both the census years 1940 and 1950, the unemployment rates of single persons and persons widowed, divorced, or married without spouse present, were consistently above those of married persons with spouse present. Moreover, in both years, the unemployment rates of male members of households other than heads were well above those of male household heads, and the unemployment rates of male heads who did not have a wife present were higher than those who did.

In both 1940 and 1950, the unemployment rates of female members of households other than wives of heads were higher than those of wives of heads, and the unemployment rates of female heads—widowed, married, or divorced—were higher than those of single female heads.

Throughout the period 1948 to 1953, unemployment rates of wage or salary workers were above the average in agriculture, forestry, and fisheries; construction; retail trade; domestic service; personal service other than domestic; amusement and recreation; and, in all but one year, in the nondurable goods manufacturing industries. Excluding government workers, unemployment rates were lowest for workers in finance, insurance and real estate, and in the professional and related services. Similarly, throughout this period and back to 1940, unemployment rates were higher than the average for the experienced labor force for nonfarm laborers and operatives, and, except for one of the seven years analyzed, for craftsmen and foremen. White collar workers tended to have below average rates.

Despite the relative stability in patterns of differential unemployment rates during the period studied, the actual composition of the jobless varied appreciably as the result of the great changes in the labor force participation rates of various population groups and the changing pattern of industrial occupational activity under the conditions of World War II and its aftermath. With the great increase in the number of women in the civilian labor force during the war and the decrease of male workers, the number of female unemployed almost equaled the male. Demobilization and contraction of the total labor force led to a decline in the proportion of females among the unemployed. But when the proportion of women in the civilian labor force increased at the time of the Korean War, their proportion of the unemployed again increased.

During the war years, great changes occurred in the age composition of the jobless, especially at the extremes of the age distribution. The increased labor force participation rates of persons under twenty and persons sixty-five years of age and over during the peak of the war effort, together with the relatively great decrease in the incidence of unemployment among the age groups between these extremes, resulted in considerable increases in the proportions of the total unemployed who were under 20 or 65 and over. Persons 20 to 24 years of age decreased as a proportion of the total jobless as the result of the transfer of males of this age from the civilian labor force to the military establishment during the war, their return to school as demobilized GI's after the war, and the withdrawal of young women from the labor force after the war as the result of the postwar rise in marriage and fertility rates.

COMPOSITION OF THE UNEMPLOYED

The data indicate that the nonwhite population contributed larger proportions of the unemployed during periods of relatively low unemployment and smaller proportions during periods of relatively high unemployment. This phenomenon may be attributable to the greater success of the white population in reducing unemployment to minimal levels under full-employment conditions or to a possibly greater nonwhite mobility in labor force participation during periods of unemployment.

Despite the relatively low unemployment rates of men with wives present, they constituted about half of the unemployed in 1940 and in 1950, reflecting their numerical domination of the labor force. The proportion of the male jobless who were single decreased slightly between 1940 and 1950. But the proportion of unemployed women who were living with their husbands more than doubled, while that of single women increased markedly. In consequence, the proportions of married and single women among the unemployed were roughly equal in 1950, while in 1940 the proportion of single women among the jobless was almost four times larger. These shifts reflect both the increased participation of married women in the labor force and the increase in the proportion of women married.

Very little difference occurred in the composition of unemployed males by relationship to head, marital status, and age between 1940 and 1950. On both dates, more than half were heads of households, generally with a wife present. A much larger proportion of the unemployed women than of the men were relatives of heads of households—about three-fourths in both years—and less than one-fifth were heads themselves. The proportion who were wives of heads was almost three times as great in 1950 as in 1940—another reflection of the changing role of the married women in the labor force.

Throughout the period studied, workers in manufacturing made up roughly one-third of the unemployed wage and salary workers, workers in wholesale and retail trade about one-fifth, workers in service industries about one-sixth, and construction workers 11 to 16 per cent. The proportion of the unemployed who were laborers (about one-fourth in 1940) decreased as the volume of unemployment decreased. The proportion of operatives and kindred workers (from one-fourth to one-third after 1940) increased during the period under observation. No pattern was evident in the variation in the proportions of other occupational groups during the period studied. Craftsmen, foremen, and kindred workers accounted for from 13 to 16 per cent of the unemployed, and service workers, from about 9 to 13 per cent after 1940.

Curiously enough, the proportion of the unemployed who were new workers (no previous full-time job) was greatest in the period of the highest unemployment (1940) and of the lowest (1944), about 10 and about 8 per cent respectively. In subsequent years they constituted from about 4 to 6 per cent. Their relatively high proportion in 1940 and 1944 reflects the influx of secondary workers to the labor force under conditions of relatively high unemployment or of national emergency in war.

CONCLUSION

The observed patterns of differential unemployment rates cannot be interpreted to indicate the differential vulnerability of employed workers to unemployment. The rates include both the unemployment resulting from disemployment (from employment to unemployment) and that resulting from a change in status from "not in the labor force" to unemployment. Unemployment rates, therefore, reflect differential patterns of labor force participation as well as differential vulnerabilities to disemployment.

The gross change statistics tabulated by the Bureau of the Census permit the separation of these two components by sex. The higher unemployment rates of women were attributable primarily to their greater movement into and out of the labor force rather than to their greater vulnerability to disemployment.

Similarly, differentials in gross changes in labor force participation may account for considerable portions of the other differentials in unemployment rates which have been observed. It would be highly desirable to have gross change data that would permit the calculation of disemployment rates for as many characteristics and as much cross tabulation, as possible. Without question, the analysis of differential disemployment rates will continue to be an important objective in further research on unemployment. It is likely that there will be considerable interest, as well, in the analysis of differentials and changes in the incidence of the portion of unemployment that originates in non-labor-force status[14] and in the status that follows reduction in unemployment.[15]

One hopes that the Bureau of the Census will be able to provide more detailed tabulations of gross changes at least on an annual basis. The small size of the sample of the Current Population Survey sets definite limits to the gross change tabulations possible. However, even if only annual tabulations were made, or two or more years' statistics were pooled to stabilize the data, highly significant knowledge could be gained about unemployment. Particularly important would be the continuation of such a series of data so that the analysis of disemployment rates could be made over a considerable period of time.

COMMENT

ELI GINZBERG, Columbia University

In meeting my assignment to discuss the paper by Phillip M. Hauser, I have taken the liberty of a loose interpretation. After commenting briefly on selected aspects, I shall comment more fully on the theme of the session and its relation to the conference as a whole.

As far as Hauser's paper is concerned, I find his concept of "disemployment" suggestive. I am not enough of a technician to know about the feasibility of collecting data that would permit one to relate a person's presently unemployed status to his previous position in the labor force. However, I am sure that from a policy point of view it is very important to know whether a currently unemployed person has been regularly attached to the labor force with a long record of steady employment, or whether he represents a new entrant, or one of the

[14] For example, between 1949 and 1952, between 21 and 29 per cent of the male additions to unemployment originated in the non-labor-force status. Among females during the same period about 53 to 57 per cent of the additions to unemployment had similar origin. Most of the males who entered unemployment from the non-labor-force status were in the category "other"; most of the females by far had been housewives. Each of the sexes contributed about the same proportion of additions to unemployment from the previous status of "in school."

[15] For example, between 1949 and 1952, about three-fourths to four-fifths of the male reductions in unemployment were accounted for by employment and most of the remaining reductions by "other" in the non-labor-force status. Among females about half of the reductions in unemployment were accounted for by employment and most of the remaining reductions by "keeping house."

many who flow in and out of the labor market in response to changes in personal and economic conditions.

Hauser's paper has also placed before us a rich body of statistical information that highlights differential unemployment according to such important characteristics as sex, age, color, marital status, and other socio-economic factors. I was particularly struck by the much higher rates of unemployment of persons who are single or in "other status" in contrast to the rates for married persons.

Now, a few general comments about the way in which this conference has approached the task of dealing with the meaurement and behavior of unemployment. My point of view, which less flatteringly could be called my prejudices, grows out of my earlier studies of unemployment.[1] It is also influenced by my current consulting work for the Secretary of Labor, which has afforded me an opportunity to see some of these problems from the vantage point of administration.

Although one-half of the conference's title deals with the behavior of unemployment, I have been impressed with the failure of the participants to recognize the importance of studying the behavior of the unemployed, which is surely the key to the study of the behavior of unemployment. Admittedly such studies are not easy to plan and carry through, and they require skills that go beyond the typical training of economists or statisticians. It is inevitable that individuals will approach research problems in terms of the theories and techniques that they control. In the present instance this simply means that economists, unless they broaden their horizons, will be unable to make significant contributions to studying the behavior of unemployment.

I believe that as economists we have a particular obligation to be concerned about the allocation of resources, including research resources. It seems to me that we have approached, if we have not already passed, the point of diminishing returns in our preoccupation with the nuances of measurement. Specifically, there is a major need to learn more than we now know about the significant groups who today comprise the unemployed, as, for instance, case studies of the unemployed in distressed areas, such as eastern Pennsylvania and New England. We ought to learn more about seasonal industries with a predominance of female employees. I suspect that new patterns of an annual work cycle are developing in response to the institutionalization of unemployment insurance and other socio-economic developments. Likewise, it would be well to look into the unemployment problem in the Southeast where we are developing new work patterns based upon a simultaneous attachment of the worker to agriculture and industry.

[1] Eli Ginzberg, *Grass on the Slag Heaps: The Story of the Welsh Miners*, Harper, 1942, and *The Unemployed*, Harper, 1943.

There is a heightened need for such studies at the present time since we are confronted with a rather modest level of unemployment. When one out of every three or four persons is unemployed, as was the case during the major depression of the 1930's, social policy can be directed toward the alleviation of a gross pathological condition. At the present time the decision whether special social action is required and what types of action are indicated depends upon a much more specific appraisal of the conditions that prevail in different parts of the country among different groups of unemployed persons.

It may not be out of place at a conference sponsored by the National Bureau of Economic Research to raise the question whether increases in statistical information, which are a necessary condition of progress in the social sciences, may not on occasion become a danger. Wesley Mitchell produced his magnum opus on business cycles in 1913, working largely by himself. After the establishment of the National Bureau, a considerable number of able co-workers devoted their energies to investigating one or another aspect of the cycle. More and more attention was devoted to improving and expanding existing measurements.

As the years passed, two contradictory developments occurred. Constant improvement in the collection and analysis of the data took place at the same time that radical changes in the structure of our economic life made it increasingly difficult to use such data as a valid basis for appraising the present and the future. Moreover, the task of improving the statistical information proved so exhausting that less and less attention was paid to the relation between the new collections of economic facts and the alternatives of economic policy.

Without further elaboration, I want to suggest that we face a danger in becoming so preoccupied with refining our measures of unemployment that we lose our sensitivity to historical change and we fail to distinguish the 1930's from the 1950's by overlooking the meaning of such major institutional changes as the raising of the school-leaving age, the increasing participation of women in the labor force, the establishment of unemployment insurance, and a host of other important developments. Finally, we are on the verge of forgetting that all measurements that do not add significantly to new knowledge have value only as they contribute to improvements in social policy.

UNEMPLOYMENT BY INDUSTRY—SOME COMMENTS ON ITS MEASUREMENT AND BEHAVIOR

DAVID L. KAPLAN

BUREAU OF THE CENSUS

As INDICATED by the title, this paper is not a comprehensive, definitive study of unemployment in relation to industry. Rather, the paper is limited to examining three selected aspects of the phenomenon, presenting some analyses and conclusions, and showing the base data for further consideration by interested readers. Each of the three selected topics is treated in a separate section, and the detailed tables and an over-all statement on the reliability of the data are given in the two appendixes. The first analytical section is concerned with the problem of measurement and offers some conceptual cautions in the use of the most common statistical measures of unemployment by industry. The second and third sections are concerned with behavior—the role of unemployment in the labor force dynamics of three major industry groups and 1940-1950 changes in the rates of unemployment in the several industries.

1. Some Conceptual Problems in Measurement

The subject of this section is whether the common measures of unemployment by industry should be accepted at face value. The question is aimed at the concepts involved, not the practical difficulties of collecting reliable statistics.

The two most frequent measures of unemployment by industry are (1) the distribution of unemployed workers by industry, and (2) the rate of unemployment for a particular industry. In both cases, unemployed workers are allocated according to the industry in which they had worked at some time in the past. This allocation may be according to their last job, their "usual" job, or another similar basis. The method of deriving the industrial distribution of the unemployed, either in absolute or percentage terms, is self-evident. The computation of the unemployment rate for a particular industry merely involves dividing the number of unemployed in the industry, by the labor force for the particular industry; the latter is the sum of the unemployed and the currently employed workers in the industry.

Note: The opinions expressed are those of the writer and not necessarily those of the Bureau of the Census.

The industrial distribution purportedly shows the kinds of workers—according to their industry—in the pool of unemployed at the given moment of time. This would seem to be essentially similar to such distributions as those by sex, race, age, and occupation in describing the currently disfranchised members of the labor force. The second measure, the unemployment rate purportedly pictures the economic fortunes of the particular industry, as expressed in terms of people. In providing information on the condition of an industry, the rate of unemployment apparently is similar to such financial indicators as profits and sales. Both the industrial distribution of the unemployed and the unemployment rate by industry are presumably useful for both time-to-time and interindustry comparisons, along the above-mentioned analytical lines.

THE INDUSTRIAL DISTRIBUTION

Taking the industrial distribution first, what aspects of the unemployed workers' actions in the labor market does it measure reliably? Past, present, future? All three? The answer is, of course, crucial to the valid use of this type of data. In the writer's opinion, the answer hinges primarily on how firmly workers are attached to an industry; or, more specifically, the strength of the bond between unemployed workers and the industry in which they worked some time in the past. If, on the average, this attachment is well established and lasting, we have a characteristic which is a significant facet of the unemployed worker's past activities and is also an important determinant of his present and future labor market actions. Industry thereby becomes a distinguishing characteristic, with the permanence or continuity of such other prime descriptive items as sex, race, age, and occupation.

If, on the other hand, the industrial attachment of the average worker is merely a happenstance, with no more significance than the number of stories in the building where he works, we have a characteristic which plays little or no part in the worker's labor market actions. The industrial distribution of the unemployed, thereby, merely pictures past events, and is of minor utility even in this respect. At some point along the broad range established by these two possibilities lies the true description of how firmly wedded the average unemployed worker is to the industry in which the statisticians have allocated him.

Appreciable numbers of workers are, of course, virtually wholly dependent on a particular industry for their livelihood, unless they are willing to make a major occupational or geographic change. For example, locomotive engineers are almost completely dependent on the railroad industry for employment because few locomotive engineers are hired by other industries. The other classic type of dependency exists where the worker lives in a "one-industry" town. For the locomotive engineer to leave the railroad industry normally means giving up the occupational skill which he spent many years to acquire. For almost any worker in a "one-industry" town to change jobs means moving his family to a different place, and perhaps learning a new trade. Prime economic motives, as well as human inertia, tend to keep such workers tied to a single industry even though unemployed for substantial periods of time.

These are certainly significant illustrations, but are they representative of the great mass of workers or only vivid exceptions to the general rule? A partial answer may be gleaned from a comparison of the industry of the unemployed worker's last job and the industry in which he obtains his next job. Table 1 presents some few data on this subject. The figures are based on fairly small samples, refer to only a scattering of ten months from 1949 to 1953, and are limited to three major industry groups. To state the obvious, these data should not be construed as definitive, even for the time and industries covered.

According to this table, about one-quarter of the unemployed whose

TABLE 1

Comparison between Major Industry Group of Last Job and of Current Job for Persons Unemployed in One Month and Employed in the Following Month, for Three Major Industry Groups and Ten Pairs of Months, 1949-1953

MAJOR INDUSTRY GROUP OF LAST JOB	PERCENTAGE DISTRIBUTION BY MAJOR INDUSTRY GROUP OF CURRENT JOB		
	Total	*Same as Last Job*	*Different[a] from Last Job*
Construction:			
Total of 10 pairs of months	100	74	26
4 pairs of months in 1949-1950	100	76	24
6 pairs of months in 1951-1953	100	72	28
Manufacturing:			
Total of 10 pairs of months	100	66	34
4 pairs of months in 1949-1950	100	67	33
6 pairs of months in 1951-1953	100	65	35
Wholesale and retail trade:			
Total of 10 pairs of months	100	54	46
4 pairs of months in 1949-1950	100	54	46
6 pairs of months in 1951-1953	100	55	45

[a] Includes all major industry groups other than the one specified; e.g. on the construction lines, "different" includes agriculture, mining, manufacturing, public utilities, trade, services, etc.

Note: Data are subject to sampling variability (see Appendix B).

Source: Current Population Survey, Bureau of the Census. See Appendix Table A-1.

last job was in construction got their next job in some other major industry group. For the unemployed whose last job was in manufacturing, around one-third got their next job in a nonmanufacturing industry. Finally, in wholesale and retail trade, almost one-half of the unemployed got their next job in another major industry group. This seems to indicate quite clearly that, at least over the 1949-1953 period, the industrial attachment of unemployed workers was not very firm, even when measured in terms of such gross groupings as construction, manufacturing, and trade. It is unlikely that the proportion of shifts is exaggerated because of the use of last job as the base rather than a longer-term concept such as usual job. First, by definition, the unemployed worker held this last job for at least two weeks. Second, general employment conditions, especially during the 1951-1953 period, were such that workers probably tended to stay away from temporary "pickup" jobs.

The data in Table 1 were subdivided into two time periods as a check on whether the magnitudes are affected by economic conditions. It appears, however, that there is no significant difference between the 1949-1950 "recession" and the 1951-1953 "prosperity." The separate monthly figures from which Table 1 was summarized are given in Appendix Table A-1. Broadly discounting seasonal variations (most pronounced in construction), the percentages in each major industry group show a surprising degree of stability. This stability is especially noteworthy because the small monthly samples could be expected to yield relatively large random fluctuations.

Further information on the extent of interindustry mobility is provided by the data in Table 2 (which, incidentally, is based on considerably larger sample frequencies than Table 1). This table presents, for the same three major industry groups and for the years 1949 to 1952, the industrial attachments in two consecutive months of persons who were employed in both months. As the table shows, of those employed in construction in one month who were also employed in the next month, around 12 or 13 per cent were in a different major industry group. For those employed in manufacturing, the proportion was about 6 per cent in a different major industry group; and for trade, about 10 per cent.

Although some few of these differences may be ascribed to changes in the industrial activity of the business establishment, the great bulk of the differences reflect job changes by people who moved with little or no intervening period of unemployment. The apparent "trends" indicated for manufacturing and trade do not seem to warrant serious discussion. However, the general levels of change for the three major

TABLE 2

Comparison of Industrial Attachment in Two Consecutive Months of Persons Employed in Both Months, for Three Major Industry Groups, 1949-1952

MAJOR INDUSTRY GROUP IN FIRST MONTH	PERCENTAGE DISTRIBUTION BY MAJOR INDUSTRY GROUP IN SECOND MONTH		
	Total	*Same as First Month*	*Different[a] from First Month*
Construction:			
1949	100	87	13
1950	100	88	12
1951	100	88	12
1952	100	87	13
Manufacturing:			
1949	100	95	5
1950	100	94	6
1951	100	93	7
1952	100	93	7
Wholesale and retail trade:			
1949	100	92	8
1950	100	91	9
1951	100	90	10
1952	100	89	11

[a] Includes all major industry groups other than the one specified; e.g. on the construction lines, "different" includes agriculture, mining, manufacturing, public utilities, trade, services, etc.

Note: Data are annual averages, each based on 12 pairs of observations. Data are subject to sampling variability (see Appendix B).

Source: Current Population Survey, Bureau of the Census.

industry groups do appear significant. The figures are quite stable even though the 1949-1952 period was fairly diverse economically. It should be emphasized that the proportions of difference shown refer to average change during a period of just a single month.

THE UNEMPLOYMENT RATE

Is the rate of unemployment for an industry an adequate indicator of the economic status of the industry, as measured in human terms? To help answer the question, a hypothetical example may be useful. The illustration developed below is unquestionably extreme but the essential point is entirely realistic.

Assume that there are two industries, A and B; the first employs 1,000 workers, the second 10,000 workers. Neither has any former workers in the ranks of the unemployed at the present time. In each case, therefore, the current rate of unemployment is zero. Suddenly, industry A fires 100 workers with only a few hours notice; at the same moment, industry B fires 1,000 workers. Assuming that all the separated workers decide to stay in the labor market and look for new jobs, it would appear that the unemployment rates for the two industries on the next day would be 10 per cent (or a shade below if any of the discharged workers got new jobs immediately).

How would these two rates stand a week later, if there were no additional firings? Is it reasonable to expect that, given similar geographic distributions, the two groups of unemployed would decline in generally similar fashion? Before offering an answer, let us examine the kinds of workers in each of the two industries.

Continuing our assumptions, industry A is in the financial field and it separated 100 of its 950 stenographers and typists; the 50 managerial workers were not touched. Industry B is in the manufacturing field and it separated 1,000 of its 9,500 production workers; the managerial workers here too were not touched. In view of the comparative employment opportunities existing in the mid-1954 labor market, it is clear that industry A's former stenographers and typists would obtain new jobs in short order. Industry B's former production workers would, in all likelihood, have a much lengthier sojourn among the unemployed. It might be expected, therefore, that within a week of the firings, the unemployment rate for industry A could be down from 10 per cent to 1 or 2 per cent. For industry B, the rate could still be around 7 or 8 per cent. Yet, both industries had reduced their work forces by equal proportions just a week before.

This example is, of course, extreme. However, the wide variations in occupational composition among the several industries, together with the marked differentials in employment opportunities for the various occupations, undoubtedly do produce distortions of the type (if not degree) illustrated here. Even within the manufacturing industries alone, there are very substantial variations in occupational composition, as shown by the 1950 population census data in Appendix Table A-2. Salaried managerial workers constituted around 1 per cent of the total employed in steel works, fabric mills, and synthetic fibers; and 6 per cent in dairy products, grain-mill products, and paints. Similarly, stenographers, typists, and secretaries made up less than 1 per cent of all persons employed in logging and saw mills, but more than 5 per cent in petroleum refining, photographic equipment, and drugs and medicines. At perhaps the other end of the occupational scale in terms of present-day employment opportunities, laborers constituted 1 per cent of the total employed in office machinery and apparel, and around 34 per cent in structural clay products. The respective unemployment rates for these three occupations—i.e. managers, stenographers, and laborers—were in the approximate ratio of 1 to 1½ to 7.

The differential impact of unemployment on the various occupation groups within the same industry is illustrated by Appendix Table A-3. Appreciable differences exist even though the comparisons are limited to the semiskilled operatives and unskilled laborers in manufacturing. At the time of the 1950 census, when unemployment was generally low, the rate was around 5 per cent for operatives and 7 per cent for laborers, taking manufacturing as a whole. For most of the individual manufacturing industries, the difference in rates for these two occupations was between 1 and 3 percentage points. In some cases, however, the spread was much greater; for example, the gap was 14 points for tobacco manufactures and 8 points for ship building. In only one case was the unemployment rate for operatives greater than for laborers; in the watch and clock industry, the rate for operatives dipped 1 percentage point below the rate for laborers.

Part of this difference is undoubtedly due to the fact that laborers are probably discharged at a higher rate than operatives. Unskilled workers represent a smaller training investment to industry, and therefore can be fired with less loss. However, a substantial part of the difference is probably due to the greater ability of the semiskilled workers to find another job.

To help complete the picture, mention should be made of two well-recognized factors which, like occupation, can cause interindustry distortions in the rate of unemployment. One is geographic location. It is obvious that discharged workers can find jobs more rapidly in prosperous areas than depressed areas. Given a more favorable geographic distribution, workers laid off from one industry can, therefore, find new employment sooner than those of another industry. As a result of this "extraneous" factor, the unemployment rates of two industries with identical proportional reductions in employment can show markedly different declines.

The second factor is class of worker. For obvious reasons, wage and salary workers are much more exposed to unemployment than self-employed workers. Identical degrees of economic misfortune suffered by industries of substantially different class-of-worker composition can, therefore, produce markedly different unemployment rates. One industry fires its workers; the other goes on a diet of lower income and underemployment. Manufacturing is probably the best example of the former and agriculture is the classic illustration of the latter. Fortunately, the class-of-worker factor can be controlled statistically quite simply, by confining the computation of the unemployment rate to the wage-and-salary worker component of the industry.

Before ending this discussion of the unemployment rate, it is worthwhile to examine its usefulness for a purpose other than to measure economic conditions in an industry. The rate for a particular industry at a specific moment in time might be viewed as an indicator of labor market conditions for workers in the industry, and, therefore, of great significance to any worker faced with loss of his job. That is, in measuring the industry's "residual" unemployment (rather than "total" separated), the rate might be construed as measuring the chances of a discharged worker getting a new job. Actually, however, the separated worker's fate will be determined essentially by elements (e.g. his occupation) which the industry's unemployment rate does not take into account. For example, a chemical engineer facing loss of his job had little to worry about in mid-1954, regardless of the unemployment rate for his industry. On the other hand, an elevator operator in the same industry had something to worry about if he lost his job.

CONCLUSIONS

In regard to the industrial distribution of the unemployed, the data presented above indicate that appreciable proportions of the unemployed get their next job in a major industry group other than the one they just left. However, at least in the three major industry groups covered, the majority do go back to the same group. It appears reasonable to state, therefore, that industry does represent a significant characteristic of unemployed workers, but not of the importance of such other characteristics as sex, age, race, and occupation. This type of data is, as a result, useful as a general descriptive measure of one aspect of the pool of unemployed workers; it should not, however, be interpreted as delimiting the future labor market activities of these workers to any substantial extent, except perhaps for some few specific industries. A practical proof of the secondary importance of industry is found in the help wanted section of any newspaper. The listings are basically subdivided by sex and occupation; age and (depending on local legal limitations) race receive frequent mention; industry, however, is rarely mentioned.

In regard to the unemployment rate, the key figure in the ratio (i.e. the number of unemployed ascribed to the industry) is only partially determined by the economic status of the industry. Although the industry itself fixes the initial size of this figure, immediately thereafter the figure is largely determined by the willingness or ability of the economy as a whole to re-employ these workers. Under ordinary conditions, perhaps the most important determinant of the rapidity with which the economy absorbs the separated workers is the occupations of these workers. (The prospective employer is not interested in merely hiring a worker; he wants someone to do a particular kind of work.) As a result, the occupational distribution of the industry's separated workers—which is essentially the resultant of the industry's occupational structure—has a prime effect on the destiny of the unemployment rate for the industry. Since there are major differences in the occupational structures of the several industries, interindustry comparisons of this rate can easily yield a deceptive picture of relative economic status at a particular moment in time.

The rate of unemployment, however, appears satisfactory as a measure of change in economic status of any single industry over time. Such time-to-time changes, moreover, can profitably be subject to interindustry comparisons. For at least two reasons, these comparisons would tend to reflect real changes in status for the several industries. First, the occupational composition of each industry normally changes quite slowly and, second, the relative vulnerability to unemployment of the various occupational groups remains fairly constant over time (see, for example, the 1940-1950 comparisons for these two factors in section 3, below).

In summary, therefore, if the figures and conclusions offered here are valid (see Appendix B), considerable restraint should be exercised in the use and interpretation of these two measures of unemployment by industry. The industrial distribution is not of prime importance as a descriptive characteristic of the unemployed, and the unemployment rate is meaningful only in limited contexts.

2. *Unemployment in the Dynamics of Three Major Industry Groups*

As many studies have shown, the character of the American labor force is dynamic rather than static. Large numbers of movements are constantly occurring as workers leave their jobs, get new jobs, leave the labor market, and come into the labor market. From the standpoint of this paper, the question can be raised whether there are industry differentials in these movements, specifically as they relate to unemployment. When workers leave their jobs, does the industry in which they worked affect the likelihood of their entering the ranks of the unemployed? And, from the point of view of worker accessions, in what proportions do the several industries draw upon the pool of unemployed?

The data used here to try to answer these questions are based on two observations of the individual worker, taken one month apart. Because the information is limited to a comparison of two points in time, it does not provide a continuous story. As a result, the data understate the number of movements made, since the figures do not include changes intermediate between the statuses shown by the two observations. In terms of the categories used, it is likely that only the unemployed group may be affected appreciably. Even in this case, however, major distortions are unlikely because the observation points average only three weeks apart.

It should be noted that these points are calendar weeks and, by definition, employment is given priority over unemployment. That is, the person must not have done any work during the survey week to be counted as unemployed. Therefore, in using these data, it should be emphasized that the "unemployed" category is essentially limited to those out of work for at least one calendar week. In addition, this category excludes those who were unemployed for one to four weeks, but whose period of unemployment fell between the monthly observation points.

The period covered by the data consists of the years 1949 to 1952. The selection of this span of time was determined by the purely practical consideration of availability of comparable data, rather than a carefully devised scientific thesis. The three major industry groups chosen for study here—construction, manufacturing, and trade—were selected on a more thoughtful basis. They include substantially more than half of the nonagricultural labor force and represent markedly different major segments of the economy. Since the data are based on a fairly small sample, they do not permit an analysis of individual industries.

In evaluating the statistics which follow, it is useful to have as a yardstick an indication of the month-to-month changes in total employment for the particular major industry group. The greater the monthly swings in employment, the greater the movements in and out of the major industry group to be expected. As shown in Appendix Table A-4, the monthly change in construction ranged between zero and 10 per cent, and, on an annual basis, averaged out at between 4 and 5 per cent. Manufacturing ranged between zero and 6 per cent, and averaged out at about 1.5 per cent. Trade presented virtually the same picture as manufacturing; the few substantial seasonal swings were balanced by marked stability during the remainder of the year.

SEPARATIONS

Data on the separations from each of the three major industry groups are given in Table 3, which shows the annual averages of the month-to-month patterns of change. As can be expected because of differentials in magnitude of seasonal variations, construction exhibits the highest monthly rate of separation, trade next, and manufacturing

TABLE 3

Persons Employed in Specified Major Industry Group in One Month Distributed According to Their Employment Status and Major Industry Group in the Following Month, for Three Major Industry Groups, 1949-1952

MAJOR INDUSTRY GROUP AND YEAR	TOTAL EMPLOYED IN SPECIFIED GROUP IN GIVEN MONTH (*per cent*)	PER CENT EMPLOYED IN SAME GROUP IN FOLLOWING MONTH	PER CENT NOT EMPLOYED IN SAME GROUP IN FOLLOWING MONTH	PERCENTAGE DISTRIBUTION OF PERSONS NOT EMPLOYED IN SAME GROUP IN FOLLOWING MONTH			
				Total	*Employed in Different*[a] *Group*	*Unemployed*	*Not in Labor Force*
Construction:							
1949	100	80.5	19.5	100	60.3	28.4	11.3
1950	100	82.3	17.7	100	65.0	20.9	14.1
1951	100	83.0	17.0	100	69.2	16.0	14.8
1952	100	82.4	17.6	100	71.1	16.2	12.7
Manufacturing:							
1949	100	91.0	9.0	100	57.6	25.8	16.6
1950	100	91.5	8.5	100	64.3	17.3	18.4
1951	100	90.3	9.7	100	66.2	11.9	21.9
1952	100	89.8	10.2	100	70.7	10.9	18.4
Wholesale and Retail Trade:							
1949	100	87.5	12.5	100	58.9	13.0	28.1
1950	100	86.2	13.8	100	62.5	10.1	27.4
1951	100	84.8	15.2	100	62.6	7.1	30.3
1952	100	84.3	15.7	100	64.4	7.0	28.6

[a] Includes all major industry groups other than the one specified; e.g. on the construction lines, "different" includes agriculture, mining, manufacturing, public utilities, trade, services, etc.

Note: Data are annual averages, each based on 12 monthly percentage distributions. Data are subject to sampling variability (see Appendix B).

Source: Current Population Survey, Bureau of the Census. See Appendix Table A-5.

the lowest. During the four-year period, approximately 18 per cent of the workers in construction left the industry group during the average month. In trade, about 14 per cent left, and in manufacturing around 9 or 10 per cent. For each of the three industry groups, the four annual figures depart from the "four-year" average by no more than 2 percentage points. There is some evidence of a trend in the annual figures for trade, but no striking conclusions appear warranted by the available data.

The size of these out-movements is worthy of notice, especially when compared with the monthly changes in total employment in these industry groups. Construction, with an average monthly change of 4 to 5 per cent in total employment, separates about four times this proportion of workers each month. Manufacturing and trade, with average monthly changes of around 1.5 per cent in total employment, separate six and ten times this proportion, respectively. Granted that response variations tend to increase the apparent size of this out-movement, still the differentials between the two sets of levels are unquestionably striking.

Given this massive monthly separation, where do all these workers go? There are three possible destinations—employment in another industry group, unemployment, and out of the labor force. (Another possibility is, of course, for the worker to die; this avenue of departure has been eliminated from these calculations.) The right-hand portion of Table 3 shows the percentages of separated workers who went to each of the three categories. Before examining the figures, it is worth repeating the earlier cautions that the "employed in different major industry group" category may be somewhat overstated because of enumeration problems, and the "unemployed" category somewhat understated because of the nature of the data.

The data show that the patterns of destination for the three industry groups are apparently affected by changing economic conditions. This seems quite clear, especially with respect to the "different industry" and "unemployed" categories. The patterns differ in this respect from the over-all separation rates, which, as mentioned above, show no clear trend, except perhaps in trade. Because of these changes through time, certain of the interindustry differentials are revealed most clearly through year-to-year comparisons among the three industry groups.

To indicate the general levels first, the "different industry" category took the majority of separated workers in all three industries. For construction and manufacturing, the proportion ranged from around 60 to 70 per cent; for trade, it ranged around 60 to 65 per cent. The unemployed category consistently ranked second in relative importance in construction, moving in the 16 to 28 per cent range. In trade, on the other hand, this category consistently ranked last, ranging from 7 to 13 per cent. In manufacturing, this category ranked last in three of the four years, moving in the 11 to 26 per cent range. The "not in labor force" category filled in the vacant second or third position and exhibited generally stable levels of around 13, 18, and 28 per cent in construction, manufacturing, and trade, respectively.

To examine the interindustry differentials more closely, let us return to the "different industry" category. Construction and manufacturing bore a consistent relationship to each other in this regard, with the former exceeding the latter by between 1 to 3 points in all four years. Trade seemed to go its own way, being on the same level as the other two in 1949 but substantially lower than construction and manufacturing by 1952.

The interindustry comparison of the unemployed levels shows construction 3 to 5 percentage points above manufacturing, and about

10 points above trade. These comparatively wide differences for unemployed among the three industry groups are largely counterbalanced by the differences in the "not in labor force" category. Here, construction was 5 to 7 points below manufacturing, and around 15 points below trade. The relative importance of these two categories in the three industry groups is probably largely the result of the proportion of females in each industry group. Women constitute about one-thirtieth of total employment in construction, one-fourth in manufacturing, and one-third in trade. To state the obvious, women are much more likely than men to leave the labor force upon separation from a job.

The movements exhibited by the data in Table 3 are worthy of notice, especially since they were quite similar for all three industry groups. As can be anticipated from the changing economic conditions over the 1949-1952 period, the unemployed category bulked largest in 1949, started to taper off in 1950, and settled to a fairly stable level in 1951 and 1952. Conversely, the "different industry" category moved in the opposite direction. The "not in labor force" group remained quite stable, apparently unaffected by economic changes. The movements shown by this last group may have some pattern, but the available information does not seem to support any firm conclusions.

In evaluating the role of unemployment as shown by these figures, it should be recognized that 1949-1952 was a generally prosperous period, and that the data tend to understate the unemployed category. It still appears striking, however, that only in 1949 (and then in only two of the three industry groups) did the unemployed category reach even close to half the size of the "different industry" category. Furthermore, allowing for some chance fluctuations, the monthly relationships are essentially similar to the annual averages. Examination of the monthly data shown in Appendix Table A-5 reveals that in only a handful of months did the unemployed exceed half the "different industry" group. Construction exhibited this characteristic in some winter months, particularly during 1949 and 1950. In manufacturing, this occurred in only three months (January and October 1949, and January 1950), out of the forty-eight months considered here. In trade, this never happened during the four-year period.

ACCESSIONS

Data on accessions to each of the three major industry groups are given in Table 4. In this table, the focus is on what the workers in an industry group in a particular month had been doing in the *previous* month. (In Table 3, on the other hand, the focus is on what the workers in an industry group in a particular month were doing in the *following* month.)

The magnitudes of the in-movements for each industry group are not especially surprising in view of, first, the size of the out-movements shown in Table 3 and, second, the trends in total employment in the three industry groups. As shown in Appendix Table A-4, the annual averages of the monthly percentage changes in total employment com-

TABLE 4

Persons Employed in Specified Major Industry Group in One Month Distributed According to Their Employment Status and Major Industry Group in the Previous Month, for Three Major Industry Groups, 1949-1952

MAJOR INDUSTRY GROUP AND YEAR	TOTAL EMPLOYED IN SPECIFIED GROUP IN GIVEN MONTH (*per cent*)	PER CENT EMPLOYED IN SAME GROUP IN PREVIOUS MONTH	PER CENT NOT EMPLOYED IN SAME GROUP IN PREVIOUS MONTH	PERCENTAGE DISTRIBUTION OF PERSONS NOT EMPLOYED IN SAME GROUP IN PREVIOUS MONTH			
				Total	*Employed in Different*[a] *Group*	*Unemployed*	*Not in Labor Force*
Construction:							
1949	100	80.5	19.5	100	62.9	26.8	10.3
1950	100	81.5	18.5	100	64.7	24.7	10.6
1951	100	82.6	17.4	100	69.3	16.0	14.7
1952	100	81.8	18.2	100	72.9	15.2	11.9
Manufacturing:							
1949	100	91.7	8.3	100	62.3	21.9	15.8
1950	100	90.6	9.4	100	62.9	20.4	16.7
1951	100	90.3	9.7	100	66.4	12.9	20.7
1952	100	89.5	10.5	100	69.2	11.6	19.2
Wholesale and Retail Trade:							
1949	100	87.3	12.7	100	59.1	12.3	28.6
1950	100	86.4	13.6	100	61.3	11.7	27.0
1951	100	84.8	15.2	100	60.4	8.1	31.5
1952	100	84.1	15.9	100	63.4	6.9	29.7

[a] Includes all major industry groups other than the one specified; e.g. on the construction lines, "different" includes agriculture, mining, manufacturing, public utilities, trade, services, etc.

Note: Data are annual averages, each based on 12 monthly percentage distributions. Data are subject to sampling variability (see Appendix B).

Source: Current Population Survey, Bureau of the Census. See Appendix Table A-6.

puted on a net (i.e. algebraic) basis did not exceed 1 per cent in any of the three industry groups over the four-year period. For construction, the average monthly net changes centered around 0.5 per cent; for trade around 0.2 per cent. For manufacturing, the 1949-1950 levels were about 0.9 per cent; the 1951-1952 levels were around 0.3 and 0.4 per cent. (The direction of trend, disregarded here in order to indicate magnitudes more clearly, is shown in Appendix Table A-4.)

Since the average monthly net changes were quite small, accessions would, of necessity, be in close balance with separations.

Looking at the sources of accessions, the pattern for each of the three industry groups is very much like the pattern of destinations shown in the separation figures. A comparison of the last three columns of Tables 3 and 4 reveals the striking similarities. Some differences do, of course, exist, especially in the unemployed category; these are largely tied to the rise and fall of total unemployment. Comparison of the monthly figures in Appendix Tables A-5 and A-6 shows greater differences than the annual averages, but this is probably largely due to seasonal variations and sporadic statistical aberrations.

The reason for this close similarity in each industry group's patterns of separation and accession is not entirely clear, at least to the writer. Although, at first glance, it might appear that the conceptual nature of the data causes this similarity, this is not so. The same sets of tabulations were used to derive the separation and accession figures, but the only overlap consists of those persons employed in the same industry group in both months. The two types of persons under immediate consideration—separations and accessions—do not overlap and, theoretically, could fall in any pattern. Accepting the fact that the similarity does not result from conceptual limitations in the data, there still remains the problem of practical limitations. It may be that the random variations to which this type of data is sensitive (see Appendix B) are sufficiently numerous to bury real differences under a blanket of spurious identity. However, despite this emphasis on problems in the data, it is still, of course, entirely possible that what the data show are the true patterns of separation and accession in construction, manufacturing, and trade.

3. Changes in Rate of Unemployment, 1940-1950

This section, which is based on the rates of unemployment for the several industries shown in the 1940 and 1950 population censuses, is concerned with the relative changes in these rates. To measure these changes, a ratio of the 1950 rate to the 1940 rate was computed for each industry; for convenience, the ratios have been multiplied by 100. Since 1940 was used as the base, the ratio moves inversely with the decline in unemployment over the decade; i.e. the smaller the ratio, the greater the relative gain.

There are, unquestionably, a number of difficulties with the census data on unemployment. One of the most important, for the present purpose, is that the 1940 industry data for the unemployed cover all workers; figures limited to wage and salary workers are not available.

The unemployment rates used here are, therefore, based on all workers rather than the wage-and-salary segment. Another difficulty is that the available data refer to "usual" job of the unemployed in 1940, and "last" job in 1950; it is unlikely, however, that this difference has substantial impact on the relationships analyzed below. On the positive side, these census data have the important virtue of providing a comprehensive and detailed story which, with care in interpretation, can be kept substantially free of distortion.

As a prelude to the analysis of the figures, it is appropriate to examine three of the previously mentioned factors which can affect comparisons of the rates. Considering the fact that we are dealing with a ten-year period with major technological changes, the apparent degree of stability in at least two of these factors is quite striking.

The broad occupational structures of the several major industry groups have not changed appreciably between 1940 and 1950. Taking manufacturing as a whole, clerical and sales workers made up 14 per cent of the total employed in both years, craftsmen 20 per cent in both years, operatives 43 per cent in 1940 and 46 per cent in 1950, and laborers 14 per cent in 1940 and 9 per cent in 1950. In construction, the 1940 and 1950 proportions were 59 and 57 per cent for craftsmen, and 21 and 19 per cent for laborers. In trade, the 1940 and 1950 proportions were 27 and 23 per cent for managerial workers, and 37 and 39 per cent for clerical and sales workers. Some industry groups showed somewhat greater differences, but the general pattern is one of stability.

The relative vulnerability to unemployment of the several major occupation groups has not changed radically. The white-collar groups still had lower unemployment rates than the manual workers. The laborers had the highest rate in both 1940 and 1950, but ranked considerably better in the latter year vis-à-vis their fellow manual workers and, especially, the service workers.

The most marked changes probably occurred in the class-of-worker composition of the several industries. In almost all cases, the percentage of wage and salary workers increased and, conversely, the percentage of self-employed workers decreased. As a result, the proportions of workers most exposed to unemployment were generally greater in 1950 than in 1940. From the point of view of industry differentials, however, the changes were not of sufficient magnitudes to cause major distortions in the relationships shown by the unemployment rates. Few, if any, of the 1950 unemployment rates are likely to be affected by as much as 0.5 percentage point relative to 1940, and the ratios are probably not affected by more than two or three points at the most.

The examination of occupational structure and comparative vulnerability to unemployment in 1940 and 1950 was, it should be emphasized, performed on broad levels only, and not intensively explored even in this respect. It appears most likely, however, that the movements described in the analysis which follows have resulted primarily from changes in the basic economic status of the several industries. Shifts in occupational structure, relative employability, and class-of-worker composition probably had only a minor role in determining the changes in the unemployment rates.

April 1940 was still largely a depression time. The war in Europe had brought appreciable amounts of work to some American industries but our own defense effort was essentially in the talking stage. April 1950 was entirely different, although again the economy was on the upturn. This time, however, we were coming out of a short and fairly shallow recession which occurred after years of wartime boom and postwar prosperity. Taking the civilian labor force as a whole, the 1940 census showed an unemployment rate of 15 per cent; the 1950 census showed 5 per cent.

MAJOR INDUSTRY GROUPS

As Table 5 indicates, the unemployment rates for the several major industry groups all decreased over the decade, but the ratios of change ranged quite widely around the over-all level of 32. At the extremes, construction exhibited the greatest gain with a ratio of 20; and personal services the smallest gain with a ratio of 48. Business and repair services and finance, on the other hand, were within a single point of the average.

The position of construction merits a word of caution. The 1940 unemployment rate for this industry (which towers above the rates for all other industries) was substantially inflated by the public emergency work programs. Included as unemployed workers attached to construction were many persons who, but for these programs, would never have been in this industry. Although construction was certainly not in an especially healthy economic condition in early 1940, its illness was not as severe as these figures indicate. And, therefore, the 1940-1950 gain in construction has not been as great as the ratio of 20 indicates.

Other industry groups with better-than-average ratios were mining (23), professional services (23), and the agriculture category (28). Industries with poorer-than-average ratios included entertainment (35), the public utilities group (38), manufacturing (40), public administration (43), and trade (43).

TABLE 5

Unemployment Rates for the Experienced Civilian Labor Force, by Major Industry Group, 1950 and 1940

MAJOR INDUSTRY GROUP	UNEMPLOYMENT RATE		RATIO[a] OF 1950 RATE TO 1940 RATE
	1950	1940[b]	
All industries[c]	3.55	11.05	32
Agriculture, forestry, and fisheries	2.03	7.28	28
Mining	4.05	17.74	23
Construction	8.08	41.39	20
Manufacturing[d]	4.06	10.07	40
Durable goods	4.09	9.42	43
Nondurable goods	3.97	10.31	39
Transportation, communication, and other public utilities	3.29	8.72	38
Wholesale and retail trade	3.51	8.08	43
Finance, insurance, and real estate	1.74	5.23	33
Business and repair services	3.81	12.14	31
Personal services	4.66	9.69	48
Entertainment and recreational services	6.10	17.36	35
Professional and related services	1.34	5.73	23
Public administration	3.07	7.17	43

[a] Actual ratio multiplied by 100.
[b] Data for 1940 not completely adjusted for differences in industrial classification with 1950 data.
[c] Excludes persons who did not report industry.
[d] Includes persons in "Not specified manufacturing industries."
Note: Data for 1940 are subject to sampling variability (see Appendix B).
Source: *Census of Population, 1950*, Bureau of the Census, Vol. II, Part 1, Table 130; 1940 Series P-14, No. 13. See Appendix Table A-7.

The ratios of change do not appear to follow any particular pattern. The extractive industries (i.e. agriculture and mining) both showed gains more marked than the average. On the other hand, among the service industry groups the ratios ranged just about from one extreme to the other. It is noteworthy, however, that at least two of the most depressed industries in 1940—mining and construction—made among the greatest relative gains.

Manufacturing apparently did a little better than trade during the decade, but both were considerably below the average in ratio of change. Within manufacturing, nondurable goods made a somewhat better gain than durable goods, the respective ratios being 39 and 43. This may be a little surprising, considering what the depression did to heavy industry. Part of the explanation may lie in the public emergency sewing projects which resulted in some inflation of the 1940 unemployment rate for nondurables.

SPECIFIC INDUSTRIES

Since some 98 per cent of the employment in the agriculture, forestry, and fisheries major group is concentrated in agriculture, it is no surprise that the total and its prime component showed the same ratio of change (28). The forestry and fisheries components, however, exhibited strikingly different trends, with ratios of 10 and 53 respectively. Too much weight should not be placed on the remarkable gain for forestry; the situation was similar to the one in construction. The 1940 unemployment rate for forestry was markedly affected by the public emergency work programs. In regard to fisheries, only about twenty-five of the more than 100 industries listed separately in Appendix Table A-7 had a lower rate of recovery.

Among the individual mining industries, there were some differences in ratio of change. Coal mining, with a ratio of 23, did as well as the industry group as a whole. Crude petroleum and natural gas did less well with 29, and metal mining worst with 33. The ratio of 14 for the residual nonmetallic group reflects, in similar fashion to construction and forestry, some 1940 public emergency work.

The individual durable goods manufacturing industries varied widely around the over-all ratio of 43. Steel works showed the greatest gain, with a ratio of 24. Structural clay products also did relatively well (28). On the other hand, the several transportation equipment industries did very poorly. The automobile and railroad equipment industries had ratios of 54 and 86, respectively. The other two industries—aircraft and ship building—actually had substantially higher unemployment rates in 1950 than in 1940; their ratios of change were 123 and 163.

Ships and airplanes were both in great demand in prewar and war periods; the postwar era saw a letdown in demand. The similarity ends there, since in 1940 the historical backgrounds of the two industries were entirely different. Aircraft was still a new industry whereas ship building was, of course, one of our oldest. In 1940, aircraft had the lowest unemployment rate of all durable goods industries. A decade later, however, this industry's position in the labor market closely approximated that of older industries, and the unemployment rate for aircraft in 1950 was exactly the same as that for durable goods manufacturing industries as a whole. Ship building, which was already feeling the war boom in early 1940, reverted to its pre-1940 ailing condition and showed the highest unemployment rate of all durable goods industries in 1950.

The ratios of change for the nondurable goods manufacturing industries did not vary as widely as the durable goods ratios. The best showings were made by apparel with a ratio of 26, and printing and publishing with a ratio of 31. (The 1940 unemployment rate for apparel, however, was inflated by the emergency sewing projects.) Among the industries which did comparatively poorly were canning (72), synthetic fibers (70), tobacco (66), and leather products other than footwear (64). The situation for synthetic fibers is somewhat analogous to that for aircraft; in 1940, synthetic fibers was still a fairly new industry, with the lowest unemployment rate of all the nondurable manufacturing industries.

There was a marked similarity in the ratios of change for the various industries in the public utilities group. With just two exceptions, the ratios were in the 30's or 40's. The two exceptions were taxicab service (54) and water transportation (72). The trucking industry made the greatest relative gain (31), despite a substantial increase in the proportion of wage and salary workers in the industry.

The wholesale and retail segments of trade showed about the same ratios of change (45 and 43, respectively). In retail trade, the greatest relative gains occurred in shoe stores (30) and dairy products stores (32). The smallest proportionate gains were in liquor stores (67) and jewelry stores (60).

In personal services, the private households, hotels, and laundering-cleaning components all had ratios in the 50's. These relatively low decreases in rate of unemployment are probably due to the basic irregularity of work in these fields. In the retail areas, five and ten cent stores, gas stations, and eating and drinking places have somewhat similar employment conditions; they also showed ratios in the 50's.

Theaters and motion pictures (40) exhibited a slightly greater gain than radio and television (43). Like some of the industries mentioned above, radio was a comparatively new industry in 1940, with a low unemployment rate. The movie and theater industry, on the other hand, continued to suffer from instability in employment, albeit on a more prosperous level; also, by 1950, the industry had already receded appreciably from its postwar boom.

Educational services had one of the greatest gains of any industry, with a ratio of 12. However, part of this gain is the result, as in construction, of public emergency work programs which tended to inflate the 1940 unemployment rate for the industry.

In public administration, the state and local component apparently showed a more substantial gain than the federal component, with respective ratios of 23 and 39. The size of the latter ratio is, however, probably overstated. Certain conceptual factors and reporting problems in the enumeration and classification of public emergency workers tended to deflate the 1940 unemployment rate for federal public administration. Postal service, uniquely, had a ratio of 114, mainly because of its abnormally low unemployment rate in 1940. A postal job during the 1930's was a sought-for haven and few left to seek other employment.

4. Conclusion

Since the three analytical sections of this paper are separate and distinct, it is not possible to present a single over-all concluding statement. For summary purposes, however, a brief statement on each section appears worthwhile.

Section 1 discussed the conceptual limitations of the two most common measures of unemployment by industry—the industrial distribution and the unemployment rate. On the basis of certain statistical indications, it was concluded that the industrial distribution is not of prime importance as a way of characterizing the unemployed; and that the unemployment rate is essentially useful for time-to-time comparisons, rather than interindustry comparisons at a single moment in time.

Section 2 presented data which showed that substantial proportions of workers moved in and out of construction, manufacturing, and trade each month during the 1949-1952 period. Unemployment, however, played a comparatively minor role in the labor market movements of the workers in these three major industry groups.

Section 3 described the changes in unemployment rates for the several industries between 1940 and 1950. For all industries combined, the 1950 rate was about one-third the 1940 rate. Some industries, however, had 1950 unemployment rates less than one-fifth their 1940 rates, while aircraft manufacturing and ship building had 1950 rates higher by one-fifth and three-fifths, respectively, than their 1940 rates.

Finally, to put this material in its proper qualitative setting, a statement on reliability of data is given in Appendix B. A perusal of this statement is earnestly recommended to the reader.

Appendix A

TABLE A-1

Comparison between Major Industry Group of Last Job and of Current Job for Persons Unemployed in One Month and Employed in the Following Month, for Three Major Industry Groups and Ten Pairs of Months, 1949-1953

MAJOR INDUSTRY GROUP OF LAST JOB, AND SURVEY MONTHS	NUMBER OF PERSONS IN SAMPLE	PERCENTAGE DISTRIBUTION BY MAJOR INDUSTRY GROUP OF CURRENT JOB		
		Total	*Same as Last Job*	*Different[a] from Last Job*
Construction:				
Total of 10 pairs of months	619	100	74	26
4 pairs of months in 1949-1950	350	100	76	24
March-April 1949	127	100	78	22
May-June 1949	86	100	74	26
September-October 1949	50	100	66	34
January-February 1950	87	100	79	21
6 pairs of months in 1951-1953	269	100	72	28
December 1951-January 1952	18	100	61	39
March-April 1952	62	100	79	21
May-June 1952	38	100	79	21
September-October 1952	16	100	81	19
January-February 1953	83	100	63	37
March-April 1953	52	100	75	25
Manufacturing:				
Total of 10 pairs of months	923	100	66	34
4 pairs of months in 1949-1950	539	100	67	33
March-April 1949	122	100	59	41
May-June 1949	157	100	62	38
September-October 1949	140	100	71	29
January-February 1950	120	100	75	25
6 pairs of months in 1951-1953	384	100	65	35
December 1951-January 1952	64	100	70	30
March-April 1952	73	100	59	41
May-June 1952	69	100	62	38
September-October 1952	54	100	69	31
January-February 1953	73	100	67	33
March-April 1953	51	100	67	33
Wholesale and retail trade:				
Total of 10 pairs of months	550	100	54	46
4 pairs of months in 1949-1950	315	100	54	46
March-April 1949	64	100	47	53
May-June 1949	108	100	52	48
September-October 1949	70	100	63	37
January-February 1950	73	100	53	47
6 pairs of months in 1951-1953	235	100	55	45
December 1951-January 1952	39	100	64	36
March-April 1952	43	100	60	40
May-June 1952	54	100	56	44
September-October 1952	31	100	52	48
January-February 1953	36	100	56	44
March-April 1953	32	100	41	59

[a] Includes all major industry groups other than the one specified; e.g. on the construction lines, "different" includes agriculture, mining, manufacturing, public utilities, trade, services, etc.

Note: Data are subject to sampling variability (see Appendix B).

Source: Current Population Survey, Bureau of the Census.

TABLE A-2

Persons in Selected Occupations as a Percentage of Total Employed in the Particular Industry, for Manufacturing Industries, 1950

Industry	*Managers, Officials, and Proprietors (n.e.c.)–Salaried*	*Stenographers, Typists, and Secretaries*	*Laborers, except Farm and Mine*
Manufacturing	2.86	2.47	8.81
Durable goods	2.46	2.44	11.27
Logging	1.07	0.12	77.44
Sawmills, planing mills, and mill work	2.15	0.67	31.34
Miscellaneous wood products	2.83	1.05	15.84
Furniture and fixtures	2.31	1.65	6.34
Glass and glass products	2.10	2.58	10.65
Cement, and concrete, gypsum, and plaster products	3.71	2.04	21.57
Structural clay products	3.34	1.57	33.97
Pottery and related products	1.89	2.00	11.95
Miscellaneous nonmetallic mineral and stone products	4.24	3.24	10.50
Blast furnaces, steel works, and rolling mills	1.46	1.56	20.63
Other primary iron and steel industries	2.32	1.52	16.39
Primary nonferrous industries	2.25	2.62	12.22
Fabricated steel products	3.07	2.95	7.15
Fabricated nonferrous metal products	3.14	2.04	4.34
Not specified metal industries	4.82	4.13	6.43
Agricultural machinery and tractors	2.63	3.04	7.00
Office and store machines and devices	3.48	4.32	1.32
Miscellaneous machinery	3.22	3.06	3.78
Electrical machinery, equipment, and supplies	2.32	3.57	3.57
Motor vehicles and motor vehicle equipment	1.78	2.09	5.58
Aircraft and parts	1.50	3.51	1.50
Ship and boat building and repairing	1.69	2.31	8.39
Railroad and miscellaneous transportation equipment	1.98	2.85	7.02
Professional equipment and supplies	3.61	4.36	1.71
Photographic equipment and supplies	2.60	5.33	3.44
Watches, clocks, and clockwork-operated devices	2.27	2.70	1.92
Miscellaneous manufacturing industries	3.38	2.91	3.25
Nondurable goods	3.30	2.45	6.01
Meat products	3.27	1.93	13.47
Dairy products	6.13	1.82	9.28
Canning and preserving fruit, vegetables, and sea foods	4.06	2.20	13.68
Grain-mill products	6.30	3.08	16.25
Bakery products	3.69	0.95	3.08
Confectionery and related products	2.57	1.94	5.43
Beverage industries	5.65	2.51	12.93
Miscellaneous food preparations and kindred products	5.54	2.29	15.15
Not specified food industries	6.50	4.90	8.99

(continued on next page)

TABLE A-2 (continued)

Industry	*Managers, Officials, and Proprietors (n.e.c.)—Salaried*	*Stenographers, Typists, and Secretaries*	*Laborers, except Farm and Mine*
Nondurable goods (cont.)			
Tobacco manufactures	2.50	1.07	7.89
Knitting mills	1.53	1.20	1.34
Dyeing and finishing textiles, except knit goods	1.77	1.55	5.21
Carpets, rugs, and other floor coverings	1.86	2.18	9.29
Yarn, thread, and fabric mills	1.37	1.03	5.28
Miscellaneous textile mill products	3.95	2.45	5.18
Apparel and accessories	1.67	1.05	0.91
Miscellaneous fabricated textile products	2.44	1.95	3.08
Pulp, paper, and paperboard mills	2.41	1.88	12.89
Paperboard containers and boxes	3.59	2.27	7.78
Miscellaneous paper and pulp products	4.20	4.43	6.76
Printing, publishing, and allied industries	5.21	4.31	1.35
Synthetic fibers	1.38	2.08	6.58
Drugs and medicines	5.57	7.03	3.41
Paints, varnishes, and related products	5.75	4.85	6.22
Miscellaneous chemicals and allied products	4.58	4.99	11.15
Petroleum refining	4.74	5.03	9.22
Miscellaneous petroleum and coal products	5.39	2.42	18.82
Rubber products	2.74	3.06	6.36
Leather: tanned, curried and finished	2.15	1.26	11.07
Footwear, except rubber	1.54	1.09	1.88
Leather products, except footwear	2.04	1.49	2.56
Not specified manufacturing industries	3.98	4.69	6.96

Note: Data subject to sampling variability. See Appendix B.
n.e.c. = not elsewhere classified.

Source: Bureau of the Census. Figures shown here based on a special summarization of 1950 Population Census data. Similar figures can be obtained from 1950 Population Census Bulletin Series P-E, No. 1c.

TABLE A-3

Unemployment Rates in Manufacturing Industries for All Persons in Industry, Operatives, and Laborers, 1950

Industry	*All Persons*	*Operatives and Kindred Workers (n.e.c.)*	*Laborers (n.e.c.)*
Manufacturing	4.06	4.94	6.95
Durable goods	4.09	4.68	6.55
Logging	9.54	..	..
Sawmills, planing mills, and mill work	3.85	3.82	5.44
Miscellaneous wood products	4.81	5.44	7.25
Furniture and fixtures	3.62	4.11	5.65
Glass and glass products	2.89	3.09	6.33
Cement, and concrete, gypsum, and plaster products	2.90	3.46	5.10
Structural clay products	3.65	4.01	4.66
Pottery and related products	3.00	2.94	5.78
Miscellaneous nonmetallic mineral and stone products	2.86	3.16	5.63
Blast furnaces, steel works, and rolling mills	2.92	2.88	5.82
Other primary iron and steel industries	4.82	5.23	7.92
Primary nonferrous industries	3.01	3.38	5.78
Fabricated steel products	3.68	4.49	6.70
Fabricated nonferrous metal products	4.24	5.35	7.75
Not specified metal industries	4.22	5.13	5.90
Agricultural machinery and tractors	1.66	1.89	3.29
Office and store machines and devices	2.81	4.13	6.47
Miscellaneous machinery	3.20	4.02	5.92
Electrical machinery, equipment, and supplies	3.03	3.64	6.68
Motor vehicles and motor vehicle equipment	5.12	6.43	7.95
Aircraft and parts	4.09	5.13	7.58
Ship and boat building and repairing	11.97	13.37	20.99
Railroad and miscellaneous transportation equipment	10.03	13.07	19.08
Professional equipment and supplies	2.89	3.77	3.92
Photographic equipment and supplies	3.03	4.71	4.81
Watches, clocks, and clockwork-operated devices	6.13	7.65	6.98
Miscellaneous manufacturing industries	5.19	6.81	7.73
Nondurable goods	3.97	5.08	7.43
Meat products	3.31	4.07	5.64
Dairy products	2.35	3.12	4.11
Canning and preserving fruits, vegetables, and sea foods	16.23	21.78	22.57
Grain-mill products	2.78	3.60	5.89
Bakery products	3.28	4.83	5.96
Confectionery and related products	6.69	8.50	9.82
Beverage industries	3.86	5.35	7.32
Miscellaneous food preparations and kindred products	5.10	6.52	9.45
Not specified food industries	4.14	6.51	8.91

(continued on next page)

TABLE A-3 (continued)

Industry	*All Persons*	*Operatives and Kindred Workers (n.e.c.)*	*Laborers (n.e.c.)*
Nondurable goods (cont.)			
Tobacco manufactures	8.84	8.80	22.71
Knitting mills	3.04	3.25	5.49
Dyeing and finishing textiles, except knit goods	3.67	4.05	4.99
Carpet, rugs, and other floor coverings	2.12	2.68	3.22
Yarn, thread, and fabric mills	4.34	4.74	6.22
Miscellaneous textile mill products	3.77	4.42	6.39
Apparel and accessories	4.92	5.06	7.87
Miscellaneous fabricated textile products	4.54	5.28	7.59
Pulp, paper, and paperboard mills	2.24	2.24	4.23
Paperboard containers and boxes	3.70	4.52	6.10
Miscellaneous paper and pulp products	2.68	3.31	5.72
Printing, publishing, and allied industries	2.35	4.27	5.09
Synthetic fibers	2.83	3.18	5.65
Drugs and medicines	1.93	2.86	3.74
Paints, varnishes, and related products	2.53	3.39	5.69
Miscellaneous chemicals and allied products	2.93	3.66	6.12
Petroleum refining	2.09	1.91	5.38
Miscellaneous petroleum and coal products	3.07	3.29	6.18
Rubber products	3.14	3.64	5.65
Leather: tanned, curried, and finished	4.67	4.63	9.18
Footwear, except rubber	4.37	4.69	7.75
Leather products, except footwear	6.54	7.77	8.46
Not specified manufacturing industries	7.36	9.67	15.48

n.e.c. = not elsewhere classified.
Source: *Census of Population, 1950,* Vol. II, Part 1, Tables 124 and 130.

TABLE A-4

Percentage Change in Employment in Construction, Manufacturing, and Wholesale and Retail Trade, 1949-1952

Major Industry Group and Month	*1949*	*1950*	*1951*	*1952*
Construction:				
January	−8.6	−10.0	−4.7	−8.1
February	−3.3	−2.0	−2.9	5.2
March	2.3	1.8	7.9	1.6
April	4.1	7.7	4.4	9.6
May	4.5	6.0	5.5	3.4
June	4.3	6.7	3.4	4.2
July	2.5	3.4	4.0	2.0
August	6.8	1.8	3.5	3.3
September	−5.4	−4.4	−6.0	−6.4
October	7.0	0.8	−0.1	−1.9
November	−4.5	1.7	−8.2	0.5
December	−6.0	−7.3	0.9	−5.5
Average gross change[a]	4.9	4.5	4.3	4.3
Average net change[b]	0.3	0.5	0.6	0.6
Manufacturing:				
January	−3.7	−0.7	0.1	−1.5
February	−1.5	2.1	0.1	−0.8
March	−1.3	−1.4	2.3	−1.3
April	−0.9	0.2	0.1	0.2
May	−1.5	2.0	−1.7	−0.1
June	0.3	2.8	0.8	0.7
July	−1.9	−0.4	−0.1	0.9
August	4.2	5.7	1.7	4.1
September	−1.3	−0.7	−3.2	−3.9
October	−1.3	−0.1	1.6	1.9
November	−1.5	1.2	1.2	2.5
December	0.8	1.0	1.7	0.4
Average gross change[a]	1.7	1.5	1.2	1.5
Average net change[b]	−0.8	1.0	0.4	0.3
Wholesale and retail trade:				
January	−3.8	−4.9	−6.1	−4.3
February	−0.2	−1.4	−0.6	0.7
March	1.2	0.1	0.0	0.8
April	−0.8	1.3	−3.7	−2.8
May	−0.1	−1.5	3.9	−0.9
June	2.0	2.8	0.4	1.7
July	1.1	0.5	3.6	0.6
August	0.2	1.3	0.1	0.3
September	0.5	−2.2	−1.7	1.3
October	1.3	1.3	0.0	0.8
November	1.1	0.5	0.3	0.7
December	1.4	3.4	1.5	4.6
Average gross change[a]	1.1	1.8	1.9	1.6
Average net change[b]	0.3	0.1	−0.2	0.3

[a] Based on arithmetic sum of 12 monthly percentages.
[b] Based on algebraic sum of 12 monthly percentages.
Note: Data show change from previous month. Data are subject to sampling variability (see Appendix B).
Source: Current Population Survey, Bureau of the Census.

TABLE A-5

Persons Employed in Specified Major Industry Group in One Month Distributed Accordin Their Employment Status and Major Industry Group in the Following Month, for Thre Major Industry Groups, 1949-1952

MAJOR INDUSTRY GROUP, MONTH AND YEAR	TOTAL EMPLOYED IN SPECIFIED GROUP IN GIVEN MONTH (*per cent*)	PER CENT EMPLOYED IN SAME GROUP IN FOLLOWING MONTH	PER CENT NOT EMPLOYED IN SAME GROUP IN FOLLOWING MONTH	PERCENTAGE DISTRIBUTION OF PERSONS NOT EMPLOYED IN SAME GROUP IN FOLLOWING MONTH			
				Total	*Employed in Different[a] Group*	*Unemployed*	*N L F*
Construction:							
1949:							
January	100	78.70	21.30	100	53.76	39.11	
February	100	79.35	20.65	100	60.95	32.90	
March	100	80.43	19.57	100	64.71	22.58	1
April	100	79.87	20.13	100	64.53	24.39	1
May	100	83.50	16.50	100	63.88	24.24	1
June	100	81.39	18.61	100	60.61	32.08	
July	100	82.77	17.23	100	69.76	24.20	
August	100	79.74	20.26	100	59.55	18.35	2
September	100	86.01	13.99	100	61.33	23.30	1
October	100	79.66	20.34	100	64.80	21.78	1
November	100	80.17	19.83	100	48.71	36.86	1
December	100	74.79	25.21	100	51.11	41.31	
1950:							
January	100	79.70	20.30	100	53.65	31.77	1
February	100	83.75	16.25	100	62.15	29.97	
March	100	82.91	17.09	100	66.16	20.78	1
April	100	83.50	16.50	100	72.00	16.00	1
May	100	85.65	14.35	100	70.43	18.34	1
June	100	82.05	17.95	100	64.57	19.78	1
July	100	81.53	18.47	100	68.33	18.19	1
August	100	80.14	19.86	100	65.43	12.58	2
September	100	81.78	18.22	100	75.14	11.91	1
October	100	85.76	14.24	100	65.03	19.52	1
November	100	81.25	18.75	100	61.60	22.99	1
December	100	79.64	20.36	100	55.68	29.19	1
1951:							
January	100	82.25	17.75	100	60.72	23.42	1
February	100	86.81	13.19	100	67.02	19.79	1
March	100	83.18	16.82	100	76.81	11.24	1
April	100	84.61	15.39	100	77.13	11.76	1
May	100	84.23	15.77	100	74.19	12.68	1
June	100	84.38	15.62	100	63.76	16.26	1
July	100	86.64	13.36	100	78.74	9.28	1
August	100	80.15	19.85	100	68.56	10.08	2
September	100	82.18	17.82	100	68.22	12.97	1
October	100	79.34	20.66	100	75.75	14.42	
November	100	84.50	15.50	100	66.65	21.10	1
December	100	77.98	22.02	100	52.54	29.65	1

(continued on next page)

TABLE A-5 (continued)

MAJOR INDUSTRY GROUP, MONTH AND YEAR	TOTAL EMPLOYED IN SPECIFIED GROUP IN GIVEN MONTH (*per cent*)	PER CENT EMPLOYED IN SAME GROUP IN FOLLOWING MONTH	PER CENT NOT EMPLOYED IN SAME GROUP IN FOLLOWING MONTH	PERCENTAGE DISTRIBUTION OF PERSONS NOT EMPLOYED IN SAME GROUP IN FOLLOWING MONTH			
				Total	*Employed in Different[a] Group*	*Unemployed*	*Not in Labor Force*
struction (cont.):							
952:							
January	100	84.28	15.72	100	68.00	22.58	9.41
February	100	83.29	16.71	100	62.78	25.25	11.97
March	100	85.25	14.75	100	73.15	15.12	11.73
April	100	81.96	18.04	100	70.01	15.74	14.25
May	100	81.74	18.26	100	77.27	11.56	11.17
June	100	84.34	15.66	100	73.31	14.50	12.20
July	100	84.24	15.76	100	73.79	13.32	12.88
August	100	77.85	22.15	100	71.42	8.98	19.59
September	100	83.04	16.96	100	79.83	9.14	11.03
October	100	83.57	16.43	100	74.98	13.69	11.32
November	100	79.24	20.76	100	69.04	16.61	14.35
December	100	80.26	19.74	100	59.80	27.80	12.41
ıufacturing:							
949:							
January	100	91.08	8.92	100	52.91	28.03	19.06
February	100	91.60	8.40	100	58.28	26.22	15.49
March	100	91.42	8.58	100	60.26	22.84	16.90
April	100	90.34	9.66	100	57.76	28.05	14.18
May	100	91.75	8.25	100	60.61	25.21	14.18
June	100	90.29	9.71	100	58.39	27.70	13.90
July	100	91.95	8.05	100	57.14	23.23	19.63
August	100	90.42	9.58	100	55.47	17.00	27.52
September	100	89.82	10.18	100	59.00	22.62	18.39
October	100	90.15	9.85	100	53.10	31.68	15.23
November	100	92.55	7.45	100	60.00	27.79	12.21
December	100	91.09	8.91	100	58.70	28.84	12.46
950:							
January	100	92.74	7.26	100	54.06	28.75	17.19
February	100	90.84	9.16	100	68.31	17.81	13.88
March	100	91.07	8.93	100	65.36	20.63	14.01
April	100	92.04	7.96	100	62.31	22.86	14.82
May	100	93.60	6.40	100	62.28	22.85	14.87
June	100	89.88	10.12	100	68.58	16.50	14.92
July	100	92.04	7.96	100	69.85	12.06	18.09
August	100	90.02	9.98	100	63.39	8.93	27.68
September	100	90.68	9.32	100	65.24	9.87	24.89
October	100	91.86	8.14	100	64.00	18.06	17.94
November	100	92.33	7.67	100	66.58	12.66	20.76
December	100	91.38	8.62	100	61.25	16.59	22.16

(continued on next page)

TABLE A-5 (continued)

MAJOR INDUSTRY GROUP, MONTH AND YEAR	TOTAL EMPLOYED IN SPECIFIED GROUP IN GIVEN MONTH (*per cent*)	PER CENT EMPLOYED IN SAME GROUP IN FOLLOWING MONTH	PER CENT NOT EMPLOYED IN SAME GROUP IN FOLLOWING MONTH	PERCENTAGE DISTRIBUTION OF PERSONS NOT EMPLOYED IN SAME GROUP IN FOLLOWING MONTH			
				Total	*Employed in Different*[a] *Group*	*Unemployed*	*No La Fo*
Manufacturing (cont.):							
1951:							
January	100	90.87	9.13	100	61.45	11.06	27
February	100	91.69	8.31	100	61.08	12.29	26
March	100	90.14	9.86	100	65.01	12.58	22
April	100	89.68	10.32	100	68.54	11.91	19
May	100	91.35	8.65	100	69.13	11.33	19
June	100	89.83	10.17	100	67.03	11.91	21
July	100	90.66	9.34	100	65.78	9.95	24
August	100	88.66	11.34	100	67.46	9.26	23
September	100	89.10	10.90	100	69.17	10.09	20
October	100	91.02	8.98	100	67.19	14.91	17
November	100	91.60	8.40	100	70.92	12.51	16
December	100	89.47	10.53	100	61.35	15.38	23
1952:							
January	100	89.85	10.15	100	69.72	11.83	18
February	100	90.18	9.82	100	72.51	9.47	18
March	100	89.65	10.35	100	68.96	11.61	19
April	100	89.47	10.53	100	73.24	11.86	14
May	100	89.27	10.73	100	74.56	10.25	15
June	100	88.95	11.05	100	66.52	13.85	19
July	100	91.08	8.92	100	68.20	13.21	18
August	100	87.60	12.40	100	63.63	10.56	25
September	100	90.00	10.00	100	72.13	7.39	20
October	100	91.06	8.94	100	74.69	7.50	17
November	100	90.27	9.73	100	73.92	9.75	16
December	100	90.59	9.41	100	70.11	13.09	16
Wholesale and retail trade:							
1949:							
January	100	88.20	11.80	100	54.87	17.27	27
February	100	89.87	10.13	100	64.36	11.85	23
March	100	87.66	12.34	100	59.56	10.37	30
April	100	86.68	13.32	100	63.59	9.91	26
May	100	88.36	11.64	100	65.72	12.37	21
June	100	87.68	12.32	100	57.92	13.24	28
July	100	87.00	13.00	100	58.38	14.00	27
August	100	86.61	13.39	100	51.79	10.37	37
September	100	86.83	13.17	100	59.26	12.29	28
October	100	87.79	12.21	100	57.30	13.69	29
November	100	89.02	10.98	100	65.03	11.75	23
December	100	84.63	15.37	100	49.32	19.06	31

(continued on next page)

TABLE A-5 (continued)

MAJOR INDUSTRY GROUP, MONTH AND YEAR	TOTAL EMPLOYED IN SPECIFIED GROUP IN GIVEN MONTH (*per cent*)	PER CENT EMPLOYED IN SAME GROUP IN FOLLOWING MONTH	PER CENT NOT EMPLOYED IN SAME GROUP IN FOLLOWING MONTH	PERCENTAGE DISTRIBUTION OF PERSONS NOT EMPLOYED IN SAME GROUP IN FOLLOWING MONTH			
				Total	*Employed in Different[a] Group*	*Unemployed*	*Not in Labor Force*
olesale and retail trade (cont.):							
950:							
January	100	86.98	13.02	100	64.67	14.44	20.89
February	100	86.72	13.28	100	60.99	11.90	27.11
March	100	87.54	12.46	100	68.54	11.32	20.14
April	100	86.03	13.97	100	60.06	11.10	28.85
May	100	88.88	11.12	100	62.50	12.68	24.82
June	100	85.58	14.42	100	66.30	9.64	24.06
July	100	85.45	14.55	100	66.78	7.08	26.13
August	100	84.23	15.77	100	57.70	5.96	36.33
September	100	85.64	14.36	100	60.79	7.17	32.03
October	100	86.69	13.31	100	67.32	8.87	23.82
November	100	88.43	11.57	100	64.74	10.37	24.89
December	100	81.89	18.11	100	49.81	11.10	39.09
951:							
January	100	85.62	14.38	100	60.22	9.46	30.32
February	100	85.12	14.88	100	63.91	7.80	28.29
March	100	82.55	17.45	100	61.63	6.93	31.44
April	100	86.49	13.51	100	67.65	5.18	27.17
May	100	85.09	14.91	100	63.69	7.45	28.86
June	100	85.57	14.43	100	65.56	9.36	25.09
July	100	85.24	14.76	100	66.73	7.05	26.22
August	100	83.28	16.72	100	52.21	5.98	41.81
September	100	83.13	16.87	100	62.48	6.34	31.18
October	100	86.31	13.69	100	66.76	6.36	26.88
November	100	86.43	13.57	100	65.17	6.77	28.06
December	100	82.31	17.69	100	54.89	6.61	38.50
952:							
January	100	84.98	15.02	100	63.38	9.99	26.63
February	100	86.45	13.55	100	70.90	6.87	22.23
March	100	83.60	16.40	100	70.24	5.18	24.57
April	100	83.50	16.50	100	66.61	5.58	27.82
May	100	83.73	16.27	100	64.29	8.42	27.29
June	100	84.22	15.78	100	64.20	9.25	26.55
July	100	84.94	15.06	100	68.39	5.91	25.70
August	100	83.22	16.78	100	55.01	5.30	39.69
September	100	84.22	15.78	100	62.70	4.69	32.62
October	100	84.06	15.94	100	67.57	8.09	24.34
November	100	86.73	13.27	100	63.75	7.84	28.41
December	100	81.45	18.55	100	55.80	6.90	37.30

Includes all major industry groups other than the one specified; e.g. on the construction lines, ferent" includes agriculture, mining, manufacturing, public utilities, trade, services, etc.
Note: Data are subject to sampling variability (see Appendix B).
ource: Current Population Survey, Bureau of the Census.

TABLE A-6

Persons Employed in Specified Major Industry Group in One Month Distributed According Their Employment Status and Major Industry Group in the Previous Month, for Three Major Industry Groups, 1949-1952

MAJOR INDUSTRY GROUP, MONTH AND YEAR	TOTAL EMPLOYED IN SPECIFIED GROUP IN GIVEN MONTH (*per cent*)	PER CENT EMPLOYED IN SAME GROUP IN PREVIOUS MONTH	PER CENT NOT EMPLOYED IN SAME GROUP IN PREVIOUS MONTH	PERCENTAGE DISTRIBUTION OF PERSONS NOT EMPLOYED IN SAME GROUP IN PREVIOUS MONTH			
				Total	*Employed in Different[a] Group*	*Unemployed*	*No La Fo*
Construction:							
1949:							
January	100	83.45	16.55	100	81.58	11.35	7
February	100	81.31	18.69	100	62.01	28.84	9
March	100	77.61	22.39	100	56.59	32.60	10
April	100	77.26	22.74	100	51.45	40.24	8
May	100	76.41	23.59	100	61.59	26.16	12
June	100	80.01	19.99	100	62.18	24.81	13
July	100	79.47	20.53	100	64.63	20.59	14
August	100	77.42	22.58	100	62.78	26.50	10
September	100	84.34	15.66	100	62.26	31.35	6
October	100	80.37	19.63	100	62.32	24.13	13
November	100	83.44	16.56	100	55.37	35.39	9
December	100	85.26	14.74	100	72.46	19.06	8
1950:							
January	100	83.08	16.92	100	66.49	19.80	13
February	100	81.38	18.62	100	51.61	37.27	11
March	100	82.24	17.76	100	52.36	38.57	9
April	100	77.16	22.84	100	60.51	32.92	6
May	100	78.75	21.25	100	56.59	31.56	11
June	100	80.25	19.75	100	56.10	28.30	15
July	100	79.35	20.65	100	66.59	20.63	12
August	100	80.01	19.99	100	67.48	17.76	14
September	100	83.60	16.40	100	80.12	12.99	6
October	100	80.67	19.33	100	67.08	23.46	9
November	100	84.00	16.00	100	79.63	12.81	7
December	100	87.29	12.71	100	72.33	19.81	7
1951:							
January	100	83.40	16.60	100	64.42	21.55	14
February	100	84.24	15.76	100	60.24	22.26	17
March	100	80.42	19.58	100	56.31	25.55	18
April	100	79.41	20.59	100	65.11	24.68	10
May	100	80.00	20.00	100	67.70	12.50	19
June	100	81.26	18.74	100	73.59	11.31	15
July	100	81.04	18.96	100	68.72	12.71	18
August	100	83.64	16.36	100	74.27	13.02	12
September	100	85.19	14.81	100	72.65	13.98	13
October	100	82.36	17.64	100	74.38	13.55	12
November	100	86.38	13.62	100	75.62	11.23	13
December	100	83.66	16.34	100	78.40	9.91	11

(continued on next page)

TABLE A-6 (continued)

MAJOR INDUSTRY GROUP, MONTH AND YEAR	TOTAL EMPLOYED IN SPECIFIED GROUP IN GIVEN MONTH (*per cent*)	PER CENT EMPLOYED IN SAME GROUP IN PREVIOUS MONTH	PER CENT NOT EMPLOYED IN SAME GROUP IN PREVIOUS MONTH	PERCENTAGE DISTRIBUTION OF PERSONS NOT EMPLOYED IN SAME GROUP IN PREVIOUS MONTH			
				Total	*Employed in Different[a] Group*	*Unemployed*	*Not in Labor Force*
Construction (cont.):							
1952:							
January	100	84.76	15.24	100	79.33	11.35	9.32
February	100	80.01	19.99	100	64.35	26.60	9.05
March	100	81.85	18.15	100	65.60	20.07	14.33
April	100	77.76	22.24	100	60.75	26.26	12.99
May	100	79.29	20.71	100	68.76	18.78	12.46
June	100	78.52	21.48	100	70.56	12.16	17.28
July	100	82.77	17.23	100	75.78	14.11	10.10
August	100	81.56	18.44	100	74.15	15.07	10.79
September	100	83.15	16.85	100	73.96	13.29	12.75
October	100	84.74	15.26	100	82.44	9.17	8.39
November	100	83.20	16.80	100	79.46	6.49	14.05
December	100	83.76	16.24	100	80.30	8.81	10.90
Manufacturing:							
1949:							
January	100	93.74	6.26	100	77.80	8.63	13.58
February	100	92.43	7.57	100	63.67	19.42	16.91
March	100	92.97	7.03	100	57.61	24.32	18.07
April	100	92.29	7.71	100	65.63	21.53	12.84
May	100	91.75	8.25	100	62.91	20.73	16.36
June	100	91.44	8.56	100	60.75	20.09	19.16
July	100	92.07	7.93	100	55.61	25.47	18.92
August	100	88.22	11.78	100	54.67	28.86	16.47
September	100	91.56	8.44	100	59.36	26.42	14.22
October	100	91.01	8.99	100	55.46	27.51	17.04
November	100	91.49	8.51	100	64.94	21.88	13.18
December	100	91.80	8.20	100	68.66	18.41	12.93
1950:							
January	100	91.74	8.26	100	65.62	21.67	12.71
February	100	90.83	9.17	100	62.75	24.62	12.64
March	100	92.14	7.86	100	58.45	25.67	15.88
April	100	90.95	9.05	100	67.18	25.75	7.07
May	100	90.25	9.75	100	56.41	29.23	14.36
June	100	91.07	8.93	100	58.34	18.70	22.96
July	100	90.26	9.74	100	60.82	20.62	18.56
August	100	87.03	12.97	100	55.20	24.44	20.35
September	100	90.51	9.49	100	68.53	16.42	15.05
October	100	90.44	9.56	100	62.93	12.98	24.08
November	100	90.47	9.53	100	67.75	11.03	21.22
December	100	91.17	8.83	100	70.52	13.38	16.10

(continued on next page)

TABLE A-6 (continued)

MAJOR INDUSTRY GROUP, MONTH AND YEAR	TOTAL EMPLOYED IN SPECIFIED GROUP IN GIVEN MONTH (*per cent*)	PER CENT EMPLOYED IN SAME GROUP IN PREVIOUS MONTH	PER CENT NOT EMPLOYED IN SAME GROUP IN PREVIOUS MONTH	PERCENTAGE DISTRIBUTION OF PERSONS NOT EMPLOYED IN SAME GROUP IN PREVIOUS MONTH			
				Total	*Employed in Different*[a] *Group*	*Unemployed*	*No La Fo*
Manufacturing (cont.):							
1951:							
January	100	91.11	8.89	100	68.24	11.04	20
February	100	90.39	9.61	100	56.82	17.59	25
March	100	89.60	10.40	100	56.87	13.83	29
April	100	89.83	10.17	100	71.39	13.37	15
May	100	91.03	8.97	100	72.13	10.59	17
June	100	90.47	9.53	100	66.49	10.92	22
July	100	89.81	10.19	100	60.75	13.64	25
August	100	89.09	10.91	100	66.45	12.01	21
September	100	91.59	8.41	100	71.67	13.69	14
October	100	90.59	9.41	100	69.04	11.06	19
November	100	89.86	10.14	100	68.74	12.23	19
December	100	89.99	10.01	100	67.96	15.37	16
1952:							
January	100	90.76	9.24	100	72.84	10.39	16
February	100	90.46	9.54	100	65.93	13.21	20
March	100	91.26	8.74	100	67.54	13.37	19
April	100	89.47	10.53	100	69.92	13.19	16
May	100	89.61	10.39	100	72.86	11.07	16
June	100	88.67	11.33	100	65.58	9.44	24
July	100	88.25	11.75	100	71.40	10.47	18
August	100	87.51	12.49	100	66.93	14.65	18
September	100	91.19	8.81	100	61.22	15.76	23
October	100	88.38	11.62	100	72.81	9.64	17
November	100	88.89	11.11	100	71.38	9.27	19
December	100	90.00	10.00	100	72.17	8.71	19
Wholesale and retail trade:							
1949:							
January	100	88.64	11.36	100	69.19	6.87	23
February	100	88.29	11.71	100	61.88	9.15	28
March	100	88.76	11.24	100	61.21	11.39	27
April	100	88.39	11.61	100	59.74	12.67	27
May	100	86.75	13.25	100	59.85	13.13	27
June	100	86.61	13.39	100	54.04	10.76	35
July	100	86.81	13.19	100	53.60	11.68	34
August	100	86.89	13.11	100	52.63	15.87	31
September	100	86.21	13.79	100	62.80	14.65	22
October	100	85.76	14.24	100	62.68	12.09	25
November	100	86.85	13.15	100	57.53	13.01	29
December	100	87.78	12.22	100	54.13	16.35	29

(continued on next page)

TABLE A-6 (continued)

MAJOR INDUSTRY GROUP, MONTH AND YEAR	TOTAL EMPLOYED IN SPECIFIED GROUP IN GIVEN MONTH (*per cent*)	PER CENT EMPLOYED IN SAME GROUP IN PREVIOUS MONTH	PER CENT NOT EMPLOYED IN SAME GROUP IN PREVIOUS MONTH	PERCENTAGE DISTRIBUTION OF PERSONS NOT EMPLOYED IN SAME GROUP IN PREVIOUS MONTH			
				Total	*Employed in Different*[a] *Group*	*Unemployed*	*Not in Labor Force*
Wholesale and retail trade (cont.):							
1950:							
January	100	89.01	10.99	100	69.88	9.28	20.84
February	100	88.28	11.72	100	61.38	12.11	26.51
March	100	86.63	13.37	100	63.72	15.56	20.72
April	100	87.81	12.19	100	71.84	17.16	11.00
May	100	87.34	12.66	100	58.29	15.56	26.15
June	100	86.41	13.59	100	52.69	10.67	36.64
July	100	85.22	14.78	100	62.58	10.28	27.13
August	100	84.36	15.64	100	58.18	11.38	30.43
September	100	85.99	14.01	100	64.84	9.70	25.46
October	100	84.22	15.78	100	57.54	10.14	32.32
November	100	86.00	14.00	100	60.93	8.64	30.43
December	100	85.29	14.71	100	54.04	9.72	36.23
1951:							
January	100	87.08	12.92	100	65.24	9.37	25.39
February	100	85.80	14.20	100	57.89	8.73	33.38
March	100	85.11	14.89	100	49.33	10.34	40.34
April	100	85.54	14.46	100	66.69	9.40	23.91
May	100	83.14	16.86	100	62.93	6.94	30.13
June	100	84.68	15.32	100	61.49	5.16	33.36
July	100	82.52	17.48	100	56.10	9.79	34.12
August	100	85.04	14.96	100	59.83	7.69	32.49
September	100	84.69	15.31	100	66.30	7.18	26.52
October	100	83.20	16.80	100	58.90	8.34	32.76
November	100	85.99	14.01	100	63.03	7.28	29.69
December	100	85.08	14.92	100	57.10	7.31	35.59
1952:							
January	100	85.98	14.02	100	67.14	6.27	26.59
February	100	84.31	15.69	100	65.11	6.12	28.76
March	100	85.67	14.33	100	70.48	7.26	22.26
April	100	86.00	14.00	100	65.86	7.36	26.79
May	100	84.30	15.70	100	65.35	5.54	29.11
June	100	82.37	17.63	100	57.57	7.94	34.49
July	100	83.79	16.21	100	63.95	8.27	27.78
August	100	84.66	15.34	100	62.39	8.74	28.88
September	100	82.15	17.85	100	61.01	7.56	31.43
October	100	83.66	16.34	100	65.69	5.08	29.24
November	100	83.54	16.46	100	58.81	4.74	36.45
December	100	82.92	17.08	100	57.20	7.96	34.84

[a] Includes all major industry groups other than the one specified; e.g. on the construction lines, "different" includes agriculture, mining, manufacturing, public utilities, trade, services, etc.
Note: Data are subject to sampling variability (see Appendix B).
Source: Current Population Survey, Bureau of the Census.

TABLE A-7

Unemployment Rates for the Experienced Civilian Labor Force, by Industry, 1950 and 1940

INDUSTRY	UNEMPLOYMENT RATES		RATIO[a] OF 1950 RATE TO 1940 RATE
	1950	*1940*[b]	
Total	4.62	13.25	34.9
Total, except industry not reported	3.55	11.05	32.1
Agriculture, forestry, and fisheries	2.03	7.28	27.9
Agriculture	1.97	7.01	28.1
Forestry	3.78	37.37	10.1
Fisheries	6.60	12.39	53.3
Mining	4.05	17.74	22.8
Metal mining	5.00	15.01	33.3
Coal mining	4.32	19.20	22.5
Crude petroleum and natural gas extraction	3.37	11.59	29.1
Nonmetallic mining and quarrying, except fuel	3.32	23.97	13.9
Construction	8.08	41.39	19.5
Manufacturing	4.06	10.07	40.3
Durable goods	4.09	9.42	43.4
Lumber and wood products, except furniture	5.15	12.62	40.8
Logging	9.54	22.07	43.2
Sawmills, planing mills, and mill work	3.85	9.99	38.5
Miscellaneous wood products	4.81	9.66	49.8
Furniture and fixtures	3.62	11.08	32.7
Stone, clay, and glass products	3.03	9.70	31.2
Glass and glass products	2.89	9.11	31.7
Cement, and concrete, gypsum, and plaster products	2.90	8.08	35.9
Structural clay products	3.65	13.13	27.8
Pottery and related products	3.00	6.16	48.7
Miscellaneous nonmetallic mineral and stone products	2.86	10.73	26.7
Metal industries	3.56	10.16	35.0
Blast furnace, steel works, and rolling mills	2.92	12.18	24.0
Other primary iron and steel industries Fabricated steel products	4.00	9.22	43.4
Primary nonferrous industries Fabricated nonferrous metal products	3.41	7.54	45.2
Not specified metal industries	4.22	11.97	35.3
Machinery, except electrical	2.96	6.37	46.5
Agricultural machinery and tractors	1.66	5.03	33.0
Office and store machines and devices	2.81	4.75	59.2
Miscellaneous machinery	3.20	6.74	47.5

(continued on next page)

TABLE A-7 (continued)

INDUSTRY	UNEMPLOYMENT RATES 1950	UNEMPLOYMENT RATES 1940[b]	RATIO[a] OF 1950 RATE TO 1940 RATE
Manufacturing (cont.)			
Durable Goods (cont.)			
Electrical machinery, equipment and supplies	3.03	7.05	43.0
Transportation equipment	6.02	8.48	71.0
Motor vehicles and motor vehicle equipment	5.12	9.42	54.4
Aircraft and parts	4.09	3.34	122.5
Ship and boat building and repairing	11.97	7.35	162.9
Railroad and miscellaneous transportation equipment	10.03	11.61	86.4
All other durable goods	4.68	8.89	52.6
Professional equipment and supplies; Photographic equipment and supplies	2.93	3.65	80.3
Watches, clocks, and clockwork-operated devices; Miscellaneous manufacturing industries	5.26	10.21	51.5
Nondurable goods	3.97	10.31	38.5
Food and kindred products	5.12	9.80	52.2
Meat products	3.31	8.35	39.6
Dairy products	2.35	5.96	39.4
Canning and preserving fruits, vegetables and sea foods	16.23	22.61	71.8
Grain-mill products	2.78	6.13	45.4
Bakery products	3.28	8.68	37.8
Confectionery and related products	6.69	12.29	54.4
Beverage industries	3.86	6.77	57.0
Miscellaneous food preparations and kindred products; Not specified food industries	4.86	11.92	40.8
Tobacco manufactures	8.84	13.38	66.1
Textile mill products	3.97	9.52	41.7
Knitting mills	3.04	7.30	41.6
Dyeing and finishing textiles, except knit goods	3.67	9.27	39.6
Carpets, rugs, and other floor coverings	2.12	5.99	35.4
Yarn, thread, and fabric mills	4.34	10.37	41.9
Miscellaneous textile mill products	3.77	8.60	43.8
Apparel and other fabricated textile products	4.89	18.58	26.3
Apparel and accessories	4.92	18.62	26.4
Miscellaneous fabricated textile products	4.54	17.96	25.3

(continued on next page)

TABLE A-7 (continued)

INDUSTRY	UNEMPLOYMENT RATES 1950	UNEMPLOYMENT RATES 1940[b]	RATIO[a] OF 1950 RATE TO 1940 RATE
Manufacturing (cont.)			
Nondurable goods (cont.)			
Paper and allied products	2.71	6.35	42.7
Pulp, paper, and paperboard mills	2.24	5.49	40.8
Paperboard containers and boxes	3.70	8.86	41.8
Miscellaneous paper and pulp products	2.68	6.29	42.6
Printing, publishing, and allied industries	2.35	7.69	30.6
Chemicals and allied products	2.80	5.75	48.7
Synthetic fibers	2.83	4.03	70.2
Paints, varnishes, and related products	2.53	5.45	46.4
Drugs and medicines; Miscellaneous chemicals and allied products	2.83	6.04	46.9
Petroleum and coal products	2.18	5.11	42.7
Petroleum refining	2.09	4.51	46.3
Miscellaneous petroleum and coal products	3.07	9.53	32.2
Rubber products	3.14	8.34	37.6
Leather and leather products	4.79	10.50	45.6
Leather: tanned, curried, and finished	4.67	12.03	38.8
Footwear, except rubber	4.37	10.24	42.7
Leather products, except footwear	6.54	10.21	64.1
Not specified manufacturing industries	7.36	19.77	37.2
Transportation, communication, and other public utilities	3.29	8.72	37.7
Transportation	4.02	10.36	38.8
Railroads and railway express service	2.88	8.31	34.7
Street railways and bus lines	1.68	4.47	37.6
Trucking service	4.80	15.46	31.0
Warehousing and storage	5.42	13.63	39.8
Taxicab service	4.56	8.38	54.4
Water transportation	11.60	16.12	72.0
Air transportation	2.95	6.76	43.6
Petroleum and gasoline pipe lines	4.00	9.31	43.0
Services incidental to transportation	3.27	8.45	38.7
Telecommunications	1.57	3.94	39.8
Telephone (wire and radio)	1.36	3.12	43.6
Telegraph (wire and radio)	4.08	8.48	48.1
Utilities and sanitary services	1.95	4.95	39.4
Electric light and power, and electric-gas utilities; Other and not specified utilities	1.65	4.26	38.7
Gas and steam supply systems	2.01	4.71	42.7
Water supply; Sanitary services	2.71	7.00	38.7

(continued on next page)

TABLE A-7 (continued)

INDUSTRY	UNEMPLOYMENT RATES 1950	UNEMPLOYMENT RATES 1940[b]	RATIO[a] OF 1950 RATE TO 1940 RATE
Wholesale and retail trade	3.51	8.08	43.4
Wholesale trade	3.03	6.74	45.0
Retail trade	3.62	8.34	43.4
Food stores, except dairy products	2.64	7.07	37.3
Dairy products stores and milk retailing	2.14	6.63	32.3
General merchandise stores	3.69	10.14	36.4
Five and ten cent stores	4.30	7.44	57.8
Apparel and accessories stores, except shoe stores	3.28	8.54	38.4
Shoe stores	2.68	9.04	29.6
Furniture and housefurnishings stores	2.57	6.61	38.9
Household appliance and radio stores	2.67	7.71	34.6
Motor vehicles and accessories retailing	2.33	5.40	43.1
Gasoline service stations	3.03	5.84	51.9
Drug stores	2.96	6.87	43.1
Eating and drinking places	6.34	11.67	54.3
Hardware and farm implement stores	1.51	3.79	39.8
Lumber and building material retailing	2.89	7.32	39.5
Liquor stores	2.82	4.23	66.7
Retail florists	2.41	5.82	41.4
Jewelry stores	2.80	4.64	60.3
Fuel and ice retailing	4.09	10.36	39.5
Miscellaneous retail stores	2.43	5.72	42.5
Not specified retail trade	4.18	13.46	31.1
Finance, insurance, and real estate	1.74	5.23	33.3
Banking and credit agencies; Security and commodity brokerage, and investment companies	1.17	4.69	24.9
Insurance	1.30	3.89	33.4
Real estate (including real estate-insurance-law offices)	2.99	7.22	41.4
Business and repair services	3.81	12.14	31.4
Advertising	3.22	9.52	33.8
Accounting, auditing, and bookkeeping services; Miscellaneous business services	3.25	9.13	35.6
Automobile repair services and garages	4.20	13.64	30.8
Miscellaneous repair services	3.82	11.37	33.6
Personal services	4.66	9.69	48.1
Private households	5.70	10.73	53.1
Hotels and lodging places	5.25	9.04	58.1
Laundering, cleaning, and dyeing services	3.85	6.84	56.3
Dressmaking shops; Shoe repair shops; Miscellaneous personal services	2.32	8.39	27.7

(continued on next page)

TABLE A-7 (continued)

INDUSTRY	UNEMPLOYMENT RATES 1950	UNEMPLOYMENT RATES 1940[b]	RATIO[a] OF 1950 RATE TO 1940 RATE
Entertainment and recreation services	6.10	17.36	35.1
Radio broadcasting and television	3.34	7.80	42.8
Theaters and motion pictures	5.62	13.96	40.3
Bowling alleys, and billiard and pool parlors; Miscellaneous entertainment and recreation services	7.04	20.58	34.2
Professional and related services	1.34	5.73	23.4
Medical and other health services, except hospitals; Hospitals	1.72	3.80	45.3
Educational services, government; Educational services, private	0.87	7.10	12.3
Welfare and religious services; Nonprofit membership organizations	1.59	2.98	53.4
Legal services; Engineering and architectural services; Miscellaneous professional and related services	1.93	7.96	24.2
Public administration	3.07	7.17	42.8
Postal service	2.06	1.80	114.4
Federal public administration	5.06	13.05	38.8
State public administration; Local public administration	1.49	6.63	22.5
Industry not reported	45.37	66.44	68.3

[a] Actual ratio multiplied by 100.

[b] Data for 1940 not completely adjusted for differences in industrial classification with 1950 data.

Note: Data for 1940 are subject to sampling variability (see Appendix B).

Source: *Census of Population, 1950,* Bureau of the Census, Vol. II, Part 1, Table 130; 1940 Series P-14, No. 13.

Appendix B

Reliability of Data

The figures used in this paper are, like most statistical information, subject to various types of errors. These figures are affected by errors arising in the collection, processing, and publication stages; and, in the case of the figures based on a sample, from sampling variability. Except for sampling variability, the quantitative effects of these errors on the data have not been firmly established. Judgment tempered with caution must, therefore, be exercised in the use of the data. As a result, relationships and movements based on small differences in the figures were not made a subject of analysis and hypothesis in this paper. The reader is urged to adopt a similar conservative approach in any further use of the data presented here. (The fact that the figures in certain tables were computed to two decimal places does not necessarily mean the data are valid to this degree of detail; rather, it merely reflects some clerical overenthusiasm.)

MONTH-TO-MONTH DATA

A special caution is necessary with regard to reliability of the "month-to-month" statistics used in Tables 1 to 4 and Appendix Tables A-1, A-5, and A-6. This fairly new body of information (frequently identified as "gross change" data) is developed by pairing the results of two successive monthly enumerations of an individual. Random response and other types of variations, which tend to compensate in the data for any single month, give rise in the month-to-month comparisons to spurious changes from one category to another. The element of greatest analytical interest in these data—the movements from one category to another—is thereby exaggerated. Whether the degree of overstatement is sufficient to distort the true relationships is not now known.

SAMPLING VARIABILITY

Except for Appendix Table A-3 and the 1950 data in Appendix Table A-7, the figures in this paper are based on samples of the population and are, therefore, subject to sampling variability. Measures of this variability are given below in terms of standard errors. The chances are about 2 out of 3 that the difference due to sampling variability between an estimate and the figure that would have been obtained from a complete count of the population is less than the standard error. The chances are about 19 out of 20 that the difference is less than twice the standard error, and 99 out of 100 that it is less than 2½ times the standard error. Linear interpolation can be used for percentages not shown in the standard error tables.

The standard error of a percentage is dependent on the size of the base on which the percentage was computed. Since virtually all of the figures in this paper are in the form of percentages, a full statement on sampling variability here would require the listing of many absolute numbers. In view of the generally broad approach taken in this paper, other (and unmeasured) types of error in the figures, and space limitations, it was deemed sufficient to present only the condensed information given below.

The approximate standard errors of the percentages shown in Table 1 and Appendix Table A-1 are as follows:

NUMBER IN SAMPLE	ESTIMATED PERCENTAGE			
	20 or 80	*30 or 70*	*40 or 60*	*50*
25	8.5	9.8	10.4	10.7
50	6.0	6.9	7.4	7.6
100	4.3	4.9	5.1	5.2
250	2.7	3.2	3.3	3.4
500	1.9	2.3	2.4	2.4
1,000	1.4	1.7	1.9	1.9

The approximate standard errors of the percentages shown in Tables 2, 3, and 4, can be obtained from the table below. (For Table 2, use the "total in major industry group" lines.) This table can also be

MAJOR INDUSTRY GROUP AND TYPE OF PERCENTAGE	ESTIMATED PERCENTAGE				
	5 or 95	*10 or 90*	*20 or 80*	*25 or 75*	*50*
Construction:					
Percentages based on total in major industry group	0.6	0.8	1.0	1.1	1.3
Percentages based on persons not in major industry group in following (or previous) month	1.3	1.8	2.4	2.7	3.0
Manufacturing:					
Percentages based on total in major industry group	0.3	0.4	0.5	0.6	0.7
Percentages based on persons not in major industry group in following (or previous) month	0.9	1.2	1.7	1.8	2.0
Wholesale and retail trade:					
Percentages based on total in major industry group	0.3	0.5	0.6	0.7	0.8
Percentages based on persons not in major industry group in following (or previous) month	0.9	1.2	1.6	1.7	1.9

used for the monthly data shown in Appendix Tables A-5 and A-6 by multiplying the standard errors by a factor of 2.

The approximate standard errors of the percentages shown in Appendix Table A-2 (except for the very few manufacturing industries with less than 50,000 workers) are less than the values shown below:

Estimated Percentage	*Maximum Value of Standard Error*
2	0.3
5	0.5
10	0.7
25	1.1
50	1.2

In Appendix Table A-4, the approximate standard errors for the monthly percentages for construction are 2.0, for manufacturing 1.0, and for trade 1.1.

In Table 5 and Appendix Table A-7, the 1940 unemployment rates are based partially on sample data. Presentation of all the pertinent information would require more detail here than seems necessary. An adequate rough approximation of the standard errors of the 1940 unemployment rates in Table 5 can be obtained by multiplying the rate by 1 per cent. For example, the unemployment rate of 17.74 for the mining major group is subject to an approximate standard error of 0.18. For the individual industries shown in Appendix Table A-7, the rate should be multiplied by 3 per cent. These approximations overstate the standard errors for the industries with large numbers of unemployed, and understate the standard errors for industries with small numbers of unemployed.

COMMENT

George F. Rohrlich, Bureau of Employment Security, Department of Labor

Despite David L. Kaplan's many reservations, his analysis of unemployment by industry, especially when studied in conjunction with Hauser's findings on differential unemployment by occupational group, offers some encouragement for undertaking further research to test the following hypothesis: Granting that the relative stability of industrial accession and separation patterns calls for an explanation of its causes and for further statistical evidence, the pattern for each industry group and subgroup—whether described by means of averages and deviations from these averages or by some other numerical or visual indexes—lends itself to systematic computation and comparison. (In the present hypothesis, it constitutes the "known" quantity.)

The stability of the industry employment turnover patterns is enhanced by another known and relatively slow-changing component: Each industry's technological basis necessitates a certain occupational composition of its work force. (On the other hand, the stability is lessened by the ups and downs of the business cycle.)

Narrowing the frame of reference from all industries to those industries covered by our federal-state unemployment insurance system, and from all employment turnover to the portion covered by that program and appearing as compensable unemployment insurance claims, one might establish industry-specific unemployment insurance claims loads and costs and, by expressing these through some ratio (e.g. to covered workers and payrolls, respectively), one might establish indexes that permit of comparison under certain conditions. Collected over a period of time, such series may add up to insured unemployment "profiles" for each covered industry over the period of one or more business cycles. Over a longer period, such time series may also reveal technological trends. Since unemployment insurance data are collected on a state-by-state basis, comparisons would be possible not only over time but also among states.

The practical objective in testing this hypothesis would be to arrive at industry-specific indexes of the insured or compensable unemployment risk under various economic conditions, chiefly the several phases of the business cycle. These indexes, in turn, could serve as the basis for the eventual construction of unemployment tables roughly comparable to—if subject to more qualification than—the life tables and disability tables commonly used in the operation of these respective branches of insurance.

While the primary use of such tables would be to refine unemployment insurance cost estimating techniques beyond their present rather crude stage of development, it is not inconceivable that the venture, if successful, may have implications of a broader economic analysis and policy nature. It is for this reason that I thought a mention of the fact that we in the Actuarial and Financial Services Division of the Bureau of Employment Security are planning to embark on such a project may be of interest to this Conference.

UNEMPLOYMENT BY LOCALITY AND INDUSTRY

LOUIS LEVINE

BUREAU OF EMPLOYMENT SECURITY

DEPARTMENT OF LABOR

1. Introduction

UNEMPLOYMENT—its level and trend, and its composition—is widely regarded as a key index to the state of economic well-being. There is a basic need for an objective measure of the number and the characteristics of the unemployed. Although general agreement exists regarding the need for and the uses of a measure of unemployment, considerable difference of opinion has developed as to who shall be counted as "unemployed" and what are the essential tests of "unemployment." There are many ways in which unemployment can be defined and each definition provides a different count of the unemployed. The definition selected must be useful for a wide variety of purposes. It must be in keeping with our free enterprise system and with the free functioning of the labor market. At the same time, it must be easily applied, be readily understood, and yield reasonably accurate counts of the unemployed.

The term "unemployed" encompasses a variety of meanings. It may describe a condition—that of being not at work; an "activity"—that of seeking work; an "attitude"—that of desiring a job under certain conditions; and a "need"—that of needing a job. The term also has other connotations and various shadings and combinations. For example, should a definition of unemployed include individuals who do not have jobs and who are not looking for work but who would accept jobs under certain conditions? Is a person unemployed who is in need of a job but because of home responsibilities is unable to look for or to accept a job? Should only those persons be counted as unemployed who are without jobs but who are breadwinners of their families? Obviously, the definition used determines the resultant count.

Within the framework of an agreed definition, difficulties arise about the interpretation of the facts which are essential elements of the unemployment definition. In the final analysis, unemployment is a subjective state which depends upon the intent and desires of the individual. Even the apparently simple determination of whether a person is "at work" can be difficult. Are the members of a farm family at work or not during the inactive months on the farm? Under what

Note: Appreciation is expressed to V. D. Chavrid, Bureau of Employment Security, for his extensive assistance in the preparation of this paper.

circumstances is the industrial worker on vacation or on strike to be classified as employed or unemployed? Is the urban worker who works a few hours a week employed or not? Does it make any difference whether he wants only a few hours of work a week or whether he wants full-time employment? Should the number of hours he works or the amount of money he earns be considered in defining unemployment? Should an individual who has been working one-half of the week and looking for work the other half be counted as unemployed? Should a person who has a job always be counted as employed, even when he is temporarily not working?

The determination of whether an individual is "seeking work" is also generally subjective. Here the problem is one of the degree of the job-seeking effort in relation to the conditions of the labor market. It can generally be concluded that an individual is seeking work if he approaches employers and registers for work with an employment agency. But questions arise about the individual who knows there are no opportunities for employment for him in his community and who, therefore, limits his search for work. Questions also arise as to the validity of the employment search on the part of workers who restrict their efforts to a limited geographic area, to a small number of establishments, or to a short period of time.

Concern with the definition and measurement of unemployment is not a mere intellectual exercise. It has practical implications for the man in the street. It has important government policy and program implications. The administration of public employment offices and the operations of unemployment insurance systems are greatly influenced by these considerations. State employment security agencies have therefore found it necessary to undertake the preparation of estimates of total unemployment.[1] For the same reasons, estimates of local area unemployment have been developed even though at times, lack of data or inadequate data made accurate estimates difficult.

Since the inception of the employment service and unemployment insurance programs, state and local employment security offices have been collecting data on the volume and composition of unemployment. Initially, these data were limited to the number and characteristics of job applicants registered for work with the employment service (active file) or to the number of persons filing for unemployment insurance benefits (insured unemployed). However, since it was necessary to know the total volume of unemployment for a wide variety of uses, local and state employment security offices (and during the war years,

[1] "Total unemployment" as used here means "all unemployed" and differs from the legal unemployment insurance concept, which uses "total unemployment" to distinguish from "partial unemployment."

War Manpower Commission offices) began to make estimates of total unemployment. At present, state agencies prepare estimates of total unemployment for all important labor market areas, and many agencies also estimate total unemployment on a state-wide basis.

While current estimates of total unemployment, based on the Bureau of the Census sample household survey (Current Population Survey) are available for the nation as a whole, no estimates can be obtained from this source for states or areas. For such areas and states, data on unemployment are available only once every ten years from the decennial census of population. State employment security agencies, which collect a great deal of data on insured unemployment for the smallest geographic area as a by-product of their operations, naturally undertook the preparation of current estimates of total unemployment by local area and state. A description of the techniques and concepts used to develop these estimates is given in sections 2 and 3. As a part of this description there is included a comparison of the estimates resulting from these techniques with data from other sources. The fact that other sources provide little data by area limited the extent to which such comparisons were possible.

Sections 4 and 5 are concerned with an analysis of the behavior of unemployment by area and industry and with the characteristics of the unemployed with respect to duration of unemployment, sex, age, and occupation. It is apparent from this analysis that national figures on unemployment, though important in providing a general indication of the status of the economy, conceal wide variations in the employment and unemployment conditions in different areas of the country. These differences are significant both as to the level of unemployment and duration of unemployment, as well as to the characteristics of the unemployed by age, sex, occupation, and industry. The causes for these differences are also varied. It is only after the specific conditions creating the unemployment problems in the various communities are known that adequate programming to solve unemployment problems is possible. Similarly, measures to reduce joblessness are dependent not only upon information regarding the volume and characteristics of the unemployed but also on other aspects of area's economy, such as its industrial facilities, water power and fuel resources, transportation facilities, the local tax structure, and proximity of raw materials and markets to the area.

2. Definition of Local Labor Market Area

The labor market, viewed as an institution, means the complex of economic and social factors involved in the process through which employers recruit workers and workers seek employment. It encompasses all the factors involving the demand and supply of labor, wage differentials, variations in hours, shifts of work, employer hiring practices, and the multitude of other working conditions which shape employer-worker job relationships.

For purposes of characterizing the structure of the labor market or for measuring its behavior, it is frequently desirable to subdivide it into at least three broad divisions—industrial, occupational, and geographic. Although these are by no means completely exclusive categories, they are indicative of different approaches that may be taken in an analysis of the labor market. Moreover, depending upon the approach taken, certain economic and social factors operating in the labor market receive greater or lesser emphasis in the analyses. For example, in the analysis of an occupational labor market, it is necessary to concentrate on the relationship between the segment of the labor force having specified occupational characteristics and industries employing significant numbers of such workers. In an industrial labor market analysis, emphasis is placed on a given industry and the employer-worker relationships affecting such industry. Finally, in local labor market analysis the complex of economic and social factors affecting and shaping employer-worker job relationships within a given geographic area constitutes the focus of study.

The definition of any of these types of labor markets is influenced by different factors. The local labor market area definition is determined to a considerable degree by differences in the geographic mobility of labor, while this factor is less important in the definitions of both the occupational and industrial labor markets.

A study of unemployment trends by locality must start from a determination of the local geographic unit which constitutes the local labor market area. The discussions and data contained in the subsequent sections of this paper are for such areas. A local labor market area may be defined as a geographic area consisting of a central city (or cities) and surrounding territory in which there is a concentration of urban economic activity or urban labor demand and in which workers can generally change jobs without changing their residence. The basic factor in this definition is, of course, the relationship between the place of residence and the place of work of the local labor supply.

Sublabor markets may also exist within such local labor market areas. These submarkets usually result from limitation of employment opportunities in terms of specific occupations, industries, or companies. However, for general labor market analyses, these submarkets do not present serious obstacles since their effects are generally encompassed and reflected in the conditions of the entire area.

The possibility of each company's employment office being a real and distinct market for labor is noted in the study by Lloyd G. Reynolds. He found that "The employed worker is attached basically to a *company* rather than to an industry or an occupation."[2] This conclusion is reached by Reynolds because his study showed that if a worker leaves one company, his movement to another company within the area is conditioned chiefly by the hiring practices of other companies. However, Reynolds also found that shifts from company to company take place within the limits of an area and that a worker's mobility beyond this area is conditioned by a reluctance to change his place of residence. A similar conclusion was reached by Myers and Shultz in their study of a New England area in 1948. They found that, despite many factors such as seniority and others which isolate individual workers in the area labor market, changes in employment opportunities in certain establishments within the labor market area affect all workers in the area. In addition, they found that "Even in the period when the local employment outlook was bleak, though, unemployed workers generally tried to get along the best they could without moving. . . ." And that "Unemployed workers remain in the community long enough to produce purely local effects."[3]

Boundaries of all the labor market areas do not encompass the same amount of territory. Important reasons are that (1) the extremities of an area's boundaries are determined, in large part, by transportation time and cost rather than by the distances involved, and (2) in certain areas, partly because of the nature of the job opportunities, people will customarily travel shorter or longer distances to work.

These factors, as well as others, arise when efforts are made to determine the boundary of a specific labor market area. Thus, though an agreement regarding the concept of the labor market area can usually be reached, it is not simple to establish a uniform procedure for delineating labor market areas. With some few exceptions, the major labor market areas now defined in the employment security system conform to the Standard Metropolitan Areas established by the Bureau of the Budget in 1948.

A number of considerations were involved in the establishment of the Standard Metropolitan Areas.[4] Most important was the need for having local economic and social statistical data collected by many government and private agencies presented in a common geographic pattern to facilitate comparative analyses and other uses of the data.

[2] Lloyd G. Reynolds, *Structure of Labor Markets*, Harper, 1951.

[3] Charles A. Myers and George P. Shultz, *The Dynamics of a Labor Market Area*, Prentice-Hall, 1951.

[4] Robert C. Klove, "The Definition of Standard Metropolitan Areas," *Economic Geography*, April 1952.

To meet this need, the areas were designed to serve a wide variety of statistical purposes, including the presentation of census statistics on population, housing, manufacturing, business, current employment and payroll data, and local labor market analyses. The definitions of necessity took into account the manner in which local data are usually available so as to ease the burden of compiling and collecting pertinent data. Commuting range was the single most important substantive element in determining the boundaries of the Standard Metropolitan Areas.

3. *Measurement of Unemployment by Locality*

STATEMENT OF PROBLEM

A study of a local labor market is usually hampered by a dearth of relevant data. This is particularly true where special surveys cannot be undertaken and only the available labor force data and other economic statistics can be used. Even where such data are available by locality, they often lack comparability over a period of time.[5] These difficulties are magnified when one concentrates on such relatively detailed data as unemployment by locality.

Data on most aspects of unemployment have only recently become available. The first attempts to collect information on a national scale on unemployment were made in conjunction with our decennial censuses but until the 1930 decade, information on the unemployed did not yield a comparable and meaningful measure of unemployment because an adequate conceptual framework with respect to the labor force and its components had not been developed. With the studies of unemployment undertaken between 1930 and 1940, there emerged the labor force concept currently accepted which permits the identification and measurement of the unemployed with some degree of consistency. This is not to say that problems of concept and definition are still not present. Nevertheless, the use of the labor force concept has permitted the development of a substantial amount of information on the unemployed and other components of the labor force. As a result, the census of 1940 and that of 1950 provide considerable information on the unemployed, not only on a national scale, but also by locality.

However, data by labor market area, as now defined, were not available in the 1940 census. Labor force information, collected in that

[5] Illustrations of the problems involved in developing and using data by locality for different time periods may be found in the discussion by Gladys L. Palmer and Ann Ratner in Appendix C, *Use of Population Census Data in the Preparation of Estimates of Labor Force and Unemployment in a Metropolitan Area,* of the booklet by Louis J. Ducoff and Margaret J. Hagood, *Labor Force Definition and Measurement: Recent Experience in the United States,* Social Science Research Council, Bull. 56, 1947.

census by metropolitan district, was not only inadequate but, more importantly, the definitions were not satisfactory for labor market analyses. The introduction of the Standard Metropolitan Area in the 1950 decennial census provides, for the first time on a national basis, local geographic labor force data that are adequate for area labor market analyses. Considerable detail on the characteristics of the various segments of the labor force is also available from this census. Information on unemployment is provided by age and sex, occupation of the experienced unemployed, industry of worker attachment, and other items in sufficient detail to satisfy many analytical needs.

Analyses on a current and continuing basis, unfortunately, cannot be made from census data. The Census Bureau's Current Population Survey (CPS) provides a national unemployment figure on a current and regular basis. Occasionally, as for example in 1947, labor force and unemployment data for selected localities have been obtained. Unemployment information on a national basis is an important indicator of economic conditions and is useful for the development of broad national economic policies. However, the national unemployment rate conceals wide differences in economic conditions among localities. The nature and importance of these differences (discussed in section 4) can be shown by comparing unemployment rates among areas in 1950 and in 1954.

The need for such local labor market information is widespread, not only for the operation of the employment security program, but for various groups concerned with local labor market conditions. The Bureau of Employment Security, in cooperation with its affiliated employment security agencies, has developed procedures for estimating unemployment by area based on data available from unemployment insurance (UI) operations. The estimates of total unemployment are based primarily on insured unemployment data.[6]

Many important considerations arise in the measurement of unemployment by locality, but fundamental to all of these is a thorough understanding of the unemployment concepts and criteria used for considering a person unemployed. Estimates of total unemployment, based upon a count of the insured unemployed derived from UI operations and in accordance with legal provisions of state laws and administrative procedures, differ in some ways from the concept of unemployment used by the Census Bureau in its CPS, and familiarity with both concepts is necessary. Review of the elements of similarity and differences in the unemployment measured by the employment security

[6] For a description of these data see "Source, Nature and Limitations of Insured Unemployment Statistics," *The Labor Market and Employment Security*, Bureau of Employment Security, April 1954.

system and the Census sample survey is therefore desirable and is presented below.[7]

BUREAU OF THE CENSUS DEFINITION

The definition of unemployment used in the CPS is based primarily on the *major activity* of the individual in the survey week (the calendar week which includes the eighth of the month). This sample survey is designed to obtain information as to the work status of the population without duplication. The determination of work status is based on a person's labor-force activity during the survey week. Thus, if a person was working during the survey week (i.e. if he did any work at all for pay or profit, or worked without pay for fifteen hours or more on a family farm or business) he is classified as "at work" and "employed." If, on the other hand, he was not "at work," but was seeking work, he is classified as "unemployed." This basic system of classification, however, although appropriate for enumeration of most persons to be included in the labor force, is not all inclusive, since it fails to take into account persons who neither worked nor sought work during the survey week but who have a strong attachment to the labor force. (Included among such persons are, for example, individuals who were inactive during the survey week only because of illness, vacations, industrial disputes, and similar factors.) Accordingly, modifications have been made to permit their inclusion. With these modifications, the problem arose as to whether to include them with the employed or the unemployed segments of the labor force. In general, an attempt is made to classify these persons as employed or unemployed according to the degree of their attachment to jobs. This means that persons are not considered unemployed unless they are exerting pressure on the labor market for employment.

Accordingly, those who are deemed to have sufficient attachment to jobs to keep them from actively seeking work are included with "employed" and designated as "with a job but not at work." This group includes persons who have jobs but who did not work at all nor looked for work during the survey week because of illness, vacations, bad weather, and various personal reasons, or because of industrial disputes at their places of employment. It also includes persons who were temporarily laid off from their jobs with definite instructions to return to work within thirty days or who were waiting to report to new jobs scheduled to begin within thirty days.

[7] Also see symposium on "How Much Unemployment?" *Review of Economics and Statistics*, February 1950, pp. 49-79 (also *Hearings before the Joint Committee on the Economic Report*, 83d Cong., 2d sess., February 1-18, 1954, pp. 230-239 and 345-348).

Just as modification was made in the "activity" concept to include as employed both those "at work" (i.e. actively employed) and those "with a job but not at work" (frequently termed the "inactive employed"), so too was modification made to include as unemployed both those actively seeking work and the so-called "inactive unemployed" group. A strict application of the activity concept would exclude from the unemployed certain groups of individuals who in any realistic sense must be regarded as unemployed even though they have not been looking for work continuously. For example, in a one-industry town, if all plants are shut down, most workers would have no alternative but to wait until the plants reopen and probably would not be actively seeking work meanwhile. The definition of unemployed persons is, therefore, expanded to include—in addition to persons actively seeking work—those who would have been seeking work except that (1) they believed that no job was available in their line of work or in their community, (2) they were temporarily ill, or (3) they were on indefinite layoff.

In the final analysis, the classification of persons as employed or unemployed by the Bureau of the Census rests on a system of priorities. The first priority is given to "at work"; the second, to "looking for work," including the "inactive" unemployed; the third, to "with a job but not at work" (inactive employed). This system of priorities is so designed that "looking for work" has priority over all other activities except "at work." Stated in other words, unless a person is "at work," he will always be classified as "unemployed" if he is actively seeking work, regardless of the degree of his attachment to a job. For example, persons who are directly involved in a labor dispute, or who have been kept from work by bad weather, or who are on an indefinite layoff, or who expect to start on a new job, are classified as unemployed rather than employed if they were looking for work during the survey week. Seeking work, therefore, is the very essence of the CPS definition of the unemployed.

The Bureau of the Census defines "looking for work" to include any effort to get a job or to establish a business or profession. Persons are reported as looking for work if in the last week they were waiting to hear the results of attempts made within the last sixty days to find a job. Examples of looking for work are: (1) registration at a public or private employment office; (2) being on call at a personnel office, at a union hiring hall, or from a nurses' register or other similar professional register; (3) meeting with or telephoning prospective employers; (4) placing or answering advertisements (5) writing letters of application; and (6) working without pay in order to get experience or training.

UI DEFINITION

Because the UI system is designed to pay benefits only to unemployed persons, it *requires* that a person to be eligible for benefits in any week must be totally or partially unemployed. So an understanding of "insured unemployment" stems from knowledge of the requirements for eligibility which have been set up under the various state laws. All of these laws require that a claimant, to receive benefits, be able to work and available for work. One evidence of availability for work is the filing of claims and regular reporting at a public employment office, required under all state laws, ordinarily on a weekly basis. Availability for work is also evidenced by registration at a local public employment office. Although not all state laws contain provisions requiring a claimant to "seek work actively" (or make a reasonably independent effort to obtain work), such requirements are contained in regulations in practically all of the states.

Essentially, therefore, for *UI purposes*, an *unemployed person* is one who is without work (or, in the case of a person partially unemployed, with earnings which are less than a certain specified amount), who is seeking work, and who is both able to work and available for work. Certain other conditions which must be met by an unemployed worker before he is deemed eligible for benefits (e.g. qualifying wages, no disqualifying acts). These do not essentially alter the underlying concept.

Except for the fact that the UI concept of unemployed includes persons who are only partially unemployed, the similarity between the two concepts is striking. Both the CPS definition and the UI laws require that a person to be considered unemployed must not have worked during the week in question. State employment security agencies in general require that a person be actively seeking work, able to work, and available for work. These requirements are at least partially met by registration with the local employment office. Similarly, the Bureau of the Census regards registration with a public employment office as one evidence of "seeking work." To be sure, there are some variations among the state laws, but such variations as do exist are relatively minor in terms of their effect on the basic definition. Aside from the treatment of partially unemployed persons, the CPS and UI definitions, conceptually, are in essential agreement. Differences arise principally from the treatment of some of the inactive employed and unemployed, as in the case of persons who do not seek work only because they are ill. Such persons would fail to meet the "ability to work" requirement of state UI laws but would be counted as unemployed in the CPS.

There are other differences which arise, however, not from lack of agreement in concept, but from differences in the method of collecting data. Thus, there are some workers who are eligible for unemployment insurance who would normally be considered as unemployed by the Bureau of the Census, but are not included with the unemployed simply because the household interview fails to reveal that they were actively looking for work in the survey week. Persons included in this category are most likely to be found among (1) persons who had been temporarily laid off from their jobs with definite instructions to return to work within thirty days of layoff; (2) workers who were temporarily separated from their jobs because of bad weather; (3) workers who had a new job or business to which they were scheduled to report within the following thirty days; and (4) workers who were on unpaid vacations (this group is included with the total group on vacations in the CPS classification). *It is important to note, however, that persons in the above-mentioned groups are considered by the Bureau of the Census as "with a job but not at work" and are so classified only if the household interview does not reveal that they were looking for work.* If the interview reveals that they were looking for work in the survey week, they are included with the unemployed.

DEFINITION USED BY EMPLOYMENT SECURITY AGENCIES IN ESTIMATING UNEMPLOYMENT

Legal and administrative factors which are intertwined with the UI program must, of course, be reflected in the definition of unemployment used by state employment security agencies. At the same time, the preceding analysis of the CPS and UI definitions suggests that a definition can be devised for employment security use which would not be seriously at variance with the CPS definition and which would also come quite close to the common conception of unemployment. With these considerations in mind, the following definition has been devised for use in labor market analyses in the employment security system:

Unemployment is defined as a count of persons who, for an entire week, did not work at all, were able to work and available for work, and were looking for work.

However, those individuals who did not actively seek work during the week would be considered unemployed if they would have looked for work except that (1) they believed no work was available in their line of work or in the community, (2) they expected to return to a job from which they had been laid off, or (3) they had a job to which they expected to report.

Persons not at work because they are directly involved in a labor-management dispute would be counted as unemployed only if they were actively looking for other work. Persons who were laid off as an indirect result of a labor-management dispute would be counted as unemployed. Persons on vacation would not be counted as unemployed unless they were actively seeking other work. Persons on sick leave would not be counted as unemployed because they are not "able to work."

The fact that a person has received a UI payment or waiting week credit is deemed adequate evidence that he was unemployed, except that claimants for partial or part-total benefits are not considered as unemployed.

AREA UNEMPLOYMENT ESTIMATING TECHNIQUE

The area unemployment estimating technique used in the employment security system may be described, in general terms, as one which starts with a count of the unemployed workers covered by the UI program and then derives estimates for the segments of the unemployed not covered by this program. This technique is described in greater detail under the following subitems: (1) unemployment related to employment covered by state UI laws; (2) unemployment related to noncovered employment (excluding entrants to the labor force); and (3) unemployed new entrants and re-entrants to the labor force.[8] The relative importance of these several groups in the total estimate of unemployment in an average industrial area would be approximately as follows: the first group will account for about 60 to 70 per cent; the second group for about 15 to 20 per cent and the third, also for 15 to 20 per cent, depending upon the time of the year for which the estimate is prepared.

UNEMPLOYMENT RELATED TO UI COVERED EMPLOYMENT

From the UI claims-taking operations data are obtained on the number of covered workers claiming unemployment insurance who are totally unemployed in a given week. This group has been usually termed the "insured unemployed." Added to this figure are data provided by the Railroad Retirement Board on the number of unemployed railroad workers.

In order to obtain data on the total number of unemployed related to UI covered employment, three other groups must be taken into account. The first group consists of workers from covered industries

[8] A detailed description of these procedures is provided in "Techniques for Estimating Unemployment" and Supplement 5, Bureau of Employment Security, July 1953.

filing initial claims; i.e. notices to the employment security offices that they have just become unemployed. Although such persons are expected to file their initial claim immediately upon becoming unemployed, there are a number who delay the filing of claims until they are unemployed for at least a full week or more. From unpublished studies conducted by the employment security agencies, data have been developed indicating the proportion of such workers. Using this information, it is possible to estimate the number of persons filing initial claims who have been unemployed for at least a full week before filing an initial claim.

The second group of unemployed, related to the UI program but not included in the insured unemployment figures, are persons who have exhausted their rights to unemployment benefits and remain unemployed. During periods of low unemployment, the number is relatively small. However, during those periods when unemployment is high and of long duration, this group becomes important. The procedures currently used for estimating this category of unemployed, although satisfactory during periods of low unemployment, may not be as satisfactory when unemployment levels are relatively high. Further work on the improvement of these estimates is now under way, and it is anticipated that procedures will be available shortly which will permit more reliable estimates of this group through all cycles of the economy.

The third group consists of persons who are disqualified from receiving UI benefits, workers in covered employment who do not earn sufficient wage credits, or have not been employed in such employment for a sufficient length of time to become eligible to receive benefits, and unemployed covered workers eligible for benefits who for some reason fail to apply for them. At present, relatively crude procedures are available for estimating the number of such unemployed based on information and special studies of the employment security agencies. This is another area where further work is under way to develop improved estimating techniques.

UNEMPLOYMENT RELATED TO NONCOVERED EMPLOYMENT

For estimating purposes the unemployed in this category are divided into two groups: (1) those from covered industries but in noncovered establishments and (2) those from noncovered industries, such as domestic workers and government workers, workers from nonprofit institutions, wage and salaried agricultural workers, and self-employed and unpaid family workers (both agricultural and nonagricultural). The method used to estimate the number in each of these groups is given below.

The estimate of the unemployed from noncovered establishments in covered industries is based upon the unemployment rates for workers in the covered segments of the same industries. From the data available in UI records, a distribution of insured unemployment by industry of employment prior to becoming unemployed is obtained. Information is also available from the UI records on total covered employment by industry. By relating insured unemployment to covered employment, industry-by-industry, unemployment rates for each of these industries may be obtained. The use of these rates in estimating unemployment from the noncovered sectors of these industries involves the assumption that the unemployment rates in the covered and noncovered segments are similar. However, even if this assumption is not completely valid, the resulting error in the estimate cannot affect the estimate of total unemployment significantly because the number of workers involved in this excluded group is relatively small (approximately 10 per cent of the total). It should also be noted that this procedure is not required in states where UI coverage applies to employers of one or more workers.

The unemployment rates for covered industries is also used to estimate unemployment in noncovered industries. The unemployment rates by industry provided by the CPS show that there are fairly constant relationships between the unemployment rates of various industries and classes of workers. For example, these data indicate that the unemployment rate for wage and salary workers in agriculture is approximately the same as the unemployment rate for wage and salary workers outside agriculture. Similarly, the data show that the incidence of unemployment among domestic-service workers is usually about the same as for wage and salary workers in "other personal services," which are covered by unemployment insurance. Thus, by using certain data for the covered industries, estimates of unemployed in all the noncovered segments may be obtained.

UNEMPLOYED NEW ENTRANTS AND RE-ENTRANTS

Unemployed new entrants and re-entrants are individuals whose present spell of unemployment has *not* been immediately preceded by employment. Unemployed new entrants may be defined as that group of individuals who have entered the labor market for the first time and have not found jobs; unemployed re-entrants are the individuals who have had prior work experience but who were out of the labor force and have re-entered the labor market but have not found jobs. The two groups taken together have been termed "unemployed entrants." Unemployed entrants appear to be significant numerically throughout the year, but there is an appreciable rise of this group when school graduations take place.

Unemployed entrants are probably one of the most difficult groups for which an estimate of unemployment must be developed. Despite the fact that the unemployed new and re-entrants may represent a significant part of total unemployment, there is insufficient information about them on a local basis. Although they are not covered by the UI program, some of this group seek employment through the employment service, including those eligible for unemployment compensation for "Korean" veterans. However, since neither this group as a whole nor any constant proportion of it seeks employment through this channel, the data cannot be used to estimate the total number of unemployed entrants. The only data that are available on the number of unemployed new entrants or re-entrants are those obtained in the CPS. By using these data, it is possible to devise a procedure for estimating the number of unemployed entrants for a local area. A study of the national data showed that there was a close relationship between unemployed entrants and the level of the civilian labor force (excluding unemployed entrants) and the level of unemployment (excluding unemployed entrants). Examination of the monthly labor force data from June 1948 to October 1952 also indicated that after adjusting for seasonal factors, unemployed entrants for any month of the year were—on the average—equal to 0.7 per cent of the civilian labor force (excluding unemployed entrants) and slightly over 11 per cent of the unemployed (excluding unemployed entrants).[9]

Although the techniques which have been developed for estimating total unemployment by area are by no means perfect, the results up to this time show that they do yield reasonably satisfactory local unemployment estimates. These procedures are inexpensive, require relatively little time once the necessary data are available, and have the advantage of using data that are available and needed in the employment security program. These techniques are, in a sense, expedients necessitated by the fact that household surveys for a local area similar to the CPS are not possible because of cost considerations and other factors.

COMPARISON OF ESTIMATES WITH OTHER DATA

The very factors, discussed earlier in this section, that necessitated the development of techniques for estimating unemployment by area also make it difficult to make direct comparisons of the estimates result-

[9] A detailed description of this procedure is given in *Estimating the Volume of Unemployed New Entrants and Re-Entrants*, Supplement 4, Bureau of Employment Security, July 1953.

ing from these techniques with unemployment estimates from other sources. Except for area data from the decennial census of 1950, only indirect comparisons which shed some light on the reasonableness of the area unemployment estimates are possible. Unfortunately, for reasons which will be noted later, completely satisfactory comparison with the 1950 census data is not possible.

As previously mentioned, the insured unemployment data from the employment security system provide the base for the area unemployment estimates and account for a large part of the unemployed total. Despite the effect of the various exclusions under the UI program, the basic fact remains that covered employment accounts for about 75 per cent of the 48 million (August 1954) employees in nonagricultural establishments—both private and public. With the extension of coverage to federal civilian employees (from January 1955) and to private firms with four or more employees (from January 1956) in accordance with the legislation passed by the 83rd Congress, the coverage will rise to over 80 per cent. The UI coverage of the private sector of the economy which is most sensitive to economic change is even greater. Today, covered employment accounts for about 85 per cent of total private employment of wage and salary workers outside of agriculture. With the extension of coverage to four or more workers this percentage will rise to 90 per cent. It is evident from this that a large segment of our economy and one which is most responsive to economic change is adequately reflected in the insured unemployment data.

The usefulness of the UI data has been questioned by some because these data flow from the state employment security operations, and are, therefore, affected by differences in the administrative and legal factors underlying the state operations. While it is true that such factors affect the data, steps can be, and have been, taken to overcome some of the consequent limitations. Notwithstanding these limitations, comparisons between the Bureau of the Census unemployment data and insured unemployment show the existence of a close relationship when adjustments for differences in coverage are made. From Chart 1 it may be seen that for most of the time during the period 1950-1953 the two adjusted series have moved in the same direction and frequently by approximately the same amount. In order to make the two series as comparable as possible, persons who were not employed in industries covered by the UI program and who never had a full-time job were subtracted from the CPS series. From the insured unemployment total the estimated numbers drawing partial or part-total benefits were also deducted, since these individuals would not have been included in the CPS count of unemployment. Persons on temporary layoff from nonagricultural jobs with definite instructions to return to work within thirty days are classified by the Bureau of the Census as employed unless they are reported as looking for other jobs. The extent to which such persons are claiming benefits is not known. It is probable that the number may be considerable at certain periods and

CHART 1

Estimates of Completely Unemployed Persons in Industries Covered By Unemployment Insurance, 1950-1953

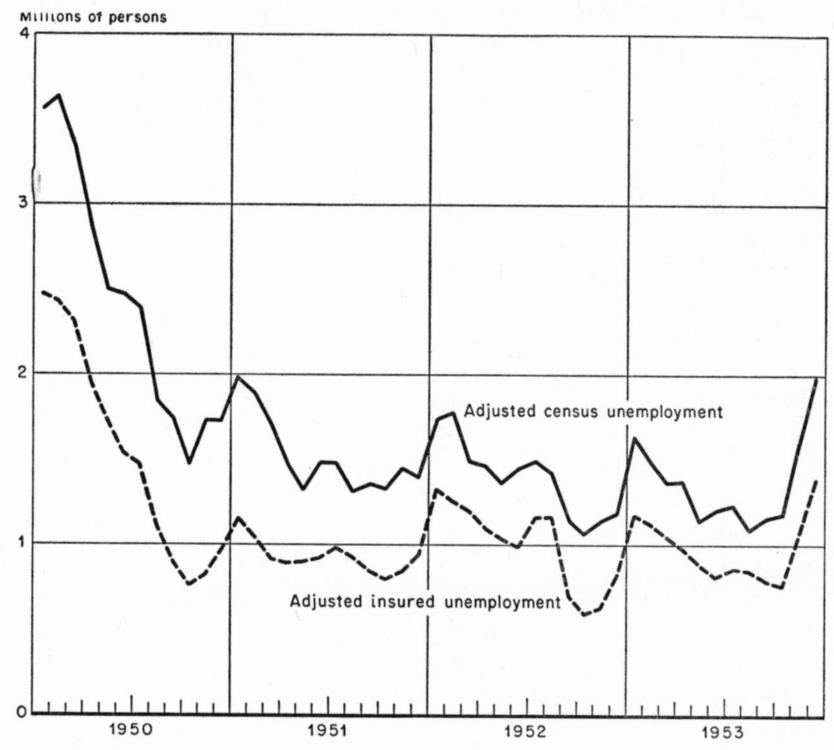

Adjustments: Census—unemployed persons minus those who never had a full-time job or whose last reported job was in agriculture, government, domestic service, self-employment, or unpaid family work; added to the unemployed are persons laid off from nonagricultural jobs with instructions to return to work at a definite date within thirty days. Census data for the last four months of 1953 have been adjusted to correspond to the 230-area sample levels.

Insured unemployment—state-insured unemployment, unemployment compensation for veterans, and railroad insured unemployment, minus the number who received less than the full weekly benefit amount due to some employment during the week (partial and part-total employment).

Source: Bureau of the Census (CPS data) and Bureau of Employment Security (UI data).

for that reason, this group has been added to the CPS figure to improve comparability.

Complete comparability between the UI and CPS data could not be obtained because it was not possible to remove from the CPS series the unemployed workers from covered industries but in noncovered establishments. This probably explains the difference in level between the adjusted CPS series and the adjusted UI series.

A further indication of the sensitiveness of the employment security data to economic developments is shown in Chart 2. This chart compares the "disemployment" rates as measured by the initial claims data of the employment security system and the additions to unemployment from nonagricultural industries from the CPS for the period 1949 through the second quarter of 1954. The comparison shows a strikingly close relationship between the two rates. The initial claims rate in the chart represents the average of initial claims for the quarter expressed as a percentage of average covered employment for the quarter. Similarly, the CPS quarterly average of additions to unemployment from all nonagricultural industries is expressed as a percentage of nonagricultural employment. (For illustrative purposes quarterly averages were used; monthly averages would have shown similar results.)

When a covered worker becomes unemployed he reports to a local office of the state employment security agency and files an initial claim —a notice to the administrative agency of the beginning of a period of unemployment for which benefits are claimed. He is usually expected to file this claim immediately after separation from his job and it is to his advantage to do so since benefit payments cannot start until an initial claim has been filed. Consequently, initial claims are the most sensitive indicators available of emerging or new unemployment among covered workers. It is clearly shown in the chart that initial claims or disemployment in the covered industries follows the same pattern as new unemployment or disemployment in all nonagricultural industries.

The preceding comparisons have been between the UI covered portion of the nonagricultural sector of the economy and the total nonagricultural sector. These comparisons are most appropriate because the unemployment estimates prepared by the employment security system are for labor market areas which are urban centers in which nonagricultural activities predominate. There are only a few major areas where nonagricultural employment accounts for less than 90 per cent of total employment according to the 1950 Census of Population.

CHART 2

Relationship between Initial Unemployment Insurance Claims and Total New Unemployment from Nonagricultural Industries, Quarterly Rates, 1949-1954

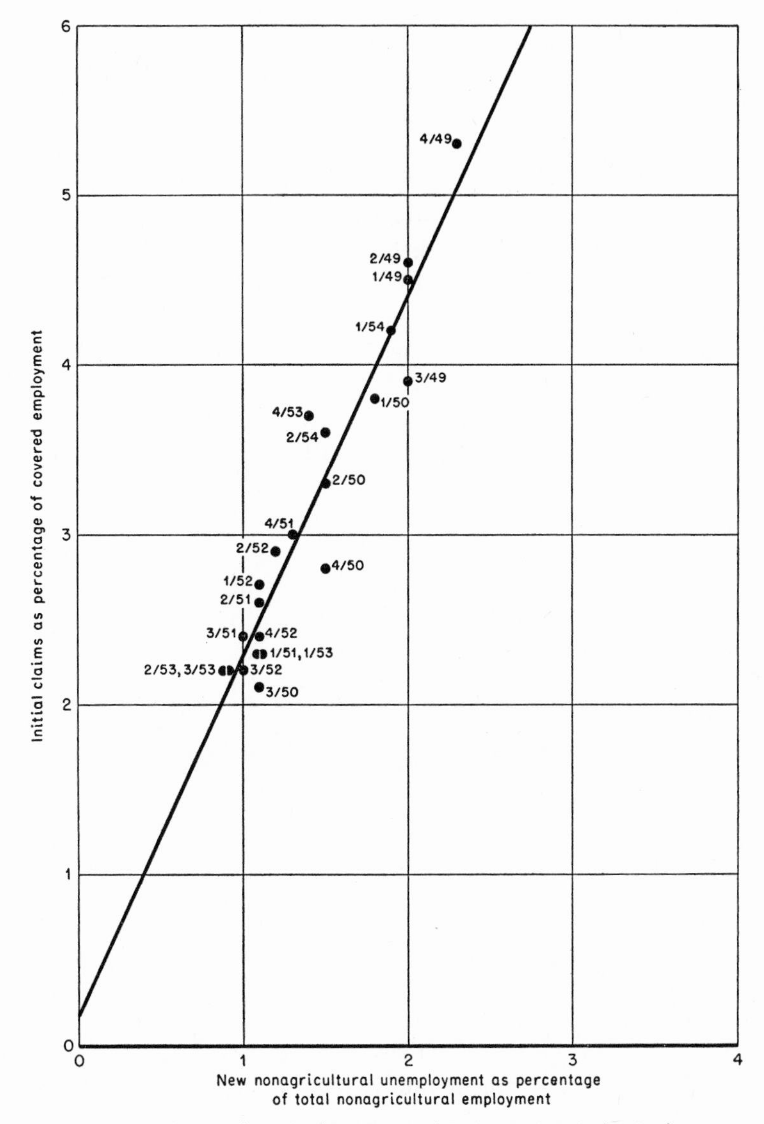

Source: Bureau of Census (CPS data) and Bureau of Employment Security (UI data).

A comparison of unemployment estimates using the Bureau of Employment Security (BES) techniques and the 1950 census figures is difficult because in the 1950 census a large proportion of unemployed workers were not reported. On a national basis the understatement amounts to about 25 per cent. Unfortunately, it cannot be assumed, however, that the 1950 census underenumeration of the unemployed is distributed evenly among all the areas. It is more reasonable to expect that in some areas the nonreporting of unemployed might have been very small, while in others it could have greatly exceeded the 25 per cent national average.

One other problem that complicates the comparison is the fact that the census enumeration was spread over a relatively long period of time so that the reference week is constantly changing. While most of the census enumerations were completed by the end of April, a significant number were still going on in May and even later. The BES data, however, relate to a specific week in April.

Since the Bureau of the Census has no information available on the underenumeration error by area, definitive conclusions with respect to the results of the comparison of the BES and census rates are not possible. However, certain interesting facts come to light when the unemployment rates for the sixteen largest labor market areas are compared.[10]

In all cases except one, the BES rate was higher than the census rate. When the comparison is made in terms of ratios of the BES rate to the census unemployment rate the following results are shown: For one area the BES rate is about 6 per cent lower than the census rate. In three areas the BES rate is between 5 and 10 per cent higher than the census rate, while for seven areas the BES rate is between 10 and 15 per cent higher. In four cases the BES rate is greater than the census rate by somewhat more than 25 per cent, while in one instance (one of the larger areas of the country), the BES rate is about 40 per cent higher. In the latter instance there appears to be no question about the fact that there was a substantial understatement in the census estimate since the number of unemployment insurance claimants reported for this area was about equal to the census estimate of total unemployment. It may also be of some significance possibly to note that when the data for these sixteen areas are aggregated the resulting BES unemployment rate is higher than the census rate for

[10] These areas are: New York, N.Y.; Newark, N.J.; Chicago, Ill.; Los Angeles, Calif.; Philadelphia, Pa.; Detroit, Mich.; Boston, Mass.; San Francisco, Calif.; Pittsburgh, Pa.; St. Louis, Mo.; Cleveland, Ohio; Washington, D.C.; Baltimore, Md.; Minneapolis–St. Paul, Minn.; Buffalo, N.Y.; and Cincinnati, Ohio.

this group by about 25 per cent, or the estimated understatement in the Census national unemployment estimate.

It is unfortunate that because of the underenumeration of the unemployed in the 1950 census, it is not possible to derive from the above comparison a clean-cut and clear evaluation of the reasonableness of the area unemployment estimates obtained by the use of the BES estimating procedure. However, from the results of the comparison the following inferences are possible:

1. The fact that the BES rates are in most instances higher than the census rates may be taken as an indication of the reasonableness of the BES estimates. Because of the nature of the reasons for the census understatement of the unemployed—incomplete reporting of the unemployment of teen-agers and women twenty-five years of age and over[11]—it is plausible to assume that there was some degree of under-reporting of the unemployed in most areas and therefore the "true figures" for these areas would be higher than the census estimates.

2. The reasonableness of the BES estimates may also be inferred from the fact that on an aggregated basis the BES unemployment rate for the sixteen areas is greater than the census rate by about 25 per cent, or a proportion similar to the estimated underenumeration of the unemployed nationally. This group of areas accounted for a large proportion (approximately 40 per cent) of the total unemployed according to the 1950 census data. Given a figure of this magnitude there is some basis for assuming that for this group of areas as a whole the percentage understatement in the number of unemployed probably would be similar to that for the census national unemployment figure.

There are other indications that the system used by the BES for estimating unemployment by area is fairly satisfactory. When the estimates for all major areas are blown up to a national total, the resulting unemployment figures come within a few per cent of the CPS estimates. Also, comparison of estimates of unemployment in individual areas with other data reflecting local economic developments such as trends and levels in employment and department store sales give credence to the reasonableness of the unemployment estimates.

4. Behavior of Unemployment by Area

TRENDS IN AREA UNEMPLOYMENT

An over-all national analysis of employment and unemployment often fails to disclose the true character of manpower problems, especially in specific local labor markets.

[11] See *Census of Population: 1950*, Bureau of the Census, Vol. II, *Characteristics of the Population*, Part I, U.S. Summary, p. 12. Also see *Census of Population Preliminary Reports*, Series PC-7, No. 2, 1950.

A national labor market exists for only a relatively few professional occupations and for selected workers as in the construction field and in agricultural employment. Despite the volume of interarea migration, it is still true that for most occupations and industries, as well as for employers and workers, the labor market has relatively narrow geographical limits. Typically, workers seek jobs and employers recruit workers in the local area which has a composite of employing establishments as labor-demand points, and worker residential sectors as labor supply points.[12]

Examination of employment by industry in the various labor market areas shows a very wide difference in the types of industries that are located in specific communities. The relative importance of manufacturing employment alone varies greatly from one community to another. In May 1954, manufacturing employment ranged from as high as 66.0 per cent of total nonagricultural employment in New Britain, Connecticut to as little as 7.8 per cent in Austin, Texas (see Appendix Table A-1). The types of manufacturing employment in different localities also vary markedly. Metalworking employment accounted for 95.6 per cent of total manufacturing employment in the Flint, Michigan area, compared with 16.6 per cent in the Lawrence, Massachusetts area. As a result of these differences, changes in demand for goods and services of a general or limited nature will have differential impacts on the economic conditions of specific areas. Therefore, an adequate appraisal of unemployment experience requires an analysis not only of the national but also of the local labor market situations.

The differences that may occur in the behavior of unemployment by area in periods of relatively similar national economic conditions are illustrated by the comparison that follows of unemployment rates in a number of areas in early 1950 and mid-1954. These were periods of readjustment in the national economy. The unemployed represented approximately 7 per cent of the civilian labor force in early 1950 and in mid-1954 the unemployment rate was 5 per cent. However, the economic sectors of weakness and strength were different in these two periods. In 1950 the major decline was in the soft goods sector of the economy while in 1954, the downturn was concentrated primarily in durable goods manufacturing. In addition, defense expenditures were lower in 1950 than in 1954. The influence of these factors is reflected in the behavior of unemployment areawise.

The effects of changes in the allocation of defense expenditures between 1950 and 1954 on the economic conditions of specific areas

[12] Louis Levine, "Some Problems in the Organization and Administration of Our Labor Markets," in *Manpower in the United States: Problems and Policies*, William Haber, *et al.*, editors, Harper, 1954.

is shown in the following instances: In the beginning of 1950 the unemployment rate in San Diego, California was in excess of 12 per cent, while rates approximating the national average for 1950 were reported for Columbus and Dayton, Ohio, and Hartford, Connecticut. However, in 1954 as the result of higher levels of defense expenditures for the aircraft and naval activities located in these communities unemployment rates well below the national average were reported for all of these areas. Hartford and Columbus had unemployment rates of less than 3 per cent while the rates in both San Diego and Dayton ranged between 3 and 5 per cent.

Substantial differences from the national unemployment level were also shown by the Des Moines, Iowa and Omaha, Nebraska areas. In mid-1954 unemployment in these localities was under 3 per cent of the labor force or about half the national average. Similarly, rates below the national average were reported in early 1950. At that time they ranged between 4 and 5 per cent. The economic strength of these areas is attributable to their importance as trading centers for the surrounding agricultural communities and in the diversification of their industrial activity. Industries such as food processing, railroad transportation, printing and publishing, and government make important contributions to the employment totals of these areas. In both 1950 and 1954 most of these activities as well as trade maintained high levels of employment.

The significance of the effects that limited economic changes such as shifts in the market position of a large firm or a segment of an industry have upon the economy of an area is strikingly illustrated in the case of South Bend, Indiana. In January 1950 it was one of the few areas showing an unemployment rate of less than 3 per cent. In contrast, in mid-1954 unemployment in South Bend was in excess of 12 per cent. Automobile production is a major activity in this area and the low unemployment rate in 1950 reflected the high levels of this activity. The unfavorable market position of certain independent producers in 1954 was reflected in the South Bend economy.

Some communities appear to have fared moderately well in both periods under consideration. In most instances, these were areas with diversified industrial activity. For example, the unemployment rate for the Chicago area was approximately 5 per cent in both 1950 and 1954. Similarly, Cleveland, another area of wide industrial diversification, had unemployment rates approximating the national average in both 1950 and 1954. The importance of diversification of industry on the economy of an area is illustrated by Utica-Rome. In 1950 this locality was seriously hit by the slump in the textile industry and by the reduction in the activity of an Air Force base maintained in this area. In 1950 the unemployment rate was in excess of 12 per cent, or almost twice the national average. Continuous efforts have been made by this community since 1950 to expand the industrial base of the area. These efforts have been partly successful. Thus, despite continued low levels in textile employment, the unemployment rate in 1954 was approximately 7 per cent or only slightly higher than the national average.

There is a final group of areas that need mention here. These are areas which have faced unemployment problems over an extended period of time because of the type of industrial activity in the area. Improvements in the level of national economic activity have little effect on unemployment in most of these communities so that unemployment rates of 5 per cent or more were not unusual even in 1953 when the national economy was functioning at exceptionally high levels. These are discussed in detail in the subsequent paragraphs.

SURPLUS LABOR MARKETS

As was true during World War II, islands of heavy unemployment existed despite the expanding national volume of business, expanding employment opportunities, and higher levels of economic activity between 1950 and 1953.[13] In a few of the nation's major production and employment centers, conditions have approximated those which generally prevailed during the depression years of the thirties. In a number of other areas where unemployment has not reached such serious proportions, it has been three or four times as high as for the country as a whole.

These centers of heavy unemployment represent a serious waste of the nation's most vital economic resource—manpower. A number of factors explain the high unemployment levels in particular areas, while the nation is generally prosperous. Although no single cause may be involved, it is possible to isolate several factors which contribute to the creation of labor surplus areas. Among these, the following can be identified: (1) depletion of natural resources, combined with dwindling markets (these largely affect coal mining and lumbering centers), (2) lack of sufficient industrialization to support a growing population and labor force, (3) technological changes, and (4) unbalanced local economy. The unbalanced economic areas can be subdivided into two categories: (a) areas which depend for their support primarily on one or two basic industries which have declining markets, or on industries which have experienced geographical shifts, and

[13] See "Idle Manpower," *The Labor Market and Employment Security*, November 1951, pp. 17-21 for further discussion on this subject.

(b) areas which depend on one or two industries which temporarily cut their employment levels because of such factors as material shortages or temporary declines in consumer demand.

A large group of areas, with relatively heavy unemployment during the last three years, are basically depressed coal mining centers. Over the years, the economies of these areas have been progressively weakened by one of three major economic forces, acting singly or in combination: (1) reduced markets, resulting from use of substitute fuels and to some extent from reduced coal exports, (2) increased mechanization which cut drastically the amount of manpower required to operate the mines, and (3) depletion of coal resources or exhaustion of the higher grade and easily accessible seams. Employment in anthracite mining especially has been declining for several decades. Three Pennsylvania anthracite areas—Scranton, Wilkes-Barre–Hazleton, and Pottsville—are among the hardest hit of all major coal mining areas.

In Tacoma, Washington, the only western area with substantial surplus labor in 1953, a diminishing supply of saw and peeler logs, resulting from depleted timber resources, was primarily responsible for increased unemployment; poor markets for plywood and cutbacks at government installations were other contributing factors.

In several areas, changing technology played a part in declining employment levels. In Cumberland, Maryland, dieselization of the area's important railroad industry reduced manpower needs, while railroad operations were also affected by a lower volume of coal shipments. Textiles, this area's other important industry, also underwent technological changes, as modernization of equipment for weaving and dyeing synthetic yarn lowered the need for workers. The jobs lost through these technological changes in Cumberland have not yet been replaced.

Declining railroad employment also affected the Altoona, Pennsylvania area with its large repair shops. In Iron Mountain, Michigan, the area's largest firm, which had been producing wooden automobile station wagon bodies, closed down as the automobile makers converted to all-metal construction, while two other important activities in the area—lumbering and iron mining—have not been prosperous in recent years.

Lack of industrialization and limited year-round job opportunities kept unemployment high in a number of areas. While some of these have a significant amount of manufacturing employment, their major industries are characterized by severe seasonal fluctuations. In two North Carolina areas—Durham and Winston-Salem—the dominant tobacco-product industry operates at a low level for about eight months each year. In Asheville, North Carolina and Atlantic City, New Jersey, extreme seasonality connected with resort activities creates an unstable economy. In both, unemployment remains at substantial levels for most of the year. Gloversville, New York has experienced declining employment for a number of years due to the problems of the local glove industry. A decline in sales of fine leather gloves and competition of foreign glove makers and manufacturers in the Middle West tended to depress the economy of this virtually one-industry area.

A large number of areas with continuous heavy unemployment have been affected by the ills of the textile, apparel, and shoe industries, particularly in New England. Declining textile employment is the dominant cause of high unemployment in Lawrence, Massachusetts. This area has consistently shown the highest unemployment rate of all the nation's major areas—a rate running between 15 and 30 per cent of the labor force. Lowell and New Bedford, Massachusetts, and Utica-Rome, New York have also been serious affected by declines in textile employment. In Providence, Rhode Island, employment reductions in the important textile industry were aggravated by declines in costume jewelry—the area's second largest manufacturing activity. Declines in employment in textiles and shoes led to excessive unemployment in Brockton, Massachusetts and Manchester, New Hampshire. Apparel by itself was the dominant cause of substantial surplus (during 1952) in only one area—Metropolitan New York.

A number of areas developed heavy labor surpluses during the period of Korean mobilization primarily as a result of restrictions on the use of scarce materials for nondefense production. Hardest hit were those producing automobiles, auto parts, household appliances, and similar metal products. The largest center so affected was Detroit, where unemployment rose from around 46,000 in April to about 122,000 in December 1951. Flint, Grand Rapids, and Bay City were other areas experiencing similar problems. Heavy unemployment in these areas was of short duration. In Detroit, for example, unemployment fell from the high of 122,000 to a minimum level of 20,000 by March 1953.

Substantial labor surpluses persisted in some areas even when economic conditions in the country generally were prosperous. In these areas, the basic industrial composition is such that it cannot be expected, either in the short or long run, to provide full employment for the area's workforce. The two most commonly mentioned solutions to unemployment problems in these areas are: (1) reduce the labor surplus by out-migration and balance the number of job seekers with the number of available jobs, and (2) bring new industries into the area and increase the utilization of the local labor supply, thereby reducing unemployment.[14]

That population does not migrate in sufficient volume to bring into balance the number of job seekers with the number of jobs is indicated by the continuous heavy unemployment in depressed areas. It could well be that the very out-migration from the areas that has occurred creates further unemployment problems as the community's economy continues to lose the purchasing power of the out-migrants. In contrast to the population increase of 22 per cent which over the decade (1940-1950) occurred in all Standard Metropolitan Areas combined, all of the chronic labor surplus areas lost population. The Scranton and Wilkes-Barre areas, for example, had net declines in population of 14.6 and 11.2 per cent, respectively.

Out-migration indirectly leads to further local hardship since in many cases the outmigrants are individuals at the best working age. This leaves families dependent on secondary workers or in some cases completely stranded. Out-migration of the more able-bodied persons also results in a decline in the labor force participation rates. While close to 80 per cent of all males fourteen years of age and over were in the labor force for all Standard Metropolitan Areas in 1950, in Scranton and Wilkes-Barre the rates were 72.2 and 72.9 per cent, respectively. A substantial proportion of those in these two areas were unemployed. Communities face other problems when out-migration occurs. Some of these include the loss of tax revenues and, therefore, the slow decay of public installations and services; the loss of payrolls and markets and, therefore, decline in real estate and other property values with their effects on the ability of local banks and other lending institutions to advance credit for new enterprises. Failure of local secondary activities, including trade and service, adds to unemployment and further detracts from the community as an attractive place for the location of new enterprises.

Without some form of planned out-migration, the community is left with the "less desirable" workforce; it is likely to have an excessive proportion of older and younger persons and fewer of the most desirable working-age group.

The objective in dealing with local area unemployment problems is, of course, to increase the utilization of the local labor supply. To bring about greater utilization of local labor supply requires the expansion of existing industries or attraction of new industries and diversification of an area's economic base. New industries, offering additional and diversified employment opportunities, provide a basic approach to

[14] See *Employment Security Review*, December 1953, for a discussion of the steps taken by various areas to attract new industry.

chronic labor surplus problems. Planned efforts to relieve the distressed areas of surplus population are an alternative when it is possible for residents to move to other more prosperous and growing communities.

The availability of manpower, its occupational composition, and local wage rates are only some of the factors which are important in locating new facilities in an area. Others are unused industrial facilities; water power and fuel resources; transportation facilities, including railroad, highway, and air; housing, educational, and recreational facilities; proximity of raw materials and markets to the area; and the local tax structure. Many of the areas with chronic unemployment do not have such facilities and, therefore, are not able to attract new industries. Nevertheless, local communities, on an organized and planned basis, must constantly search for means of inducing private enterprise to select labor surplus areas as sites for expansion.

AREA LABOR MARKET CLASSIFICATIONS

Area classifications according to relative adequacy of labor supply, prepared by the BES, are intended to provide a quick, convenient tool to measure comparative differences in the availability of labor (and general economic well-being) of the nation's major production and employment centers. These indicators of area labor market conditions have been widely used by government agencies and private organizations in the introduction, administration, and evaluation of manpower programs, as well as of other programs that affect employment opportunities ever since the area classification program was first initiated in the early days of World War II. Table 1 gives a summary of area classifications for selected periods and includes a distribution of wage and salaried employment in each classification group.

LABOR FORCE PARTICIPATION

The extent of labor force participation has an important bearing on the well-being of the area's economy.[15] The degree of labor force participation of both men and women varies greatly among areas. According to the 1950 census, some areas had as high as 87 per cent of their male population, fourteen years of age and over, in the labor force (Columbus, Georgia), while others had no more than 71 per cent (Tampa–St. Petersburg, Florida). Labor force participation rates for women ran as high as 42 and 41 per cent in Washington, D.C. and New Bedford, Massachusetts to as low as 19 per cent in Johnstown, Pennsylvania (see Appendix Table A-1).

The extent of participation by the population in the labor force

[15] See *Labor Force Participation, Its Significance to Labor Market Analysis*, Bureau of Employment Security, June 1952.

TABLE 1

Distribution of Areas, and Nonagricultural Wage and Salary Employment and Unemployment, by Classification Group, July 1953, May and July 1954

	NUMBER OF AREAS		PER CENT OF WAGE AND SALARY EMPLOYMENT		PER CENT OF UNEMPLOYMENT	
CLASSIFICATION[a]	*July 1954*	*July 1953*	*May 1954*	*May 1953*	*May 1954*	*May 1953*
Total	145	145	100.0	100.0	100.0	100.0
Group I	0	5	0.0	1.4	0.0	0.6
Group II	16	65	7.4	44.8	3.5	27.9
Group III	80	62	66.6	50.8	59.2	64.4
Group IV	49	13	26.0	3.0	37.3	7.1
IV-A	42	b	24.0	b	31.8	b
IV-B	7	b	2.0	b	5.5	b

[a] See Appendix A, Table A-2, note b for an explanation of the classification groupings.
[b] In 1953, Group IV areas were not subdivided into A and B.

depends upon many factors, the more important of which are the age and color composition of the population, the type of industries in the area, and the general health of the area's economy. Areas which have industries in which large numbers of women can be employed have a much higher female labor force participation rate, as for instance, Washington, D.C. and New Bedford, Massachusetts. On the other hand, areas such as Johnstown and Pittsburgh, Pennsylvania whose basic economies are dependent, in a large measure, on such heavy industries as production of steel and coal mining have very low rates. The age composition of the population is also an important factor in the labor force participation of both men and women. In Tampa–St. Petersburg, Florida, which has a disproportionately large older population, the participation rates are the lowest among all of the Standard Metropolitan Areas. On the other hand, areas which have experienced a large inmigration of workers because of their expanding economies have attracted a proportionately larger number of persons in the working-age groups. These communities have considerably higher-than-the-national-average labor force participation rates.

5. *Industrial and Other Characteristics of the Unemployed*

SOURCES OF DATA

Because of the dynamic nature of the labor market, current information on the characteristics of the unemployed is extremely important, particularly when unemployment reaches major proportions. Evaluation of the significance of unemployment data and the development of measures to reduce joblessness and to attract new business to the area are dependent upon detailed information regarding the kinds of workers who are unemployed. The more important characteristics for which there is a need for data are the duration of unemployment, age and sex, and occupation and industry of attachment. Other than the decennial census enumerations which provide data on some of these characteristics, there is no current comprehensive information on a uniform basis for all of the major labor market areas. The decennial censuses quickly become much too old for analysis of the current characteristics of the unemployed.

Aside from the broad categories of data available from the CPS, the only source of current information consists of the reports emanating from employment security operations. At present, regularly prepared reports of insured unemployment provide a breakdown by sex, and sex and veteran status is available for all jobseekers. A number of states also prepare reports on the previous industrial attachment of unemployment insurance beneficiaries. The only regular current employment security source on duration of unemployment covers the number of weeks of benefits received by claimants exhausting their benefit rights.

While no regularly reported data on many of the characteristics of unemployed workers are being made available, such basic information does exist. This information has not been utilized up to now primarily because of lack of funds. The existing employment security records could, however, yield more detailed statistics on such characteristics of the unemployed as age, sex, veteran status, industry of attachment, occupation, duration of unemployment, marital status, past earnings, education, previous work history, duration of stay in most recent area of residence, number of dependents, and physical handicaps. These basic data are available for all job seekers and benefit claimants at public employment offices and could be obtained not only for the nation as a whole but for individual states and areas.

The importance of the information on the characteristics of the unemployed in individual areas cannot be overemphasized. For example, unemployment in any one area at any specific time may be low; duration of unemployment, however, could conceivably be quite long. In such a case, a low unemployment figure could present problems which are more serious than when unemployment is high but is of short duration. More information is needed to carry out the necessary programs to assist older workers. Similarly, industry of attachment and the occupation of the unemployed is of vital importance in planning programs to alleviate unemployment.

To the extent to which job applicants at public employment offices are representative of total unemployment, they furnish a valuable measure of the characteristics of the unemployed at any time in any area. In April 1950, the BES sponsored a ninety-area survey of job applicants at public employment offices.[16] Characteristics of job applicants were tabulated according to age, sex, occupation, veteran status, unemployment insurance claimant status and length of time seeking work through the local office. In order to make possible a comparison of information on job applicants with information on total unemployment, the job applicant survey was scheduled for the same period as the 1950 Census of Population. Occupational groupings insofar as possible, intervals of length of time seeking work, and age groups were selected for the survey so as to be reasonably consistent with the groupings used by the Bureau of the Census.

Some differences still remained in definitions and coverage between the job applicant survey and the census. The job applicant survey included some persons who were seeking work through the employment service even though they may have had other jobs. There were also differences in the definitions of the "occupations" used in the survey and those used by the Bureau of the Census. Strict comparability was not possible between the "skilled and semiskilled" categories in the job applicant survey and the census' titles of "craftsmen, foremen and kindred workers." However, when the two former groups are combined the differences in definitions become relatively small. Another problem making comparisons by occupational group difficult was the very substantial number of unemployed in the census data for which occupation was not reported. For the country as a whole, the "occupation not reported" group accounted for over 20 per cent. In nearly all areas, these percentages were of approximately the same magnitude. The results, however, of the comparison between the census and the job applicant survey data for the country as a whole and for individual areas, as, for example, the Baltimore area, indicates that despite the differences between the two studies in certain specifics, there is a remarkable similarity in many over-all aspects.

The April 1950 job applicant survey data aggregated for the ninety areas revealed that these industrial centers accounted for over 2 million local office job applicants. For this month the CPS reported total unemployment as 3,515,000. The major difference between the job applicant survey and the 1950 census data occurred in the number of women and young job seekers included in the employment office files. Women appeared to be somewhat over-represented when compared with the census enumeration, while job seekers under twenty years of age were underrepresented in the employment office data. Young job

[16] *Job Seekers at Public Employment Offices*, Bureau of Employment Security, April 1950.

seekers constitute a higher proportion of the total unemployed than of applicants at the local public employment offices because they lack wage credits under unemployment insurance programs, and therefore, do not use the employment service to the same extent as more experienced workers. The proportion of individuals in other age brackets was, of course, influenced by this difference in the lower age brackets.

A very close correlation by age, however, was found when those under twenty years of age were removed from both the census and the job applicant survey data. For the United States as a whole the census data show 45 per cent to be unemployed in the twenty-five and under forty-five age group as against 49 per cent in the BES data. For the Baltimore area, these percentages were 50 and 52. For those between forty-five and sixty-five, the ninety-area survey showed 29 per cent as against 30 per cent in the census, while in Baltimore, the similar percentages were 27 and 27. For the sixty-five years of age and over group, census data showed 5.4 per cent as against 6 per cent in the job applicant survey and in Baltimore these percentages were 3.8 and 5.7. Both sources showed a relatively smaller number of unemployed older women; about one-half the rate for men of the same age. In the group of women twenty and under twenty-five, the census data had 19 per cent as against 16.5 in the job applicant survey, while in Baltimore similar percentages were 19.5 and 15.4. Thus, both surveys clearly point up the well-known facts that women withdraw from the job market at a much earlier age than do men, that the greatest bulk of job seekers are between the ages of twenty-five and forty-five, and that the next largest group is between forty-five and sixty-five.

Comparison by occupation of the job applicants and the total unemployed as reported by the census was extremely difficult because of the afore-mentioned fact that the census data did not report occupation for a large group of the unemployed. It is believed that a large proportion of individuals for whom occupation was not reported would fall in the "unskilled" category, but there is no evidence to verify this. Nationally, excluding unemployed farm workers, "occupation not reported" was 24 per cent and for Baltimore 22 per cent.

If it is assumed that the census "not reported" group was distributed in the same proportion as those for whom occupations were reported, the job applicant survey has a somewhat smaller proportion for nearly all the occupational groups except the "unskilled." For the "unskilled" group, the job applicant survey shows a substantially higher percentage—for example, percentages in Baltimore were 31.7 per cent as against 17.3 per cent shown by the census. On the other hand, the census reported a substantially higher number of domestic service workers unemployed than did the job applicant survey. It is quite likely that in many local offices domestic service workers are referred to available work without the formality of registration.

A strikingly close agreement on the data from the two sources is shown if it is assumed that the greater bulk of the "group not reported" in the census data are unskilled workers. Thus, the proper distribution of the "occupation not reported" exerts an almost decisive influence on the extent of the correspondence of data from the two sources. In general, it can be concluded, however, that the distribution of job applicants by occupation agrees fairly well with the occupational distribution of the experienced unemployed as reported by the census.

DURATION OF UNEMPLOYMENT

Analyses of the severity of unemployment require data on the length of time that the unemployed have been out of work. At times information on the duration of unemployment is even more significant to the analysis of the unemployment problem than the data on the total number of the unemployed. Unemployment may be low at any one time, but its duration long. Usually, however, high unemployment produces long spells of unemployment.

The most recent comprehensive information on the duration of unemployment for local areas was obtained in the April 1950 job applicant survey.[17] Analyses of these data indicate wide differences in the duration of unemployment among local areas. As might be expected in areas with relatively large volume of unemployment, applicants had been looking for work much longer than in areas with tight labor supply. Thus, in areas with unemployment in excess of 12 per cent of the labor force, on the average, 20 per cent of applicants had been unemployed for more than twenty weeks, while only 27 per cent of the applicants sought work for less than four weeks. On the other hand, in areas with unemployment of less than 3 per cent, 48 per cent looked for work for less than four weeks and only 5 per cent for more than twenty weeks. South Bend, Indiana, for example, one of the tightest labor market areas in the country in 1950, had only 2.6 per cent of its applicants unemployed for over twenty weeks while almost 56 per cent were unemployed less than four weeks. In contrast, Scranton, Pennsylvania had close to 28 per cent of its job applicants seeking work for over twenty weeks and only 24 per cent unemployed for less than four weeks.

Another important source of data on duration of unemployment is found in the surveys of individuals who have exhausted unemployment insurance benefits. These studies are made by the state employment security agencies to determine the adequacy of benefits under state

[17] *Ibid.*

unemployment insurance laws. Many of such surveys conducted in 1949-1950[18] indicate that a significant proportion of workers were unemployed for very long periods. In Connecticut,[19] for example, in 1949 when unemployment rose sharply and some 154,000 workers drew unemployment insurance benefits, the number of persons who exhausted benefits totaled 50,200; 45,900 still resided in the state during the survey week, the end of January 1950. The survey revealed that the majority of exhaustees were not re-employed after exhaustion of benefits. Of those who found jobs, only 10 per cent did so within a week after exhaustion of benefits while 26 per cent did not find jobs until sixteen weeks later. The average (median) duration of unemployment from exhaustion of benefits to first job was nine weeks. This is in addition to an average of sixteen and eight-tenths weeks of unemployment while drawing benefits. Of the 25,000 who were not re-employed after exhaustion, 9,300 dropped out of the labor market and 15,700 were looking for work at the time of the survey. Those who were looking for work had an average (median) duration of unemployment of nineteen weeks from the time they exhausted benefits, with a significant 15 per cent looking for work for over thirty-five weeks. These periods of unemployment were in addition to an average of sixteen and nine-tenths weeks of unemployment while in benefit status. Relatively more women than men exhausted benefits, and relatively more of the older workers than the workers in the age group thirty-five to forty-four. Significantly, however, about the same proportion of women as of men who had exhausted benefits were working during the survey week, while more women and older workers dropped out of the labor market.

Areas with heavier unemployment had a larger number of individuals exhausting benefits than those with better job opportunities. In Bridgeport, for instance, where many layoffs occurred, the ratio of exhaustions to covered workers was 9.3 per cent, whereas in Hartford where employment opportunities were relatively good the ratio stood at 4.1 per cent.

The age of applicants has a considerable bearing on duration of unemployment. Most areas showed a steadily increasing proportion in older age categories who were in the "seeking work over 20 weeks" group. In Houston, Texas, for example, 12.3 per cent of applicants, forty-five to sixty-four years of age, looked for work for "over 20 weeks"

[18] *Adequacy of Benefits under Unemployment Insurance*, Bureau of Employment Security, September 1952.

[19] "What Happens after Exhaustion of Benefits," *The Labor Market and Employment Security*, May 1950. Based in part on a *Study of Persons Who Exhausted Unemployment Compensation Benefits in Connecticut during 1949*, Connecticut Department of Labor, Employment Security Division, March 1950.

and 22.7 per cent of those sixty-five years of age and over as against 8 per cent of all the applicants.

SEX AND AGE CHARACTERISTICS

While the unemployment rate markedly affects the duration of unemployment, it does not appear to directly influence the sex composition of unemployment. Women constituted 35 per cent of all applicants in ninety areas surveyed by employment offices in 1950. While there were significant differences by area in the proportion of women applicants to the total, the difference could not be attributed to the relative volume of unemployment. Some areas with low unemployment had a relatively small proportion of women looking for work —as, for instance, Des Moines, Iowa (25 per cent)—while others with the same low volume of unemployment had a high proportion of women job seekers—as, for instance, South Bend (40 per cent). Similar differences were found in areas of heavy unemployment. The proportion of women job seekers in Scranton, Pennsylvania and Utica-Rome, New York was 26 per cent and 38 per cent, respectively. The industrial composition of the area, the degree of labor force participation by women, and the types of industries which released workers were the major factors that determined the relative severity of unemployment among women.

By age, 47 per cent of the applicants were in the most employable age bracket (twenty-five to forty-four), 33 per cent were forty-five or older, with an appreciable 6 per cent in the difficult-to-place over-sixty-five category. The distribution varied by area. Although the overall average showed 33 per cent of the applicants to be forty-five and older, in more than half the areas a smaller proportion fell into this older age group.

Men, who constituted 65 per cent of all applicants, were in the majority in all age groups. However, their proportion of the total ranged from 56 per cent in the eighteen- to nineteen-year group to 84 per cent in the sixty-five-and-over group.

INDUSTRIAL AND OCCUPATIONAL CHARACTERISTICS

Divergence in the industrial characteristics of various areas introduces marked differences in the occupational distribution.[20] In Los Angeles, 8.5 per cent of the 139,600 job applicants had professional or managerial backgrounds, clerical and sales categories accounted for 21.4 per cent, and about 52 per cent of the total were quite evenly divided among skilled, semiskilled, and unskilled occupations. But in

[20] *Job Seekers at Public Employment Offices*, as cited.

Philadelphia, with a far greater concentration of manufacturing establishments, only 3.4 per cent of the 124,400 job seekers were recorded in professional and managerial categories and but 12.1 per cent in clerical and sales; semiskilled occupations accounted for 28.1 per cent, and the skilled and unskilled groups each made up over a fifth of the total.

Current data on industry of attachment of the unemployed are generally lacking. Only the decennial census of population provides comprehensive information on this subject. These data are valuable for historic analysis of the unemployed but they cannot be used in the analysis of the current problems.

One approach to the analysis of unemployment by industry is the evaluation of the changes in employment from one period to another (see Appendix Table A-2). This, however, can be done only for short periods of time since a sizable number of the unemployed are likely to shift to other industries where job opportunities develop. In the analyses of the current unemployment situation, there is little question but that the growth in unemployment between 1953 and 1954 was primarily due to reduction in employment in durable goods industries. The increase in unemployment over the year in Detroit, for instance, was about the same as the reduction in employment in the durable goods industry. Many of the workers in Detroit who were released by the automobile industry left the area, while others entered the local labor force but did not find jobs.

While the data are not generally published, many of the state agencies tabulate information on the industry of attachment of unemployment insurance claimants for administrative uses. These data are often shown by sex and in some states, as in New York, information is provided for individual labor market areas. While these data are not representative of total unemployment, they are extremely valuable in the analysis of the most volatile and important industrial segment of our economy. Regardless of the size-of-firm coverage of the unemployment insurance laws, almost all manufacturing industry is covered.

TABLE A-1

Population and Labor Force, 1950, and Nonagricultural Wage and Salary Employment, by Area, May 1954

	1950				May 1954				
			Per Cent 14 and over in Labor Force						
STATE AND AREA	*Population (thousands)*	*Per Cent Increase in Population over 1940*	*Men*	*Women*	*Total Nonagricultural Wage and Salary Employment*	*Per Cent of Total in Manufacturing*	*Per Cent of Total in Metalworking*[a]	*Per Cent of Manufacturing in Metal working*	*Women as Per Cent of Total*
Alabama:									
Birmingham	558.9	21.5	80.0	28.7	187.4	32.4	21.9	67.5	24.6
Mobile	231.1	62.8	80.3	33.9	75.9	21.2	4.3	20.4	27.6
Arizona:									
Phoenix	331.8	78.2	75.1	27.8	97.4	15.9	9.3	58.4	30.0
Arkansas:									
Little Rock–North Little Rock	196.7	26.0	75.4	34.6	67.7	18.6	5.1	27.4	37.0
California:									
Fresno	276.5	54.9	78.1	25.7	66.2	18.3	5.4	29.3	31.4
Los Angeles	4,367.9	49.8	78.2	32.2	1,814.6	34.9	20.4	58.5	32.3
Sacramento	277.1	62.7	78.4	33.6	113.5	10.0	1.4	13.6	32.1
San Bernardino–Riverside	451.7	69.4	74.0	25.0	127.6	20.5	11.1	54.2	30.0
San Diego	556.8	92.4	81.1	27.4	178.2	28.6	24.0	83.9	32.6
San Francisco–Oakland	2,240.8	53.3	79.7	34.0	855.7	23.3	10.6	45.4	32.9
San Jose	290.5	66.1	73.7	29.1	89.2	26.5	9.9	37.3	31.6
Stockton	200.8	49.6	77.9	28.9	54.0	21.7	3.7	17.1	29.3
Colorado:									
Denver	563.8	38.3	79.1	32.6	223.5	19.1	2.8	14.5	38.4

(continued on next page)

TABLE A-1 (continued)

STATE AND AREA	1950				May 1954				
	Population (thousands)	Per Cent Increase in Population over 1940	Per Cent 14 and over in Labor Force		Total Nonagricultural Wage and Salary Employment	Per Cent of Total in Manufacturing	Per Cent of Total in Metalworking[a]	Per Cent of Manufacturing in Metal working	Women as Per Cent of Total
			Men	Women					
Connecticut:									
Bridgeport[b]	258.1	21.4	81.3	33.7	116.2	58.7	43.4	73.9	33.0
Hartford[b]	358.1	21.1	81.6	38.6	196.1	38.8	31.1	80.1	35.8
New Britain[b]	147.0	16.0	83.5	37.1	42.1	66.0	58.6	88.8	32.1
New Haven[b]	264.6	9.9	75.9	34.2	117.5	39.1	20.8	53.0	35.9
Stamford–Norwalk[b]	196.0	22.3	81.7	34.4	72.9	45.0	22.9	50.9	34.6
Waterbury[b]	154.7	11.4	82.6	36.4	67.1	63.9	31.4	49.2	34.0
Delaware:									
Wilmington[b]	268.4	21.0	80.1	30.0	98.8	43.7	13.0	29.6	27.8
District of Columbia:									
Washington	1,464.1	51.3	81.1	42.5	600.9	4.3	0.8	19.3	39.3
Florida:									
Jacksonville	304.0	44.7	81.6	34.3	114.7	15.7	2.1	13.3	31.4
Miami	495.1	84.9	76.9	33.6	202.4	12.0	1.4	11.9	32.7
Tampa–St. Petersburg	409.1	50.4	70.9	29.6	122.4	18.8	1.8	9.8	35.1
Georgia:									
Atlanta	671.8	29.7	78.6	36.6	296.4	26.4	9.2	34.8	34.1
Columbus	170.5	34.9	87.1	37.1	42.7	40.5	2.9	7.0	38.3
Macon	135.0	42.0	82.1	36.0	54.4	23.0	4.3	18.7	32.1
Savannah	151.5	28.4	81.1	33.4	48.8	27.7	2.5	9.2	26.6

(continued on next page)

TABLE A-1 (continued)

STATE AND AREA	1950				May 1954				
	Population (thousands)	*Per Cent Increase in Population over 1940*	*Per Cent 14 and over in Labor Force*		*Total Nonagricultural Wage and Salary Employment*	*Per Cent of Total in Manufacturing*	*Per Cent of Total in Metalworking*[a]	*Per Cent of Manufacturing in Metal working*	*Women as Per Cent of Total*
			Men	*Women*					
Illinois:									
Aurora	80.5	16.0	84.8[c]	34.0[c]	30.1	52.5	31.5	60.0	37.0
Chicago[b]	5,031.5	12.8	82.2	35.2	2,263.3	39.3	21.3	54.3	30.8
Davenport–Rock Island–Moline	234.3	18.3	81.6	29.6	89.6	47.3	36.4	76.9	30.7
Joliet	134.3	17.6	75.4	25.6	47.0	46.4	21.8	47.0	30.5
Peoria	250.5	18.3	81.9	29.2	86.3	45.9	31.9	69.5	28.6
Rockford	152.4	25.8	85.8	33.5	63.4	58.4	48.1	82.5	29.2
Indiana:									
Evansville	160.4	22.7	81.8	29.6	66.3	47.7	32.5	68.1	28.8
Fort Wayne	183.7	18.5	92.2	32.7	73.4	47.8	36.1	75.5	33.8
Indianapolis	555.2	19.7	82.9	35.0	267.3	38.5	25.3	65.6	33.2
South Bend	205.1	26.7	81.7	31.1	74.1	49.3	30.4	61.8	33.2
Terre Haute	105.2	5.5	75.6	29.1	34.2	31.3	8.1	25.9	28.9
Iowa:									
Cedar Rapids	104.3	17.0	83.0	32.8	41.9	44.4	25.5	57.5	31.6
Des Moines	226.0	15.4	80.9	35.1	90.3	24.1	5.8	23.9	33.6
Kansas:									
Wichita	222.2	55.1	83.0	30.6	115.0	44.9	36.7	81.9	32.3
Kentucky:									
Louisville	576.9	27.8	80.5	30.8	218.2	41.0	15.6	38.0	34.9

(continued on next page)

TABLE A-1 (continued)

STATE AND AREA	1950				MAY 1954				
	Population (thousands)	Per Cent Increase in Population over 1940	Per Cent 14 and over in Labor Force: Men	Per Cent 14 and over in Labor Force: Women	Total Nonagricultural Wage and Salary Employment	Per Cent of Total in Manufacturing	Per Cent of Total in Metalworking[a]	Per Cent of Manufacturing in Metal working	Women as Per Cent of Total
Louisiana:									
Baton Rouge	158.2	79.0	74.8	30.1	56.5	32.7	1.0	3.1	24.8
New Orleans	685.4	24.1	78.8	30.9	266.2	20.2	6.2	30.9	27.3
Shreveport	176.5	17.5	79.3	33.6	51.0	14.3	3.2	22.6	28.4
Maine:									
Portland	119.9	12.6	78.3	31.8	51.9	26.0	4.9	19.0	31.2
Maryland:									
Baltimore	1,337.4	23.5	81.0	32.5	548.5	34.6	18.9	54.8	31.5
Massachusetts:									
Boston[b]	2,370.0	8.8	76.1	32.4	932.0	33.1	14.6	44.0	n.a.
Brockton[b]	129.4	8.5	74.4	31.7	42.2	47.9	8.6	18.0	41.9
Fall River[b]	137.3	1.6	77.6	41.1	47.2	59.3	1.8	3.0	45.5
Lawrence	125.9	0.9	79.8	42.3	33.5	50.7	8.4	16.6	36.7
Lowell[b]	133.9	2.2	73.7	34.5	39.6	51.8	4.7	9.1	40.0
New Bedford[b]	137.5	2.3	78.4	41.1	52.0	54.6	15.3	28.1	40.7
Springfield-Holyoke[b]	407.3	11.7	80.1	34.3	157.7	49.6	22.9	46.1	32.0
Worcester[b]	276.3	9.3	74.4	30.1	103.8	48.2	24.6	51.0	34.1
Michigan:									
Battle Creek	120.8	28.2	78.1	32.9	40.0	53.2	29.0	54.5	29.8
Detroit	3,016.2	26.9	83.3	28.9	1,242.0	50.4	41.5	82.4	27.8
Flint	271.0	18.9	85.1	28.3	122.3	65.2	62.4	95.6	21.3

(continued on next page)

TABLE A-1 (continued)

STATE AND AREA	1950				MAY 1954				
	Population (thousands)	Per Cent Increase in Population over 1940	Per Cent 14 and over in Labor Force: Men	Per Cent 14 and over in Labor Force: Women	Total Nonagricultural Wage and Salary Employment	Per Cent of Total in Manufacturing	Per Cent of Total in Metalworking[a]	Per Cent of Manufacturing in Metal working	Women as Per Cent of Total
Michigan (cont):									
Grand Rapids	288.3	17.0	81.6	30.3	104.3	50.3	27.4	54.5	32.4
Kalamazoo	126.7	26.6	77.4	30.8	44.3	54.2	16.9	31.2	30.5
Lansing	172.9	32.4	74.8	31.5	73.9	44.0	41.0	93.2	26.7
Muskegon	121.5	28.6	82.5	25.3	40.2	63.4	50.0	78.8	23.4
Saginaw	153.5	17.7	82.1	26.5	50.5	52.5	45.0	85.7	21.0
Minnesota:									
Duluth–Superior[b]	252.8	–0.5	78.4	28.1	50.9	21.8	11.7	53.5	33.2
Minneapolis–St. Paul	1,116.5	18.7	79.3	35.6	457.9	30.2	14.1	46.8	37.0
Mississippi:									
Jackson[b]	142.2	32.5	80.0	37.8	45.0	19.8	2.0	10.1	34.9
Missouri:									
Kansas City	814.4	18.6	80.5	33.3	364.6	30.6	14.2	46.4	29.4
St. Louis	1,681.3	17.4	80.2	31.6	703.5	37.9	17.0	44.8	31.0
Nebraska:									
Omaha	366.4	12.7	79.8	31.7	139.8	22.6	3.7	16.3	33.5
New Hampshire:									
Manchester	88.4	7.9	79.7	42.2	38.5	48.6	4.5	9.4	44.2
New Jersey:									
Atlantic City[b]	132.4	6.7	76.3	31.5	42.0	14.0	0.5	3.4	35.8

(continued on next page)

TABLE A-1 (continued)

STATE AND AREA	1950				MAY 1954				
	Population (thousands)	Per Cent Increase in Population over 1940	Per Cent 14 and over in Labor Force		Total Nonagricultural Wage and Salary Employment	Per Cent of Total in Manufacturing	Per Cent of Total in Metalworking[a]	Per Cent of Manufacturing in Metal working	Women as Per Cent of Total
			Men	Women					
New Jersey (cont.):									
Newark	1,743.1	7.9	81.4[d]	32.8[d]	748.2	44.6	21.1	47.3	31.0
Paterson	1,040.6	17.6	[d]	[d]	343.7	52.3	19.4	37.1	29.8
Perth Amboy	241.3	21.1	[d]	[d]	104.0	59.0	21.7	36.8	30.4
Trenton[b]	229.8	16.5	75.4	36.3	121.0	43.2	21.8	50.5	36.1
New Mexico:									
Albuquerque	145.7	109.9	78.9	26.6	53.2	16.4	11.1	68.2	25.9
New York:									
Albany–Schenectady–Troy	514.5	10.5	78.2	31.5	206.2	39.9	24.3	60.9	30.0
Binghamton	184.7	11.4	79.2	33.9	75.5	54.3	21.9	40.2	34.8
Buffalo	1,089.2	13.6	80.6	28.4	432.7	46.5	29.0	62.2	26.0
New York[b]	9,555.9	9.8	79.0	33.5	3,959.9	27.2	6.7	24.7	n.a.
Rochester	487.6	11.3	79.4	34.3	208.9	52.7	14.2	27.0	35.1
Syracuse	341.7	15.8	77.6	33.2	139.3	42.1	30.5	72.4	30.4
Utica-Rome	284.3	8.0	76.4	31.1	95.0	46.3	27.4	59.1	35.0
North Carolina:									
Asheville	124.4	14.4	74.2	31.6	36.1	31.3	[e]	[e]	33.2
Charlotte	197.1	29.8	83.4	41.8	80.8	26.0	3.8	14.7	40.5
Durham	101.6	26.7	74.1	42.3	35.0	33.7	1.6	4.8	41.2
Greensboro–High Point	191.1	24.1	82.4	41.5	78.0	49.5	3.6	7.3	35.6
Winston-Salem	146.1	15.5	80.8	39.2	60.3	50.7	11.0	21.7	39.9

(continued on next page)

TABLE A-1 (continued)

STATE AND AREA	1950				MAY 1954				
	Population (thousands)	Per Cent Increase in Population over 1940	Per Cent 14 and over in Labor Force		Total Nonagricultural Wage and Salary Employment	Per Cent of Total in Manufacturing	Per Cent of Total in Metalworking[a]	Per Cent of Manufacturing in Metal working	Women as Per Cent of Total
			Men	Women					
Ohio:									
Akron	410.0	20.8	82.4	29.0	168.0	55.0	14.9	27.1	28.9
Canton	283.2	20.6	82.3	26.6	110.7	52.4	38.9	74.3	29.2
Cincinnati	904.4	14.9	79.9	30.7	374.4	42.8	21.8	51.0	29.6
Cleveland	1,465.5	15.6	82.9	32.6	643.8	47.7	32.8	68.7	30.8
Columbus	503.4	29.5	75.5	34.1	225.5	31.8	18.9	59.3	36.7
Dayton	457.3	38.0	81.4	31.4	201.9	47.1	34.4	73.2	29.1
Hamilton–Middletown	147.2	22.4	79.0	27.1	55.7	58.2	51.1	87.8	24.2
Lorain–Elyria	148.2	31.8	83.4	25.1	50.4	59.1	53.8	90.9	23.2
Toledo[b]	395.6	14.9	81.7	30.9	151.7	44.2	27.2	61.5	28.8
Youngstown	528.5	11.6	82.1	25.0	181.1	55.8	47.4	85.0	30.5
Oklahoma:									
Oklahoma City	325.4	33.3	82.0	33.6	133.8	12.0	3.1	26.0	30.1
Tulsa	251.7	30.2	80.2	32.1	114.0	25.6	16.3	63.7	28.4
Oregon:									
Portland	704.8	40.6	79.0	32.0	236.6	24.3	6.2	25.5	30.0
Pennsylvania:									
Allentown-Bethlehem	437.8	10.4	79.7	32.7	167.2	56.4	27.3	48.5	29.9
Altoona	139.5	—0.6	76.0	22.0	38.6	35.8	16.3	45.7	27.5
Erie	219.4	21.3	80.6	30.1	77.0	53.0	36.0	67.9	29.0
Harrisburg	292.2	15.9	79.4	32.2	120.8	25.3	10.3	40.7	35.1

(continued on next page)

TABLE A-1 (continued)

STATE AND AREA	1950				MAY 1954				
	Population (thousands)	Per Cent Increase in Population over 1940	Per Cent 14 and over in Labor Force: Men	Per Cent 14 and over in Labor Force: Women	Total Nonagricultural Wage and Salary Employment	Per Cent of Total in Manufacturing	Per Cent of Total in Metalworking[a]	Per Cent of Manufacturing in Metal working	Women as Per Cent of Total
Pennsylvania (cont.):									
Johnstown	291.4	–2.4	74.1	19.4	71.2	32.0	21.9	68.4	22.4
Lancaster	234.7	10.5	82.2	32.8	81.0	52.3	16.1	30.8	35.4
Philadelphia	3,671.0	14.7	78.7	31.6	1,392.5	41.6	17.6	42.4	30.8
Pittsburgh	2,213.2	6.3	78.7	24.4	768.6	42.9	31.8	74.0	24.5
Reading	255.7	5.7	82.2	33.9	91.9	52.7	21.1	40.0	33.3
Scranton	257.4	–14.6	72.2	28.8	78.4	38.4	9.4	24.6	37.6
Wilkes-Barre–Hazleton	392.2	–11.2	72.9	27.7	107.1	31.7	3.6	11.4	41.7
York	207.7	13.9	83.7	32.6	79.1	58.2	23.1	39.8	32.2
Rhode Island:									
Providence	737.2	8.9	78.0	36.0	271.8	47.7	11.7	24.4	38.4
South Carolina:									
Aiken-Augusta[a]	179.3	18.0	81.2	35.5	71.8	32.5	0.2	0.7	29.5
Charleston	164.9	36.1	79.1	33.3	48.7	32.0	15.9	49.7	30.6
Greenville	168.2	23.1	80.8	38.4	57.4	48.8	2.4	4.8	40.7
Tennessee:									
Chattanooga	246.5	16.5	78.6	32.5	87.3	46.8	13.9	29.6	32.0
Knoxville	337.1	37.0	75.4	26.7	116.3	37.5	7.5	20.1	27.2
Memphis	482.4	34.7	82.1	35.6	165.6	25.5	3.6	14.0	30.1
Nashville	321.8	25.1	74.8	35.0	120.2	28.1	5.0	17.6	35.8

(continued on next page)

TABLE A-1 (continued)

STATE AND AREA	1950				MAY 1954				
	Population (thousands)	*Per Cent Increase in Population over 1940*	*Per Cent 14 and over in Labor Force*		*Total Nonagricultural Wage and Salary Employment*	*Per Cent of Total in Manufacturing*	*Per Cent of Total in Metalworking*[a]	*Per Cent of Manufacturing in Metal working*	*Women as Per Cent of Total*
			Men	*Women*					
Texas:									
Austin	161.0	45.0	68.2	33.3	49.9	7.8	0.7	8.9	38.5
Beaumont–Port Arthur	195.1	34.2	83.4	28.6	66.2	39.6	5.7	14.5	22.5
Corpus Christi	165.5	78.6	84.8	27.5	51.8	14.9	2.2	14.7	26.6
Dallas	614.8	54.3	83.3	38.2	262.2	28.1	13.8	49.3	34.5
El Paso	195.0	48.8	82.2	28.5	61.1	17.0	3.4	20.2	31.8
Fort Worth	361.3	60.2	83.1	32.9	151.8	34.2	20.3	59.4	29.0
Houston	806.7	52.5	83.2	32.0	307.5	25.6	10.0	39.1	27.6
San Antonio	500.5	48.0	80.5	28.6	150.7	12.5	2.1	16.6	32.7
Utah:									
Salt Lake City[b]	274.9	29.9	80.4	29.4	104.5	15.3	5.7	37.5	27.8
Virginia:									
Hampton–Newport News–Warwick	143.2	69.5	81.6	30.7	52.3	36.1	29.9	82.8	28.1
Norfolk–Portsmouth	446.2	72.3	87.4	30.5	134.2	22.2	12.9	58.2	30.2
Richmond	328.1	24.7	80.1	38.6	144.6	24.5	2.3	9.3	34.8
Roanoke	133.4	18.9	77.1	32.1	49.8	25.1	3.9	15.4	32.0
Washington:									
Seattle	733.0	45.2	78.7	32.6	279.8	28.4	19.0	66.9	36.1
Spokane	221.6	34.6	75.5	28.7	66.8	19.9	8.9	44.6	30.4
Tacoma	275.9	51.5	80.3	26.5	69.0	24.6	5.3	21.5	30.1

(continued on next page)

TABLE A-1 (continued)

STATE AND AREA	1950				MAY 1954				
	Population (thousands)	*Per Cent Increase in Population over 1940*	*Per Cent 14 and over in Labor Force*		*Total Nonagricultural Wage and Salary Employment*	*Per Cent of Total in Manufacturing*	*Per Cent of Total in Metalworking*[a]	*Per Cent of Manufacturing in Metal working*	*Women as Per Cent of Total*
			Men	*Women*					
West Virginia:									
Charleston	322.1	16.6	76.7	22.3	89.4	28.9	4.4	15.1	23.6
Huntington–Ashland	245.8	8.9	73.6	23.1	63.6	37.4	16.3	43.5	28.2
Wheeling–Steubenville	354.1	−2.8	77.5	23.8	109.4	48.4	31.2	64.3	24.0
Wisconsin:									
Kenosha	75.2	18.5	86.5	28.2	21.0	62.9	39.9	63.4	26.5
Madison	169.4	29.6	74.8	36.0	51.6	25.8	7.9	30.6	40.8
Milwaukee	871.0	13.6	82.1	33.5	365.0	50.5	33.3	65.8	28.8
Racine	109.6	16.5	83.9	29.6	37.4	57.5	42.6	74.1	33.9

[a] Metalworking industries are defined to include the following industrial groups covered by the *Standard Industrial Classification Manual* (Bureau of the Budget, November 1945): Ordnance; primary metal industries; fabricated metal products; machinery (except electrical); electrical machinery, equipment, and supplies; transportation equipment.

[b] Geographic area covered for 1950 not strictly comparable with area covered for May 1954.

[c] Geographic area covered for per cent 14 and over in labor force not strictly comparable with area covered for all other data.

[d] Data shown for per cent 14 and over in labor force relate to entire New Jersey portion of New York–Northern New Jersey Standard Metropolitan Area.

[e] Data not shown to avoid disclosing figures for individual establishments.

n.a. = not available.

Source: Population and labor force, Bureau of the Census; nonagricultural wage and salary employment, Bureau of Employment Security, Department of Labor, based on regular bimonthly reports received from affiliated state employment security agencies.

TABLE A-2

Changes in Nonagricultural Wage and Salary Employment between May 1953 and May 1954, and Labor Market Classifications, July 1953 and July 1954, by Area

STATE AND AREA	TOTAL NONAGRICULTURAL WAGE AND SALARY EMPLOYMENT	MANUFACTURING EMPLOYMENT		METALWORKING[a] EMPLOYMENT		CLASSIFICATION[b]	
	Change from May 1953 (per cent)	*May 1954 (thousands)*	*Change from May 1953 (per cent)*	*May 1954 (thousands)*	*Change from May 1953 (per cent)*	*July 1954*	*July 1953*
Alabama:							
Birmingham	−1.8	60.7	−3.1	41.0	−4.0	III	III
Mobile	−0.5	16.1	+2.1	3.3	+7.2	III	III
Arizona:							
Phoenix	+1.2	15.5	−4.9	9.0	−2.7	III	III
Arkansas:							
Little Rock–North Little Rock	−2.1	12.6	−3.4	3.4	−9.2	III	III
California:							
Fresno	−2.0	12.1	−1.0	3.6	+8.4	III	III
Los Angeles	−0.8	633.3	−2.6	370.4	−2.2	III	III
Sacramento	−0.4	11.4	+0.9	1.6	+3.3	III	II
San Bernardino–Riverside	−1.8	26.2	+4.8	14.2	+6.0	III	III
San Diego	−2.8	50.9	−2.5	42.7	−2.7	III	II
San Francisco–Oakland	−3.3	199.2	−5.8	90.4	−8.4	III	III
San Jose	+2.4	23.6	+1.5	8.8	−3.3	III	III
Stockton	−3.2	11.7	−0.8	2.0	−20.0	III	III
Colorado:							
Denver	−3.3	42.8	−6.1	6.2	0.0	II	II

(continued on next page)

TABLE A-2 (continued)

STATE AND AREA	TOTAL NONAGRICULTURAL WAGE AND SALARY EMPLOYMENT	MANUFACTURING EMPLOYMENT		METALWORKING[a] EMPLOYMENT		CLASSIFICATION[b]	
	Change from May 1953 (per cent)	*May 1954 (thousands)*	*Change from May 1953 (per cent)*	*May 1954 (thousands)*	*Change from May 1953 (per cent)*	*July 1954*	*July 1953*
Connecticut:							
Bridgeport	−6.0	68.2	−9.8	50.4	−10.5	III	II
Hartford	+0.5	76.1	−1.6	61.0	−1.4	II	I
New Britain	−3.4	27.8	−5.4	24.7	−4.1	III	II
New Haven	−2.2	46.0	−7.3	24.4	−9.3	II	II
Stamford–Norwalk	−4.8	32.8	−10.6	16.7	−6.4	III	II
Waterbury	−7.3	42.9	−11.7	21.1	−10.2	III	II
Delaware:							
Wilmington	−4.2	43.2	−9.9	12.8	−22.3	III	II
District of Columbia:							
Washington	−4.5	25.7	−3.0	5.0	−1.0	III	III
Florida:							
Jacksonville	+3.6	18.0	+1.1	2.4	−5.9	II	II
Miami	+6.4	24.3	+6.6	2.9	−12.1	III	III
Tampa–St. Petersburg	+7.0	23.0	+1.8	2.2	+15.4	III	III
Georgia:							
Atlanta	−0.4	78.2	−0.2	27.2	+8.2	II	II
Columbus	−6.2	17.3	−8.3	1.2	−17.7	IV-A	III
Macon	−2.5	12.5	−4.7	2.3	0.0	III	II
Savannah	−3.8	13.5	−5.3	1.2	−24.8	III	III

(continued on next page)

TABLE A-2 (continued)

STATE AND AREA	TOTAL NONAGRICULTURAL WAGE AND SALARY EMPLOYMENT	MANUFACTURING EMPLOYMENT		METALWORKING[a] EMPLOYMENT		CLASSIFICATION[b]	
	Change from May 1953 (per cent)	*May 1954 (thousands)*	*Change from May 1953 (per cent)*	*May 1954 (thousands)*	*Change from May 1953 (per cent)*	*July 1954*	*July 1953*
Illinois:							
Aurora	−6.7	15.8	−11.5	9.5	−15.4	IV-A	II
Chicago	−3.5	889.6	−8.9	482.8	−12.4	III	II
Davenport–Rock Island–Moline	−9.2	42.4	−15.0	32.6	−16.8	IV-A	II
Joliet	−15.8	21.8	−22.1	10.2	−29.9	IV-A	I
Peoria	−7.2	39.6	−13.2	27.5	−17.2	IV-A	II
Rockford	−8.1	37.0	−11.5	30.5	−10.6	III	II
Indiana:							
Evansville	−18.7	31.6	−32.2	21.5	−40.2	IV-A	III
Fort Wayne	−10.6	35.1	−16.4	26.5	−17.6	IV-A	II
Indianapolis	−5.4	103.0	−9.1	67.5	−12.0	III	II
South Bend	−24.8	36.5	−37.4	22.5	−47.7	IV-A	II
Terre Haute	−6.9	10.7	−10.7	2.8	−12.6	IV-A	IV
Iowa:							
Cedar Rapids	+0.9	18.6	−0.1	10.7	−4.0	II	II
Des Moines	0.0	21.8	−4.6	5.2	−9.6	II	II
Kansas:							
Wichita	−3.0	51.6	−7.0	42.2	−8.7	II	I
Kentucky:							
Louisville	−6.8	89.5	−11.5	34.0	−14.0	III	II

(continued on next page)

TABLE A-2 (continued)

STATE AND AREA	TOTAL NONAGRICULTURAL WAGE AND SALARY EMPLOYMENT	MANUFACTURING EMPLOYMENT		METALWORKING[a] EMPLOYMENT		CLASSIFICATION[b]	
	Change from May 1953 (per cent)	*May 1954 (thousands)*	*Change from May 1953 (per cent)*	*May 1954 (thousands)*	*Change from May 1953 (per cent)*	*July 1954*	*July 1953*
Louisiana:							
Baton Rouge	−4.6	18.5	−4.0	0.6	−59.9	III	III
New Orleans	−0.9	53.8	−3.7	16.6	−10.1	III	III
Shreveport	−2.9	7.3	−13.3	1.6	−30.5	III	III
Maine:							
Portland	+0.9	13.5	−0.1	2.6	+14.8	III	III
Maryland:							
Baltimore	−1.8	189.7	−6.1	103.9	−6.8	III	II
Massachusetts:							
Boston	−2.9	308.9	−6.1	136.0	−8.6	III	III
Brockton	−0.6	20.2	−3.8	3.6	−4.5	III	III
Fall River	−5.5	28.0	−7.1	0.8	−17.0	IV-A	III
Lawrence	−16.8	17.0	−26.8	2.8	−3.1	IV-B	IV
Lowell	−7.2	20.5	−12.9	1.9	+28.3	IV-A	IV
New Bedford	−9.5	28.4	−14.6	8.0	−22.3	IV-A	III
Springfield–Holyoke	−4.9	78.2	−10.6	36.0	−14.5	III	III
Worcester	−3.4	50.0	−8.9	25.5	−10.0	III	III
Michigan:							
Battle Creek	−18.2	21.3	−22.3	11.6	−35.6	IV-A	I
Detroit	−9.2	626.0	−19.8	516.0	−22.8	IV-A	II

(continued on next page)

TABLE A-2 (continued)

STATE AND AREA	TOTAL NONAGRICULTURAL WAGE AND SALARY EMPLOYMENT	MANUFACTURING EMPLOYMENT		METALWORKING[a] EMPLOYMENT		CLASSIFICATION[b]	
	Change from May 1953 (per cent)	*May 1954 (thousands)*	*Change from May 1953 (per cent)*	*May 1954 (thousands)*	*Change from May 1953 (per cent)*	*July 1954*	*July 1953*
Michigan (cont.):							
Flint	+10.9	79.8	+9.0	76.3	+9.5	II	II
Grand Rapids	−3.2	52.5	−4.5	28.6	−6.2	III	II
Kalamazoo	−5.1	24.0	−3.6	7.5	−10.7	III	II
Lansing	−2.9	32.5	−7.9	30.3	−8.2	III	II
Muskegon	−14.1	25.5	−18.5	20.1	−21.8	IV-A	II
Saginaw	−1.2	26.5	−4.7	22.7	−4.6	III	I
Minnesota:							
Duluth–Superior	−2.7	11.1	−8.9	5.9	−9.3	IV-A	III
Minneapolis–St. Paul	−2.4	138.4	−8.7	64.7	−13.7	III	II
Mississippi:							
Jackson	−0.8	8.9	−5.5	0.9	−6.6	IV-A	III
Missouri:							
Kansas City	−3.2	111.7	−8.3	51.8	−9.9	III	II
St. Louis	−5.1	266.5	−11.8	119.4	−19.7	IV-A	II
Nebraska:							
Omaha	−0.1	31.6	+1.8	5.2	−7.3	III	II
New Hampshire:							
Manchester	−3.9	18.7	−7.6	1.8	+29.6	III	III

(continued on next page)

TABLE A-2 (continued)

STATE AND AREA	TOTAL NONAGRICULTURAL WAGE AND SALARY EMPLOYMENT	MANUFACTURING EMPLOYMENT		METALWORKING[a] EMPLOYMENT		CLASSIFICATION[b]	
	Change from May 1953 (per cent)	*May 1954 (thousands)*	*Change from May 1953 (per cent)*	*May 1954 (thousands)*	*Change from May 1953 (per cent)*	*July 1954*	*July 1953*
New Jersey:							
Atlantic City	+3.3	5.9	−2.1	0.2	0.0	IV-A	IV
Newark	−3.2	333.6	−7.5	157.8	−10.9	III	III
Paterson	−3.8	179.7	−7.3	66.6	+4.9	IV-A	III
Perth Amboy	−3.3	61.4	−7.1	22.6	−9.6	III	II
Trenton	−4.9	52.3	−12.4	26.4	−15.8	III	II
New Mexico:							
Albuquerque	−1.9	8.7	−0.5	5.9	+5.7	IV-A	III
New York:							
Albany–Schenectady–Troy	−8.1	82.2	−14.8	50.1	−18.4	IV-A	III
Binghamton	−1.7	41.0	−3.0	16.5	−0.9	III	II
Buffalo	−4.9	201.4	−8.1	125.3	−9.3	IV-A	II
New York	−1.9	1,077.6	−7.7	266.1	−7.6	III	III
Rochester	−1.6	110.0	−3.9	29.7	−10.0	II	II
Syracuse	+0.7	58.7	+1.7	42.5	+2.7	III	II
Utica–Rome	−5.2	44.0	−8.3	26.0	−5.9	IV-A	III
North Carolina:							
Asheville	+0.6	11.3	0.0	c		IV-A	IV
Charlotte	+0.1	21.0	−1.6	3.1	−5.8	III	II
Durham	−0.5	11.8	−4.1	0.6	−23.5	IV-A	IV
Greensboro–High Point	−1.4	38.6	−2.2	2.8	+1.6	III	III
Winston-Salem	+0.8	30.6	−1.8	6.7	−2.5	IV-A	IV

(continued on next page)

TABLE A-2 (continued)

STATE AND AREA	TOTAL NONAGRICULTURAL WAGE AND SALARY EMPLOYMENT	MANUFACTURING EMPLOYMENT		METALWORKING[a] EMPLOYMENT		CLASSIFICATION[b]	
	Change from May 1953 (per cent)	*May 1954 (thousands)*	*Change from May 1953 (per cent)*	*May 1954 (thousands)*	*Change from May 1953 (per cent)*	*July 1954*	*July 1953*
Ohio:							
Akron	—4.8	92.4	—11.6	25.0	—6.6	III	II
Canton	—12.1	58.0	—15.9	43.1	—20.9	IV-A	II
Cincinnati	—3.9	160.3	—8.5	81.7	—13.0	III	II
Cleveland	—4.2	307.2	—9.5	211.2	—12.5	III	II
Columbus	—3.0	71.8	—9.1	42.6	—9.0	III	II
Dayton	—3.0	95.0	—5.6	69.5	—6.5	II	II
Hamilton–Middletown	—0.6	32.4	—1.3	28.4	—0.7	II	II
Lorain–Elyria	—11.0	29.8	—17.0	27.1	—18.1	III	II
Toledo	—7.7	67.1	—16.2	41.3	—22.7	IV-A	II
Youngstown	—8.2	101.1	—13.2	85.9	—12.5	III	II
Oklahoma:							
Oklahoma City	—2.6	16.1	+1.6	4.2	—3.0	III	II
Tulsa	—0.7	29.2	—4.4	18.6	—6.9	II	II
Oregon:							
Portland	—2.7	57.6	—5.6	14.7	—9.8	IV-A	III
Pennsylvania:							
Allentown–Bethlehem	—4.7	94.3	—9.3	45.7	—13.0	III	II
Altoona	—14.9	13.8	—31.6	6.3	—48.8	IV-B	IV
Erie	—9.7	40.8	—16.8	27.7	—19.4	IV-A	III

(continued on next page)

TABLE A-2 (continued)

STATE AND AREA	TOTAL NONAGRICULTURAL WAGE AND SALARY EMPLOYMENT	MANUFACTURING EMPLOYMENT		METALWORKING[a] EMPLOYMENT		CLASSIFICATION[b]	
	Change from May 1953 (per cent)	*May 1954 (thousands)*	*Change from May 1953 (per cent)*	*May 1954 (thousands)*	*Change from May 1953 (per cent)*	*July 1954*	*July 1953*
Pennsylvania (cont.):							
Harrisburg	–5.6	30.6	–11.2	12.4	–25.9	III	II
Johnstown	–12.4	22.8	–17.8	15.6	–23.9	IV-B	IV
Lancaster	–2.8	42.4	–4.2	13.0	–3.0	III	II
Philadelphia	–4.0	578.7	–11.3	245.1	–14.9	IV-A	III
Pittsburgh	–7.7	329.8	–12.1	244.1	–13.5	IV-A	III
Reading	–6.7	48.4	–11.2	19.4	–15.3	IV-A	III
Scranton	–5.9	30.1	–4.1	7.4	+2.1	IV-B	IV
Wilkes-Barre–Hazleton	–9.5	33.9	–11.9	3.8	–27.4	IV-B	IV
York	–3.3	46.0	–5.0	18.3	–5.9	III	II
Rhode Island:							
Providence	–9.0	129.7	–16.2	31.7	–20.8	IV-B	IV
South Carolina:							
Aiken-Augusta	–16.0	23.3	+7.6	0.2	–10.5	III	II
Charleston	–6.1	15.6	–10.6	7.8	–14.8	III	III
Greenville	–3.0	28.0	–6.8	1.4	–15.6	III	III
Tennessee:							
Chattanooga	–6.1	40.9	–9.9	12.1	–14.3	IV-A	III
Knoxville	+3.1	43.6	–2.6	8.8	–9.7	IV-A	III
Memphis	–3.2	42.2	–6.1	5.9	–3.3	III	III
Nashville	–2.9	33.8	–10.2	6.0	–33.1	III	III

(continued on next page)

TABLE A-2 (continued)

STATE AND AREA	TOTAL NONAGRICULTURAL WAGE AND SALARY EMPLOYMENT	MANUFACTURING EMPLOYMENT		METALWORKING[a] EMPLOYMENT		CLASSIFICATION[b]	
	Change from May 1953 (*per cent*)	*May 1954* (*thousands*)	*Change from May 1953* (*per cent*)	*May 1954* (*thousands*)	*Change from May 1953* (*per cent*)	*July 1954*	*July 1953*
Texas:							
Austin	+1.9	3.9	+1.8	0.3	+14.9	III	III
Beaumont–Port Arthur	–1.8	26.2	–1.0	3.8	–3.7	III	III
Corpus Christi	–0.3	7.7	+6.5	1.1	+13.1	III	III
Dallas	–0.2	73.6	–0.3	36.3	+1.6	II	II
El Paso	+2.2	10.4	+3.3	2.1	–5.1	III	III
Fort Worth	+0.9	51.9	–0.6	30.8	–0.2	III	III
Houston	–0.5	78.8	–5.1	30.8	–11.0	III	II
San Antonio	–6.9	18.9	–4.4	3.1	+1.8	IV-A	III
Utah:							
Salt Lake City	–1.2	16.0	–1.7	6.0	+3.8	III	III
Virginia:							
Hampton–Newport News–Warwick	–3.2	18.9	–5.4	15.6	–5.2	III	II
Norfolk–Portsmouth	–3.5	29.8	–8.7	17.4	–10.6	III	II
Richmond	–1.9	35.4	–5.1	3.3	+6.5	II	II
Roanoke	–3.4	12.5	–9.7	1.9	–10.7	III	III
Washington:							
Seattle	+3.0	79.5	+13.8	53.2	+24.5	III	III
Spokane	–5.9	13.3	–9.5	5.9	–12.4	III	III
Tacoma	–4.4	17.0	–6.6	3.7	–8.0	IV-A	IV

(continued on next page)

TABLE A-2 (continued)

STATE AND AREA	TOTAL NONAGRICULTURAL WAGE AND SALARY EMPLOYMENT	MANUFACTURING EMPLOYMENT		METALWORKING[a] EMPLOYMENT		CLASSIFICATION[b]	
	Change from May 1953 (per cent)	*May 1954 (thousands)*	*Change from May 1953 (per cent)*	*May 1954 (thousands)*	*Change from May 1953 (per cent)*	*July 1954*	*July 1953*
West Virginia:							
Charleston	−7.4	25.8	−8.2	3.9	−18.8	IV-A	III
Huntington–Ashland	−7.0	23.8	−11.9	10.4	−16.9	IV-A	III
Wheeling–Steubenville	−5.4	53.0	−6.4	34.1	−7.8	IV-A	III
Wisconsin							
Kenosha	−26.8	13.2	−34.0	8.4	−41.0	IV-B	III
Madison	+0.4	13.3	−6.6	4.1	−4.6	II	II
Milwaukee	−5.0	184.5	−11.0	121.4	−12.8	III	II
Racine	−9.3	21.5	−14.2	15.9	−17.6	IV-A	III

[a] Metalworking industries are defined to include the following industrial groups covered by the *Standard Industrial Classification Manual* (Bureau of the Budget, November 1945): Ordnance; primary metal industries; fabricated metal products; machinery (except electrical); electrical machinery, equipment, and supplies; transportation equipment.

[b] Area classifications according to relative adequacy of local labor supply are assigned by the Bureau of Employment Security according to uniformly applied criteria and are based on labor market information submitted by affiliated state employment security agencies. While several factors are taken into account, the extent of unemployment in a particular area is a key factor in determining the appropriate classification assigned to each locality. Unemployment criteria are: Group I—1.5 per cent or less of total labor force, Group II—1.5 to 3 per cent of total labor force, Group III—3 to 6 per cent of total labor force, Group IV-A—6 to 12 per cent of total labor force, Group IV-B—12 per cent or more of total labor force. The division of the Group IV classification category into two groupings (IV-A and IV-B) was instituted with the May 1954 labor market area classification.

[c] Data not shown to avoid disclosing figures for individual establishments.

Source: Bureau of Employment Security, based on regular bimonthly reports received from affiliated state employment security agencies.

COMMENT

E. J. EBERLING, Vanderbilt University

The unemployment insurance system in the United States has been a primary contributor to the development of employment and unemployment data by industry and locality, as is evident from the paper presented by Louis Levine. With respect to information about employment, it might be pointed out that state "covered" employment data are used as bench marks for the development of current monthly estimates of nonagricultural employment for classified labor market areas, for the states, and for the nation as a whole.[1] This series which is sponsored jointly by the Bureau of Labor Statistics, the Bureau of Employment Security, and affiliated state employment security agencies is of considerable value in the preparation of total unemployment estimates by industry and locality.

Interest in the current measures of both employment and unemployment increased greatly during the early months of 1954 as economic activity slackened and unemployment levels rose sharply in certain areas of the country. Since the monthly unemployment estimates prepared by the Bureau of the Census (Monthly Report on the Labor Force) do not provide such information for the states or local labor market areas and make available only limited data by industry, it was not possible by using this series to identify the local areas most severely affected by the rising unemployment nor to measure its extent by area in terms of either total volume or industries affected. Furthermore, there was some evidence during 1953 that this series was not recording reliably the extent of the decline for the nation as a whole.

The question concerning the reliability of this series which arose in 1953 caused attention to be focused on area and industry estimates of unemployment as prepared by employment security agencies. The sharp impact of the cutback in government defense spending was immediately reflected in a rising volume of unemployment claims from workers laid off by industries which had incurred cancellation of contracts. The areas and industries thus affected were clearly identified by the nature and volume of the claims load. The extent of this increase in unemployment was also clearly indicated in the national aggregates. Corroborating evidence of the nature and extent of this decline was reflected in the monthly estimates of nonagricultural employment prepared under the current employment statistics program mentioned above.

[1] See Ernest J. Eberling and Charles S. Bullock, Jr., "Employment Statistics and Manpower," *Industrial and Labor Relations Review*, January 1952.

Efforts to reconcile the trends and levels of unemployment as recorded by the census data series and the employment security data resulted in considerable controversy and also confusion. It is, of course, well known that controversy and discussion concerning the nature and validity of unemployment estimates always intensifies during a period of economic slump.

A number of significant developments occurred as a result of the increased attention given to unemployment estimates:

1. A Committee for Review of Labor Force Concepts was established by the Office of Statistical Standards of the Bureau of the Budget to review the definitions of employment and unemployment used by governmental agencies, to investigate the methods of presentation and interpretation, and to point up gaps in the data.

2. The Bureau of Employment Security set up a Work Committee on Unemployment Estimates and Related Problems.

3. The Committee on Research and Reporting of the Interstate Conference of Employment Security Agencies made an excellent report on employment and unemployment estimates, pointing out reasons for major discrepancies between the census estimates and the insured unemployment data and presenting recommendations for improvement of the latter estimates.[2]

4. The confusion resulting from the conflicting data on unemployment released by the federal agencies led to the institution of a joint release by the Departments of Labor and Commerce each month on employment and unemployment.[3]

There are several facts which stand out in appraising the importance and value of the current total unemployment estimates prepared by employment security agencies for localities by industry:

1. They are the only data available which indicate unemployment levels and trends by area.

2. They have as their base unemployment as indicated by persons filing claims for benefits. In spite of differences in laws and administrative procedures, claims data reflect accurately the level and trends of unemployment within the limits of the coverage of the unemployment insurance program in each state. Generally, this component represents 50 to 70 per cent of the total unemployment in a state. Even more important is the fact that the coverage of this component is very close to 100 per cent of the segment of employment in which an economic change usually first becomes manifest, namely, manufacturing.

[2] See Report of the Second Meeting of the Committee on Research and Reporting, July 13-15, 1954, Chap. IV.

[3] "Combined Employment and Unemployment Release," Depts. of Commerce and Labor.

One factor which should not be overlooked with respect to claims data is that they are available on a week-to-week basis. There is no other series in the country that gives an indication as immediate as this of changes in the volume of unemployment. In addition, claims data can be classified by industry, sex, area, and many other characteristics.

3. Unemployment insurance statistics [of unemployment] are largely cost free since they are by-products of the operation of the UI system. Hence, it is possible to expand at a low cost unemployment estimates based upon UI data. Further, the day-to-day contact of the system with claimants and other unemployed workers makes possible a wide variety of special studies on unemployment at low cost and with little inconvenience to the worker.

As pointed out in Levine's paper, total unemployment estimates for a given labor market area begin with the solid core of "insured unemployed," that is, the number of covered workers claiming unemployment insurance benefits who are totally unemployed in a given week. Data supplied by the Railroad Retirement Board on the number of unemployed railroad workers are added to this figure. So far, there are no particular difficulties in compiling the estimates.

Insured unemployment data exclude several classes of workers, however, whose unemployment is properly related to the UI program. One class includes workers from covered industries who file initial claims (notice of separation from their jobs), but who for various reasons may wait to file their claims until after a week or more of total unemployment has elapsed. The proportion who do this can be fairly well determined from the claims determinations made by the agency (comparison of date of separation with date of filing claim). Hence, estimates of unemployment among this group are made by the agency and added to the base figure of insured unemployment.

A much more difficult problem of estimating is presented by a second class of unemployed, namely, those claimants who have exhausted their benefits. The number of such claimants and the length of their unemployment after exhausting their benefit rights will vary with unemployment levels. At present the UI agencies make adjustments for this group based upon such sample studies as they have made from time to time. Actually, in many cases, such adjustments may be quite arbitrary and based upon inadequate information. This is an area which needs considerable study of ways and means to improve the quality of the estimates.

Finally, there is a third group of claimants for which estimates have to be made. It includes claimants who have been disqualified from receiving benefits and workers who are eligible but fail to apply for benefits. Here, too, information so far developed is fragmentary and arbitrary adjustments are made.

Insured unemployment plus the adjustments for these three latter groups comprise what is termed "unemployment related to unemployment insurance covered employment." The ratio of total UI unemployment to total UI covered employment is then obtained. This unemployment rate may be further refined by the development of separate industry rates. In any event, this rate (or rates) constitutes the key to the further development of the estimates to include an additional group, namely, "unemployment related to noncovered employment." This group is divided into two subdivisions: (1) unemployment from noncovered establishments in covered industries, and (2) unemployment from noncovered industries.

For this first subgroup, it is assumed that the unemployment rates will be similar to those obtained for the covered establishments by the procedures outlined above. Hence, the "UI covered unemployment rate" is applied to the *current employment* for each industry and a total unemployment figure is thus obtained for all unemployment from both covered and noncovered establishments in covered industries.[4]

The second subgroup, the unemployed in noncovered industries, includes agricultural wage and salaried workers, domestics, government workers, and unpaid family workers. Current employment data are not compiled for this group with the exception of government workers. Hence, estimates of unemployment relating to this group must be based on arbitrary assumptions such as carrying forward the figures on employment for agricultural workers, domestics, etc. as constants from the 1950 census. The UI covered unemployment rate is then applied (with some adjustments in certain cases) to these estimated employment figures; that is, for example, the unemployment rate for agricultural wage and salaried workers is assumed to be the same as that for UI covered nonagricultural wage and salaried workers. This assumption is based, as Levine points out, on an analysis of the Census Bureau's Monthly Report on the Labor Force showing unemployment rates by industry. Of course, this assumption when applied to a given local area may be wide of the mark. Seasonal differences, weather, and a number of factors could cause a wide variation from the results obtained under this assumption. Indeed, since the total number of agricultural wage and salaried workers is not accurately known to begin with, the chances of error in this segment of the unemployment are greatly increased. The

[4] Current employment estimates are obtained for all non-agricultural workers except domestic, self-employed, and unpaid family workers, from the Bureau of Labor Statistics–State Employment Security Program of "Current Employment Statistics" (see p. I).

same point could be made with respect to the other groups in this category. With respect to the effects of errors in estimating unemployment for agricultural workers, it should be emphasized that since total unemployment estimates are prepared for the most part for local areas which are quite highly industrialized, the segment of the estimates relating to agricultural unemployment would ordinarily be relatively small.

But as Levine indicates, even greater difficulties are encountered in making unemployment estimates for the final group which must be included before it can be assumed that total unemployment in an area has been accounted for. This is the group known as unemployed new entrants and re-entrants, that is, those individuals whose current spell of unemployment was not preceded by employment. Information about this group is very limited. Based on data developed from the Monthly Report on the Labor Force, monthly rates for unemployed entrants related to the civilian labor force and to the total of all other unemployed have been developed. These rates, however, were developed on the basis of national data and hence may or may not apply to local area situations.

In summary then, total unemployment estimates for local areas as developed by state employment security agencies have as their base "insured unemployment" data. As indicated previously, there can be little doubt about the reliability of this series. Then too, since insured unemployment will include upwards of 50 per cent or more of total unemployment and nearly 100 per cent of manufacturing employment, this series provides a reliable picture of unemployment trends and a sound base from which to develop total unemployment estimates. When, however, these data are expanded to include all unemployment related to covered employment, it is necessary to make adjustments which are at times quite arbitrary and which are subject to considerable chance of error.

Moreover, when it becomes necessary to make estimates for the unemployment not covered by the program, even wider margins of error can creep into the data. The Bureau of Employment Security and state technicians have been working for over a decade on the problems involved in preparing reliable total unemployment estimates by area. One advantage inherent in the preparation of these estimates is that they are made at the local and state level and, therefore, are susceptible of some validation through the application of supplemental data and judgment factors derived from local data. This is not possible for estimates made at the national level. The recent action of Congress in providing for coverage of federal civilian employees and for all establishments in covered industries having four or more employees will certainly aid in improving the quality of local unemployment estimates.

There is general agreement among technicians in this field that much remains to be done by way of exploration and study of means of improving these estimates of total unemployment. In this connection, the conclusions of the Research and Reporting Committee of the Interstate Conference of Employment Security Agencies are in point:

> "A cooperative Bureau of the Census-Bureau of Employment Security-State Employment Security Agencies experiment should be set up to develop improved techniques for estimating total unemployment from unemployment insurance claims. This experiment would provide for detailed studies of new entrant and re-entrant unemployment, unemployment among persons having exhausted their unemployment insurance and unemployment among various groups not covered by unemployment insurance. These studies would be aimed at providing information on the variation in these factors by geographical area and under differing economic conditions."[5]

Levine's paper gives an excellent account of the development of techniques for preparing estimates of total unemployment by area and industry. Much of this development has been in the nature of a pioneering effort. In spite of the weaknesses which still exist in the estimating procedures, the information developed under this program has been invaluable in the administration of employment security and in the solution of manpower problems. Through the development of manuals by the Bureau of Employment Security providing uniform estimating procedures, constant improvement is being made in the comparability of these estimates—area by area and state by state. It is to be hoped that the widespread interest and attention now being given to the problem of unemployment estimating by government agencies and private organizations will lead to intensified efforts on the part of technicians, both in government and in universities to study the various aspects of this problem thoroughly. Unemployment estimates developed from employment security data constitute a research frontier where much further refinement and improvement of the data should be expected in the next few years. The work of the Universities–National Bureau Committee for Economic Research is a most constructive step in this direction.

WILLIAM HABER, University of Michigan

It is significant to note the difference in the problems which face economists and statisticians concerned with the measurement of un-

[5] *Op.cit.*, p. 9.

employment now, in 1954, with those they faced twenty years ago. Then our major concern was with the paucity of statistical data. Estimates of unemployment were derived from other data and the results often varied widely. Since unemployment then, as now, was a political issue as well as an economic and statistical problem, organizations which had a political interest in the problem produced their own estimate and published the results. Thus, the A.F. of L., the C.I.O., and the National Industrial Conference Board, among others, provided monthly unemployment estimates. The Communist party found these estimates of the number of jobless too conservative and published its own series, invariably indicating far more unemployment than that estimated by the labor organizations, the Conference Board, or the Bureau of Labor Statistics. Even private persons, like Robert R. Nathan, provided a monthly series on the number of jobless.

It is well to remember how woefully inadequate our data on employment and unemployment really were only a short two decades ago. And it was on the basis of such data that we built our plans for public works and unemployment relief and carried on the vigorous controversies on public policy in dealing with the depression.

Reference to this brief historical note should allay our concern with the controversies concerning measurement of unemployment today. We now seem to be disturbed with the fact that we have too much data. We dispute the details of the sampling procedure and we question the value of industry and area data. Our shortcomings in measurement of unemployment today are far less important than was the case a decade or two decades ago. Phenomenal progress has been made. Vast areas of knowledge about our labor force have been illuminated.

The papers on unemployment by industry and locality prepared by David L. Kaplan and Louis Levine emphasize both the limitations and the contributions of such information. National data such as are provided by the decennial census and the monthly changes in the labor force are not adequate for many purposes. Such data do not even describe the true character of the national problem. To comprehend that, we need more detailed information on unemployment by industry and locality. National figures often hide dramatic changes that can only be ascertained by industry and area analysis. Both papers show the wide variations that often exist between industries and localities. I am impressed by Kaplan's emphasis on the limitations of industry data and that he considers it useful only as a general descriptive measure of one aspect of unemployment. His data on mobility and on the proportion of an industry's employees who get their next job in an industry other than the one they just left are useful in emphasizing that the absorption of the unemployed depends upon the general health of the economy rather than on the health of a particular industry.

Levine's paper calls special attention to the particular problems of labor market administration. The employment security program of the states and the federal government requires the current availability of employment and unemployment information applicable to a particular labor market area. Such data are essential to the efficient administration of the unemployment insurance and employment service in each locality. Industry data on a national basis or unemployment in aggregate national terms provide only the roughest approximation of the situation in a particular state or area. Such national totals do not expose islands of local unemployment. The variations among localities are not reflected in average figures or national totals. Area data is therefore indispensable for local administration for determining staffing and budget needs.

In addition, much labor market information is a by-product of the employment security operations. Claims for unemployment insurance, exhaustion ratios, employment service registrations, and placement—these measures, while covering but a segment of the local labor force, throw considerable light on the nature of the local unemployment. As Levine indicates, fuller coverage under the unemployment insurance program would provide more comprehensive measures of employment and unemployment and this will in time be achieved.

Even if limited, however, area labor market data is indispensable to the administrators of employment security and provides a necessary addition to the national data derived from the sample methods now employed. While such data may be less valuable for economic analysis, they are indispensable for short-run decisions and local and state planning. Every effort to refine and improve the area data must be made, for even the most accurate national estimates are often inadequate for local purposes.

LABOR FORCE MATERIALS FOR THE STUDY OF UNEMPLOYMENT IN THE SOVIET UNION

WARREN W. EASON
PRINCETON UNIVERSITY

1. Introduction

IN THE Soviet Union, a conference on the "measurement and behavior of unemployment" could be concerned only with other countries, because in the official view unemployment at home simply does not exist. "In 1953, as in preceding years, there has been no unemployment,"[1] is typical of pronouncements which have appeared repeatedly in Soviet publications since the abolition of unemployment insurance on October 9, 1930.

Unemployment in capitalist countries, on the other hand, is found to be on a large scale. For example, a Soviet source reports the number of "fully and partially unemployed" in the United States in 1952 as 13 million, which is calculated by adding to the number of fully unemployed (about 2 million) the number of persons working less than thirty-five hours per week. The latter are called "unemployed," in the Soviet view, because "the overwhelming majority work less than half a week, and their meager salary places them in a situation which can be distinguished only in small degree from that of the unemployed."[2] The alleged high degree of unemployment in capitalist countries and the absence of unemployment at home are frequently contrasted in the Soviet press.

It is quite conceivable on the face of it that a planned society such as the Soviet Union, undergoing rapid economic expansion, would

[1] *Pravda*, January 31, 1954.

[2] Akademiia nauk SSSR, *Ekonomika kapitalisticheskikh stran posle vtoroi mirovoi voiny: statisticheskii sbornik*, Moscow, 1953, pp. 238-239, 251-252 and 262-263. The *Monthly Labor Review*, No. 3, 1950, 1951 and 1952, is given as the source for data on the fully unemployed and the number working less than thirty-five hours.

The following comments on official U.S. unemployment data are also offered: "Bourgeois statisticians employ other diverse contrivances in order to understate the number of unemployed. As a rule, only the number of insured unemployed are included, while persons seeking work for the first time are not—this concerns a great mass of youth and women. Also not included are beggars, hobos, etc., a significant stratum of declassed, degraded people, spawned continuously by capitalism. . . . in addition, American bourgeois statisticians resort even to such tricks as excluding the number with a job but not working; and of these there is a large number." (p. 239.)

eliminate unemployment, at least of the type associated with the business cycle and with the failure of the economy to grow (and the demand for labor to increase) rapidly enough to absorb the services of an expanding labor force. In addition, if planning itself were a success, other types of unemployment, stemming from frictions, seasonality, labor immobility, etc., would tend toward an irreducible minimum.

This general view would seem to be the basis for the "right to work" enjoyed by every Soviet citizen according to Article 118 of the Soviet Constitution:

> "Citizens of the U.S.S.R. have the right to work, that is, are guaranteed the right to employment and payment for their work in accordance with its quantity and quality.
>
> "The right to work is insured by the socialist organization of the national economy, the steady growth of the productive forces of Soviet society, the elimination of the possibility of economic crises, and the abolition of unemployment."

In the sense that a citizen has the opportunity to work at going wage rates and under existing working conditions, there is little evidence that this guarantee is not carried out in practice, although it should be noted that existing working conditions may include the particularly severe conditions prevailing in the remote areas of the U.S.S.R. Furthermore, persons may be restricted from certain types of work for political reasons, work for which they are otherwise qualified. However, beyond a certain point political considerations can subject the individual to forced labor.

Prior to the abolition of unemployment insurance at the end of 1930, unemployment varied from a low of 0.2 million in 1922 to a high of 1.7 million in 1929. At the peak, the unemployed were about 2 per cent of the civilian labor force, but 18 per cent of the labor force of wage and salary workers.[3] (The overwhelming majority of the civilian labor force was "self-employed" on family farms.)

The first question is whether the rate of economic growth under the Five-Year Plans could have led to a sufficient increase in the demand for labor to have eliminated this unemployment and to have kept abreast or ahead of the increases in the labor force. In general, this seems to have been the case: National income has been growing since 1928 at an average rate of from 5 to 10 per cent per year,[4] while the

[3] Data on unemployment are from Soviet sources in S. M. Schwarz, *Labor in the Soviet Union,* Praeger, 1952, p. 38. Data on the labor force are adapted from Table 1 (1926), below.

[4] Gregory Grossman, "National Income," in *Soviet Economic Growth: Conditions and Perspectives,* Abram Bergson, editor, Row, Peterson, 1953, pp. 5-11.

growth of the labor force has averaged less than 2 per cent per year.[5] The expansion of output, together with the relatively high rate of investment, would seem to have been adequate for the full employment of the labor force.

The prospect for unemployment under the Five-Year Plans therefore arises in connection not with the fundamental growth characteristics of the economy, but with the problems of resources allocation within the broad outlines of the Plans, and in connection with the planning technique itself.

Soviet attempts to solve this problem include the method of balanced estimates, incorporated into the Plans.[6] Among others, there is a manpower balance (*balans rabochei sily*) in which the supply of labor by geographical areas and the labor requirements of respective industries are brought into line with each other.[7] Assuming that the balanced estimates are accurately drawn, in both real and money terms, and that prices and wages reflect the supply and demand conditions of the Plan, fulfillment requires that managers of enterprises not only meet the planned output but conduct their operations, including the hiring (and firing) of labor, on the basis of strict financial accountability. Fulfillment also requires that labor's services be provided according to the projected manpower balance. Failure of any or all conditions to be satisfied could lead to imbalance in the operation and fulfillment of the Plan, i.e. to a less than optimum allocation of resources from the standpoint of the Plan, including the theoretical possibility of unemployment at some points while the demand for labor was unsatisfied at others.

A particularly significant departure from optimum conditions appears where the manager of an industrial enterprise or collective farm acquires or retains labor in excess of that warranted by strict financial or economic considerations, motivated perhaps by greater concern for the fulfillment of output goals than for real or money costs or, in the case of the collective farm, by the difficulty of getting collective farm members to work an adequate number of days. Labor hired beyond the point dictated by economic rationality has been said to represent "hidden unemployment."[8]

[5] Warren W. Eason, "Population and Labor Force," in *ibid.*, p. 121.

[6] For a discussion of the method of balanced estimates, see Alexander Baykov, *The Development of the Soviet Economic System: An Essay on the Experience of Planning in the U.S.S.R.*, Macmillan, 1946, pp. 444ff.

[7] For example, B. Babynin, "Voprosy balansa rabochei sily," *Planovoe khoziaistvo*, No. 9, 1939, pp. 56-70.

[8] Alfred R. Oxenfeldt and Ernest van den Haag, "Unemployment in Planned and Capitalist Economies," *Quarterly Journal of Economics*, February 1954, pp. 43-60.

The expression "hidden *unemployment*" is suggested because the general economic effect of the excess hired labor is the same as with unemployment proper, namely, a less-than-optimum utilization of labor resources from the standpoint of productivity in the economy as a whole. It is considered "hidden" because the distinguishing feature of unemployment, an excess of labor supplied over labor demanded at going wage rates, has been eliminated.

To conceive in this way of one manifestation of the less-than-optimum utilization of labor in terms of an explicit characteristic (unemployment) of another manifestation is a useful descriptive device, but it does not move us very far toward a real understanding of a very complex construct of interrelationships. Furthermore, the problem of expressing the less-than-optimum utilization of labor quantitatively in unemployment equivalents is a formidable if not impossible task.[9]

In any event, the aim of this paper falls short of such an ambitious undertaking. As far as unemployment is concerned, attention will be given to several instances in which explicit unemployment might be expected to exist, as suggested by available data on employment and on the population; and some further remarks will be made on the subject of "hidden unemployment" in connection with specific examples.

The principal purpose of the paper is to discuss the impact of Soviet planning and economic expansion on the supply of labor, with particular attention to the proportion of the population in the labor force and the distribution by economic sectors, and to examine trends in the percentage of full-time participation of the labor force.

The introduction of economic planning after 1928 modified the operation of the Soviet labor market, and together with the program of rapid industrialization and economic expansion, brought about marked changes in the composition of the labor force. On the eve of the Five-Year Plans, at the time of the 1926 census, more than 85 per cent of

[9] As Oxenfeldt and van den Haag express it (*ibid.*, pp. 58-59) ". . . we must therefore measure . . . hidden unemployment through . . . productivity. . . . Since it is impossible to isolate hidden unemployment from other factors affecting productivity, we cannot hope to measure it accurately."

Incidentally, the Soviet source cited in note 2, above, has the following to say about "hidden unemployment" in the United States, in a discussion of the implications of "partial unemployment," by which is meant persons working less than thirty-five hours per week:

> "Partial unemployment is a characteristic of the general crisis of capitalism; it is one of the signs of the rotting of the capitalist economy, the growth of unutilized productive capacity, and the increasing impoverishment of the proletariat. Enterprises working with a large amount of unutilized capacity frequently prefer not to discharge workers, but to shorten the workweek. By this means, capitalists endeavor to shift the burden of unemployment to as large a number of wage and salary workers as possible, and at the same time to conceal the true amount of unemployment" (p. 239).

the civilian labor force were self-employed or unpaid family workers, and of these, the overwhelming majority were occupied in agriculture. Wage and salary workers comprised only 11.5 per cent of the civilian labor force, the unemployed 1.2 per cent, and the number working as members of producer cooperatives and collective farms, between 1 and 2 per cent.

The consequences of the introduction of the Five-Year Plans were a large increase in the number of wage and salary workers, the transfer of most of the agricultural labor force from the status of self-employed and unpaid family workers to membership in collective farms while permitting the retention of small homestead garden plots, the widening of the producer cooperative network within the handicrafts sector, and the increased use of forced labor. The most important development was the increase in the number of wage and salary workers, linked with the expansion of industry, which will be discussed in this paper by way of comparison with changes in the other economic sectors.

Of special interest is the fact that in spite of the increase in the socialized sectors of the labor force (wage and salary workers, collective farmers, cooperative handicraftsmen, and the military), to include by the late 1930's between 75 and 80 per cent of the total labor force estimated from reported data, the majority of the labor force still retains at least a part-time link with what is strictly a "self-employed and unpaid family worker" status. This link is through the homestead farm operated by all collective farmers and by a certain number of wage and salary workers, especially in rural areas, and through the continued existence of a small number of private farmers and artisans.

Finally, the yearly average number of persons "working" or "employed" in all sectors as a percentage of the total reported labor force is seen to display a substantial increase by the late 1930's, the result of the increase in the number of wage and salary workers, the relative decline of the agricultural labor force, and widened demands on the available labor time of the collective farmer and his family. This development forms the basis for a general discussion of trends in "labor utilization."

The paper is divided into three parts. The first deals with the overall relationship of the labor force to the population and the second, with the distribution of the labor force by economic sectors. The third part discusses labor utilization and includes summary remarks on unemployment.

2. *Relationship of Labor Force to Population*

At the time of the 1926 census, two years before the start of the Five-Year Plans, 86.2 million persons, or 58.7 per cent of the total population, were "economically active"[10] (see Table 1). Of these, 84.4 million were gainfully occupied, unemployed, or in the military and the remainder (1.9 million) were dependents of institutions and persons receiving "unearned income."[11] Borrowing terminology now current in the United States, the sum of the gainfully occupied and the unemployed will be called the "civilian labor force," and including the military, the "total labor force."[12]

The overwhelming majority of the civilian labor force in 1926 consisted of self-employed or unpaid family workers—73.1 million, or 87.3 per cent; and of these, 70.5 million were in agriculture. In other words, the dominant economic unit in the Soviet economy before the Five-Year Plans, at least in terms of the labor force, was the family farm. The remainder of the civilian labor force was made up of wage and salary workers, mostly nonagricultural, and the unemployed (see Table 1).

Unpaid family workers comprised 48.5 million or 57.4 per cent of the civilian labor force, with all but a negligible number (349,000) in agriculture; and among unpaid family workers, 32.2 million or 66.4 per cent were females. The percentage of females in other groups was lower

[10] "Economically active" (*samodeiatel'nye*) under the census is defined to include all persons receiving wages or other income, as well as unpaid family workers, plus dependents of State and other institutions and persons receiving so-called "unearned income." In other words, "noneconomically active" are persons dependent on other individuals for their source of livelihood.

[11] Under the census, persons "having an occupation" included wage earners (*rabochie*), salaried employees (*sluzhashchie*), professionals (*litsa svobodnykh professii*), proprietors with hired labor (*khoziaeva s naemnymi rabochimi*), proprietors working only with members of their families, and members of artels (*khoziaeva, rabotaiushchiesia tol'ko s chlenami sem'i i chleny arteli*), persons working alone (*odinochki*), and family members helping in the occupation (*chleny sem'i, pomogaiushchie v zaniatii*). Listed separately are the unemployed (*bezrabotnye*), the military (*voennosluzhashchie*), and economically active persons not having or not indicating an occupation (*litsa, ne imeiushchie ili ne ukazavshie zaniatii*).

[12] Soviet censuses have no concept strictly analogous to our "labor force," i.e. referring to the number of persons working or wanting work during a given week. The category of "having an occupation" of the 1926 Census is more or less equivalent to that of the "gainful worker" used by the U.S. Census prior to 1940, and indicates one's general occupational status without reference to any particular period of time.

The section on "occupations" from the Soviet censuses of 1937 and 1939 was similar to that of the 1926 Census. However, data have been released only for 1939 and only from the section on "social groups," which is based on a substantial modification of the principle of "occupational status," tending to inflate the proportion of the population associated with State as distinct from cooperative and private economic activity (see I. V. Sautin, *Vsesoiuznaia perepis' naseleniia 1939 goda*, Moscow, 1939, pp. 55-60).

In the general field of Soviet labor statistics the expression "*rabochaia sila*," usually translated "manpower," refers to the available stock of labor in the sense of the number of persons expected to work (see, for example, M. Sonin, *Voprosy balansa rabochei sily*, Moscow, 1949, *passim*).

The Labor Force and the Economically Active, U.S.S.R., [illegible]

(*number in thousands*)

LABOR FORCE STATUS	BOTH SEXES			MALE			FEMALE			FEMALE AS A PERCENTAGE OF BOTH SEXES		
	Total	*Agri-culture*	*Nonagri-culture*	*Total*	*Agri-culture*	*Nonagri-culture*	*Total*	*Agri-culture*	*Nonagri-culture*	*Total*	*Agri-culture*	*Nonagri-culture*
Wage and salary workers	9,583	1,201	8,382	6,637	836	5,801	2,946	365	2,581	30.7	30.4	30.8
Self-employed and unpaid family workers	73,129	70,533	2,596	37,351	35,335	2,016	35,778	35,198	580	48.9	49.9	22.3
Self-employed workers[a]	24,666	22,419	2,247	21,078	19,269	1,809	3,588	3,150	438	14.5	14.1	19.5
Unpaid family workers	48,463	48,114	349	16,273	16,066	207	32,190	32,048	142	66.4	66.6	40.7
Unemployed[b]	1,014	119	895	599	79	520	415	40	375	40.9	33.6	41.9
Total Civilian Labor Force	83,726	71,853	11,873	44,587	36,250	8,337	39,139	35,603	3,536	46.7	49.5	29.8
Military	631	0	631	631	0	631	[c]	0	[c]			
Total Labor Force	84,357	71,853	12,504	45,218	36,250	8,968	39,139	35,603	3,536	46.4	49.5	28.3
Dependents of institutions and persons receiving "unearned income"	1,863			996			867			46.5		
Total economically active	86,220			46,214			40,006			46.4		

Percentage Distribution of the Civilian Labor Force, by Labor Force Status

LABOR FORCE STATUS	BOTH SEXES			MALE			FEMALE			NONAGRICULTURE AS A PERCENTAGE OF TOTAL		
	Total	*Agri-culture*	*Nonagri-culture*	*Total*	*Agri-culture*	*Nonagri-culture*	*Total*	*Agri-culture*	*Nonagri-culture*	*Both*	*Male*	*Female*
Wage and salary workers	11.5	1.7	70.6	14.9	2.3	69.6	7.5	1.0	73.0	87.5	87.4	87.6
Self-employed and unpaid family workers	87.3	98.2	21.9	83.8	97.5	24.2	91.4	98.9	16.4	3.5	5.4	1.6
Self-employed workers	29.4	31.2	18.9	47.3	53.2	21.7	9.2	8.9	12.4	9.1	8.6	12.2
Unpaid family workers	57.9	67.0	3.0	36.5	44.3	2.5	82.2	90.0	4.0	0.7	1.3	0.4
Unemployed	1.2	0.1	7.5	1.3	0.2	6.2	1.1	0.1	10.6	88.3	86.8	90.4
Total Civilian Labor Force	100.0	100.0	100.0	100.0	100.0	100.0	100.0	100.0	100.0	14.2	18.7	9.0

(notes on next page)

Notes to Table 1

[a] Including a small number of cooperative handicraftsmen, not enumerated separately by the census.

[b] Since the census does not give a distribution by agriculture and nonagriculture for the unemployed, the distribution by rural and urban is used.

[c] Less than 500.

Source: *Vsesoiuznaia perepis' naseleniia 1926 goda,* Moscow, TsSU, 1928-1931, Vol. XXXIV, pp. 2-3 and 8-12.

(14.5 per cent of self-employed workers, 30.7 per cent of wage and salary workers and 40.9 per cent of the unemployed); but taken together, females constituted almost half (46.7 per cent) of the civilian labor force.

The relatively high percentage of females reflects in part the deficit in the number of males relative to females in the adult population—5.3 million in the total population sixteen years and over and 4.8 million in the rural.[13] The deficit appears to have been an effect of World War I, the Revolution, and the Civil War, since the population at the time of the 1897 census showed almost no deficit.[14]

More important is the fact that the proportion of the female population in the labor force was exceptionally high. As shown in Table 2, 75.5 per cent of the female population age sixteen to fifty-nine were in the labor force. The percentage was much higher for the population dependent on agricultural than on nonagricultural occupations. Of the female population age sixteen to fifty-nine dependent on agricultural occupations, 87.9 per cent were in the labor force, compared to 36.7 per cent of the female population age sixteen to fifty-nine dependent on nonagricultural occupations.

The percentage of the total female population in the labor force exceeds that for all other countries listed in a recent compendium of the United Nations,[15] where in no case is the proportion of females age twenty to sixty-four who are "economically active" greater than 49.9 (Japan). Only in certain eastern European countries does the proportion approach that of the U.S.S.R.[16]

The high labor force percentages among Soviet males shown in Table 2, on the other hand, are not exceptional.[17] In 1926, 98.6 per cent of the male population age sixteen to fifty-nine dependent on agricul-

[13] *Vsesoiuznaia perepis' naseleniia 1926 goda,* Volume XVII.

[14] *Pervaia vseobshchaia perepis' naseleniia Rossiiskoi imperii 1897 goda,* St. Petersburg, TsSK, 1905, Summary Volume.

[15] *Demographic Yearbook 1948,* United Nations, 1949, pp. 232-233.

[16] "A Comparison of the Gainfully Occupied Population by Sex and Age in the Various Countries of the World," *International Labour Review,* May 1940, pp. 541-550.

[17] *Ibid.*

TABLE 2

The Labor Force and the Economically Active as a Percentage of the Corresponding Population, by Age and Sex, U.S.S.R., 1926

	LABOR FORCE					ECONOMICALLY ACTIVE		
GE AND SEX	*Total*	*Rural*	*Urban*	*Agri-culture*	*Nonagri-culture*	*Total*	*Rural*	*Urban*
oth sexes:								
10-15	58.2	66.8	9.1	69.3	12.8	59.5	67.5	14.6
16-59	85.0	91.4	60.8	92.9	65.4	86.4	91.7	66.3
60 and over	54.6	59.1	29.3	60.7	36.8	58.4	60.5	46.5
0 and over	57.5	61.1	41.0	62.9	43.1	58.7	61.4	45.9
ale:								
10-15	60.6	69.1	9.7	71.8	16.2	62.0	69.9	15.9
16-59	95.6	98.2	86.3	98.6	93.5	97.2	98.5	92.9
60 and over	74.9	77.5	57.9	78.6	71.7	78.3	78.6	76.1
0 and over	63.7	64.8	58.6	66.2	62.3	65.1	65.3	64.1
emale:								
10-15	55.9	64.4	8.4	66.8	8.9	57.3	65.0	13.3
16-59	75.5	85.5	35.7	87.9	36.7	76.6	85.8	40.1
60 and over	38.6	44.0	11.4	45.7	15.0	42.8	45.6	28.1
0 and over	51.6	57.5	24.0	59.9	24.2	52.6	57.8	28.4

Source: *Vsesoiuznaia perepis' naseleniia 1926 goda*, Moscow, TsSU, 1928-1931, Vol. XXXIV.

tural occupations were in the labor force, and 93.0 per cent of those dependent on nonagricultural occupations.

The high labor force percentages for females reflect a distinguishing feature of the economic life of the countryside in pre-Soviet Russia as well as in the Soviet Union of the preplan era, namely, that women worked in the fields alongside their husbands. Indeed, most able-bodied members of the family, regardless of age, did a share of the work when the season required it.[18] Nevertheless, the indicated percentages are so high that a question is raised whether they may include some persons who should really be classed as dependents within the meaning of the census instructions.

According to the instructions, the word of the respondent sufficed to indicate an occupation, including work as an unpaid family member, except that in the latter case, work was supposed to have been "regular" and in connection with the principal occupation of the head of the family. There was no precise frame of reference, from the standpoint either of measuring period, amount of income or hours of work. In other words, "having an occupation" referred to one's general or usual status.[19]

[18] For example, John Maynard, *The Russian Peasant: and Other Studies*, Gollancz, 1947, p. 22.

[19] For comments on the subject of "occupation" in Soviet labor force analysis,

One did not have to be working at the time of the census (December 17, 1926) in order to be counted as having an occupation, providing seasonal work was reported "of a permanent character [which] occurs year after year."[20] This held not only for cases where the family was the economic unit, but also where persons worked (seasonally) for hire; for example, "construction workers [*rabochie*] must indicate their summer work . . . even though at the moment of the census they are not so occupied." In the case of persons with more than one occupation, a summer seasonal job bringing the major income for the year was listed as the principal occupation, even though the individual was otherwise occupied at the time of the census.

Persons "completely without work and seeking it" at the time of the census, including those who never worked before, were registered as "unemployed." However, judging from tables on principal and secondary occupations, persons reporting seasonal summer work but seeking work in December, were registered as "occupied" in the summer job and not as unemployed.[21]

The absence of a quantitative standard in terms of money earned or hours worked raises the possibility that persons working relatively little throughout the year would nevertheless be counted as occupied. The possibility is especially evident with respect to unpaid family workers, although the clear intent of the census is to include only those who "help" in the fullest sense of the word:[22]

> "In the category of family members helping in the occupation are included those who regularly [*postoianno*] help the head of their own family by their work in his craft or occupation; and as helping family members in agriculture, persons, regardless of age, who take part in the principal agricultural work (field work, threshing, pasturage of cattle, etc.), even though also working in the home."

---

see note 12, above; and for a general discussion of methods and concepts in this field, see A. J. Jaffe and Charles D. Stewart, *Manpower Resources and Utilization: Principles of Working Force Analysis*, Wiley, 1951.

[20] *Vsesoiuznaia perepis' naseleniia 1926 goda*, Supplement to Volumes XVIII-XXXIV, pp. 10-11.

[21] *Ibid.*, Volume XXXIV, pp. 118-119. This may explain why the census total of unemployed (1,014,000) is less than the yearly average number registered in fiscal year 1926-1927 (1,242,000) as well as the number on April 1, 1927 (1,478,000), although seasonal factors distinguishing December from April may also be involved. Unemployment data from Soviet sources in Schwarz, *op.cit.*, p. 38. It seems probable, furthermore, that the census underenumerated persons with a seasonal occupation for hire in agriculture but not working (and not unemployed) at the time of the census (see Warren W. Eason, "The Agricultural Labor Force and Population of the U.S.S.R., 1926-1941," Rand Corporation, hectographed, RM-1248, May 4, 1954).

[22] *Vsesoiuznaia perepis' naseleniia 1926 goda*, Supplement to Volumes XVIII-XXXIV, p. 10.

The difficulty of delineating regular work from irregular or occasional, and housework from farm work, is recognized in another section of the instructions:[23]

> "Members of the family helping in the occupation introduce elements characteristic, chiefly, of the peasant economy, and to a certain degree of trade and handicrafts. In this group is included wives and daughters and sons who have not left the household, regularly helping the head of the family in the principal agricultural work; and also the sons of artisans working together with the father in the handicraft as an apprentice, as well as wives working over the counter in the shops of their husbands.
>
> "For the most part, we have here a case of labor which is insufficiently differentiated, and which stands on the border between professional labor and the home economy (female work and peasant economy). The fact that they are actually working, under the direction of a primary person, places them in the production process, but the filial or marital connection with the head of the economic unit makes their social position different from the position of persons working for hire."

It will be noticed that the emphasis is on *regular* participation in the *principal* work of the head of the family, and the census goes further to demand a straightforward indication to the enumerator of help in the principal occupation on the part of the family member.

It is clear that the census instructions were formulated to include in the labor force only persons with more than a transient or casual relationship to it, although not necessarily working a full year, or even a full agricultural year. In fact, since the demand for labor in agriculture is concentrated in a few months of the year, it would seem that relatively little work on an annual basis would suffice for compliance with the spirit of the instructions. Subject to the qualification that the results may embody wide variation in the amount of work per year and per day in the given case, therefore, the census probably gives a fairly accurate measure of the number of persons "having an occupation."

We now ask what effect the Plans may have had on the percentage of the population in the labor force. Unfortunately, comprehensive figures on the total labor force of the U.S.S.R. have not been released since the Five-Year Plans began. The 1937 census was officially abrogated shortly after it was taken;[24] and although tabulation was subsequently completed,[25] the results have never admittedly been pub-

[23] *Ibid.*, p. 12.

[24] *Izvestiia*, September 26, 1937.

[25] Testimony of a former Soviet demographer now in this country.

lished. Releases from the 1939 census, on the other hand, have been confined to population data with partial detail, including a classification by "social groups" which is only of indirect aid in deriving labor force figures. Soviet estimates of the total labor force after 1929 from non-census sources have never been published. In the absence of adequate data on the total labor force, therefore, any indication of the change in the percentage of the population in the labor force must be to a certain extent speculative.

Under the conditions of the Five-Year Plans, certain factors would appear to have increased the percentage of the population in the labor force and others to have decreased it; but on balance, the effect has probably been to decrease the percentage to some degree. Tending to decrease it would be the increase in the number of students and the large-scale migration of females from rural to urban areas. Tending to increase it would be the efforts of the Soviet government to get the maximum proportion of the adult population into the labor force; the increase in the population age sixteen to fifty-nine relative to other groups; and possibly the indirect effects of the fall in real wages, which were low before the Plans and which apparently remained below the 1928 level until as recently as 1952.[26] These factors will now be considered briefly, and an indication will be given of their effect on the percentage in the labor force at the time of the 1939 census.

Increase in School Attendance. The number of students, excluding those in universities, rose from 41.5 per cent of the population age eight to sixteen in 1928-1929 to 89.6 per cent in 1938-1939,[27] which would imply that the contribution of youths to the labor force at the same time decreased. However, for comparability with the concepts of the 1926 census, students continuing to supply seasonal labor would be considered occupied. Although urban youths attending school may not as a rule have worked during the summer[28]—as seems to have been the case even in 1926, judging by the relatively small percentage in the labor force[29]—youths from collective farms (as well as other rural

[26] Janet G. Chapman, "Real Wages in the Soviet Union, 1928-1952," *The Review of Economics and Statistics*, May 1954, pp. 134-156.

[27] The number of students in 1928-1929 (12,548,000) relative to the population age 8-16 from the 1926 census (30,257,000); the number of students in 1938-1939 (32,711,000) relative to the population age 8-16 from the 1939 census (36,519,000) as adjusted by Lorimer (Frank Lorimer, *The Population of the Soviet Union: History and Prospects*, Geneva, League of Nations, 1946, p. 141). Children entered school officially at 8 years of age during this period.

[28] From time to time, however, special circumstances may have existed. For example, during and shortly after World War II, a large number of urban youths were pressed into working in rural areas during harvest time (see Schwarz, *op.cit.*, p. 122).

[29] In 1926, 9.1 per cent of urban youths age 10-15 were in the labor force, com-

youths) probably did work, either for the collective farm or on the homestead farm of the household. The increase in school attendance would thus appear to have had no marked effect on the over-all percentage of youths having an occupation, within the concept of the 1926 census.

Specifically, it would seem that the percentage of the population age twelve to fifteen in the labor force (by rural and urban areas) remained unchanged from 1926, although the percentage of children age ten to eleven probably fell to negligible proportions.[30]

Rural-Urban Migration of Females. In 1926, 85.5 per cent of the rural female population age sixteen to fifty-nine and 40.1 per cent of the urban were in the labor force. A differential of this magnitude maintained throughout the 1930's would mean that rural-urban migration of between 11 and 14 million females by 1939,[31] including a relatively high percentage of adults, would have a downward effect on the percentage of the total female population age sixteen to fifty-nine economically active.

It is felt that the percentage of the *rural* population age sixteen to fifty-nine in the labor force has not changed significantly since 1926. This conclusion is reached by ruling out, for different reasons, the possibility of an increase or decrease. An increase is ruled out because the 1926 percentage (85.5) would seem to represent more or less an upper limit consonant with a minimum number of females attending full time to home and family obligations. A decrease is ruled out on the grounds that certain basic conditions of rural economic life had not changed, namely, the low standard of living and family type agriculture retained in the form of the homestead garden plot. Finally, it may be noted that only a fraction of the total number of dependents of institutions and persons receiving "unearned income" were in rural areas.[32] It is therefore assumed that 85.5 per cent of the rural female population age sixteen to fifty-nine were in the labor force in 1939.

---

pared to 66.8 per cent of rural (*Vsesoiuznaia perepis' naseleniia 1926 goda,* Volume XXXIV).

[30] The evidence for an unchanged percentage of the rural population age 12-15 in the labor force is the relatively large number of youths age 12-15 earning labor-days on collective farms (see Eason, "The Agricultural Labor Force and Population of the U.S.S.R., 1926-1941," p. 25). The evidence for assuming a negligible number age 10-11 is, first, that the percentage of children age 10-11 in the labor force in 1926 must have been very small (but cannot be determined exactly because the age-group 10-14 is reported as a unit); and, second, that all discussion of the labor of children and youths on the collective farms during the 1930's was confined to those age 12-15 (although there was no age limit on the earning of labor-days).

[31] Eason, "Population and Labor Force," Appendix B, p. 30.

[32] Of 1.9 million in this group (see Table 1), 1.5 million were in urban areas.

In the case of *urban* females age sixteen to fifty-nine, it is generally presumed that the percentage in the labor force increased during the Five-Year Plans in response to the efforts by the government to get females into the wage and salary group. The presumption seems to be borne out by the reported increase in the number of female wage and salary workers, from 2.9 million at the time of the 1926 census to 10.7 million on January 1, 1939, or from 30.7 to 37.4 per cent of both sexes (see Table 3, below).

However, this increase arose not only from an increase in the percentage of the urban female population in the labor force, but also from the absolute increase in the urban female population and from the proportionate shift of females in the labor force from a nonhired to a hired status. The last two factors alone could have accounted for almost all of the increase in the number of wage and salary workers between 1926 and 1939, if it is assumed (1) that the rural-urban distribution of the reported number of female wage and salary workers in nonagricultural sectors was the same in 1939 as in 1926 and (2) that the proportion of the urban labor force in nonhired occupations was relatively small. On this basis, it may be assumed that about 40 per cent of the urban female population age sixteen to fifty-nine in 1939 was in the labor force, compared to 35.7 per cent in 1926.[33]

However, if in fact the percentage was higher than 40 in 1939, it

[33] In 1926, 72 per cent of female wage and salary workers lived in urban areas (*Vsesoiuznaia perepis' naseleniia 1926 goda*, Vol. XXXIV). The same proportion in 1939 would mean that 7.4 million female wage and salary workers lived in urban areas. On the assumption that 40 per cent of the urban female population age 16-59 were in the labor force, this would be about 85 per cent of the urban female labor force, while if 50 per cent of the urban female population age 16-59 were in the labor force, the proportion of female wage and salary workers in the urban female labor force would be about 65 per cent.

In 1926, 52 per cent of the urban female labor force were wage and salary workers. The percentage would be expected to be higher in 1939 through the switch of certain occupations from a nonhired to hired status. Data on the nonagricultural nonhired labor force for 1939 are very poor, but the impression conveyed in Soviet sources is that the number was proportionately much smaller than in 1926. According to this, the proportion of the urban (female) labor force in the wage and salary group was relatively large, which would be more consistent with the higher estimate above (85) than the lower (65). The assumption that 40 per cent of the urban female population age 16-59 in 1939 were in the labor force is made on this basis.

The assumption is obviously not well supported, but it conforms to available evidence better than any alternative. The principal weakness lies in the grounds for assuming that the number of persons in the nonhired urban labor force was relatively small; in fact, the percentage could have been higher than the Soviets are willing to admit. Furthermore, it must be kept in mind that the estimates of the urban population for 1939 by age-groups are subject to a considerable margin of error.

would imply one or more of the following conditions: (1) a higher proportion of female nonagricultural wage and salary workers residing in urban areas in 1939 than in 1926, (2) a larger number of female private artisans (noncooperative handicraftsmen) than indicated by partial information presently available, (3) a relatively large number of females temporarily unemployed or not in the labor force, or (4) a relatively large number in urban nonreported sectors. Except for (1), which is felt to be unlikely on the basis of indirect evidence,[34] and the inadequate fragmentary data on (2), there is no direct information on these categories in Soviet sources.

Government Efforts and General Conditions Operating to Increase Percentage of Population in Labor Force. The existence of these pressures has already been indicated and need not be elaborated.[35] The salient factor concerning their effect is that the percentage of the population in the labor force in 1926 was already very high, and in the case of rural areas, high enough to leave little room for expansion. The percentage of the rural male population age sixteen to fifty-nine in the labor force (98.2) could exclude only those physically and mentally incapable of work, and, as noted above, the percentage of the female (85.5) would seem to exclude only the minimum number required for household and family duties. For all practical purposes, therefore, an increase in the percentage of the adult rural population in the labor force does not seem plausible.

In urban areas, the percentage of the male population age sixteen to fifty-nine in the labor force is assumed to have increased from the 1926 level (86.3) to 97.1, an estimated figure which purports to include all those physically and mentally capable of work (see Appendix Table A-1). The percentage of the urban female population age sixteen to fifty-nine in the labor force, as discussed above, is assumed equal to 40. The percentage of males and females sixty years of age and over in the labor force (rural and urban) is assumed unchanged.

The foregoing discussion suggests possible change in the age-specific proportion of the urban and rural population in the labor force under the Five-Year Plans. In Appendix C and Table 4, the proportions assumed above are applied to the urban and rural population by age

[34] If anything, the proportion of the female nonagricultural wage and salary workers living in urban areas may have declined by 1939, or, in other words, the proportion in rural areas may have increased. This observation is based on the fact that the nonagricultural proportion of the total rural population apparently increased between 1926 and 1939 (see Warren W. Eason, "Population Growth and Economic Development in the U.S.S.R.," to be published in the proceedings of the World Population Conference, 1954).

[35] For a further discussion of the subject, see Schwarz, *op.cit.*, Chap. II.

and sex to derive a hypothetical labor force at the time of the 1939 census. The results, compared to 1926, are as follows:

	1926 (census)	*1939 (hypothetical)*	*Percentage Increase*
Both sexes:			
Labor force (thousands)	84,357	94,019	11.5
Labor force as per cent of population	57.5	55.2	
Male:			
Labor force (thousands)	45,218	52,938	17.1
Labor force as per cent of male population	63.7	64.8	
Female:			
Labor force (thousands)	39,139	41,081	5.0
Labor force as per cent of female population	51.6	46.3	

The higher percentage of the male population in the labor force in 1939 reflects predominantly the assumption of a higher percentage of the urban male population age sixteen to fifty-nine in the labor force. The lower percentage of the female population in the labor force shows the effect of rural-urban migration only partly balanced by the assumption of an increase in the percentage of urban females age sixteen to fifty-nine in the labor force. The percentage increase in the total labor force (11.5) is somewhat less than the percentage increase in the population (15.9), in spite of the larger proportion of adults in the population, because of the assumptions concerning the percentage of children age ten to eleven and youths age twelve to fifteen in the labor force and the net effect of rural-urban migration.

3. *Labor Force by Reported Groups*

Although information is not available on the total labor force under the Five-Year Plans, as discussed in the preceding section, data by certain of the most important occupation groups have been reported, but with diminishing frequency and consistency. During the intercensal period, the following were the major developments in the size and distribution of the labor force by these groups:

1. The number of wage and salary workers tripled, from 9.6 million according to principal occupation at the time of the 1926 census, to 28.6 million employed on January 1, 1939. The expansion of industry, construction, transportation, education, and administration, carried out by state enterprises working with hired labor, accounted for virtually all of the increase. The number of wage and salary workers in agriculture (after the early 1930's these were associated with state farms

and machine-tractor stations) declined from 13 per cent of the total in 1926 to 7 per cent in 1939.

2. The number of self-employed and unpaid family workers was drastically reduced by the collectivization of agriculture and the expansion of the producer cooperative network, as well as by the movement of labor into the wage and salary group. The number of self-employed fell from 72.1 million in 1926 to less than 4 million individual farmers and a relatively small number of private artisans in 1939. Within the collective farm organization, however, the existence of the individual homestead garden plot, attracting considerable full- and part-time labor from the members of the household, has meant the continuation *de facto* of a relatively large amount of "self-employment," principally among females.

3. There was an increase in the number of persons earning "labor shares," especially the number earning *trudodni* (labor-days) as collective farmers, but also those earning *zarabotki* as members of producer cooperatives. By 1939, roughly half of the total labor force earned one or more labor shares during the year, although a large number of collective farmers also earned wages (from work outside the collective farm) and self-employment income (from work on the homestead farm).

4. The number of persons on active duty with the military increased after the middle 1930's, and by early 1939 (before the widening of military activity later in the year) was near 1.6 million, or almost triple the level at the time of the 1926 census.[36]

These over-all trends did not develop in a regular fashion. On the contrary, the growth of the various sectors was extremely irregular, related to fundamental changes in the economic system. In describing the salient features of the period, the following stages may be differentiated: 1928-1930, inclusive; the year 1931; 1932-1936, inclusive; and 1937 until the annexation of territory and the start of World War II in 1939.

From the beginning of the first Five-Year Plan to the end of 1930, the total number of wage and salary workers increased by an amount somewhat greater than projected by the Plan, reaching 15.6 million on January 1, 1931, as against 13.8 million planned for fiscal year 1930-1931.[37] The planned increase in the number of wage and salary workers, incidentally, was deliberately set below the average annual increase over the preceding five years.

[36] Eason, "Population and Labor Force," as cited, p. 108 and Appendix A, Table A-1.

[37] *Piatiletnii plan narodno-khoziaistvennogo stroitel'stva*, Moscow, Gosplan, 1930, Volume II, Part 2, p. 165.

The number of registered unemployed increased initially during the Plan, from 1.4 million on October 1, 1928 to 1.7 million on April 1, 1929, and then decreased to 1.1 million on April 1, 1930.[38]

In spite of some correspondence between the planned and actual increases in the number of wage and salary workers from 1928 through 1930, and the continued existence of unemployment, labor shortages apparently developed in certain areas. Measures to get the unemployed to work and to ensure adequate manpower for expanding industry were discussed with increasing frequency.[39] To this end, on October 9, 1930, unemployment insurance was abolished, and the state labor exchanges were told to "take all steps necessary to put the unemployed to work at once,"[40] even though this meant accepting work outside one's specialty which might have been refused given the alternative of insurance. From that moment to the present, unemployment has officially not existed in the U.S.S.R.

Immediately thereafter—although only partly if at all due to the abolition of unemployment insurance—the number of wage and salary workers rose sharply. As shown in Table 3, the increase during 1931 was 6.3 million, starting from 15.6 million on January 1 and reaching 21.5 million on October 1 and 21.9 million on January 1 of the next year. This increase by more than 30 per cent in one year was equal in absolute terms to that over the preceding four.

The exceptional growth in the number of wage and salary workers during 1931 was undoubtedly an indirect result of the major and irreversible moves toward collectivization in agriculture which took place at the end of 1930 and throughout 1931. The adverse reaction of many of the peasants to collectivization would appear to have motivated a large number to seek work in the cities. Following a sharp rise and fall in early 1930,[41] the number of collective farms grew from 85,000 on July 1, 1930, to 230,000 a year and a half later. The related increase in the number of collectivized households did not begin until 1931, when in the course of the year it went from 6.6 million to 15.4 million, or from 26.4 to 62.6 per cent of all households in agriculture.[42] The population of collective farms increased from 4.8 million in 1929 to 68.7 million in 1932, and the number of able-bodied members sixteen years of age and over, from 2.3 million to 42.1 million.[43]

[38] See note 21.

[39] See Schwarz, *op.cit.*, Chap. II.

[40] *Izvestiia*, October 11, 1930.

[41] Between February and March, 1930, the number of collective farms increased from 87,500 to 110,200, and the number of collective farm households from 8 million to 14 million; then, responding to official objections to the speed of collectivization, the respective numbers fell by May to below the February levels (see Eason, "The Agricultural Labor Force and Population of the U.S.S.R., 1926-1941," Table B-1 in Appendix B, p. 122).

[42] *Ibid.*

[43] *Ibid.*, pp. 17 and 22.

TABLE 3

Wage and Salary Workers, U.S.S.R., 1926-1939
(*thousands*)

MONTH AND YEAR[a]	BOTH SEXES			MALE			FEMALE			FEMALE AS A PERCENTAGE OF BOTH SEXES		
	Total	*Agri-culture*	*Nonagri-culture*	*Total*	*Agri-culture*	*Nonagri-culture*	*Total*	*Agri-culture*	*Nonagri-culture*	*Total*	*Agri-culture*	*Nonagri-culture*
1926 census	9,583	1,201	8,382	6,637	836	5,801	2,946	365	2,581	30.7	30.4	30.8
1926-1927 yearly av.	10,944	..	..	..	..	..	..	..	..	..	..	..
1928 yearly av.	11,599	1,676	9,923	..	..	..	..	..	..	..	..	..
1929 yearly av.	12,168	1,576	10,592	8,864	1,135	7,729	3,304	441	2,863	27.2	28.0	27.0
1930 yearly av.	14,531	1,552	12,979	10,654	1,127	9,527	3,877	425	3,452	26.7	27.4	26.6
1931:												
January	15,602	957	14,645	11,405	736	10,669	4,197	221	3,976	26.9	23.1	27.1
April	..	..	..	..	..	..	..	..	..	..	..	..
July	..	..	..	..	..	..	..	..	..	..	..	..
October	21,494	..	..	..	..	..	..	..	..	..	..	..
yearly av.	18,990	2,060	16,930	..	..	..	..	..	..	..	..	..
1932:												
January	21,923	1,850	20,073	15,916	1,456	14,460	6,007	394	5,613	27.4	21.3	28.0
April	20,827	..	..	15,120	..	..	5,707	..	..	27.4	..	..
July	24,064	3,736	20,328	16,797	2,269	14,528	7,267	1,267	6,000	30.2	33.9	29.5
October	24,131	..	..	16,771	..	..	7,360	..	..	30.5	..	..
yearly av.	22,943	2,858	20.085	16,190	..	..	6,753	..	..	29.4	..	..
1933:												
January	22,649	2,099	20,550	15,741	1,591	14,150	6,908	508	6,400	30.5	24.2	31.1
April	21,517	2,227	19,290	14,945	..	..	6,563	..	..	30.5	..	..
July	22,141	3,458	18,683	14,989	2,250	12,739	7,152	1,208	5,944	32.3	34.9	31.8
October	22,776	3,323	19,453	15,556	..	..	7,220	..	..	31.7	..	..
yearly av.	22,325	2,819	19,506	15,292	1,979	13,313	7,033	840	6,193	31.5	29.9	31.7

(continued on next page)

TABLE 3 (continued)
(*thousands*)

MONTH AND YEAR[a]	BOTH SEXES			MALE			FEMALE			FEMALE AS A PERCENTAGE OF BOTH SEXES		
	Total	*Agri-culture*	*Nonagri-culture*	*Total*	*Agri-culture*	*Nonagri-culture*	*Total*	*Agri-culture*	*Nonagri-culture*	*Total*	*Agri-culture*	*Nonagri-culture*
1934:												
January	22,726	2,382	20,344	15,522	1,777	13,745	7,204	605	6,599	31.7	25.4	32.4
April	21,595	2,450	19,145	14,749	..	..	6,846	..	..	31.7	..	..
July	24,814	3,725	21,089	16,402	2,384	14,018	8,412	1,341	7,071	33.9	36.0	33.5
October	24,294	3,496	20,798	16,180	..	..	8,114	..	..	33.4	..	..
yearly av.	23,681	3,094	20,587	15,856	2,096	13,760	7,825	998	6,827	33.0	32.3	33.2
1935:												
January	23,844	2,489	21,355	15,880	1,817	14,063	7,964	672	7,292	33.4	27.0	34.1
April	23,130	2,503	20,627	15,405	..	..	7,725	..	..	33.4	..	..
July	25,837	3,592	22,245	16,768	2,319	14.449	9,069	1,273	7,796	35.1	35.4	35.0
October	24,996	3,230	21,766	16,497	..	..	8,499	..	..	34.0	..	..
yearly av.	24,770	2,974	21,796	16,300	2,030	14,270	8,470	944	7,526	34.2	31.7	34.5
1936:												
January	24,976	2,379	22,597	16,484	1,751	14,733	8,492	628	7,864	34.0	26.4	34.8
April	24,247	2,321	21,926	16,003	..	..	8,244	..	..	34.0	..	..
July	26,375	3,015	23,360	17,038	1,983	15,055	9,337	1,032	8,305	35.4	34.2	35.6
October	26,239	..	..	16,950	..	..	9,289	..	..	35.4	..	..
yearly av.	25,771	2,615	23,159	16,765	1,808	14,957	9,009	807	8,202	35.0	30.9	35.4
1937:												
January	26,432	2,121	24,311	17,075	1,576	15,499	9,357	545	8,812	35.4	25.7	36.2
April	26,005	..	..	16,799	..	..	9,206	..	..	35.4	..	..
July	27,922	2,907	25,015	17,703	1,933	15,770	10,219	974	9,245	36.6	33.5	37.0
October	26,830	..	..	17,064	..	..	9,766	..	..	36.4	..	..
yearly av.	26,990	2,483	24,507	17,262	1,734	15,528	9,728	749	8,979	36.0	30.2	36.6

(continued on next page)

TABLE 3 (continued)
(*thousands*)

MONTH AND YEAR[a]	BOTH SEXES			MALE			FEMALE			FEMALE AS A PERCENTAGE OF BOTH SEXES		
	Total	*Agriculture*	*Nonagriculture*	*Total*	*Agriculture*	*Nonagriculture*	*Total*	*Agriculture*	*Nonagriculture*	*Total*	*Agriculture*	*Nonagriculture*
1938:												
January	26,830	2,039	24,791	17,228	1,535	15,693	9,602	504	9,098	36.4	24.7	36.7
April	26,401	..	..	16,791	..	..	9,610	..	..	36.4	..	..
July	28,175	2,361	25,814	17,581	1,619	15,962	10,594	743	9,851	37.6	31.4	38.2
October	28,610	..	..	17,910	..	..	10,700	..	..	37.4	..	..
yearly av.	27,800	2,142	25,658	17,500	1,524	15,976	10,300	618	9,682	37.1	28.9	37.7
1939:												
January	28,610	1,808	26,802	17,910	1,386	16,524	10,700	422	10,278	37.4	23.3	38.3
April	28,152	..	..	17,623	..	..	10,529	..	..	37.4	..	..
July	29,427	..	..	18,039	..	..	11,388	..	..	38.7	..	..

[a] Monthly data are the first of each month; yearly averages are calendar year except 1926-1927, which is fiscal year (October-September).

Source: Appendix B.

Rural-urban migration statistics and data on the growth of the population also show a pattern of concentration in 1931:

Urban Population, 1928-1934
(*thousands*)

Year	*January 1*[a]	*Increase during Year*	*Rural-Urban Migration*[b]
1928	27,571	59	1,062
1929	27,630	3,270	1,392
1930	30,900	1,100	2,633
1931	32,000	4,340	4,100
1932	36,340	3,399	2,719
1933	39,739	1,361	772
1934	41,100		

[a] Warren Eason, "Population Growth and Economic Development in the U.S.S.R.," to be published in the proceedings of the World Population Conference, Table 2.
[b] *Sotsialisticheskoe stroitel'stvo SSSR, 1936*, Moscow, TsUNKhU, 1936, p. 545.

The several years following 1931 were relatively stable. The average number of wage and salary workers was lower in 1933 than in 1932, but increased by somewhat over 1 million per year thereafter until 1939. The number in nonagriculture fell off after 1931 and then recovered; however, it did not rise significantly above the level of January 1, 1932, until 1937 (see Table 3).

The number of wage and salary workers in agriculture, i.e. on state farms and machine-tractor stations,[44] had grown more rapidly in 1931 than the number in nonagriculture. This growth continued in the 1931-1934 period, when the number of nonagricultural wage and salary workers remained more or less constant, and reflected the planned effort to widen the share of state relative to collective and individual farming. By the mid-1930's, however, the poor record of state farms had led to a process of contraction,[45] which appears as an absolute decline in the number of wage and salary workers in agriculture after 1934, to the 1931 level by 1939.

In collectivized agriculture, following 1931 the absolute number of collective farm households did not increase again until the beginning

[44] Only the permanent staff of the Machine-Tractor Stations is included, seasonal labor being supplied by collective farms, for the most part, and paid in labor-days. Through the summer of 1932, the number of wage and salary workers in agriculture included a significant number working for hire on individual farms (see *ibid.*, Appendix C, p. 143).

[45] Naum Jasny, *The Socialized Agriculture of the U.S.S.R.: Plans and Performance*, Stanford University Press, 1949, p. 254ff.

of 1935.[46] However, collectivized households as a percentage of the total (in agriculture) continued to increase as a result of the decrease in the number of individual farm households. This led, through the movement of population into existing collective farm households and a rise in the average population per household, to a continuous increase in the collective farm population, reaching a prewar peak near 100 million in 1936.[47]

Following 1936, for reasons which are not entirely clear, the labor force and population of collective farms dropped sharply, primarily through a decline in the number of males sixteen years of age and over. The number fell from 25.3 million in 1936 to 20 million in 1937 and 18.5 million in 1938, for an over-all decline of almost 7 million in two years, while the corresponding number of females changed very little. The number of males earning labor-days fell by 4 million—less than the decrease in the total because fewer were earning no labor-days.[48]

In an attempt to explain the drop in the number of males, the following factors are considered relevant, although they do not necessarily add up to a completely satisfactory explanation:

1. Because 1936 was a year of relatively poor harvest, a large number of males may have moved from the farms to the cities. If this were true, however, one would expect to see an increase in the number of male wage and salary workers; and although there was an increase, it was a modest one. Between the end of 1936 and the beginning of 1939, the number of male wage and salary workers increased by less than 1 million.

2. Theoretically, expansion of the military could account for a certain number, but the increase prior to 1939 was only about 580,000 and took place during 1934-1935.[49]

3. During 1937 and 1938, many official protests were registered concerning large-scale expulsions from collective farms the year before for "trivial" reasons. Laws were established stipulating the conditions for expulsion and listing the relatively minor offenses which could not thereafter be considered as valid.[50] Here too, one would expect a rise in other sectors of the labor force, unless the expulsions, however "trivial," justified imprisonment—and we have no data on the size of the prison population.

[46] Eason, "The Agricultural Labor Force and Population of the U.S.S.R., 1926-1941," Table B-1 in Appendix B, p. 122.

[47] *Ibid.*, p. 17. [48] *Ibid.*, p. 25.

[49] Eason, "Population and Labor Force," Appendix A, p. 2, note g.

[50] Eason, "The Agricultural Labor Force and Population of the U.S.S.R., 1926-1941," p. 29.

4. Entering the group sixteen years of age and older between 1933 and 1937 were persons born during World War I, the Revolution, and the Civil War, when the birth rate was low.[51] This presumably could have at least slowed down the rate of natural increase of the collective farm population sixteen years of age and older, although it does not explain the differential change between males and females.

5. Finally, it should be noted that where the decline involved persons already working much of the year for hire outside the collective farm, their quitting the farm entirely and working full time for hire would have a relatively small effect on the yearly average number of wage and salary workers. Perhaps 1 or 2 million persons fell into this category.[52]

In any event, during 1939 and 1940 the number of males on collective farms continued to decline, by about 1 million each year; but in these years there was a parallel increase in the number of male wage and salary workers and in the military.

Turning once again to the intercensal period as a whole, what general conclusions can be reached concerning the labor force trends outlined above?

First, we may aggregate the data by reported groups as of January, 1939, and, allowing for double counting and seasonal fluctuations, arrive at a total which is conceptually more or less consistent with that of the 1926 census. This total, which will be called the "reported labor force" for 1939, is 84.3 million (see Table 4)—almost identical to the total labor force in 1926. The number of males is about 1 million greater than in 1926 and the number of females 1 million less.

The fact that the "reported labor force" in 1939 is not very different from the total labor force in 1926 does not necessarily imply a rejection of the hypothetical increase in the labor force proposed in the preceding section, from 84 million to 94 million. The difference of 10 million between the reported and the hypothetical totals for 1939 could be due to statistical shortcomings in the original data, to estimating and aggregating errors, and to the nonreporting of certain sectors, notably forced labor.[53]

[51] Lorimer, *op.cit.*, p. 41.

[52] Between 1936 and 1937, of the total decline of 5.3 million in the number of able-bodied males 16 years of age and over, more than 3 million occurred in groups earning *more* than 51 labor-days per year. The latter are generally not considered to work for hire to any great extent, if at all, and many persons earning less than 51 labor-days do not work much for hire (Eason, "The Agricultural Labor Force and Population of the U.S.S.R., 1926-1941," pp. 27 and 181-192).

[53] Attempts to measure these factors are not very successful. Possibilities in this

This makes it difficult to establish and analyze certain basic trends in the growth of the Soviet labor force. Consider, for example, the shift from agricultural to nonagricultural employment. Using the reported labor force for 1939, the increase in the nonagricultural sectors of about 17 million compared to 1926, is balanced by an equal decline in the agricultural sectors.[54] Using the hypothetical labor force, on the other hand, which would mean increasing both the agricultural and nonagricultural components (relative to the reported labor force) by, say, 5 million,[55] the absolute increase in the nonagricultural component over the intercensal period, rather than being equal to the decline in the agricultural, would be almost twice as great in absolute terms.

We can minimize such difficulties arising from our inability to estimate the total labor force accurately and at the same time gain some insight into the fundamental growth relationships of the labor force under the Five-Year Plans by concentrating attention on wage and salary workers. The wage and salary sector, since it includes the bulk of the industrial labor force and has been a priority sector from the standpoint of manpower allocation, is an important index of the impact of industrialization on the growth and distribution of the labor force.

We shall therefore compare trends in the number of wage and salary workers with those of nonwage and nonsalary workers as a group, and with trends in the growth and age-sex composition of the population. The statistical problems are minimized by this procedure because data on wage and salary workers seem to be more reliable than for other reported groups.

The expansion of the industrial sector of the economy under the Plans increased the demand for wage and salary workers. The demand was satisfied during the 1930's partly by the available supplies of manpower already in the urban areas, consisting of both the unemployed and persons in other categories of the urban labor force; partly by the large-scale migration of labor from rural to urban areas; and partly by the drawing of persons into the labor force. Of these, rural-urban migration and the transformation of formerly rural communities

---

connection are discussed in Eason, "Population and Labor Force," Appendix A, pp. 1-7.

[54] The data are from the section on the labor force in Table 4, including the number of wage and salary workers in agriculture from Eason, "Agricultural Labor Force and Population of the U.S.S.R., 1926-1941," p. 55.

[55] This is but one of many conceivable ways of making the distribution between agriculture and nonagriculture. In particular, it should be noted that the distribution with respect to nonreported sectors (including forced labor) could involve both nonagriculture and agriculture, or the rural economy (e.g. forestry).

into urban areas appear to have accounted for more than 80 per cent of the increase in the labor supply of the urban areas.[56]

At the same time, the adult population was growing, although the average rate of growth during the intercensal period was less than projected (from 1926) on the basis of pre-Plan survival ratios.[57] The events of the early 1930's had caused a temporary but marked decline in population growth, including a low birth rate and high death rate for several years.[58] Nevertheless, the absolute increase in the adult population age sixteen to fifty-nine between 1926 and 1939 was at a rate of 1.5 per cent per year, for a total increase of 16.5 million, compared to 18.4 million for wage and salary workers. Allowing for a certain number of females not entering the labor force, the absolute increase in the adult population accounts for almost two-thirds of the increase in the number of wage and salary workers.

Since population growth would therefore seem to have been no deterrent to the expansion of the wage and salary sector, it is difficult to explain the pattern of growth in the sector, specifically in the case of males. Almost the entire intercensal increase of 10.6 million male wage and salary workers in nonagricultural employment took place by the end of 1931. During 1931 alone, the number increased from 10.7 to 14.5 million, or by 40 per cent, after which it declined somewhat and then rose again to the 1932 level; but it did not increase above 15 million until the end of 1936, and it increased by only 500,000 during 1937 and 1938.

The increase in the number of female wage and salary workers was proportionate to males through 1931, i.e. the distribution of the sexes remained more or less unchanged. But thereafter, in the five-year period during which the number of males did not increase, the number of females increased by more than 2 million or 40 per cent; and even after 1936, the rate of increase of females was greater than that of males.

An explanation for the relatively low rate of increase of male wage and salary workers is difficult to find in other reported labor force data. The number of males in the collective farm labor force declined sharply after 1936, as shown above; and the individual farm labor force, as judged by the number of individual farm households, was declining throughout the 1930's. In each case, the release of males to work for hire is implied.

It may also be noted that in the period from 1939 to 1950, the increase in the number of male wage and salary workers was less by 4

[56] S. I. Sul'kevich, *Territoriia i naselenie SSSR*, Moscow, 1940, p. 30.

[57] Lorimer, *op.cit.*, p. 113.

[58] Eason, "Population Growth and Economic Development in the U.S.S.R."

million than the estimated increase in the male population age sixteen to fifty-nine, which includes a relatively high allowance for military deaths during the war. Thus, over the period 1926-1950 as a whole, the increase in the number of male wage and salary workers was no greater than the absolute increase in the male population age sixteen to fifty-nine.

The irregularity of the rate of growth of the industrial labor force during the 1930's appears as evidence of "hidden unemployment" in the Soviet economy. It may be argued that if industrial enterprise managers had been economically prudent, payrolls would not have increased by such a large amount in one year (1931) and remained more or less unchanged for several years thereafter. The mass exodus to the cities in 1931 would seem necessarily to have led to unemployment under "normal" conditions.

On the other hand, it is possible to view the "hiding" of manpower in these years as an investment in training, or at least "indoctrination." One of the big problems facing the Soviet leaders during the 1930's was the acclimatization of the peasant migrant to industrial life. In this sense his inclusion on the payrolls, rather than being left unemployed and forced to return to the countryside, may be viewed as a contribution tending to balance the negative effects in terms of per capita productivity.

For later years, the rate of growth of the number of wage and salary workers gives no clear indication of the existence of "hidden unemployment," except perhaps in the case of the fourth Five-Year Plan (1945-1950). There the planned increase was overfulfilled by 75 per cent,[59] but this could have been the result of an incorrect estimate of the needs of industry (in recovering from the war and in further expansion) on the part of the planners, as much as of the excessive hiring of labor.

4. *Percentage Utilization of the Labor Force*

The discussion thus far has been concerned primarily with trends in the size and distribution of the "labor force," defined to include the number of persons having an occupational status. According to this definition, it will be recalled, persons in agriculture, for example, were considered "occupied" even though actually working only a fraction of the year because of seasonal variation in work requirements.

The labor force by occupational status would thus normally be greater than the average number of persons actually working or employed at any one time during the year; and in a predominantly agricultural economy such as the Soviet Union before the Five-Year

[59] Eason, "Population and Labor Force," p. 112.

Plans, the difference between the two figures could be large. This part of the paper presents a measure of the average number of persons working or employed in the Soviet Union in 1926 and in 1938, and examines the trends in the percentage utilization of the labor force which the measures reveal. The question of unemployment is also discussed.

According to a survey of peasant households for the year 1924-1925 (March-February), the average number of persons working per day during the year, calculated from primary data on days of labor, was equal to 55.3 per cent of the total labor supply of individual peasants and wage and salary workers (in agriculture).[60] Working time is exclusive of housework, but includes in addition to agriculture, nonagricultural pursuits within the rural economy. These are supplementary to agriculture, for the most part, such as handicrafts, but also include work for hire. The average number of persons working in agriculture alone was equal to 34.8 per cent of the total.

If we apply the average percentages by sex calculated from the survey to the labor force principally in agriculture according to the 1926 census (Table 1),[61] and add the number of wage and salary workers and self-employed and family workers principally occupied in nonagricultural employment, as well as the military—on the assumption that persons in nonagricultural employment were by and large "working" or "employed" throughout the year—the result is an estimate of the average number of persons working or employed during 1926 of 50.4 million, equal to 59.7 per cent of the total labor force.

The Soviet government has tried to increase the percentage utilization of the total labor supply, in addition to increasing the supply as a percentage of the population, through the movement of labor from agriculture to industry, and through the reduction of seasonal variation in agricultural labor requirements (by mechanization and improved organization). In the process much of the labor force has been

[60] L. E. Mints, *Agrarnoe perenaselenie i rynok truda SSSR*, Moscow-Leningrad, 1929, pp. 22-31.

[61] This method of applying percentages from the survey to the number of persons from the census may be supported as follows: About 63 per cent of total time worked according to the survey (34.8/55.3) was in agriculture proper; however, almost 93 per cent of the rural population according to the census received their principal source of livelihood from agriculture. In other words, activities supplementary to agriculture and those strictly nonagricultural performed by members of the peasant household, although occupying a substantial portion of total time worked, constituted by and large a secondary source of livelihood. It is for this reason that the percentage of total labor going to agriculture from the total labor supply according to the survey may be used to estimate the number of persons "working" among the labor force having a *principal* occupation in agriculture according to the census.

"socialized," as seen in the increase in the number of wage and salary workers (of state enterprises), the collectivization of agriculture, and the widening of the producer cooperative network; while the number of persons occupied solely in private economic activity has declined. The homestead garden plot of collective farmers, tolerated by the government to avoid further repercussions over collectivization, has always been considered by the government as subordinate to the work of the collective farm, although it still attracts a large proportion of the collective farmer's time; and it was Stalin's view that the homestead plot would ultimately be eliminated in favor of "communalizing" all of agriculture.[62]

A measure of the average number of persons working or employed within the reported groups in the late 1930's would include the following: (1) the average number employed in the reported socialized sectors, defined as the number earning wages and salaries, labor-days (collective farmers), *zarabotki* (cooperative handicraftsmen) or military stipends; and (2) the average number working in the reported private sectors, i.e. on the homestead farm and the private farm and as private handicraftsmen. A measure of this type for 1938 is constructed as follows:

Socialized Sectors. The average number of persons earning labor-days is estimated on the basis of data from a special survey of a small number of collective farms, converted into all-U.S.S.R. equivalents (see Appendix Table D-2). The result is then aggregated directly with employment data from other reported socialized sectors—i.e. the number of wage and salary workers, which is reported as a yearly average (from periodic enterprise payroll data); the number of persons *hired* by collective farms during July and August, which may be converted into a yearly average; and the number of cooperative handicraftsmen and the military, who are assumed "employed" throughout the year.

Private Sectors. The average number of persons working on the homestead farms is estimated from survey data giving the distribution of the labor time of members of collective farm households.[63] The average number working on private farms and as private handicraftsmen is assumed the same percentage of the labor force (by sex) as in 1926.

The resulting aggregate average number of persons employed (in socialized sectors) or working (in private sectors) for 1938 is 60.9

[62] J. V. Stalin, "Economic Problems of Socialism in the U.S.S.R.," *Bol'shevik*, No. 18, 1952, translated in *The Current Digest of the Soviet Press*, April 18, 1952.

[63] *Proizvoditel'nost' i ispol'zovanie truda v kolkhozakh vo vtoroi piatiletke*, Moscow and Leningrad, TsUNKhU, 1939, pp. 67-68; and I. Merinov, "Trudovye resursy kolkhozov i ikh ispol'zovanie," *Sotsialisticheskoe sel'skoe khoziaistvo*, No. 3, 1941, pp. 17-19.

million or 72.3 per cent of the reported labor force (see Table 4). In 1926, the average number of persons working or employed in all sectors was equal to 59.7 per cent of the total labor force.

The reason for the higher rate of participation in 1938 is, first, the larger proportion of wage and salary workers, which was 8 per cent

TABLE 4

The Labor Force and the Average Number Working or Employed, by Principal Occupation, U.S.S.R., end of 1938

(number in thousands)

PRINCIPAL OCCUPATION	BOTH SEXES		MALE		FEMALE	
	Number	*Per Cent of Total*	*Number*	*Per Cent of Total*	*Number*	*Per Cent of Total*
			Labor Force			
Wage and salary workers	27,983	33.2	17,283	37.5	10,700	28.1
Collective farmers	32,893	39.1	17,089	37.1	15,894	41.7
Collective farm hired laborers	2,228	2.6	1,524	3.3	704	1.8
Co-op handicraftsmen	1,650	2.0	1,229	2.7	421	1.1
Military	1,550	1.9	1,550	3.3	0	
Socialized sectors	66,394	78.8	38,675	83.9	27,719	72.7
Homestead farmers (collective farm)	13,429	15.9	5,087	11.0	8,342	21.9
Private farmers	3,863	4.6	1,935	4.2	1,928	5.1
Private handicraftsmen	569	0.7	424	0.9	145	0.3
Private sectors	17,861	21.2	7,446	16.1	10,415	27.3
Total	84,255	100.0	46,121	100.0	38,134	100.0
			Average Number Working or Employed			
Wage and salary workers	27,800	45.6	17,500	49.0	10,300	40.8
Collective farmers	19,087	31.3	11,482	32.2	7,605	30.1
Collective farm hired laborers	371	0.6	254	0.7	117	0.5
Co-op handicraftsmen	1,650	2.7	1,229	3.4	421	1.7
Military	1,550	2.6	1,550	4.3	0	0
Socialized sectors	50,458	82.8	32,015	89.7	18,443	73.1
Homestead farmers (collective farm)	7,808	12.8	1,961	5.5	5,847	23.2
Private farmers	2,090	3.4	1,300	3.6	790	3.1
Private handicraftsmen	569	1.0	424	1.2	145	0.6
Private sectors	10,467	17.2	3,685	10.3	6,782	26.9
Total	60,925	100.0	35,700	100.0	25,225	100.0
			Average Number Working or Employed as a Percentage of the Labor Force, 1926 and 1938			
1926		59.7		72.4		45.0
1938		72.3		77.4		66.1

Source: Appendix C.

of the total labor force in 1926 and 33 per cent of the reported labor force in 1938. Most of this increase took place in nonagricultural employment, largely by drawing labor from agricultural sectors where the average rate of participation was relatively low.

Second, the rate of participation in collective and homestead farm agriculture in 1938 was higher than in private agriculture (and the related rural economy) in 1926. The average number of persons sixteen years of age and over earning labor-days or working on the homestead farm in 1938 was 69 per cent of the total labor force sixteen and over from collective farm households; while in 1926, the average number of persons working from peasant households was 55 per cent of the total. The combined demands of collective and homestead farm agriculture seem to have attracted a higher percentage of work time in 1938 than the demands of private agriculture in 1926. However, the average number employed on the collective farm alone was equal to only 48 per cent of the total.

The indicated increase in the number of wage and salary workers and the higher rate of participation in agriculture was relatively greater among females. That is, while the average number of males working or employed in all reported sectors rose slightly, from 72 per cent of the labor force in 1926 to 77 per cent of the reported labor force in 1938, the average number of females rose from 45 to 66 per cent.

In collective and homestead farming, a relatively greater share of the labor time of males went to the collective farm proper, and of females to the homestead farm. According to the survey data on which the estimates in Table 4 are based, adult females spent about 25 per cent of their available time on the homestead farm, compared to about 7 per cent for males. This relationship appears in Table 4 as an estimated average of 5.8 million females working on the homestead farm compared to 2.0 million males.

On the other hand, males spent about 75 per cent of their time earning labor-days and females about 35 per cent. This relationship appears in Table 4 as an estimated average of 11.5 million males earning labor-days compared to 7.6 million females. However, the number of males principally occupied on the collective farm, i.e. earning more than fifty labor-days during the year, was only slightly higher than the number of females—17.1 million compared to 15.9 million; while the number of males earning one or more labor-days was less than the number of females—20.3 million compared to 21.6 million.[64] In other words, males were in the minority among the total number of persons

[64] Eason, "The Agricultural Labor Force and Population of the U.S.S.R., 1926-1941," p. 84.

earning one or more labor-days but, because of a higher rate of participation, contributed about 50 per cent more in total labor time to the collective farm.[65]

The major portion of time (in days) not spent on the collective farm or homestead farm, for males, was spent working for hire outside of the collective farm, such that only about 5 per cent of available time remained "nonutilized," according to the survey. Females, on the other hand, spent less time working for hire, and as a result about 30 per cent of available time was "nonutilized."

The major portion of the "nonutilized" labor time of females was probably taken up with the activities of the household. In any event, for both males and females, "nonutilized" time would seem to be spent neither working (outside the household) nor, in all probability, seeking work.[66]

The over-all increase in the percentage utilization of the labor force, as pointed out, is traceable in part to the relative increase in the socialized sectors. Nevertheless, the socialized sectors in Table 4 are considerably smaller, and the private sectors considerably larger, as a percentage of the total, than the Soviet government would have us believe is the case. For example, according to the classification of the population by "social groups" in the 1939 census, only 3.4 per cent of the population was listed in private sectors or other marginal groups, while in Table 4, 21.2 per cent of the reported labor force by principal occupation, and 17.2 per cent of the average number working or employed, were in the private sector. The percentages in Table 4 are higher because homestead farming is listed as private economic activity. The census treated it as "subsidiary agriculture" and classified such persons either as collective farmers or, if the case warranted, as wage and salary workers. In addition, the number of private farmers is minimized by the census, since only those with no occupation other than private agriculture were included, while in Table 4 this category is based on the reported number of individual peasant households.[67]

[65] The same relationships hold on a month-by-month basis, as may be seen by comparing Appendix Table D-1 with Table D-2. More females earned one or more labor-days per month in the summer months, and more males in the winter (D-1); but the average number of males earning labor-days per day by months was higher every month of the year (D-2).

[66] It is customary for collective farmers seeking work for hire and unable to find it in the vicinity of the farm, to leave the household temporarily and to live away (to be in *otkhod*) while working (or seeking work). Since absence from the collective farm is reckoned as "utilized" time in the survey, it may be concluded that persons living on the collective farm and not working (on the collective or homestead farm or for hire) would also not be seeking work.

[67] The difference between the reported labor force and the hypothetical labor force (11 million), when "distributed" between socialized and private sectors,

The question of "explicit" unemployment (as distinct from "hidden" unemployment) in the Soviet Union centers on the seasonal and frictional varieties. Incidentally, a former employee of a Soviet census bureau currently writing as a refugee in Europe, insists on the existence of temporary unemployment in the Soviet Union and refers to provisions which were taken in the 1937 census to register it.[68]

Seasonal labor outside of agriculture is supplied primarily by persons from collective farm households. Other sources, including private farm and other rural households, can not be insignificant, however, because in 1939 about 25 per cent of the rural population was noncollective farm.[69]

In 1938, 4 million males and 1.5 million females from collective farm households worked for hire (outside the collective farm) at one or another time during the year, although not all of this work was for seasonal industries. Nevertheless, the variety of seasonal industries (e.g. forestry in the winter, construction in the summer) means that a substantial fraction of aggregate labor working outside the collective farm was so engaged throughout the year.

Seasonal labor is included in the manpower balance referred to in the introduction to this paper. In order to link the labor supply (by areas) with seasonal labor requirements, furthermore, collective farmers were required to contract for work for hire through the collective farm manager. Absence from the collective farm without the manager's permission was declared illegal. Nevertheless, in spite of these regulations, by the late 1930's a major share of labor outside the collective farms was contracted for on an individual basis, beyond direct or indirect controls.[70]

A certain amount of temporary unemployment would therefore seem to be inevitable in the market for seasonal labor, with such a large portion of the market outside effective controls. Unfortunately, the data do not permit us even to estimate the number of people involved at a given time.

The evidence of frictional unemployment during the 1930's centers on the relatively high rate of labor turnover, as seen in the following

---

could affect the over-all distribution. However, the percentage in private sectors would still be significantly larger than that shown by the census, for the reasons given.

[68] P. Galin, *Kak proizvodilis' perepisi naseleniia v SSSR*, Munich, 1951, p. 18.

[69] Eason, "The Agricultural Labor Force and Population of the U.S.S.R., 1926-1941," p. 105.

[70] N. Aristov, "Organizovannyi nabor rabochei sily," *Planovoe khoziaistvo*, No. 11, 1939, pp. 93ff.

data for production workers in large-scale industry (turnover as a percentage of the yearly average number of production workers):

Year	*Entries*	*Departures*
1928	100.8	92.4
1929	122.4	115.2
1930	176.4	152.4
1931	151.2	136.8
1932	127.1	135.3
1933	124.9	122.4
1934	100.5	96.7
1935	91.6	86.1
1938	66.0	68.4
1939	84.0	96.0

Source: 1928-1935, from *Sotsialistieheskoe stroitel'stvo SSSR, 1936*, Moscow, TsUNKhU, 1936, p. 531; 1936-1937, not available; 1938-1939, derived from monthly data for 1938 and the first half of 1939, in S. Trubnikov, "Istochniki komplektovaniia rabochei sily v SSSR," *Problemy ekonomiki*, No. 6, 1939, p. 138.

Considering that the average number of production workers in large-scale industry at the end of the 1930's was more than 9 million, labor turnover represents an equivalent of about 8 million persons. Of course, labor turnover does not necessarily connote frictional unemployment. But if each instance of turnover were to involve on the average one month off the payrolls (and looking for work), it would be equivalent to an average of more than 600,000 persons frictionally unemployed with respect to large-scale industry at all times. This number is more than 2 per cent of the total of wage and salary workers (28 million).

Efforts to curb labor turnover and to channel and retain graduates where they were needed in industry were stepped up markedly in the late 1930's,[71] but the effect on labor turnover cannot be learned from available information.

This paper has dealt almost exclusively with the period of the 1930's, because postwar data are inadequate for the type of analysis presented. Nevertheless, the transformation of Soviet society under the impact of the Plans, as seen in the collectivization of agriculture and the expansion of state and other cooperative enterprises, had progressed sufficiently far by the end of the 1930's, that many of the impressions conveyed by the discussion would hold for the more recent period.

However, just before the war, several developments took place which may have had a significant effect on the utilization of labor: (1) the requirement of an obligatory minimum number of labor-days

[71] Schwarz, *op.cit.*, Chap. III.

on the collective farm and (2) the measures prohibiting wage and salary workers from quitting work without permission.

Starting in 1939, collective farmers were ordered to work a minimum number of labor-days or face possible expulsion from the collective farm.[72] This may have raised the rate of participation in collective farm work, but whether it has been at the expense of other activities (homestead farm or work for hire) or has led to a further increase in the over-all rate of participation in all types of economic activity is impossible to say.

In 1940, it was decreed that wage and salary workers could not quit a job (sickness and retirement excepted) or take a new one without the permission of plant management.[73] The decree was designed to strengthen labor discipline and reduce labor turnover.

It is unfortunate that we cannot measure the effectiveness of either decree, but the results of postwar collective farm budget surveys such as for the prewar used in this paper, have not been released, and there are no data on labor turnover. The decrees are directed at increasing and stabilizing the rate of participation of the labor force. The dearth of information about their results leaves an important gap in our understanding of trends in the utilization of labor in the Soviet Union.

[72] *Postanovlenie TsK VKP(b) i SNK SSSR*, May 27, 1939.
[73] Portions of the decree are reproduced in Schwarz, *op.cit.*, pp. 106-107.

Appendix A

TABLE A-1

Calculation of Hypothetical Labor Force, U.S.S.R., January 17, 1939
(*number in thousands*)

	AGE 12-15			AGE 16-59			AGE 60 AND OVER			AGE 12 AND OVER
	Total	*Rural*	*Urban*	*Total*	*Rural*	*Urban*	*Total*	*Rural*	*Urban*	*Total*
Both sexes:										
Labor force	10,848	10,486	362	77,762	51,275	26,487	5,409	4,396	1,013	94,019
Male:										
Population	8,519	6,800	1,719	45,268	26,487	18,781	4,369	3,064	1,305	
Hypothetical labor force percentage	65.2	78.9	11.2	97.7	98.2	97.1	71.7	77.5	57.9	
Labor force	5,558	5,365	193	44,249	26,010	18,239	3,131	2,375	756	52,938
Female:										
Population	8,455	6,729	1,726	50,169	29,550	20,619	6,847	4,594	2,253	
Hypothetical labor force percentage	62.6	76.1	9.8	66.8	85.5	40.0	33.3	44.0	11.4	
Labor force	5,290	5,121	169	33,513	25,265	8,248	2,278	2,021	257	41,081

Source: Population data are from the 1939 census, as adjusted by Warren W. Eason, "Population and Labor Force," in *Soviet Economic Growth: Conditions and Perspectives*, Abram Bergson, editor, Row, Peterson, 1953, Appendix B, pp. 25 and 34. Labor force percentages by age, sex, and rural-urban distribution are taken directly from the 1926 census, as in Table 2, except for the following: (1) age 12-15, which is estimated from 1926 census data reported by age groups 10-14 and 15; (2) urban females age 16-59, which is hypothetical on grounds discussed in footnote 33; and (3) urban males age 16-59, estimated by means of a calculation of the absolute number excluded from the labor force as physically and mentally incapable of work. For details on the latter, see *ibid.*, Appendix A, pp. 2-3.

Appendix B:
Sources of and Commentary to Table 3

The data in Table 3 are from Soviet sources and by estimation, as summarized below. Sources report the yearly average number of wage and salary workers for most of the 1930's, as well as selected quarterly figures. In estimating the number for certain dates, an equation is used which sets the reported yearly average for a given year (calculated by Soviet statisticians from daily or monthly payroll data) equal to the average of the number on January 1 of the given year and the following year, April 1, October 1, and twice the number on July 1. The assumption is that the average of the quarterly figures is approximately equal to the reported yearly average, which can be shown to be the case in agriculture, where the data are adequate (Warren W. Eason, "The Agricultural Labor Force and Population of the U.S.S.R.," Appendix C, p. 135), although it cannot be shown for the total because a complete set of data is not available for any one year. Since the yearly average and quarterly number are reported separately in Soviet sources, the question must be raised as to whether the data are comparable to each other; as to whether, for example, the yearly average number of wage and salary workers for a given year covers the same enterprises and institutions as the number for January 1. Unfortunately, except for the data for April 1, 1934-1936, the sum of sector data, where given, falls short of the reported total by at least a few hundred thousand, even when the two appear in the same source. However, a reasonably careful, although preliminary, sector-by-sector comparison of the data grouping the seasonal and nonseasonal sectors separately, too detailed to be presented here, indicates that differences are a function of seasonal and secular movements, and cannot (at least to any measurable degree) be attributed to varying degrees of comprehensiveness.

Sources and derivations of the data may be listed by the columns of Table 3:

Total

Yearly average. Both sexes: 1928-1935, *Trud v SSSR, statisticheskii spravochnik*, Moscow, TsUNKhU, 1936, p. 10; 1936, Ia. Joffe, *SSSR i kapitalisticheskie strany*, Moscow, 1939, p. 90; 1937, *Bol'shaia sovetskaia entsiklopediia*, Moscow, 1947, col. 68; 1938, preliminary figure, *Sotsialisticheskoe stroitel'stvo SSSR, 1933-1938*, Moscow and Leningrad, TsUNKhU, 1939, p. 20. Males: derived from the equation relating yearly average to quarterly data (above). Females: both sexes minus males.

January 1. Both sexes: 1931-1937, E. Orlikova, "Zhenskii trud v SSSR," *Planovoe khoziaistvo*, 1939, No. 10, p. 113; 1938, assumed 1.016 of April 1 (relationship from corresponding dates for 1937) and derived simultaneously with it, by means of equation relating yearly average to quarterly data (above); 1939, *Gornyi zhurnal*, 1940, No. 3, p. 4. Males: 1931-1937 and 1939, same sources as both sexes; 1938, on basis of percentage of females interpolated between January 1, 1937 and 1939. Females: both sexes minus males.

April 1. Both sexes: 1932 and 1933, assumed .95 of the respective January 1 figure (relationship taken from data for 1934); 1934, derived from the monthly average for March, 1934 (21,704,000), as given in TsUNKhU, *Trud v SSSR, 1934, ezhegodnik*, Moscow, 1935, p. 42, by assuming the same percentage differential with respect to the March average (.995) as given for 1935 and 1936; 1935, *Trud v SSSR . . .* (1936), p. 31; 1936, *Chislennost' i zarabotnaia plata rabochikh i sluzhashchikh v SSSR*, Moscow, TsUNKhU, 1936, p. 13; 1937, derived from Trade Union data in *Handbook on the Soviet Trade Unions*, A. Lozovsky, editor, Moscow, Cooperative Publication Society of Foreign Workers in the U.S.S.R., 1937, p. 19 (see comment below on utilization of Trade Union data); 1938 and 1939, assumed .984 (1/1.016) of respective January 1 figure (relationship taken from data for 1937), and in case of April 1, 1938, derived simultaneously with January 1, 1938 (see January 1, above). Males and females: derived below.

July 1. Both sexes: 1932-1935 and 1937, derived from equation relating yearly average to quarterly data (above); 1936, assumed 1.056 of January 1 (relationship taken from 1937); 1938 and 1939, derived from following type of Trade Union information in VTsSPS, *Statisticheskii spravochnik*, Moscow, 1939, Vypusk III, pp. 4-13:

	July 1, 1939
Total number of wage and salary workers	28,581,600
Members of unions, among wage and salary workers	22,828,800
Total members of unions, including students	24,338,200
Per cent of members of unions among wage and salary workers	82.7%

It is seen that the indicated per cent does not follow from any of the absolute figures, i.e., wage and salary workers who are members of Unions (22,828,800) is 79.9 per cent of the total number of wage and salary workers (28,581,600); and total Union members including students (24,338,200) is 85.2 per cent of the total number of wage and salary workers.

The explanation apparently lies in a footnote to the original table, concerning the comprehensiveness of the data, which states that the total number of wage and salary workers is from VTsSPS (All-Union Central Council of Trade Unions), the compiler of the book in which the figures appear, and that it is less than the number for the corresponding date in the TsUNKhU series, by 700,000-800,000. Since all other possibilities can be ruled out as inconsistent with one or another aspect of the given data, the given percentage must relate the total union membership to the number of wage and salary workers according to TsUNKhU. The latter is therefore derived as 29,427,000 (24,338,200 ÷ .827), or 845,000 greater than the total given by VTsSPS.

A similar calculation for July 1, 1938, using similar data in the same source, yields 28,175,000 as the TsUNKhU figure, which is 665,000 greater than the total according to VTsSPS (27,510,000).

Males and females (July 1): derived below.

October 1. Both sexes: 1931-1935, derived from Trade Union data in *Trud v SSSR* . . . (1936), p. 56, in the manner described above (July 1); 1936, derived from the equation relating yearly average to quarterly data (above); 1937 and 1938, assumed equal to the number on subsequent January 1, from an inspection of corresponding data for 1935 and 1936. Males and females: derived below.

Agriculture

All data under these columns are from Eason, "The Agricultural Labor Force and Population of the U.S.S.R., 1926-1941," Appendix C.

Nonagriculture

All data in these columns are obtained by subtracting the number in agriculture from the total.

Males and Females

Except as indicated for particular cases above, the data in these columns are derived as follows:

The total number of wage and salary workers by sex is available, after 1930, only for January 1, 1931-1937 and 1939 (and in addition, for several years after 1939). The yearly average number of female wage and salary workers is not given after 1930, nor is the number for dates other than January 1. However, the distribution of the sexes *by certain sectors* of the wage and salary group is available with varying frequency for dates other than January 1 (but even in these cases, not the yearly average). Sufficient of the sector data are available for July 1, 1935, to construct an estimate of the number of male and female wage and salary workers for that date. The calculations are too detailed to be summarized here, but the result is 16,768,000 males and 9,069,000 females, with females 35.1 per cent of both sexes. The latter percentage is greater than for January 1, 1935 (33.4) or January 1, 1936 (34.0), showing, in other words, a seasonal increase in the per cent of females for 1935. A straight-line increase between the two January 1 percentages would give 33.7 per cent for July 1, 1935. The estimated per cent (35.1) is thus 1.04 times the straight-line per cent based on January 1 data.

With the per cent of females given for January 1, each year after 1930, the per cent of females for July 1 of years other than 1935 is estimated arbitrarily therefrom, as follows: (1) The per cent for July 1, 1931-1934, inclusive, is assumed to be 1.04 times the calculated straight-line increase between consecutive January 1 figures. (2) The per cent for July 1, 1936-1939, inclusive, is assumed to be 1.02 times the calculated straight-line increase between consecutive January 1 figures, a factor (1.02) which is less than that for 1935 (1.04), by an arbitrary degree, in order to reflect the fact that the absolute seasonal increase in the number of wage and salary workers in agriculture (a major share of the seasonal sector in the wage and salary worker series) dropped sharply between 1935 and 1936, signifying a secular decline.

The per cent of females on October 1 and April 1 is assumed the same as given for the nearest January 1.

Given the number for both sexes the number of males and females for the first of each quarter is derived from the percentages just discussed.

Appendix C: *Sources and Commentary to Table 4*

Table 4 presents the results of aggregating the reported labor force data according to (1) an estimated distribution by principal occupation and (2) an estimate of the average number working or unemployed in each sector. The steps used in the aggregation may be summarized by the rows of Table 4:

Labor Force by Principal Occupation

Wage and Salary Workers. Number on January 1, 1939 (Table 3) minus (1) an estimate of those included whose principal occupation is collective farmer, plus (2) an estimate of those not included whose principal occupation is wage and salary worker. (1) and (2) are estimated from the number of collective farmers also working for hire. The assumption is that, on the average, one-quarter of those principally in collective and homestead farm agriculture (4,249,000) were working for hire at any given time during the year (1,062,000), and under (1) are subtracted from the number of wage and salary workers; and that one-quarter of those principally working for hire (1,743,000) were not actually doing so at any given time during the year (435,000), and under (2) are added to the number of wage and salary workers. The evidence is that the share of time working for hire is roughly the same throughout the year (*Proizvoditel'nost'* . . . , pp. 67-68; and I. Merinov, "Trudovye resursy kolkhozov i ikh ispol'zovanie," *Sotsialisticheskoe sel'skoe khoziaistvo*, No. 3, 1941, pp. 17-19), although the assumed proportion (one quarter/three quarters) is arbitrary, to conform to the notion of a "principal" occupation, i.e., that which brings in from one-half to total income.

Collective Farmers. Number earning fifty-one or more labor-days during the year (Eason, "The Agricultural Labor Force and Population of the U.S.S.R., 1926-1941," p. 84).

Collective Farm Hired Laborers. Number working in July and August, on the assumption that they had no other source of income (*ibid.*, pp. 198-200).

Cooperative Handicraftsmen and Military. Estimated from Soviet sources (Eason, "Population and Labor Force," Appendix A, p. 2).

Homestead Farmers (Collective Farm). Those with a principal occupation in collective *and* homestead agriculture but earning less than fifty-one labor-days (Eason, "The Agricultural Labor Force and Population of the U.S.S.R., 1926-1941," p. 84).

Private Farmers. Estimated from the reported number of individual peasant households (*ibid.*, pp. 201-203).

Private Handicraftsmen. Estimated from the population by "social groups" in the 1939 census (Eason, "Population and Labor Force," Appendix A, p. 2).

Average Number Working or Employed

Wage and Salary Workers. Yearly average number for 1938 (Table 3).

Collective Farmers. Average number earning labor-days per day (Appendix Table D-2).

Collective Farm Hired Laborers. Annual average equivalent of the number working in July and August.

Cooperative Handicraftsmen and Military. Same as the labor force.

Homestead Farmers (Collective Farm). Estimated as 5.7 per cent of total males sixteen and over from collective farm households (18,946,000) and 24.1 per cent of total females (20,713,000). (Percentage data from *Proizvoditel'nost'* . . . , *op. cit.*, pp. 67-68; absolute numbers from Eason, "The Agricultural Labor Force and Population of the U.S.S.R., 1926-1941," p. 25). Average number working age twelve to fifteen is assumed same percentage (19.7) of total number from collective farm households (8,946,000) as in private agriculture according to the survey of 1924-1925 (Mints, *op.cit.*, pp. 22-31).

Private Farmers. Assumed same percentage of the labor force as in 1926.

Private Handicraftsmen. Same as the labor force.

Appendix D

TABLE D-1

Collective Farmers Earning Labor-Days to Any Extent During Each Month and During Year, by Sex, U.S.S.R., 1938

	AGE 12-15			AGE 16 AND OVER			AGE 12 AND OVER		
ONTH	*Both Sexes*	*Male*	*Female*	*Both Sexes*	*Male*	*Female*	*Both Sexes*	*Male*	*Female*
				Number in Thousands					
nuary	861	448	413	15,410	10,068	5,342	16,271	10,516	5,755
bruary	887	461	426	16,275	10,437	5,838	17,162	10,898	6,264
arch	1,141	593	548	19,374	11,667	7,707	20,515	12,260	8,255
ril	1,556	809	747	23,466	12,897	10,569	25,022	13,706	11,316
ay	2,464	1,281	1,183	27,430	13,618	13,812	29,894	14,899	14,995
ne	3,761	1,956	1,805	29,187	14,250	14,937	32,948	16,206	16,742
ly	4,223	2,196	2,027	30,862	15,181	15,681	35,085	17,377	17,708
gust	3,839	1,996	1,843	30,020	15,006	15,014	33,859	17,002	16,857
ptember	2,661	1,384	1,277	28,025	14,022	14,003	30,686	15,406	15,280
tober	2,433	1,265	1,168	26,851	13,459	13,392	29,284	14,724	14,560
vember	1,940	1,009	931	22,848	11,860	10,988	24,788	12,869	11,919
cember	1,427	742	685	19,895	11,368	8,527	21,322	12,110	9,212
arly av.	2,226	1,178	1,088	24,137	12,819	11,318	26,403	13,997	12,406
Total	5,188	2,698	2,490	36,648	17,571	19,077	41,836	20,269	21,567
				Percentage Distribution of Sexes[a]					
nuary				100	65.3	34.7	100	64.6	35.4
bruary				100	64.1	35.9	100	63.5	36.5
arch				100	60.2	39.8	100	59.8	40.2
ril				100	54.9	45.1	100	54.8	45.2
ay				100	49.6	50.4	100	49.8	50.2
ne				100	48.8	51.2	100	49.2	50.8
ly				100	49.2	50.8	100	49.5	50.5
gust				100	50.0	50.0	100	50.2	49.8
ptember				100	50.0	50.0	100	50.2	49.8
ctober				100	50.1	49.9	100	50.3	49.7
ovember				100	51.9	48.1	100	51.9	48.1
ecember				100	57.1	42.9	100	56.8	43.2
arly av.				100	53.1	46.9	100	53.0	47.0
Total	100	52.0	48.0	100	47.9	52.1	100	48.4	51.6

[a] Percentage distribution for persons age 12-15 by months and for yearly average assumed e same as for total.

Source: Figures other than total derived from data in a survey of a small number of collective rms, in *Proizvoditel'nost'* . . . , Moscow and Leningrad, TsUNKhU, 1939, pp. 77-126. The rvey gives the number of persons per on-hand household earning labor-days to any extent ch month of the year, as well as for the year as a whole. Monthly data as a percentage of nual are then multiplied by the total, above, for all collective farms to derive monthly data this table.

TABLE D-2

Collective Farmers Earning Labor-Days per Day during Each Month and during Year, by Sex, U.S.S.R., 1938

MONTH	AGE 12-15			AGE 16 AND OVER			AGE 12 AND OVER		
	Both Sexes	*Male*	*Female*	*Both Sexes*	*Male*	*Female*	*Both Sexes*	*Male*	*Fem*
				Number in Thousands					
January	231	120	111	10,661	7,860	2,801	10,892	7,980	2,9
February	232	121	111	10,609	7,729	2,880	10,841	7,850	2,9
March	288	150	138	13,085	9,312	3,773	13,373	9,462	3,9
April	391	203	188	16,854	11,232	5,622	17,245	11,435	5,8
May	563	293	270	21,324	12,082	9,242	21,887	12,375	9,5
June	853	443	410	23,135	12,588	10,547	23,988	13,031	10,9
July	948	493	455	27,508	14,864	12,644	28,456	15,357	13,0
August	856	445	411	25,452	14,210	11,242	26,308	14,655	11,5
September	645	335	310	22,831	12,823	10,008	23,476	13,158	10,3
October	574	299	275	20,870	11,952	8,918	21,444	12,251	9,1
November	416	216	200	15,397	9,753	5,644	15,813	9,969	5,8
December	334	172	162	13,842	9,492	4,350	14,176	9,664	4,5
Yearly av.	623	324	299	18,464	11,158	7,306	19,087	11,482	7,6
				Percentage Distribution of Sexes[a]					
January				100	73.7	26.3	100	73.3	26
February				100	72.9	27.1	100	72.4	27
March				100	71.2	28.8	100	70.8	29
April				100	66.6	33.4	100	66.3	33
May				100	56.7	43.3	100	56.5	43
June				100	54.4	45.6	100	54.3	45
July				100	54.0	46.0	100	54.0	46
August				100	55.8	44.2	100	55.7	44
September				100	56.2	43.8	100	56.0	44
October				100	57.3	42.7	100	57.1	42
November				100	63.3	36.7	100	63.0	37
December				100	68.6	31.4	100	68.2	31
Yearly av.	100	52.0	48.0	100	60.4	39.6	100	60.1	39

[a] Percentage distribution for persons age 12-15 by months and for yearly average assum the same as for total in Table D-1.

Source: Data in this table are derived from survey of a small number of collective far in *Proizvoditel'nost'* . . . , Moscow and Leningrad, TsUNKhU, 1939, pp. 77-126. The surv gives the number of days worked per on-hand household each month and total for year, as w as total number of persons working any days. Percentage relationships between the three typ of data are then converted to all-U.S.S.R. equivalents, given the total number of persons worki one or more labor-days from all collective farms (Appendix Table D-1).

COMMENT

EUGENE M. KULISCHER, Library of Congress

On the eve of World War II, the Soviet government was continuing its efforts to include in the ranks of the workers and employees (wage and salary earners) as many housewives as possible, but at the same time the Soviet authorities were the first to acknowledge that there was a surplus of 5 million unused people in the agricultural labor force. We will gain a better understanding of this paradox if we approach it as incidental to the industrial revolution that has taken place in Russia since the end of the nineteenth century.

Russia's rapidly progressing industrialization was interrupted when the Communists seized power. With the introduction of the Five-Year Plans, industrialization was vigorously resumed in a new form—ruthless state capitalism covered by Socialist verbiage about the interests of the working class. With regard to employment, the industrial revolution pursued two intrinsically connected goals: to provide manpower for industrial development and to liquidate agrarian overpopulation—a form of hidden unemployment. Hidden unemployment due to agrarian overpopulation in Russia dates back to the time before the liberation of the serfs. In 1923-1926, i.e. in a period when industrialization had regressed compared with the World War I situation, estimates of excess persons in agriculture (based mainly on a comprehensive inquiry of the Research Institute for Colonization) went as high as 10 to 20 million. In the early 1930's, hastened industrialization and compulsory collectivization seemed to have put an end to agrarian overpopulation.

Soon it appeared, however, that the same processes of industrialization and collectivization that earlier had helped to absorb excess persons in agriculture were now beginning to produce new rural labor surpluses. For as mechanization of agriculture progressed (the only positive aspect of collectivization), manpower requirements were reduced, and such reductions built up a group of superfluous *kolkhozians*. In spite of millions absorbed by industry and additional millions who had perished from famine, there was in the *kolkhozes* (according to an official estimate of 1940) a surplus labor force of 5 million. Communist terror against well-to-do peasants and famine (resulting from enforced collectivization), drove millions of peasants to urban centers, where they found employment in industries which developed rapidly with the help of capital investment squeezed out of the rural economy.

I quote from an article of Sonin, a leading Soviet planner (*Problemy Economiki*, 1940):

Editor's Note: Members of the Conference deeply regret Mr. Kulischer's death on April 2, 1956.

"Owing to industrialization and socialist reconstruction of agriculture, unemployment and agrarian overpopulation were definitely liquidated as early as in 1930. In consequence of a high degree of mechanization and rapid increase of labor prductivity in socialist agriculture, there is in the kolkhozes a surplus labor force (due to its better utilization) that can shift to employment in industry and construction or move from regions with not enough arable land to those having much land. The number of such kolkhozians runs for the whole Soviet Union to about 5 million."

The mass of rural people who streamed to the new industrial centers in search of employment were unskilled workers, and they could be utilized since there also was an influx of skilled workers from the old Russian industrial areas. As a Frenchman would say, "Avec un cadre de travailleurs qualifiés on peut encadrer de nombres beaucoup plus grands de la manoeuvre non-qualifiée." But when, in certain cases, the flow of skilled workers ceased, there was no work for the rough rural inmigrants, at least for a time. So, such activities as roadbuilding were organized in the Urals to employ them during the very period of industrialization boom. In other words, there was structural unemployment which ultimately led to a sort of Works Progress Administration.

However, this was the industrial machine thrown temporarily out of gear. The broad effort to industrialize was continued and intensified. As an indication of the degree to which these efforts were pursued one needs only to consider the frantic efforts of the Soviet government to enlist a marginal group among the wage and salary earners—housewives, a part of whom formerly were semiemployed as helpers to their husbands, small shopkeepers and artisans. There was indeed a substantial increase of female workers and employees, promoted both by the necessity to contribute to the earnings of the husband, insufficient for the family budget, and by the expansion of child care facilities. To round out the perfect paradox, on the eve of the war, with 5 million superfluous agricultural hands, the enlistment of women among wage and salary earners had reached an all-time high and was still being vigorously pushed.

At present there is no more superfluous labor force in the *kolkhozes*; there is rather a deficiency of farm labor. How was the pre-World War II hidden unemployment liquidated?

Huge military and civilian casualties in the war with Germany reduced the manpower base mainly of the rural areas of the German-occupied territory, for evacuation of personnel and equipment was almost entirely from urban areas. In the postwar years, after a relatively short period of reconstruction, the cities picked up where they had left off. As before the war, the magnet of industrialization was strong enough to attract a sum of migrants equivalent to the entire natural increase of the rural population. In 1939 the adult agricultural labor force numbered 39 million collective and independent farmers (excluding *kolkhozians* who worked only on their own plots) and 4 million agricultural and related wage and salary earners; adding 7 million in the subsequently annexed territories, we obtain 50 million who before the war worked in agriculture on what was to be Soviet territory. In 1950 the corresponding total was about 46 million, almost all of the decrease having occurred in the male contingent.

The hidden unemployment in agriculture, formerly so large, has been liquidated not by peculiar planning magic but by changes of the two elements of the economico-demographical relation, both changes tending to the same result—an increase of available nonagricultural jobs and a physical decimation of people looking for jobs. However, there is hidden unemployment produced by another factor—not mechanization, but ineffective planning. Unlike the former, the latter is essentially a characteristic of urban economy.

Oxenfeldt and van den Haag have made a detailed study of various other factors that obstruct a full utilization of the available labor force in the Soviet Union, juxtaposing situations under planned and market economies that tend to favor unemployment. The authors observe that in Soviet economy nonutilization of resources appears mostly not as unemployment, but as low productivity (in essence our old friend hidden unemployment). Planned economy experiences a real depression if output goals are set so low as to leave available resources, goods, or workers unutilized. On the other hand, managers are eager to reduce the risk of underfulfilling their output goals; consequently, they tend to hoard raw materials and workers. The result is again labor productivity reduced through excess of workers (hidden unemployment).

Yet a convinced adherent of planned economy would not be silenced by such shortcomings. He would say that in all these cases unemployment is due to defects in planning. If honest, he would add that these defects show only that Russia is not ripe for planned economy. And I must admit, I think too, if—Heaven forbid—we had here in the United States a planned economy, several of the mistakes leading to hidden unemployment would be avoided.

The Soviet Union—as well as the capitalist world—has been unable to eliminate frictional unemployment originating from labor turnover. Certainly the Soviet worker is by far not as free to leave his work as the Western worker. Still, the stronger legal ties to the working place are combined with chronic dissatisfactions over working conditions and the human urge to find something better. As a matter of fact, turnover is probably even higher in the U.S.S.R. than in the free West.

There are many other such specific differences, but when it comes to the question of unemployment in its broadest sense, we must not forget the great *similarity* between the problems faced by the Soviet Union and the Western World. And in this connection, I think we have lost perspective. I do not believe that Adam Smith would have been as concerned as we have become with the differing results of the planned versus the monetary economy. We look condescendingly upon Adam Smith and other founders of political economy when they introduce a Robinson or a primitive fisherman in order to lay open the nucleus of an economic process. We have lost interest for the economic *Ding an Sich.* Since Keynes, monetary economy has become for us an organism where everything is explained by the functioning of the system. It is wholesome to be reminded from time to time that it is neither the monetary system nor Socialist planning, but production, distribution, and consumption that are by themselves as well as in their relation to population the basic components of the economico-demographic equation.

A. David Redding, Council on Foreign Relations

Warren W. Eason's paper provided much new information, especially on the labor force in Soviet agriculture. It is a careful, scholarly study of high quality, rich in empirical research. However, because the Soviet data were inaccurate and incomplete and were often withheld by Soviet authorities, Eason found it necessary to lean heavily on assumptions in making some estimates. He was careful to point this out in evaluating the difference between his estimates of the total and reported labor force in 1939—largely because of interest in the "residual" as a basis for estimating the extent of forced labor. I wondered, therefore, why he appeared to overlook the "explanation" of statistical deficiencies in other parts of his paper and, consequently, to make in one instance what seemed to me to be a less reasonable estimate than could have been made on the basis of the evidence he cited.

For example, it does not seem unreasonable, a priori, to suggest that Soviet statisticians may have overestimated the number of collective farmers in 1936. This possibility deserves at least explicit rejection by Eason, especially since other explanations were unsatisfactory to him.

More important, in rejecting a higher labor force–population ratio for urban females in 1939 (than in 1926), Eason did not consider the possibility of statistical deficiencies accounting for what he considered would be an unreasonable phenomenon: namely, "a substantial number of non-worker-and-employee females economically active in urban areas, principally in the non co-op handicrafts sector. . . ."* He assumed, in the absence of evidence, that the same percentage (72 per cent) of female nonagricultural workers and employees lived in urban areas in 1939 as in 1926. If, however, that percentage were raised to (say) 80 per cent, his estimate of 7.4 million female nonagricultural workers and employees would be raised to 8.2 million; and these workers would represent 92 (instead of 85) per cent of *his estimate* (itself subject to sizable error) of the urban female labor force in 1939—leaving only a small number to be accounted for as "female private artisans." A labor force–population ratio for urban females greater in 1939 than in 1926 thus would not be inconsistent with the evidence on employment cited by Eason; and, further, it seems indicated by other evidence cited by him on the greater participation of urban females in economic activities in the later year.

Use of a higher labor force–population ratio in computing the number of females in the urban labor force in 1939 would, it should be noted, result in a larger total labor force in that year and a larger discrepancy between the total and reported labor force. The extent of the increase in both magnitudes would depend, of course, on the adjustments made to the ratio in question.

I am aware of the need for "numbers" in this field where data have been notably inadequate. Eason's estimates are indeed a valuable contribution to our knowledge; and, therefore, I should like to express again my appreciation and admiration for the magnitude and high quality of his work. However, I feel I should also stress the sharp limitations to those estimates which are based (necessarily) on inadequate data. Awareness of the limitations is especially important to readers who might otherwise use the estimates as a basis for still further estimates or conclusions, which would in many instances be unwarranted by the underlying statistics.

* Editor's Note: The comment is as given originally; in his revised paper Eason uses a higher labor force–population ratio.

but of non-workers and employees (families economically active in urban areas, principally in the non-[illegible] regions. [illegible] assumed, in the absence of [illegible], that the same [illegible] of [illegible] workers and employees lived in urban areas [illegible] 1959 [illegible] 1959, [illegible] percent [illegible] female [illegible] workers and employees [illegible] 2 million, and [illegible] percent of the [illegible] (likely subject to [illegible]) of the urban [illegible] labor force in 1959 [illegible] only a small number [illegible] [illegible]. A labor force-population ratio for urban females greater in 1959 than in 1926 [illegible] [illegible] [illegible] [illegible] indicated by other [illegible] [illegible] [illegible] urban females in economic activities in the later [illegible].

[illegible] population [illegible] the number of females in the urban labor force in 1959 [illegible] [illegible] [illegible] [illegible] reported labor force. [illegible] of the increase in both [illegible] [illegible] and [illegible] make [illegible] the ratio in question.

[illegible] of the [illegible] in [illegible] where data have [illegible], [illegible] [illegible] available [illegible] of our knowledge and, therefore, [illegible] [illegible] [illegible] [illegible] [illegible] which [illegible] [illegible] [illegible]

[illegible] [illegible] in the underlying statistics.

[illegible]

INTERNATIONAL COMPARISON OF UNEMPLOYMENT RATES

WALTER GALENSON

UNIVERSITY OF CALIFORNIA, BERKELEY

AND

ARNOLD ZELLNER

UNIVERSITY OF WASHINGTON

1. Introduction

ANYONE who has followed the recent controversy over American unemployment statistics is aware of the definitional and technical pitfalls involved in the preparation of a single unemployment series, to say nothing of the problems involved in comparing several series for the same country emanating from different sources. Such difficulties are thrice compounded in international comparisons in which the data to be compared have no common basis in economic structure and political and social institutions. On its face, unemployment among industrial workers appears to be a fairly simple concept. In fact, it is a complex multi-dimensional phenomenon, imperfectly measured even in the industrial nations of the West. Nevertheless, interest in unemployment, both as an aspect of the comparative development of national economies and as a factor powerfully influencing the role of nations in the world economy, has stimulated efforts in the past to secure some measure of unemployment going beyond national boundary lines. The most ambitious attempt was the construction of an international index of unemployment by John Lindberg of the International Labour Office.[1] Successive international conferences of labor statisticians have agreed upon the importance of altering statistical practice to the end of facilitating international comparison, but actual progress in this direction has been slow.[2] Helpful in this respect have been several

Note: The authors wish to express their appreciation to Professor Clarence D. Long and to Mrs. Ruth P. Mack for a helpful reading of the first draft of this paper. The Institute of Industrial Relations, University of California, Berkeley, provided material assistance in the preparation of the paper.

[1] This index was computed by averaging percentages of unemployment for 15 countries, weighted by occupied industrial population as indicated by census data. The figures are available for the years 1929 to 1938. For the details of method and calculation, see John Lindberg, "An Attempt to Construct International Measures of Unemployment" (October 1932, p. 491), "Some Problems in the Construction of Index Numbers of Unemployment" (April 1934, p. 472), "World Index Numbers of Unemployment" (January 1939, p. 118), and "World Level of Unemployment" (June 1939, p. 812), in the *International Labour Review.*

[2] See *The Second International Conference of Labour Statisticians*, Interna-

reports of the ILO dealing with specific problems involved in reconciling unemployment statistics on an international basis.[3]

The procedure we have adopted for the purposes of this paper is in some respects more ambitious than previous endeavors, in others much less so. We have attempted to assemble unemployment data for some ten countries, all of them relatively industrialized, for the period 1900-1950, insofar as relevant data were available. The choice of countries was governed (1) by the availability of unemployment statistics, (2) by the availability to us of a minimum of material describing and evaluating these statistics, and (3) by the amount of time at our disposal. Thus, for example, Italy was ruled out by the unsuitable character of its unemployment statistics for much of the period in which we are interested. The United States and the Soviet Union were excluded on the ground that they were to be the subjects of special papers at the Conference.

For each of the countries with which we deal, we have endeavored to prepare a statement setting forth the available unemployment series. The purpose was to secure some basis for judging the degree to which available data express adequately the extent of unemployment, defined as indicated below. Heavy reliance has been placed in each case upon published evaluations of the data by government statisticians, parliamentary commissions, and private economists and statisticians of the countries concerned.

From the available series, we have either selected the one which appeared to us most appropriate for purposes of international comparison, or constructed a new series on the basis of existing ones. Adjustments were made wherever feasible to bring the national data into closer conformance to one another. However, no attempt was made at fine adjustment to an ideal standard, a project which would have required considerably greater resources than we had at our disposal, if indeed it were possible at all. For example, a correction factor was applied to the official Australian unemployment series to eliminate unemployment due to illness and causes other than lack of work, but no adjustment was made to reconcile the Australian definition of unemployment due to lack of work with that, say, of Great Britain.

---

tional Labour Office, Studies and Reports, Series N, No. 8, 1925, pp. 48-64; *The Sixth International Congress of Labour Statisticians*, New Series, No. 7, 1948.

[3] Cf. the following International Labour Office Studies and Reports: *Methods of Compiling Statistics of Unemployment*, Series C, No. 7, 1922; *Methods of Statistics of Unemployment*, Series N, No. 7, 1925; *The International Standardization of Labour Statistics*, Series N, No. 25, 1943; *Employment, Unemployment and Labour Force Statistics*, New Series, No. 7, Part 1, 1948.

The resultant unemployment series, expressed in percentages representing the ratio of the unemployed to the number of persons subject to the risk of unemployment, are then brought together and compared. It is at this point that the national expert is apt to throw up his hands in horror. Yet we feel that the results are not without significance. We are not concerned with pinpointing small international differences in the levels of unemployment at particular points of time, but rather with the gross behavior of the data over half a century. We are seeking to detect differences in unemployment rates, secularly and internationally, which appear to be of such magnitude as to render unlikely the legitimate ascription of cause to differences in definition and measurement techniques. In the final analysis, this must remain a matter for individual judgment until a great deal more work has been done on detailed international reconciliation of concepts. In our view, even the brief review that we have undertaken of the statistics of individual countries provides the basis for the exercise of far more informed judgment than would otherwise be possible.[4]

2. *Definition of Unemployment*

The 1925 International Conference of Labour Statisticians resolved that each participating country should investigate the representative qualities of its unemployment statistics in relation to the following criteria:

> "(1) that the ideal population 'field' to which the statistics should relate should be all persons whose normal means of livelihood is employment under contract of service, as well as those persons not hitherto wage earners who seek to become so;
>
> "(2) that the unemployment measured should exclude that due to sickness, invalidity, participation in trade disputes, or voluntary absence from work, and should be limited to unemployment due to lack of employment or to lack of work while in employment.
>
> "(3) that the necessary and sufficing condition for being enumerated as unemployed is that the individual must have been not at work for one day at least."[5]

The next Conference to consider the question, that of 1947, resolved in favor of a considerably different definition. The population at risk

[4] We are by no means the first to engage upon such an undertaking. For previous attempts, see Paul H. Douglas and Aaron Director, *The Problem of Unemployment*, Macmillan, 1931, Chaps. III, IV; *Unemployment: An International Problem*, London, Royal Institute of International Affairs, 1935, Chaps. III-V; Wladimir S. Woytinsky, *Three Sources of Unemployment*, International Labour Office, Studies and Reports, Series C, No. 20, 1935.

[5] *The Second International Conference of Labour Statisticians*, 1925, p. 72.

was broadened to include employers, the self-employed, and unpaid family workers. All persons "able to take a job if offered one, who are out of a job on a given day and have remained out of a job and seeking work for a specified minimum period not exceeding one week" were to be counted as unemployed.[6] Some members of the Conference maintained that a minimum period of one week would serve to understate the "true" level of unemployment, but the majority was of the opinion that "the procedures currently in use, as well as the requirement of maximum accuracy in the count of the unemployed, necessitated the use of a period longer than one day."[7] It may be noted parenthetically that an ILO staff report submitted to the Conference suggested that it would be consonant with usual practice to count as unemployed all persons seeking work "on a given day who are not employed but are able to take a job if offered one."[8]

Unfortunately for our purposes, such resolutions had little effect upon actual practice for the period with which we are concerned.[9] No two countries defined unemployment in precisely the same manner. With reference to time, for example, an unemployed person in Australia was one who had been out of work for three days or more during a specified survey week; in Sweden, it was one who had less than twenty-four hours of employment in a week in his regular trade, or a person working outside his regular trade whose weekly earnings were below those paid in his own trade. The remaining countries, however, appear to have measured unemployment status with reference to a particular day, the precise day depending upon the operating requirements of the institution from which the statistics emanated.[10] Differences also pre-

[6] *The Sixth International Conference of Labour Statisticians*, 1948, Part 4, p. 54.

[7] *Ibid.*, p. 17.

[8] *Employment, Unemployment and Labour Force Statistics*, p. 12. The report stated, in part:

"For the basic definition, the time reference should be of a given day. The reason for this is not only that it is the common practice in most countries, but also that, as far as unemployment and employment statistics are concerned, it yields an unimpeachable result; furthermore, the different sources when compared will be compared on the basis of the same definition instead of a series of different definitions. The basic difficulty in the choice of a week or a month is not the length of the period, but the error involved if the condition is imposed that the status of employment or of unemployment must last throughout that period, or that the status of employment and unemployment must be counted if it appears at any time during the period. The clear definition of the numbers employed or unemployed, therefore, requires the time reference to a given day" (*ibid.*, p. 71).

[9] Particularly since 1945, a number of countries have revised their methods of tabulating unemployment. The changes, however, have not been concerned so much with the definition of unemployment as with the collection of data from different sources.

[10] For a discussion of this point, see *Employment, Unemployment and Labour Force Statistics*, pp. 14-18.

vailed with respect to industrial and occupational coverage, the causes of unemployment taken into account, the treatment of temporary and partial unemployment, and the treatment of persons engaged in emergency public works.

However, the statistics exhibit greater uniformity of definition than the above list of variables might suggest. The cause may be ascribed to a more or less uniform development of the economic and social institutions which permitted the accumulation of unemployment statistics in the first place. For example, in most countries of the West the earliest statistics of unemployment were compiled by trade unions as a by-product of their activities. The development of the organized labor movement exhibits a remarkable uniformity: skilled craftsmen almost always organize before semiskilled factory workers; certain industries, such as building and mining, tend to be early in the timetable of organization; and white collar and farm workers are generally the last to organize, if indeed they organize at all. Thus, coverage of trade union unemployment statistics is generally confined at first to the skilled trades and then gradually broadened to the remainder of manufacturing, mining, transportation, and communication, with commercial and agricultural coverage coming much later. With respect to the registration of unemployment by trade unions, there are usually two major motives involved: the payment of out of work benefits, either entirely from union funds or pursuant to some variant of the Ghent system of unemployment insurance, and the waiver of dues payments during unemployment. There are numerous possibilities of definition, depending upon the precise statutes of the union involved, but imitation among union movements and the choice of simple methods owing to the limited time available to the average union secretary to process his data combine to produce greater uniformity than is commonly believed.

The definition of unemployment which is used appears to us most closely to approach the norm actually employed in practice. This is by no means an "ideal" definition, nor necessarily a modal definition, but rather that definition about which the various available unemployment series tend to cluster and toward which it seemed practicable to work in making our adjustments. In selecting among the various series available for purposes of international comparison, where a choice was possible, this normative definition also played an important role.

TIME PERIOD

As already indicated, most unemployment series are based upon the employment status of the individual worker on a single day. This is the simplest statistic to prepare; the trade union secretary or the employment exchange manager need merely tabulate the number of persons receiving benefits, or registered for work, on a particular day. Where the Ghent system of unemployment insurance is well developed, as in Belgium, Denmark, and Holland, detailed figures on total man-days of unemployment during a period may be available as a by-product of reports that must be made to the supervising authorities, but in the more usual case there is only the one-day count. The current United States Census definition has virtually no counterpart in most of the earlier statistics, for the distinction between no work at all and some work, no matter how little, during a week was not relevant to the operations of trade unions, employment exchanges, or relief authorities.

Some effort has been made in the past to separate from the unemployed those persons who were on temporary layoff. Canadian retrospective estimates for the years 1931-1950 attempted to exclude persons on a maximum thirty-day layoff with definite instructions to return, but earlier Canadian unemployment series made no such distinction. The British unemployment insurance statistics recorded separately temporarily unemployed persons, that is, persons who had a definite expectation of being re-engaged within six weeks, together with persons employed on a part-time schedule, as *temporarily stopped.* In the Belgian unemployment insurance statistics, workers who had not definitely broken their employment contract with their employer were distinguished from those wholly unemployed. In general, however, persons on temporary layoffs would have been treated as unemployed for most purposes in the countries under review.

It is clear that as the minimum period for which a man must be unemployed in order to be counted lengthens, the less will be the reported amount of unemployment, but little can be said beyond this.[11] A ratio of, say, full weeks of unemployment to single days of unemployment for one country would not necessarily hold true for another, since the relationship is dependent upon the pattern of work force reduction undertaken during periods of recession. For example, if in country A work sharing were more commonly practiced than in country B, the ratio of a full week to a single day of unemployment would tend to be smaller in country A than in B.

EMPLOYMENT STATUS

Historically, statistics of unemployment are usually limited to wage earners, that is, persons working for hire in manual jobs. "Independent

[11] This subject is discussed by Louis J. Ducoff and Margaret J. Hagood, in *Labor Force Definitions and Measurement: Recent Experience in the United States,* Social Science Research Council, Bull. No. 56, New York, 1947.

workers, shopkeepers, handicraftsmen, farmers, the liberal professions, etc., are generally excluded; so also as a rule are salaried employees."[12] In the case of trade union data, the reason is obvious. Unemployment insurance schemes were generally limited to wage earners until recent years, while labor exchanges have usually catered to industrial wage earners (though in some countries they have long been an important factor in the farm labor market).

This generalization is not without exceptions. In Australia, Denmark, and Sweden, organization of white collar workers resulted in their inclusion in unemployment statistics in increasing numbers for the past quarter of a century, though less than in proportion to their labor force strength. In Germany and Great Britain, salaried employees earning less than specified amounts have been insured for some time against unemployment and therefore included in the statistics of unemployment based upon this source. The labor force survey technique that has been adopted by several countries since World War II generally results in full coverage of salaried employees and the self-employed, which is one reason for exercising considerable care in comparing such data with the traditional unemployment statistics.

One other type of person who may be mentioned is the new entrant to the labor market who cannot immediately find a job. Since he was not ordinarily eligible for union membership or qualified for unemployment insurance benefits, he was usually excluded from unemployment series of this character. However, freedom of access to labor exchanges meant that he was often counted among the number of job seekers, as well as among the unemployed in the newer labor force surveys. Exclusion was sometimes accomplished by eliminating individuals below a certain age both from the labor force count and the count of the unemployed.[13]

INDUSTRIAL COVERAGE

There is less uniformity in this respect than on either of the two preceding points, but the situation is by no means hopeless. The general practice has been well summarized as follows:

> "agriculture is either wholly excluded or but feebly represented. . . . Mining is generally included where this branch of economic activity is of practical importance. . . . Transport and communications, banking, commerce, etc., are unevenly represented, but are not, as

[12] Lindberg, "Some Problems in the Construction of Index Numbers of Unemployment," p. 484.

[13] Before the war, for example, in Belgium, persons under 15 years of age were not eligible for unemployment insurance, while those between 15 and 18 years were eligible only if they had worked for an employer for at least six months.

a rule, numerically strong. By far the most important group is 'industry' (including building and mining). And, very broadly speaking, the existing statistics can be said to represent conditions among industrial workers. The fact that some categories of nonindustrial workers are included is not likely to affect the comparisons much."[14]

The source of the particular unemployment series has largely determined the scope of industrial coverage. Since trade unionism traditionally made scant inroads into agriculture, domestic service, commercial pursuits, and government employment, these areas are poorly represented, if at all.[15] Unemployment insurance statistics usually commenced on a narrow industrial base and broadened out in the course of time to include most industries; the British statistics are a case in point. In other countries, however, agriculture, domestic service, and government are excluded from the unemployment insurance system, and therefore from the statistics.

Changes in coverage over time complicate the problem. While one might plot a general trend of industrial coverage, beginning with segments of mining, manufacturing and building, and expanding gradually to the rest of manufacturing and the nonmanufacturing industries, the difficulty is that there is no uniformity either in the precise time of change or in the rate of change internationally. In consequence, even if there was close correspondence between the unemployment series of two countries, at a particular point in time, there would not necessarily be a similar degree of correspondence either earlier or later. Since there is considerable variation in unemployment rates among industries—for example, unemployment is normally much lower among government and commercial employees than among manufacturing wage earners—this factor must be kept in mind in any international comparison of rates of unemployment.

OTHER ELEMENTS IN THE DEFINITION

It has been general practice to limit the concept of unemployment to involuntary idleness due to lack of work, excluding idleness due to

[14] Lindberg, "Some Problems in the Construction of Index Numbers for Unemployment," p. 484.

[15] The fact that in many countries, the railroads and the telephone and telegraph system are nationally owned, and their employees civil servants like our own postal workers, has often meant the exclusion of a large portion of transportation, and virtually all of communications, from unemployment statistics. Trucking has generally been included, though for much of the period under consideration it did not play an important role. No generalization can be made with respect to the maritime trades; exclusion, where it occurred, was based upon the special character of hiring and contract practices in that industry.

labor disputes, illness, and vacations. Where idleness due to any of the latter causes is included in the general unemployment data, as in Australia, it is usually possible to correct the series on the basis of accompanying classifications of the causes of unemployment.

The usual intent has been to keep total and partial unemployment separate, i.e. a worker on short time on the census day will not ordinarily be counted as unemployed. On the other hand, a worker employed intermittently rather than for a reduced number of hours each day would generally be included among the unemployed if an off-day happened to coincide with the census day. Moreover, there is not always a consistent concept of part-time employment; "persons are often included among the unemployed who either are performing various odd jobs or are working on such a reduced schedule of hours that for social reasons they are admitted to relief and are included among the unemployed."[16] It may be noted that a consequence of the adoption of a calendar week as the census unit of time, as in the United States monthly labor force survey, is that partial unemployment does not appear, except insofar as it may be of the skip-a-week type as practiced, for example, by some New England textile firms.

To summarize the foregoing, the concept of unemployment which has been taken as normative for the purposes of this paper is total (as distinguished from partial) involuntary idleness due to lack of work on a particular day, regardless of layoff status, among wage earners whose normal occupation is in manufacturing or mining and who held jobs previous to the inception of unemployment. It is scarcely necessary to add that none of the series considered below conforms precisely to this definition. Nevertheless, the definition conveys the sense of what is being compared when we juxtapose available unemployment series internationally more proximately than any alternative definition that we have been able to construct.

3. *Sources of Unemployment Statistics*

It is not our purpose to present a disquisition on the sources of unemployment statistics. The subject has been dealt with adequately elsewhere.[17] However, it is necessary to consider the question briefly in order that the statistical material dealt with below shall be more intelligible, and also because our conclusions regarding the value of the statistics are somewhat at variance with those of other commentators.

[16] Lindberg, "Some Problems in the Construction of Index Numbers for Unemployment," p. 477.

[17] See the sources cited [*supra*] in notes 1, 2, and 3.

TRADE UNION AND TRADE UNION UNEMPLOYMENT FUND STATISTICS

For anyone who desires to study trends of unemployment going back any distance into the past, the statistics relating to unemployment among members of trade unions constitute an invaluable source of information. These data, for all their faults, constitute the first systematic record of unemployment in most of the industrial nations of the West.

The trade union statistics are subject to numerous and serious deficiencies:

1. The sample of workers which they represent is not a random one; usually skilled craftsmen have been the first to organize, so that they are disproportionately heavily represented in the earlier years. Since skilled workers tend to be less subject to the risk of unemployment, the argument runs, there is an upward bias in trade union unemployment percentages as the labor movement embraces a progressively larger portion of the labor force.[18]

2. Certain industries, such as building construction and the metal trades, which tend to come relatively early in the timetable of trade union organization, are unusually sensitive to cyclical movements, and an index of unemployment in which they figure prominently is less stable than would be one representing the entire population.

3. Some of the trade union statistics are compiled by union secretaries who are simultaneously administering insurance funds, and are thus apt to be reasonably accurate; but in the absence of accompanying insurance schemes, the data may be mere rough estimates rather than careful observations.[19]

4. The trade union statistics typically exclude certain industries, such as agriculture, government service, and rail transport, in which employment tends to be relatively stable.

5. In some countries the number of reporting trade unions has not been held constant, and there is some evidence that the errors in this respect may vary systematically with the business cycle.[20]

Notwithstanding these objections, we have been obliged to rely heavily upon the trade union unemployment statistics. For a number of countries (e.g. Australia, Canada, Denmark, the Netherlands, Nor-

[18] See *Employment, Unemployment and Labour Force Statistics*, p. 87.

[19] *Methods of Statistics of Unemployment*, p. 24.

[20] "The real drawback is that from month to month the number of unions reporting their unemployment varies, and more particularly that the sample reporting varies in kind according to employment conditions. When employment is on the up-grade the reports of the union seem to be fairly representative; when it is on the down-grade there is a clearly marked tendency for the reporting unions to have better employment conditions than the non-reporting unions" (*Seventh Census of Canada, 1931*, Monographs, *Unemployment*, Vol. XIII, 1942, p. 222).

way, and Sweden) they have been the principal if not the exclusive source of information on unemployment until recent years. For the other countries with which we have dealt (France, Germany, and Great Britain) they provided the sole source of information for earlier years, and an important supplementary source more recently.

Necessity has not been the only consideration, however. Upon closer examination, the trade union series do not appear to be as objectionable in particular as they seem in general. In the first place, it is widely conceded that they did provide a fairly accurate index of the trend, as opposed to the absolute level, of unemployment over shorter periods. There are greater reservations with respect to longer periods. For example, a Swedish parliamentary commission came to the conclusion that until the 1930's, the Swedish trade union unemployment series was biased in the direction of greater unemployment over time because of changes in coverage. However, a similar widely held belief regarding the Danish statistics was not substantiated by a special study conducted in 1934. The Dutch trade union statistics were considered without such bias up to 1935 at least, while the Australian and Norwegian statistics do not suffer from this defect. The German and British trade union series have long been regarded as good indexes of the trend of unemployment.[21]

Even when one considers absolute levels of unemployment, the trade union statistics do not come off as badly as might be supposed from the character of the criticism noted above. The Australian series, which has been widely based for many years, differed substantially from the results of the Australian census of 1921, but checked fairly closely with the censuses of 1933 and 1947. Years of criticism have not caused the discontinuation of the series as the principal measure of Australian unemployment, and it is currently regarded by the Commonwealth Statistician as a good measure of trends and as a measure of absolute employment if used "with caution." The voluntary trade union–unemployment insurance statistics of pre-World War II Belgium checked closely with several censuses, though the same could not be said of the pre-World War I data. A comprehensive estimate of Canadian unemployment from 1920 to 1940 by the Bureau of Statistics revealed a significant divergence between this series and the trade union series from 1932 to 1940; during this period, average unemployment was 15 per cent according to the trade union series and 17.8 per cent according to the Bureau's estimates. The trade union unemployment insurance statistics of Denmark are regarded in that country as a satisfactory index of the level of unemployment. While before World

[21] The assertions in this paragraph are based upon the findings contained in the respective appendixes below.

War I, the German trade union statistics appeared significantly to understate unemployment, the data for 1919 to 1933 appear to have been quite satisfactory. The French trade union data are among the least satisfactory of those with which we have dealt, but then the same statement may be made of French unemployment statistics in general. Early adoption of a national unemployment insurance scheme in Great Britain, independent of the trade unions, rendered less necessary reliance upon trade union returns. For the years in which both the unemployment insurance and the trade union unemployment percentages were available, it was found that much better agreement existed than had been anticipated. The trade union unemployment insurance statistics of the Netherlands "could safely be considered as representative up to the 1930's. After 1935, however, they presented in all probability a too unfavorable picture of the size of unemployment."[22] The Norwegian trade union data, despite a somewhat limited base, were found by comparison with the 1930 census to be representative of the unemployment situation among all industrial wage earners at the time. During the subsequent decades, the trade union data are believed to have exaggerated the extent of unemployment, though the facts are difficult to ascertain in the absence of bench-mark data. The conclusion was reached with respect to the Swedish trade union data that they provided a good index of unemployment in the country after 1920 for the industries they covered but were less reliable prior to World War I.[23]

The fact that the trade union unemployment statistics, despite their defects, do not come off so badly after all may be ascribed to the following factors:

1. In some cases the sample of employment covered is relatively large (e.g. 25 per cent of all male employment in Australia as early as 1912, 65 per cent of all Danish wage earners in 1930). This renders the problem of error in collection and sampling less critical.

2. Given the difficulties involved in defining unemployment to begin with, there are certain advantages in having the initial collection and processing of the data done by experts. The local trade union secretary, particularly if he is concurrently operating an unemployment insurance fund, is uniquely in a position to know the state of trade in his area and to appraise the employment status of each individual worker. By contrast, the labor force survey enumerator is often not well pre-

[22] Letter to the authors from Dr. Ph. J. Idenburg, Director General of Statistics, The Netherlands, July 29, 1953.

[23] The statements in this paragraph summarize the relevant findings of Appendixes A to J.

pared, and the informant not always cognizant of the precise employment status of the person under investigation.[24]

3. One of the limitations of certain types of unemployment statistics (e.g. those emanating from public employment offices) is that reporting is incomplete because of lack of incentive of the unemployed worker to report himself as such. In the case of trade union statistics, reporting may be of personal advantage to the unemployed on one or more of three counts: he may be eligible for unemployment benefits, he may be excused from paying his union dues, and he may be able to secure a new job by referral from the union in the event that unemployment registers are kept. In a specific situation, the greater the advantage that accrues to the worker from registering, the more complete the count of unemployment is apt to be.

UNEMPLOYMENT INSURANCE STATISTICS

In those countries in which the Ghent system of unemployment insurance prevails, there is generally a combined set of trade union–unemployment insurance statistics based upon the voluntary unemployment insurance societies closely allied, in the main, with local trade unions.[25] Where there is a national system of unemployment insurance, however, the two types of statistics are always separate.

The limitations of unemployment insurance data for measuring unemployment, and particularly for comparing rates of unemployment, are too well known to require extensive comment. The principal problems arise out of variations in the qualifying formulas, the exhaustion factor, waiting periods, failure to file, and other factors. Here again, however, it seems to us that often too great stress is placed upon differences and not enough upon uniformity. An ILO study published in 1925, when unemployment insurance covered a much smaller proportion of the working population of most countries than it does now, and when benefits were much more limited in scope, mapped out certain principles of coverage and benefit payment which were of quite general application.[26] As the systems became more complete, initial differences tended to disappear.

Unemployment insurance statistics have the unique advantage of permitting the calculation of the total volume of compensable unemployment during a specified period, thus avoiding some of the problems involved in selecting a time period for which to measure

[24] See, e.g. Gertrude Bancroft, "The Census Bureau Estimates of Unemployment," *The Review of Economics and Statistics*, February 1950, p. 60.

[25] This is not universally true, however. In Sweden, for example, the trade unions issue one set of statistics and the unemployment insurance funds another.

[26] *Unemployment Insurance*, International Labour Office, Studies and Reports, Series C, No. 10, 1925.

unemployment. Thus, Danish and Dutch series are available showing the relationship of the number of days lost per annum due to unemployment to the potential number of days worked by all persons covered by the statistics.

We do not mean to suggest that it is possible blithely to compare unemployment insurance data over time, or internationally, on the assumption that they are always sufficiently similar to eliminate the possibility of substantial error. The problem in making comparisons is to determine the limits within which observed differences in the data may be due to the institutions of the unemployment insurance system.

EMPLOYMENT EXCHANGE AND RELIEF STATISTICS

When registration at an employment exchange is a compulsory qualifying prerequisite for unemployment insurance benefits, unemployment exchange registration is likely to parallel closely the unemployment insurance figures. Even there, however, differences may arise because of registration of employed persons seeking to change jobs, or continued registration by unemployed workers who have exhausted benefits. However, when registration is voluntary, employment exchange data are of much more limited value. In such cases rates of unemployment calculated from them cannot be compared internationally; they can only be used to measure differences in trend from a common base year for which comparative rates of unemployment are available from other sources. For our purposes, these statistics have been useful primarily for intranational comparison. Serious divergence between, say, the unemployment insurance series and the employment exchange series would at least serve to raise some question about the representativeness of the former at a particular point in time.

Statistics of unemployment relief were of little value for the purpose at hand. As has been well stated:

> "To a much greater extent than the statistics of compulsory insurance, those obtained from relief institutions are lacking in comparability at different dates owing to changes in the conditions under which relief has been granted, changes which have been much more frequent than in the case of insurance schemes. . . . It may be concluded that despite their imperfections and limitations, these statistics, in the absence of other sources of information, have been of some value in indicating the general movement of unemployment. . . ."[27]

[27] *Methods of Statistics of Unemployment*, pp. 16-17.

LABOR FORCE SURVEYS AND CENSUSES

The periodic labor force survey technique, which was pioneered by the United States and is currently being used in several other countries, would clearly come at the head of the list if the subject under discussion were current rather than historical international unemployment rate comparisons. Given a uniform definition of unemployment, the results of such surveys are likely to be directly comparable with little adjustment, since virtual universal coverage appears to be characteristic of them.[28] For historical purposes, however, labor force surveys do not enter into the picture except in the case of Canada.

Census information is invaluable in providing bench-mark data from which to evaluate the various series of unemployment enumerated above. However, since such information usually relates to a single day of the year, and is available only at long intervals, it is obviously of little value for annual international comparisons of unemployment.

4. *Statistics of Unemployment*

Statistics of unemployment for nine countries, based upon Appendixes A to J, and stated in terms of rates of unemployment, are shown in Table 1 and Chart 1. The French unemployment rates are not included, since they are rough estimates. The series were selected, and in some cases constructed, from available data according to the criteria considered above. The data go as far back to the starting year of 1900 as possible, but only for the United Kingdom did it prove feasible actually to begin with that year. Gaps appear in several cases for wartime years because of the lack of published information.

LEVELS OF UNEMPLOYMENT DURING SIX MAJOR PERIODS

The half century 1900-1950 is not an historically homogeneous time period. Rather it is an era containing several fairly well-defined periods marked off by great historical events, the effects of which penetrated all national boundaries. This is not to say that the course of historical development in these subperiods was independent of what occurred in past periods or had no influence on developments in following periods. Certainly the histories of the countries considered displayed important elements of continuity in their development over the whole period 1900-1950. It is true, however, that in certain time periods the world economy was subjected to the action of major forces which were

[28] This would appear to be true, at least, of the figures for the United States and Canada. We have not examined the data for France (commencing 1950), Denmark (commencing 1951) or Sweden (under contemplation) with sufficient care to be able to render any judgments on their comparability.

CHART 1
Unemployment Rates, Nine Countries, 1900-1950

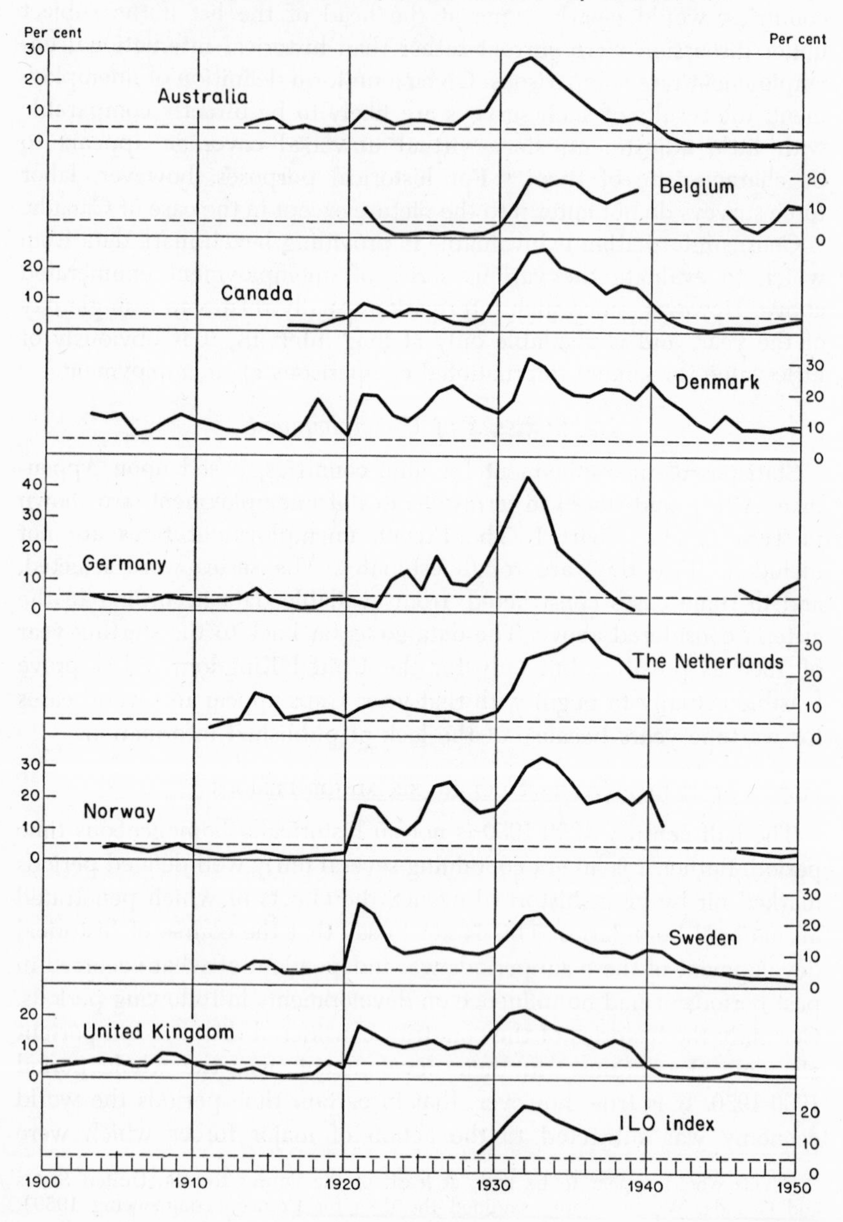

TABLE 1

Unemployment Rates, Nine Countries, 1900-1950

(*per cent*)

ar	*Australia*	*Belgium*	*Canada*	*Denmark*	*Germany*	*The Nether-lands*	*Norway*	*Sweden*	*United Kingdom*
00									2.5
01									3.3
02									4.0
03				13.0	4.7				4.7
04				12.0	3.6		3.9		6.0
05				13.0	3.0		4.4		5.0
06				6.0	2.7		3.2		3.6
07				7.0	2.9		2.5		3.7
08				11.0	4.4		3.7		7.8
09				13.0	4.3		5.0		7.7
10				10.7	3.5		2.9		4.7
11				9.5	3.1	2.5	1.9	5.6	3.0
12				7.6	3.2	4.0	1.3	5.4	3.2
13	5.4			7.5	4.2	5.0	1.7	4.4	2.1
14	7.4			9.9	7.2	13.8	2.3	7.3	3.3
15	8.3			8.1	3.2	12.0	1.9	7.2	1.1
16	4.8		1.9	5.1	2.2	5.1	0.9	4.0	0.4
17	6.1		1.9	9.7	1.0	6.5	0.9	4.0	0.7
18	4.6		1.3	18.1	1.2	7.5	1.5	4.6	1.3
19	4.6		3.4	10.9	3.7	7.7	1.7	5.5	5.2
20	5.5		4.6	6.1	3.8	5.8	2.3	5.4	3.2
21	10.4	9.7	8.9	19.7	2.8	9.0	17.7	26.6	17.0
22	8.5	3.1	7.1	19.3	1.5	11.0	17.1	22.9	14.3
23	6.2	1.0	4.9	12.7	10.2	11.2	10.7	12.5	11.7
24	7.8	1.0	7.1	10.7	13.1	8.8	8.5	10.1	10.3
25	7.8	1.5	7.0	14.7	6.8	8.1	13.2	11.0	11.3
26	6.3	1.4	4.7	20.7	18.0	7.3	24.3	12.2	12.5
27	6.2	1.8	2.9	22.5	8.8	7.5	25.4	12.0	9.7
28	10.0	0.9	2.6	18.5	8.6	5.6	19.2	10.6	10.8
29	10.2	1.3	4.2	15.5	13.3	5.9	15.4	10.2	10.4
30	18.4	3.6	12.9	13.7	22.7	7.8	16.6	11.9	16.1
31	26.5	10.9	17.4	17.9	34.3	14.8	22.3	16.8	21.3
32	28.1	19.0	26.0	31.7	43.8	25.3	30.8	22.4	22.1
33	24.2	16.9	26.6	28.8	36.2	26.9	33.4	23.3	19.9
34	19.6	18.9	20.6	22.2	20.5	28.0	30.7	18.0	16.7
35	15.6	17.8	19.1	19.7	16.2	31.7	25.3	15.0	15.5
36	11.3	13.5	16.7	19.3	12.0	32.7	18.8	12.7	13.1
37	8.4	11.5	12.5	21.9	6.9	26.9	20.0	10.8	10.8
38	7.8	14.0	15.1	21.5	3.2	25.0	22.0	10.9	12.9
39	8.8	15.9	14.1	18.4	0.9	19.9	18.3	9.2	10.5

(continued on next page)

TABLE 1 (continued)
(*per cent*)

Year	*Australia*	*Belgium*	*Canada*	*Denmark*	*Germany*	*The Nether-lands*	*Norway*	*Sweden*	*Unite Kingdo*
1940	7.1		9.3	23.9		19.8	23.1	11.8	5.0
1941	2.8		4.5	18.4			11.4	11.3	1.5
1942	0.7		2.2	15.1				7.5	1.0
1943	0.2		0.8	10.7				5.7	0.5
1944	0.3		0.5	8.3				4.9	0.5
1945	0.3	9.1	1.4	13.4				4.5	1.0
1946	0.5	3.9	1.4	8.9	7.5		3.6	3.2	2.5
1947	0.3	2.2	1.3	8.9	5.0		3.1	2.8	2.0
1948	0.3	5.3	2.2	8.6	4.2		2.7	2.8	1.6
1949	1.4	11.1	3.0	9.6	8.3		2.2	2.7	1.6
1950	0.4	10.1	3.8	8.7	10.2		2.7	2.2	1.6

Source:

Australia: Reports of trade unions, corrected to eliminate unemployment due to caus other than nonavailability of work. See Table A-2.

Belgium: 1921-1939, official statistics of the voluntary unemployment insurance societi 1945-1950, same, corrected to eliminate extensions in coverage effected after World War See Table B-3.

Canada: 1916-1920, reports of trade unions; 1921-1940, estimates of the Dominion Bure of Statistics, based on trade union reports; 1941-1950, trade union reports. See Table C-1.

Denmark: Reports of trade union unemployment insurance funds. See Table D-1.

Germany: 1903-1913, trade union reports, corrected for understatement of seasonal u employment; 1914-1932, trade union reports; 1933-1939, our estimates, based upon employme exchange statistics; 1946-1950, employment exchange statistics. See Tables F-1, F-5, F-6.

The Netherlands: Reports of trade union unemployment insurance funds. See Table G-1.

Norway: Trade union reports. See Table H-1.

Sweden: Trade union reports. See Table I-1.

United Kingdom: 1900-1917, trade union reports; 1918-1950, unemployment insuran statistics. See Tables J-1, J-5, J-7.

inoperative in other periods; the action of these forces delineated certain periods to such an extent that detailed study of them is justified. Of course, in each subperiod there was important variation in the experience of different countries. Unfortunately, it is impossible to isolate the effects of international influences from those produced by forces which were confined within the boundaries of particular nations.

It is generally agreed that in many respects the first World War marked the end of one era and the beginning of another. Fundamental changes occurred in the relative power of nations, the patterns and nature of international trade, and the rates of industrial expansion. We have selected 1904 to 1913 as the first period in which to attempt to measure the average level of unemployment in the countries whose statistics extend back that far. The choice of 1904 as the initial year of this period was determined by the availability of unemployment statistics. The Norwegian statistics began in 1904, while the German statistics which began in 1903 appeared for only three-quarters of that year.

In the period 1904-1913, with the exception only of Denmark, the averages of the annual unemployment rates shown in Table 2 and displayed graphically in Chart 2, were all below 5 per cent. Even though the annual German trade union figures have been corrected for an understatement of seasonal unemployment, their average, 3.5 per cent, was well below 5 per cent and more than one percentage point below the British average of 4.7 per cent. A study in a report of the British Committee on Industry and Trade[29] which attempted to compare British and German levels of unemployment before World War I also concluded that the German level of unemployment was somewhat lower than the British. While continuous series for France and Belgium could not be constructed for this period, the data available suggest that the average level of unemployment in these two countries was below 5 per cent. Unemployment in Australia for the years 1906-1913 (1906 marking the beginning of the Australian trade union series) averaged 5.7 per cent according to the trade union percentages. This figure, however, is subject to a downward bias since the annual unemployment figures were for periods of low unemployment during each year, rather than annual averages. On the other hand, the high percentage for Denmark (an average of 9.7 per cent unemployed for the years 1904-1913) contains an upward bias which is difficult to evaluate quantitatively.

The second period which we have marked out, 1914-1920, embraces the years most directly influenced by the effects of the war. Since the inclusion of two postwar years, during which some countries were recovering from the ravages of war while others were faced with serious problems of inflation and reconversion, may unduly influence the period averages, the analysis will be extended to cover subdivisions of this period as well as the entire period. For the entire period, the disruption of world economic relations caused by the war was responsible for high levels of unemployment in several countries. For example, Denmark's recorded average level of unemployment was 9.7 per cent, while the Netherlands had 8.3 per cent. For Belgium, there is no satisfactory series available for these years. However, the results of the unemployment census of February-March 1915 and the behavior of the Ghent trade union series indicate that the level of unemployment in Belgium during this period was extremely high. The levels of un-

[29] *Survey of Industrial Relations*, London, Committee on Industry and Trade, 1926, pp. 246-250.

CHART 2

Average Unemployment Rates, Nine Countries, Six Major Periods, 1904-1950

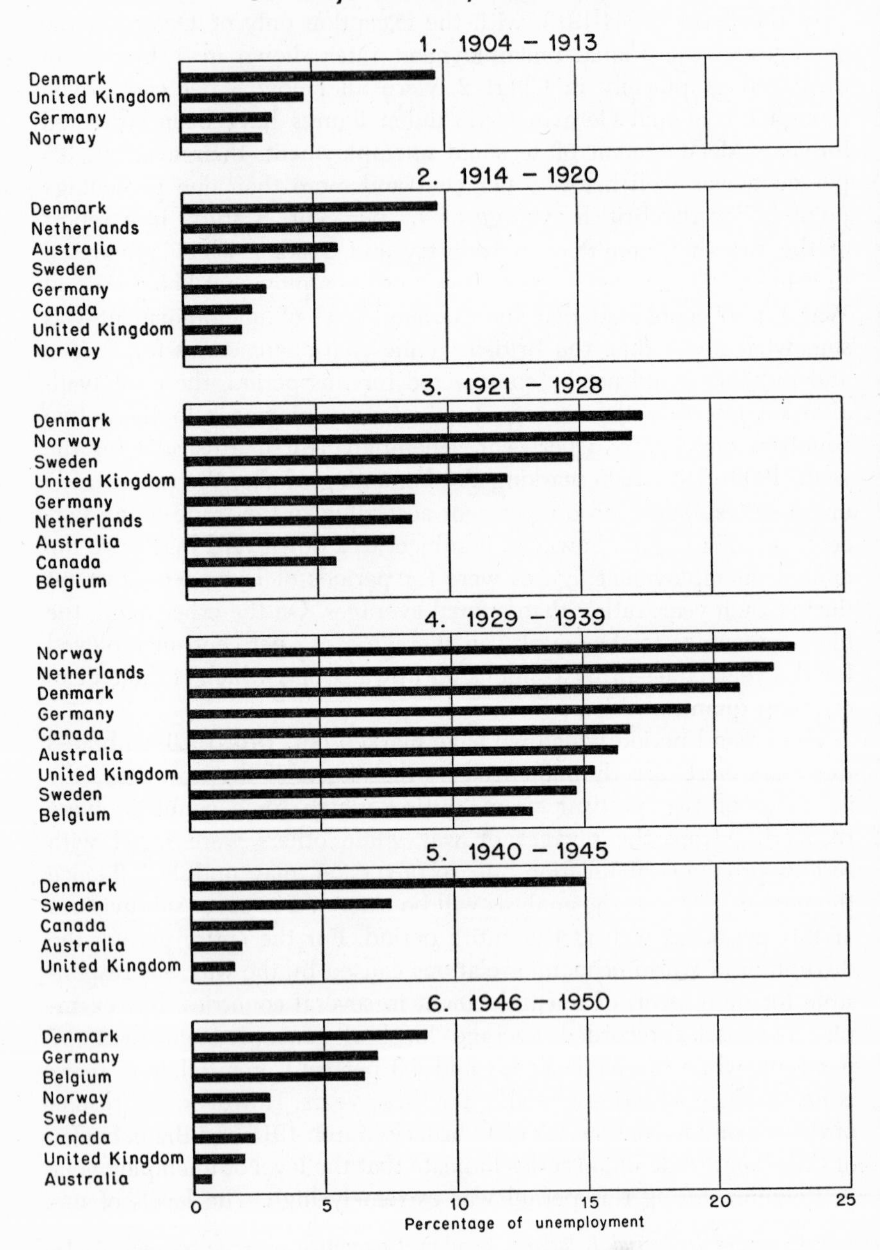

TABLE 2

Average Unemployment Rates, Nine Countries, Six Major Periods, 1904-1950[a]

(*per cent*)

Period	*Australia*	*Belgium*	*Canada*	*Denmark*	*Germany*	*The Netherlands*	*Norway*	*Sweden*	*United Kingdom*
1904-1913				9.7 (0.23)	3.5 (0.15)		3.1 (0.32)		4.7 (0.34)
1914-1920	5.9 (0.20)		2.6[b] (0.42)	9.7 (0.29)	3.2 (0.47)	8.3 (0.31)	1.6 (0.31)	5.4 (0.20)	2.2 (0.68)
1921-1928	7.9 (0.16)	2.6 (0.77)	5.7 (0.33)	17.4 (0.20)	8.7 (0.44)	8.6 (0.16)	17.0 (0.28)	14.7 (0.34)	12.2 (0.15)
1929-1939	16.3 (0.40)	13.0 (0.33)	16.8 (0.27)	21.0 (0.19)	19.1 (0.59)	22.3 (0.33)	23.1 (0.22)	14.7 (0.27)	15.4 (0.23)
1940-1945	1.9 (1.05)		3.1 (0.81)	15.0 (0.25)				7.6 (0.34)	1.6 (0.75)
1946-1950	0.6 (0.50)	6.5 (0.51)	2.3 (0.35)	8.9 (0.02)	7.0 (0.29)		2.9 (0.17)	2.7 (0.07)	1.9 (0.16)

[a] Figures in parentheses are means of absolute deviations from the period averages divided by the period averages.

[b] 1916-1920.

employment in Australia and Sweden, 5.9 and 5.4 per cent respectively, were moderate while those for the United Kingdom, Germany, Norway, and Canada (1916-1920) were all below 3.2 per cent, the average for Germany.

Countries with unemployment percentages greater than 5.4 during the war years showed decreases in unemployment in the 1919-1920 period, while those with unemployment percentages of 5.4 or lower during the war showed increases in 1919-1920 (see Table 3). The

TABLE 3

Average Unemployment Rates, Eight Countries, 1914-1918 and 1919-1920
(*per cent*)

	Australia	*Canada*	*Denmark*	*Germany*	*The Netherlands*	*Norway*	*Sweden*	*United Kingdom*
1914-1918	6.2	1.7[a]	10.2	3.0	9.0	1.5	5.4	1.4
1919-1920	5.1	4.0	8.5	3.8	6.8	2.0	5.5	4.2

[a] 1916-1918.

average wartime level of unemployment in Germany, given as 3.0 per cent above, is somewhat high because of the relatively high unemployment percentage in 1914 which resulted principally from panic conditions following the institution of certain monetary policies. The average for 1915-1918 is 1.9 per cent. The 1919-1920 United Kingdom figure, 4.2 per cent, is very approximate since the statistics for 1919 are incomplete, but there is no question that unemployment in these two years was higher than during the war years.

The unemployment statistics of the third period we have considered, 1921-1928, reveal a condition of great diversity. Average levels of unemployment for certain countries (17.4 per cent for Denmark, 17.0 per cent for Norway, 14.7 per cent for Sweden, and 12.2 per cent for the United Kingdom) approached those experienced by many countries during the following period, 1929-1939, a period of international crisis. Other countries (notably Belgium with an average of 2.6 per cent, and France) exhibited average levels of unemployment paralleling the low pre-World War I levels. The remaining countries suffered unemployment levels which appreciably exceeded their previous peacetime levels (Germany 8.7 per cent, the Netherlands 8.6 per cent, Australia 7.9 per cent, and Canada 5.7 per cent). In sum, levels of unemployment reached heights rarely recorded before in the majority of nations.

The years of world-wide economic crisis, 1929-1939, constitute the fourth period of our study. In these years, no country escaped the scourge of extensive unemployment. Average levels of unemployment ranged from a high of 23.1 per cent for Norway to a low of 13.0 per cent for Belgium (see Table 2). For every country except Sweden, the average level of unemployment was greater than in the preceding period.

Countries with relatively low levels of unemployment in the years 1921-1928 exhibited the greatest relative and absolute increases in the years 1929-1939. If the countries are ranked in both periods according to the absolute level of unemployment, the rank coefficient of correlation is —.679. A ranking based upon the percentage change in unemployment between the two countries yields a coefficient of —.867. The significance of this finding is considered below.

Belgium's average level of unemployment increased fivefold between the two periods, those of Canada and the Netherlands nearly threefold, and those of Australia and Germany more than doubled. The countries which had experienced high unemployment in the period 1921-1928 (Denmark, Norway, and the United Kingdom) showed an increase of about one-quarter. In absolute terms, the general level of unemployment in the 1929-1939 period exceeded that of the 1921-1928 period by about 10 percentage points for Belgium, Canada, Australia, and Germany, by about 14 percentage points for the Netherlands, and by about 3 to 6 percentage points for Denmark, Norway, and the United Kingdom. Sweden alone had little increase. While precise data are lacking for France, it is probable that the average levels of unemployment in these two periods most closely resembled those of Belgium.

Another point of some interest, which may be in part a function of the foregoing finding, is that the dispersion of the unemployment percentages is less in the period 1929-1939 than in 1921-1928. Using as a relative measure of intercountry dispersion the mean of the absolute deviations from the period average divided by the period average, the result is a figure of 0.17 for 1929-1939 and 0.41 for 1921-1928. Why there should have been so great a compression of rates is difficult to determine. It may have been that the high absolute levels of unemployment in the thirties caused an understatement in the reported unemployment due to the phenomena of declining trade union membership and increasing unemployment insurance benefit exhaustions. However, the extent of the compression is so great as to suggest that real forces were at work, that as unemployment rises, economic and institutional factors operate to set limits to the extent of the rise.

The advent of World War II radically changed employment conditions in virtually all nations. The United Kingdom, Australia, and Canada, with average unemployment rates of 1.6, 1.9, and 3.1 per cent, respectively, displayed the lowest unemployment in the period 1940-1945. The seemingly high average for Canada reflects the relatively high unemployment rates of 9.3 in 1940 and 4.5 in 1941. Similarly for the United Kingdom, the adaptation of its peacetime economy to a wartime full-employment basis took time as evidenced by unemployment rates of 5.0 in 1940 and 1.5 in 1941. Denmark with an average unemployment rate of 15.0, and Sweden with an average of 7.6 per cent for the period 1940-1945, present good examples of the dislocating effects which the war had on the economies of countries not directly engaged in actual combat.

In the postwar period, 1946-1950, the average rate of unemployment was low in all countries with the exception of Denmark, Germany, and Belgium where the averages stood at from 7.0 to 8.0 per cent. Australia's average unemployment, 0.6 per cent, represents the lowest national level for the period. Unemployment in Canada, Norway, Sweden, and the United Kingdom ranged from levels of 2 to 3 per cent. The available evidence for France, the behavior of the series of the number of unplaced applicants for work and of the number of unemployed in receipt of relief as well as the results of sampling surveys of the Institut National de la Statistique et des Études Économiques, indicate that postwar unemployment in France has been low, undoubtedly below 2.5 per cent and probably below 2.0 per cent.

Some mention should be made of the dispersion of the annual unemployment percentages in each period for each country, as an indication of the extent to which the period averages really approximate different levels of unemployment. We have again used the mean of the absolute deviations from the period average divided by the period average as a relative measure of dispersion. In Table 2 the values of this relative coefficient of dispersion are presented in parentheses below each period average. The coefficient values are of most interest for the periods 1904-1913, 1921-1928, and 1929-1939. In the first of these periods, the data for the United Kingdom and Norway show the greatest variation. The coefficient values are 0.34 for the British series and 0.32 for the Norwegian series. One of the major sources of variation in both these series arose from unemployment percentages much above the period averages recorded in 1908 and 1909. In the period 1921-1928, the Belgian data exhibit the greatest variation, giving rise to a coefficient of 0.77. While the Belgian variation took place about a low level of unemployment, such was not the case with Germany, the country whose data display the next greatest degree of variation. During the 1920's the countries whose annual unemployment rates show the least dispersion are the United Kingdom, the Netherlands, Denmark, and Australia whose coefficient values are

0.15, 0.16, 0.20, and 0.16, respectively. The degree of variation in the data of individual countries for the 1929-1939 period is largely determined by the extent to which the peak unemployment exceeded the period average and by the degree and rate of recovery achieved. Since both Germany and Australia experienced sharp and sizable rises in unemployment coupled with very rapid and extensive recoveries, the data for these two countries show the greatest degree of variation. The countries showing the lowest coefficient values for this period, ranging from 0.19 to 0.23, are Denmark, Norway, and the United Kingdom.

THE TREND OF UNEMPLOYMENT IN INDIVIDUAL COUNTRIES

In considering the course of unemployment in the several countries for which we have gathered statistics, no effort will be made to determine the specific *causes* of unemployment in each case. This would involve a major essay in economic history and is obviously beyond the scope of the present paper. Any analysis of this nature requires a framework broad enough to include the multitude of factors affecting the supply of and demand for labor in each country. On the supply side, study would have to be made of the development and growth of the labor force of each country, which would require detailed consideration of demographic factors; factors determining the supply of female, juvenile, and aged workers; the effects of changing economic conditions, particularly wage levels and the availability of work, on the number of persons seeking work; the growth of trade unionism; the influence of various institutions for combating unemployment; and the operation of factors determining the proportion of skilled and unskilled labor in the labor force. For consideration of the demand for labor in each country, no less than a general explanation of the level and composition of output would suffice. In addition to the variables included in the usual short-run, closed-economy, Keynesian, and classical analyses, it would be necessary to consider for each country the stage of economic development, the rate of industrial growth, the nature and magnitude of cyclical and seasonal fluctuations, the changing structure of industry with special reference to national policies governing trusts and cartels, the path of technological progress with its effects on productivity and on the kinds of labor demanded, the internal effects of changing patterns of world trade and of national policies regulating international trade, and the destructive and dislocating effects of war. This lengthy enumeration, undoubtedly incomplete, provides a basis for appreciating the difficulty inherent in any attempt to isolate the specific causes of unemployment in each country.

The major studies of unemployment that have been made are generally limited to single countries,[30] or if they are international in scope, do very little in the way of true international comparison.[31] Moreover, serious work in the field generally dates back to the early 1930's when unemployment was a pressing question involving immediate governmental action. The students of that period were writing against a background of thirty years of secularly rising unemployment and did not have our vantage point of a much longer sweep of time, with a sharp reversal of the previous trend during and after World War II.

All that we hope to do in what follows is to indicate for each of the countries with which we deal its general position in the spectrum of unemployment rates, and to assess the validity of our conclusions in each case in the light of our knowledge of the particular unemployment series involved.

1. Australia. During the pre-World War I years, Australian unemployment was relatively high (see Appendix A). This conclusion is reinforced by the fact that the Australian data shown in Table A-1 for the years prior to 1913 are for periods of low unemployment during the year, rather than annual averages. In the interwar years unemployment remained relatively low but rose rapidly beginning in 1929 to reach a maximum of 28.1 per cent in 1932 (see Table A-2). The recovery after 1932 was remarkably rapid and persistent, however. For no country with the exception of Germany (and the German figures are suspect for this period) was the drop in unemployment from 1932 to 1938 as sharp as that for Australia. By 1938 recorded unemployment was under 8 per cent, less than for any of our countries except Germany.

There was a slight increase in unemployment in 1939, a year later than the secondary peak of the 1930's for most of the other countries. With the entrance of Australia into the war, however, unemployment declined almost to the zero level, and remained extraordinarily low until 1951, the end of the period studied. While the post-World War II Australian unemployment percentages may be understated somewhat because of the application of an arbitrary correction factor to eliminate unemployment for causes other than lack of work, there can be little doubt of the extreme tightness of the Australian labor market since 1940 compared with those of most countries of Western Europe.

2. Belgium. The pre-World War I statistics of unemployment, though incomplete, indicate that unemployment was low up to the depression

[30] See particularly W. H. Beveridge, *Unemployment—A Problem of Industry,* Longmans, 1930; Douglas and Director, *op.cit.*

[31] *Unemployment—An International Problem,* is perhaps the best single study of unemployment internationally.

year of 1908 (see Appendix B). From 1908 up to the outbreak of World War I, there is evidence that Belgium experienced a somewhat higher level of unemployment. During the wartime German occupation of Belgium, unemployment reached extremely high levels as evidenced by the finding of the unemployment census of February-March 1915 that the number of unemployed amounted to a little less than 50 per cent of the number of workers enumerated in the census of 1910. While the exact percentage unemployed is not known, since the accuracy of the unemployment census is questionable on certain grounds, there can be no doubt that unemployment was high at the time of the 1915 census.

The first postwar statistics of the newly formed voluntary unemployment insurance scheme showed 9.7 per cent unemployed in 1921 and 3.1 per cent unemployed in 1922 (see Table B-3). The experience of the next eight years, during which Belgian unemployment did not exceed 2.0 per cent and even dropped below 1.0 per cent in 1928, stands in sharp contrast to the experience of virtually every other one of the countries studied. It should be noted that the Belgian unemployment statistics were very satisfactory in this period since they covered a large number of workers and agreed closely with the unemployment percentages recorded by the censuses of 1930 and 1937.

Depression unemployment in the 1930's reached a peak of 19.0 per cent in 1932, a relatively low peak internationally. Unemployment dipped slightly in 1933, only to rise again in 1934 to 18.9 per cent. Thereafter, unemployment started downward, the descent having been reversed temporarily by the 1938 recession.

Unemployment statistics are not available for the war period. In the postwar period the level of unemployment has been relatively high, in contrast with the prewar experience, averaging 6.5 per cent for the years 1946-1950. The postwar percentages refer only to workers in mining, manufacturing, transportation, and construction, with all other occupations insured under the postwar compulsory unemployment insurance scheme excluded insofar as is possible. This limitation of coverage makes the figures more comparable with the prewar series.

3. *Canada.* The history of unemployment in Canada is in many ways parallel to that of Australia (see Appendix C). Canadian unemployment statistics go back only as far as December 1915, so that no comparison can be made for the pre-World War I period. Beginning in 1919, however, and until 1926, Canadian and Australian unemployment moved together with remarkable precision.

From 1926 to 1928, when Australian unemployment was on the rise, Canadian unemployment declined to what was for the time an extremely low level, reaching a low of 2.6 per cent in 1928, only to rise to a maximum of 26.6 per cent in 1933, slightly lower than the Australian maximum and later by one year to reach the peak (see Table C-1). The Canadian recovery, as measured by the decline in unemployment, was at about the average rate for the countries studied, with a fairly sharp retardation in 1938. Immediately after World War II, Canadian unemployment was below the 2 per cent mark, but from 1948 to 1950 a progressive increase brought the level in the latter year to 3.8 per cent (see Table C-2). However, postwar Canada must certainly be included among the countries with low unemployment.

4. *France*. The course of unemployment in France can be traced only in a very approximate fashion because of incomplete statistics (see Appendix E). Before World War I, the unemployment data of four quinquennial censuses, each relating to a single day of March of the census year, provide some basis for asserting that there was a low level of unemployment. Trade union data indicating somewhat higher percentages of unemployment, on the order of from 6 to 8 per cent for years in the first decade of the century, are suspect for a variety of reasons.

The tightness of the French labor market in the 1920's, apart from "the not very intense crises of 1921-1922 and 1926-1927,"[32] is indicated by the fact that large numbers of foreign workers were imported to supplement the French labor force, which had been depleted by war losses.

The precise levels of unemployment prevailing during the depression years of the 1930's are difficult to ascertain from the available statistics. Our estimates, which are shown in Table E-8, must be interpreted with caution; in fact, so approximate do we regard them that we have excluded them from Table 1. They suggest that French unemployment remained relatively low during this period, in fact, lower than for any country studied. The several estimates that are available tend to support the conclusion of relatively low unemployment. A similar conclusion appears to be justified for the postwar years, though the nature of the data renders precise comparison with other countries hazardous. France, it may be noted, provides an apparent exception to our finding that relatively low unemployment during the 1920's tended to be followed by relatively high unemployment during the following decade.

5. *Germany*. Unemployment in Germany before World War I was low according to the fairly reliable trade union unemployment percentages (see Appendix F). Except for a relatively high level of

[32] "Le chômage en France de 1930 à 1936," Institut de Recherches Économiques et Sociales, Paris, 1938, p. 11.

unemployment in 1914, unemployment in Germany was also extremely low during World War I and in the inflationary period following the war (see Table F-1). In 1923, a sharp increase, from 1.5 per cent unemployed in 1922 to 10.2 per cent in 1923, was indicated by the trade union series. Thereafter, unemployment increased to 13.1 per cent in 1924, fell sharply in 1925, and then spiralled up to 18.0 per cent in 1926. The sharpness of the 1926 peak was unique for Germany, although Norway and Denmark, and to a lesser extent Great Britain, were subject to increasing unemployment during this year. In 1927 the level of unemployment fell about 10 points below the 1926 peak where it remained until the first effects of the Great Depression took hold in Germany. It is clear that instability was one of the distinguishing features of the German labor market in the 1920's, as was the case in Scandinavia. The high average level of unemployment in Germany during these years contrasts sharply with the low levels experienced in Belgium and France.

The Great Depression struck Germany with unusual severity. Unemployment by 1932 had reached a pinnacle of 43.8 per cent. This peak is the highest attained by any of the countries studied. That this percentage is no statistical mirage is evidenced by the fact that the census of 1933 recorded 37.3 per cent of the workers and employees in manufacturing, mining, and construction unemployed. After 1932, the statistics of the number of registered unemployed (Table F-4), as well as those of the number of applicants seeking work, give evidence of an extensive and swift recovery. In 1934, 20.5 per cent of the workers and employees in manufacturing, mining, and construction are estimated to have been unemployed, while by 1938, this percentage had decreased to 3.2. The introduction of forced labor and other Nazi practices renders the figures somewhat suspect for the 1933-1940 period, though the main outlines of the trend in unemployment seem clear enough.

After World War II, the statistics of unemployment reveal a substantial volume of unemployment in Germany, similar to the Belgian and Danish experience. Unemployment percentages for the United States and British occupation zones showed a fall from 7.5 per cent of the total wage and salary earning labor force unemployed in 1946 to 4.7 per cent in 1948, and then a steep rise to 8.1 per cent in 1949 (see Table F-6). Similar percentages for the German Federal Republic also display a sharp increase from 4.2 per cent unemployed in 1948 to 8.3 per cent in 1949. Unemployment rose still further in 1950, reaching 10.2 per cent.

6. *The Netherlands.* The unemployment picture of the Netherlands

is quite atypical (see Appendix G). In the immediate post-World War I years, 1918 to 1923, unemployment was relatively high. However, from 1923 to 1929, when most other countries had at least one cycle of unemployment, the Dutch level of unemployment declined almost steadily (see Table G-1). In this respect, the Dutch experience was reminiscent of the Belgian, though the absolute level of unemployment in the latter country was considerably below that of Holland.

In 1929, Dutch unemployment began to rise, relatively slowly at first, and then more rapidly as the depression deepened. The unusual feature of the Dutch unemployment trend, however, was that the peak was not reached until 1936, four years later than the modal peak year of 1932. Moreover, while Dutch unemployment declined after 1936, it remained almost until the outbreak of the war at a higher level (percentagewise) than that of any of the countries studied. Part of this excess is in all probability a statistical rather than a real phenomenon, but nonetheless it is probably true that during the later thirties, the Netherlands experienced an abnormally high rate of unemployment. On the other hand, the 1938 recession had no repercussions in Holland in terms of unemployment.

Percentages of unemployment are not available for the Netherlands after 1940. However, employment exchange statistics indicate that after World War II, unemployment was far below the immediate prewar level. For example, whereas some 235,600 persons were registered as totally unemployed in 1939, the 1950 total was only 57,000 (see Table G-2). In all probability, Dutch unemployment from 1946 to 1950 was at a lower level than at any peacetime quinquennium in its recorded unemployment history.

7. *Scandinavia.* The proximity and close economic ties of the Scandinavian countries, Denmark, Norway, and Sweden, have made for certain similarities in their unemployment histories, although in many ways it is the differences among them that are the more interesting (see Appendixes D, H, and I). Recorded unemployment for Denmark was very high throughout the entire half century (see Table D-1). However, at least until World War I, the Danish statistics were relatively overstated, and it is doubtful that average unemployment in Denmark from 1904 to 1913 was twice as high, on the average, as that of Great Britain, as the figures in Table 1 suggest. Throughout this same period Norwegian unemployment was undoubtedly much lower than that of Denmark (see Table H-1), and somewhat lower than Swedish unemployment as well, for the Swedish figures are in all probability understated.

Although all the Scandinavian countries were neutral in World

War I, the Danish economy was subject to the greatest adverse effects of the war, as indicated by the rise of unemployment to 18 per cent in 1918, whereas Norway and Sweden experienced much lower rates, 1.5 per cent and 4.6 per cent respectively, in the same year (see Table I-1).

The Scandinavian unemployment pattern of the 1920's is of particular interest. While unemployment rose in most countries from 1920 to 1921, the increase was particularly sharp for the three Scandinavian countries. Only the United Kingdom showed a rise of comparable magnitude. Swedish unemployment, until that time always moderate, reached the highest peak thereto recorded in any of our countries, 26.6 per cent, although there is some reason to believe that the increase shown by the data exceeded the real rise. Norwegian unemployment, which had averaged 3.1 per cent from 1904 to 1913, rose to 17.7 per cent in 1921. Denmark was intermediate with 19.7 per cent of insured workers unemployed, and the United Kingdom figure was just short of the Norwegian.

Scandinavian unemployment remained at record levels in 1922 and then fell sharply until 1924, when it was roughly comparable to the British level. In 1925, however, at a time when unemployment in all of our countries with the exception of Germany was either stable or declining, a sharp rise in the Danish and Norwegian levels set in, culminating in peaks of 22.5 per cent and 25.4 per cent, respectively, in 1927. This time Swedish unemployment did not follow suit, remaining on a par with the relatively high but stable British level. Thus, during the 1920's Denmark and Norway had two major cycles of unemployment, and Sweden one, quite in contrast with what was happening elsewhere.

Denmark and Norway were very badly hit by the Great Depression, with only Germany exhibiting more unemployment. The Norwegian peak of 33.4 per cent must in all probability be discounted, for the composition of the Norwegian unemployment index was such as to make it unduly volatile. Nevertheless, it is difficult to escape the conclusion that a major change in the structural characteristics of the Norwegian labor market occurred after World War I. Unemployment remained high in both Denmark and Norway right up to the beginning of World War II, only the Netherlands exhibiting a greater degree of unemployment in the late 1930's.

The effects of the Great Depression upon the Swedish economy were not nearly so drastic. Reaching a maximum of 23.3 per cent in 1933, unemployment declined steadily until 1940; the 1937-1938 unemployment increase in Denmark and Norway had no counterpart in the Swedish economy.

Swedish neutrality during World War II was reflected in a somewhat higher unemployment rate than that which prevailed in the belligerent nations (the wartime figures shown for Denmark were due to the extraordinary conditions of the German occupation). From 1946 to 1950, unemployment in Norway averaged 2.9 per cent and in Sweden around 2.7 per cent, a situation of "overfull" employment. By way of contrast, the Danish labor market was much looser, with unemployment remaining fairly steady at about 9 per cent, about the same average level as that which prevailed from 1904 to 1913. In 1950, Denmark, along with Belgium and Germany, was one of the relatively high unemployment countries of Europe, while Norway and Sweden were down at the low British level.

8. *United Kingdom.* Unemployment in the United Kingdom was only roughly measured in the pre-World War I period by the trade union percentages of unemployment (see Appendix J). The average of the trade union figures for the years 1900-1913 is 4.4 per cent, which, according to most authorities, is a satisfactory estimate. The highest pre-World War I trade union percentage, 7.8, was observed for 1908 (see Table J-1). While this high percentage may be biased upward on account of overrepresentation of certain groups of workers in cyclically sensitive trades, it is probable that the overstatement is not great.

During World War I, unemployment fell to very low levels, reaching 0.4 per cent in 1916. Directly after the war, however, unemployment rose severely. The unemployment insurance data for 1919 are incomplete, while the trade union percentage, 2.4, does not properly portray the extent of unemployment in the demobilization period. We have estimated unemployment in 1919 rather roughly at about 5.2 per cent (see Table J-3). In 1921, the unemployment insurance rate curve for the United Kingdom shows a very sharp peak of 17.0 per cent followed by a percentage of 14.3 for 1922. The height of this peak was exceeded only by those of similar peaks occurring in Scandinavian unemployment. During the remaining years of the 1920's, the level of unemployment displayed remarkable stability, varying between a high of 12.5 in 1926, partly influenced by the coal strike of that year, to a low of 9.7 in 1927 (see Table J-7). The average level of unemployment for the years 1921-1928, 12.2 per cent, is exceeded only by the averages for the Scandinavian countries.

Starting from a level of 10.4 per cent in 1929, unemployment increased to a peak of 22.1 per cent in 1932 and declined thereafter. However, the decline was far from complete for the 1939 unemployment percentage was still 10.5.

As in World War I, unemployment rates in World War II were low. In the postwar years 1946-1950, recorded unemployment averaged 1.9 per cent. This percentage is somewhat too low to use in making comparisons with the prewar averages, primarily because of the greater scope of the postwar unemployment insurance schemes. If all the additional persons covered by unemployment insurance in the postwar period are excluded from the denominator used in the calculation of percentages in the postwar period and no change is made in the numbers unemployed, the maximum difference in the postwar percentages due to changes in coverage of the unemployment insurance schemes can be obtained. The results of this calculation indicate that an upward correction of about 0.6 percentage points would be the maximum correction needed to make the postwar percentages comparable to the prewar percentages with respect to coverage. Actually the correction should be smaller, since it was assumed that in excluding persons from the denominator, none of them was unemployed. Probably a postwar average of 2.2 per cent is about right for comparisons with the prewar date.

9. *The ILO World Index of Unemployment.*[33] For the years 1929 to 1938, the International Labour Organization calculated a world index of unemployment based upon the statistics of some fifteen countries.[34] Several alternate systems of weights were tried, including totally gainfully occupied, and totally gainfully occupied in mining, manufacturing, transport, and commerce, without producing great variations in the results. Two indexes, one including the National Industrial Conference Board unemployment estimates for the United States, and the other the higher American Federation of Labor estimates for the United States, are shown in Table 4.

The ILO unemployment percentages are below those shown for most of our countries during the entire period, Belgium excepted (see Table 1). The explanation for this discrepancy appears to lie chiefly in the inclusion in the ILO index of several countries with relatively low unemployment with which we have not dealt, namely, Japan, Poland, and Czechoslovakia. Reported Japanese unemployment for 1929 to 1937 averaged only 5.0 per cent, while Poland averaged 12.6 per cent, and Czechoslovakia, 11.2 per cent. While the ILO index figures for the countries we have covered do not agree with our figures in every particular, there is substantial agreement between them.

[33] For details regarding this measure, see the sources cited above in note 1.

[34] France, Italy, and the Soviet Union were the only countries of industrial importance excluded from the index.

TABLE 4

ILO World Unemployment Rates, 1929-1938

(*per cent*)

Year	*Series 1*	*Series 2*
1929	5.4	6.2
1930	10.3	10.8
1931	16.2	16.5
1932	21.1	21.5
1933	20.1	20.7
1934	16.3	17.1
1935	14.8	15.3
1936	12.4	13.2
1937	10.1	10.8
1938	11.4	11.6

Note: Series 1 and Series 2 differ only with respect to the unemployment estimates used for the United States.

Source: *International Labour Review*, June, 1939, p. 813.

5. *Conclusions*

In the foregoing pages we have presented statistical information on the course of unemployment in ten countries during the first half of this century. The problem of measurement in itself is a difficult one and yet represents only an initial step toward a fuller understanding of the causes of unemployment. The few generalizations which do emerge from the data must be regarded as tentative in character, in part statements of hypotheses rather than of fact.

1. There are striking differences in the general levels of unemployment characterizing different periods during the past fifty years. The interwar years were years of relatively high unemployment, while the first and fifth decades had relatively little unemployment.

2. There is important variation among the unemployment records of various countries, variation so pronounced in many cases that it cannot be ascribed to elements of incomparability in the available statistics. Among the peculiar developments that stand out are the relatively low level of Belgian unemployment during the 1920's, and its contrastingly high post-World War II level; the "extra" cycles of unemployment in Scandinavia during the 1920's, and the transformation of Norway from a "low" to a "high," then back to a "low" unemployment country; the consistently high level of unemployment in the Netherlands from 1932 to 1940, compared with earlier experience; and the extraordinarily high rate of German unemployment in 1932, followed by a very rapid recovery.

3. In the period 1921-1928, average unemployment rates for the

countries studied show much more dispersion than do those of the 1929-1939 period. Relative coefficients of dispersion for the two periods are 0.41 and 0.17.[35] The two lowest average rates for the 1921-1928 period, those of Belgium, 2.6, and Canada, 5.7, contrast sharply with those of Sweden, 17.4, and Norway, 17.0, the two highest. Average rates, 1929-1939, range from Belgium's low of 13.0 to Norway's high of 23.1.

4. We have found an inverse international relationship between the average rates of unemployment during the years 1921-1928 and the changes in average rates between the 1921-1928 and 1929-1939 periods.[36] This relationship may be purely fortuitous, or it may have a genuine economic basis. For example, one might set up the hypothesis that the level of investment relative to gross national product was low in countries with relatively high levels of unemployment in the 1920's, and higher in countries of lower unemployment. Since net investment has a floor (where disinvestment equals depreciation), the impact of the depression could have resulted in a greater fall in investment in the countries with the higher levels of investment (and lower rates of unemployment). This means that the negative multiplier effects in the 1930's would have been greater in these countries. For example, consider the two possibilities for a given country:

a. In the 1920's unemployment was fairly low and investment high. Investment could fall, under the impact of the depression, from the high level to a negative value equal to, but no lower than, depreciation. The multiplier effect would produce a large fall in gross national product with a concomitant large rise in unemployment.

b. In the 1920's unemployment was fairly high and the level of investment low. The shock of the depression could then produce only a relatively small decrease in investment; therefore gross national product would fall less than in case a and the increase in unemployment would be smaller.

5. A positive rank correlation, 0.679, was found between peak unemployment rates in the 1930's and the extent to which unemployment diminished thereafter, as measured by the difference between the peak and the minimum rates observed in the 1930's.[37] This correlation may be merely due to chance or perhaps to a peculiar combination of biases in the data. If the relationship is indeed a real one, it suggests that countries hardest hit by unemployment did the most to alleviate the

[35] This coefficient is the average of absolute deviations from the general period average (the unweighted average of the individual countries' period averages) divided by the general period average.

[36] See p. 461.

[37] The Netherlands' peak unemployment did not occur until 1936. All other peaks occurred either in 1932 or 1933. Exclusion of the Netherlands from this calculation raises the correlation coefficient to 0.804.

problem. Certainly the extreme case of Germany, the country exhibiting the highest peak unemployment and the most extensive recovery, fits in well with the above hypothesis.[38]

6. To test whether the data give any indication that the extent of recovery in the 1930's is related in some fashion to conditions responsible for levels of unemployment in the 1920's, two calculations were performed. Average levels of unemployment, 1921-1928, were correlated with peak minus minimum rates of the 1930's, a measure of the extent of recovery. A rank correlation coefficient equal to 0.179 (0.103 upon exclusion of the Netherlands) was obtained. A similar calculation involving 1921-1928 average rates and minimum rates in the 1930's produced a positive correlation of only 0.200. These rather weak correlations, while not disproving the hypothesis under inspection, provide no substantial support for it.

7. Progress toward more refined and accurate measures of unemployment and more uniform and conceptually complete definitions of unemployment was observed to be related to the stage of development of institutions concerned with combating unemployment and its effects. The establishment of state-supported trade union unemployment funds was a first step in the direction of standardizing and refining the preexisting trade union statistics. National systems of unemployment insurance resulted in the broadening of coverage, as well as in further standardization of definitions. Employment exchange statistics have been less useful to us than other types as a result of the form in which they generally appear but provided a useful supplementary source of information on unemployment trends. Finally, the most recent type of statistic developed, the labor force sample survey, reflects a heightened interest in the exact state of the labor market by the community and particularly by national governments, which have in large part assumed responsibility for offsetting unfavorable developments.

Our study, limited as it is to a single gross measure of unemployment, provides only a rough index of the relative intensity of unemployment in the countries studied. It is our impression that a more intensive examination of the available data on a comparative basis, including a study of seasonality, industrial, and geographical distribution of unemployment, and its incidence among various segments of the labor force, would, in conjunction with supplementary studies, provide a basis for testing more refined and significant hypotheses concerning the causes of unemployment and the mechanism by which it is transmitted across national boundaries.

[38] Values of the rank correlation coefficient required for significance when calculated from samples of 8 cases are 0.63 at the 90 per cent level and 0.71 at the 95 per cent level. It should be noted that the correlation coefficient above, 0.679, is based on samples with 9 cases. Tables for $n = 9$ are not available (see Helen M. Walker and Joseph Lev, *Statistical Inference*, Holt, 1953, pp. 282 and 478).

Appendix A: Australia

Any historical analysis of Australian unemployment must be based upon figures reported over a long period by trade unions. The currently available unemployment insurance data under the Unemployment and Sickness Benefits Act began only on July 1, 1945. The trade union series has the following characteristics:

1. Beginning with the year 1913, quarterly figures on unemployment were collected from a number of trade unions. For selected years from 1891 to 1912, the Commonwealth Bureau of Census and Statistics endeavored to obtain retrospective estimates of unemployment from a number of trade unions as of the end of the year only. These figures are shown, together with the number of reporting unions and membership of reporting unions, in Table A-1.

TABLE A-1

Unemployment Rates Reported by Trade Unions, Australia, Selected Years, 1891-1912

Year	*Number of Reporting Unions*	*Membership of Reporting Unions*	*Per Cent of Members Unemployed at End of Year*
1891	25	6,445	9.29
1896	25	4,227	10.81
1901	39	8,710	6.59
1906	47	11,299	6.67
1907	51	13,179	5.74
1908	68	18,685	5.98
1909	84	21,122	5.79
1910	109	32,995	5.63
1911	160	67,961	4.67
1912	464	224,023	5.55

Source: *Trade Unionism, Unemployment, Wages, Prices, and Cost of Living in Australia, 1891 to 1912,* Melbourne, Commonwealth Bureau of Census and Statistics, 1913.

Since few trade unions paid any form of unemployment benefit in the earlier years, accurate records of unemployment were difficult to obtain, and returns were not available for the same unions throughout the period. Moreover, since the data are year-end data, they cannot be taken to represent average unemployment for the specified year.

The data for 1912 represented 75 per cent of the total number of local unions existing at the time and 52 per cent of union membership. However, coverage drops off rapidly as we go backward from 1912. Thus, in 1891, only 20 per cent of the local unions with 12 per cent of total union membership were covered. The corresponding figures for

1896 were: 19 and 8 per cent; for 1901, 20 and 9 per cent; and for 1906, 16 and 6 per cent.[1] It was estimated that for 1912, 44 per cent of all male employees and 8.4 per cent of all female employees, in all professions, trades, and occupations in the Commonwealth, were members of trade unions.[2] If it is assumed that all trade union members were males,[3] coverage among male employees in 1912 would have been about 25 per cent.

The Bureau of Census was of the opinion that the particular industries covered in this sample did not result either in upward or downward bias. The building and metal trades were heavily represented, while such comparatively stable industries as railways were not represented at all. Unskilled casual labor was poorly represented. "Thus, for some reasons, the percentage given is likely to be greater, and for other reasons less, than the true average percentage unemployed throughout the country."[4] Moreover, the following comparisons with census returns were adduced in favor of the reliability of the data:[5]

	PER CENT UNEMPLOYED		
	1891	*1901*	*1911*
Trade union returns	9.29	6.59	4.67
Census returns[a]	7.46[b]	6.50	4.53

[a] All male wage earners, excluding "professional" occupations.
[b] New South Wales and Victoria only.

The difference shown for 1891 was ascribed to the fact that the census was taken in March while the trade union data were for the year end, the intervening months having witnessed a depression following upon a long strike of maritime workers and sheep shearers.

The validity of these observations has been challenged, however. It has been asserted that since the two series were for different dates in the year any resemblance in the results "is only an accident and does not support a claim that the trade union returns are representative of the state of unemployment in Australia."[6] The relatively small membership of the reporting unions in each of the census years is another limiting factor.

[1] *Trade Unionism, Unemployment, Wages, Prices, and Cost of Living in Australia, 1891 to 1912*, Melbourne, Commonwealth Bureau of Census and Statistics, 1913, pp. 13, 18.

[2] *Ibid.*, p. 12.

[3] In fact, some 96 per cent of trade union members were males in 1912 (*ibid.*, p. 11).

[4] *Ibid.*, p. 18. [5] *Ibid.*

[6] J. K. L. Gifford, *Economic Statistics for Australian Arbitration Courts*, Melbourne, Macmillan, 1928, p. 7.

As to the first objection, it may be noted that for the years 1913 to 1920, for which quarterly trade union data are available (for the last week in the months of February, May, August, and November), and which, except for 1914, were years in which unemployment was comparable absolutely to that reported for the years 1901-1912, the percentage of unemployment in the fourth quarter of any year was within one percentage point of unemployment in the first quarter of the following year.[7] The first and fourth quarters of the year normally mark the period of lowest unemployment in Australia. Since the census date was in the first quarter, and the trade union report was at the end of the fourth quarter (prior to 1913), the possibility of divergence between the two was not so great as implied by the above quotation. However, neither the census nor the trade union figures prior to 1913 accurately represent average unemployment throughout the year, precisely because they were both in quarters of lowest unemployment.

2. The quarterly trade union data collected since 1913 represent unemployment in the last weeks of the months of February, May, August, and November. Annual averages derived from them are shown in Table A-2.

These figures have certain limitations, of which the following are the most important.

a. Coverage. The relative size of the sample of workers represented by the series is indicated by the following data:[8]

Year	*Per Cent of Trade Union Members in Sample*	*Estimated Per Cent of All Male Wage and Salary Earners*
1921	51.4	31.1
1933	56.2	35.0
1939	48.2	31.6
1947	53.6	40.0
1950	52[a]	25-30[a]

[a] These figures are from *Labour Report*, 1950, No. 39, p. 122. The last figure is the ratio of reporting membership to all wage earners, including women.

[7] The average difference for the years 1913 to 1920 inclusive was 0.9 per cent. In five of the seven years, unemployment in the first quarter was higher than in the preceding quarter (by an average of 0.7 per cent), while in the two remaining years, the reverse was true (by an average of 1.4 per cent).

[8] The data are from various issues of *Labour Report*, Commonwealth Bureau of Census and Statistics. The years chosen are those for which census data are available. For the earlier years, the omission of female wage and salary earners did not constitute a serious distorting factor in indicating degree of coverage, since the labor force participation of women was low. For later years, however, and particularly since the war, the greatly increased labor force participation of women, plus the smaller extent to which they are unionized, produce quite different results if they are included in the comparison. Thus, for 1947, the ratio of covered trade union membership to *all* wage and salary earners is only 29 per cent, compared with the 40 per cent ratio to *male* wage and salary earners shown in the table.

TABLE A-2

Unemployment Rates Reported by Trade Unions, Australia, Annual Average, 1913-1951

(*per cent unemployed*)

Year	*Due to Lack of Work Only*	*All Causes*	*Year*	*Due to Lack of Work Only*	*All Causes*
1913	5.4	6.5	1933	24.2	25.1
1914	7.4	8.3	1934	19.6	20.5
1915	8.3	9.3	1935	15.6	16.5
1916	4.8	5.8	1936	11.3	12.2
1917	6.1	7.1	1937	8.4	9.3
1918	4.6	5.8	1938	7.8	8.7
1919	4.6	6.6	1939	8.8	9.7
1920	5.5	6.5	1940	7.1	8.0
1921	10.4	11.2	1941	2.8	3.7
1922	8.5	9.3	1942	0.7	1.6
1923	6.2	7.1	1943	0.2	1.1
1924	7.8	8.9	1944	0.3	1.2
1925	7.8	8.8	1945	0.3	1.2
1926	6.3	7.1	1946	0.5	1.4
1927	6.2	7.0	1947	0.3	1.2
1928	10.0	10.8	1948	0.3	0.9
1929	10.2	11.1	1949	1.4	2.0
1930	18.4	19.3	1950	0.4	0.8
1931	26.5	27.4	1951	0.3	0.7
1932	28.1	29.0			

Note: For the years up to and including 1929, a special sample of unemployment by cause is shown separately in the annual *Labour Reports.* For some years, however, total unemployment for all causes shown in this special sample differs from total unemployment for all causes for all reporting unions. In making the adjustment, the ratio of unemployment due to lack of work to unemployment for all causes, derived from the special restricted sample, was applied to the global unemployment figure derived from the total reporting population.

From 1929 to 1947 the *Labour Reports* simply note that the percentage of unemployment due to (1) sickness and accident and (2) all other causes except lack of work remained uniform at 0.7 per cent and 0.2 per cent, respectively. Thus, a constant factor of 0.9 per cent has been deducted from the global unemployment percentages to adjust for these years. Beginning with 1948, the adjustment factor was put at 0.6 per cent for accident and illness, and "insignificant" for other causes; for the years 1948-1951, therefore, a 0.6 per cent adjustment factor has been deducted.

Source: *Labour Reports,* Commonwealth Bureau of Census and Statistics, *passim.*

It is apparent that because of the high degree of union organization, the trade union unemployment series has long covered a remarkably large proportion of the Australian labor market, in comparison to similar types of statistics of other countries.

The principal omissions in industrial coverage are for the pastoral and agricultural trades, for industries in which workers have permanency of employment (such as railway and tramway employees and civil servants), and for such casual trades as longshoremen's work. However, there appears to be no reason to suspect any particular bias toward greater or less unemployment for the industrial fields covered, which include, in addition to manufacturing, mining, building construction, land transport other than railways, and domestic service. Salaried individuals as well as wage earners appear to be represented in the sample, though whether to the same relative extent cannot be determined from the data.

b. Methods of Collecting Information. The basic reports are prepared quarterly by local trade union secretaries and submitted to the Bureau of the Census for processing. The Bureau has made the following observations regarding the reporting mechanism:

> "Very few unions pay unemployment benefits, but the majority of the larger organizations have permanent secretaries and organizers who are in close touch with the members and with the state of trade in their particular industries. In many cases unemployment registers are kept, and employers apply to the union officials when labor is required. Provision is also made in the rules for members out of work to pay reduced subscriptions."[9]

An intensive examination of the reporting procedure in thirty reporting unions yielded the following conclusions:

> "Some kept unemployment registers, which members signed when they became unemployed. In unions paying unemployment benefit, such a record would probably be fairly accurate, but in others, the majority, where there is no advantage in registering, for a time at least, the records and the returns based on them would obviously be liable to error. There would be no reliable check on members working in other occupations, up to one or two years at least, when they are removed from the register . . . some unions try to allow for these errors by guessing the probable numbers affected. Such returns are based on records plus guesswork. Other unions keep no record at all, and simply send in a return based on 'general observation.' The character of the occupations represented by some unions, e.g. seasonal work, prevents any accurate record being kept. Some unions return men on relief work as employed, while others, probably the majority, do not. Generally speaking, the information which unions have about unemployment amongst their own members is, in a few

[9] *Labour Reports*, No. 27, 1936, p. 108.

cases, fairly complete, and in the majority approximate to very dubious."[10]

In addition to these difficulties, the reporting system sometimes conceals unemployment if the unions are seeking wage increases through a court of arbitration and at other times exaggerates unemployment in order to justify restrictions on entry to the trade.[11]

Notwithstanding these imperfections, the Commonwealth Statistician thinks that the trade union series provides a good measure of the trend of unemployment, even though the absolute figures must be used with caution, apparently on the theory that the errors cancel out, in a rough way.[12]

c. Definitions. A person is recorded as unemployed if he is out of work for three days or more during the specified survey week. Part-time unemployment is not reported separately; the particular work pattern of the individual on less than full time determines whether he is classified as employed or unemployed.

Persons who are out of work due to direct involvement in a strike or lockout are not counted as unemployed, but those in other industries who are indirectly affected are considered unemployed.[13] However, persons unemployed for any other cause, such as illness and accident, are included among the unemployed. Fortunately, data were collected for a number of years from some of the reporting unions which permitted a breakdown of unemployment by cause. These data have been used to correct the global unemployment percentages by eliminating unemployment for all causes other than lack of work. The corrected series is also shown in Table A-2.

3. The trade union unemployment data may be checked against census data for 1921, 1933, and 1947. The comparisons are shown in Table A-3. The substantial difference between the figures in 1921 led to the observation that "the trade union unemployment percentages for those unemployed through scarcity of work very much exaggerated the amount of unemployment due to scarcity of work."[14] However, the close correspondence between them in 1933, when the census figure was, if anything, higher than the trade union data, indicates that at least in periods of very high unemployment, the trade union data mirrored with considerable accuracy the prevailing level of unemploy-

[10] E. E. Ward, "A Sample of Unemployment in Victoria," *Economic Record*, June 1938, p. 23.

[11] Gifford, *op.cit.*, p. 5.

[12] E. Ronald Walker, *Unemployment Policy*, Sydney, Angus and Robinson, 1936, pp. 64-65.

[13] *Labour Reports*, No. 30, 1939, p. 103.

[14] Gifford, *op.cit.*, p. 9.

TABLE A-3

Comparison of Unemployment Rates Due to Lack of Work as Shown by Census and Trade Union Returns, Australia, 1921, 1933, and 1947

YEAR	TYPE OF WORKER COVERED	CENSUS *Per Cent Unemployed*	CENSUS *Date*	TRADE UNION *Per Cent Unemployed*	TRADE UNION *Date*
1921	Male workers	6.0[a]	April 4	10.4	1st quarter
1933	Male workers	24.9[b]	June 30	24.8	2nd quarter
1947	Male and female workers	1.3	June 30	0.4	2nd quarter

[a] The corresponding figure for males and females together is 5.0 per cent.

[b] The corresponding figure for males and females together is 22.4 per cent. This percentage makes no allowance for youths and girls who would normally have been wage and salary earners but who were never employed on account of the depression and were thus not classified as wage and salary earners. Such an allowance would raise the percentage of unemployment.

Source: 1921—J. L. K. Gifford, *Economic Statistics for Australian Arbitration Courts,* Melbourne, Macmillan, 1928, p. 9. 1933—*Census of the Commonwealth of Australia,* June 30, 1933, Vol. II. 1947—*Year Book of the Commonwealth of Australia,* 1953, p. 549.

ment. The same, of course, would be true when unemployment was very low, as indicated by the data for 1947.

A comparison of unemployment in Queensland for the years 1925-1927, based upon unemployment insurance statistics in that state, yielded the conclusion that

> "the trade union percentage very much exaggerated at certain times the amount of unemployment due to lack of work, though at other times it fell below the percentage based on the Department [of Labour] statistics. From August to November, 1924, from February to May, 1925, from May to August, 1926, and from August to November, 1926, even the direction of movement of the two series was different, and in general the trade union percentage fluctuated more than the other."[15]

A more careful and elaborate study of unemployment in Victoria in 1937 indicated that of a sample of 2,000 men receiving public assistance, only 12 per cent were or ever had been members of unions, reporting or otherwise, whereas the reporting unions constituted a sample of 20 to 25 per cent of the wage and salary earners in Victoria at the time. In fact, only about 6 per cent of the group studied were currently registered as unemployed with reporting unions. Despite this great discrepancy, total unemployment in Victoria was estimated at 10 per cent from public labor exchange data, and 9.3 per cent on the basis of the trade union reports. This fairly close correspondence

[15] *Ibid.,* p. 11.

is attributed to "a fortuitous cancelling of errors which may or may not persist."[16]

CONCLUSIONS

The only series of unemployment other than the trade union reports available for Australia is that emanating from the unemployment insurance system, commencing in 1945. For each year between 1945 and 1952, *the direction of movement* was the same for the two series; but the absolute level of unemployment shown by the two series cannot be compared, since there are qualifications for the receipt of unemployment benefits, including a means test, which restrict the coverage of the unemployment insurance data.

The trade union series, therefore, must be used for Australian unemployment statistics for any considerable period of time. Even with corrections to eliminate unemployment for causes other than lack of work, this series has certain drawbacks. To an outside observer it seems that much of the criticism of the series was made by individuals who were attempting to make out the strongest possible case against it. The sample is, and has been for many years, substantial; industrial coverage has been wide, and not obviously biased; and several tests of the trade union data against census and other bench marks have revealed fairly close correspondence between the two, with the conspicuous and important exception of the year 1921. It cannot be said prima facie, that the trade union series either "overstated" or "understated" unemployment as compared with some theoretical norm of perfection, on the basis of the available evidence. All things considered, the Australian trade union series appears to be one of the better of the unemployment series, when compared with the character of the data available for other countries.

Appendix B:
Belgium

The principal series yielding information on unemployment in Belgium are (1) early trade union, communal fund, and employment exchange statistics, (2) voluntary unemployment insurance statistics, and (3) compulsory unemployment insurance statistics.

EARLY TRADE UNION, COMMUNAL FUND, AND EMPLOYMENT EXCHANGE STATISTICS

The Ghent trade union rates of unemployment were the first official unemployment statistics to appear. They were published monthly in

[16] Ward, *op.cit.*

the *Revue du travail* beginning in December 1895. The unions covered were classified in ten groups: clerical workers, commercial agents, and foremen; workers in printing; textiles; building; wood; metals; food; clothing; transport; and a miscellaneous group. The size of the Ghent sample increased from 13,591 members in twenty-nine unions in the first year of operation to 19,028 members in forty-nine unions in 1907 (see Table B-1).

Reporting was on a voluntary basis in the years before the creation of the Ghent Communal Unemployment Fund[1] in 1901. After the fund

TABLE B-1

Trade Union and Communal Fund Unemployment Rates, Belgium, 1896-1918
(*per cent*)

	GHENT TRADE UNIONS[a]			
YEAR	*All Members*	*Excluding Clerks*	NATIONAL TRADE UNIONS[b]	COMMUNAL FUNDS[b]
1896	3.5	4.3		
1897	2.8	3.6		
1898	3.1	3.9		
1899	2.4			
1900	2.9	2.7		
1901	2.7	2.9		
1902	2.9	3.3		
1903	2.6	3.6	3.4	
1904	2.8	3.4	3.0	
1905	2.2	2.9	2.1	
1906	1.9	2.3	1.8	
1907	1.6	2.1	2.2	
1908	2.9		5.8	
1909	3.1		3.3	3.0
1910	1.9		2.0	3.6
1911	1.5		1.9	4.4
1912	1.2		1.3	4.8
1913	1.5		2.0	
1914	13.5			
1915	32.3			
1916	59.3			
1917	58.4			
1918	53.7			

[a] 1896-1913: Averages of monthly percentages appearing in the *Revue du travail*. Rates, excluding clerks, commercial travelers, and foremen, were calculated from annual data (based on twelve months from December through November) appearing in the *Revue du travail* through 1907.

1914-1918: Calculated from data in Ernest Mahaim, *Le secours de chômage en Belgique pendant l'occupation Allemande*, Yale University Press, 1926, pp. 152-153.

[b] Averages of monthly data appearing in the *Revue du travail*.

[1] Ernest Mahaim states: "The Ghent unemployment fund was the best organized institution of unemployment insurance before the war" (*Le secours de chômage*

came into operation, participating unions, receiving communal unemployment subsidies, were required to submit monthly statements of the amount of unemployment to a special communal comptroller. Close controls by the communal authorities, as well as supervision by individual unions, insured accurate reporting.

The industrial distribution of workers covered by the Ghent scheme is compared below with that of all workers in the commune of Ghent and of industrial wage earners in Belgium. While the industrial classifications may not be perfectly comparable, it is evident that the Ghent sample underrepresented workers in building, food and tobacco, and clothing, and overrepresented workers in textiles and metals. Other important groups, workers in ceramics, mining, quarrying, and transport (after 1904) were not represented in the sample at all. In addition, the published Ghent percentages are based upon a sample which includes a considerable number of clerical workers, sales agents, and foremen.

INDUSTRY	GHENT TRADE UNION SAMPLE		CENSUS OF 1910	
	1902	*1907*	*Ghent Commune*	*Entire Country*
Book	2.8	3.0	2.2	[a]
Textile	61.7	53.4	46.2	18.9
Building	4.0	6.8	7.6	9.5
Wood	6.3	7.9	7.1	6.8
Metal	15.7	17.3	9.6	14.8
Food and tobacco	2.3	2.6	3.6	5.1
Clothing	2.8	2.8	9.3	7.7
Transport	0.7	0.0	14.4 (Transport and Other)	3.6
Other	3.7	6.2		33.6
	100.0	100.0	100.0	100.0
Total (thousands)	14.1[b]	16.1[b]	43.8	1,270.0

[a] Included in "Other" group.

[b] Union totals exclude clerical workers, sales agents, and foremen, 2,513 persons in nine unions in 1902 and 2,924 persons in nine unions in 1907.

Source: Ghent trade union statistics from annual reports appearing in issues of the *Revue du travail*; census data from *Recensement de l'industrie et du commerce*, 1910, Vol. I, p. 519 and 554.

With the spread of trade union unemployment plans, the *Revue du travail* began in 1902 to publish National Trade Union percentages of unemployment. They first covered 115 unions with 29,920 members, but by 1912, the coverage had expanded to include 276 unions with

en Belgique pendant l'occupation Allemande, Paris, Les Presses Universitaires de France, Publications de la Donation Carnegie pour la Paix, Yale University Press, 1926, p. 150).

77,526 members (see Table B-1). Since the trade union unemployment schemes developed to meet the needs of special trades, unions, and localities, it is not surprising to find that there were many differences among them.[2] Definitions of unemployment were far from uniform and conditions governing the payment of unemployment benefit varied considerably. However, it appears likely that the usual short duration of benefit payments, coupled with stringent eligibility requirements, produced a downward bias in the trade union unemployment percentages, particularly in times of depression.

From 1909 through 1912, monthly unemployment statistics of the communal unemployment funds were published in the *Revue du travail* as part of the annual report on communal and provincial unemployment subsidies (see Table B-1, column 3). In 1909, the percentages were based on the reports of 310 trade unions affiliated with communal funds whose members numbered 58,413. By 1912, coverage had extended to include 370 unions with a membership of 103,537. The communal fund statistics included wage earners in mining, transportation, and manufacturing, and salary earners. Since the majority of communal funds were modeled after the Ghent fund, their operations exhibited some degree of uniformity. Study of the industrial distribution of workers included in the communal fund statistics in December 1910, the month of the census, reveals that workers in construction, mining, and clothing were underrepresented, while those in textiles, wood and furniture, printing, and arts and crafts were overrepresented.

Public and subsidized private employment exchange statistics are available beginning with 1896. They provide data on the number of applications for work, of vacancies, and of placements. The early figures are poor since the number of exchanges was small and reporting was irregular. In 1904, only ten exchanges were in operation. By 1914, the number had increased to fifty. While useful as a rough indicator of fluctuations in the labor market, the statistics do not provide anything approaching a suitable measure of the number of unemployed persons. Many unemployed persons registered at more than one exchange and were therefore included in the statistics twice. Other unemployed persons did not use the exchanges when seeking work. The limited number of employment exchanges in the early years meant that many of the unemployed did not have the services of an employment exchange at their disposal. Later, when the statistics became more comprehensive, the far better unemployment insurance statistics make it unnecessary to refer to them for a measure of unemployment (see Table B-2).

[2] See Constance A. Kiehel, *Unemployment Insurance in Belgium*, Industrial Relations Counselors, 1932, pp. 117-119.

TABLE B-2

Public and Subsidized Private Employment Exchange Statistics, Belgium, 1896-1930[a]

Year	Number of Exchanges (thousands)	Applications (thousands)	Vacancies (thousands)	Placements (thousands)	Vacancies per 100 Applicants[b]
1896		13.1	16.8	4.3	128
1897		12.0	16.7	6.4	139
1898		13.5	16.4	6.3	121
1899		10.9	16.7	6.7	153
1900		10.0	16.5	8.2	165
1901		14.1	13.1	7.7	93
1902		17.0	11.1	6.4	65
1903		23.4	12.4	7.1	53
1904	10	20.5	13.3	8.0	65
1905	10	17.2	14.9	8.2	87
1906	10	19.2	16.3	10.6	85
1907	12	23.8	18.5	11.9	78
1908	14	39.9	21.6	15.1	54
1909	17	51.6	28.0	18.7	54
1910	31	60.1	40.8	24.9	68
1911	39	69.7	56.0	31.7	80
1912	43	71.2	64.8	36.1	91
1913	49	88.2	74.7	43.7	85
1914[c]	50	88.6	54.9	34.0	62
1919[d, e]	47	92.2	26.8	14.9	29
1920	38	141.6	90.2	57.4	64
1921[f]		181.3	96.8	71.4	53
1922[f]		192.3	136.9	89.8	71
1923	30	161.3	144.3	93.2	89
1924	33	168.9	125.5	86.0	74
1925	36	166.0	101.6	74.1	61
1926	37	179.5	98.0	73.0	55
1927	40	176.8	107.8	75.8	61
1928	42	148.5	143.3	89.5	97
1929	42	141.2	146.1	89.2	103
1930	44	190.1	100.8	72.9	53

[a] From 1896 to 1907, figures were particularly poor. Failure to report and typographical errors which cannot be corrected were frequent.

[b] Calculated for years 1896-1906, 1914, and 1919; *Revue du travail* for other years.

[c] First seven months.

[d] No data available 1915-1918.

[e] Last six months; exchanges not in operation during first six months.

[f] No reports from subsidized private exchanges.

Source: 1896-1906, 1914 and 1919—Constance A. Kiehel, *Unemployment Insurance in Belgium*, Industrial Relations Counselors, 1932, p. 62. 1907-1930, excluding 1914 and 1919—*Revue du travail*, February 1931, p. 334.

INTERNATIONAL COMPARISON OF RATES

There are available two unemployment censuses which afford an opportunity to gauge the value of the trade union and communal fund unemployment rates. The results of the first census, that of October 31, 1896, were marred by several methodological defects.[3] In particular, workers' returns understated the amount of unemployment in certain seasonal trades, counted as unemployed some persons who were sick, and included among the unemployed some older persons who were not looking for work. Data in the census report suggest that between 4 and 5 per cent of the total number of industrial wage earners were unemployed on the date of the census.

The percentages unemployed reported in the second census of December 31, 1910,[4] are shown below:

	Industry	*Commerce*	*Industry and Commerce*
Wage earners[a]	6.3	6.9	6.3
Salary earners[b]	1.3	3.2	2.0
Wage and salary earners[a, b]	6.0	4.8	5.9

[a] 5,242 wage earners on strike, included among the unemployed in the census, have been excluded.

[b] 23 salary earners on strike, included among the unemployed in the census, have been excluded.

A comparison of the trade union and communal fund unemployment percentages with those of the censuses follows:

	UNEMPLOYMENT PERCENTAGES[a]			
DATE	*Census*[b]	*Ghent Trade Unions*	*National Trade Unions*	*Communal Funds*
October 31, 1896	4.5	2.9 (3.5)		
December 31, 1910	6.3	2.2 (1.9)	1.8 (2.0)	4.2 (3.6)

[a] Percentages in parentheses are annual averages.

[b] Percentage of industrial wage earners unemployed.

It is apparent that the differences encountered above are substantial. Some of the reasons for them have already been mentioned: the local nature of the Ghent statistics, diversities in trade union practices and definitions, and unrepresentative small samples.

[3] See *Recensement général des industries et des métiers (31 octobre 1896)*, Vol. 18, p. 424; Max E. Waxweiler, "Le statistique des ouvriers industriels sans travail en Belgique" in *Compte rendu de la Conference Internationale du Chômage*, Vol. II, report No. 8, 1910, pp. 1-15; B. Seebohm Rowntree, *Land and Labour, Lessons from Belgium*, London, Macmillan, 1910, pp. 502-503; Kiehel, *op.cit.*, p. 41.

[4] *Recensement de l'industrie et du commerce*, Vol. 8, p. 37 and Vol. 2, p. 1414.

What then may be said of the level of unemployment in Belgium before World War I? Rowntree, in an admittedly rough approximation, employed the trend in the Ghent trade union series in conjunction with the census of 1896 in order to estimate the level of unemployment in the years from 1896 through 1907. After remarking that the Belgian economy prospered in the closing years of the nineteenth century and in the early years of the twentieth century, he writes:

> "Thus, the percentage of men out of work, which was shown by the census to have been 4½ per cent in 1896, has been considerably smaller since then. If it has declined in the same ratio as the percentage of unemployed in Ghent, it will have averaged 3½ per cent for the seven years 1896 to 1902, and 2¾ per cent from 1903 to 1907. . . . These are the only statistics upon which any estimate of the amount of unemployment in Belgium can be based. So far as they go, they appear to show that, taking an average of years, the percentage of unemployed workers in Belgium is somewhere about 3 per cent, but for reasons given on p. 503, this figure can only be taken as approximately correct."[5]

Rowntree cites personal communications from M. Louis Varlez, director of the Ghent unemployment fund, M. Vandervelde, leader of the Belgian Labor Party, and M. De Leener, a Belgian economist, to the effect that 3 per cent is a good estimate of the average level of unemployment in Belgium for the period from 1896 through 1907.

The depression of 1908 is undoubtedly not adequately reflected in the trade union series. Many workers exhausted their unemployment benefits, and, though still unemployed, did not appear in the statistics. The Ghent percentage rose only to 2.9 in 1908 and then to 3.1 in 1909. In 1910, when the census put normal average unemployment at about 5 per cent,[6] the Ghent percentage stood at 1.9. The National Trade Union percentage reached a peak of 12.0 in January 1908, while the annual average for 1908 was 5.8, followed by percentages of 3.3 and 2.0 for 1909 and 1910, respectively.

Several rough calculations indicate that the level of unemployment in 1908 and 1909 was about 6 to 9 per cent for industrial wage earners.[7] For the years 1910 to the beginning of World War I, the level of unemployment probably fluctuated between 3 and 6 per cent.

[5] Rowntree, *op.cit.*, p. 504.

[6] *Recensement de l'industrie et du commerce*, Vol. 8, p. 22.

[7] Two calculations were performed. In the first, the ratio of the census estimate of normal unemployment in 1910 to the Ghent percentage for 1910 was applied to earlier Ghent percentages. The second calculation employed unemployment percentages for the industrial groups in the Ghent sample and weights derived from the census of 1910.

During World War I, with the German invasion and occupation, unemployment rose to extraordinary heights. The Ghent trade union series, the only one which continued to appear, represented relief more than unemployment figures and reached very high levels (see Table B-1). The unemployment census of February-March 1915, which was limited to occupied Belgium, showed that a little less than 50 per cent of the total number of wage and salary earners, as given by the 1910 census, were unemployed.[8] While the accuracy of the census is questionable since it was not carefully planned and was rushed to completion under the disturbing influence of an occupying power, there can be little doubt but that there actually existed an extremely high level of unemployment at the time of the census and throughout the war years.

VOLUNTARY UNEMPLOYMENT INSURANCE STATISTICS[9]

After World War I, steps were taken to form a system of voluntary unemployment insurance societies to replace relief measures which had been instituted during the war. In spite of difficulties encountered in the depression of 1920-1921, this program was a success. By the end of 1920, 627 communes had formed eighty-four communal and intercommunal unemployment funds and total membership in the unemployment insurance societies increased from 126,300 in 1913 to 668,000.

State supervision, in addition to requiring uniformity of operation, entailed a more careful and uniform definition of involuntary unemployment. Persons incapable of working, on strike or locked out, and those definitely dismissed from their previous employment who refused to accept suitable work under customary working conditions (as determined by the employment exchange authorities with the help of the executive committees of the unemployment funds) were excluded from benefit and hence not considered unemployed. Registration at an employment exchange was required on the first day of unemployment. A person was considered as wholly unemployed (*chômeur complet*) if he met the above conditions and if his employment were definitely terminated for an indeterminate period or for a limited period of more than one month.

The statistics of the voluntary unemployment insurance societies, published monthly in the *Revue du travail*, covered workers above fifteen years of age engaged in mining, manufacturing, building, transport, etc., but excluded those in agriculture, fishing, and personal

[8] Mahaim, *op.cit.*, p. 50.

[9] Source: *Revue du travail; Yearbook 1934-1935*, International Labour Organization, Vol. II, p. 171; Kiehel, *op.cit.*, Chaps. 3 and 9-14, pp. 41-51 and 138-298.

service. The inclusion of persons under eighteen was qualified, however, since such persons received benefit only if they had been working for an employer for at least six months and had been insured for at least twelve months. In October 1930, persons over sixty-five years of age were excluded from benefit. Persons in their waiting period, or having exhausted their right to benefit, or receiving relief from emergency relief funds (*fonds de crise*), were counted as unemployed (see Table B-3).

The results of two censuses, those of December 31, 1930, and of February 27, 1937, provide information which is of great value in

TABLE B-3
Unemployment Insurance Statistics, Belgium, 1921-1952

	VOLUNTARY UNEMPLOYMENT INSURANCE			COMPULSORY UNEMPLOYMENT INSURANCE		
					Wholly Unemployed (per cent)	
YEAR	*Membership (thousands)*	*Wholly Unemployed*[a] *(per cent)*	YEAR	*Membership*[b] *(thousands)*	*All Industry*	*Selected Industry*[c]
1921	688	9.7	1945	1,554	7.4	9.1
1922	705	3.1	1946	1,880	3.2	3.9
1923	654	1.0	1947	1,995	1.8	2.2
1924	607	1.0	1948	2,004	4.3	5.3
1925	598	1.5	1949	2,047	8.7	11.1
1926	611	1.4	1950	2,047	8.4	10.1
1927	629	1.8	1951	2,095	7.5	8.6
1928	632	0.9	1952	2,098	8.2[d]	
1929	640	1.3				
1930	693	3.6				
1931	761	10.9				
1932	920	19.0				
1933	980	16.9				
1934	955	18.9				
1935	900	17.8				
1936	911	13.4				
1937	916	11.5				
1938	987	14.0				
1939	1,016	15.9				

[a] Percentages calculated from monthly data. The monthly percentages are formed by comparing the daily average of the registered unemployed with the total number of insured persons.

[b] June of indicated years.

[c] The following groups are excluded: agriculture, forestry, hunting, fishing, hotels, restaurants, personal and welfare services, salary earners, artists, and domestic service.

[d] 10 months.

Source: *Revue du travail* and *Yearbooks of Labour Statistics*, ILO.

assessing the accuracy of the voluntary unemployment insurance percentages of unemployment. In Table B-4, the industrial distribution of insured wage earners is compared with that of the total population of industrial wage earners. The comparison reveals that the insurance sample's industrial representation closely approximated that of the total population of industrial wage earners.

Table B-5 indicates that the insurance sample included a preponderance of industrial wage earners. Percentage wise, the representation of salary earners and wage and salary earners in commerce was much

TABLE B-4

Comparison of the Industrial Distribution of Insured Wage Earners with That of Census Wage Earners in Industry, Belgium, December 31, 1930

INDUSTRY	PERCENTAGE OF THE TOTAL NUMBER OF: *Insured Industrial Wage Earners*	*Industrial Wage Earners*
Fishing	0.4	0.1
Mining	9.8	10.9
Quarrying	3.1	2.4
Metal	21.3	19.7
Ceramics	2.6	2.5
Glass	1.8	1.8
Chemical	2.9	3.6
Food	2.7	4.7
Textile	21.4	15.2
Clothing	1.3	5.3
Construction	9.2	10.9
Wood and furnishing	6.5	6.8
Hides and leather	2.7	2.8
Tobacco	1.2	0.9
Paper	1.0	1.1
Book	1.7	1.4
Art and crafts	3.3	2.5
Transport	7.0	7.4
Total	100.0	100.0
Total numbers	610,886	1,480,753

Note: Details may not add up to totals because of rounding.
Source: *Revue du travail,* June 1934, pp. 760-761.

smaller than in the total population of wage and salary earners. Males represented 86.6 per cent of the total insurance sample, while in the census males accounted for 81.3 per cent of the total number enumerated.

On the basis of this analysis of the insurance sample, it would appear that the insurance percentages can be taken to represent the level of

TABLE B-5

Comparison of Proportion of Wage Earners, Salary Earners, and Males and Females in the Insurance Sample and Census, Belgium, December 31, 1930

A. Percentage of Wage and Salary Earners Who Were in Industry and Commerce, and Number in Each Sample

	Industry	*Commerce*	*Unassigned*	*Total*	*Total Number*
Wage earners:					
Insurance	98.6	1.4	a	100.0	619,584
Census	95.9	4.1	a	100.0	1,545,377
Salary earners:					
Insurance	76.8	23.2	a	100.0	35,636
Census	60.6	39.0	0.4	100.0	304,895
Total wage and salary earners:					
Insurance	97.4	2.6	a	100.0	655,230
Census	90.0	9.9	0.1	100.0	1,850,272

B. Percentage in Industry and Commerce Who Were Wage and Salary Earners, and Number in Each Sample

	Wage Earners	*Salary Earners*	*Total*	*Total Number*
Industry:				
Insurance	95.8	4.2	100.0	638,222[b]
Census	88.9	11.1	100.0	1,665,603[c]
Commerce:				
Insurance	51.0	49.0	100.0	16,927[b]
Census	34.9	65.1	100.0	182,804[c]
Industry and commerce:				
Insurance	94.5	5.5	100.0	655,230
Census	83.5	16.5	100.0	1,850,272

C. Percentage of Males and Females in Industry and Commerce Who Were Wage and Salary Earners, and Number in Each Sample

	Male	*Female*	*Total*	*Total Number*
Industry and commerce:				
Wage earners				
Insurance	86.7	13.3	100.0	619,584
Census	81.9	18.1	100.0	1,545,377
Wage and salary earners				
Insurance	86.6	13.4	100.0	655,230
Census	81.3	18.7	100.0	1,850,272

[a] Less than 0.05.

[b] Excluding 26 insured salary earners and 55 insured wage earners who could not be definitely assigned to industry or commerce.

[c] Excluding 1,059 census salary earners and 806 census wage earners who could not be definitely assigned to industry or commerce.

Source: *Revue du travail*, June 1934, pp. 722-725.

unemployment among industrial wage earners subject to the following biases:

1. The inclusion of some salary earners in industry (4.2 per cent of the number insured in industry) should produce a downward bias since salary earners usually experience lower unemployment rates than industrial wage earners.

2. The inclusion of a small number of wage and salary earners in commerce (2.6 per cent of the total insurance sample) should act to lower the insurance percentage relative to the "true" percentage for industrial wage earners.

3. The overrepresentation of males in the insurance sample should tend to raise the insurance percentage, since male unemployment rates usually exceed those of females.

On the two census dates, it is possible to compare the insurance unemployment rates with the census rates. The data, presented below, reveal that on December 31, 1930, the insurance unemployment percentage, based on the total number of insured persons, was 0.5 percentage points below that of the census percentage for industrial wage earners; on February 27, 1937, the insurance percentage exceeded the census percentage for industrial wage earners by 2.0 percentage points.[10]

That the insurance percentage stood below the census percentage in 1930 and above it in 1937 may be attributable to the operation of the biases listed above. In 1930, the difference between male and female industrial wage earners' unemployment rates, as given by the census, was much smaller than in 1937. This implies that the bias due to the overrepresentation of males operated more strongly in 1937 than in 1930. Further, unemployment rates for salary earners and for wage and salary earners in commerce were both lower than the rates for industrial wage earners in 1930 than in 1937 according to the censuses (see Table B-6). This means that the biases arising from the inclusion of some salary earners and a small number of wage and salary earners in commerce in the insurance sample probably influenced the insurance percentages more in 1930 than in 1937. Since the

10

DATE	INSURANCE PERCENTAGES (WHOLLY UNEMPLOYED)	CENSUS UNEMPLOYMENT PERCENTAGES FOR INDUSTRIAL WAGE EARNERS		
		Male	*Female*	*Total*
December 31, 1930	9.2	10.1	7.8	9.7
February 27, 1937	13.7	13.6	3.3	11.7

Source: Table B-6 and *Revue du travail.*

TABLE B-6

Unemployment Rates of Wage and Salary Earners, by Sex, Belgium, Census of December 31, 1930, and February 27, 1937[a]

(*per cent*)

	WAGE EARNERS		SALARY EARNERS		WAGE AND SALARY EARNERS	
	1930	*1937*	*1930*	*1937*	*1930*	*1937*
Industry:						
Male	10.1	13.6	1.7	4.0	9.1	12.4
Female	7.8	3.0	1.9	3.1	7.3	3.0
Both sexes	9.7	11.7	1.7	3.9	8.8	10.8
Commerce:						
Male	5.9	11.4	2.9	6.9	4.1	9.3
Female	4.8	5.7	2.5	4.4	3.0	4.9
Both sexes	5.7	10.1	2.8	6.0	3.8	8.0
Industry and commerce:						
Male	9.9[b]	13.5	2.3[c]	5.0	8.7[b, c]	12.1
Female	7.7[b]	3.3	2.5[c]	3.9	6.7[b, c]	3.4
Both sexes	9.5[b]	11.6	2.3[c]	4.7	8.3[b, c]	10.4

[a] Helpers (*aidants*), none of whom were listed as unemployed in either census, are excluded.

[b] Including 806 wage earners (663 males of whom 373 were unemployed and 143 females of whom 33 were unemployed) who were not able to be assigned to industry or commerce.

[c] Including 1,059 salary earners (761 males of whom 474 were unemployed and 298 females of whom 158 were unemployed) who were not able to be assigned to industry or commerce.

Source: 1930 census—*Revue du travail*, June 1934, pp. 758-759. 1937 census—*Annuaire statistique de la Belgique et du Congo Belge*, Vol. 70, 1950, pp. 128-129.

first two biases act to depress the insurance percentage while the third acts to raise it, all relative to the "true" rate for industrial wage earners, the combined action of all of them may be responsible for the differences between the insurance percentages and the census percentages for industrial wage earners on these two dates.

COMPULSORY UNEMPLOYMENT INSURANCE STATISTICS[11]

After World War II, Belgium instituted compulsory unemployment insurance for all wage and salary earners in all lines of economic activity except civil servants appointed permanently by the state, the provinces, and the municipalities; employees of the Societé Nationale des Chemins de Fer Belges with the exception of temporary workers; persons performing military service; family helpers; apprentices; and

[11] Source: "Rapport sur la possibilité d'une coordination et d'une comparaison des statistiques du chômage dans les pays de Benelux," Commission de Coordination des Statistiques, Groupe de travail: Statistiques du chômage, 1952; *Revue du travail; International Labour Review*, December 1948, pp. 827-828.

private domestic servants (except in Eupen, Malmedy, and Saint Vith). Also excluded are unemployed persons who have a right to old age pensions (sixty-five years old and over in general) or who receive a pension from public authorities.

Counted as unemployed in the statistics are unemployed persons who must register at an unemployment exchange in order to receive benefit and wholly unemployed persons seeking work who voluntarily register. A person is counted as unemployed from the day he registers at an employment exchange. An unemployed person who does not keep up his registration (whether because he has found a job or for any other reason) is immediately excluded from the series. Since the right to unemployment benefits is of unlimited duration, the problem of unemployed persons exhausting their right to benefit and hence possibly not being motivated to register at an employment exchange does not arise.

Partial unemployment, which is differentiated from total unemployment, is defined as a period of unemployment alternating regularly with periods of employment. Accidental unemployment refers to unemployment resulting from floods, freezing weather, lack of power, machinery breakdown, etc. Unemployment rates, published in the *Revue du travail,* are calculated for the wholly unemployed and for the partially or accidentally unemployed.

In order to establish a rate of unemployment comparable to the prewar percentages, the compulsory insurance data, presented in Table B-3, have been subjected to the following adjustments:

1. For the years 1947 and on, unemployed persons in the following groups have been excluded from the monthly totals of wholly unemployed persons: agriculture, forestry, hunting, fishing, hotels, restaurants, personal and welfare services, salary earners, artists, and domestic service. The monthly numbers of remaining wholly unemployed persons were averaged to obtain an annual average.

2. Annual estimates of the total number of insured persons outside the groups listed above were constructed by excluding persons in these groups from the total number insured on December 31, 1946. On this date the total number insured was 1,880,268. After excluding the aforementioned groups, there remained 1,242,000 insured persons. To obtain estimates for following years, it was assumed that this group of insured persons, 1,242,000 persons in 1946, grew at the same rate as did the total number of insured persons.

3. From the annual averages of wholly unemployed persons developed in (1) and from estimates derived in (2), annual unemployment percentages were calculated.

The unemployment percentages, calculated in the manner described above,[12] are probably not strictly comparable with the pre-World War II percentages of the voluntary unemployment insurance societies. However, they do provide a better basis for comparing post- and pre-World War II levels of unemployment for industrial wage earners than do the unaltered compulsory unemployment insurance percentages. This is so because the postwar insurance system includes many persons outside industry not included in the prewar voluntary unemployment insurance sample.

SUMMARY

Before 1921, the available unemployment statistics are too fragmentary to derive reliable annual percentages of unemployment. The Ghent Trade Union series, relating to a limited geographical region, cannot be assumed to represent the level of unemployment in the whole of Belgium. The National Trade Union series, based on the returns of unions with extremely diverse unemployment benefit schemes embodying varying definitions of unemployment, is of little or no value as a measure of unemployment. Finally, the unemployment percentages of the trade unions affiliated with communal funds cover only a few years and are based on a sample which was rapidly changing.

After 1920, the unemployment insurance statistics, with wide coverage in all years, provide an excellent measure of unemployment in Belgium. The unemployment percentages of the voluntary unemployment insurance scheme can be taken to approximate closely the level of unemployment among industrial wage earners. The data of the more inclusive compulsory unemployment insurance system, available for the post-World War II period, have been adjusted to obtain unemployment percentages as comparable as possible to the prewar percentages.

Appendix C: Canada

Canadian unemployment statistics go back only as far as December 1915, when the government began to compile and publish data relating to unemployment among trade union members. This series was published quarterly until 1920, monthly from 1920 to 1943, and quarterly

[12] Data are not available to perform this calculation for 1945 and 1946. The calculated percentages for 1947-1951 bear a fairly constant relationship to the published percentages for the wholly unemployed for all insured persons. For 1947, the ratio of the calculated percentage to the percentage based on the total number insured is 1.22, and for following years is 1.23, 1.21, 1.37, 1.19, and 1.15. The average of these ratios, 1.23, was used to obtain percentages for 1945 and 1946.

from 1944 to June 1950, when it was discontinued. The principal characteristics and limitations of the series are as follows:[1]

1. There has been variation from month to month in coverage. Local unions, which supplied the basic data, were not always faithful in submitting returns. In 1950 there were 2,643 local unions with 570,600 members submitting returns (the total numbers of paid workers in nonagricultural industry on June 1, 1950, was estimated at 3,378,000), but neither the extent nor the industrial scope of the coverage in that year typified the situation at any other time. Roughly speaking, the trade union sample included between 10 and 20 per cent of the total number of nonagricultural wage earners in Canada.

2. The representative nature of the sample was found to vary with business conditions. When employment was rising, the trade union data were found to approximate more closely the degree of unemployment as measured by more comprehensive censuses than when employment was declining, since there was a tendency for the reporting unions to have better employment conditions than the nonreporting unions. Moreover, persons dropping out of unions on the downswing of the cycle were more apt to be unemployed than those remaining in the unions.

3. The industrial coverage of the trade union data included fishing, lumbering, mining, manufacturing, transportation, communications, trade, and services. Among major occupational groups only agriculture was excluded.

4. Only wage earners (or paid workers, the terms being used almost interchangeably in Canadian statistics) were included in the reports. For purposes of international comparison such a limitation is an advantage rather than a disadvantage.

5. Persons engaged in work other than their own trade or idle because of illness were not considered as unemployed, and unions engaged in industrial disputes were excluded from the tabulation. From the nature of the returns, persons who had never held nonagricultural jobs, and were therefore not likely to have joined a union, would not have been covered.

6. M. C. McLean, who was largely responsible for the excellent monograph on unemployment which accompanied the 1931 census, had the following to say of the trade union series:

> "The objection that the organization of labor unions brings about employment conditions different from those prevailing among the generality of wage-earners is here regarded as frivolous. If we could

[1] A detailed analysis of the trade union series may be found in *Seventh Census of Canada, 1931*, Monographs, *Unemployment*, Vol. XIII, 1942, pp. 222-228.

obtain an estimate of unemployment as close to the truth as the difference caused by labor union organization we should have not only the best estimate in the world, but also figures better than those of any census, since definitions of employment are subject to very wide variations. This is not the trouble with the labor union figures. The real drawback is that from month to month the number of unions reporting their unemployment varies, and more particularly that the sample reporting varies in kind according to employment conditions. When employment is on the up-grade the reports of the unions seem to be fairly representative; when it is on the down-grade there is a clearly marked tendency for the reporting unions to have better employment conditions than the non-reporting unions."[2]

Annual unemployment percentages derived by arithmetical average from the quarterly or monthly trade union statistics are shown in Table C-1, column 1.

In an effort to eliminate some of the deficiencies of the trade union data, the Dominion Bureau of Statistics adjusted them for variation in the size of the sample and for decline in trade union membership during periods of recession, for the years 1920-1935. The corrected data are shown in Table C-1, column 2. A comparison of the two series reveals that only in 1921 and 1932 (both years of considerable unemployment) did the two series differ by more than 2 percentage points of unemployment.

To secure unemployment statistics free of the limitations inherent in the trade union data, the Dominion Bureau of Statistics, on the basis of the 1931 census, an index of employment based upon monthly reports of business concerns,[3] and the trade union data as corrected, prepared independent estimates for the years 1920-1940. Annual unemployment rates, derived from the monthly data of these estimates, are contained in Table C-1, column 3.

An unemployed was defined for the purpose of these estimates as "the person who could tell a census enumerator that he had worked as a wage earner or that he had a wage-earning occupation, but is at present out of work (not through illness, accident, strike or lockout, etc.)." Under this definition youths of working age who had never held steady jobs, as well as those on farms who might have been wage earners under better employment conditions, were excluded from the unemployment census.

[2] *Ibid.*, p. 222.

[3] The Bureau of Statistics' index of employment varied in coverage from year to year, including 36 per cent of all wage earners in 1921 and 45 per cent in 1931. Because of sharp variations in the size of the labor force at risk, this index alone could serve only as a very rough indicator of unemployment.

TABLE C-1

Annual Unemployment Rates among Wage Earners, Canada, 1915-1950
(*per cent*)

Year	*Reported by Trade Unions* (1)	*Reported by Trade Unions, Corrected for Variation in Size of Sample and Membership* (2)	*Estimated by the Bureau of Statistics* (3)
1915	7.9[a]		
1916	1.9		
1917	1.9		
1918	1.3		
1919	3.4		
1920	4.6	3.8[a]	3.8[b]
1921	12.6	8.9	8.9
1922	7.1	7.1	7.1
1923	4.9	4.9	4.9
1924	7.2	7.1	7.1
1925	6.4	7.0	7.0
1926	5.1	4.7	4.7
1927	4.9	2.9	2.9
1928	4.5	2.6	2.6
1929	5.7	4.2	4.2
1930	11.0	12.7	12.9
1931	16.9	17.5	17.4
1932	22.0	24.4	26.0
1933	22.3	24.1	26.6
1934	18.2	18.9	20.6
1935	15.4	16.0	19.1
1936	13.2		16.7
1937	10.7		12.5
1938	13.1		15.1
1939	12.2		14.1
1940	7.8		9.3
1941	4.5		
1942	2.2		
1943	0.8		
1944	0.5		
1945	1.4		
1946	1.4		
1947	1.3		
1948	2.2		
1949	3.0		
1950	3.8[c]		

[a] December only. [b] June to December. [c] March and June only.

Column — Source

1 1915-1919, W. A. Berridge, *Report on Employment and Income of Labor in Canada, 1910-1931*, World Social Economic Congress, 1931, p. 6. 1920-1935, *Seventh Census of Canada, Unemployment*, pp. 283-285. 1936-1950, *Labour Gazette, passim.*

2 1920-1935, *Seventh Census of Canada, Unemployment*, pp. 285-287.

3 1920-1936, *Seventh Census of Canada, Unemployment*, pp. 274-276. 1936-1937, *Canada's Unemployment Problem*, L. Richter, editor, Toronto, Macmillan, 1939, p. 9. 1938-1940, *Statistics Relating to Labor Supply under War Conditions*, Ottawa, Dominion Bureau of Statistics, 1941, p. 14.

Several of the problems encountered in the preparation of these estimates are worthy of special note:

1. There was found to be a considerable amount of migration between the wage earner and the independent worker groups during the period studied. This was attributed to the rapid industrialization which Canada was then undergoing. For example, according to the 1921 census, there were 3,173,000 gainfully employed persons; in 1931, there were 3,927,000, an increase of 23.8 per cent. The number of wage earners employed rose from 1,789,000 in 1921 to 2,133,000 in 1931, or 19.2 per cent. If the ratio of wage earners to gainfully employed population in 1931 had remained unchanged from 1921 (62.1 per cent), there would have been in 1931 some 2,439,000 wage earners, and unemployment would have been 12.5 per cent. In fact, the 1931 census revealed that there were 2,570,000 wage earners in that year, so that 17 per cent were without jobs. Consequently, estimates of the labor force based upon census projections were hazardous, and indexes of *employment* were only of limited value in estimating unemployment.

2. Large-scale immigration to and emigration from Canada, depending upon the phase of the business cycle, were additional complicating factors.

> "The immigration occurred during low unemployment but kept up until unemployment rose almost to a peak. Emigration then started and it was accompanied (or followed) by decreasing unemployment. This, of course, introduces a widely different concept of unemployment from that generally accepted, *viz.* that unemployment is merely the opposite of employment. Unemployment only partly declined with increasing employment. As noticed it also *increased with increasing numbers of wage earners and decreased with decreasing numbers of wage earners.*"[4]

Recently, the Dominion Bureau of Statistics prepared an estimate of the labor force for the period 1931 to 1950, based in part upon the quarterly survey of the labor force which was initiated in November 1945. However, these estimates, from which unemployment percentages may be derived, differ substantially from the earlier statistics in concept and coverage:

1. The new series includes agriculture as well as nonagricultural industry. While the agricultural labor force is shown separately, no separate figure is given for agricultural unemployment.

2. As far as the labor force is concerned, paid workers (wage earners) and the self-employed (including unpaid family workers) are shown separately, but again no separation is made for the unemployed.

[4] *Seventh Census of Canada, 1931 Unemployment*, p. 15.

3. The labor force survey includes in the labor force (i.e. in the denominator of the unemployment ratio)

> "those who were at work during any part of the [survey] week, or had jobs from which they were temporarily absent, or were looking for work . . . while those who did not work for pay or profit during the survey week and had no job and were not looking for work, are classed as not in the labor force (as either permanently unable or too old to work, keeping house, going to school, retired or voluntarily idle, or other)."[5]

4. Persons temporarily laid off with definite instructions to return to work within thirty days are regarded as *employed* by the labor force survey, but as *unemployed* under earlier definitions. This tends toward a relative understatement of unemployment under the labor force concept. Offsetting this is the fact that persons who have never worked but are looking for work are counted as in the labor force and unemployed by the labor force survey, and (in theory) as neither gainfully occupied nor unemployed under the earlier census concept.

5. The Bureau of Statistics, in its estimates, linked the post-1945 labor force survey data to the pre-1945 census data by adjusting the latter to the former concept.[6] The estimates were made as of June 1 for each year beginning with 1931, to take advantage of the fact that this was the population census day in 1931 and 1941.[7]

Two sets of unemployment rates derived from these estimates are presented in Table C-2. In the first set, persons without jobs and seeking work are related to the entire civilian labor force. From 1931 to 1939 the resultant unemployment percentages are below any of the other series considered above, because while unemployment is normally restricted to the paid-worker group, the labor force at risk here includes a substantial number of employees, self-employed, and unpaid family workers. After 1939, however, this series follows closely the uncorrected trade union percentage, being slightly above the latter up to 1947 and slightly below it from 1948 to 1950.

The second series in Table C-2 relates persons without jobs and seeking work to the total of paid workers with jobs and persons without jobs. This series runs consistently higher than any other series, caused no doubt by the fact that the unemployment data include farm workers and some self-employed, whereas the labor force at risk excludes these categories.

[5] *Canadian Labor Force Estimates 1931-1950*, Dominion Bureau of Statistics, Reference Paper No. 23, 1951, p. 2.

[6] For the war years, employment service data were used in making the estimates (*ibid.*, p. 10).

[7] The actual day for 1941 was June 2.

For purposes of international comparison, the best of the unemployment series is that in Table C-1, column 3. Coverage is inclusive, with only agriculture excluded; it is limited to wage earners, avoiding the

TABLE C-2

Estimated Unemployment Rates Derived from Labor Force Survey Data and Projected Back to 1931 by the Bureau of Statistics, Canada, 1931-1950

Year	*Unemployed as Per Cent of Total Labor Force*	*Unemployed as Per Cent of Paid Workers plus Persons without Jobs*
1931	11.6	19.1
1932	17.6	28.6
1933	19.3	32.5
1934	14.5	24.6
1935	14.2	24.3
1936	12.8	22.3
1937	9.1	16.3
1938	11.4	20.1
1939	11.4	20.3
1940	9.2	16.1
1941	4.4	7.1
1942	3.0	4.6
1943	1.7	2.5
1944	1.4	2.1
1945	1.6	2.4
1946	2.6	4.1
1947	1.9	2.8
1948	1.6	2.5
1949	2.0	3.0
1950	2.6	3.8

Source: *Canadian Labor Force Estimates*, Dominion Bureau of Statistics, p. 15.

pitfalls of attempting to measure unemployment among other groups; persons on temporary layoff are counted as unemployed, while those who have never worked are excluded from the count; and persons engaged primarily in keeping house, with part-time employment outside, are similarly handled.

Unfortunately, this series is available only for the period 1920 to 1940. The only series which presents data prior to 1920 is the trade union series, which has the additional advantage of continuing unbroken until 1950. The trade union data diverge significantly from the Bureau of Statistics estimates from 1932 to 1940; during these years, average unemployment was 15 per cent according to the trade union series and 17.8 per cent in the Bureau estimates. The maximum divergence was 4 percentage points in 1933, the year of greatest unemployment. The years before 1920 and after 1940 were years of relatively low unemployment. On the basis of the behavior of the two series—and indeed, all available series[8]—in such periods, it does not seem unreasonable to link to the Bureau estimates the trade union series for the pre-1920 and post-1940 years. It was not necessary to average the series for the two years in which they were linked, since they were quite close together in those years (0.8 percentage points in 1920, 1.5 percentage points in 1940). For 1950, the trade union series is extrapolated on the basis of the labor force survey series. The resultant series is shown in Table 1.

Appendix D: Denmark

There is only one major source of information on Danish unemployment, namely, the statistics emanating from the operation of the unemployment insurance system. Denmark has the Ghent system of unemployment insurance, under which the state subsidizes and supervises unemployment insurance societies operated by trade unions. The early establishment of the system (subsidies were paid as early as 1907) and its relative liberality combine to render the unemployment statistics derived from it a generally accepted measure of unemployment in the country.

The rates of unemployment derived from this source are shown in Table D-1, for the years 1903-1950. The specific characteristics of the series are as follows:

1. Prior to 1910, the data were calculated by the trade unions directly. Beginning in that year, the task of assembling and publishing the data was taken over by the Danish Statistical Department, a governmental agency. The basic reports come from unemployment insurance societies, covering persons aged eighteen or over, who are able to work and seeking work.

Because Danish unemployment insurance provisions have always been relatively liberal, particularly with respect to duration of benefits, the degree of unemployment registration is probably higher than in most other countries.[1] This would be particularly true of the earlier

[8] From 1941 to 1949 inclusive, the labor force survey series yields average unemployment of 2.2 per cent compared with 1.9 per cent as shown by the trade union data.

[1] Under the Danish system of unemployment insurance, reporting is virtually mandatory even for those who may not immediately qualify for benefits. Long duration of benefits, plus the additional fact that persons who exhaust benefits are still "controlled" as long as they retain membership in the insurance society, make for full reporting.

TABLE D-1

Unemployment Rates and Working Days Lost Due to Unemployment among Insured Workers, Denmark, Annual Average, 1903-1950

Year	*Rates*	*Days Lost*	*Year*	*Rates*	*Days Lost*	*Year*	*Rates*	*Days Lost*
1903	13.0		1919	10.9	30.4	1935	19.7	59.7
1904	12.0		1920	6.1	17.4	1936	19.3	58.1
1905	13.0		1921	19.7	56.7	1937	21.9	64.5
1906	6.0		1922	19.3	57.4	1938	21.5	65.6
1907	7.0		1923	12.7	36.9	1939	18.4	56.1
1908	11.0		1924	10.7	32.2	1940	23.9	71.7
1909	13.0		1925	14.7	42.2	1941	18.4	
1910	10.7	27.4	1926	20.7	62.0	1942	15.1	
1911	9.5	23.9	1927	22.5	68.3	1943	10.7	
1912	7.6	20.0	1928	18.5	56.2	1944	8.3	
1913	7.5	18.8	1929	15.5	47.0	1945	13.4	
1914	9.9	24.7	1930	13.7	40.9	1946	8.9	
1915	8.1	20.5	1931	17.9	53.7	1947	8.9	
1916	5.1	13.1	1932	31.7	95.9	1948	8.6	
1917	9.7	23.7	1933	28.8	88.6	1949	9.6	
1918	18.1	48.5	1934	22.2	67.3	1950	8.7	

Source: *Unemployment rates*: 1903-1908—F. Zeuthen, "Arbejdsløsheden," *Socialt Tidsskrift*, 1932, Vol. VIII, p. 305. 1909-1940—K. Vedel-Petersen, *Danmarks Statistik*, Copenhagen, 1946, p. 418. 1941-1950—*Statistiske Meddelelser*, 4 Raekke, 144 Bind, 2 Haefte, *Arbejdsløsheden 1950*, p. 13.

Working days lost: The following volumes of *Statistiske Meddelelser*—4 R., 48 B., 5 H.; 4 R., 61 B., 4 H.; 4 R., 74 B., 2 H.; 4 R., 88 B., 4 H.; 4 R., 100 B., 2 H.; 4 R., 115 B., 4 H.

years of the century, because of the comparatively early development of the Danish unemployment insurance system.[2]

2. The unemployment rates are derived by comparing the number of persons registered as unemployed on a particular day of the month (in recent years, at least, the count day has been the last Friday in each month) with the total numbers of persons insured.[3] Since records are kept on the basis of actual days of unemployment suffered, data are also available on the number of working days lost due to this cause (see Table D-1). Statistics on the potential number of working days are not published, so that it is not possible to express the latter series in percentage form. However, when the two series are compared, it is

[2] Thus Professor Zeuthen has noted: "The [unemployment] figures appear to have been relatively high for Denmark earlier; but a large part of this difference disappeared later, partly on the basis of more complete statistics in other countries after the introduction of unemployment insurance." F. Zeuthen, *Arbejdsløn og Arbejdsløshed*, Copenhagen, Nyt Nordisk Forlag, 1939, p. 245.

[3] K. Vedel-Petersen, *Danmarks Statistik*, Copenhagen, 1946, p. 418. It should be emphasized that the number of persons reporting themselves as unemployed, not the number receiving benefits, is used in calculating the rate of unemployment.

clear that they move very closely together. This is not unexpected, in view of the common source, but it does indicate that basing the calculation of the unemployment percentage on an end-month count does not introduce any serious bias, as compared with a daily count.

3. The degree of coverage has varied considerably over time. The total number of members of unemployment insurance societies was as follows:[4]

Year	*Members*	*Year*	*Members*
1910	101,462	1930	288,939
1914	127,685	1935	386,080
1915	141,090	1940	501,426
1920	306,919	1950	645,000
1925	269,238		

These figures may be compared with the following statistics of employment, derived from census data. The figures exclude the self-employed, higher supervisory personnel, and those unemployed at the time of the census, and are limited to manufacturing, construction, and retail and wholesale trade.

Census Year	*Manufacturing and Construction*	*Commerce*	*Total*
1914	262,000	n.a.	
1925	309,000	114,000	423,000
1935	353,000	123,000	476,000

n.a. = not available.

Thus, in 1914, when insurance was limited almost exclusively to skilled workers in manufacturing and construction, the coverage was less than 50 per cent of this group. From 1914 to 1920, the insured group expanded considerably as a consequence of a more liberal policy of admission to funds, but the next five years witnessed a sharp decline in unemployment insurance society membership. Nevertheless, coverage in 1925 was much greater than in 1914, particularly when it is realized that the number of insured among commercial employees was very small.

An estimate of unemployment insurance coverage for 1930 indicated that 65 per cent of all wage earners and 20 per cent of salaried employees were society members, with virtually no membership among supervisory personnel and domestic employees. The wage-earner group

[4] *Statistiske Meddelelser*, 4R., 115B., 4H.; 4R., 114B., 2H.

included apprentices not eligible for membership, and agricultural workers.[5] Excluding these two groups raised the coverage of wage earners to 79 per cent. Moreover, since many of the commercial employees were young people, receiving help at home and only marginally attached to the labor market, the actual coverage among commercial employees was probably understated.[6]

The figures for 1935 indicate increased coverage, though conceptual differences between the census and unemployment insurance figures render hazardous the determination of a precise percentage of coverage. The following statement regarding coverage in 1952 indicates roughly the degree of coverage since the war: "In Denmark the overwhelming majority of the insured are urban workers in crafts and industries where the coverage approaches 90 per cent of all workers. In the rural districts and among salaried employees, on the other hand, coverage does not exceed 20 per cent."[7]

4. At the beginning of the century, unemployment insurance coverage was confined largely to skilled workers in manufacturing. The subsequent extension of coverage resulted, first, in bringing in unskilled and semiskilled wage earners (who in Denmark are organized in a large multi-industrial union), and secondly, in embracing many employees in retail and wholesale establishments. There has been considerable discussion in the Danish literature of the possible bias imparted to the unemployment figures by this extension of coverage.

It was generally assumed that the effect of growing coverage was to impart an upward bias to unemployment statistics, on the assumption that the newer recruits were more unemployment-prone than the older members; that the closer coverage reached 100 per cent for each trade or industry, the greater would be the reported unemployment, other things being equal. This effect was particularly feared during the rapid increase in unemployment society membership from 1930 to 1935. However, a special study conducted in June 1934, indicated that newly enrolled members were *less* subject to unemployment than older members.

The chief explanation appears to have been that a substantial proportion of the new members enrolled between 1930 and 1934 were recent migrants from the countryside into industry, who because of age and other characteristics were able to displace older insured workers.[8]

[5] About 20 per cent of wage earners in agriculture and fishing were covered.

[6] J. S. Dich, "Arbejdsløshedstallene og Arbejdsløsheden," *Socialt Tidsskrift*, January 1932, p. 16.

[7] The Ministries of Social Affairs of Denmark, Finland, Iceland, Norway, and Sweden, *Freedom and Welfare*, 1953, p. 414.

[8] Vedel-Petersen, *op.cit.*, p. 243.

Nevertheless, the belief persists that in the long run, increased coverage, and in particular the greater coverage of unskilled and semiskilled workers, has tended to result in an increase in reported unemployment, though precise estimates of the degree of the bias are not available.[9]

5. Low coverage among agricultural laborers, domestic servants, and commercial employees, as well as the exclusion of civil servants, results in an overstatement of reported unemployment in comparison with the unemployment for the entire labor force, since by and large the excluded groups tend to have a lower rate of unemployment than the covered groups. It was estimated that for 1930, the published data would have to be reduced by one-sixth to take the noninsured labor force into account.[10]

CONCLUSION

On the basis of the foregoing observations, it may be concluded that the Danish statistics of unemployment derived from the unemployment insurance system provide a good index of unemployment among wage earners in manufacturing and construction. They would appear to be more reliable than similar data for other countries for the following reasons: (1) the early development of unemployment insurance in Denmark, which meant less of an upward bias in the data as coverage broadened; (2) the high degree of coverage in manufacturing and construction in recent years; (3) the high intensity of reporting due to the liberality of the benefit system; and (4) the decentralization of administration, and particularly the fact that registration of the unemployed and the payment of benefits are handled by persons completely familiar with the employment situation in the trade concerned. There has probably been some upward bias in the absolute size of the figures over the years, although this may have been reversed in recent years because of the spread of unemployment society membership among wholesale and retail employees. However, no measure of this bias is available.

Compared with other countries, it is probable that, particularly for the first quarter of the century, the Danish unemployment statistics were relatively overstated because of relative completeness of reporting and a high degree of coverage. This factor has undoubtedly diminished in importance, but the Danish unemployment statistics still remain among the most comprehensive of the several countries studied.

[9] Zeuthen, *op.cit.*, pp. 240-243. See also Jørgen S. Dich, *Arbejdsløshedsproblemet i Danmark 1930-1938*, Copenhagen, Socialministeriets Økonomisk-Statistiske Undersøgelser Nr. 4, 1939, pp. 3-49, for a discussion of this factor, and of the effect of more stringent controls over registration of unemployed introduced during the nineteen-thirties.

[10] J. S. Dich, *op.cit.*

Appendix E:
France

AVAILABLE STATISTICAL INFORMATION CONCERNING UNEMPLOYMENT

Quinquennial Censuses of Unemployment.[1] Since 1896, the quinquennial censuses, embracing the total population of France, have included questions concerning the employment status of all persons who work under the direction of or in the service of another, with the exception of homeworkers. Wage and salary earners in all lines of activity came within the scope of the censuses. In Table E-1, the results

TABLE E-1

Unemployment According to the Quinquennial Censuses, France, 1896-1936

DATE	WAGE AND SALARY EARNERS UNEMPLOYED (*thousands*)	PER CENT OF WAGE AND SALARY EARNERS UNEMPLOYED			INDUSTRIAL WAGE AND SALARY EARNERS[a] UNEMPLOYED (*thousands*)	PER CENT OF INDUSTRIAL WAGE AND SALARY EARNERS UNEMPLOYED		
		Both Sexes	*Male*	*Female*		*Both Sexes*	*Male*	*Female*
Mar. 29, 1896	267	3.0	3.2	2.7	170	4.3	4.3	4.3
Mar. 3, 1901	315	3.5	3.8	3.0	199	4.6	4.7	4.4
Mar. 4, 1906	239	2.6	2.8	2.3	166	3.8	3.8	3.9
Mar. 5, 1911	209	1.9	n.a.	n.a.	b	b	b	b
Mar. 6, 1921	537	5.1	4.6	5.9	426	7.6	6.2	11.6
Mar. 7, 1926	243	2.2	2.2	2.1	168	2.6	2.6	2.7
Mar. 8, 1931	453	4.0	4.0	4.0	330	5.0	4.8	5.7
Mar. 8, 1936	864	7.5	7.8	6.9	638	11.6	11.8	11.0

[a] Wage and salary earners in mining, quarrying, building, manufacturing, communications, and transportation.

[b] Change in the system of industrial classification makes data not comparable to that for other years.

n.a. = not available.

Source: 1911: *Bulletin du Ministère du Travail*, October-December 1932, p. 381. 1936: *Annuaire statistique*, Vol. 56, Paris 1946, p. 143. Other years: *Recense général de la population (8 mars 1931)*, Vol. 1, Part 3, Paris 1935, pp. 67-68.

of these censuses are presented. The unemployment percentages refer to both wage and salary earners. It is not possible to calculate percentages for wage earners alone since in all the censuses, the number of unemployed (*sans emploi*) is not given for wage and salary earners separately.

While the census returns generally excluded those unemployed because of sickness from the total number unemployed, this is not

[1] See Census Reports: *Le chômage en France d'après les recensements professionals*, Paris, Bulletin du Ministère du Travail, October-December 1932, pp. 377-385; Alexander de Lavergne and L. Paul Henry, *Le chômage*, Paris, Marcel Rivière, 1910, p. 66.

true for the two earliest censuses. In the census of 1896, 62,407 of the 266,875 persons reporting themselves unemployed failed to indicate the cause of their unemployment. In the 1901 census questionnaire, no question concerning the cause of unemployment was included. The following censuses queried the unemployed to determine whether their unemployment was due to sickness.

The census unemployment figures refer to wage and salary earners of all ages. A breakdown of the unemployed by age is available in the 1911 census report and in earlier ones, but is not available in reports following 1911.

Trade Union Unemployment Statistics.[2] The trade union series, shown in Table E-2, which extends from 1895 through 1913 is based on trade union replies made monthly to inquiries of the Office du Travail which asked for the number of workers belonging to the union on a specified day of the month and the number of these members

TABLE E-2

Unemployment Rates among Trade Union Members, France, 1895-1913

Year	*Total Sample of Union Members*	*Total Sample Excluding Miners*	*Union Members in Industry and Commerce*[a]
1895	7.0	n.a.	n.a.
1896	6.7	n.a.	n.a.
1897	6.9	n.a.	n.a.
1898	7.3	n.a.	n.a.
1899	6.6	n.a.	n.a.
1900	6.8	8.0	n.a.
1901	7.8	9.9	n.a.
1902	9.9	10.9	n.a.
1903	9.4	10.2	9.1
1904	10.2	11.3	10.7
1905	9.0	10.0	8.7
1906	7.6	8.4	7.4
1907	7.0	7.6	6.8
1908	8.6	9.6	9.2
1909	7.3	8.1	7.1
1910	5.8	6.5	5.8
1911	5.7	6.2	5.4
1912	5.4	6.1	5.6
1913	4.7	n.a.	n.a.

[a] Excluding union members in mining, agriculture, and wood-cutting.
n.a. = not available.
Source: *Annuaire statistique*, Paris 1913, p. 183. *Bulletin de l'Office du Travail*, February 1908, p. 130, and February 1913, p. 123.

[2] See *Le chômage en France de 1900 à 1907*, Bulletin de l'Office du Travail, February 1908, pp. 128-134; annual reports entitled, *Le chômage en France en 19--*, which appeared in the Bulletin through 1913; Lavergne and Henry, *op.cit.*, p. 53.

without work (*sans ouvrage*) or without a job (*sans place*) on the above date. In order to make the meaning of the word unemployed more precise, those not at work because of sickness or workers who were on strike were not counted as unemployed. At about the fifteenth of each month, the Labor Ministry sent a questionnaire to all unions whose existence was known to the Ministry. These included unions paying out of work benefits as well as those not paying such benefits. In 1900, of 2,754 unions known to the Ministry and to whom questionnaires were sent, 626 unions (22.7 per cent) replied. The responding unions had a membership of 141,000 which was 29.3 per cent of the membership of all known unions. By 1907, 1,059 of a total of 5,475 unions (19.3 per cent) responded. These unions had a membership of 207,000 which was 23.2 per cent of the total number of union members in France. In all the years from 1900 on, the union sample included about 20 to 25 per cent of the total number of unionists (see Table E-3). However, the number of trade unionists covered by

TABLE E-3

Coverage of Trade Union Unemployment Series, France, 1900-1912

	NUMBER OF UNIONS			MEMBERSHIP OF UNIONS (*thousands*)		
YEAR	*In Existence*	*Responding*	*Per Cent Responding*	*All Unions*	*Responding Unions*	*Responding as Per Cent of All*
1900	2,754	626	22.7	480	141	29.3
1901	3,448	822	23.8	578	143	24.7
1902	3,833	887	23.1	614	146	23.7
1903	4,089	1,004	24.6	642	157	24.5
1904	4,361	1,004	23.0	717	173	24.2
1905	4,768	980	20.1	772	174	22.6
1906	4,996	1,143	22.9	818	203	24.9
1907	5,475	1,059	19.3	892	207	23.2
1908	n.a.	986		n.a.	200	
1909		1,034			222	
1910		1,009			232	
1911		912			221	
1912		814			211	

n.a. = not available.

Source: *Bulletin de l'Office du Travail*, February 1908, p. 129, and February 1913, p. 122.

the returns represented only about 5 per cent of the total number of wage and salary earners in manufacturing, mining, building, and transportation.

The industrial groups represented in the trade union returns were agriculture, forestry, food, hides and leather, books, textiles, wood, metal, mining, building, and salary earners. The miners' union of Pas-de-Calais with a membership of 20,000 to 30,000 was generally excluded in calculation of the percentages published in the *Bulletin* since this union reported irregularly. Annual percentages including miners, 1895-1913, appeared in *Annuaire statistique* of 1913. From 1903-1912, a separate percentage for industry and commerce, that is excluding workers in agriculture, wood-cutting, fishing and mining, was published in the *Bulletin* (see Table E-3).

Public Relief Fund Statistics.[3] Since August 1914, when the state began to subsidize unemployment relief funds, monthly statistics of the number of wholly unemployed persons in receipt of relief from departmental, communal and intercommunal unemployment relief funds have appeared. Annual averages of the monthly data for 1915 and following years are shown in Table E-4.

In spite of the fact that local unemployment fund operations have been required to conform to conditions embodied in state decrees, far from complete uniformity of operation has resulted. In general, relief has been extended to those who are involuntarily unemployed, that is, to workers who have terminated their relation with their former employer and who have satisfied certain additional conditions. To be eligible for receipt of relief, the involuntarily unemployed person had to be capable of working and ready and willing to accept a job. As evidence of willingness to work, unemployed workers were required to register at an employment exchange. Further, an unemployed person had to satisfy certain residence requirements and to show proof of previous employment in the period directly preceding his period of unemployment. Those unemployed on account of strikes and lockouts, misbehavior, and seasonal causes, as well as those pensioned off or retired, were generally denied relief.

The effect of these restrictions on the grant of relief has been to keep the recorded number of unemployed in receipt of relief considerably below the actual number of unemployed. This understatement is further magnified for several other reasons. Since the relief payments were very small, many unemployed persons, although eligible for relief payments, did not apply for them. Furthermore, other eligible

[3] See *Le chômage en France d'après les statistiques des Institutes Publiques d'Assistance aux Chômeurs et des Offices Publics de Placement*, Bulletin du Ministère du Travail, January-March 1933, pp. 1-10; *ILO Yearbook*, 1934-1935, p. 175; *Note Française sur la reglementation du chômage et ses rapports avec l'élaboration des statistiques*, Commission Permanente de l'Organisation du Traité de Bruxelles, 3ème Session du Groupe de Travail des Statisticiens, Document A/1690; *International Labour Review*, December 1948, p. 830.

TABLE E-4

Unemployed in Receipt of Public Relief, France, 1915-1952

Year	Unemployed in Receipt of Relief (thousands)	Year	Unemployed in Receipt of Relief (thousands)
1915	174	1935	427
1916	72	1936	432
1917	28	1937	355
1918	13	1938	374
1919	52	1939	382[b]
1920	6	1940	n.a.
1921	47	1941	293
1922	5	1942	70
1923	2	1943	20
1924	1	1944	n.a.
1925	1	1945	16
1926	2	1946	16
1927	34	1947	7
1928	5	1948	17
1929	1	1949	40
1930	3	1950	52
1931	45	1951	40
1932	273[a]	1952	39
1933	274		
1934	345		

[a] From July 1932 on, unemployed in receipt of relief from the welfare offices are included.

[b] Average of months January through August.

n.a. = not available.

Source: 1915-1926: Calculated from monthly data in *Bulletin du Ministère du Travail*, January-March 1933, p. 6. 1927-1952: International Labour Organisation's *Yearbooks of Labour Statistics.*

unemployed persons who were unwilling to submit to questioning by the relief authorities or who felt that the acceptance of relief involved a certain social humiliation did not apply for relief. For the above reasons, the series of the number of unemployed in receipt of relief is of extremely limited value as a measure of the true volume of unemployment in France.

Employment Exchange Statistics.[4] These statistics, covering all lines of activity, relate to persons seeking work who register at employment exchanges. The monthly figures show the number of unfilled applications for work at the end of the week ending nearest the end of the month. The law requires that employment offices be created in all departments and all towns with more than 10,000 inhabitants; however, in normal times many unemployed workers who prefer to seek

[4] See note 3.

work on their own do not register with the employment exchanges. In times of economic crisis, the registration is more complete since payment of unemployment relief is subject to such registration. Annual averages of the number of unplaced applicants for work are presented in Table E-5.

TABLE E-5

Unplaced Applicants for Work, France, 1921-1952

Year	*Number of Unplaced Applicants for Work (thousands)*	*Year*	*Number of Unplaced Applicants for Work (thousands)*
1921	28	1940	n.a.
1922	13	1941	395
1923	10	1942	124
1924	10	1943	42
1925	11	1944	n.a.
1926	12	1945	68
1927	47[a]	1946	57
1928	15	1947	46
1929	10	1948	78
1930	14	1949	131
1931	64	1950	153
1932	308	1951	120
1933	305	1952	132
1934	376		
1935	464		
1936	475		
1937	380		
1938	402		
1939	418[b]		

[a] From February 1927 onward, these figures include unemployed persons in receipt of public relief.

[b] Average of months January through August.

n.a. = not available.

Source: 1921-1926—Calculated from monthly data presented by Adolf Agthe, "Statistische Übersicht der Arbeitslosigkeit in der Welt," in *Die Arbeitslosigkeit der Gegenwart*, Manuel Saitzew, editor, Verein für Sozialpolitik, Vol. 185, No. 1, p. 157. 1927-1952—International Labour Organisation's *Yearbooks of Labour Statistics*.

Employment Surveys.[5] In April 1950, and twice each year since then, the Institut National de la Statistique et des Études Économiques has conducted employment surveys (*les enquêtes par sondage sur l'emploi*), based on a stratified sample of dwellings, in an attempt to ascertain the level of unemployment and to gain other information

[5] See *Une enquête par sondage sur l'emploi*, Institut National de la Statistique et des Études Économiques, Bulletin Mensuel de Statistique, Supplement, January-March 1951, pp. 1-24.

pertaining to employment and unemployment. (In December 1951, the sample consisted of 10,314 dwellings obtained from the census of 1946. The sample was constructed as follows: France was divided into eight regions which were each further subdivided into ten subregions. The subregions were weighted in the random drawing of dwelling places by the number of persons in agriculture for rural communes and by the number of inhabitants for urban communes. First a random drawing of communes was made, each commune being weighted as described above, and then a random selection of dwelling places within each commune was drawn.)

All persons fourteen years of age and over living in the selected dwelling places are questioned. The unemployed are defined as persons not having employment, having already worked, physically able to perform the work for which they are qualified, and actively seeking work. Excluded from the surveys are persons living in convents, barracks, hospitals, prisons, and other institutions. In addition, the surveys do not include the island of Corsica.

The results of two of these inquiries, together with the number of unemployed in receipt of public relief and the number of unplaced applicants for work, are shown below (in thousands):

Date	*Unemployed as Estimated by Surveys*	*Unplaced Applicants for Work*	*Unemployed in Receipt of Public Relief*
April 1950	290	175	61
October 1950	190	139	45

Source: *Bulletin mensuel de statistique*, Supplement, January-March 1951, p. 6, and International Labour Organisation, *Yearbook of Labour Statistics*, 1953, p. 87.

As had been anticipated, the estimate of the total number of unemployed persons was much larger than either of the two other categories.

Employment Indexes. Since 1930, returns made by industrial establishments to the provincial offices of the Factory Inspectorate have provided information affording an employment index.[6] The first index, using 1930 as a base, covered all establishments employing 100 persons or over in mining, manufacturing, commerce, and transportation. In the early 1930's, the chain index covered about 2.5 million wage earners with almost 90 per cent in mining and manufacturing. A second employment index, employing April 1939 as a base, was constructed from the returns of establishments employing 10 or more

[6] Later information was obtained from surveys of a representative sample of establishments.

workers. This index, which has been carried back to 1937, came to cover approximately 6.8 million workers in 1947 (see Table E-6).

TABLE E-6

Index of the General Level of Employment, France, 1930-1950

Year	*Old Index*[a]	*New Index*[b]	*Year*	*New Index*[b]
1930	100.0		1941	91.7
1931	92.5		1942	93.2[c]
1932	80.9		1943	97.0[d]
1933	79.4		1944	92.1
1934	76.9		1945	93.8
1935	73.5		1946	99.2
1936	74.1		1947	104.9
1937	78.6	100.0	1948	107.7
1938	81.2	102.7	1949	109.5
1939	83.4[e]	104.0[e]	1950	110.0
1940	n.a.	n.a.		

[a] Relates to establishments employing 100 or more persons.
[b] Relates to establishments employing 10 or more persons.
[c] January-June, September, and December.
[d] Figures commencing 1943 are averages of quarterly figures except: 1944, average of March and December; 1945, average of March, June, and September.
[e] January-July.
n.a. = not available.
Source: Old index: *Yearbook of Labour Statistics, 1941,* International Labour Organisation, p. 29. New Index: *Yearbook of Labour Statistics, 1949-1950,* International Labour Organisation, p. 44.

EVALUATION OF FRENCH UNEMPLOYMENT STATISTICS

Because French unemployment statistics are singularly incomplete, it is extremely difficult to develop a satisfactory continuous measure of unemployment. The only pre-World War I continuous series is that of the trade unions. The percentage figures shown for this series, when compared with the results of the quinquennial censuses, appear to overstate the volume of unemployment. The table at the top of the next page reveals the magnitude of this overstatement.

To single out the particular factors responsible for the differences between the census and trade union percentages of unemployment is a task beset with uncertainties. Possibly the trade unions that answered the inquiries were experiencing high rates of unemployment and did not constitute a representative sample. Further, since it is generally maintained that unions with systems of unemployment payments report more accurately than unions without such arrangements, the accuracy of the French trade union unemployment statistics, not limited to unions with such systems, is open to question. But most important is the fact that the sample of unionists covered by the

DATE	CENSUS PERCENTAGE		TRADE UNION PERCENTAGE	
	Total	*Industry*	*Total*	*Industry and Commerce*
March 1896	3.0	4.3	6.7[a]	n.a.
March 1901	3.5	4.6	7.8[a]	n.a.
March 1906	2.6	3.8	9.4	8.6
March 1911	1.9	[b]	6.3	5.8

[a] Annual figures including miners. Other trade union figures are for March of the census years and exclude miners.

[b] A change of industrial classification in the census of 1911 makes it incomparable to earlier and later censuses.

n.a. = not available.

Source: Tables E-1, E-2, and *Bulletin de l'Office du Travail, passim.*

returns was exceedingly small. That the census percentages did not understate the level of unemployment is difficult to establish with certainty. It should be noted, however, that in spite of the slow growth of the French labor force, the index of industrial production rose continuously, without a fall in any year, from a level of 63 in 1901 to one of 100 in 1913.[7] If no large changes in productivity occurred, it would appear that France was experiencing a low level of unemployment in these years.[8]

In the interwar period, the statistics of the employment exchanges and of the unemployment relief funds understate the amount of unemployment for reasons set forth above. The extent of this understatement can be appreciated by comparison with the numbers reported unemployed in the quinquennial censuses (in thousands):

Date	*Unemployed According to Census*	*Unemployed in Receipt of Relief*	*Unplaced Applicants for Work*[a]
March 1921	537	70	32
March 1926	243	0.4	9
March 1931	453	41	57
March 1936	864	465	509

[a] Before February 1927, these figures do not include the number of unemployed in receipt of relief.

Source: Table E-1; Adolf Agthe, "Statistische Übersicht der Arbeitslosigkeit in der Welt," in *Die Arbeitslosigkeit der Gegenwart*, Manuel Saitzew, editor, Verein für Sozialpolitik, Vol. 185, No. 1, p. 157; and *Bulletin de l'Office du Travail, passim.*

In view of the unsatisfactory nature of the available statistics, various estimates of unemployment in France in the interwar period

[7] *Résumé rétrospectif, annuaire statistique*, Vol. 57, 1946, p. 99.

[8] See statement of *l'Institut de Recherches Économiques et Sociales* quoted below.

will be consulted in an effort to gain some idea of the actual amount of unemployment during these years. The Institut de Recherches Économiques et Sociales in the opening paragraph of its study, *Le chômage en France de 1930 à 1936*, states:

"From the beginning of the century to the year 1930, France—except at the beginning of hostilities in 1914 and during the short and not very intense crises of 1921-22 and 1926-27—barely suffered from any unemployment except seasonal unemployment. In normal periods, it was the scarcity of manual labor and not its superabundance which was feared; in the years of prosperity which followed the war it was necessary to call in foreign workers at great expense in order to fill up the vacancies left in the economically active population."[9]

The low level of unemployment in the 1920's, referred to above, is reflected in the following estimates of unemployment which Adolf Agthe[10] constructed on the basis of the census results and the series of unplaced applicants for work (in thousands):

Year	*Average Number Wholly Unemployed*	*Year*	*Average Number Wholly Unemployed*
1921	362	1927	1,085
1922	182	1928	383
1923	142	1929	127
1924	240	1930	163
1925	266	1931	845
1926	278	end 1931	1,381

According to the 1926 census, there were 12.25 million wage and salary earners in France, including 2.4 million in agriculture, forestry, and fishing. Thus, if the above estimates are accurate, it is seen that (except for 1921 and 1927) the level of unemployment during the 1920's probably hovered about the "irreducible minimum."

With the advent of the depression of the 1930's, unemployment increased to levels not properly reflected in the inadequate statistics of the period. A number of estimates have been gathered and are presented on the next page.

The estimates of Agthe have been described above. Cahill constructed his estimate "on the basis of the Census and other official returns."[11] Gilbert, Chief of the First Bureau, Directorate of Labor,

[9] *Le chômage en France de 1930 à 1936*, Paris, Institut Scientifique de Recherches Économiques et Sociales, 1938, p. 11.

[10] Adolf Agthe, "Statistische Übersicht der Arbeitslosigkeit in der Welt," in *Die Arbeitslosigkeit der Gegenwart*, Manuel Saitzew, editor, Verein für Sozialpolitik, Vol. 185, No. 1, pp. 137-174, especially p. 148.

[11] Cahill, *op.cit.*, p. 37.

Date	Authority	Number Wholly Unemployed (thousands)	
1930	Agthe[a]	163	
1931	Agthe[a]	845	
March 1931	Census[b]	453	
End 1931	Agthe[a]	1,381	
1932	Woytinsky[c]	1,300	
1934	Cahill[d]	700-800	
February 1935	Institut Scientifique de Recherches Économiques et Sociales (ISRES)[e]	more than 1,089[f]	(1,140)
February 1935	Gilbert[g]	2,000	
April 1935	Gilbert[g]	1,900	
October 1935	ISRES[e]	722[f]	(758)
March 1936	Census[b]	864	
October 1937	ISRES[e]	559[f]	(587)
1937	Clark[h]	about 24 per cent of the *non-agricultural* occupied population	

[a] Adolf Agthe, "Statistische Übersicht der Arbeitslosigkeit in der Welt," in *Die Arbeitslosigkeit der Gegenwart*, Manuel Saitzew, editor, Verein für Sozialpolitik, Vol. 185, No. 1, p. 148.

[b] Table E-1.

[c] Wladimir S. Woytinsky, *Three Sources of Unemployment*, ILO Studies and Reports, Series C, No. 20, Geneva, 1935, p. 114.

[d] Sir Robert Cahill, *Economic Conditions in France*, Department of Overseas Trade, H.M.S.O., 1934, p. 37.

[e] *Ibid.*, p. 37 and p. 62.

[f] These estimates were made employing the provisional figure of 823,803 unemployed for the census of 1936. Figures in parentheses have been calculated using the actual 1936 census figure, 864,170.

[g] A. Gilbert, "Public Employment Office Administration and Unemployment Insurance in France," in *Administration of Public Employment Offices and Unemployment Insurance*, Industrial Relations Counselors, 1935, pp. 106-107.

[h] Colin Clark, *Conditions of Economic Progress*, Macmillan and Co., London 1940, p. 70.

Ministry of Labor, presented his figures without explanation. Clark described his estimate as follows, "The figure for 1937 is roughly computed from the decline in the statistics of employment, compilation of which began in 1930."[12] The 1936 census enumerated 20.3 million persons gainfully occupied, with 7.1 million in agriculture and forestry. Thus the nonagricultural occupied population was about 13 million. Of these 13 million, 9.6 million were wage and salary earners; therefore 24 per cent of this latter number would yield approximately 2.3 million unemployed in 1937 according to Clark's estimate (on the assumption that the number occupied did not vary appreciably between 1936 and 1937).

[12] Clark, *op.cit.*, p. 71.

Woytinsky constructed his estimate of unemployment in 1932 in the following manner. He assumed that the normal level of unemployment was 240,000 (the result of the 1926 census). From his careful comparison of the amount of work performed and the course of industrial production, he concluded that the fall of over 31 per cent in industrial production between 1926 and 1932 should have led to the dismissal of 1.7 million workers in industry; in commerce and transport, he estimated that staffs were cut down by about 10 per cent (i.e. by 200,000 wage earners) by 1932. The reduction in the average hours of work, according to Woytinsky, saved some 500,000 workers from dismissal. Further, account must be taken of the fall in the number of wage earners mainly due to a net exodus of foreign workers which he estimated at from 400 to 500 thousand. Thus Woytinsky's estimate incorporates the following items:[13]

Item	*Estimate (thousands)*
Normal unemployment	240
Decrease in employment in industry	1,700
Decrease in employment in commerce and transport	200
Decrease in employment in other occupations	60
Total	2,200
Number saved from dismissal by shortening hours of work	—500
Decrease in the number of wage earners	—400
Total wholly unemployed	1,300

The estimates of the Institut Scientifique de Recherches Économiques et Sociales were made with many reservations and a complete awareness of the difficulties involved in constructing such estimates. The Institute calculated that the number of unplaced applicants for work represented 15.8 per cent of the number of unemployed reported in the census of 1931 and 61.7 per cent of the number reported unemployed in the census of 1936. To estimate unemployment in February 1935, the date at which unemployment reached its peak (according to the figures of unplaced applicants for work), the Institute assumed that the number of unplaced applicants for work represented 50 per cent of the actual number of unemployed. Since there were 544,567 unplaced applicants for work in February 1935, the total number of unemployed on the above assumption must have been "more than 1,089,000."[14] The estimates for October 1935 and

[13] Woytinsky, *op.cit.*, p. 113.

[14] This calculation employed the provisional results of the census of 1936. On the basis of the actual results of this census, this figure is calculated to be 1,140,000.

October 1937 were constructed in a similar way on the assumption that the number of unplaced applicants for work represented 58.0 and 61.7 per cent, respectively, of the actual number of unemployed in these two months.

The problem of picking one's way through these various estimates in order to arrive at reasonable figures approximating the actual number unemployed in each year is a thorny one. This task is made doubly difficult by several complicating features of the French labor market. During the 1930's there was a large exodus of foreign workers from France which is only partially shown in the statistics of emigration and immigration (see Table E-7). Cahill, commenting on the exodus of foreign workers, wrote:

TABLE E-7

Controlled Admissions and Departures of Foreign Workers, France, 1922-1938

(thousands)

Year	*Admissions*	*Departures*[a]	*Excess or Deficit (—) of Admissions*
1922	182	50	132
1923	263	60	203
1924	265	48	218
1925	176	54	122
1926	162	49	113
1927	64	90	—26
1928	98	54	44
1929	179	39	140
1930	222	44	178
1931	102	93	9
1932	69	109	—40
1933	75	49	26
1934	72	40	32
1935	57	67	—10
1936	41	46	—5
1937	68	21	47
1938	46	21	25

[a] "While the number of controlled admissions is a close approximation to the actual number of foreign workers entering France, because of the strict regulations regarding entry, this is by no means the case as far as departures are concerned. It seems likely that the number of uncontrolled departures is twice as many as the controlled, or rather that the actual number of departures is three times the number given herewith." A. Gilbert, "Public Employment Office Administration and Unemployment Insurance in France," in *Administration of Public Employment Offices and Unemployment Insurance*, Industrial Relations Counselors, 1935, p. 102.

Source: 1922-1933: *ibid.* 1934-1938: *Yearbook of Labour Statistics, 1939*, International Labour Organisation, p. 198.

"The total number of foreigners resident in France at the census of March, 1931, was 2,890,923 (of whom 1,258,000 wage earners), as against 2,485,047 in 1926 (1,096,000 wage earners). . . . In view of the large number of departures from the latter half of 1931 onwards, consequent upon the general depression and the stricter limitation on the entry of foreign labour, it is possible that by the end of 1933 this total had declined to about 2,200,000 . . . the central federation of the metallurgical and mining industries in February, 1934, assumed that the effective total of departures was threefold that of the recorded departures, and the total net exodus for the three years since early in 1931 was between 450,000 and 500,000 workers. An official figure of December, 1933, calculated the net excess of departures over arrivals of foreign workers since the March 1931 census at 418,000."[15]

The estimate of a net exodus of about 450,000 for the years 1931-1934 seems too high in the light of the census results. These show that in 1931 there were about 1,289,000 foreign wage and salary earners (employed and unemployed) in France (see below). The 1936 census showed 911,000. The decrease in the number of foreign wage and salary earners is thus 378,000 between the years 1931 and 1936. That this smaller number is not the result of a net influx between 1934 and 1936 is easily established since the unaltered statistics of immigration and emigration show a net exodus for 1935 and 1936 in spite of the afore-mentioned understatement of departures.

Other complications are brought out in the following excerpt from the British *Ministry of Labour Gazette*:

"On the basis of the employment returns it would appear that the total reduction in the numbers employed between September, 1930, and September, 1934, was nearly 1½ million, whereas the number registered at the Employment Exchanges in September, 1934, was only 357,672. The French Ministry of Labour states that this difference is largely due to an exodus of about 450,000 foreign workers, coupled with the withdrawal from gainful occupation of persons who are not obliged to earn a living, and the return to agricultural employment, which is not covered by the monthly employment returns."[16]

The suggested shift to agricultural employment can be examined in the light of the census returns. In 1931, there were 7,704,000 occupied in agriculture, forestry, and fishing (5,532,000 employers and inde-

[15] Cahill, *op.cit.*, pp. 29-30.
[16] *Ministry of Labour Gazette*, March 1935, p. 96.

pendent workers, 6,500 salaried employees, 2,141,000 wage earners, and 24,900 unemployed). In 1936, there were 7,204,000 occupied in agriculture, forestry, and fishing (5,260,000 employers and independent workers, 1,898,000 wage and salary earners, and 45,600 unemployed). Thus the total number occupied in agriculture, forestry, and fishing actually decreased by about 500,000. Some of this decrease may be explained by the exodus of foreign workers and withdrawal from gainful occupation. The data, however, do not suggest that any appreciable shift to agricultural employment occurred.

As regards the above-mentioned withdrawal from gainful occupation, there does appear to be a significant decrease in the number gainfully occupied between 1931 and 1936. The 1931 census listed 21,612,000 persons gainfully occupied (including the unemployed) while the 1936 census listed only 20,260,000. Thus the decrease amounted to 1,352,000. The composition of this decrease is revealed below (in thousands):

YEAR	GAINFULLY OCCUPIED		WAGE AND SALARY EARNERS		WAGE AND SALARY EARNERS EXCLUDING AGRICULTURE, FORESTRY, AND FISHING	
	Total	*Foreigners*	*Total*	*Foreigners*	*Total*	*Foreigners*
1931	21,612	1,599	12,621	1,289	10,449	1,135
1936	20,260	1,245	11,562	911	9,619	748
Decrease:	1,352	354	1,059	378	830	387

For wage and salary earners (omitting agriculture, forestry, and fishing), the total decrease was 830,000 of which 387,000 represented a decrease in the number of foreigners. Thus there remains a net decrease in this group of 443,000 which may constitute the group which the French Ministry of Labor said withdrew from gainful occupation.

It is clear that the task of constructing unemployment rates for France is not easy. Any derived percentages must, from the nature of the data, be subject to a large degree of uncertainty. The percentages presented in Table E-8 represent crude estimates of the level of unemployment among wage and salary earners in manufacturing, construction, and mining. The estimates for 1921-1930 were derived as follows: Agthe's estimates of unemployment, presented above, were compared with the 12.25 million wage and salary earners enumerated in the census of 1926 to obtain annual unemployment percentages. Since both Agthe's estimates and the census figure include workers

TABLE E-8

Estimated Unemployment Rates among Wage and Salary Earners in Manufacturing, Mining, and Construction, France, 1921-1939

Year	*Per Cent Unemployed*	*Year*	*Per Cent Unemployed*
1921	5.0	1930	2.0
1922	2.0	1931	6.5
1923	2.0	1932	15.4
1924	3.0	1933	14.1
1925	3.0	1934	13.8
1926	3.0	1935	14.5
1927	11.0	1936	10.4
1928	4.0	1937	7.4
1929	1.0	1938	7.8
		1939	8.1[a]

[a] January-August.

outside manufacturing, construction, and mining, a correction factor was applied to raise the percentages. The correction factor was obtained by comparing the census unemployment rate for wage and salary earners in industry (see Table E-1) with the unemployment rate for all workers and assuming that the value of this ratio varied linearly between censuses. The values of the ratio for the censuses of 1921, 1926, and 1931 were calculated to be 1.49, 1.18, and 1.25, respectively.

The estimates for 1931-1936 were derived in the following manner: The census of March 1931 enumerated 5,385,000 wage and salary earners in employment in manufacturing, construction, and mining.[17] On the assumption that the employment index for industrial establishments employing 100 or more workers can be taken to represent the trend of employment in manufacturing, construction, and mining,[18] the annual figure of the number employed in manufacturing, construction, and mining in 1931 was calculated to be 5,265,000. The employment index was further used to obtain estimates for other years. The estimate for 1936, 4,218,000, is in good agreement with the number of employed wage and salary earners in manufacturing, mining, and construction, namely, 4,223,000. The total number of wage and salary earners, employed and unemployed, was 5,630,000 in the census of 1931 and 4,710,000 in the census of 1936. The lower figure for 1936 reflects both the exodus of foreign workers and the withdrawal from

[17] In 1931, according to the census, there were 556,000 employed salary earners (*employés*) in manufacturing, mining, and construction.

[18] As mentioned above, almost 90 per cent of the workers covered by the returns upon which the employment index was calculated were engaged in manufacturing and mining.

gainful occupation mentioned above. Lack of data permits no course other than to assume that the variation between the census dates was a linear decrease. The number unemployed was then estimated by subtracting the estimated number employed from the estimated total number of wage and salary earners. The resulting estimates of French wage and salary earners in manufacturing, mining, and construction from 1931 to 1936 are tabulated below (in thousands):

Year	*Total Number*	*Number Employed*	*Number Unemployed*
1931	5,630	5,265	365
1932	5,446	4,605	841
1933	5,262	4,519	743
1934	5,078	4,377	701
1935	4,894	4,184	710
1936	4,710	4,218	492

The estimates for the years 1937-1939 were not constructed in the same manner since there is some difficulty in estimating the total number of wage and salary earners in these years. Instead, the assumption, employed by the Institut Scientifique de Recherches Économiques et Sociales, that the number of unplaced applicants for work represented about 61.7 per cent of the actual number of unemployed in all lines of activity was adopted. It was then assumed that the number unemployed in all occupations bore the same relation to the number unemployed in manufacturing, mining, and construction as in the census of 1936.[19] The total numbers unemployed given by this calculation are 616,000 in 1937, 652,000 in 1938, and 678,000 for January through August of 1939. On the basis of the second assumption, the estimated numbers unemployed in manufacturing, mining, and construction are 347,000 in 1937, 368,000 in 1938, and 382,000 in 1939 (January-August). To calculate percentages, it was assumed that the number of wage and salary earners in manufacturing, mining, and construction remained at 4,710,000, the number given in the census of 1936.[20]

The census of March 1931 showed 4.3 per cent of the wage and salary earners in manufacturing, mining, and construction unemployed. While this is below the estimate of 6.5 per cent presented in Table E-8 for 1931, the difference can be explained by the worsening of unemployment in the months after March. For example, Agthe estimated 1,381,000 unemployed in all lines of activity at the end of 1931, a much

[19] The census recorded a total of 864,000 unemployed wage and salary earners of whom 487,000 were in manufacturing, mining, and construction.

[20] This assumption, when used in conjunction with the method of deriving the estimates of unemployment for 1931-1936, led to unreasonably low estimates of unemployment for 1937-1939.

higher figure than the 453,000 recorded by the census in March. The estimate of 492,000 unemployed in manufacturing, mining, and construction in 1936 agrees quite closely with the 1936 census figure of 487,000.

Woytinsky's estimate of 1,300,000 unemployed in 1932 included 260,000 in commerce, transport, and occupations other than manufacturing, mining, and construction. Subtraction of these leaves 1,040,000 unemployed. Also included in this latter number is a figure for normal unemployment before the depression, 240,000, which Woytinsky obtained from the 1926 census. This census listed about 160,000 unemployed in manufacturing, mining, and construction. Thus 80,000 of the 240,000 in normal unemployment must be subtracted from Woytinsky's estimate. When this is done, there remains 960,000 unemployed. This figure compared with the estimated number of wage and salary earners in manufacturing, mining, and construction in 1932, 5,446,000, yields an unemployment percentage of 17.6. In view of the crude nature of the estimates, the agreement with the estimate above, 841,000 unemployed or 15.4 per cent unemployed, is quite satisfactory.

None of the other estimates presented above were as explicitly derived as was Woytinsky's and therefore it is difficult to make direct comparisons. Cahill's estimate of 700 to 800 thousand unemployed in all lines of activity in 1934 seems to be too low in view of the fact that the employment index fell four points from 80.9 in 1932 to 76.9 in 1934. Of course, because of the departure of foreign workers and the withdrawal from gainful occupation, as well as for other reasons, the employment index alone can not be taken as an indicator of the level of unemployment. However, when Cahill's estimate is viewed both in relation to the fall of the index and in relation to the other estimates presented above, it seems to be low. The estimates of the Institut Scientifique de Recherches Économiques et Sociales and those of Gilbert for 1935 differ considerably. Gilbert's estimates suggest that the estimate of 14.5 per cent unemployed in manufacturing, mining, and construction may be too low a figure. On the other hand, the Institute's estimates for 1935, which are slightly lower than Woytinsky's estimate for 1932, are in agreement in this respect with the estimates presented in Table E-8. If it is assumed that the unemployed in manufacturing, mining, and construction represented 60 per cent of the total number unemployed,[21] then, on the basis of the Institute's estimates for 1935, there were over 684,000 unemployed in these industries in February and 455,000 in October. On the basis of Gilbert's estimate of 2 million unemployed in February, there were

[21] This percentage was 56.4 according to the results of the census of 1936.

1.2 million unemployed in manufacturing, mining, and construction in this month. The estimate of 710,000 unemployed in these activities in 1935, derived above, does not seem unreasonable compared with the results of these calculations. For 1937, Clark's estimate, amounting to about 2.3 million unemployed, is far above the Institute's estimate for October of 1937 which was 587,000. Since the census of March 1936 showed a total of 864,000 unemployed and since there was an improvement of economic conditions between 1936 and 1937, it appears that Clark's estimate is much too high.

In the post World War II years what statistical information is available indicates that unemployment rates have been very low. In 1950 it was estimated on the basis of surveys that 290,000 persons were unemployed in April and 190,000 in October (see above). These figures which include persons in all activities, when compared with the total number of wage and salary earners enumerated in the census of 1946, about 13.4 million, suggest very low unemployment rates. In 1950 the number of unplaced applicants for work was 153,000 and the number of unemployed in receipt of public relief was 52,000 (see Tables E-4 and E-5). Since both these latter figures are peak values for the postwar years, the conclusion that unemployment was quite low in the postwar years appears reasonable.

Appendix F:
Germany

TRADE UNION SERIES

Percentages of unemployment for members of trade unions which paid unemployment benefit first appeared in 1903 as the result of an agreement between the Imperial Statistical Office and the statistical offices of these trade unions. From 1903 to June 1906, these percentages were given quarterly; from then until 1933 when the series terminated, the percentages appeared monthly, based on reports relating to the end of each month. The annual trade union rates, averages of the monthly data, are presented in Table F-1.

The trade unions covered by the series reported the total number of members, the number of wholly unemployed members whether in receipt of benefit or not (*unterstützte und nichtunterstützte*), the number of members working short time, and information concerning the number of hours worked in the last week of each month.[1] Since unemployed trade union members were reported whether in receipt of benefit or not, differences in the unemployment benefit schemes of

[1] See monthly reports in the *Reichsarbeitsblatt.*

TABLE F-1

Unemployment Rates among Members of Reporting Trade Unions, Germany, 1903-1932

Year	*Membership of Reporting Unions*[a] *(thousands)*	*Per Cent Wholly Unemployed*[b]	*Corrected Per Cent Wholly Unemployed*[c]
1903	429	2.9	4.7
1904	642	2.1	3.6
1905	1,082	1.6	3.0
1906	1,367	1.2	2.7
1907	1,294	1.6	2.9
1908	1,262	2.9	4.4
1909	1,387	2.8	4.3
1910	1,688	2.0	3.5
1911	1,975	1.9	3.1
1912	2,100	2.0	3.2
1913	1,980	2.9	4.2
1914	1,265	7.2[d]	
1915	830	3.2	
1916	804	2.2	
1917	1,078	1.0	
1918	1,601	1.2	
1919	4,497	3.7	
1920	5,545	3.8	
1921	6,076	2.8	
1922	6,455	1.5	
1923	4,625	10.2	
1924	3,483	13.1	
1925	3,639	6.8	
1926	3,420	18.0	
1927	4,039	8.8	
1928	4,484	8.6	
1929	4,583	13.3	
1930	4,445	22.7	
1931	3,968	34.3	
1932	3,347	43.8	

[a] Figures refer to the last quarter of each year until 1919; for 1919 and later years, the figures relate to the last day of December of each year.

[b] Average of quarterly figures for 1903-1906 and monthly averages thereafter. The figure for 1903 is based on an average of percentages for the last three quarters.

[c] See text for discussion of correction.

[d] The high percentage recorded in 1914 is in part due to the panic conditions which accompanied the German decree of August 4, 1914, affecting the basis of the currency system.

Source: *Reichsarbeitsblatt* and *Statistisches Jahrbuch.*

reporting unions probably did not materially affect the statistics. The numbers reported unemployed did not include invalids who were no longer able to perform work and persons on strike, locked out, or sick.[2]

The numerical coverage of the series shown in Table F-1 expanded rapidly in the first few years. At the end of 1903, 429,000 trade unionists were covered by the returns. By the end of 1905, this figure had increased to 1,082,000, and at the end of 1912, it exceeded 2 million. After World War I, the percentages came to be based on a much greater number of trade unionists, 6,076,000 at the end of 1921, 3,639,000 at the end of 1925, and 3,347,000 at the end of 1932, or about one-half or more of all trade unionists in Germany. During the 1920's and early 1930's, from about one-third to one-half of the total number of wage earners in manufacturing, mining, and construction were included in the trade union sample.

The trade union returns covered workers in manufacturing, mining, building, and transportation. Industrial representation in the trade union sample at several dates is shown in Table F-2 together with the

TABLE F-2

Percentage Distribution of Industrial Workers in Trade Union Sample, 1912-1929, and Censuses of 1925 and 1933, Germany

INDUSTRY	TRADE UNION SAMPLE				CENSUS	
	1912[a]	*1922*[b]	*1925*[c]	*1929*[b]	*1925*[d]	*1933*[d]
Mining	5.6	e	e	3.3	7.5	6.2
Stone and earthwork	7.6	2.5	2.5	5.7	5.7	5.0
Machine construction and metals	25.6	27.9	23.0	22.6	21.9	17.8
Textiles	8.9	13.4	10.9	8.3	9.0	9.0
Book and paper	1.6	1.5	1.5	2.7	4.1 (Book and paper, and Printing)	4.0 (Book and paper, and Printing)
Printing	6.1	2.2	3.4	3.3		
Leather and shoemaking	4.4	2.8	4.0	0.2	1.2[f]	1.1[f]
Wood and woodworking	10.3	7.4	8.4	7.0	6.7	6.0
Food, tobacco, and drink	6.0	4.8	5.6	6.8	7.6	9.5
Clothing	0.7	1.7	2.9	3.6	8.1	8.3
Building	0.3	10.5	13.6	15.9	12.7	15.2
Transportation	10.8	8.8	6.7	8.3	7.0	7.0
Other	12.1	16.5	17.5	12.3	8.5	10.9
	100.0	100.0	100.0	100.0	100.0	100.0

[a] Fourth quarter. [b] End of October. [c] End of June. [d] June 16.
[e] Including linoleum. [f] Included in "Other" group.

Source: *Reichsarbeitsblatt* for trade union data and *Statistisches Jahrbuch für des Deutsches Reichs*, 1930, Vol. 49, pp. 19-21 and 1935, Vol. 54, pp. 20-21 for census data.

[2] Wladimir S. Woytinsky, "Arbeitslosigkeit und Kurzarbeit," *Jahrbücher für Nationalökonomie und Statistik*, Vol. 79, 1931, p. 18.

industrial distribution of all workers (*arbeiter*) in these groups as given in the censuses of 1925 and 1933. The data show that there was no gross over- or underrepresentation of particular groups, with the exception of clothing workers, during the 1920's. In 1912, workers in building and clothing were very much under represented.

Before World War I, there is very little statistical information available to gauge the validity of the trade union unemployment figures. The only nationwide unemployment census (that of 1895) took place before the trade union percentages appeared. While no direct comparison can thus be made between the census results and the trade union figures, the census results do give some indication of the level of unemployment in what has been described as a year of "fairly good trade."[3] Since the census count was made both in June and in December of 1895, its results also shed some light on the variation of seasonal unemployment.

On June 18, 1895, the census found 97,782 workers in mining and industry (excluding agriculture, transport, commerce, household service, public service, and the professions) unemployed.[4] On December 2, 1895, 274,625 workers in mining and industry were unemployed. These figures, which excluded those unemployed on account of sickness, represented 1.5 and 4.2 per cent, respectively, of the total number of workers in industry and mining. The average of these percentages (2.9), it will be noted, is almost equal to the trade union percentages in the years of two cyclical lows (1903 and 1908). This suggests that the trade union percentages may have understated the actual amount of unemployment in Germany in the early years of the series.

The suggested understatement of the level of unemployment by the trade union percentages is also indicated by the magnitude of their seasonal variation. The pre-World War I percentages for June and December of each year are given below:

Month	*1903*	*1904*	*1905*	*1906*	*1907*	*1908*	*1909*	*1910*	*1911*	*1912*	*1913*
June	3.2	2.1	1.5	1.2	1.4	2.9	2.8	2.0	1.6	1.7	2.7
December	2.6	2.4	1.8	1.8	2.7	4.4	2.6	2.1	2.4	2.8	4.8

Source: *Reichsarbeitsblatt, passim.*

Whereas the census unemployment percentage for December (4.2) exceeded the percentage for June (1.5) by 2.7 percentage points in a year of recovery from the depression of 1894,[5] the trade union per-

[3] Otto Most, *The Problem of Unemployment in Germany*, London, Cassell, 1910, p. 16.

[4] Census data from *ibid.*, p. 20.

[5] Hubert Post, *Untersuchungen über den Umfang der Erwerbslosigkeit* in *Sammlung Nationalökonomischer und Abhandlungen*, Jena, G. Fischer, 1914, Vol. 70. p. 16.

centages reveal no seasonal variation of this magnitude in any of the years, 1903-1913. This may be the result of the afore-mentioned under-representation of building workers in the union sample. For the good years 1905, 1906, 1907, 1911, and 1912, the trade union percentages for June are quite similar to the percentage of unemployment recorded in the census of June 1895.

More direct evidence revealing the understatement of seasonal unemployment by the trade union figures is afforded by the unemployment censuses taken by various municipalities in the winter of 1908-1909 (see Table F-3). These censuses showed that there was a total

TABLE F-3

Number and Per Cent Unemployed According to the Unemployment Censuses of Various Municipalities, Germany, 1908-1909

Date of Census	*Municipality*	*Number Unemployed*[a]	*Per Cent of Workers Unemployed*
Nov. 18, 1908	Berlin	28,006	5.1
Mar. 31, 1909	Bochum	420	1.4
Jan. 20, 1909	Brunswick	575	1.8
Nov. 18, 1908	Charlottenburg	1,948	2.5
Jan. 15, 1909	Chemnitz	1,862	2.4
Jan. 24, 1909	Cologne	3,478	3.4
Feb. 28, 1909	Dortmund	1,078	2.1
Nov. 28, 1908	Dresden	5,004	4.2
Feb. 14, 1908	Elberfeld	703	1.7
Oct. 15, 1908	Halle-on-the-Saal	2,917	7.8
Dec. 13, 1908	Kiel	1,960	5.3
Nov. 29, 1908	Magdeburg	2,208	3.9
Feb. 1, 1909	Mannheim	1,511	3.4
Dec. 10, 1908	Nuremberg	2,513	2.7
Nov. 18, 1908	Rixdorf	3,681	7.2
Feb. 14, 1909	Shoeneberg	2,659	10.2
Nov. 17, 1908	Stuttgart	1,001	1.6
Nov. 3, 1908	Wiesbaden	596	2.8

[a] Excluding those incapable of working because of illness or causes other than lack of work.

Source: Otto Most, *The Problem of Unemployment in Germany*, London, Cassell, 1910, p. 16.

of 62,120 workers unemployed, or 4.1 per cent of the number of workers residing in these cities. After careful consideration of the methods employed in these censuses and of criticisms which have been made of the results, Most concluded: "It is notorious, however, that this figure [4.1 per cent] is very considerably less than the reality, and according to careful estimates must be increased by about one-half, so that the average of these towns would in reality be about 6 per cent."[6]

[6] Most, *op.cit.*, p. 22.

This estimate of about 6 per cent for the winter of 1908 is considerably higher than the trade union percentage for December 1908 (4.4), which was the highest recorded in the winter of 1908-1909. The difference between the trade union percentage of June 1908 (2.9) and Most's estimate of about 6 per cent unemployed in the winter of 1908-1909 is 3.1 percentage points, not far different from the seasonal variation exhibited in the census of 1895 (2.7 percentage points).

To take account of seasonal variation, a rough correction can be made. The June trade union percentages are assumed to be correct. The seasonal variation, assumed to be 2.9 percentage points, is added to the June figure to yield a figure approximating winter unemployment. Rough annual rates can then be obtained by averaging the June figures and the winter figures. While far from being entirely satisfactory estimates, it is probable that percentages calculated in this fashion (see Table F-1) more nearly approach the actual level of unemployment in Germany before World War I than do the unadjusted figures.

After World War I, when the trade union percentages came to be based on reports covering a considerable number of workers, there does not seem to be much doubt but that they represent good measures of the level of unemployment. Wiggs points out that the low percentages for the inflationary period, 1918-1923, represent a valid picture of the unemployment situation: "This [the broad coverage] means that there is little danger of the low 1922 figures having been an underestimation. The feature of the period from 1918 to 1923 was the lowness of unemployment and the nonappearance of seasonal fluctuations, in spite of the existence of statistics which would certainly have revealed them had they existed."[7]

Woytinsky, evaluating the trade union percentages for the 1920's, dismissed the contention that the trade unionists represented a select group and thus did not constitute a good sample as follows: "This consideration does not hold up however. The modern unions are not associations of the working class aristocracy, but much more are they industrial unions which encompass all occupations rather uniformly and in which the unskilled and partially skilled are just as well represented as the skilled."[8] He then went on to write: "I believe to have proved that the unemployment figures of the unions reflect rather exactly the situation on the whole labor market. The usual extrapolation of these figures is thus warranted. The accounts of the unions concerning unemployment and short-time among their members are characteristic of all industry."[9]

[7] Kenneth I. Wiggs, *Unemployment in Germany since the War*, London, King, 1933, pp. 31-32.

[8] Woytinsky, *op.cit.*, p. 22.

[9] *Ibid.*, p. 23.

Woytinsky's conclusion is borne out by the results of the censuses of June 16, 1925 and of June 16, 1933, shown below:

WORKERS AND EMPLOYEES	MANUFACTURING, MINING, AND CONSTRUCTION		TRADE, COMMERCE, AND TRANSPORTATION		TOTAL	
	1925	*1933*	*1925*	*1933*	*1925*	*1933*
Total number[a] (*thousands*)	11,766	11,240	3,055	3,632	14,821	14,872
Number unemployed (*thousands*)	421	4,197	130	922	551	5,119
Per cent unemployed	3.6	37.3	4.3	25.4	3.7	34.4

[a] *Arbeiter* and *Angestellte*. The figures for 1925 included a small number of public officials (*Beamte*). It was assumed that the number of officials in 1925 was the same as the number enumerated in these groups in 1933.

Source: *Die Erwerbstätigkeit der Reichsbevölkerung*, Statistik des Deutsches Reichs, Berlin, 1936, Bd. 453, Heft 2, p. 16.

On June 16, 1925, 3.6 per cent of the workers and employees in manufacturing, mining, and construction were unemployed.[10] For the end of the same month, the trade union percentage for the wholly unemployed was 3.5 (3.6 at the end of May 1925). The census of June 16, 1933 showed 37.3 per cent of the workers and employees in the above named activities unemployed. The trade union rate was 40.3 at the end of June 1933 (44.7 at the end of May).[11] These comparisons lend support to the claim that the trade union rates were valid measures of the volume of unemployment among workers in manufacturing, mining, and construction.

EMPLOYMENT EXCHANGE STATISTICS BEFORE WORLD WAR II

Reports of employment exchanges have been published monthly in the *Reichsarbeitsblatt* since 1907. Before the Employment Exchanges Act of 1922, which established an employment exchange in every commune and district of local administration, the published statistics (giving the number of persons seeking work, the number of vacancies, and an index of the number of workers seeking work per hundred

[10] Those enumerated as unemployed in the census were all persons capable of working who before the census count were occupied as workers and employees and who were without employment at the time of the census because of lack of work (see *Einführung in die Berufszählung Systematische und Alphabetische Verzeichnisse zur Berufszählung 1933*, Berlin, Statistik des Deutsches Reichs, 1936, Bd. 453, Heft 1, pp. 6-7).

[11] Trade union rates, with the exception of June 1933, from *Reichsarbeitsblatt*. The June 1933 figure was obtained from Oscar Weigert, *Placement and Unemployment Insurance in Germany*, Industrial Relations Counselors, 1934, p. 25.

vacancies) covered only a few exchanges and for this reason are of limited value.

Later employment exchange returns listed the number of registered unemployed as well as the numbers seeking work. Until November 1926, the monthly statistics of the applicants for work referred to the middle of each month. After November 1926, these figures were given for the end of each month and later also for the middle of each month. The number of registered unemployed referred to the end of each month. These statistics covered all lines of activity.

The *registered unemployed* figures (see Table F-4) included all unemployed persons registered at the employment exchanges, whether in receipt of unemployment insurance or relief benefit or not.[12] For

TABLE F-4

Registered Unemployed, Germany, 1925-1940

(*thousands*)

Year	*Registered Unemployed*	*Year*	*Registered Unemployed*
1925	687	1935	2,151[b]
1926	2,028	1936	1,593
1927	1,336	1937	912
1928	1,376	1938	429
1929	1,899	1939	119[c]
1930	3,076	1940	52[c]
1931	4,520		
1932	5,575		
1933	4,804[a]		
1934	2,718		

[a] The figures for July 31, 1933 and following months excluded persons employed in labor camps. In July 1933 the number excluded amounted to 150,000.

[b] Including registered unemployed persons in the Saar Territory after April 1935.

[c] Excluding unemployed in East Prussia, Upper Silesia, and the German Sudetenland.

Source: 1925-1927—Wladimir S. Woytinsky, *Three Sources of Unemployment*, ILO Studies and Reports, Series C, No. 20, Geneva, 1935, p. 80. 1928-1940—*Statistisches Jahrbuch* and ILO *Yearbooks of Labour Statistics.*

[12] After World War I, there were frequent changes in the form of unemployment relief. A comprehensive scheme of relief was introduced during the demobilization period. In February 1924, the scope of the scheme was limited to cover only those unemployed who had already completed a prescribed period as employed persons. On October 1, 1927, the relief system was superseded by a system of unemployment insurance which covered all occupations. Emergency benefit, originally supplementary to unemployment relief, was embodied in the unemployment insurance scheme. Under the strain of the widespread unemployment of the great depression, the insurance and emergency benefit schemes proved unequal to the task of providing for the masses of unemployed workers. Therefore, the poor relief system evolved into a third form of unemployment relief for those unemployed persons who, for a variety of reasons, were no longer covered by either unemployment insurance or emergency benefit.

example, the composition of the number of registered unemployed at the end of January 1933 was as follows:

Recipients of standard benefit	953,117
Recipients of emergency benefit	1,418,949
Able-bodied unemployed in receipt of poor relief	2,366,259
Unemployed not in receipt of any form of relief	1,275,287
Total registered unemployed	6,013,612

There is ample evidence that during the 1930's the figures of the registered unemployed did not measure the full extent of unemployment. Many persons who lost all hope of finding work at the exchanges or who had no claim to benefits of any kind, failed to register at employment exchanges. Estimates of the numbers of such persons (i.e. of so-called *invisible unemployment*), based on incomplete statistics, are quite divergent. For example, the German Institute for Business Research, in a discussion of estimates of the extent of invisible unemployment made by the *Economist*,[13] concluded that the *Economist's* estimates of 2,537,000 for June 1933 and 2,418,000 for June 1935 were much too high. The Institute's own estimates for these two dates were 799,000 and 722,000. Woytinsky's estimate for the summer of 1932 was 2,100,000.[14] Since there is no way of reconciling these estimates or of making more reliable ones, the actual number of unemployed persons in Germany during the 1930's is only very approximately known.

The figures of the registered unemployed (covering all occupations and subject to the shortcomings touched upon above) cannot be used directly to obtain unemployment percentages for workers in manufacturing, mining, and construction. Perhaps the best that can be done is to use the result of the census of June 16, 1933[15] in conjunction with the trend of the registered unemployed series to obtain percentages of unemployment applicable to the above group of workers. Percentages constructed in this manner (see Table F-5) agree fairly

[13] *Weekly Report of the German Institute for Business Research*, Berlin, August 22, 1935.

[14] Wladimir S. Woytinsky, *Three Sources of Unemployment*, Geneva, International Labour Organisation, Studies and Reports, Series C, No. 20, 1935, p. 97. Woytinsky's and the other estimates depended upon the Health Insurance statistics for an estimate of employment and estimates of the total number of workers.

[15] The census of June 16, 1933 found 37.3 per cent of the workers and employees in manufacturing, construction, and mining unemployed. By use of the monthly registered unemployed figures, the annual rate is found to be 36.2. The figures in Table F-4 serve to provide a basis for calculating percentages for other years. For June 1925, the month of the census, the calculated percentage is 3.1 compared with the census rate of 3.6, shown above, for manufacturing, mining, and construction.

TABLE F-5

Estimated Unemployment Rates for Workers and Employees in Manufacturing, Mining, and Construction, Germany, 1925-1939

Year	Per Cent Unemployed[a]	Year	Per Cent Unemployed[a]
1925	5.2	1933	36.2
1926	15.3	1934	20.5
1927	10.1	1935	16.2
1928	10.4	1936	12.0
1929	14.3	1937	6.9
1930	23.2	1938	3.2
1931	34.1	1939	0.9
1932	42.0		

[a] Estimates constructed as described in text. The estimates have been taken back to 1925 to afford comparison with the trade union percentages in the years 1925-1932.

closely with the trade union figures for 1925 to 1932 and with the result of the 1925 census. For the later 1930's the calculated percentages are somewhat higher than those published in the ILO's *Yearbooks of Labour Statistics* since these latter percentages apply to workers and employees (approximately 21 million) in all lines of activity, including agriculture, personal and domestic service, and public administration. Further, it is not clear how the problem of invisible unemployment was dealt with in calculating the ILO percentages.

POST-WORLD WAR II UNEMPLOYMENT STATISTICS

After World War II, quarterly unemployment statistics for occupied Germany first appeared for March 1946, and quarterly figures for the German Federal Republic, for March 1948.[16] For the United States and British occupation zones, the series showed the number of unemployed as a percentage of the total number of wage and salary earners (see Table F-6). In 1946, and through March 1947, the unemployed were defined to be persons not working and considered available for work under the Allied Control Council's Order No. 3 of 1946. Under this order, all persons (1) in employment, (2) unemployed and seeking work, and (3) all other males between the ages of fourteen and sixty-five and all other females between the ages of fifteen and fifty were required to register at local employment offices. Persons in this last group who were physically or mentally incapacitated, mothers of young children, housewives, or students were considered as not available for work; all other persons in this group, in addition to those in

[16] Source: *Report of the Military Governor, Statistical Annex*; Office of the Military Government for Germany (U.S. Zone), *International Labour Review*, December 1948, p. 830.

TABLE F-6

Unemployment Rates, United States and British Occupation Zones and German Federal Republic, 1946-1952

	UNEMPLOYED AS PER CENT OF WAGE- AND SALARY-EARNING LABOR FORCE[a]	
YEAR	*U.S. and British Occupation Zones*	*German Federal Republic*
1946	7.5[b]	
1947	5.0[b]	
1948	4.7	4.2
1949	8.1	8.3
1950		10.2
1951		9.0
1952		8.4

[a] Averages of quarterly data.

[b] The unemployed in 1946 and through March 1947 were persons not working and available for work within the meaning of Control Council Order No. 3 (see text). Files of the unemployed thereafter were gradually purged of unplaceables. June 1948 and later figures show only persons not working and registered as seeking work.

Source: Office of the Military Government for Germany (U.S. Zone), *Report of the Military Governor, Statistical Annex*, No. XXVII, May 1949, p. 75. *Yearbook of Labour Statistics, 1953*, International Labour Organisation, p. 87.

groups (1) and (2), were considered as available for work and came to be counted among the unemployed whether seeking work or not.

In mid-1948, and thereafter, both the unemployment statistics of the United States and British occupation zones and of the German Federal Republic include as unemployed only persons registered at employment exchanges as seeking work. The wage- and salary-earning labor force, which serves as a base for calculating unemployment rates, is equal to the sum of the number of registered unemployed seeking work and the number of employed wage and salary earners. Wage and salary earners in all occupations are covered by the statistics.

SUMMARY

Before World War I, the trade union unemployment percentages probably understated the actual level of unemployment in Germany. For the most part, this understatement is presumed to have arisen because certain seasonal trades, particularly building, were not sufficiently represented in the trade union sample. To overcome this shortcoming, a rather rough correction (described above) was applied to the trade union percentages for the years 1903-1913.

The trade union percentages for the years 1914-1932, based on a large sample of union members in which industrial groups received approximately appropriate weights, represent good measures of the extent of unemployment among workers in mining, manufacturing, construction, and transportation.

A calculation based on the census results of June 16, 1933 and on the trend of the numbers of registered unemployed, provides unemployment rates for the years 1933-1939. These, when carried back before 1933, are in fair agreement with both the trade union percentages for 1925-1932 and with the results of the census of June 16, 1925.

In the post-World War II years, unemployment rates covering all wage and salary earners are available from 1946 on. These rates are probably lower than unemployment percentages for only wage earners in manufacturing, mining, and construction. The amount of the probable understatement for the years 1946-1948 is somewhat lessened because some persons who were not seeking work were included among the numbers unemployed.

Appendix G:
The Netherlands

The information that we have been able to secure on Dutch unemployment statistics is insufficient to provide the basis for a thorough critical evaluation. It has therefore been necessary to confine this section to a presentation of the available statistics with as full a description as the material at our disposal allowed.

The principal unemployment series for the Netherlands were those emanating from trade union unemployment insurance funds, commencing in 1911 and terminating in 1941 (see Table G-1). The first series (in column 1) represents the ratio of unemployed workers to those insured in voluntary union funds.[1] The data were compiled on a weekly basis, no distinction being made with respect to the number of days per week for which benefits were paid (i.e. a worker was counted as being unemployed once in a week whether he lost one day or the entire week). Workers with separate spells of unemployment in a single week were similarly counted just once.[2] The series shown in column 2 represents the ratio of the precise number of

[1] The data include also "a small number of workers who, although belonging to unions having [unemployment] funds, are excluded from benefit on account of age, and workers who belong to unions having no unemployment funds." *The I.L.O. Yearbook 1934-35*, International Labour Office, Vol. II, p. 180. It was reported in 1925 that only 7,000 workers whose employment status was reported on were in unions not having unemployment funds compared with some 270,000 thus covered.

[2] *Methods of Compiling Statistics of Unemployment*, International Labour Office, Studies and Reports, Series C, 1922, pp. 71-77.

TABLE G-1

Unemployment Rates among Insured Trade Unionists, the Netherlands, 1911-1940

Year	Per Cent of Workers Unemployed (1)	Ratio of Days Lost Due to Unemployment to Potential Working Days of Insured Workers (2)	Year	Per Cent of Workers Unemployed (1)	Ratio of Days Lost Due to Unemployment to Potential Working Days of Insured Workers (2)
1911	2.7	2.5	1926	8.7	7.3
1912	4.2	4.0	1927	9.0	7.5
1913	5.1	5.0	1928	6.9	5.6
1914	16.2	13.8	1929	7.1	5.9
1915	14.6	12.0	1930	9.7	7.8
1916	5.8	5.1	1931	18.1	14.8
1917	9.6	6.5	1932	29.5	25.3
1918	10.0	7.5	1933	31.0	26.9
1919	8.9	7.7	1934	32.1	28.0
1920	7.2	5.8	1935	36.3	31.7
1921	10.9	9.0	1936	36.3	32.7
1922	12.6	11.0	1937	29.2	26.9
1923	12.8	11.2	1938	27.2	25.0
1924	10.2	8.8	1939	21.7	19.9
1925	9.5	8.1	1940	22.9	19.8

Source: *Maandschrift van het Centraal Bureau voor de Statistiek, passim.*

man-days of unemployment to the maximum number of days at risk of unemployment (i.e. six times the membership of the reporting organizations).

The major characteristics of these data may be outlined as follows:

1. It is obvious that the index in column 2 is more accurate than that in column 1 in measuring the total volume of unemployment. The weekly percentage of unemployed workers would be unaffected, for example, by changes in the average duration of unemployment per week, whereas the percentage of man-days unemployed would reflect such a change. The difference between the two series reflects changes in the number of days per week of average unemployment. The two percentages would be the same, for example, if all unemployed workers during a particular week were unemployed for six days. As the average number of days of unemployment per week declines, the difference between the two percentages widens.

The relationship of the two series is thus dependent upon the form that unemployment takes. If it is concentrated on a particular group of individuals, the percentages would correspond closely; if available work were spread among the work force, in the form either of a reduction in the number of days worked per week or the number of hours worked per day,[3] the second series would depart from the first. The largest percentage difference in the spread between the two series came in the years 1917 and 1918, whereas during the Great Depression, the spread did not widen greatly (in percentage terms).

2. The industrial coverage of the data appears to have been quite broad, including, in addition to manufacturing, building construction, agriculture, fishing, the retail trades, and commercial work. However, manufacturing and building appear to have been most fully represented in the sample. The insured population in 1925 was said to constitute 90 per cent of the total number of organized workers in the Netherlands, so that the data presented "a very accurate idea both of the fluctuation in unemployment and of the absolute extent of unemployment among insured persons."[4] At the time, however, some 65 per cent of the industrial labor force was not organized, so that the data could not be said to be representative necessarily of unemployment generally.[5] The absolute number of workers covered by the statistics rose from 275,000 in 1925 to a high of 525,000 in 1933, declined to 468,000 in 1936, and rose again to 511,000 in 1940.[6] The reporting base was fairly substantial from the start, having been 65,000 in 1913 and 106,000 by 1915.

3. The method of collecting the statistics was calculated to insure a considerable degree of accuracy. The trade union unemployment insurance funds, as a condition for the receipt of state aid, were required to maintain comprehensive membership registers, and to record not only the days of unemployment for which benefits were paid, but also the number of benefitless days of unemployment. The funds received from the state a per capita allowance per week to cover administrative costs, including the preparation of statistics. Although persons who had exhausted their benefits sometimes failed to keep their registration as unemployed current, it was believed that this did not constitute a serious source of error.[7]

4. Persons out of work due to labor disputes, illness, accidents, or other causes than lack of work, were not counted as unemployed.

5. The following statement was made by the Director General of Statistics with respect to the representative character of the series:

[3] It would appear that days of less than full employment were tabulated as such. However, we have been able to find no precise statement to this effect.

[4] *The Second International Conference of Labour Statisticians*, International Labour Office, Studies and Reports, Series N, No. 8, 1925, p. 51, note 1.

[5] Estimated from *Jaarcijfers von Nederland, passim.* The number of trade union members on January 1, 1925, was compared with the average of the number of industrial and transport workers in 1920 and 1930.

[6] These figures are from Central Bureau Voor De Statistiek, *Jaarcijfers von Nederland, passim.*

[7] *The Second International Conference of Labour Statisticians*, p. 51, note 1.

"These percentages could safely be considered as representative up to the 1930's. After 1935, however, they presented in all probability a too unfavorable picture of the size of unemployment."[8]

The only other series of unemployment going back over a long period is that relating to the operation of public employment offices. Prior to the 1930's these data were incomplete, since there was no widespread registration of the unemployed by these offices. However, with the growth of unemployment during the depression, registration was made compulsory for all unemployed in receipt of relief and unemployment benefits, and those employed on public works. Registration is voluntary for others.

Coverage is quite broad. It is believed that all manual workers register, as a rule, and maintain their registration even after their right to benefits has expired. Clerical workers not in receipt of benefits often do not register, however. Young workers seeking their first jobs are included in the registration, but persons formerly self-employed who are seeking employment are not. Married women who are not the sole support of their families are not included among the unemployed, even though they may be willing and able to work. Figures for unemployed agricultural workers are not considered complete.[9] The enumeration takes place on the last day of each month, and the annual figures are an average of the monthly tallies.

This series is shown in Table G-2.[10] In two respects the prewar and postwar data are not comparable:

1. The so-called "frost unemployed" (persons laid off in extremely cold weather) were included up to 1940 but excluded thereafter. These persons constituted some 15 per cent of the total unemployed during the months of December and January and, on an annual basis, increased reported unemployment by perhaps 3 per cent.

2. Up to and including 1948, the unemployed aged sixty-five and over were included among the unemployed, but were omitted thereafter. It is estimated that the over sixty-five-year age group constituted about 1.5 per cent of the total number of persons out of work.

In general, persons who are partially unemployed are excluded from the count of unemployment. A person without a labor contract must be willing and able to work for a full day in order to be included. Persons on temporary layoff are not included among the unemployed unless they did not perform any labor during the entire week in which the census day falls.

[8] Letter to the authors from Dr. Ph. J. Idenburg, Director General of Statistics of the Netherlands, July 29, 1953.

[9] *The Netherlands*, United States Bureau of Labor Statistics, Catalogue of Labor Statistics Series, mimeographed, June 1952.

[10] Data for the years of German occupation of the Netherlands are omitted.

TABLE G-2
Persons Registered at End of Month as Unemployed at Public Employment Offices, the Netherlands, Annual Average, 1933-1952
(*thousands*)

Year	*Totally Unemployed*	*Employed on Public Works*	*Unemployed but Receiving Pay from Employers*	*Total*
1933	274.8	48.1	a	322.9
1934	281.8	51.0	a	332.8
1935	328.8	55.9	a	384.7
1936	368.5	46.0	a	414.5
1937	324.0	44.9	a	368.9
1938	303.4	50.2	a	353.6
1939	235.6	60.0	a	295.6
1945[b]	97.4	39.8	60.1	197.3
1946	53.1	35.7	4.3	93.1
1947	30.7	15.2	1.1	47.0
1948	29.0	13.4	0.8	43.2
1949	42.1	20.2	0.8	63.1
1950	57.7	21.4	1.1	80.2
1951	67.7	25.0	0.6	93.3
1952	104.3	31.8	1.5	137.6

[a] Not significant.
[b] Covers the months June-December only.
Source: *Jaarcijfers voor Nederland,* Centraal Bureau voor Statistiek, *passim.*

If the data in Table G-2 are converted into index form with 1933 as a base, and the resultant index applied to the 1933 percentage of unemployment indicated under the man-days lost series of the trade union data, it appears that the two series corresponded closely until 1935, but after that time the employment exchange data showed a persistently higher level of unemployment than the union data.[11] This may have been because the former were becoming progressively more complete during the 1930's as the result of stricter registration requirements.

The only unemployment data available for the postwar years are the employment exchanges statistics of Table G-2.[12] They indicate a level of unemployment much lower than that of the 1930's. If one were to extrapolate the prewar unemployment percentages on the basis of this series, unemployment would average about 5 per cent from 1946 to 1950 inclusive. However, assigning specific percentages

[11] However, the trend was similar from 1936 to 1939; the principal divergence came between 1935 and 1936, when the employment exchange series moved up more rapidly than the trade union series.

[12] Beginning with July 1952, a new series based upon the Unemployment Act of 1949 was initiated. These data are of too recent origin to warrant consideration here.

for particular years does not appear to be warranted on the basis of such an extrapolation in view of the nature of the relationship between the two series during the years 1933-1939.

CONCLUSIONS

The only statistics of unemployment for the Netherlands that are appropriate for purposes of international comparison for the period with which we are concerned are those shown in Table G-1. As between the two series contained therein, that in column 2, showing the ratio of days lost due to unemployment to potential working days of insured workers, would appear to be the one which is the more consistent with our normative definition.

This series has the usual defects of this type of statistics. Nevertheless, the Dutch statistical authorities consider it as generally representative of unemployment in the country until 1935, after which it probably overstated unemployment somewhat. No unemployment percentages are available for the postwar period, but it is clear from the data in Table G-2 that the postwar level of unemployment was considerably below the prewar level.

Appendix H:
Norway

TRADE UNION STATISTICS

The major source of unemployment statistics in Norway is provided by trade union reports to the Central Bureau of Statistics, beginning with July 1903, and continuing up to the present time. The percentages of unemployment thus derived are shown in Table H-1.

The characteristics of this series are as follows:

1. The data cover the national trade unions in the following industries and trades: metalworking (including shipbuilding); molders; printing; bookbinding; shoe manufacture; baking; bricklaying; the remaining building trades; sawmills; and woodworking. Coverage has been limited consistently to these ten organizations, all of which operated their own unemployment funds until 1939, when a national compulsory unemployment system was adopted.

2. In July, 1903, when the first reports were made, they covered 162 local unions with 10,200 members. At that time there were 350 local unions with 15,000 total membership.[1] Coverage for subsequent years was as follows:[2]

[1] Tillaegshefte 2 til *Statistiske Meddelelser*, Norway, Statistisk Centralbyrå, 1920, p. 18.
[2] *Ibid.*

Year	*Number of Members (thousands)*
1906	14.5
1909	18.0
1912	27.0
1915	30.0
1918	35.7

In 1918, when total trade union membership was 116,000 coverage was less representative of trade union unemployment, though not necessarily of total unemployment, than at the outset. In 1939, the ten reporting unions had 96,000 members out of a total union membership of 357,000, or about 27 per cent.[3] The corresponding figures for December 31, 1949 were 139,000 covered out of a total trade union

TABLE H-1

Unemployment Rates among Members of Reporting Trade Unions, Norway, 1904-1941, 1946-1951

Year	*Per Cent Unemployed*	*Year*	*Per Cent Unemployed*
1904	3.9	1927	25.4
1905	4.4	1928	19.2
1906	3.2	1929	15.4
1907	2.5	1930	16.6
1908	3.7	1931	22.3
1909	5.0	1932	30.8
1910	2.9	1933	33.4
1911	1.9	1934	30.7
1912	1.3	1935	25.3
1913	1.7	1936	18.8
1914	2.3	1937	20.0
1915	1.9	1938	22.0
1916	0.9	1939	18.3
1917	0.9	1940	23.1
1918	1.5	1941	11.4
1919	1.7		
1920	2.3	1946	3.6
1921	17.7	1947	3.1
1922	17.1	1948	2.7
1923	10.7	1949	2.2
1924	8.5[a]	1950	2.7
1925	13.2	1951	3.6
1926	24.3		

[a] Data for this year affected by a general work stoppage in the metal trades.

Source: 1904-1947—Statistisk Centralbyrå, *Statistiske Oversikter*, 1948, p. 363. 1948-1951—*Statistisk Årbok for Norge*, 1952, p. 223.

[3] This total includes only unions affiliated with the Norwegian Federation of Labor. However, unaffiliated trade-union membership was insignificant at this time.

membership of 474,000 or 29 per cent. The percentage covered in 1949 was roughly equal to that prevailing in 1918.

3. The statistics were gathered by trade union secretaries in charge of union unemployment funds and were considered to be fairly reliable insofar as reporting was concerned, since the unemployed individual had a strong incentive to report his status. An individual was counted as unemployed only once each month regardless of the number of spells of unemployment suffered. One limitation on completeness was the fact that when the right to benefits ceased, many individuals ceased reporting, thus tending to understate the degree of unemployment during periods of severe recession.[4]

4. The most serious deficiency of the trade union series appears to be the fact that it is heavily weighted with industries which are very sensitive to cyclical fluctuations. Five of the ten unions reporting are in capital goods industries; two unions, those in the metal and building trades, alone accounted for from 70 to 80 per cent of total reporting membership. The following conclusion emerged from an analysis of this aspect of the series:

> "The percentage of unemployment for the 10 trade unions thus cannot be said to give a representative picture of unemployment in the nation—not even for industry, since among others such important groups as the cellulose and paper industry, mining, the electrometallurgical and electrochemical industry, the textile and clothing industries, and food processing, apart from baking, are excluded. To this should be added the fact that it covers only organized workers."[5]

A comparison of the published trade union series with an apparently unpublished series covering working days lost due to unemployment in some twenty-five to twenty-nine trade unions indicates that the latter group has absolutely lower and less severely fluctuating unemployment. These percentages, which were read off a chart and are therefore approximate, are shown in Table H-2. For example, at the height of the depression in 1933, when the ten-union series showed 33.4 per cent unemployment, the twenty-nine-union series showed only about 22 per cent. The fact that the more comprehensive data have not been published, however, must indicate a lack of confidence in it by the Central Bureau of Statistics, perhaps because many of the unions had no unemployment funds which would ensure full reporting by the unemployed.

5. A census of unemployment taken on December 1, 1930 provided

[4] Tillaegshefte 2 til *Statistiske Meddelelser*, 1920, p. 18.

[5] Morton Tuveng, *Arbeidsløshet og Beskjeftigelse i Norge Før og Under Krigen*, Bergen, J. Grieg, 1946, p. 40.

TABLE H-2

Unemployment Rates among Members of from 25 to 29 Trade Unions, Norway, 1920-1939

Year	*Per Cent Unemployed*	*Year*	*Per Cent Unemployed*
1920	2.0	1930	16.0
1921	14.0	1931	21.0
1922	12.5	1932	21.5
1923	8.0	1933	22.0
1924	5.0	1934	20.0
1925	9.0	1935	19.0
1926	16.5	1936	18.0
1927	19.0	1937	17.0
1928	14.0	1938	20.0
1929	13.0	1939	20.0

Source: Figure 2 in Morton Tuveng, *Arbeidsløshet og Beskjeftigelse i Norge Før og Under Krigen*, Bergen, 1946, p. 35. No published source other than this chart has been found for these data.

an opportunity to test the validity of the trade union series. This census included all wage earners in industrial and agricultural occupations, except that fishermen and the self-employed other than artisans in manufacturing were excluded. Newly entering young persons who had not secured permanent employment but were looking for work were included among the unemployed.

The percentage of unemployment among men was 14.6 per cent (for women it was much lower, 2.7 per cent). The rate of unemployment among the ten reporting trade unions at the end of November 1930, was 21.4 per cent, considerably higher than the over-all census figure (virtually all the reporting trade union membership was male). However, the census percentage of male wage earner unemployment in industry, excluding transportation, agriculture, and the forest trades, was 17.8 per cent; for *urban* industrial wage earners, it was 22.6 per cent. This close correspondence seemed to indicate that the trade union rates of unemployment were representative of unemployment among all industrial wage earners.[6]

LABOR EXCHANGE DATA (TO 1939)

The only other Norwegian unemployment data available for any considerable time period are those emanating from the public employment exchanges. Table H-3 shows the excess of job seekers over vacancies at the exchanges, from 1919 to 1939. A drastic change in the reporting system adopted in 1940 makes it impossible to com-

[6] "Arbeidsledigheten efter folketellingen, 1930," *Statistiske Meddelelser, Det Statistiske Centralbyrå*, 1933, p. 74.

pare the data for that year and subsequent years with the series in Table H-3.

TABLE H-3

Excess of Job Seekers over Vacancies at Public Employment Exchanges, Norway, 1919-1939

Year	*Excess*	*Year*	*Excess*
1919	110	1930	19,353
1920	1,726	1931	27,478
1921	17,375	1932	33,831
1922	19,492	1933	36,279
1923	14,425	1934	36,339
1924	11,263	1935	36,103
1925	14,956	1936	32,643
1926	23,467	1937	28,520
1927	23,889	1938	28,923
1928	21,759	1939	26,777
1929	19,089		

Source: Morton Tuveng, *Arbeidsløshet og Beskjeftigelse i Norge Før og Under Krigen*, Bergen, 1946, p. 40.

The deficiencies of the labor exchange data, even apart from the manner in which they are expressed, render them of use only for comparative purposes with other Norwegian data. The number of exchanges reporting has varied over time; agricultural as well as industrial job seekers were included; registration was entirely voluntary, except where required as a condition for obtaining relief, where the relief laws influenced registration; and a relatively small number of job vacancies were reported to the public exchanges.[7]

While the general movements of the two series are similar, the amplitude of the cyclical changes in the trade union series is considerably greater. The movement of the labor exchange data is closer to that of the special union series shown in Table H-2 during the period 1929-1939, though from 1920-1929 the latter exhibited greater swings.

LABOR EXCHANGE DATA (SINCE 1945)

Beginning in 1938, applicants for unemployment insurance were required to report to the labor exchanges as a condition of securing unemployment benefits. Moreover, a law enacted in 1947 required all employers who had in their employ persons subject to the insurance law (which includes virtually all workers except those in fishing, domestic service, and civil service) to notify the labor exchanges of all vacancies.[8] For these reasons, the labor exchange data of the last

[7] See *Arbeidsmarkedet*, Arbeidsdirektorat, No. 6, 1952, p. 178; Johan Hvidsten, "Unemployment in Norway," *International Labour Review*, February-March 1923, p. 231; *Statistiske Meddelelser*, 1926, p. 82.

[8] *Sosial Håndbok for Norge*, Oslo, Norsk Forening for Sosialt Arbeide, 1953, Vol. II, p. 26.

decade are likely to be more representative than the earlier statistics. It must be borne in mind, however, that employees who are either not covered by the unemployment insurance system, or are not eligible for benefits, although covered, are not required to report.

These data, shown in Table H-4, confirm the fact that there has been a very low rate of unemployment in Norway since the war.

TABLE H-4

Unemployment Indicated by Labor Exchange Data, Norway, 1946-1951

Year	*Job Seekers*	*Vacancies*	*Excess(+) or Deficit(−) of Job Seekers over Vacancies*
1946	196,243	225,621	−29,378
1947	191,121	219,259	−28,138
1948	198,612	223,011	−24,399
1949	200,095	234,673	−34,578
1950	219,759	244,781	−25,022
1951	384,369	351,870	+32,499

Source: *Statistisk Årbok for Norge, passim.*

Their movement does not follow in detail the trade union series of Table H-1, which is not unexpected because of the nature of the data and the low levels of employment involved. Both sets of data, however, show an increase in unemployment in 1951, perhaps the only significant movement during the period 1946-1951.

CONCLUSION

Despite its inadequacies, the trade union series provides the only useable index of Norwegian unemployment over any considerable period of time. Its most serious defect is the exaggerated swing during the depression of the 1930's because of the heavy weighting accorded to business cycle-sensitive industries. The data in Table H-2 indicate that some of the extreme figures shown for this period should be discounted, but the information necessary for making this correction is lacking.

Appendix I:
Sweden

There are two published series measuring unemployment for Sweden which go back to the first decade of this century: one based upon reports of trade unions, the other upon reports of labor exchanges. A series based upon unemployment insurance statistics is available only since 1936.

TRADE UNION STATISTICS

These data, which are shown in Table I-1, are based upon reports submitted by trade unions to the Royal Social Board. An exhaustive analysis of their validity as a general gauge of unemployment pre-

TABLE I-1

Unemployment Rates among Members of Reporting Trade Unions, Sweden, 1911-1952

Year	*Per Cent Unemployed*	*Year*	*Per Cent Unemployed*
1911	5.6	1932	22.4
1912	5.4	1933	23.3
1913	4.4	1934	18.0
1914	7.3	1935	15.0
1915	7.2	1936	12.7
1916	4.0	1937	10.8
1917	4.0	1938	10.9
1918	4.6	1939	9.2
1919	5.5	1940	11.8
1920	5.4	1941	11.3
1921	26.6	1942	7.5
1922	22.9	1943	5.7
1923	12.5	1944	4.9
1924	10.1	1945	4.5
1925	11.0	1946	3.2
1926	12.2	1947	2.8
1927	12.0	1948	2.8
1928	10.6	1949	2.7
1929	10.2	1950	2.2
1930	11.9	1951	1.8
1931	16.8	1952	2.4

Source: 1911-1929—*Statens Offentliga Utredningar 1931*, No. 20, p. 58. 1930-1952—*Sociala Meddelanden, passim.*

sented in 1931 by a governmental commission,[1] resulted in the following findings:

1. The trade union series is based upon reports submitted by co-operating trade unions to the Royal Social Board, first commencing in 1911. At the outset, about thirty national unions with members in manufacturing, transportation, building, and commerce reported. This included virtually all the trade unions in these branches of the economy. Unions of agricultural workers, railroad workers, seamen, and, until 1920, lumber workers, did not report, however.

2. Since reporting was voluntary, not all locals of these national

[1] *Arbetslöshetens Omfattning, Karaktär och Orsaker*, Statens Offentliga Utredningar, Stockholm, Socialdepartementet, No. 20, 1931.

unions submitted reports each month. In 1911, 64 per cent of the members of reporting national unions were accounted for in the reports submitted. The proportion declined to a low of 42 in 1920, but rose thereafter to 69 per cent in 1929 and 87 per cent in 1940. At the end of 1949, the percentage of the membership covered by reports was 97.5 per cent.

3. A special study made in 1923 of twenty-seven reporting national unions (the percentage of membership covered in 1923 was 49 per cent) indicated that in only three cases—the bricklayers, painters, and miners—did the reporting locals appear to be unrepresentative of unemployment in the union as a whole. "With regard to other unions the data seem quite accurately to portray changes in unemployment for the organized members, and when the data for the various unions are combined, the average unemployment percentage appears quite accurately to represent the situation in the trade unions."[2] The high reporting percentages during the 1930's and 1940's would tend to reinforce the conclusion that the trade union data were representative of unemployment *among trade union members.*

4. The trade unions report the total number of members and the number unemployed on the last day of each month, the monthly data being averaged to secure an annual figure. As a rule, unemployment comes to the notice of the local union secretary because unemployed members are exempted from the payment of union dues, the so-called "free-stamping" of their membership cards. "The right of free-stamping due to unemployment is general in the case of total absence from work because of lack of work; it is sometimes given when employment is less than twenty-four hours a week, sometimes when a man has work outside the trade and his weekly earnings do not amount to more than twenty-four hours of work at the rate of pay provided in the collective agreement."[3] Since in addition to this right some unions have long paid unemployment insurance benefits, there has been considerable incentive for the unemployed trade unionist to report himself as such. The union secretary may seek to verify the claim, or he may simply accept the statement of the worker, depending upon the circumstances. The local union has no obligation to pay per capita tax to the national union for "free-stamped" workers, but the national union must continue its per capita to the Federation of Labor, so that it has an incentive to police the system. In some unions the local officer is personally liable for underpayment to the national union, serving to

[2] *Ibid.,* p. 50.

[3] *Ibid.,* p. 45. We have seen no suggestion to the effect that the right of free-stamping accorded to underemployed was so widespread as seriously to affect the unemployment figures.

offset a tendency to grant "free-stamping" on account of age, partial unemployment, or personal reasons.

Although the "free-stamping" rules were found to vary in detail among unions, the Commission found a rough uniformity to exist. However, no distinction was made between voluntary and involuntary unemployment. Also, some unions were less representative because they maintained a closed door policy to new members.

5. The principal drawbacks which the Commission found in the trade union statistics stemmed from changes in absolute numbers and the composition of trade union membership. As a consequence of a disastrous general strike in 1909, Swedish trade union membership fell drastically, and did not again attain what the Commission considered to be a representative magnitude until after World War I,[4] though this is a matter of judgment rather than of proof. After World War I, however, there can be little question that the Swedish trade unions were representative within the economic sector which they covered. By 1929, the unions include over half of all persons employed in manufacturing, commerce, transport, and communications. For manufacturing alone, the coverage was two-thirds. The 1950 organization in manufacturing, building, and transportation has been estimated at 95 per cent of the labor force.[5]

When unemployment reporting first started, the Swedish trade union movement was largely craft in character. With the spread of organization to factory industry, as well as with increasing organization of women and youths, groups which were more unemployment-prone were represented in the statistics to a greater extent. As a consequence, at least until the 1930's, the trade union unemployment series is subject to a bias over time in the direction of greater unemployment, though no estimate of the magnitude of the bias is available.

6. Nor is there any specific information on the effects upon representativeness of cyclical movements in employment. It is generally true that during severe downswings in employment, trade union unemployment statistics do not fully reflect the degree of unemployment because of withdrawals or exclusion of unemployed members. This phenomenon was noted in 1931,[6] but specific information on this point is not available for later periods.

7. The growth of trade unions, while it has had the effect of making them more representative of the labor force at large, has had an offsetting effect in that it becomes more difficult to verify claims of unemployment, due to the greater burden of work upon union officials.

[4] *Ibid.*, p. 97.
[5] Walter Galenson, *Comparative Labor Movements*, Prentice-Hall, 1952, p. 119.
[6] *Statens Offentliga Utredningar*, No. 20, 1931, p. 50.

An inquiry into the operation of three unions in the 1920's revealed that, on occasion, persons who were not working because of age or illness, or those working on their own account, were included with the unemployed. Married women not looking for jobs were sometimes retained as members and accorded "free-stamping" and were thus included among the unemployed. However, better training of union officials, and more important, the increasing importance of trade union unemployment funds, tended to make for stricter control.

8. On the basis of the foregoing factors, the Commission reached the conclusion that "the data based upon the trade union unemployment series yield too low a result for the prewar (World War I) period and that the post-1920 data better reflect unemployment than the prewar figures. The errors discovered for the years after 1920 are difficult to measure precisely, but they appear to increase the magnitude to some extent. However, the data can be used to describe changes in unemployment during the latter period."[7]

9. Several attempts have been made to check the trade union unemployment data against special censuses of unemployment. A census of May 5, 1927, when appropriately adjusted to the trade union concept, indicated a considerably lower rate of unemployment than that shown by the trade union statistics.[8] Better results were obtained with respect to an unemployment census of March 2, 1936. It was estimated that for the entire country, 211,000 persons were unemployed on that date. However, since white collar workers and women were not well represented in the trade union statistics, the appropriate figure to compare with the latter was an estimated 175,000 male manual workers unemployed. At that time, the unions reported unemployment of 96,000, which was adjusted upward to 123,000 to take into account the nonreporting unions. In addition, 58,000 persons in urban communities applied for unemployment relief, of whom between 38,000 and 43,000 were estimated *not* to belong to trade unions. Thus total unemployment by this method was from 161,000 to 166,000, and male worker unemployed from 150,000 to 155,000. The difference of 20,000 to 25,000 in unemployment among male workers indicated by the two

[7] *Ibid.*, p. 61. Bagge has commented on the data as follows: "The prewar figures are probably somewhat too low in relation to the postwar figures, but as a general picture of the development of unemployment the above-mentioned conclusion that the general level of unemployment during the period 1922-23 to 1929-30 was about twice as high as before the war will hold good." Gösta Bagge, "Wages and Unemployment in Sweden 1920-30," *Economic Essays in Honor of Gustav Cassel*, London, G. Allen, 1933, p. 691.

[8] *Ibid.*, p. 94. The discrepancy appears to have been due largely to the failure of the census adequately to enumerate the unemployed (see Harrison Clark, *Swedish Unemployment Policy—1914 to 1940*, American Council on Public Affairs, 1941, p. 66).

methods was attributed to unemployment among nonunion workers who had not applied for relief. The most important discrepancy was for agricultural workers, of whom perhaps 20,000 were subject to seasonal unemployment.[9]

EMPLOYMENT EXCHANGE STATISTICS

The only other unemployment series dating back as far as the trade union series is that compiled by the employment exchange system. About ten labor exchanges were established in the major cities between 1902 and 1906. The system grew thereafter into a network of offices covering the entire country. Until 1934, the local employment exchanges were autonomous, although they had to meet certain operating requirements in order to secure state aid. In 1934 the entire system was unified under the direct supervision of the Unemployment Commission (which became the Employment Commission in 1940 and the Employment Board in 1948). In 1952 there were 210 employment offices operating under twenty-five provincial employment boards.[10] In 1913, the employment exchanges filled 118,000 vacancies, in 1951, 1,200,000. It is estimated that about one-third of all the vacancies in manufacturing and commerce are filled by the public employment exchanges.[11]

The data relating to the work of the labor exchanges show the number of job applications per month in relation to each 100 vacancies of which the exchanges are notified. Each job applicant is counted only once a year in the annual averages, regardless of the number of separate job applications made during the year. Similar practice is followed in averaging vacancies: whereas during each month the total number of unfilled vacancies is counted in, regardless of the fact that some vacancies carry over from month to month, the annual averages count each carried over unfilled vacancy just once. The annual averages are shown in Table I-2.

These data, while useful for checking the trade union series, have certain deficiencies both with respect to the measurement of unemployment and for our specific purposes. Not all persons seeking jobs at the exchanges are unemployed: some want to change their jobs, others may be seeking seasonal work. Since persons seeking unemployment relief are generally required to register with the employment exchanges, changes in relief qualifications influence reporting. Strikers, and other persons not working for reasons other than unemployment,

[9] See *Sociala Meddelanden*, No. 5, 1939, p. 339.

[10] *Social Sweden*, Stockholm, Social Welfare Board, 1952, p. 412, and Harrison Clark, *op.cit.*, Chap. VII.

[11] *Ibid.*

TABLE I-2

Number of Job Applicants per 100 Vacancies at Employment Exchanges, Sweden, 1910-1949

Year	*Applications per 100 Vacancies*	*Year*	*Applications per 100 Vacancies*
1910	138	1930	183
1911	132	1931	251
1912	125	1932	487
1913	116	1933	685
1914	131	1934	479
1915	137	1935	365
1916	98	1936	262[a]
1917	102	1937	187
1918	139	1938	196
1919	116	1939	173
1920	107	1940	182
1921	282	1941	198
1922	296	1942	147
1923	186	1943	131
1924	171	1944	136
1925	198	1945	131
1926	201	1946	116
1927	210[a]	1947	111
1928	201	1948	118
1929	174	1949	134

[a] Beginning with 1936, vacancies were redefined to exclude state unemployment reserve work, whereas prior to that year such work was included among the vacancies. The effect of this change was to reduce the number of vacancies and thus increase the relative, particularly during the depression years. The relatives under the new concept were calculated back to 1927, and are shown here. The old series from 1927 to 1934 was as follows:

1927	198	1931	236
1928	192	1932	413
1929	169	1933	545
1930	178	1934	392

See *Sociala Meddelanden*, 1936, No. 2, p. 73.

Source: 1910-1914—*Sociala Meddelanden*, 1915, No. 3, p. 267. 1915-1920—*Ibid., passim.* 1921-1926—*Ibid.*, 1936, No. 2, p. 73. 1927-1936—*Ibid.*, 1937, No. 2, p. 82. 1937-1950—*Ibid., passim.*

may also register at the exchanges. Nor do the published figures permit the computation of a rate of unemployment, since the number of job seekers is related to vacancies reported by employers[12] rather than to the employed population catered to by the exchanges.

When the year-to-year *trend* of unemployment indicated by the

[12] It should also be noted that employer notification of vacancies may vary cyclically. In periods of manpower shortage there is apt to be more adequate notification than during periods of unemployment, when the employer can rehire old employees at the gate.

employment exchanges data is compared with the trade union series, it appears that except for the period 1920-1923, the two series have moved in much the same manner,[13] although the drop in unemployment from 1933 to 1937 was relatively greater according to the employment exchange data. From 1920 to 1921, however, the relative increase in unemployment as indicated by the trade union series was much greater than according to the employment exchange series, and similarly with the decline in unemployment from 1921 to 1923. The reasons for this divergence have not been established. A possible source of discrepancy is the fact that from 1920 to 1923, state relief work was included with vacancies (see note to Table I-2), so that while union members on relief work would normally have been reported unemployed, they would not have affected the supply-demand ratio at the labor exchanges. Nevertheless, the magnitude of the discrepancy does throw some doubt upon the validity of the very high unemployment rates for 1921 and 1922 in the trade union series.

UNEMPLOYMENT INSURANCE DATA

The Swedish unemployment insurance system is organized along the lines of the Ghent System, with the basic operating units being state-subsidized trade union unemployment funds. The present state system first came into effect in 1934, although many trade unions had previously operated funds without state assistance. In that year the funds were opened, on a voluntary basis, to all persons working in the particular trade.[14] In order to receive benefits, an unemployed person must register for work with a public employment exchange. In 1950 some 1,100,000 persons were insured under the state scheme, a great increase over the 181,000 workers covered in 1938.

The unemployment fund rates of unemployment represent the relationship between the total number of weeks of unemployment during a month and the total possible weeks of work during that month (i.e. the membership of the fund multiplied by elapsed weeks). An unemployed worker is exempted from the payment of his normal contribution to the unemployment fund, and it is this number of "free-stamped" weeks which is reported as weeks of unemployment. In most cases, the fund secretary, who is usually also the local union secretary, makes the determination as to an individual's unemployment status. Registration at an employment exchange is *not* required for "free stamping," though it is required for the receipt of benefits.

[13] The correspondence is a rough one at best. There are variations for individual years in addition to those indicated in the text.

[14] *Social Sweden*, p. 420.

Since these statistics are based upon "free stamping" of the unemployment books rather than upon weeks of benefit payment, they tend to be more comprehensive than the usual unemployment insurance statistics. While in general they are based upon the same principle as the trade union unemployment series, there are some differences:

1. The coverage of the unemployment fund statistics is somewhat broader than that of the trade union series, including musicians, barbers, commercial white collar workers, hotel and restaurant personnel, foremen, and other groups not included in the trade union reports.

2. There is an eight-week period of grace for the payment of the unemployment fund contribution, so that there is a lag in the reporting of unemployment, since the weeks of employment are reported in the accounting period when "free stamping" is granted. This lag is more significant for the monthly than for the annual averages.[15]

The unemployment insurance fund percentages are shown in Table I-3 for the period 1936-1951. Comparison of these figures with the

TABLE I-3

Percentage of Member-Weeks of Unemployment among Members of the Unemployment Insurance System, Sweden, 1936-1951

Year	*Per Cent of Unemployment*	Year	*Per Cent of Unemployment*
1936	11.4	1945	5.1
1937	8.9	1946	4.0
1938	7.2	1947	3.9
1939	6.4	1948	4.4
		1949	3.9
1940	7.9		
1941	8.6	1950	3.5
1942	5.2	1951	2.7
1943	4.9		
1944	5.1		

Source: *Sociala Meddelanden.*

trade union data reveals that from 1936 to 1943 they were somewhat lower than the latter; the maximum divergence was 3.9 per cent in 1940, and the average divergence for the period was 2.4 per cent of unemployment. From 1944 to 1951 the unemployment insurance fund percentage consistently exceeded the trade union unemployment percentages, the average excess for the period being 1.0 per cent of unemployment.

[15] See *Sociala Meddelanden*, No. 4, 1942, p. 322.

OTHER STATISTICS

Beginning with 1922, data on the number of unemployment relief applicants were collected on a systematic basis. The difficulty with these data, however, is that the local administration of relief has varied considerably. ". . . the number of applications for relief at the local committees has always been strongly affected by the prospects of getting relief. If the committee has a reputation for generosity, many will come who are not really in need, and the reverse is also true."[16] Relief rolls were often padded by local communities in order to qualify for or increase the subsidy from the central government. The conclusion has been reached that the relief statistics do not represent "either the number of unemployed or the number needing relief."[17]

There are several employment series published regularly. The Royal Social Board has published monthly since 1939 an index of employment in manufacturing, which continued an annual series beginning in 1911. There is also an older series, no longer published, representing evaluations of employment conditions by employers, ranked in five grades from poor to good. These employment series are not suitable for the measurement of unemployment.

SUMMARY

The trade union series constitutes the best long-term index of Swedish unemployment. With respect to international comparison, it has the following characteristics:

1. For recent years only, the coverage goes beyond manufacturing, mining, and building. It includes in addition those unions covering commerce, municipal workers, and trucking. The weight of the latter groups (in terms of reported membership) was 20 per cent at the end of 1950.

2. The returns have not been confined to unions which pay unemployment benefits, though since 1934 the process of reporting unemployed members and weeks of unemployment among insured members has been closely parallel.

3. In general, unemployment due to labor disputes and illness is excluded.

4. The trade union percentages are generally believed by Swedish economists to constitute a good index of unemployment for the sector of the economy covered and within the definition of unemployment used.

[16] Clark, *op.cit.*, p. 73.
[17] *Ibid.*, p. 72.

Appendix J: *The United Kingdom*

The three major continuous unemployment series available for the United Kingdom are the trade union series, the unemployment insurance series, and the series giving the number of unemployed persons on the registers of the employment exchanges.

TRADE UNION SERIES

The trade union unemployment series was constructed from monthly reports, submitted in the early years to the Board of Trade and later to the Ministry of Labour, by trade unions paying out-of-work benefits. In these monthly returns, the trade unions reported (1) the total number of their members and (2) the number of members wholly unemployed at the end of the month whether in receipt of unemployment benefit or not. With this information at their disposal, the authorities were able to calculate monthly unemployment percentages by comparing the number of trade unionists reported unemployed with the membership of the reporting unions. Annual trade union percentages (1881-1926), averages of the monthly percentages, are presented in Table J-1. The series, which extends back to 1851, was discontinued in 1926. Some further characteristics of the series are set forth below.

1. The trade union unemployment reports excluded workers who were sick, superannuated, on strike, or locked out from the total number reported unemployed each month. In addition to being excluded from the numbers unemployed, persons on strike or locked out were also excluded from the membership figures used in calculating percentages.

2. The accuracy of the union reports is generally held to be quite good. Beveridge described the caliber of the reporting as follows:

> "The unions making returns are asked to include all their unemployed members whether in receipt of benefit or not. The great bulk of them continue their payments for periods so considerable that those who at any time have run out of benefit are a very small fraction of all the unemployed. Even as to these the obligation to register generally remains; the rules almost invariably provide that all members out of work must sign the vacant book regularly whether in receipt of benefit or not. Nor is the obligation to register merely formal. In a good many unions, even after the actual allowance has come to an end, members continuing to sign the books are excused from payment of their contributions. . . .

"There is, therefore, no reason to doubt the substantial completeness of the returns made, at least as to the members who are wholly unemployed."[1]

TABLE J-1

Unemployment among Trade Union Members, United Kingdom, 1881-1926

YEAR	COVERAGE (*thousands*)	PER CENT UNEMPLOYED[a]	
		Uncorrected	*Corrected*[b]
1881	140	3.5	3.55
1882	151	2.3	2.35
1883	160	2.6	2.6
1884	167	8.1	7.15
1885	169	9.3	8.55
1886	168	10.2	9.55
1887	164	7.6	7.15
1888	168	4.9	4.15
1889	188	2.1	2.05
1890	213	2.1	2.1
1891	229	3.5	3.4
1892	234	6.3	6.2
1893	329	7.5	7.7
1894	368	6.9	7.2
1895	391	5.8	6.0
1896	423	3.3	3.35
1897	458	3.3	3.45
1898	458	2.8	2.95
1899	494	2.0	2.05
1900	525	2.5	2.45
1901	531	3.3	3.35
1902	538	4.0	4.2
1903	550	4.7	5.0
1904	567	6.0	6.4
1905	569	5.0	5.25
1906	586	3.6	3.7
1907	661	3.7	3.95
1908	689	7.8	8.65
1909	698	7.7	8.7
1910	703	4.7	5.1
1911	759	3.0	3.05
1912	834	3.2	
1913	922	2.1	
1914	993	3.3	
1915	922	1.1	
1916	939	0.4	
1917	950	0.7	
1918	1,117	0.8	
1919	1,334	2.4	

(continued on next page)

[1] William H. Beveridge, *Unemployment, a Problem of Industry*, London, Longmans, 1909, p. 19.

TABLE J-1 (continued)

YEAR	COVERAGE (*thousands*)	PER CENT UNEMPLOYED[a]	
		Uncorrected	*Corrected*[b]
1920	1,603	2.4	
1921	1,235	14.8[c, d]	
1922	1,360	15.2	
1923	1,145	11.3	
1924	1,084	8.1[d]	
1925	978	10.5	
1926	833	12.2[c]	

[a] Trade union percentages based on returns collected by the Board of Trade and the Ministry of Labour from various trade unions which paid unemployment benefit; persons on strike or locked out, sick or superannuated are excluded. Percentages for some of the earlier years are partly computed from the expenditure of the several unions on unemployment benefit.

[b] The nature of the correction applied by the Board of Trade is discussed in the text.

[c] Affected by general coal mining stoppage.

[d] Figures from 1921 on exclude pottery trade operatives. From July 1924 building trade operatives are also excluded from the general average.

Source: *Fourteenth Abstract of Labour Statistics*, London, Board of Trade, 1911, p. 2. *Twenty-second Abstract of Labour Statistics*, London, Ministry of Labour, 1937, p. 48.

Further, since the labor unions served in many instances as labor exchanges, unemployed members who sought work at the labor union offices were brought to the attention of the union secretaries. Thus, to abide by union rules, to collect benefit, to be excused from payment of contributions, and to find work, unemployed members had good reason to make their unemployment known to the union officials charged with submitting the monthly unemployment reports to the authorities.

3. The membership of the reporting trade unions (see Table J-1) expanded from 140,000 in 1881 to 525,000 in 1900. By 1910, the number covered by the returns had reached 703,000, followed by coverage of well over a million in the years 1918-1924. After reaching a peak of 1,603,000 in 1920, the number covered contracted until in 1926, the last year of the series, membership in the reporting unions stood at 833,000. From 1900 to the outbreak of World War I, the membership of the reporting unions included about one-fourth of the total membership of trade unions and other employees' associations in Great Britain and Northern Ireland.[2] After the war, this fraction fluctuated from about one-sixth to about one-fifth.

[2] *Twenty-second Abstract of Labour Statistics*, London, Ministry of Labour, 1937, p. 137. The statistics relate to all organizations of employees, including those

The census of 1921 for Great Britain enumerated approximately 7.74 million employees with occupations in manufacturing, mining, quarrying, and building. Included in this figure are 555,660 general laborers or other unskilled workers. The union sample therefore represented from approximately one-fifth to a little over one-tenth of the total number of employees enumerated in the above named activities in 1921. Unfortunately, the census figures do not show wage and salary earners separately, therefore it is not possible to compare the membership of the reporting trade unions with the number of wage earners alone.

4. The industrial coverage of the trade union sample depended upon the development of trade union schemes providing for the payment of unemployment benefits in the various trades. Since out-of-work payments were first instituted among unions in the engineering, shipbuilding, and metal trades, unionists in these trades are more heavily represented in the union sample in the earlier years of the series. In the years 1881-1890, these groups accounted for nearly 60 per cent of the total membership represented in the returns. For 1894, 1908, and 1921, the industrial percentage distribution of the trade union sample in the United Kingdom was:

Trade	*1894*	*January 1908*		*December 1921*	
Building	21	9.4	14.8	6.8	13.1
Woodworking and furnishing		5.4		6.3	
Coal mining	19	19.5		12.7	
Engineering and shipbuilding	46	34.2	39.1	37.4	42.6
Other metal		4.9		5.2	
Printing, bookbinding, and paper	10	8.7		7.1	
Textiles	3	14.5		11.4	
Clothing	0	0		9.6	
Pottery	0	0		2.4	
Miscellaneous	1	3.4		1.1	
Total	100	100		100	

Sources: 1894 and 1908—William H. Beveridge, *Unemployment, a Problem of Industry*, London, Longmans, 1909, p. 19. 1921—*Ministry of Labour Gazette.*

The trade union sample was drawn mainly from manufacturing, mining, and building with workers in agriculture, transportation, communications, domestic service, government, and commerce excluded.

of salaried and professional workers, as well as those of manual wage earners, which are known to include among their functions that of negotiating with employers about regulating the conditions of employment of their members.

Of the trades covered by the returns, the shipbuilding, engineering, and metal (three highly fluctuating trades) were overrepresented.

5. Since the composition of the trade union sample changed over time, the Board of Trade, in an effort to put the percentages on a comparable basis, constructed "corrected" trade union unemployment percentages. This was done by averaging the unemployment rate for the engineering, shipbuilding, and metal groups, taken together, and the mean of the unemployment rates for all other groups (see Table J-1).[3] In the years 1881-1911, the maximum deviation between the corrected percentages and the unadjusted percentages was 1.0 percentage point. In thirteen of these 31 years, the deviations were 0.1 percentage point or less. For nine of the years, the unadjusted percentages exceeded the corrected, for two there was no difference, and for the remaining years, the corrected percentages stood slightly above the unadjusted figures. The conclusion indicated by this comparison is that the correction which the Board of Trade applied did not affect the trade union percentages to any significant degree in the years 1881-1911. Furthermore, the arbitrary system of averaging which the Board of Trade adopted does not in the least insure that the "corrected" percentages represent a more correct estimate of unemployment than do the unadjusted figures.

6. A memorandum of the Ministry of Labour in the *Survey of Industrial Relations* referred to one other property of the trade union sample as follows: "Moreover, unskilled and casual labour is insufficiently represented in the returns, which relate mainly to skilled workmen."[4] For example, in the tobacco trade, unionists represented in the returns were largely cigar makers, while in the building trades, they were mostly carpenters and joiners.

7. The trade union percentages are considered to be a valid index of unemployment for the years covered by the series. The Committee on Industry and Trade stated that this had been confirmed by certain calculations of Bowley in 1912 and by the figures provided by the introduction of unemployment insurance.[5]

8. Several analyses indicate that the trade union rates of unemploy-

[3] For example, in 1908 the unemployment percentage for the engineering, shipbuilding, and metal trades was 12.5 while for all other unionists covered by the returns it was 4.8. Therefore the "corrected" percentage was 8.65 for this year. In the same year the unadjusted trade union rate was 7.8, the highest annual rate for the years between 1900 and 1914 (see *Fifteenth Abstract of Labour Statistics*, London, Board of Trade, 1912, p. 2).

[4] *Survey of Industrial Relations*, London, Committee on Industry and Trade, 1926, p. 218.

[5] *Ibid.*, p. 245.

ment did not substantially falsify the level of unemployment of wholly unemployed persons in the trades covered by the union returns.

Beveridge has presented a detailed analysis of the trade union series in an effort to determine, "how far the unemployment rate derived from trade union returns before 1914 can be taken as a guide, not merely to the direction in which unemployment was moving at any moment, that is to say its rise or fall, but also to the general level of unemployment over a period of years."[6] His analysis takes account of the following factors:

1. Coverage of the trade union series was limited to trade unionists in the trades covered. He concluded that a reduction of one-sixth, i.e. from 4.8 (the average for the years 1883-1913), to 4.0 should correct for this point.

2. Unemployment insurance records after World War I covered a greater variety of industries. No correction is needed here since in Beveridge's words: "It is safest to regard the occupations covered by the trade union returns, as having had on an average much the same general level of unemployment as all occupations taken together, though less in good times and more in bad times. That is to say, no correction either way should be made on account of the narrower occupational basis of the trade union unemployment rate."

3. The bases of the trade union and of the unemployment insurance schemes were not only different from one another but each of them changed from time to time. Beveridge suggested that an upward correction of 1 percentage point be applied to the trade union average, raising it to 5 per cent.

4. To account for the more complete recording of unemployment by the insurance statistics, Beveridge raised the union average by another percentage point to 6 per cent. Here the major part of the correction was attributed to the fact that the trade union rates did not include those working short time. Also included was allowance for the fact that some unemployment of short duration and some of extremely long duration failed to be included in the union returns.

Beveridge concluded his analysis with the suggestion that 6.0 per cent is the most probable rate of prewar unemployment to use for comparison with interwar unemployment rates. However, he admitted that this figure could be anywhere from 4.8, the actual recorded trade union average, to 7.0 per cent.

In the final report of the Royal Commission on Unemployment Insurance, there appeared the following evaluation of the average level of unemployment before World War I:

[6] William H. Beveridge, *Full Employment in a Free Society*, London, G. Allen, 1945, pp. 328-335.

"... there is, however, little doubt that the postwar average figure of 13 per cent is much higher than would have been shown by prewar experience had corresponding statistics been available. The experience of the trade unions which gave unemployment benefit was examined when the 1911 and 1920 Acts were prepared, and the estimate then reached of unemployment for the industries at present included in the insurance scheme in the twenty years before the war was an average of about 4 per cent."[7]

Actually the average of the trade union rates for the twenty years before the war (1894-1913) was 4.3 per cent.

Thus these two analyses appear to confirm the validity of the trade union percentages as a measure of the average level of unemployment over a period of years. The Royal Commission cited an estimate of about 4 per cent for the twenty years before World War I, only 0.3 percentage points below the trade union average for these years. Beveridge's estimate of approximately 6 per cent for the years 1883-1913 includes a correction for short time. If only total unemployment be counted, Beveridge's figure would be about 5.5 per cent. The average of the trade union rates, 1883-1913, was 4.8, just 0.7 percentage points below Beveridge's figure.

9. The only statistical information available to gauge the value of the trade union series as an absolute measure of unemployment at particular times is the unemployment statistics of the unemployment insurance schemes from the last months of 1912 through 1926, the year in which the trade union series terminated. In Table J-2 the annual averages of the trade union percentages and of the unemployment insurance unemployment percentages for these years are compared.

John Hilton, former Director of Statistics, Ministry of Labour, who compared the monthly trade union percentages with those of the unemployment insurance schemes for the months September 1912 through December 1922, concluded:

"The experience which has been gained since the records of the proportions unemployed among insured workpeople became available, suggests that in times of good employment the Trade Union percentage has approximated very closely to the general percentage unemployed, but that in times of serious depression the over representation of the engineering and shipbuilding trades in the figures has (as was believed to be the case) tended to raise the general percentage for all unions included to a level appreciably too high

[7] *Final Report of the Royal Commission on Unemployment Insurance*, London, 1932, pp. 85-86.

TABLE J-2

Comparison of Trade Union and Unemployment Insurance Unemployment Rates, United Kingdom, 1912-1926

(per cent)

	TRADE UNION UNEMPLOYMENT		UNEMPLOYMENT INSURANCE UNEMPLOYMENT[a]	
YEAR	*Unadjusted*[b]	*Adjusted*[c]	*Wholly Unemployed*[d]	*Wholly and Temporarily Unemployed*[e]
1912	3.2	3.3		
1913	2.1	2.1	3.6	
1914	3.3	3.3	4.2	
1915	1.1	1.1	1.2	
1916	0.4	0.4	0.6	
1917	0.7	0.6	0.7	
1918	0.8	0.8	1.3	
1919	2.4[f]	2.1[f]	5.2[g]	
1920	2.4	2.0	3.2[h]	
1921[i]	14.8	13.5	13.8	17.0
1922	15.2	12.8	13.3	14.3
1923	11.3		11.4[j]	11.7
1924	8.1		n.a.	10.3
1925	10.5		n.a.	11.3
1926	12.2[k]		8.9[k]	12.5[k]

[a] Coverage of the unemployment insurance statistics expanded in 1916 and in 1920.

[b] Data from Table J-1.

[c] John Hilton, "Statistics Derived from the Working of the Unemployment Insurance Acts," *Journal of the Royal Statistical Society*, March 1923, pp. 190-191. Hilton weighted the trade union percentages for various industrial groups by the estimated number of workers in each, instead of in the proportions in which each group was represented in the trade union returns. The annual figures above are averages of Hilton's monthly data.

[d] 1913-1922—Hilton, *op. cit.*, pp. 190-191. Averages of monthly data. 1923-1926—*Ministry of Labour Gazette*.

[e] Data from Table J-5.

[f] Trade union rates did not adequately reflect unemployment among workers in general in this year. Out-of-work donation records, the records of the scheme which temporarily replaced unemployment insurance during 1919, showed a rise from 365,000 at the beginning of January 1919 to a maximum of 790,000 early in March. For discussion of unemployment in 1919, see Hilton, *op. cit.*, pp. 183-184, and Arthur C. Pigou, *Aspects of British Economic History, 1918-1925*, London, Macmillan, 1947, pp. 9-21.

[g] The average of unemployment insurance rates for January, February, November, and December of 1919 is 8.2. Since data are not available for other months, it was assumed that the average for these months bore the same relation to the annual average as in 1920.

[h] Average of eleven months.

[i] Before December 1921, the figures relate to Great Britain and Ireland; after this date they relate to Great Britain and Northern Ireland.

[j] January-October.

[k] Affected by coal mining strike.

> to represent accurately the average proportion of workpeople unemployed in the country as a whole."[8]

In this conclusion, Hilton refers to *all workers*, including those in agriculture, railroads, domestic service, and government. Undoubtedly the overstatement in bad times, referred to above as appreciable, would be somewhat less pronounced if the comparison were limited to workers in manufacturing, building, and mining.

The Committee on Industry and Trade in its report of 1926 commented as follows:

> "The other check upon the trade union index is that which has recently been made possible by the institution of Unemployment Insurance. It will be seen from reference to p. 33 that a comparison between the percentage of insured workpeople unemployed with the trade union figure indicates that the latter is not only a fairly reliable index but even a tolerable measure of unemployment."[9]

The years after 1900 up to World War I, except for 1908 and 1909, were years of good employment. If Hilton's conclusion to the effect that the trade union percentages approximate very closely the level of unemployment in times of good employment can be carried back this far (he studied the period 1912-1922), the trade union percentages can be taken to approximate, perhaps rather roughly at times, the level of unemployment in these years. For the years 1908 and 1909, there may be some overstatement of the level of unemployment because of the overrepresentation of the engineering, shipbuilding, and metal groups. Several considerations indicate that this overstatement could not have been very serious. Comparison with the unemployment insurance statistics revealed that in the depression of the early 1920's, much more severe than that of 1908-1909, the maximum divergence between the trade union percentages and the unemployment insurance percentages was 1.9 percentage points (Table J-2). In 1921, the shipbuilding, engineering, and metal groups constituted 42.6 per cent of the union sample, whereas in 1908 it constituted 39.1 per cent. Further, as revealed in Table J-3, in the 1920's the unemployment percentages of this group stood higher relative to those of other groups than in 1908-1909 and therefore influenced the average for all groups more in the 1920's than in 1908-1909. Therefore, there is reason to suppose that the overstatement in 1908-1909 was not as great as in 1921.[10]

[8] Hilton, *op.cit.*, p. 182.

[9] *Survey of Industrial Relations*, p. 245.

[10] William A. Berridge in his article, "Employment and the Business Cycle," *The Review of Economic Statistics*, January 1922, pp. 12-51, compared cycles derived from the trade union percentages, 1903-1914, for all trades with those de-

TABLE J-3

Trade Union Unemployment Rates for Various Industrial Groups, United Kingdom, Selected Years, 1907-1926

Year	*All Unions*	*Engineering, Shipbulding, and Metal*	*Carpenters and Joiners*	*Other Wood-working and Finishing*	*Printing and Bookbinding*
1907	3.7	4.9	7.3	4.6	4.3
1908	7.8	12.5	11.6	8.3	5.5
1909	7.7	13.0	11.7	7.6	5.6
1921[a]	14.8[b]	22.1	3.9	9.4	7.3
1922	15.2	27.0	7.5[c]	7.6	6.6
1923	11.3	20.6	5.0[c]	5.8	4.7
1924[b]	8.1	13.8	1.9[c]	4.5	3.3
1925	10.5	13.5	2.2[c]	4.4	2.8
1926[a]	12.2	18.2	5.2[c]	8.2	4.3

[a] Affected by general coal mining stoppage.

[b] Figures from 1921 onward exclude pottery trade operatives. From July 1924 onward building trade operatives are excluded from the general average.

[c] Average of quarters.

Source: *Twentieth Abstract of Labour Statistics*, London, Ministry of Labour, 1931, p. 72.

UNEMPLOYMENT INSURANCE STATISTICS[11]

Since the enactment of the first National Unemployment Insurance Act of 1911, unemployment percentages are available for persons compulsorily insured against unemployment. These statistics are described below.

1. The coverage of the unemployment insurance statistics, shown in Table J-4, has expanded with the broadening of the unemployment insurance schemes. At the time when the first act came into operation in 1912, the statistics included about 2.1 million workers, sixteen years of age or older, engaged in the following lines of activity: building, construction of works, shipbuilding, engineering, construction of vehicles, and sawmilling.[12] The scope of the statistics was extended by the acts of 1916 and of 1920. The former act, which brought approximately 1.5 million additional persons under unemployment insurance, covered workers occupied in machine woodwork, the repair of metal goods, the manufacture of munitions, chemicals, meats, rubber and rubber products, leather and leather products, bricks, cement, wooden

rived by combining the cycles for four leading industrial groups (engineering, shipbuilding and metals; building; woodworking, etc.; and printing, etc.) both in weighted and unweighted averages. "The three curves agree so closely that it is unnecessary to present them for inspection" (p. 42).

[11] Occasionally these statistics are called employment exchange statistics since the employment exchange authorities administered unemployment insurance.

[12] See page 568 for this footnote.

TABLE J-4

Persons Insured under Unemployment Insurance Schemes, United Kingdom, 1913-1952

(thousands)

Year	*Number*[a]	*Year*	*Number*
1913	2,070	1935[c]	13,058[d] 14,003[e]
1914	2,326	1936[f]	14,285[g] 14,909[h]
1915	2,078	1937	15,334
1916	2,029	1938[i]	15,501[j] 15,743[k]
1917	3,632	1939	15,898
1918	3,922	1940[l]	15,194[m] 15,154[n]
1919	3,721	1941	14,918[o] 15,282[p]
1920	4,197	1942	15,438
1921	11,338	1943	15,003
1922	11,432	1944	14,514
1923	11,486	1945	14,000
1924	11,664	1946	15,572
1925	11,892	1947	15,930
1926	12,041	1948[q, r]	16,147[s] 20,820[t]
1927[b]	12,131	1949	20,870
1928	11,882	1950	21,120
1929	12,094	1951	21,216
1930	12,406	1952	21,266
1931	12,772		
1932	12,810		
1933	12,885		
1934	12,960		

[a] July of each year. The figures for 1913-1921 include all of Ireland, while later figures relate to Great Britain and Northern Ireland.

[b] Ages 16 and over through 1927 and 16-64 from 1928 on.

[c] Persons 14-16 became insurable.

[d] Includes those 16-64.

[e] Relates to ages 14-64.

[f] Persons in agriculture came under unemployment insurance in 1936.

[g] Excludes agriculture.

[h] Includes agriculture.

[i] Some classes of domestic workers first insured.

[j] Excludes domestic workers.

[k] Includes domestic workers.

[l] Women aged 60-64 ceased to be insurable in 1940.

[m] Includes women aged 60-64.

[n] Excludes women aged 60-64.

[o] Excludes nonmanual workers earning £250 and not more than £420 per year, who first became insurable in 1940.

[p] Includes nonmanual workers earning £250 and not more than £420 per year.

[q] School-leaving age raised from 14 to 15 in 1947. Figures for 1948 relate to those 15 and over.

[r] Change caused by institution of national insurance.

[s] Insured under Unemployment Insurance Scheme.

[t] Insured under National Insurance Scheme.

Source: *Report on National Unemployment Insurance to July 1923*, 1924, p. 23; *Nineteenth Abstract of Labour Statistics*, 1928, p. 78 and *Twenty-second Abstract of Labour Statistics*, 1937, p. 14 (all London, Ministry of Labour); and *Statistical Abstract for the United Kingdom*, London, Board of Trade, various dates, *passim*.

cases, artificial stone, and other artificial building materials. The act of 1920 was responsible for a large expansion of coverage. It increased the number of persons insured to well over 11 million by applying unemployment insurance to all persons, sixteen years of age or over, who were employed under a contract of service or apprenticeship (except apprentices without money payments) and, if nonmanual workers, received remuneration not exceeding £250 a year. The principal persons excluded from the scheme were those occupied in agriculture, forestry, horticulture, and private domestic service.[13] Thus the total number insured under the Act of 1920 included nonmanual workers earning less than £250 a year and engaged in an insurable trade, workers in manufacturing, mining, transportation, fishing, gas, water, electricity, the distributive trades, commerce, banking, insurance and finance.[14] Table J-6 below shows the industrial distribution of the insured population together with the census count of the number of insurable persons engaged in these industries on April 27, 1931.[15] The industrial classification employed in the insurance statistics was the same as that employed in the census.

[12] Industrial representation in the insurance year 1913-1914 was as follows:

Trade	*Number Insured*	*Proportion*
Building	812,659	35.0
Construction of works	144,231	6.2
Shipbuilding	264,217	11.3
Engineering	817,931	35.2
Construction of vehicles	209,985	9.0
Sawmilling	12,029	0.5
Others	64,546	2.8
Total	2,325,598	100.0

Source: *Nineteenth Abstract of Labour Statistics*, London, Ministry of Labour, 1928, p. 33.

[13] Also excluded were (1) persons in military service, (2) permanent members of any police force, (3) teachers, (4) agents paid by commission or fees, or a share in the profits, who are mainly dependent on earnings from some other occupation or who are ordinarily employed as agents for more than one agency, (5) nonmanual workers earning over £250 a year (note that for manual laborers, coverage is independent of the rate of remuneration), (6) casual workers occupied other than for the purposes of the employer's trade or business, (7) workers coming under special orders who are engaged in certain subsidiary employments which are not their principal means of livelihood, (8) crews of fishing vessels wholly remunerated by shares of profits or gross earnings, and (9) female nurses.

[14] These last three groups were included under Special Schemes.

[15] The term *insurable person* refers to those persons meeting the necessary requirements to be covered by unemployment insurance. The census data are adjusted to this concept by excluding those under 16 years of age, those 65 years of age and over, and those listed as managers, all of whom did not qualify for unemployment insurance coverage in 1931.

As from May 4, 1936, persons in agricultural occupations (except private gardeners who were not included until February 1937) were included in the statistics. In April 1938, certain classes of domestic employments were brought under the insurance schemes, while in September 1940, nonmanual workers with a rate of remuneration exceeding £250 but not exceeding £420 were also included.

The base of the statistics was further enlarged with the enactment of the National Insurance Scheme of 1948. Under this scheme, the total number of persons, aged fifteen or over, who work for pay or gain or who register themselves available for such work became insurable. The statistics came to include private indoor domestic servants and nonmanual workers with a rate of remuneration exceeding £420, two groups which were formerly uninsurable.

2. The age groups included in the statistics have shown some variation. Until 1928, the persons included were aged sixteen and over. In 1928, persons sixty-five and over were excluded. In 1934, the minimum age of persons covered by the statistics was lowered from sixteen years to the age (not less than fourteen years) at which juveniles were no longer required by law to attend school. Women aged sixty and under sixty-five were excluded in 1940. In 1947, when the school leaving age was raised from fourteen to fifteen, the age groups included were fifteen through sixty-four for males and fifteen through fifty-nine for females. After mid-1948, all persons over fifteen came to be included in the statistics.

3. The count of the total number of insured persons is made in conjunction with the renewal of the unemployment insurance books which are issued to all insured persons. Formerly, such a count was made once a year in July. In 1948, insurance books of different colors (marked A, B, C, and D) were issued at random and all cards of the same color are now exchanged at quarterly dates. Thus the count of the insured is now based on random 25 per cent samples at the end of each quarter.

4. Upon becoming unemployed, insured persons are required to lodge their books at an employment exchange in order to claim benefit and to seek new employment. Upon resumption of employment, the insurance book is removed and deposited with the new employer. The determination of the number of insured persons unemployed, which was the figure used in computing percentages before mid-1948, was accomplished by counting the number of books lodged at the employment exchanges on the Monday nearest the middle of the month. Persons sick, incapacitated, disqualified from benefit under the trade dispute regulation, or who refused a suitable offer of employment

were excluded. Before September, 1937, the following groups constituted the number of insured unemployed:

a. Persons whose claims had been admitted for insurance benefit
b. Persons whose applications had been authorized for unemployment allowances
c. Persons whose claims were under consideration
d. Other insured persons not in receipt of allowances but who maintained registration at an employment exchange
e. Persons under the Special Schemes for banking, insurance, and, after 1936, agriculture, with claims to benefit
f. Persons whose books were in the "two months file"[16]

Usually, the persons in categories a and e constituted the major part of the total number of insured unemployed. The numbers in category f were generally not large.

The system of counting the insured unemployed was altered on several occasions. The effects and nature of these changes are shown below:[17]

MONTH AND YEAR	NATURE OF THE CHANGE IN COUNTING THE NUMBER OF INSURED UNEMPLOYED	NUMBER OF INSURED UNEMPLOYED IN GREAT BRITAIN (THOUSANDS)	
		Old Count	*New Count*
September 1937	Before this date, all persons with books lodged on the Monday of the count were included; after this date, all persons who, during the week subsequent to the count, were found to have actually been in employment on the Monday of the count, even though their books remained lodged at an exchange, were excluded.	1,420	1,373
January 1939	Before this date, the figures related to persons who were maintaining registration at the exchanges and to persons whose books were in the "two months file"; after this date, the latter group was excluded.	2,125	2,035
January 1941	From this date, the figures excluded persons who had been classified as unsuitable for ordinary employment.	681	653
June 1948	A new procedure for counting the unemployed, described below, was instituted in July. The *Labour Gazette* gave the results of counting by the old and new methods for June.	274	286

[16] This file contained the books of persons for whom no information was available as to whether they were sick, deceased, had emigrated, or had obtained em-

The effect of each of these changes[18] on the unemployment percentages (based on some 12 to 15 million insured persons in the 1930's and about 15 to 16 million in the 1940's until 1948) is small. However, it must be recognized that in making comparisons of the percentages for the postwar period up to 1948, with those before 1937, changes in the methods of counting have tended to reduce the former relative to the latter. The change which occurred in mid-1948 is described as follows in the *Labour Gazette*:

> "Hitherto the published figures of unemployment have represented the numbers of persons insured under the Unemployment Insurance Acts who were registered at the Employment Exchanges as unemployed, i.e. who had fallen out of insurable employment. The number of persons insured under the new scheme who register for employment at Employment Exchanges may include in addition to those who have fallen out of work, some nonemployed insured persons registered for their first job. . . . It has therefore been decided to include in the statistics of unemployment all persons registered at Employment Exchanges with the exception of (a) persons in employment who are registering for a change of job and (b) registered disabled persons who require employment under sheltered conditions."[19]

As shown above, this change added 12,000 persons to the number unemployed in June 1948.

5. For most years of the unemployment insurance series, which is shown in Table J-5, separate figures are given for the numbers wholly unemployed and temporarily unemployed. The *Labour Gazette* defined temporary unemployment as follows:

> "The figures under the heading 'temporary stoppages' include those persons recorded as unemployed on the date of the return who were either on short time or were otherwise stood off or suspended

ployment in an uninsured trade. Such books were included in the count of the insured unemployed for a period of up to two months from the date the person had last been in contact with the employment exchange. Regular form letters were sent to persons losing contact with the exchange in an effort to ascertain their employment status.

[17] R. B. Ainsworth, "Labour Statistics," in *Sources and Nature of the Statistics of the United Kingdom*, Maurice G. Kendall, Editor, London, Oliver & Boyd, 1952, Vol. 1, p. 80. The data for June 1948 were obtained from the *Ministry of Labour Gazette*, January 1949, p. 2.

[18] One further change which took place in July 1940 was the exclusion of men in attendance at government training centers, who were unemployed when they entered the centers.

[19] *Ministry of Labour Gazette*, August 1948, p. 260.

TABLE J-5

Unemployment Rates, Insured Population, United Kingdom, 1921-1952

YEAR	WHOLLY AND TEMPORARILY UNEMPLOYED		WHOLLY UNEMPLOYED	
	Excluding Agriculture[a]	*Including Agriculture*[b]	*Excluding Agriculture*[c]	*Including Agriculture*[b]
1921[d]	17.0		13.8	
1922	14.3		13.3	
1923	11.7		11.4[e]	
1924	10.3		n.a.	
1925	11.3		n.a.	
1926	12.5[f]		8.9[f]	
1927	9.7		7.4	
1928	10.8		8.2	
1929	10.4		8.2	
1930	16.1		11.8	
1931	21.3		16.7	
1932	22.1		17.6	
1933	19.9		16.4	
1934	16.7		13.9	
1935	15.5		13.1	
1936	13.1		11.2	
1937	10.8	10.0	9.3	8.5
1938	12.9	11.0		9.5
1939	10.5	9.5		8.0
1940		6.0		5.0
1941		2.0		1.5
1942		1.0		1.0
1943		0.5		0.5
1944		0.5		0.5
1945		1.0		1.0
1946		2.5		2.5
1947		3.0		2.0
1948		1.6[g, h]		1.6[g, h]
1949		1.6		1.6
1950		1.6		1.6
1951		1.3		1.2
1952		2.1		1.7

[a] 1921-1927—16 years of age and over; 1928-1939—16-65 years of age.

[b] 1937-1939—14-65 years of age; 1940-1947—males aged 14-65 and females aged 14-60; 1948-1952—15 years of age and over.

[c] 1921-1927—16 years of age and over; 1928-1937—16-65 years of age.

[d] Great Britain and Ireland to December 1921; Great Britain and Northern Ireland thereafter.

[e] January-October. [f] Affected by the coal mining strike.

[g] For 1948 and on the rates relate to all registered unemployed insured under the National Insurance Scheme, 15 and over, excluding only registered disabled persons requiring employment under sheltered conditions.

[h] July-December.

Source: *Ministry of Labour Gazette*, January 1940, p. 2; International Labour Organisation's *Yearbooks of Labour Statistics.*

on the definite understanding that they were to return to their former employment within a period of six weeks from the date of suspension. In cases where there was no definite prospect of return within six weeks, the individuals have been included in the statistics as 'wholly unemployed.' "[20]

Thus, the classification "temporarily stopped" or "temporarily unemployed" embraces certain types of partial unemployment, partial both in the sense that the work week is shortened and that the employment contract is not definitely broken.

6. At mid-1948, there was the following change in the method of calculating the unemployment percentages:

"Hitherto the percentage rate of unemployment has been obtained by expressing the insured registered unemployed as a percentage of the estimated total insured under the Unemployment Insurance Acts. Because the unemployment statistics now cover a wider field, the percentage rate of unemployment will in the future be obtained by expressing the total number of unemployed persons on the registers as a percentage of the estimated total industrial population (i.e. the estimated total in civil employment together with the registered unemployed).[21]

The effects of this change on the unemployment percentages can be appreciated by noting that in July 1948, there were 15.76 million persons insurable under the old Unemployment Insurance Acts in Great Britain,[22] whereas the number in civil employment and the registered unemployed amounted to 19.4 million.[23]

7. Since unemployed insured persons have been included in the count of the insured unemployed, *whether receiving unemployment benefit or not,* as long as they maintained registration at an employment exchange, the effects of exhaustion of the right to unemployment benefit do not influence the percentages to any great extent. In the depression years of the 1930's, the *Labour Gazette* pointed out that the unemployed maintained registration at an employment exchange for the following reasons:[24]

a. To receive unemployment benefit
b. To obtain assistance in obtaining employment

[20] *Ibid.*, February 1926, p. 54.
[21] *Ibid.*, August 1948, p. 260.
[22] *Ibid.*, February 1949, p. 41. Of the total, 183,000 males and 173,000 females were under 16 years of age.
[23] *Ibid.*, October 1948, p. 329.
[24] *Ibid.*, April 1932, p. 129.

c. To have their health insurance cards franked during unemployment so as to avoid payment of health insurance
d. To meet the condition for receipt of public assistance imposed in the cases of all able-bodied applicants by the Public Assistance Authorities

Thus most unemployed insured persons came to register at an employment exchange and are therefore included in the count of the unemployed.

This assertion is confirmed by the results of the census of April 27, 1931, insofar as it relates to the industries wholly covered by unemployment insurance. The data in Table J-6 show that for April 27, 1931, the number of insured males wholly and temporarily unemployed was 1,491,000 (1,101,000 wholly unemployed and 390,000 temporarily unemployed) for the industries shown in the upper part of the table. For the same group of industries on the same date, the census count showed 1,270,000 males out of work.[25] The figures diverge somewhat because some persons temporarily stopped, that is who were working short time or had promise of employment within six weeks, did not report themselves out of work to the census, but were counted among the insured unemployed. The figures for females are at variance, the insurance total being larger than the census total, for reasons discussed below. Thus this comparison of the census and insurance figures indicates that the number of insured unemployed at this date include the total number of unemployed persons in the industries covered and did not understate unemployment because of nonregistration of those who may have exhausted their right to benefit. For other dates, there is no way of explicitly determining the extent to which nonregistration affected the statistics; however, in view of the various provisions for extended benefit during the 1920's and 1930's[26] and of the other reasons for the unemployed to register pointed out above, it does not appear likely that much long term unemployment went unrecorded.

8. Estimates are available which furnish some information on the quantitative effects which certain legislative and administrative changes have had on the numbers of unemployed recorded in the series.[27] These are given below:

[25] Arthur L. Bowley, *Studies in the National Income*, London, Cambridge University Press, 1942, p. 104. The census out-of-work figures have been adjusted by Bowley to include an estimate for Northern Ireland and to exclude persons under 16 years of age and those 65 and over.

[26] See *Nineteenth Abstract of Labour Statistics*, London, Ministry of Labour, 1928, pp. 70-73, and *Twenty-second Abstract of Labour Statistics*, London, Ministry of Labour, 1937, pp. 68-71.

[27] *Ministry of Labour Gazette*, February 1930, p. 50, and March 1935, p. 85.

Date	Nature of Change	Estimated Increase (+) or Decrease (−) Caused in the Live Register[a]
February 1924	Removal of certain special restrictions on the grant of extended benefit	+13,500
August 1924	Relaxation of certain conditions for the receipt of both standard and extended benefit	+70,000
August 1925	Restoration of the special conditions for extended benefit which were removed in February, 1924	−10,000
January 1928	Persons aged 65 and over ceased to be insured under the Unemployment Acts	−25,000
April 1928	Relaxation of conditions for the receipt of benefit	+40,000
July 1928	Institution of the system of franking Health Insurance cards of persons registered at employment exchanges	+25,000
March 1935	Introduction of the Unemployment Assistance Scheme	+10,000 to 20,000

[a] The "Live Register," a term referring to the numbers registered at the employment exchanges, is more inclusive than the number of insured unemployed registered at the exchanges in that it includes uninsured persons as well as insured; however, it does not include those in the "two months file." See below.

Two quantitatively more important changes not appearing above occurred in 1930 and in 1931. The Unemployment Insurance Act of 1930, which came into operation on March 13 of that year, repealed the condition for receipt of benefit "under which a claimant was required to prove that he was genuinely seeking work but unable to obtain suitable employment, and the Transitional condition (c) under which a claimant who had paid 30 contributions in the previous two years had to prove that during that period he had been employed in an insurable employment to such an extent as was reasonable."[28] This relaxation of the "genuinely seeking work" condition caused a number of persons, mostly married women, to register as unemployed to receive benefit when they were not really seeking employment. The effects of this change on the unemployment insurance percentages can be roughly estimated from a comparison of the unemployment rates for males with that of females. Assuming that the female rate was normally 54 per cent of the male rate in these years[29] and that the

[28] *Ministry of Labour Gazette*, June 1930, p. 221.

[29] In "An Analysis of Unemployment III," by William H. Beveridge (*Economica*, May 1937), this figure is suggested since, "In five years 1932-1936 during which there have been no major changes of the insurance scheme affecting the

TABLE J-6

Census of Population and Unemployment Insurance Statistics, United Kingdom, 1931

(thousands)

INDUSTRY	NUMBER OF PERSONS OF INSURABLE AGE				NUMBER UNEMPLOYED					
	Males		*Females*		*Males*			*Females*		
						Insured			*Insured*	
	Census[a]	*Insured*	*Census*[a]	*Insured*	*Census*	*Wholly*	*Temporarily*	*Census*	*Wholly*	*Temporarily*
Coal	1,084	1,046	6	6	216	181	97	1	1	0
Other mining	109	105	3	2	20	18	5	0	0	0
Mining products	56	46	3	3	11	9	2	0	0	0
Bricks, glass, earthenware	152	153	56	59	24	21	11	9	10	9
Chemicals	164	156	52	58	25	23	3	4	5	1
Engineering	629	687	104	113	485	405	166	37	47	15
Vehicles	316	291	39	30						
Ships	276	249	5	4						
Metals and metal trades	721	620	137	160						
Cotton	196	192	354	361	50	42	28	100	96	49
Wool	94	96	132	144	13	12	11	16	21	18
Other textiles	221	210	313	320	35	35	30	41	56	34
Leather	49	42	26	24	8	6	2	4	4	1
Clothing	228	194	437	408	31	21	10	29	27	12
Food	265	201	176	173	35	25	2	23	25	2
Drink	95	86	23	26	11	9	1	2	4	0
Tobacco	19	16	32	32	1	1	0	1	3	1
Wood	224	191	31	34	42	32	4	3	4	1
Paper	71	69	64	62	6	5	3	5	6	2

(continued on next page)

TABLE J-6 (continued)
(*thousands*)

	NUMBER OF PERSONS OF INSURABLE AGE				NUMBER UNEMPLOYED					
	Males		Females		Males			Females		
						Insured			Insured	
INDUSTRY	Census[a]	Insured	Census[a]	Insured	Census	Wholly	Temporarily	Census	Wholly	Temporarily
Printing	203	180	90	97	19	15	1	8	10	1
Miscellaneous	129	99	72	59	22	15	4	8	8	2
Building	963	1,096	13	11	196	212	8	1	1	0
Gas, etc.	229	165	7	7	20	14	1	0	0	0
Subtotal	6,493	6,190	2,175	2,193	1,270	1,101	390	292	330	151
Transport	1,304	827	48	35	154	176	5	3	3	0
Commerce	1,580	1,282	809	806	173	144	6	62	69	4
Fishing	44	29	2	1	10	5	0	0	0	0
Government	1,188	403	402	43	103	51	3	8	2	0
Professions	227	75	266	56	11	5	0	13	2	0
Entertainments	112	59	54	31	24	12	0	10	6	0
Other	136	105	43	37	96	42	1	28	4	1
Subtotal	4,591	2,780	1,624	1,009	571	435	15	124	86	5
Agriculture	635	0	58	0	62	0	0	3	0	0
Personal service	524	165	1,649	360	64	26	0	137	50	3
Grand total	12,243	9,135	5,506	3,562	1,967	1,562	406	557	466	159

[a] Includes those out of work and excludes managers, etc., and persons under 16 or over 65 years of age. An estimate for Northern Ireland is included.

Source: Arthur L. Bowley, *Studies in the National Income*, London, Cambridge University Press, 1942, pp. 104-105.

male rate was not much affected (see results of the census of 1931 in Table J-6), a simple calculation shows that, on these assumptions, the rates for males and females, taken together, were 14.4 in 1930 and 19.6 in 1931. These rates are slightly low in view of the fact that the new regulations were not operative over the whole of 1930 and 1931. Taking this into account, it is probable that the recorded rates for 1930 and 1931 (16.1 and 21.3 respectively) overstated the amount of unemployment by about a maximum of 1.5 percentage points.

The above estimate of the overstatement in 1930 and 1931 is reasonable in the light of the estimate made by the Ministry of Labour of the decrease in the unemployment insurance percentages brought about by the tightening of the conditions for receipt of benefit which occurred in late 1931 and which reversed the policy of the 1930 Act:

> "the reduction in the number of insured persons recorded as unemployed due to all the recent changes was about 65,000 at 25th January, 100,000 at 22nd February, and 129,000 at 21st March, 1932. If these persons had been included in the figures of insured persons recorded as unemployed at 21st March, the percentage rate of unemployment among insured persons would have been increased by about 1.0."[30]

Thus, at a time when unemployed insured persons and other insured persons were probably most respondent to changes in the conditions governing the payment of benefit, the unemployment percentages were influenced to the extent of only 1.0 to 1.5 percentage points. It does not seem unwarranted to conclude that these 1.0 to 1.5 percentage points represent the maximum effect which changes in the regulations governing conditions of the right to benefit have had on the insurance unemployment rates.

9. The unemployment rates in Table J-7 include only the wholly unemployed and apply to insured persons engaged in manufacturing, construction, and mining.[31] Insured persons in the following groups have been excluded in calculating these percentages: agriculture; fishing; gas, water, and electricity supply industries; distributive trades; commerce, banking, insurance, and finance; transport; and miscellaneous trades and services. Because of deficiencies in the data and

---

relation of male and female unemployment the general rate for females has averaged 54 per cent of the rate for males. This perhaps may be taken as the normal relation on the present basis of insurance" (p. 168). In an earlier article, "An Analysis of Unemployment I" (*Economica*, November 1936, p. 358), Beveridge presented the data upon which he based this statement.

[30] *Ministry of Labour Gazette*, April 1932, p. 129.

[31] Averages of quarterly data.

TABLE J-7

Insured Persons Wholly Unemployed, Manufacturing, Construction, and Mining, United Kingdom, 1927-1939

Year	*Number of Insured Persons Included*[a] *(thousands)*	*Per Cent Wholly Unemployed*
1927	7,937[b]	8.3[b]
1928	7,935	8.8
1929	8,007	8.7
1930	8,143	12.1
1931	8,227	18.6
1932	8,157	19.8
1933	8,046	18.7
1934	8,146	15.0
1935	8,168	13.9
1936	8,332	11.6
1937	8,596	9.2
1938	8,724	10.1
1939	8,864	9.0

[a] Excluded from the total number of insured persons are those engaged in (1) agriculture, (2) fishing, (3) gas, water, and electricity supply industries, (4) distributive trades, (5) commerce, banking, insurance, and finance, (6) transport, and (7) miscellaneous trades and services. Unemployed insured persons in these groups have been excluded from the total number of insured unemployed for January, April, July, and October of each year; the quarterly figures were then averaged, and this average was divided by the number of insured persons in groups excluding the above to obtain the rates presented above.

[b] Ages 16 and over for 1927 and 16-65 for following years. These figures are for July of each year.

Source: *Twentieth Abstract of Labour Statistics,* London, Ministry of Labour, 1931, pp. 34-41. *Twenty-first Abstract of Labour Statistics,* 1935, pp. 28-35. *Twenty-second Abstract of Labour Statistics,* 1937, pp. 18-27. *Ministry of Labour Gazette, passim.*

changes in industrial classification, these rates have been calculated only for the years 1927-1939.

Comparison with the percentages of the wholly unemployed (see Table J-5) reveals that the calculated rates for manufacturing, mining, and construction move in close agreement with the percentages based on the total insurance sample. The calculated rates are slightly above the percentages for the wholly unemployed, based on the entire sample, and somewhat below those for the wholly and temporarily unemployed.

STATISTICS OF NUMBERS SEEKING EMPLOYMENT AT EMPLOYMENT EXCHANGES

These statistics are available from 1910 when the national system of employment exchanges, created by the Labour Exchanges Act of 1909, came into operation. Sometimes referred to as the "live register" figures of unemployment, these statistics have borne a close relation to those of the numbers of unemployed insured persons. As pointed out above, after mid-1948 the count of the number of persons registered as unemployed at employment exchanges, subject to certain exclusions, forms the basis for calculation of unemployment rates. Before 1948, the relation between the number of persons on the "live register" and the number of unemployed insured persons registered at employment exchanges is brought out by the following table:[32]

1. Unemployment insurance claims admitted	2,244,477
2. Unemployment insurance claims under consideration	79,337
3. Insured persons not entitled to benefit	274,167
4. Uninsured persons on register	130,430
5. "Two months" file	181,001
6. Insured unemployed under Special Schemes	5,290
Persons on "live register," lines 1-4	2,728,411
Unemployed insured persons, lines 1-3, 5 and 6	2,784,272

The number on the "live register" included some uninsured persons and excluded two categories of insured persons. In contrast to the insurance statistics which are formed on a known base (the total number of insured persons), there is no suitable base with which to relate the statistics of the numbers on the "live register." For this reason, the weekly "live register" figures are less useful than the unemployed insured figures.[33]

SUMMARY

1. From 1900 to World War I, the trade union unemployment rates constitute the only continuous measure of unemployment. Comparison with later unemployment insurance statistics indicates that in times of good employment they were a fairly reliable measure of the level of unemployment among industrial wage earners. In times of poor employment, they may have overstated unemployment somewhat because of the overrepresentation of certain cyclically sensitive groups in the union sample. Further, it must be recognized that for particular dates the trade union percentages may not have been a completely reliable measure of unemployment.

2. The unemployment insurance percentages with very broad coverage after 1920 represent a good measure of unemployment. While these statistics have been subject to certain changes, the effects of

[32] *Ministry of Labour Gazette*, February 1932, p. 64.

[33] The statistics also list the number of placements and vacancies and, for most dates, separate the wholly unemployed from the temporarily unemployed.

the changes (1921-1947) have not greatly affected the continuity of the series.

3. Expansion of the base upon which rates are calculated in 1948 has tended to lower following rates relative to those preceding 1948. The maximum amount by which this expansion of coverage could have lowered the unemployment rates for the years 1948-1952 relative to the rate for 1947 is approximately one-half of a percentage point.[34]

COMMENT

GLADYS L. PALMER, University of Pennsylvania

In connection with the paper by Walter Galenson and Arnold Zellner—several international statistical organizations have struggled with the problem of securing greater comparability in unemployment rates between countries. In 1950, the Manpower Council of the Organization for European Economic Cooperation and the International Labour Office sponsored a "working party" to conduct a field study and recommend policy. This group concluded that periodic sample surveys of the labor force would yield more reliable, if less detailed, data and more comparable unemployment rates than could possibly be obtained from the records of existing national unemployment insurance systems. Largely as a result of their recommendations, several international conferences of manpower statisticians were held to discuss standard concepts of measurement, and France, Italy, and Denmark have initiated programs of periodic or occasional labor force surveys.

Variations in the coverage of European unemployment insurance systems are not the only factor that militates against making valid statistical comparisons of unemployment rates between countries. Administrative regulations with respect to the receipt of unemployment benefits also differ widely and they may account for some of the discrepancies in levels or trends noted in the paper.

ANGUS MCMORRAN, Dominion Bureau of Statistics, Canada

Walter Galenson and Arnold Zellner set themselves a very difficult task when they undertook the preparation of a set of unemployment rates that would lend themselves to international comparison. We are

[34] In 1947, with unemployment at 2.0 per cent, the base was approximately 16 million (see Tables J-4 and J-5). Expansion of the base to 21 million, under the assumption that none of the additional persons brought in were unemployed, decreases the unemployment rate from 2.0 to 1.5. The actual fall in the unemployment rate for the wholly unemployed between 1947 and 1948 was from 2.0 to 1.6.

all aware of the difficulty of preparing a measure of unemployment in only one country that is acceptable to the various elements in that country and comparable over time. The problems are increased immeasurably when we seek valid comparisons between countries. The handling of the available material has been most skillful and I find it difficult to make any real contribution to the problem within the scope laid down by the paper.

The series used in preparing an historical study in this field may not be the one considered best for each country. Of necessity, it must be the series that appears most common to all the countries and is available for the period under review. For these reasons, the series presented in this paper rely heavily on trade union statistics since they are the principal and, in some cases, the exclusive source of unemployment information until recent years. The writers point out that trade union statistics are subject to numerous and serious deficiencies. But on close examination, they find them less objectionable than such statistics would at first appear when used in particular situations such as the estimation of short-term trends. Finally, they concluded that even for absolute levels of unemployment, the trade union statistics are better than one might suppose for the following reasons.

1. In some cases coverage is relatively large. (This may be true of recent times but I feel that it would not be true over time.)

2. There are advantages to having the initial collection and processing of data done by experts like trade union secretaries as opposed to labor force enumerators, on the grounds that the latter are often ill-prepared. (I would submit that the differences in these collection procedures make such a comparison of little use.)

3. Reporting may be more complete in the case of trade union statistics because of a personal advantage, usually monetary, to the unemployed person. (For just this reason, reporting under these circumstances may be *over* complete.)

With this in mind, I return to comments made at the beginning of the paper. Data for international comparisons have no common basis in economic structure or in political and social institutions. I wonder at the usefulness of these data, having due regard to the need for them or the lack of them, and to the inherent qualifications. One wonders whether so much effort might not have been applied to greater advantage in other directions.

For example, the usefulness of *historical* comparisons between nations on a somewhat insecure basis does not appear so great as the usefulness of *current* comparisons on a firmer basis. Comparisons can be made on the more all-inclusive basis of labor force concepts between the United States and Canada. Similar material is becoming available from other countries—Italy, France, West Germany, and Denmark—and is contemplated in others—Sweden, Norway, and Australia. I would suggest that analysis of these data would yield more useful comparisons. Even here the differences in economic and social climate may be too much for the data.

ADDITIONAL COMMENTS

WILLIAM A. BERRIDGE, Metropolitan Life Insurance Company

Although my participation in the field of unemployment and employment statistics in any active way ended a quarter-century back, I had spent more than a decade before that doing some modest pioneering in the development and use of such data for business cycle measurement. Inasmuch as my first main efforts in this field go almost as far back as the end of World War I, I hope that some of my references to the genetics of employment and unemployment measurement may prove to be of some interest and value to the many younger people who now delve in this field.

For example, when you bemoan present-day uncertainty as to the exact number unemployed—however unemployment be defined—you forget how lucky you are to have a direct measure of it available to you at all. Those of us who made unemployment estimates long ago had to content ourselves with far less, as the following reminiscences will make plain.

The 1921 President's Conference on Unemployment was organized by Herbert Hoover while he was Secretary of Commerce, and it gave the National Bureau of Economic Research its first important claim to fame. The Conference had a small subcommittee charged with developing an estimate of the number then unemployed, which consisted of the late revered Wesley Mitchell, founder of the Bureau, another intellectual giant, Allyn A. Young of Harvard, and two young technicians, Ernest S. Bradford and myself (with occasional visits by Walter W. Willcox of Cornell, as I recall). As a result of earlier studies, this committee decided to use the downswing of factory employment and of a few other employments as the prime basis for its unemployment estimation—along with a posited unemployment estimate for the peak of the previous boom. That estimate had to be arrived at "by guess and by God." Now it seems corroborated, as a by-product, by Stanley Lebergott's study which uses the much better test data now available—not only on subsequent depressions and recessions, but even on that of 1921 itself.[1] As a surviving and active member of that

[1] Few present workers in this field seem to appreciate fully how inferior to the present were our current data—not only on unemployment but also on employment—at the time of that incident in 1921. Not until two years later did I succeed in persuading anyone (Dr. Walter W. Stewart of the Federal Reserve Board) to finance me in constructing the first employment index that eliminated biases and yielded truly dependable amplitudes from peak to trough in the net number of workers displaced (*Federal Reserve Bulletin*, December 1923, pp. 1272-1279).

That index, first done for factory workers, was later extended and otherwise

ancient body, I, on its behalf, express appreciation for this support after a third of a century.[2]

Indeed, the progress in measuring unemployment has been so vast that present students make exaggerated charges about discrepancies between agencies, and within different samplings by the same agency, that are really unwarranted when these are seen in historical perspective. Now the problem of discrepancy will doubtless always be with us. But you do not know what discrepancy really is if you are not familiar (by actual participation or by delving into the detailed reports and commentaries) with the much wider dispersions of a relatively few years ago. At a time when unemployment is low, does a discrepancy between 3.1 and 2.4 million warrant a wringing of hands? Not that I favor accepting the old standards. It is good that such discrepancies are being studied and that the very competent Stephan-Frankel-Teper Committee was set up (and so promptly) by Census Director Burgess to look into their origins and remedies. All that I have heard and seen of its report makes it seem a sound appraisal.[3] Why not view our greatly improved data situation with a reasonable patience?[4] Above all, let us not permit anyone to misinterpret or misuse the present minor controversies or to make them an entering wedge for discrediting sampling as such.

Not only am I a friend of small samplings but was one many years ago when small samplings had very few friends indeed. Though recog-

---

improved by Woodlief Thomas, then by Aryness Joy. Finally the Bureau of Labor Statistics (under new management) was prevailed upon to adopt the improved methods, whose results we all take for granted now.

[2] *Report of the President's Conference on Unemployment*, published in 1921. The specific section above referred to is on pages 52-57, but the same topic is adverted to variously in the general division concerned (Part II, "Unemployment Statistics," pp. 37-58, *passim*).

Also germane is Ernest S. Bradford's nearly contemporary note on "Methods Used in Measuring Unemployment" (*Journal of the American Statistical Association*, December 1921, pp. 983-994).

When that Conference and the National Bureau of Economic Research jointly issued, in 1923, the book resulting from their report and recommendations, *Business Cycles and Unemployment*, it bore three ground-breaking chapters of special interest to members of our present Conference: Chapter VI on volume of employment by Willford I. King, Chapter V on underemployment by Paul Brissenden, and Chapter XVIII on unemployment insurance by Leo Wolman. I, too, had a paper in the volume, Chapter IV, "What the Present Statistics of Unemployment Show."

[3] That very favorable opinion is confirmed by study of the report and appendixes, available in full since our Conference.

[4] In respect to the part of the problem that concerns disagreements between the Bureau of Employment Security data and either of the Census Bureau's figures, we all seem impressed by the mutual tolerance and understanding repeatedly expressed here by representatives of the two agencies.

nizing that some of these unemployment studies and many elsewhere have been based on small-size samples, I think more could well be, not only on unemployment but on such intimately related variables as employment itself. This conviction arose many years ago, during a study of employment returns. I even tried to wager Ethelbert Stewart, then Commissioner of Labor Statistics, that he could develop virtually as good a general index from a sample of, say, 10 or 5 per cent (i.e. the first quarter or eighth of his returns) as from his full standard sample (which, he always felt, should be 40 per cent).

The conviction became even stronger in the late 1920's when I was watching the returns gathered in the pilot project on labor turnover (transferred to Bureau of Labor Statistics in 1929). When a simple control was set up to guard against the explosive effect of large-employer returns, I saw samples of 5 per cent, 1 per cent, or even smaller, yield astonishingly reliable results, days and weeks ahead of the final result.[5]

A recommendation of experimental small samplings was included by the American Statistical Association's Labor Statistics Committee in its handbook nearly thirty years ago.[6] Little practical action resulted then. But now in the 1950's—with higher costs, with better knowledge and experience on sampling techniques, and with more demand for expediting results—experiments looking toward smaller samples in routine reporting, as in special studies, seem even more appropriate than ever before.

Several papers and discussions in this volume have dealt with part-time employment (or unemployment) and hidden or "disguised" unemployment both within the labor force and outside it in the so-called "secondary labor force." Opinions on this complex are difficult or impossible to synthesize, but it does seem that the case for counting

[5] For a recent handy summary of the result, see my "Technical Note" in *Monthly Labor Review*, August 1954, pp. 887-890.

If wider turnover reporting is undertaken than at present, it would seem warranted only on grounds *other* than the validity of the sample size as such, within the industries covered. It is surprising to note a seemingly contrary view in the testimony by Arthur F. Burns, Chairman of the President's Council of Economic Advisers, before the Joint Committee on the Economic Report's Subcommittee on Economic Statistics (July 12, 1954, p. 166).

[6] "Reliable statistics could probably be compiled on the basis of samples smaller than 40 per cent. [In fact some members of the committee hold that a properly selected sample of 15 per cent or even less would be adequate for some industries.] . . . Probably one-third is a feasible proportion at which to aim. Forty per cent of the workers in any industry would appear to be in general an upper limit of the quota needed; and frequently a much smaller proportion may be found ample." *Employment Statistics for the United States*, Committee on Governmental Labor Statistics, Ralph G. Hurlin and William A. Berridge, editors, Russell Sage Foundation, 1926, p. 65.

persons in all of these states as unemployed should be declared "not proven" if not "disproved." Surely 2 million people on half-time work do not form the same problem—economically, socially, or politically—as 1 million wholly without work. Any such mathematical equating can only pad the rolls of the unemployed in a deceptive and meaningless way. So would the counting of, say, farmers' or others' inaction within employment; such measuring seems mere stop-watch engineering or accounting, hardly economics.

To count as constructively unemployed those school pupils, housewives, and others who might be at work if various circumstances were different seems altogether too subjective. Hypothetical questions are not good standard practice for unemployment or labor force inquiries. After all, one need not call all inaction unemployment. Surely it is not the only problem in the world. Nor is a gainful job necessarily the *summum bonum* for every person, time, place, and circumstance. "Full employment" can become, if it is not already, a monomania. In both long and short run, it may be better for many to be at school or housework than at jobs; indeed, many on jobs right now might far better be at school, or managing home or children. Perhaps some of us have so intensively cultivated the field of unemployment that we have passed well out into the zone of diminishing returns and should transfer some part of our technical talent to the measurement and behavior of other problems—such as "unschoolment."

"Disemployment," as defined and used by Philip Hauser, seems a good and useful term, and I hope it will gain wide currency. Unemployment, in whatever scope of meaning, has come to be far less an economic than a "political" word, as Robert Nathan so aptly said at the Conference. The concept lends itself only too well to rabble rousing, it may fairly be said to embody poor semantics, and it concentrates attention unduly on "the hole rather than the doughnut." The much larger and economically more significant "positive" mass of employment deserves greater emphasis.

However, unemployment statistics are as accurate as employment statistics and as reliable as business-cycle gauges. True, the statistics of unemployment may have very inaccurately measured the actual volume of unemployment (by whatever definition, broad or narrow). But that is not a conclusive test. When not their absolute size but their relative fluctuations are examined, unemployment statistics have proved highly reliable.

This was true even for the supposedly poor statistics gathered by trade union secretaries in two states as long as a half century or so ago. Such data were among the few working materials available on the historical course of employment variations for my doctoral thesis in 1922. For a test period covering approximately 1900 to 1915, the unemployment variations were highly correlated with long-accepted business indexes. Indeed, a measure based more on unemployment than on the meager employment statistics then available showed a higher correlation with one widely accepted economic composite than did the latter's several components.[7] Those results surprised me as much as they did Wesley Mitchell and Warren Persons; even those thorough workmen had ignored the few unemployment and employment statistics available. With so much latent cyclical accuracy in the data then, how much better should be the vastly improved data on present unemployment. That bit of history shows that, however inferior unemployment may be to employment, semantically or otherwise, it was measured by data that could and did measure economic cycles as reliably as data on employment or even as other economic gauges more widely accepted at that time.

It is pleasant to have the term "labor float" used here again, partly because I apparently was first to use it and partly because the first person who took it over applied it incorrectly to all unemployment, not as I have occasionally used it, to mean substantially the same thing as the perhaps clumsier or less descriptive "frictional unemployment" (i.e. labor in suspense while en route from one employment to another, analogous to "bank float" or "money float").

I close by paying tribute to the members of the Dominion Bureau of Statistics for their unique contribution to this Conference in their treatment of the terms "unemployment" and "labor force." They have been formulating a clear and clever definition of labor force which does not once say either "unemployment" or "unemployed." It has been good to know, from their other contributions as well, that Canada is fully on the alert to problems of unemployment measurement and behavior.

I hope that my attempt at a retrospective view, synthesizing briefly some pertinent developments in the history of employment- and unemployment-measurement since the early 1920's, will have helped you do what methodologists in any field could well profit by doing more—namely, to study methodology from a genetic point of view.

[7] A less abridged summary of these correlations, etc., may if desired be found in *Review of Economic Statistics*, January 1922, especially pp. 34-35. So far as I can recall, this demonstration has not been "spelled out" more fully anywhere else, except in the thesis itself, "Employment and the Business Cycle," unpublished, Harvard University Library, pp. 196-211, *passim*.

ADDITIONAL COMMENTS

ABRAHAM L. GITLOW, New York University

The questions of underemployment raised by Louis L. Ducoff and Margaret J. Hagood, however interesting and valuable, really involve questions of the economy's structure and resource allocation among alternative uses rather than the measurement of unemployment and its behavior. We should concentrate on the latter; the former involves matters that would only divert us. Not quite so strong, but similar in nature, is my reaction to Richard C. Wilcock's paper on the secondary labor force.

One of the real, current measurement problems—clearly revealed in Gertrude Bancroft's paper—is that involving "fringe" persons in the labor force. If we expand the current measurement by the Census Bureau (in the Monthly Report on the Labor Force) to include the secondary labor force, we shall compound these difficulties and produce something that invites public confusion. Miss Bancroft's suggestion that a new category of partially unemployed ("economic" or "involuntary" part-time workers) be introduced into the MRLF would strike a responsive chord in my mind if it indicated how persons partially employed ("voluntary" part-time workers) would be identified. Otherwise, it seems more a response to some rather vocal, organized criticisms than a substantive matter. These people are counted now. What do we really change by altering the name? If, however, she intends to distinguish the partially unemployed from the partially employed my response becomes more favorable. She also suggests the monthly collection of data on the reasons for part-time work. I favor this.

I cannot be certain, but I get the impression that Miss Bancroft is distressed by definitions of unemployment which embrace *attitudes*, inclining more strictly toward an *activity* definition (see page 78 and point 1 on page 97). If we accept Louis Levine's definitions of activity (seeking work) and attitude (desiring a job under certain conditions), I would not go so far as she does in eliminating the latter from the MRLF. Her suggestion that the MRLF drop those not actively seeking work because of their belief that no job is available in their regular line of work seems all right. Instead of completely dropping those unemployed because of illness, however, it would seem more accurate to set some time limit (e.g. one month) during which they would be counted as unemployed rather than as being in the nonlabor force. In a more basic sense, I wonder if it is really desirable or possible to divorce activity from attitude. What is "full-time" activity? Does it not reflect certain attitudes of a society? If people are *voluntarily* employed part time, are they also partially unemployed? In such a case, I am inclined to give their attitudes great weight.

ELIZABETH J. SLOTKIN, Illinois Department of Labor

One of the elementary principles of scientific method is that the results of any research program depend primarily upon the original question which the research was designed to answer. Unfortunately, in proceeding from the stage where the question is posed to the definition of the problem and the concepts to be used, and from there to the collection of data, the original question is often lost sight of.

In reviewing the labor force concepts, I tried to work my way back to that original research question. After I had studied the concepts, I became more and more convinced that it had been: "How many jobs do we need to provide to employ our labor force more fully?" Consequently, I was very much interested to find some confirmation in Gertrude Bancroft's paper. On page 65, she points to the interest in determining "the number for whom jobs should be provided," as being one of the motivating forces behind the census concepts. Although she described the solution of the problem as being "middle of the road," I believe that the "current activity test" for unemployment comes closer to being a device for answering the question stated above than for answering any other single question.

I think much of the current controversy derives from the fact that we are today asking a different question and looking to census data to answer it. We are asking that our employment statistics give us a measure of the state of health of our economy. Increased employment brings with it increased purchasing power. Increased unemployment diminishes purchasing power, and whether one is a Keynesian economist or not, one cannot deny that purchasing power is required to make effective the demand for goods and services.

It is still true, of course, that we want to know how the people in our economy are being affected by the changes that are taking place in that economy. We should recognize at least two questions in need of data for their answers and should try to make our statistics conform to this double-headed problem. I believe this would result if an operational definition were adopted for employment as well as for unemployment. In other words, I think the acid test for employment is payment, and the group of workers with a job but not at work who are counted as employed should be limited to those who were paid by their employer for the week in question. Those who think they have a job to return to or to report to at some future date within the next thirty days should be counted separately. Whether they are put in a separate category or whether they are counted among the unemployed does not particularly matter. My own inclination would be to count them among the unemployed, but possibly that is because I have known too many people whose statement that they had a job to report to proved to be a fantasy on their part, and I have also known too many plants to lay off workers for a two-week period that stretched out for many more weeks.

If my suggestion were adopted, I think a series of data that would react more sensitively to economic change would result. The research question would be: "Of those participating in our economy, how many were receiving or were due to receive payment for their activity during the census week and how many were not so rewarded for their efforts?"

It has been suggested at these meetings that we need not be concerned with unemployment except as it affects primary breadwinners. Those of us who have worked directly with labor market problems know that there is no orderly procession in and out of employment, with secondary workers hired last and laid off first. Consequently, to advocate that we concern ourselves only with the unemployment of primary breadwinners takes the question of the measurement of unemployment out of the realm of economics and at the same time calls for the imposition of labor market controls to assure a minimum of unemployed primary breadwinners. Labor surpluses would have to be reduced by forcing early retirement of excess male workers and by driving women out of the labor force by such slogans as "*Küche, Kirche, Kinder.*" Adequate supplies of labor would have to be assured at other times by reversing these procedures. I think it is important to bear in mind that a definition of the term "unemployment," even though presumably designed for statistical measurement only, may have inherent in it a program of action which is inconsistent with our traditional labor market practices.

CONRAD TAEUBER, Bureau of the Census

There has been a good deal of emphasis in these papers on the desirability of having more detailed information about the unemployed as well as about the persons who move into and out of the labor force. The desire for additional information is one which we of the Bureau of the Census are striving to meet and it is our plan to make available more information about the characteristics of the unemployed than has been recently available.

However, some of the new groupings (or regroupings), that have been discussed seem to have policy implications that call for careful consideration before the new groupings are generally used. For example, there are difficulties in classifying individuals as "primary" and "secondary" workers. Even if those difficulties of classification are satisfactorily disposed of, a series on the unemployment of primary workers would provide only a part of the needed information.

Great stress has recently been laid on the production and distribution of durable consumer goods and on the importance of maintaining a broad base of purchasing power to permit the movement of such goods. Insofar as the maintenance of a high level of business activity depends on decisions to buy or not to buy, it may well be that an increase in the unemployment of secondary workers might have a disproportionate effect on the economy. To illustrate, the statistics on family income show that approximately two-thirds of the families with incomes of $6,000 to $10,000 have more than one earner, and it may well be that the ability of these families to maintain a high level of consumption is dependent on the continued earning of the secondary worker.

It is our intention to provide statistics on the unemployment of family heads. The users of such statistics should recognize their limitations in an economy whose level of activity is dependent less on the provision of the minimum essentials for the maintenance of life and more on the provision of goods and services which people can forego without immediate danger to the maintenance of life.

MORRIS H. HANSEN, Bureau of the Census

The demand for more data on unemployment has been not so much for data that could be used immediately to make decisions on economic policy as for data that could be used in analytic studies of the unemployed and of unemployment. An economical way to obtain some of the data required from the monthly labor force surveys of the Bureau of the Census would be to cumulate information from successive surveys. Estimates that are too unreliable to publish from a single month's enumeration might become publishable on a quarterly, semi-annual, or annual basis.

A word of caution is needed in connection with what has come to be known as "gross change analysis" as used in the papers by David L. Kaplan and Philip M. Hauser. The problem in interpreting these tabulations was recognized in these papers but deserves some additional emphasis. Gross change analyses are the tabulations of the month-to-month changes in labor force status of identical individuals (i.e. of persons who are included in the survey during the months under study). Our investigations of the accuracy and reliability of enumerative surveys suggest the hypothesis that substantial proportions of the gross changes from month to month may be simply response errors or "response differences." The evidence we have gathered to date suggests that 5 to 30 per cent of the individual responses to specific labor force inquiries may vary (without any change in the characteristic under inquiry) from interview to interview.[1] Some characteristics can be measured with considerably greater stability than others. The available evidence also suggests that such gross response variability usually has little effect on the summary statistics themselves—the totals and proportions. There seems to be considerable cancellation of errors. Gross change analysis, however, can not take as much advantage of the phenomenon of cancellation.

The collection of economic data is itself an activity of an economic character. The costs of producing statistics and the value of the statistics to those who use them should somehow be commensurate. This point of view has important implications for the design and conduct of data-collection activities. Not the least of these implications is that the "specifications" for a set of statistics should not only indicate the kinds of data that are required but also should consider the costs involved in various levels of inaccuracy that these data may possess. Where substantial amounts of public funds are involved, it is not enough to specify that the data should be "useful for micrometric analysis" or should be "reasonably accurate" or should be "consistent indicators of changes in the cycle." Nor is it adequate to specify that statistics should be "as accurate as possible."

Economists and other users of data must begin to examine critically how they use the data that are provided for them so that the requirements for the investment of public funds in statistics can become somewhat more rationally determined than is now feasible.

PAUL S. TAYLOR, University of California

We suffer at times from a tendency to define our task by the tools we use. We focus on arriving at one perfect statistical series. (In deference to the Bureaus of the Census and of Employment Security ought I to say two perfect series?) But our problems are not so confined and uniform in nature that they will all yield to dissection by the same tool. The people who leave Illinois industry to "go to the hills" are "out" for the Illinois Department of Labor's statistical purposes, but they are "in" for the United States Department of Agriculture. We do not ask a single question and get a single answer. At what point along the curve of unemployment do we "get worried"? Have we enough reserve manpower for our periods of greatest exertion, for example, war?

[1] Our results are generally consistent with those reported by Gladys L. Palmer in "Factors in the Variability of Response in Enumerative Studies," *Journal of the American Statistical Association*, June 1943, pp. 143-152.

Even this question is not simple, as we step up to bridle it with a single statistical measure. In preparing estimates of the adequacy of the agricultural labor supply during the defense period just prior to World War II, I came across the reports of Thorstein Veblen on the adequacy of the agricultural labor supply during World War I. In his view, the definition of available labor reserve was greatly affected by the sharp eye he cast upon the nature of economic institutions in agricultural areas, and he saw far greater labor reserves than most. Who is to say that under sufficient emergency pressure, more observers might not look twice at the corners of the economy to which he pointed?

In considering what is adequate as a statistical measure, we do not entirely escape the binding force of our institutional arrangements. Our mores are involved at times as well as our economics. The solution of our problem of measurement, it seems to me, lies in diversity of statistical series; in special studies as well as in continuous series. When unemployment and underemployment become conspicuous in, say, the anthracite industry or in agriculture, we need special studies there. When special aspects of unemployment become prominent, as for example, long duration creating a "hard-core of unemployed," we need special statistical studies that will give the dimensions of this disturbing human problem. Our problems do not lack for diversity, and our measurements ought not to be sought in the singular, but rather in the plural.

A. Ross Eckler, Bureau of the Census

There are two types of research that I think will be helpful in contributing to the eventual solution of some of the problems discussed in this volume. First, the Bureau of the Census is undertaking a considerably expanded program of research on its Current Population Survey, primarily as a result of suggestions in the report of the Stephan Committee on employment statistics. This research will take a number of forms and should bear directly on many of the subjects discussed. It will involve some exploration of conceptual problems to see whether improvements can be made in the present labor force categories. It will involve studies of questionnaire design and interview procedures to determine whether more consistent measures can be obtained. Important emphasis will be placed on quality control procedures to insure that the performance of all units of the organization is being maintained at the levels required. Greater knowledge of the dynamics of the labor force is to be expected as a result of extension of month-to-month gross change analyses and the development of gross change analysis on a year-to-year basis. We expect that the papers presented here, together with the comments, will be fully taken into account as we carry out some of this research work.

Second, I should like to suggest the desirability of steps to determine more accurately the relationship between the Bureau of the Census and the Bureau of Employment Security unemployment data. We agree, I take it, that the two sets of data serve important purposes and complement each other in a significant way. I should like to urge that efforts be made to carry out matching studies in order to learn more about the composition of each series in relation to the other. The difficulties are admittedly great, and each agency must operate carefully because of the provisions on confidential material contained in the laws and regulations governing each agency. However, the need for better understanding of the differences is so great that I hope real progress can be made by the two agencies in carrying out the matching studies necessary for a better understanding of basic statistics on unemployment.

JAMES TOBIN, Yale University

I shall discuss briefly three topics which have dominated much of this conference: the problem of ascertaining the labor force attachment of individuals of working age, the problem of ascertaining the employment status of members of the labor force, and the relation of measures of unemployment to economic policy.

LABOR FORCE STATUS

When is an individual in the labor force? The line between being unemployed and being outside the labor force is a hard one to draw, and objections can be raised to almost any criteria. There are three kinds of criteria either in current use or under discussion.

Past Job-Holding or Job-Seeking Activity. Some job-seeking activity in the most recent week is normally a requirement for being counted as unemployed rather than as outside the labor force in the Census Bureau's monthly survey. But what of individuals who did not seek jobs in the past week because they knew none were available in the locality? These the Census Bureau now counts as unemployed, but, according to Gertrude Bancroft, the monthly survey counts them quite imperfectly. On the other hand, what of individuals—married women, say—who have never been employed but have recently carried on a casual and desultory search for a job with ideal specifications? These questions suggest that activity during the most recent week is not by itself an adequate criterion. One way to supplement it is to obtain a longer history: Has the individual regularly held or sought jobs during his adult life? Richard C. Wilcock suggests an affirmative answer to such an inquiry as one way of qualifying for his "primary labor force." Regularity in the past may, however, be a poor guide to the labor force status of the young, the old, and many in between whose circumstances and attitudes change.

Both current job-seeking activity, at least in the sense of willingness to accept employment, and job-holding in the past are necessary to be counted as unemployed in connection with unemployment insurance plans. But not all persons who meet these conditions are counted. Herbert S. Parnes has expounded the omissions very thoroughly. Insurance data are nevertheless extremely valuable as a source of local estimates of unemployment.

Attitudes and Intentions. Skepticism is justified concerning the validity of hypothetical questions, "Would you take a job if . . . ?" But this does not mean that there is no way of getting a more subjective indicator of labor force status than the answers to historical questions. The Census Bureau's sample design is admirably suited to experimentation with questions about future plans and intentions because each respondent is reinterviewed a number of times. A question about what the respondent intends to do during the coming year (or quarter or month)—seek a job, stay home, go to school, or what—is not subject to the defects of hypothetical questions. People will not, of course, faithfully carry out their expressed intentions. But experience in the Federal Reserve's Surveys of Consumer Finances shows that intentions data in the aggregate can nevertheless be indicative of changes if not of levels. Analysis at the Survey Research Center shows that reinterviews can shed a great deal of light on the characteristics of those who fulfill their plans and of those who do not.

Another experimental possibility is to have the individual who does not have a job classify himself as "unemployed" or as "not in the labor force." The distinction by now probably has meaning for the vast majority of people. It is true that the meaning will not be the same from one person to another. But for many policy purposes, and for many political purposes, the important thing may be the number of persons who consider themselves unemployed, rather than the number who by some uniform objective criterion are so classified.

Demographic Characteristics. The usefulness of an individual's statements about his past and his future will be enhanced by combining them with demographic information. For example, there is a strong presumption that able-bodied males between eighteen and sixty-five are in the labor force whatever they may have been doing last week.

The same is true of males and females who are heads of spending units. Married women, especially those with children, may be expected to be less stable in their labor force attachment; and it is no cause for surprise if their answers to questions about their past or future give variable results.

Paying attention to the demographic characteristics of persons who classify themselves in or out of the labor force does not imply that unemployment of one kind of person is a less serious social problem than unemployment of another kind of person. Gladys L. Palmer and Elizabeth J. Slotkin are right to warn of the dangers of a policy that worries only about the employment status of male breadwinners. But these fears should not prevent the use of demographic data to assist in understanding and measuring unemployment and labor force participation. This was Wilcock's objective, although the terms "primary" and "secondary" may have connotations for policy that he did not intend.

EMPLOYMENT STATUS

The other line-drawing problem involved in measuring unemployment is determining the employment status of a member of the labor force. A number of difficulties have been discussed in these papers.

Partial Unemployment. One difficulty is connected with the practice of counting employment and unemployment in units of men instead of in man-hours. A man may work fewer hours than he would like or than he customarily has worked and still be counted as employed. A part-time worker who loses his job gets counted as a full unit of unemployment. Albert Rees' ingenious calculations indicate that the second kind of error outweighs the first, so that present methods of counting exaggerate the amplitude of fluctuations in unemployment. His findings are confirmed by some calculations of Gertrude Bancroft. In any event there is doubtless unanimous concurrence in Miss Bancroft's recommendations for monthly collection of data on partial unemployment.

Self-Employment and Disguised Unemployment. Self-employed individuals, including farm operators, fit poorly a conceptual scheme designed mainly for hired workers. Likewise secondary members of households headed by farmers or other business proprietors may be hard to classify. Lack of job opportunities may result not in idleness and job seeking but in unproductive self-employment or participation in the family enterprise. It is natural to seek, as Louis J. Ducoff and Margaret J. Hagood do, a way of counting these results as the equivalent of the more obvious symptom of the same disease, unemployment. Unfortunately, the phenomenon does not seem to be one for which the either/or categories of labor force and unemployment statistics are appropriate. If people are at unproductive work, whether as hired wage earners, family farm hands, or self-employed, the best statistical symptom of this social malady is low per capita income, not unemployment.

Duration of Unemployment. Unemployment is, usually, a "snapshot" concept. We speak of the amount of unemployment *existing at a moment of time*, rather than, say, the number of man-days lost *during a certain period of time*. But it would be absurd to let the employment status of an individual at a certain time depend literally only on his condition at that moment; it must depend also on his recent history. How long a history should be considered in classifying him? Does a single day without work make a man "unemployed," as in many of the European statistics reported by Walter Galenson and Arnold Zellner? Or does it take a week, as in our Census Bureau definition? How far is the single-day concept responsible for the strikingly high levels Galenson and Zellner show for European unemployment ratios over a long period of time before World War II?

Rees has argued very convincingly that long-duration unemployment is the real social malady. One-day or one-week unemployment we can easily afford, and a certain amount is inevitable in a dynamic economy. The Census Bureau is besieged with suggestions of interesting dimensions to be added to its measure of unemployment, and one hesitates to lengthen the list. But high priority should be given to the distribution of unemployment by duration. This might be done semiannually, as it is probably neither practical nor necessary to do it monthly.

MEASURES OF UNEMPLOYMENT IN RELATION TO ECONOMIC POLICY

Employment and labor force statistics are not the only kind of information an economic policy maker needs, and he needs more than one dimension even of that information. The economics profession has been all too susceptible to the belief that there is one single index of economic health that can be used as a guide to policy. Sometimes it has been a price index, sometimes gross national product, sometimes the unemployment ratio. The economy is too complex to be described or controlled by a single number. Unemployment is not the only social malady, and unemployment itself is better described by a set of numbers than by a single total.

Is it obvious that the cyclically most sensitive measure of unemployment is the most relevant for policy? Such appears to be the assumption of Rees and other of the writers. Yet it is conceivable that the components that fluctuate most violently are those of least public concern. We should decide what measures of unemployment we want and need and then see how they compare with other economic series in cyclical amplitude and timing. To do the reverse, to choose deliberately series that agree with others in cyclical pattern, is to reduce the information available for the policy maker rather than to increase it.

Should "full employment" be defined so that it is an acceptable single goal of policy? Rees seeks such a definition, and consequently he has to allow within it for desiderata other than low unemployment, principally price level stability. Would it not be better to define "full employment" unambiguously in terms of labor market data alone and to recognize that it is not an absolute goal? Wilcock's concept of "maximum desired employment," for example, would probably entail price level consequences that few policy makers would wish to accept. My difference here with Rees is largely terminological. His paper contributes mightily to answering the important questions: What dimensions of employment and unemployment are useful policy guides? How compatible are goals of low unemployment with other objectives of economic policy?

Finally, I would like to add a postscript regarding Eli Ginzberg's complaint that human behavior is not among the kinds of "behavior" this Conference considered. It is true that economists have traditionally attributed "behavior" to statistics of prices, interest rates, employment, etc., while other social scientists have maintained that only human beings, or at most only animals, behave. Aside from this terminological difference, Ginzberg's remarks are a reminder that hypotheses about human behavior are at least implicit in the concepts and methods used to measure unemployment and in the uses to which the measures are put. The "additional workers" controversy and the question of the wage elasticity of the supply of labor are only the most prominent of many indications of the need to understand more about the labor force participation decisions of households. The Census Bureau surveys, as well as other surveys of households made for different purposes, offer great opportunities for research on this aspect of human behavior.

AUTHOR INDEX

SUBJECT INDEX